GLOBAL IS 98/99

MW00964966

98/99

Fourteenth Edition

Editor

Robert M. Jackson

California State University, Chico

Robert M. Jackson is a professor of political science, director of the Center for International Studies, and acting dean of the Graduate School of California State University, Chico. In addition to teaching, he has published articles on the international political economy, international relations simulations, and political behavior. His special research interest is in the way northern California is becoming increasingly linked to the Pacific Basin. His travels include China, Japan, Hong Kong, Taiwan, Singapore, Malaysia, Portugal, Spain, Morocco, Costa Rica, El Salvador, Honduras, Guatemala, Mexico, Germany, Belgium, the Netherlands, Russia, and Czechoslovakia.

A Library of Information from the Public Press

Dushkin/McGraw·Hill

Sluice Dock, Guilford, Connecticut 06437

Visit us on the Internet—http://www.dushkin.com/

This map has been developed to give you a graphic picture of where the countries of the world are located, the relationship they have with their region and neighbors, and their positions relative to the superpowers and power blocs. We have focused on certain areas to more clearly illustrate these crowded regions.

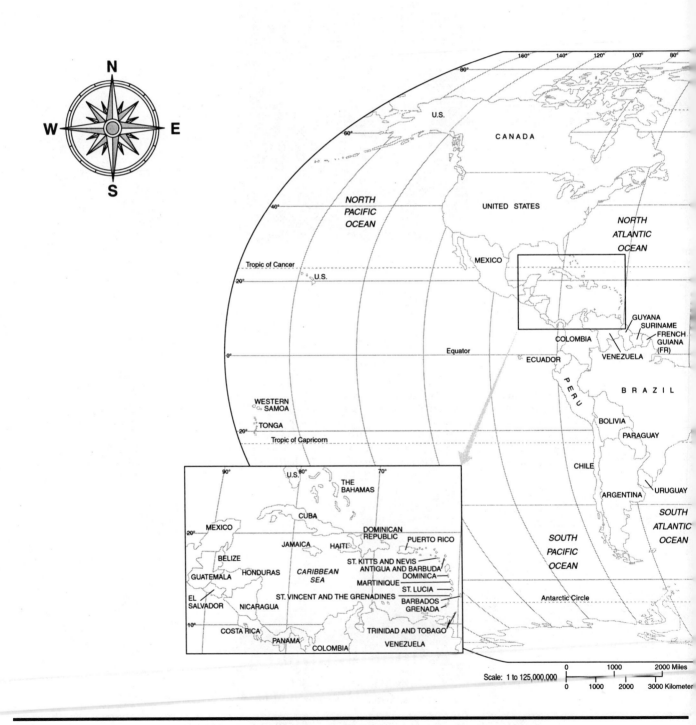

Scale: 1 to 125,000,000

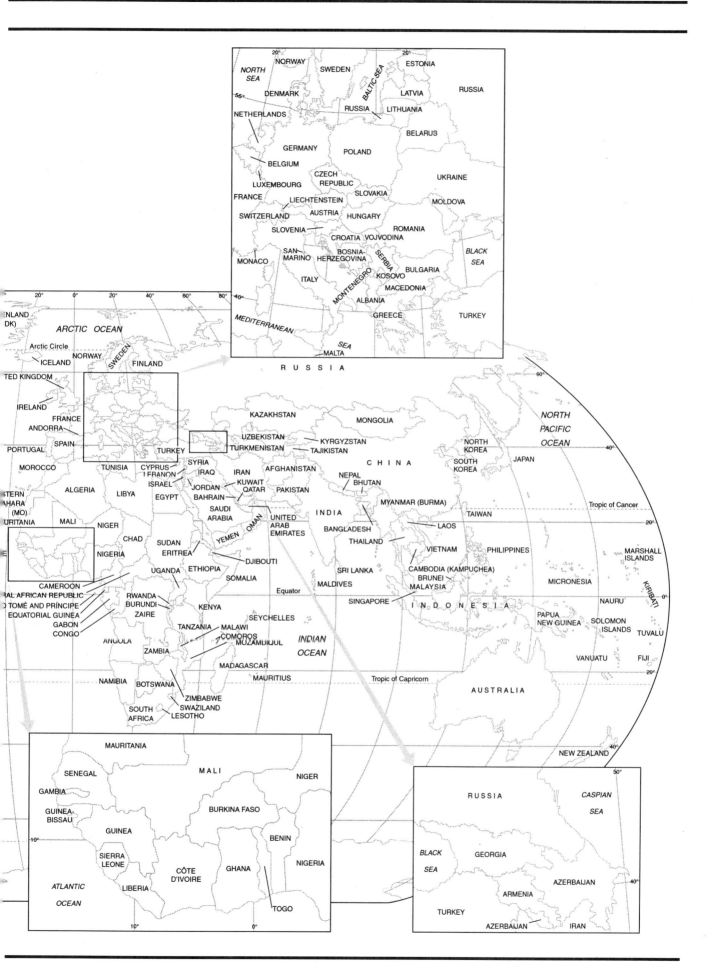

The Annual Editions Series

ANNUAL EDITIONS, including GLOBAL STUDIES, consist of over 70 volumes designed to provide the reader with convenient, low-cost access to a wide range of current, carefully selected articles from some of the most important magazines, newspapers, and journals published today. ANNUAL EDITIONS are updated on an annual basis through a continuous monitoring of over 300 periodical sources. All ANNUAL EDITIONS have a number of features that are designed to make them particularly useful, including topic guides, annotated tables of contents, unit overviews, and indexes. For the teacher using ANNUAL EDITIONS in the classroom, an Instructor's Resource Guide with test questions is available for each volume. GLOBAL STUDIES titles provide comprehensive background information and selected world press articles on the regions and countries of the world.

VOLUMES AVAILABLE

ANNUAL EDITIONS

Abnormal Psychology
Accounting
Adolescent Psychology
Aging
American Foreign Policy
American Government
American History, Pre-Civil War
American History, Post-Civil War
American Public Policy
Anthropology
Archaeology
Astronomy
Biopsychology
Business Ethics
Canadian Politics
Child Growth and Development
Comparative Politics
Computers in Education
Computers in Society
Criminal Justice
Criminology
Developing World
Deviant Behavior
Drugs, Society, and Behavior
Dying, Death, and Bereavement

Early Childhood Education
Economics
Educating Exceptional Children
Education
Educational Psychology
Environment
Geography
Geology
Global Issues
Health
Human Development
Human Resources
Human Sexuality
International Business
Macroeconomics
Management
Marketing
Marriage and Family
Mass Media
Microeconomics
Multicultural Education
Nutrition
Personal Growth and Behavior
Physical Anthropology
Psychology
Public Administration
Race and Ethnic Relations

Social Problems
Social Psychology
Sociology
State and Local Government
Teaching English as a Second
     Language
Urban Society
Violence and Terrorism
Western Civilization, Pre-Reformation
Western Civilization, Post-Reformation
Women's Health
World History, Pre-Modern
World History, Modern
World Politics

GLOBAL STUDIES

Africa
China
India and South Asia
Japan and the Pacific Rim
Latin America
Middle East
Russia, the Eurasian Republics, and
     Central/Eastern Europe
Western Europe

Cataloging in Publication Data
Main entry under title: Annual Editions: Global Issues. 1998/99.
     1. Civilization, Modern—20th century—Periodicals. 2. Social prediction—
Periodicals. 3. Social problems—20th century—Periodicals. I. Jackson, Robert, *comp.* II.
Title: Global Issues.
ISBN 0–697–39187–6   909.82'05   85–658006   ISSN 1093–278X

Fourteenth Edition

Cover image © 1998 PhotoDisc, Inc.

Printed in the United States of America   1234567890BAHBAH901234098

Printed on Recycled Paper

Editors/Advisory Board

Members of the Advisory Board are instrumental in the final selection of articles for each edition of ANNUAL EDITIONS. Their review of articles for content, level, currentness, and appropriateness provides critical direction to the editor and staff. We think that you will find their careful consideration well reflected in this volume.

EDITOR

Robert M. Jackson
California State University, Chico

ADVISORY BOARD

Thomas E. Arcaro
Elon College

Diane N. Barnes
University of Southern Maine

Leonard Cardenas
Southwest Texas State University

H. Thomas Collins
Project LINKS
George Washington University

E. Gene DeFelice
Purdue University
Calumet

Robert L. Delorme
California State University
Long Beach

Dennis R. Gordon
Santa Clara University

James E. Harf
Ohio State University

Hlib S. Hayuk
Towson University

Asad Husain
Northeastern Illinois University

D. Gregory Jeane
Samford University

Karl H. Kahrs
California State University
Fullerton

Sadat Kazi
Vanier College

Sondra King
Northern Illinois University

Steven L. Lamy
University of Southern California

T. David Mason
University of Memphis

Alexander Nadesan
Bemidji State University

Louis L. Ortmayer
Davidson College

Guy Poitras
Trinity University

Helen E. Purkitt
U.S. Naval Academy

Nicholas J. Smith-Sebasto
University of Illinois
Urbana–Champaign

Christian Søe
California State University
Long Beach

Kenneth P. Thomas
University of Missouri
St. Louis

Kenneth L. Wise
Creighton University

Rodger Yeager
West Virginia University

Staff

Ian A. Nielsen, Publisher

To the Reader

In publishing ANNUAL EDITIONS we recognize the enormous role played by the magazines, newspapers, and journals of the *public press* in providing current, first-rate educational information in a broad spectrum of interest areas. Many of these articles are appropriate for students, researchers, and professionals seeking accurate, current material to help bridge the gap between principles and theories and the real world. These articles, however, become more useful for study when those of lasting value are carefully *collected, organized, indexed,* and *reproduced* in a *low-cost format,* which provides easy and permanent access when the material is needed. That is the role played by ANNUAL EDITIONS. Under the direction of each volume's *academic editor,* who is an expert in the subject area, and with the guidance of an *Advisory Board,* each year we seek to provide in each ANNUAL EDITION a current, well-balanced, carefully selected collection of the best of the public press for your study and enjoyment. We think that you will find this volume useful, and we hope that you will take a moment to let us know what you think.

As the twentieth century draws to a close, the issues confronting humanity are increasingly more complex and diverse.

While the mass media may focus on the latest crisis for a few days or weeks, the broad forces that are shaping the world of the twenty-first century are seldom given the in-depth analysis that they warrant. Scholarly research about these historic change factors can be found in a wide variety of publications, but these are not readily accessible. In addition, the student just beginning to study global issues can be discouraged by the terminology and abstract concepts that characterize much of the scholarly literature. In selecting and organizing the materials for this book, we have been mindful of the needs of beginning students, that is, to select articles that invite the student into the subject matter.

Each unit begins with an introductory article providing a broad overview of the area to be explored. The remaining articles examine in more detail some of the issues presented. The unit then concludes with an article (or two) that not only identifies a problem but suggests positive steps that are being taken to improve the situation. The world faces many serious issues, the magnitude of which would discourage even the most stouthearted individual. Though identifying problems is easier than solving them, it is encouraging to know that many of the issues are being successfully addressed.

Perhaps the most striking feature of the study of contemporary global issues is the absence of any single, widely held theory that explains what is taking place. Therefore, we have made a conscious effort to present a wide variety of ideologies and theories. The most important consideration has been to present global issues from an international perspective, rather than from a purely American or Western point of view. By encompassing materials originally published in many different countries and written by authors of various nationalities, the anthology represents the great diversity of opinions that people hold on important global issues. Two writers examining the same phenomenon may reach very different conclusions. It is not a question of who is right and who is wrong. What is important to understand is that people from different vantage points have differing perceptions of issues.

Another major consideration when organizing these materials was to explore the complex interrelationship of factors that produce social problems such as poverty. Too often, discussions of this problem (and others like it) are reduced to arguments about the fallacies of not following the correct economic policy or not having the correct form of government. As a result, many people overlook the interplay of historic, cultural, environmental, economic, and political factors that form a complex web bringing about problems such as poverty. Here, every effort has been made to select materials that illustrate this complex interaction of factors, stimulating the beginning student to consider realistic rather than overly simplistic approaches to the pressing problems that threaten the existence of civilization.

Finally, we selected the materials in this book for both their intellectual insights and their readability. Timely and well-written materials should stimulate good classroom lectures and discussions. I hope that students and teachers will enjoy using this book. Readers can have input into the next edition by completing and returning the postage-paid *article rating form* in the back of the book.

New to this edition of *Annual Editions: Global Issues* are *World Wide Web* sites that can be used to further explore topics addressed in the articles. These sites are cross-referenced in the *topic guide.*

I would like to give special thanks to Ian Nielsen. I am grateful for his encouragement and helpful suggestions in the selection of materials for *Annual Editions: Global Issues 98/99*. It is my continuing goal to encourage the readers of this book to have a greater appreciation of the world in which we live. I hope each of you will be motivated to further explore the complex issues faced by the world as we approach the twenty-first century.

Robert M. Jackson
Editor

Contents

UNIT 1

A Clash of Views

The three articles in this section present distinct views on the present and future state of life on Earth.

UNIT 2

Population

Five articles in this section discuss the contributing factors of culture, politics, environmental degradation, disease, and migration on the world's population growth.

The concepts in bold italics are developed in the article. For further expansion please refer to the Topic Guide, the Glossary, and the Index.

UNIT 3

Natural Resources

Thirteen selections divided into four subsections—international dimensions, raw materials, food and hunger, and energy—discuss natural resources and their effects on the world community.

The concepts in bold italics are developed in the article. For further expansion please refer to the Topic Guide, the Glossary, and the Index.

The concepts in bold italics are developed in the article. For further expansion please refer to the Topic Guide, the Glossary, and the Index.

UNIT 4

Political Economy

Thirteen articles divided into two subsections present various views on economic and social development in the nonindustrial and industrial nations.

The concepts in bold italics are developed in the article. For further expansion please refer to the Topic Guide, the Glossary, and the Index.

UNIT 5

Conflict

Seven articles in this section discuss the basis for world conflict and the current state of peace in the international community.

The concepts in bold italics are developed in the article. For further expansion please refer to the Topic Guide, the Glossary, and the Index.

1

UNIT 6

Cooperation

Five selections in this section examine patterns of international cooperation and the social structures that support this cooperation.

UNIT 7

Values and Visions

Four articles discuss human rights, ethics, values, and new ideas.

The concepts in bold italics are developed in the article. For further expansion please refer to the Topic Guide, the Glossary, and the Index.

Topic Guide

This topic guide suggests how the selections in this book relate to topics of traditional concern to students and professionals involved in the study of global issues. It is useful for locating articles that relate to each other for reading and research. The guide is arranged alphabetically according to topic. Articles may, of course, treat topics that do not appear in the topic guide. In turn, entries in the topic guide do not necessarily constitute a comprehensive listing of all the contents of each selection. **In addition, relevant Web sites, which are annotated on pages 6 and 7, are noted in bold italics under the topic articles.**

TOPIC AREA	TREATED IN	TOPIC AREA	TREATED IN
Agriculture, Food, and Hunger	3. Redefining Security 4. Can Humanity Survive Unrestricted Population Growth? 14. We Can Build a Sustainable Economy 15. Global Population and the Nitrogen Cycle 16. How Much Food Will We Need in the 21st Century? 17. Fish Crisis 18. Angling for 'Aquaculture' *(5, 6, 7, 8, 12, 13, 14)*	**Development: Economic and Social (cont.)**	12. Mining the Oceans 14. We Can Build a Sustainable Economy 21. Here Comes the Sun 22. Complexities and Contradictions of Globalization 23. Spreading the Wealth 24. Prosper or Perish? 25. Illusion for Our Time 27. Piling into Central Europe 30. No More Free Lunch 31. New Tiger 32. Village Banking 33. Child Labour 34. Burden of Womanhood 47. Universal Human Values 48. Women in Power 50. Reassessing the Economic Assumption *(5, 6, 7, 8, 9, 11, 12, 13, 14, 16, 17, 20, 21, 30, 31, 32, 33, 34, 35)*
Communications	2. Many Faces of the Future 22. Complexities and Contradictions of Globalization		
Cultural Customs and Values	2. Many Faces of the Future 6. Refugees: The Rising Tide 8. How Many People Can the Earth Support? 13. Greenwatch 14. We Can Build a Sustainable Economy 19. Future of Energy 22. Complexities and Contradictions of Globalization 23. Spreading the Wealth 26. High Noon in Europe 30. No More Free Lunch 32. Village Banking 33. Child Labour 34. Burden of Womanhood 42. First Fifty Years 47. Universal Human Values 48. Women in Power 49. End of the Hunting Season in History 50. Reassessing the Economic Assumption *(1, 2, 3, 4, 7, 9, 16, 32, 33, 34)*	**Economics**	1. Preparing for the 21st Century 8. How Many People Can the Earth Support? 10. Global Warning 11. Fire in the Sky 12. Mining the Oceans 13. Greenwatch 14. We Can Build a Sustainable Economy 19. Future of Energy 20. How to Divvy Up Caspian Bonanza 21. Here Comes the Sun 22. Complexities and Contradictions of Globalization 23. Spreading the Wealth 24. Prosper or Perish? 26. High Noon in Europe 27. Piling Into Central Europe 28. Where Asia Goes from Here 29. Ignored Warnings 30. No More Free Lunch 31. New Tiger 32. Village Banking 33. Child Labour 34. Burden of Womanhood 50. Reassessing the Economic Assumption *(3, 4, 5, 6, 7, 8, 9, 12, 14, 16, 17, 19, 20, 22, 34)*
Developing World	4. Can Humanity Survive Unrestricted Population Growth? 5. Worldwide Development or Population Explosion 13. Greenwatch 23. Spreading the Wealth 24. Prosper or Perish? 31. New Tiger 32. Village Banking 33. Child Labour 34. Burden of Womanhood *(1, 2, 5, 6, 7, 8, 9, 10, 11, 16)*	**Energy: Exploration, Production, Research, and Politics**	14. We Can Build a Sustainable Economy 19. Future of Energy 20. How to Divvy Up Caspian Bonanza 21. Here Comes the Sun *(13, 14, 15, 17, 21, 24)*
Development: Economic and Social	1. Preparing for the 21st Century 3. Redefining Security 4. Can Humanity Survive Unrestricted Population Growth? 5. Worldwide Development or Population Explosion 8. How Many People Can the Earth Support? 9. Global Challenge 10. Global Warning 11. Fire in the Sky		

4

TOPIC AREA	TREATED IN	TOPIC AREA	TREATED IN
Environment, Ecology, and Conservation	5. Worldwide Development or Population Explosion 8. How Many People Can the Earth Support? 9. Global Challenge 10. Global Warning 11. Fire in the Sky 12. Mining the Oceans 13. Greenwatch 14. We Can Build a Sustainable Economy 15. Global Population and the Nitrogen Cycle 17. Fish Crisis 18. Angling for 'Aquaculture' 19. Future of Energy 21. Here Comes the Sun *(6, 7, 8, 12, 13, 14, 15, 16, 17, 18, 19, 35)*	**Military: Warfare and Terrorism**	35. New Arms Race 36. Organized Chaos 38. Uncertainty, Insecurity, and China's Military Power 39. Russian Foreign Policy in the Near Abroad and Beyond 40. Nuclear Deterrence and Regional Proliferators 41. Taking Nuclear Weapons Off Hair-Trigger Alert 43. Watchful Eye 46. Peace Prize Goes to Land-Mine Opponents 49. End of the Hunting Season in History *(23, 24, 25, 26)*
Future, The	1. Preparing for the 21st Century 2. Many Faces of the Future 3. Redefining Security 4. Can Humanity Survive Unrestricted Population Growth? 5. Worldwide Development or Population Explosion 6. Refugees: The Rising Tide 7. Water-Borne Killers 8. How Many People Can the Earth Support? 9. Global Challenge 10. Global Warning 12. Mining the Oceans 14. We Can Build a Sustainable Economy 15. Global Population and the Nitrogen Cycle 17. Fish Crisis 19. Future of Energy 20. How to Divvy Up Caspian Bonanza 21. Here Comes the Sun 22. Complexities and Contradictions of Globalization 24. Prosper or Perish? 28. Where Asia Goes from Here 31. New Tiger 38. Uncertainty, Insecurity, and China's Military Power 44. Like No Other Parliament on Earth 49. End of the Hunting Season 50. Reassessing the Economic Assumption *(1, 2, 4, 6, 7, 8, 9, 10, 11, 12, 13, 14, 15, 16, 17, 18, 19, 20, 21, 32, 33, 34, 35)*	**Natural Resources**	9. Global Challenge 10. Global Warning 11. Fire in the Sky 12. Mining the Oceans 13. Greenwatch 14. We Can Build a Sustainable Economy 17. Fish Crisis 19. Future of Energy 20. How to Divvy Up Caspian Bonanza 21. Here Comes the Sun *(12, 13, 14, 15, 16, 17, 35)*
		Political and Legal Global Issues	6. Refugees: The Rising Tide 9. Global Challenge 10. Global Warning 12. Mining the Oceans 20. How to Divvy Up Caspian Bonanza 28. Where Asia Goes from Here 29. Ignored Warnings 42. First Fifty Years 43. Watchful Eye 44. Like No Other Parliament on Earth 45. From GATT to WTO 46. Peace Prize Goes to Land-Mine Opponents *(1, 2, 4, 7, 17, 18, 19, 20, 21, 22, 32, 33, 34, 35)*
Industrial Economics	1. Preparing for the 21st Century 9. Global Challenge 10. Global Warning 14. We Can Build a Sustainable Economy 19. Future of Energy 23. Spreading the Wealth 26. High Noon in Europe *(6, 7, 8, 9, 18, 19, 20, 21, 22, 33)*	**Population and Demographics (Quality of Life Indicators)**	1. Preparing for the 21st Century 3. Redefining Security 4. Can Humanity Survive Unrestricted Population Growth? 5. Worldwide Development or Population Explosion 6. Refugees: The Rising Tide 7. Water-Borne Killers 8. How Many People Can the Earth Support? *(9, 10, 11, 12, 13, 16, 17, 30, 33)*
International Economics, Trade, Aid, and Dependencies	10. Global Warning 12. Mining the Oceans 13. Greenwatch 20. How to Divvy Up Caspian Bonanza 22. Complexities and Contradictions of Globalization 23. Spreading the Wealth 24. Prosper or Perish? 25. Illusion for Our Time 26. High Noon in Europe 27. Piling into Central Europe 28. Where Asia Goes from Here 31. New Tiger 45. From GATT to WTO *(5, 6, 7, 8, 12, 17, 18, 19, 21, 22, 28, 29)*	**Science, Technology, and Research and Development**	4. Can Humanity Survive Unrestricted Population Growth? 7. Water-Borne Killers 10. Global Warning 12. Mining the Oceans 13. Greenwatch 14. We Can Build a Sustainable Economy 18. Angling for 'Aquaculture' 21. Here Comes the Sun *(5, 6, 8, 12, 13, 14, 15, 16, 17, 18, 19, 20)*

5

Selected World Wide Web Sites for
Annual Editions: Global Issues

All of these Web sites are hot-linked through the *Annual Editions* home page:
http://www.dushkin.com/annualeditions (just click on this book's title). In addition, these sites are
referenced by number and appear where relevant in the Topic Guide on the previous two pages.

Some Web sites are continually changing their structure and content, so the information listed may not always be available.

General Sources

1. U.S. Information Agency (USIA)–*http://www.usia.gov/usis.html*–This interesting and wide-ranging USIA home page provides definition, related documentation, and discussion of topics of concern to students of global issues. The site addresses today's Hot Topics as well as ongoing issues that form the foundation of the field. Many Web links are provided.

2. World Wide Web Virtual Library: International Affairs Resources–*http://info.pitt.edu/~ian/ianres.html*–Surf this site and its extensive links to learn about specific countries and regions; to research various think tanks and international organizations; and to study such vital topics as international law, development, the international economy, human rights, and peacekeeping.

A Clash of Views

3. The Henry L. Stimson Center–*http://www.stimson.org/*–Stimson, a nonprofit and (self-described) nonpartisan organization, focuses on issues where policy, technology, and politics intersect. Use this site to find varying assessments of U.S. foreign policy in the post–cold war world and to research many other topics.

4. The Heritage Foundation–*http://www.heritage.org/*–This page offers discussion about and links to many sites having to do with foreign policy and foreign affairs, including news and commentary, policy review, events, and a resource bank.

5. The Hunger Project–*http://www.thp.org/*–Browse through this nonprofit organization's site to explore the ways in which it attempts to achieve its goal: the sustainable end to global hunger through leadership at all levels of society. The Hunger Project contends that the persistence of hunger is at the heart of the major security issues threatening our planet.

6. IISDnet–*http://iisd1.iisd.ca/*–This site of the International Institute for Sustainable Development, a Canadian organization, presents information through links to business and sustainable development, developing ideas, and Hot Topics. Linkages is its multimedia resource for environment and development policymakers.

7. The North-South Institute–*http://www.nsi-ins.ca/info.html*–Searching this site of the North-South Institute–which works to strengthen international development cooperation and enhance gender and social equity–will help you find information and debates on a variety of global issues.

8. WWW-LARCH-LK Archive: Sustainability–*http://www.clr.toronto.edu/ARCHIVES/HMAIL/larchl/0737.html*–This site gives you the opportunity to read–and respond to–a discourse on sustainability, with many different opinions and viewpoints represented.

Population

9. Penns Library: Resources by Subject–*http://www.library.upenn.edu/resources/websitest.html*–This vast site is rich in links to information about subjects of interest to students of global issues. Its extensive population and demography resources address such concerns as migration, family planning, and health and nutrition in various world regions.

10. World Health Organization–*http://www.who.ch/Welcome.html*–This home page of the World Health Organization will provide you with links to a wealth of statistical and analytical information about health and the environment in the developing world.

11. WWW Virtual Library: Demography & Population Studies–*http://coombs.anu.edu.au/ResFacilities/DemographyPage.html*–A definitive guide to demography and population studies can be found at this site. It contains a multitude of important links to information about global poverty and hunger.

Natural Resources

12. Friends of the Earth–*http://www.foe.co.uk/index.html*–This nonprofit organization, based in the United Kingdom, pursues a number of campaigns to protect Earth and its living creatures. This site has links to many environmental sites, covering such broad topics as ozone depletion, soil erosion, and biodiversity.

13. National Geographic Society–*http://www.nationalgeographic.com/*–This site provides links to National Geographic's huge archive of maps, articles, and other documents. There is a great deal of material related to the atmosphere, the oceans, and other environmental topics.

14. National Oceanic and Atmospheric Administration (NOAA)–*http://www.noaa.gov/*–Through this home page of NOAA, part of the U.S. Department of Commerce, you can find information about coastal issues, fisheries, climate, and more. The site provides many links to research materials and other Web resources related to environmental concerns.

15. Public Utilities Commission of Ohio (PUCO)–*http://www.puc.state.oh.us/consumer/gcc/index.html*–PUCO aims for this site to serve as a clearinghouse of information about global climate change. Its links provide for explanation of the science and chronology of global climate change, acronyms, definitions, and more.

16. SocioSite: Sociological Subject Areas–*http://www.pscw.uva.nl/sociosite/TOPICS/*–This huge site provides many references of interest to those interested in global issues, such as links to information on ecology and the impact of consumerism.

17. United Nations Environment Programme (UNEP)–*http://www.unep.ch/*–Consult this home page of UNEP for links to critical topics of concern to students of global issues, including desertification, migratory species, and the impact of trade on the environment. The site will direct you to useful databases and global resource information.

Political Economy

18. Belfer Center for Science and International Affairs (BCSIA)—*http://ksgwww.harvard.edu/csia/*—BCSIA is the hub of Harvard University's John F. Kennedy School of Government's research, teaching, and training in international affairs related to security, environment, and technology. This site provides insight into the development of leadership in policy making.

19. Communications for a Sustainable Future—*gopher://csf.colorado.edu/*—Information on topics in international environmental sustainability is available on this Gopher site. It pays particular attention to the political economics of protecting the environment.

20. U.S. Agency for International Development—*http://www.info.usaid.gov/*—Broad and overlapping issues such as democracy, population and health, economic growth, and development are covered on this Web site. It provides specific information about different regions and countries.

21. Virtual Seminar in Global Political Economy/Global Cities & Social Movements—*http://csf.colorado.edu/gpe/gpe95b/resources.html*—This site of Internet resources is rich in links to subjects of interest in regional environmental studies, covering topics such as sustainable cities, megacities, and urban planning. Links to many international nongovernmental organizations are included.

22. World Bank—*http://www.worldbank.org/*—News (e.g., press releases, summaries of new projects, speeches); publications; and coverage of numerous topics regarding development, countries, and regions are provided at this World Bank site. It also contains links to other important global financial organizations.

Conflict

23. DefenseLINK—*http://www.defenselink.mil/*—Learn about security news and research related publications at this U.S. Department of Defense site. Links to related sites of interest, among other things, are provided. The information systems BosniaLINK and GulfLINK can also be found here. Use the search function to investigate such issues as land mines.

24. Federation of American Scientists (FAS)—*http://www.fas.org/*—FAS, a nonprofit policy organization, maintains this site to provide coverage of and links to such topics as global security, peace and security, and governance in the post–cold war world. It notes a variety of resources of value to students of global issues.

25. ISN International Relations and Security Network—*http://www.isn.ethz.ch/*—This site, maintained by the Center for Security Studies and Conflict Research, is a clearinghouse for information on international relations and security policy. Topics are listed by category (Traditional Dimensions of Security, New Dimensions of Security, and Related Fields) and by major world region.

26. The NATO Integrated Data Service (NIDS)—*http://www.nato.int/structur/nids/nids.htm*—NIDS was created to bring information on security-related matters to within easy reach of the widest possible audience. Check out this Web site to review North Atlantic Treaty Organization documentation of all kinds, to read *NATO Review,* and to explore key issues in the field of European security and transatlantic cooperation.

Cooperation

27. Carnegie Endowment for International Peace—*http://www.ceip.org/*—An important goal of this organization is to stimulate discussion and learning among both experts and the public at large on a wide range of international issues. The site provides links to the well-respected journal *Foreign Policy,* to the Moscow Center, to descriptions of various programs, and much more.

28. Commission on Global Governance—*http://www.cgg.ch/*—This site provides access to *The Report of the Commission on Global Governance,* produced by an international group of leaders who want to find ways in which the global community can better manage its affairs. Reform of the United Nation is a goal.

29. DiploNet—*http://www.clark.net/pub/diplonet/DiploNet.html*—DiploNet is a network uniquely concerned with the needs of diplomats in the post–cold war era. It provides avenues of research into negotiation and diplomacy. It also addresses conflict management and resolution, peacemaking, and multilateral diplomacy.

30. OCED/FDI Statistics—*http://www.oecd.org/daf/cmis/fdi/statist.htm*—Explore world trade and investment trends and statistics on this site from the Organization for Economic Cooperation and Development. It provides links to many related topics and addresses the issue on a country-by-country basis.

31. U.S. Institute of Peace—*http://www.usip.org/*—USIP, which was created by the U.S. Congress to promote peaceful resolution of international conflicts, seeks to educate people and to disseminate information on how to achieve peace. Click on Highlights, Publications, Grants, Fellowships, Events, Education and Training, Research Areas, Library and Links, and About the Institute.

Values and Visions

32. Human Rights Web—*http://www.hrweb.org/*—The history of the human rights movement, text on seminal figures, landmark legal and political documents, and ideas on how individuals can get involved in helping to protect human rights around the world can be found in this valuable site.

33. InterAction—*http://www.interaction.org/advocacy/advocacy.html*—InterAction encourages grassroots action and engages government bodies and policymakers on various advocacy issues. The organization's Advocacy Committee provides this site to inform people on its initiatives to expand international humanitarian relief, refugee, and development-assistance programs.

34. RAND—*http://www.rand.org/*—RAND is a nonprofit institution that works to improve public policy through research and analysis. Links offered on this home page provide for keyword searches of certain topics and descriptions of RAND activities and major research areas (such as international relations and strategic defense policy).

35. World Wildlife Federation (WWF)—*http://www.wwf.org/*—This page will lead you to an extensive array of links to information about endangered species, wildlife management and preservation, and more. It provides many suggestions for how individuals can take an active part in protecting the biosphere.

We highly recommend that you review our Web site for expanded information and our other product lines. We are continually updating and adding links to our Web site in order to offer you the most usable and useful information that will support and expand the value of your Annual Editions. You can reach us at: *http://www. dushkin.com/annualeditions/.*

A Clash of Views

Imagine a clear, round, inflated balloon. Now imagine that a person begins to brush yellow paint onto this miniature globe; symbolically, the color yellow represents *people*. In many ways the study of global issues is ultimately the study of people. Today, there are more people occupying Earth than ever before. In addition, the world is in the midst of a period of unprecedented population growth. Not only are there many countries where the majority of people are under age 16, but because of improved health care, there are also more older people alive than ever before. The effect of a growing global population, however, goes beyond sheer numbers, for a growing population has unprecedented impacts on natural resources and social services. Population issues, then, are an appropriate place to begin the study of global issues.

Imagine that our fictional artist dips the brush into a container of blue paint to represent the world of *nature*. The natural world plays an important role in setting the international agenda. Shortages of raw materials, drought and crop failures, and pollution of waterways are just a few examples of how natural resources can have global implications.

Adding blue paint to the balloon also reveals one of the most important concepts found in this book of readings. Although the balloon originally was covered by yellow and blue paint (people and nature as separate conceptual entities), the two combined produce an entirely different color: green. Talking about nature as a separate entity or about people as though they were somehow removed from the forces of the natural world is a serious intellectual error. The people-nature relationship is one of the keys to understanding many of today's most important global issues.

The third color added to the balloon is red. It represents the *meta* component (i.e., those qualities that make human beings more than mere animals). These include new ideas and inventions, culture and values, religion and spirituality, and art and literature. The addition of the red paint immediately changes the color green to brown, again emphasizing the relationship among all three factors.

The fourth and final color added is white. This color represents *social structures*. Factors such as whether a so-

ciety is urban or rural, industrial or agrarian, planned or decentralized, and consumer-oriented or dedicated to the needs of the state fall into this category. The relationship between this component and the others is extremely important. The impact of political decisions on the environment, for example, is one of the most unusual features of the contemporary world. Historically, the forces of nature determined which species survived or perished. Today, survival depends on political decisions—or indecision. Will the whales or bald eagles survive? The answer to this question will depend on governmental activities, not evolutionary forces.

Understanding this relationship between social structure and nature (known as "ecopolitics") is important to the study of global issues.

If the painter continues to ply the paintbrush over the miniature globe, a marbling effect will become evident. In some areas, the shading will vary because one element is greater than another. The miniature system appears dynamic. Nothing is static; relationships are continually changing. This leads to a number of theoretical insights: (1) there is no such thing as separate elements, only connections or relationships; (2) changes in one area (such as the weather) will result in changes in all other areas; and (3) complex relationships make it difficult to predict events accurately, so observers are often surprised by unexpected processes and outcomes.

This book is organized along the basic lines of the balloon allegory. The first unit explores a variety of perspectives on the forces that are shaping the world of the twenty-first century. Unit 2 focuses on population. Unit 3 examines the environment and related issues (e.g., agriculture and energy). The next three units look at different aspects of the world's social structures. They explore issues of economics, national security, conflict, and international cooperation. In the final unit, a number of "meta" factors are discussed. However, the reader should be aware that, just as it was impossible to keep the individual colors from blending into new colors on the balloon, it also is impossible to separate these factors into discrete chapters in a book. Any discussion of agriculture, for example, must take into account the impact of a growing popula-

Rather than being based on the ideology and interests of the two superpowers, new political, economic, and environmental factors are interacting in an unprecedented fashion. Rapid population growth, environmental decline, and uneven economic growth are all parts of a complex situation for which there is no historic parallel. As we approach the twenty-first century, signs abound that we are entering a new era. In the words of Abraham Lincoln, "As our case is new, so we must think anew." Compounding this situation, however, is a whole series of old problems such as ethnic and religious rivalries.

The authors in this first unit provide a variety of perspectives on the trends that they believe are the most important to understanding the historic changes at work at the global level. This discussion is then pursued in greater detail in the following units.

It is important for the reader to note that although the authors look at the same world, they often come to different conclusions. This raises an important issue of values and beliefs, for it can be argued that there really is no objective reality, only differing perspectives. In short, the study of global issues will challenge each thoughtful reader to examine her or his own values and beliefs.

Looking Ahead: Challenge Questions

Do the analyses of any of the authors in this section employ the assumptions implicit in the allegory of the balloon? If so, how? If not, how are the assumptions of the authors different?

All the authors point to interactions among different factors. What are some of the relationships that they cite? How do the authors differ in terms of the relationships they emphasize?

What assets that did not exist 100 years ago do people now have to solve problems?

What events during the twentieth century have had the greatest impact on shaping the realities of contemporary international affairs?

What do you consider to be the five most pressing global problems of today? How do your answers compare to those of your family, friends, and classmates?

tion on soil and water resources, as well as new scientific breakthroughs in food production. Therefore, the organization of this book focuses attention on issue areas; it does not mean to imply that these factors are somehow separate.

With the collapse of the Soviet empire and the end of the cold war, the outlines of a new global agenda are beginning to emerge.

Preparing for the 21st Century: Winners and Losers

Paul Kennedy

Paul Kennedy is Professor of History and Director of the International Security Program at Yale University. He is the author of The Rise and Fall of the Great Powers, *among many other books.* Preparing for the Twenty-First Century, *from which this article is drawn, is published by Random House.*

1.

Everyone with an interest in international affairs must be aware that broad, global forces for change are bearing down upon humankind in both rich and poor societies alike. New technologies are challenging traditional assumptions about the way we make, trade, and even grow things. Automated workplaces in Japan intimate the end of the "factory system" that first arose in Britain's Industrial Revolution and spread around the world. Genetically engineered crops, cultivated in biotech laboratories, threaten to replace naturally grown sugar, vanilla, coconut oil, and other staple farm produce, and perhaps undermine field-based agriculture as we know it. An electronically driven, twenty-four-hour-a-day financial trading system has created a global market in, say, yen futures over which nobody really has control. The globalization of industry and services permits multinationals to switch production from one country to another (where it is usually

cheaper), benefitting the latter and hurting the former.

In addition to facing these technology-driven forces for change, human society is grappling with the effects of fast-growing demographic imbalances throughout the world. Whereas birthrates in richer societies plunge well below the rates that would replace their populations, poorer countries are experiencing a population explosion that may double or even treble their numbers over the next few decades. As these fast-swelling populations press upon the surrounding forests, grazing lands, and water supplies, they inflict dreadful damage upon local environments and may also be contributing to that process of global warming first created by the industrialization of the North a century and a half ago. With overpopulation and resource depletion undermining the social order, and with a global telecommunications revolution bringing television programs like *Dallas* and *Brideshead Revisited* to viewers everywhere from Central America to the Balkans, a vast illegal migration is under way as millions of families from the developing world strive to enter Europe and North America.

Although very different in form, these various trends from global warming to twenty-four-hour-a-day trading are *transnational* in character, crossing borders all over our planet, affecting local communities and dis-

tant societies at the same time, and reminding us that the earth, for all its divisions, is a single unit. Every country is challenged by these global forces for change, to a greater or lesser extent, and most are beginning to sense the need to prepare themselves for the coming twenty-first century. Whether *any* society is at present "well prepared" for the future is an open question;[1] but what is clear is that the regions of the globe most affected by the twin impacts of technology and demography lie in the developing world. Whether they succeed in harnessing the new technologies in an environmentally prudent fashion, and at the same time go through a demographic transition, will probably affect the prospects of global peace in the next century more than any other factor. What, then, are their chances?

Before that question can be answered, the sharp contrasts among the developing countries in the world's different regions need to be noted here.[2] Perhaps nothing better illustrates those differences than the fact that, in the 1960s, South Korea had a per capita GNP exactly the same as Ghana's (US $230), whereas today it is ten to twelve times more prosperous.[3] Both possessed a predominantly agrarian economy and had endured a half-century or more of colonial rule. Upon independence, each faced innumerable handicaps in their effort to "catch up" with the West, and although Korea possessed a greater historical and cultural coherence, its chances may have seemed less promising, since it had few natural resources (apart from tungsten) and suffered heavily during the 1950–1953 fighting.

Decades later, however, West African states remain among the most poverty-stricken countries in the world—the per capita gross national products of Niger, Sierra Leone, and Chad today, for example, are less than $500[4]—while Korea is entering the ranks of the high-income economies. Already the world's thirteenth largest trading nation, Korea is planning to become one of the richest countries of all in the twenty-first century,[5] whereas the nations of West Africa face a future, at least in the near term, of chronic poverty, malnutrition, poor health, and underdevelopment. Finally, while Korea's rising prosperity is attended by a decrease in population growth, most African countries still face a demographic explosion that erodes any gains in national output.

This divergence is not new, for there have always been richer and poorer societies; the prosperity gap in the seventeenth century—between, say, Amsterdam and the west coast of Ireland, or between such bustling Indian ports as Surat and Calcutta[6] and the inhabitants of New Guinean hill villages—must have been marked, although it probably did not equal the gulf between rich and poor nations today. The difference is that the twentieth-century global communications revolution has made such disparities widely known. This can breed resentments by poorer peoples against prosperous societies, but it can also provide a desire to emulate (as Korea emulated Japan). The key issue here is: What does it take to turn a "have not" into a "have" nation? Does it simply require imitating economic techniques, or does it involve such intangibles as culture, social structure, and attitudes toward foreign practices?

This discrepancy in performance between East Asia and sub-Saharan Africa clearly makes the term "third world" misleading. However useful the expression might have been in the 1950s, when poor, nonaligned, and recently decolonized states were at-

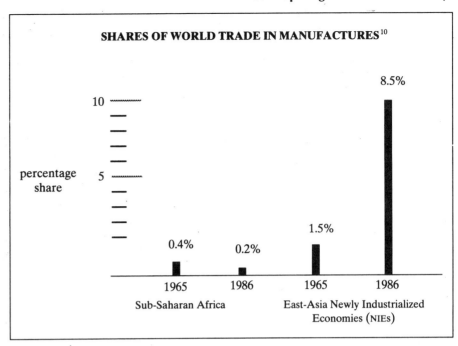

SHARES OF WORLD TRADE IN MANUFACTURES[10]

percentage share

8.5%

1.5%

0.4%   0.2%

| 1965 | 1986 | 1965 | 1986 |

Sub-Saharan Africa

East-Asia Newly Industrialized Economies (NIEs)

tempting to remain independent of the two superpower blocs,[7] the rise of super-rich oil-producing countries a decade later already made the term questionable. Now that prosperous East Asian societies—Korea, Taiwan, and Singapore—possess higher per capita GNPs than Russia, Eastern Europe, and even West European states like Portugal, the word seems less suitable than ever. With Taiwanese or Korean corporations establishing assembly plants in the Philippines, or creating distribution networks within the European Community, we need to recognize the differences that exist among non-Western economies. Some scholars now categorize *five* separate types of "developing" countries in assessing the varied potential of societies in Asia, Africa, and Latin America.[8]

Relative national growth in the 1980s confirms these differences. Whereas East Asian economies grew on average at an impressive annual rate of 7.4 percent, those in Africa and Latin America gained only 1.8 and 1.7 percent respectively[9]—and since their populations grew faster, the net result was that they slipped backward, absolutely and relatively. Differences of economic structure also grew in this decade, with African and other primary commodity-producing countries eager for higher raw-material prices, whereas the export-oriented manufacturing nations of East Asia sought

to keep commodity prices low. The most dramatic difference occurred in the shares of world trade in manufactures, a key indicator of economic competitiveness (see chart above). Thus, while some scholars still refer to a dual world economy[11] of rich and poor countries, what is emerging is increasing differentiation. Why is this so?

The developing countries most successfully catching up with the West are the trading states of the Pacific and East Asia. Except for Communist regimes there, the Pacific rim countries (including the western provinces of Canada and the United States, and in part Australia) have enjoyed a lengthy boom in manufacturing, trade, and investment; but the center of that boom is on the *Asian* side of the Pacific, chiefly fuelled by Japan's own spectacular growth and the stimulus given to neighboring economies and trans-Pacific trade. According to one source:

In 1962 the Western Pacific (notably East Asia) accounted for around 9 percent of world GNP, North America for 30 percent, and Western Europe for 31 percent. Twenty years later, the Western Pacific share had climbed to more than 15 percent, while North America's had fallen to 28 percent and Europe's to 27 percent. By the year 2000 it is likely that the Western Pacific will account for around one-quarter of world GNP, with the whole Pacific region increasing its share from just over 43 percent to around half of world GNP.[12]

East Asia's present boom is not, of course, uniform, and scholars distinguish between the different stages of economic and technological development in this vast region. Roughly speaking, the divisions would be as follows:

(a) Japan, now the world's largest or second largest financial center and, increasingly, the most innovative high-tech nation in the nonmilitary field;

(b) the four East Asian "tigers" or "dragons," the Newly Industrialized Economies (NIEs) of Singapore, Hong Kong, Taiwan, and South Korea, of which the latter two possess bigger populations and territories than the two port-city states, but all of which have enjoyed export-led growth in recent decades;

(c) the larger Southeast Asian states of Thailand, Malaysia, and Indonesia which, stimulated by foreign (chiefly Japanese) investment, are becoming involved in manufacturing, assembly, and export—it is doubtful whether the Philippines should be included in this group;

(d) finally, the stunted and impoverished Communist societies of Vietnam, Cambodia, and North Korea, as well as isolationist Myanmar pursuing its "Burmese Way to Socialism."

Because of this staggered level of development, economists in East Asia invoke the image of the "flying geese," with Japan the lead bird, followed by the East Asian NIEs, the larger Southeast Asian states, and so on. What Japan produced in one decade—relatively low-priced toys, kitchenware, electrical goods—will be imitated by the next wave of "geese" in the decade following, and by the third wave in the decade after that. However accurate the metaphor individually, the overall picture is clear; these birds are flying, purposefully and onward, to an attractive destination.

Of those states, it is the East Asian NIEs that have provided the clearest example of successful transformation. Although distant observers may regard them as similar, there are notable differences in size, population,[13] history, and political system. Even the economic structures are distinct; for example, Korea, which began its expansion at least a decade later than Taiwan (and democratized itself even more slowly), is heavily dependent upon a few enormous industrial conglomerates, or *chaebol*, of whom the top four alone (Samsung, Hyundai, Lucky-Goldstar, and Daewoo) have sales equal to half Korea's GNP. By contrast, Taiwan possesses many small companies, specializing in one or two kinds of products. While Taiwanese are concerned that their firms may lose out to foreign giants, Koreans worry that the *chaebol* will find it increasingly difficult to compete in large-scale industries like petrochemicals and semiconductors and shipbuilding at the same time.[14]

Despite such structural differences, these societies each contain certain basic characteristics, which, *taken together*, help to explain their decade-upon-decade growth. The first, and perhaps the most important, is the emphasis upon education. This derives from Confucian traditions of competitive examinations and respect for learning, reinforced daily by the mother of the family who complements what is taught at school.

To Western eyes, this process—like Japan's—appears to concentrate on rote learning and the acquisition of technical skills, and emphasizes consensus instead of encouraging individual talent and the habit of questioning authority. Even if some East Asian educators would nowadays admit that criticism, most believe that their own educational mores create social harmony and a well-trained work force. Moreover, the uniformity of the system does not exclude intense individual competitiveness; in Taiwan (where, incidentally, twelve members of the fourteen-member cabinet of 1989 had acquired Ph.D.s abroad), only the top one third of each year's 110,000 students taking the national university entrance examinations are selected, to emphasize the importance of college education.[15]

Perhaps nothing better illustrates this stress upon learning than the fact that Korea (43 million population) has around 1.4 million students in higher education, compared with 145,000 in Iran (54 million), 15,000 in Ethiopia (46 million), and 159,000 in Vietnam (64 million); or the further fact that

already by 1980 "as many engineering students were graduating from Korean institutions as in the United Kingdom, West Germany and Sweden combined."[16]

The second common characteristic of these countries is their high level of national savings. By employing fiscal measures, taxes, and import controls to encourage personal savings, large amounts of low-interest capital were made available for investment in manufacture and commerce. During the first few decades of growth, personal consumption was constrained and living standards controlled—by restrictions upon moving capital abroad, or importing foreign luxury goods—in order to funnel resources into industrial growth. While average prosperity rose, most of the fruits of economic success were plowed back into further expansion. Only when economic "take-off" was well under way has the system begun to alter; increased consumption, foreign purchases, capital investment in new homes, all allow internal demand to play a larger role in the country's growth. In such circumstances, one would expect to see overall savings ratios decline. Even in the late 1980s, however, the East Asian NIEs still had high national savings rates:

COMPARATIVE SAVINGS RATIOS, 1987[17]	
Taiwan	38.8%
Malaysia	37.8%
Korea	37.0%
Japan	32.3%
Indonesia	29.1%
US	12.7%

The third feature has been a strong political system within which economic growth is fostered. While entrepreneurship and private property are encouraged, the "tigers" never followed a laissez-faire model. Industries targeted for growth were given a variety of supports—export subsidies, training grants, tariff protection from foreign competitors. As noted above, the fiscal system was arranged to produce high savings ratios. Taxes assisted the business sector, as did energy policy. Trade unions operated under restrictions. Democracy was constrained by the governor of Hong Kong, *dirigiste* administrations in Singapore, and the military regimes in Taiwan and Korea. Only lately have free elections and party politics been permitted. Defenders of this system argued that it was necessary to restrain libertarian impulses while concentrating on economic growth, and that democratic reforms are a "reward" for the people's patience. The point is that domestic politics were unlike those in the West yet did not hurt commercial expansion.

The fourth feature was the commitment to exports, in contrast to the policies of India, which emphasize locally produced substitutes for imports, and the consumer-driven policies of the United States. This was traditional for a small, bustling trading state like Hong Kong, but it involved substantial restructuring in Taiwan and Korea, where managers and workers had to be trained to produce what foreign customers wanted. In all cases, the value of the currency was kept low, to increase exports and decrease imports. Moreover, the newly industrialized economies of East Asia took advantage of favorable global circumstances: labor costs were much lower than in North America and Europe, and they benefitted from an open international trading order, created and protected by the United States, while shielding their own industries from foreign competition.

Eventually, this led to large trade surpluses and threats of retaliation from European and American governments, reminding us of the NIEs' heavy dependence upon the current international economic system. The important thing, however, is that they targeted export-led growth in manufactures, whereas other developing nations continued to rely upon commodity exports and made little effort to cater to foreign consumers' tastes.[18] Given this emphasis on trade, it is not surprising to learn that Asia now contains seven of the world's twelve largest ports.

Finally, the East Asian NIEs possess a local model, namely Japan, which Yemen, Guatemala, and Burkina Faso simply do not have. For four decades East Asian peoples have observed the dramatic success of a non-Western neighbor, based upon its educational and technical skills, high savings ratios, long-term, state-guided targeting of industries and markets, and deter-mination to compete on world markets, though this admiration of Japan is nowadays mixed with a certain alarm at becoming members of a yen block dominated by Tokyo. While the Japanese domestic market is extremely important for the East Asian NIEs, and they benefit from Japanese investments, assembly plants, engineers, and expertise, they have little enthusiasm for a new Greater East Asia co-prosperity sphere.[19]

The benefits of economic success are seen not merely in East Asia's steadily rising standards of living. Its children are on average four or five inches taller than they were in the 1940s, and grow up in some of the world's healthiest countries:

A Taiwanese child born in 1988 could expect to live 74 years, only a year less than an American or a West German, and 15 years longer than a Taiwanese born in 1952; a South Korean born in 1988 could expect 70 years on earth, up from 58 in 1965. In 1988 the Taiwanese took in 50 percent more calories each day than they had done 35 years earlier. They had 200 times as many televisions, telephones and cars per household; in Korea the rise in the possession of these goods was even higher.[20]

In addition, the East Asian NIEs enjoy some of today's highest literacy rates, once again confirming that they are altogether closer to "first" world nations than poor, developing countries (see chart below).

Will this progress last into the twenty-first century? Politically, Hong Kong's future is completely uncertain, and many companies are relocating their headquarters elsewhere; Taiwan remains a diplomatic pariah-state because of Beijing's traditional claims; and South Korea still worries about the unpredictable, militarized regime in the north. The future of China—and of Siberia—is uncertain, and causes concern. The 1980s rise in Asian stock-market prices (driven by vast increases in the money supply) was excessive and speculative, and destined to tumble. Protectionist tendencies in the developed world threaten the trading states even more than external pressures to abandon price supports for local farmers. A rise in the value of the Korean and Taiwanese currencies has cut export earnings and reduced their overall rate of growth. Some Japanese competitors have moved production to neighboring low-cost countries such as Thailand or southern China. Sharp rises in oil prices increase the import bills. High wage awards (in Korea they increased by an average 14 percent in 1988, and by 17 percent in 1989) affect labor costs and competitiveness. The social peace, precarious in these recent democracies, is damaged by bouts of student and industrial unrest.[22]

On the other hand, these may simply be growing pains. Savings ratios are still extremely high. Large numbers of new engineers and technicians pour out of college each year. The workers' enhanced purchasing power has created a booming domestic market, and governments are investing more in housing, infrastructure, and public facilities. The labor force will not grow as swiftly as before because of the demographic slowdown, but it will be

COMPARATIVE LIVING STANDARDS[21]			
	Life Expectancy at Birth (years), 1987	Adult Literacy Rate (%), 1985	GNP per capita, 1988 US$
Niger	45	14	300
Togo	54	41	310
India	59	43	340
SINGAPORE	73	86	9,070
SOUTH KOREA	70	95	5,000
Spain	77	95	7,740
New Zealand	75	99	10,000

better educated and spend more.[23] A surge in overseas investments is assisting the long-term balance of payments. As the populous markets of Indonesia, Thailand, and Malaysia grow at double-digit rates, there is plenty of work for the trading states. A hardening of the currency can be met by greater commitment to quality exports, high rates of industrial investment, and a move into newer, high-technology manufacture—in imitation of the 1980s re-tooling of Japanese industry when its currency hardened swiftly. Nowhere else in the world would growth rates of "only" 5 or 6 percent be considered worrying, or a harbinger of decline. Barring a war in East Asia, or a widespread global slump, the signs are that the four "tigers" are better structured than most to grow in wealth and health.

2.

For confirmation of that remark, one need only consider the present difficult condition of Latin America, which lost ground in the 1980s just as East Asia was gaining it. Here again, distinctions have to be made between various countries within the continent, with its more than 400 million people in an area almost 7 million square miles stretching from the Rio Grande to Antarctica, and with a range of political cultures and socioeconomic structures. Argentina, which around 1900 had a standard of living suggesting that it was a "developed" economy, is very different from Honduras and Guyana. Similarly, population change in Latin America occurs in three distinct forms: such nations as Bolivia, the Dominican Republic, and Haiti have high fertility rates and lower life expectancies; a middle group—Brazil, Colombia, Mexico, Venezuela, Costa Rica, and Panama—is beginning to experience declines in fertility and longer life expectancy; and the temperate-zone countries of Argentina, Chile, and Uruguay have the demographic characteristics of developed countries.[24]

Despite this diversity, there are reasons for considering Latin America's prospects as a whole: the economic challenges confronting the region are similar, as are its domestic politics—in particular, the fragility of its recently emerged democracies; and each is affected by its relationship with the developed world, especially the United States.

Several decades ago, Latin America's future appeared encouraging. Sharing in the post-1950 global boom, benefitting from demand for its coffee, timber, beef, oil, and minerals, and enjoying foreign investments in its agriculture, industry, and infrastructure, the region was moving upward. In the thirty years after 1945, its production of steel multiplied twenty times, and its output of electric energy, metals, and machinery grew more than tenfold.[25] Real gross domestic product (GDP) per person rose at an annual average of 2.8 percent during the 1960s and spurted to an annual average increase of 3.4 percent in the 1970s. Unfortunately, the growth then reversed itself, and between 1980 and 1988

Latin America's real GDP per person steadily fell by an annual average of 0.9 percent.[26] In some states, such as Peru and Argentina, real income dropped by as much as one quarter during the 1980s. With very few exceptions (Chile, Colombia, the Dominican Republic, Barbados, the Bahamas), most Latin American countries now have per capita GDPs lower than they were a decade earlier, or even two decades earlier (see chart above).

The reasons for this reversal offer a striking contrast to the East Asian NIEs. Instead of encouraging industrialists to target foreign markets and stimulate the economy through export-led growth, many Latin American governments pursued a policy of import substitution, creating their own steel, cement, paper, automobiles, and electronic-goods industries, which were given protective tariffs, government

PER CAPITA GDP OF LATIN AMERICAN COUNTRIES [27]
(1988 US Dollars)

Country	1960	1970	1980	1988
Chile	1,845	2,236	2,448	2,518
Argentina	2,384	3,075	3,359	2,862
Uruguay	2,352	2,478	3,221	2,989
Brazil	1,013	1,372	2,481	2,449
Paraguay	779	931	1,612	1,557
Bolivia	634	818	983	724
Peru	1,233	1,554	1,716	1,503
Ecuador	771	904	1,581	1,477
Colombia	927	1,157	1,595	1,739
Venezuela	3,879	4,941	5,225	4,544
Guyana	1,008	1,111	1,215	995
Suriname	887	2,337	3,722	3,420
Mexico	1,425	2,022	2,872	2,588
Guatemala	1,100	1,420	1,866	1,502
Honduras	619	782	954	851
El Salvador	832	1,032	1,125	995
Nicaragua	1,055	1,495	1,147	819
Costa Rica	1,435	1,825	2,394	2,235
Panama	1,264	2,017	2,622	2,229
Dominican Republic	823	987	1,497	1,509
Haiti	331	292	386	319
Jamaica	1,610	2,364	1,880	1,843
Trinidad & Tobago	3,848	4,927	8,116	5,510
Barbados	2,000	3,530	3,994	4,233
Bahamas	8,448	10,737	10,631	11,317

GROWTH OF LATIN AMERICAN INDEBTEDNESS (SELECTED COUNTRIES)[31]						
Country	Total External Debt (billion US $)			Long-Term Public Debt As A Percentage of GNP		
	1977	1982	1987	1977	1982	1987
Argentina	8.1	32.4	53.9	10	31	62
Brazil	28.3	68.7	109.4	13	20	29
Chile	4.9	8.5	18.7	28	23	89
Guyana	0.4	0.9	1.2	100	158	353
Honduras	0.6	1.6	3.1	29	53	71
Jamaica	1.1	2.7	4.3	31	69	139
Mexico	26.6	78.0	93.7	25	32	59
Venezuela	9.8	27.0	29.0	10	16	52

subsidies, and tax-breaks to insulate them from international competition. As a result, their products became less attractive abroad.[28] Moreover, while it was relatively easy to create a basic iron and steel industry, it proved harder to establish high-tech industries like computers, aerospace, machine-tools, and pharmaceuticals—most of these states therefore still depend on imported manufactured goods, whereas exports chiefly consist of raw materials like oil, coffee, and soybeans.[29]

Secondly, economic growth was accompanied by lax financial policies and an increasing reliance upon foreign borrowings. Governments poured money not only into infrastructure and schools but also into state-owned enterprises, large bureaucracies, and oversized armed forces, paying for them by printing money and raising loans from Western (chiefly US) banks and international agencies. The result was that public spending's share of GDP soared, price inflation accelerated, and was further increased by index-linked rises in salaries and wages. Inflation became so large that it was difficult to comprehend, let alone to combat. According to the 1990 *World Resources* report, "in 1989, for example, annual inflation in Nicaragua was more than 3,400 percent; in Argentina inflation reached 3,700 percent, in Brazil almost 1,500 percent, and in Peru nearly 3,000 percent. Ecuador, with only 60 percent in-

flation, did comparatively well."[30] In such circumstances the currency becomes worthless, as does the idea of seeking to raise national savings rates for long-term capital investment.

Another result is that some Latin American countries find themselves among the most indebted in the world, as the chart below shows. Total Latin American indebtedness now equals about $1,000 for every man, woman, and child. But instead of being directed into productive investment, that money has been wasted domestically or disappeared as "capital flight" to private accounts in United States and European banks. This has left most countries incapable of repaying even the interest on their loans. Defaults on loans (or suspension of interest payments) then produced a drying up of capital from indignant Western banks and a net capital *outflow* from Latin America just when it needed capital to aid economic growth.[32] Starved of foreign funds and with currencies made worthless by hyperinflation, many countries are in a far worse position than could have been imagined twenty-five years ago.[33] For a while, it was even feared that the region's financial problems might undermine parts of the international banking system. It now appears that the chief damage will be in the continent itself, where 180 million people (40 percent) are living in poverty—a rise of 50 million alone in the 1980s.

Given such profligacy, and the conservative, "anti–big government" incumbents in the White House during the 1980s, it was predictable that Latin America would come under pressure—from the World Bank, the IMF, private bankers, Washington itself—to slash public spending, control inflation, and repay debts. Such demands were easier said than done in the existing circumstances. Islands of democracy (e.g., Costa Rica) did exist, but many states were ruled by right-wing military dictatorships or social revolutionaries; internal guerrilla wars, military *coups d'état*, labor unrest were common. Even as democracy began to reassert itself in the 1980s, the new leaders found themselves in a near-impossible situation: inheritors of the high external debts contracted by the outgoing regimes, legatees in many cases of inflationary index-linked wage systems, targets of landowner resentment and/or of guerrilla attacks, frustrated by elaborate and often corrupt bureaucracies, and deficient in trained personnel. While grappling with these weaknesses, they discovered that the Western world, which applauded the return to democracy, was unsympathetic to fresh lending, increasingly inclined to protectionism, and demanding unilateral measures (e.g., in the Amazon rain forests) to stop global warming.

Two other weaknesses have also slowed any hoped-for recovery. One is the unimpressive accomplishments of the educational systems. This is not due to an absence of schools and universities, as in parts of Africa. Many Latin American countries have extensive public education, dozens of universities, and high adult literacy rates; Brazil, for example, has sixty-eight universities, Argentina forty-one.[34] The real problem is neglect and under-investment. One citizen bemoaned the collapse in Argentina as follows:

Education, which kept illiteracy at bay for more than a century, lies in ruins. The universities are unheated and many public schools lack panes for their window frames. Last summer [1990] an elementary school teacher with ten years' experience earned less than $110 a month. An associate professor at the Universidad de Buenos Aires, teaching ten hours a week, was paid $37 a month. A doctor's salary at a municipal hospital was $120 a month.... At times, teachers took turns teaching, or cut their class hours, because they and their students could not afford transportation.[35]

Presumably, if resources were available, those decaying educational and health-care structures could be resuscitated, helping national recovery; but where the capital can be raised in present circumstances is difficult to see. Moreover, in the strife-torn countries of Central America there is little education to begin with; in Guatemala, the latest census estimated that 63 percent of those ten years of age and older were illiterate, while in Honduras the illiteracy rate was 40 percent.[36] Unfortunately, it is in the educationally most deprived Latin American countries that resources are being eroded by swift population increases.

Despite these disadvantages, recent reports on Latin America have suggested that the "lost decade" of the 1980s will be followed by a period of recovery. The coming of democratic regimes, the compromises emerging from protracted debt-recycling talks, the stiff economic reforms (cutting public spending, abandoning indexation) to reduce inflation rates, the replacement of "state protectionism with import liberalization and privatization,"[37] the conversion of budget deficits into surpluses — all this has caused the Inter-American Development Bank to argue that "a decisive and genuine takeoff" is at hand, provided the new policies are sustained.[38] Growth has resumed in Argentina, Mexico, and Venezuela. Even investment bankers are reported to be returning to the continent.

Whether these changes are going to be enough remains uncertain, especially since the newly elected governments face widespread resentment at the proposed reforms. As one commentator put it, "Much of Latin America is entering the 1990s in a race between economic deterioration and political progress."[39] Whereas Spain, Portugal, and Greece moved to democracy while enjoying reasonable prosperity, Latin America (like Eastern Europe) has to make that change as its economies flounder—which

places immense responsibilities upon the political leadership.

Although it can be argued that the region's future is in its own hands, it will also be heavily influenced by the United States. In many ways, the US–Latin America leadership is similar to that between Japan and the East Asian NIEs, which are heavily dependent upon Japan as their major market and source of capital.[40] Yet there is more to this relationship than Latin America's economic dependence upon the United States, whose banking system has also suffered because of Latin American indebtedness. United States exports, which are fifty times larger to this region than to Eastern Europe, were badly hurt by Latin America's economic difficulties, and they would benefit greatly from a resumption of growth. The United States' own environment may now be threatened by the diminution of the Amazon and Central American rain forests. Its awful drug problem, driven by domestic demand, is fuelled by Latin American supplies—more than 80 percent of the cocaine and 90 percent of the marijuana entering the United States are produced or move through this region.

Finally, the population of the United States is being altered by migration from Mexico, the Caribbean, and Central America; if there should be a widespread socioeconomic collapse south of the Rio Grande, the "spillover" effects will be felt across the United States. Instead of being marginalized by the end of the cold war, Latin America may present Washington with formidable and growing challenges—social, environmental, financial, and ultimately political.[41] Thus, while the region's own politicians and citizens have to bear the major responsibility for recovery, richer nations—especially the United States—may find it in their own best interest to lend a hand.

3.

If these remarks disappoint readers in Brazil or Peru, they may care to glance, in grim consolation, at the world of Islam. It is one thing to face population pressures, shortage of resources, educational/technological deficiencies, and regional conflicts, which would challenge the wisest governments. But it is another when

regimes themselves stand in angry resentment of global forces for change instead of (as in East Asia) selectively responding to such trends. Far from preparing for the twenty-first century, much of the Arab and Muslim world appears to have difficulty in coming to terms with the nineteenth century, with its composite legacy of secularization, democracy, laissez-faire economics, industrial and commercial linkages among different nations, social change, and intellectual questioning. If one needed an example of the importance of cultural attitudes in explaining a society's response to change, contemporary Islam provides it.

Before analyzing the distinctive role of Islamic culture, one should first note the danger of generalizing about a region that contains such variety. After all, it is not even clear what *name* should be used to describe this part of the earth. To term it the "Middle East"[42] is, apart from its Atlantic-centered bias, to leave out such North African states as Libya, Tunisia, Algeria, and Morocco. To term it the "Arab World"[43] is to exclude Iran (and, of course, Israel), the Kurds, and the non-Muslim tribes of southern Sudan and Mauritania. Even the nomenclature Islam, or the Muslim world, disguises the fact that millions of Catholics, Copts, and Jews live in these lands, and that Islamic societies extend from West Africa to Indonesia.[44]

In addition, the uneven location of oil in the Middle East has created a division between super-rich and dreadfully poor societies that has no equivalent in Central America or sub-Saharan African.[45] Countries like Kuwait (2 million), the United Arab Emirates (1.3 million), and Saudi Arabia (11.5 million) enjoy some of the world's highest incomes, but exist alongside populous neighbors one third as rich (Jordan, Iran, Iraq) or even one tenth as rich (Egypt, Yemen). The gap is accentuated by different political systems: conservative, antidemocratic, traditionalist in the Gulf sheikdoms; demagogic, populist, militarized in countries such as Libya, Syria, Iraq, and Iran.

The 1990 Iraqi attack upon Kuwait, and the different responses of the Saudi elites on the one hand and the street masses in Amman or Rabat on the other, illustrated this divide between "haves" and "have-nots" in the Muslim world. The presence of millions of Egyptian, Yemeni, Jordanian, and Palestinian *Gastarbeiter* in the oil-rich states simply increased the mutual resentments, while the Saudi and Emirate habit of giving extensive aid to Iraq during its war against Iran, or to Egypt to assist its economic needs, reinforces the impression of wealthy but precarious regimes seeking to achieve security by bribing their larger, jealous neighbors.[46] Is it any wonder that the unemployed, badly housed urban masses, despairing of their own secular advancement, are attracted to religious leaders or "strongmen" appealing to Islamic pride, a sense of identity, and resistance to foreign powers and their local lackeys?

More than in any other developing region, then, the future of the Middle East and North Africa is affected by issues of war and conflict. The region probably contains more soldiers, aircraft, missiles, and other weapons than anywhere else in the world, with billions of dollars of armaments having been supplied by Western, Soviet, and Chinese producers during the past few decades. In view of the range and destructiveness of these weapons, another Arab-Israeli war would be a nightmare, yet many Muslim states still regard Israel with acute hostility. Even if the Arab-Israeli antagonism did not exist, the region is full of other rivalries, between Syria and Iraq, Libya and Egypt, Iran and Iraq, and so on. Vicious one-man dictatorships glare threateningly at arch-conservative, antidemocratic, feudal sheikdoms. Fundamentalist regimes exist from Iran to the Sudan. Terrorist groups in exile threaten to eliminate their foes. Unrest among the masses puts a question mark over the future of Egypt, Algeria, Morocco, Jordan.[47] The recent fate of Lebanon, instead of serving as a warning against sectarian fanaticism, is more often viewed as a lesson in power politics, that the strong will devour the weak.

To the Western observer brought up in Enlightenment traditions—or, for that matter, to economic rationalists preaching the virtues of the borderless world—the answer to the Muslim nations' problems would appear to be a vast program of *education*, not simply in the technical, skills-acquiring sense

but also to advance parliamentary discourse, pluralism, and a secular civic culture. Is that not the reason, after all, for the political stability and economic success of Scandinavia or Japan today?

If that argument is correct, then such an observer would find few of those features in contemporary Islam. In countries where fundamentalism is strong, there is (obviously) little prospect of education or advancement for the female half of the population.[48] Where engineers and technicians exist, their expertise has all too often been mobilized for war purposes, as in Iraq. Tragically, Egypt possesses a large and bustling university system but a totally inadequate number of jobs for graduates and skilled workers, so that millions of both are underemployed. In Yemen, to take an extreme example, the state of education is dismal. By contrast, the oil-rich states have poured huge resources into schools, technical institutes, and universities, but these alone are insufficient to create an "enterprise culture" that would produce export-led manufacturing along East Asian lines. Ironically, possession of vast oil reserves could be a disadvantage, since it reduces the incentive to rely upon the skills and quality of the people, as occurs in countries (Japan, Switzerland) with few natural resources. Such discouraging circumstances may also explain why many educated and entrepreneurial Arabs, who passionately wanted their societies to borrow from the West, have emigrated.

It is difficult to know whether the reason for the Muslim world's troubled condition is cultural or historical. Western critics pointing to the region's religious intolerance, technological backwardness, and feudal cast of mind often forget that, centuries before the Reformation, Islam led the world in mathematics, cartography, medicine, and many other aspects of science and industry; and contained libraries, universities, and observatories, when Japan and America possessed none and Europe only a few. These assets were later sacrificed to a revival of traditionalist thought and the sectarian split between Shi'ite and Sunni Muslims, but Islam's retreat into itself—its being "out of step with History," as one author termed it[49]—

was probably also a response to the rise of a successful, expansionist Europe.

Sailing along the Arab littoral, assisting in the demise of the Mughal Empire, penetrating strategic points with railways, canals, and ports, steadily moving into North Africa, the Nile Valley, the Persian Gulf, the Levant, and then Arabia itself, dividing the Middle East along unnatural boundaries as part of a post–First World War diplomatic bargain, developing American power to buttress and then replace European influences, inserting an Israeli state in the midst of Arab peoples, instigating coups against local popular leaders, and usually indicating that this part of the globe was important only for its oil—the Western nations may have contributed more to turning the Muslim world into what it is today than outside commentators are willing to recognize.[50] Clearly, the nations of Islam suffer many self-inflicted problems. But if much of their angry, confrontational attitudes toward the international order today are due to a long-held fear of being swallowed up by the West, little in the way of change can be expected until that fear is dissipated.

4.

The condition of sub-Saharan Africa—"the third world's third world," as it has been described—is even more desperate.[51] When one considers recent developments such as perestroika in the former Soviet Union, the coming integration of Europe, and the economic miracle of Japan and the East Asian NIEs, remarked a former president of Nigeria, General Olusegun Obasanjo, and "contrasting all this with what is taking place in Africa, it is difficult to believe that we inhabit the same historical time."[52] Recent reports upon the continent's plight are extraordinarily gloomy, describing Africa as "a human and environmental disaster area," as "moribund," "marginalized," and "peripheral to the rest of the world," and having so many intractable problems that some foreign development experts are abandoning it to work elsewhere. In the view of the World Bank, virtually everywhere else in the world is likely to experience a decline in poverty by the year 2000 *except* Africa, where things will only get worse.[53] "Sub-Saharan Africa," concludes one economist, "suffers from a combination of economic, social, political, institutional and environmental handicaps which have so far largely defied development efforts by the African countries and their donors."[54] How, an empathetic study asks, can Africa survive?[55]

The unanimity of views is remarkable, given the enormous variety among the forty-five states that comprise sub-Saharan Africa.[56] Nine of them have fewer than one million people each, whereas Nigeria contains about 110 million. Some lie in the desert, some in tropical rain forests. Many are rich in mineral deposits, others have only scrubland. While a number (Botswana, Cameroun, Congo, Gabon, Kenya) have seen significant increases in living standards since independence, they are the exception—suggesting that the obstacles to growth on East Asian lines are so deep-rooted and resistant to the "development strategies" of foreign experts and/or their own leaders that it may require profound changes in attitude to achieve recovery.

This was not the mood thirty years ago, when the peoples of Africa were gaining their independence. True, there was economic backwardness, but this was assumed to have been caused by decades of foreign rule, leading to dependency upon a single metropolitan market, monoculture, lack of access to capital, and so on. Now that Africans had control of their destinies, they could build industries, develop cities, airports, and infrastructure, and attract foreign investment and aid from either Western powers or the USSR and its partners. The boom in world trade during the 1950s and 1960s, and demand for commodities, strengthened this optimism. Although some regions were in need, Africa as a whole was self-sufficient in food and, in fact, a net food exporter. Externally, African states were of increasing importance at the United Nations and other world bodies.

What went wrong? The unhappy answer is "lots of things." The first, and perhaps most serious, was that over the following three decades the population mushroomed as imported medical techniques and a reduction in malaria-borne mosquitoes drastically curtailed infant mortality. Africa's population was already increasing at an average annual rate of 2.6 percent in the 1960s, jumped to 2.9 percent during the 1970s, and increased to over 3 percent by the late 1980s, implying a doubling in size every twenty-two years; this was, therefore, the highest rate for any region in the world.[57]

In certain countries, the increases were staggering. Between 1960 and 1990, Kenya's population quadrupled, from 6.3 million to 25.1 million, and Côte d'Ivoire's jumped from 3.8 million to 12.6 million. Altogether Africa's population—including the North African states—leapt from 281 to 647 million in three decades.[58] Moreover, while the majority of Africans inhabit rural settlements, the continent has been becoming urban at a dizzying speed. Vast shanty-cities have already emerged on the edges of national capitals (such as Accra in Ghana, Monrovia in Liberia, and Lilongwe in Malawi). By 2025, urban dwellers are predicted to make up 55 percent of Africa's total population.

The worst news is that the increase is unlikely to diminish in the near future. Although most African countries spend less than 1 percent of GNP on health care and consequently have the highest infant mortality rates in the world—in Mali, for example, there are 169 infant deaths for every 1,000 live births—those rates are substantially less than they were a quarter century ago and will tumble further in the future, which is why demographers forecast that Africa's population in 2025 will be nearly three times that of today.[59]

There remains one random and tragic factor which may significantly affect all these (late 1980s) population projections—the AIDS epidemic, which is especially prevalent in Africa. Each new general study has raised the global total of people who are already HIV positive. For example, in June 1991, the World Health Organization abandoned its earlier estimate that 25–30 million people throughout the world would be infected by the year 2000, and suggested instead that the total could be closer to 40 million, and even that may be a gross underestimate.[60] Without question, Africa is the continent most deeply affected by AIDS, with entire families suffering from the disease. Tests of pregnant women in certain African families reveal that 25–30 percent are now HIV positive.[61] Obviously, this epidemic would alter the earlier projections of a doubling or trebling of Africa's total population over the next few decades—and in the worst possible way: family sizes would still be much larger than in most other regions of the globe, but tens of millions of Africans would be dying of AIDS, further crushing the world's most disadvantaged continent.

The basic reason why the present demographic boom will not otherwise be halted swiftly is traditional African belief-systems concerning fecundity, children, ancestors, and the role of women. Acutely aware of the invisible but pervasive presence of their ancestors, determined to expand their lineage, regarding childlessness or small families as the work of evil spirits, most Africans seek to have as many children as possible; a woman's virtue and usefulness are measured by the number of offspring she can bear. "Desired family size," according to polls of African women, ranges from five to nine children. The social attitudes that lead women in North America, Europe, and Japan to delay childbearing—education, career ambitions, desire for independence—scarcely exist in African societies; where such emerge, they are swiftly suppressed by familial pressures.[62]

This population growth has not been accompanied by equal or larger increases in Africa's productivity, which would of course transform the picture. During the 1960s, farm output was rising by around 3 percent each year, keeping pace with the population, but since 1970 agricultural production has grown at only half that rate. Part of this decline was caused by the drought, hitting countries south of the Sahara. Furthermore, existing agricultural resources have been badly eroded by overgrazing—caused by the sharp rise in the number of cattle and goats—as well as by deforestation in order to provide fuel and shelter for the growing population. When rain falls, the water runs off the denuded fields, taking the top-soil with it.

None of this was helped by changes in agricultural production, with farmers encouraged to grow tea, coffee, cocoa, palm oil, and rubber for export rather than food for domestic consumption. After benefitting from high commodity prices in the early stages, producers suffered a number of blows. Heavy taxation on cash crops, plus mandatory governmental marketing, reduced the incentives to increase output; competition grew from Asian and Latin American producers; many African currencies were overvalued, which hurt exports; and in the mid-1970s, world commodity prices tumbled. Yet the cost of imported manufactures and foodstuffs remained high, and sub-Saharan Africa was badly hurt by the quadrupling of oil prices.[63]

These blows increased Africa's indebtedness in ways that were qualitatively new. Early, postcolonial borrowings were driven by the desire for modernization, as money was poured into cement works, steel plants, airports, harbors, national airlines, electrification schemes, and telephone networks. Much of it, encouraged from afar by international bodies like the World Bank, suffered from bureaucratic interference, a lack of skilled personnel, unrealistic planning, and inadequate basic facilities, and now lies half-finished or (where completed) suffers from lack of upkeep. But borrowing to pay for imported oil, or to feed half the nation's population, means that indebtedness rises without any possible return on the borrowed funds. In consequence, Africa's total debt expanded from $14 billion in 1973 to $125 billion in 1987, when its capacity to repay was dropping fast; by the mid-1980s, payments on loans consumed about half of Africa's export earnings, a proportion even greater than for Latin American debtor nations. Following repeated debt reschedulings, Western bankers—never enthusiastic to begin with—virtually abandoned private loans to Africa.[64]

As a result, Africa's economy is in a far worse condition now than at independence, apart from a few countries like Botswana and Mauritius. Perhaps the most startling illustration of its plight is the fact that "excluding South Africa, the nations of sub-Saharan Africa with their 450 million people have a total GDP less than that of Belgium's 11 million people"; in fact, the entire continent generates roughly 1 percent of the world GDP.[65] Africa's share of world markets has shriveled just as East Asia's share has risen fast.

Plans for modernization lie unrealized. Manufacturing still represents only 11 percent of Africa's economic activity—scarcely up from the 9 percent share in 1965; and only 12 percent of the continent's exports is composed of manufactures (compared with Korea's 90 percent). There is a marked increase in the signs of decay: crumbling infrastructure, power failures, broken-down communications, abandoned projects, and everywhere the pressure of providing for increasing populations. Already Africa needs to import 15 million tons of maize a year to achieve minimal levels of food consumption, but with population increasing faster than agricultural output, that total could multiply over the next decade—implying an even greater diversion of funds from investment and infrastructure.[66]

Two further characteristics worsen Africa's condition. The first is the prevalence of wars, *coups d'état*, and political instability. This is partly the legacy of the European "carve-up" of Africa, when colonial boundaries were drawn without regard for the differing tribes and ethnic groups,[67] or even of earlier conquests by successful tribes of neighboring lands and peoples; Ethiopia, for example, is said to contain 76 ethnic groups and 286 languages.[68] While it is generally accepted that those boundaries cannot be unscrambled, most of them are clearly artificial. In extreme cases like Somalia, the "state" has ceased to exist. And in most other African countries, governments do not attract the loyalty of citizens (except perhaps kinsmen of the group in power), and ethnic tensions have produced innumerable civil wars—from Biafra's attempt to secede from Nigeria, to the conflict between Arab north and African south in the Sudan, to Eritrean struggles to escape from Ethiopia, to the Tutsi-Hutu struggle in Burundi, to clashes and suppressions and guerrilla campaigns from Uganda to the Western Sahara, from Angola to Mozambique.[69]

These antagonisms have often been worsened by struggles over ideology and government authority. The rulers of many new African states rapidly switched either to a personal dictatorship, or single-party rule. They also embraced a Soviet or Maoist political

economy, instituting price controls, production targets, forced industrialization, the takeover of private enterprises, and other features of "scientific socialism" that—unknown to them—were destroying the Soviet economy. Agriculture was neglected, while bureaucracy flourished. The result was the disappearance of agricultural surpluses, inattention to manufacturing for the world market, and the expansion of party and government bureaucracies, exacerbating the region's problems.

The second weakness was the wholly inadequate investment in human resources and in developing a culture of entrepreneurship, scientific inquiry, and technical prowess. According to one survey, Africa has been spending less than $1 each year on research and development per head of population, whereas the United States was spending $200 per head. Consequently, Africa's scientific population has always trailed the rest of the world:

NUMBERS OF SCIENTISTS AND ENGINEERS PER MILLION OF POPULATION[70]	
Japan	3,548
US	2,685
Europe	1,632
Latin America	209
Arab States	202
Asia (minus Japan)	99
Africa	53

In many African countries—Malawi, Zambia, Lesotho—government spending on education has fallen, so that, after some decades of advance, a smaller share of children are now in school. While there is a hunger for learning, it cannot be satisfied beyond the secondary level except for a small minority. Angola, for example, had 2.4 million pupils in primary schools in 1982–1983, but only 153,000 in secondary schools and a mere 4,700 in higher education.[71] By contrast, Sweden, with a slightly smaller total population, had 570,000 in secondary education and 179,000 in higher education.[72]

Despite these relative weaknesses, some observers claim to have detected signs of a turnaround. With the exception of intransigent African socialists,[73] many leaders are now attempting to institute reforms. In return for "structural adjustments," that is, measures to encourage free enterprise, certain African societies have secured additional loans from Western nations and the World Bank. The latter organization has identified past errors (many of them urged on African governments and funded by itself), and encouraged economic reforms. Mozambique, Ghana, and Zambia have all claimed recent successes in reversing negative growth, albeit at considerable social cost.

Democratic principles are also returning to the continent: the dismantling of apartheid in South Africa, the cease-fire in Angola, the independence of Namibia, the success of Botswana's record of democracy and prosperity, the cries for reforms in Gabon, Kenya, and Zaire, the rising awareness among African intellectuals of the transformations in East Asia, may all help—so the argument goes—to change attitudes, which is the prerequisite for recovery.[74] Moreover, there are local examples of economic self-improvement, cooperative ventures to halt erosion and improve yields, and village-based schemes of improvement.[75] This is, after all, a continent of enormous agricultural and mineral resources, provided they can be sensibly exploited.

Despite such signs of promise, conditions are likely to stay poor. Population increases countered only by the growing toll of AIDS victims, the diminution of grazing lands and food supplies, the burdens of indebtedness, the decay of infrastructures and reduced spending on health care and education, the residual strength of animist religions and traditional belief-systems, the powerful hold of corrupt bureaucracies and ethnic loyalties... all those tilt against the relatively few African political leaders, educators, scientists, and economists who perceive the need for changes.

What does this mean for Africa's future? As the Somalian disaster unfolds, some observers suggest that parts of the continent may be taken over and administered from the outside, rather like the post–1919 League of Nations mandates. By contrast, other experts argue that disengagement by developed countries might have the positive effect of compelling

Africans to begin a *self-driven* recovery, as well as ending the misuse of aid monies.[76] Still others feel that Africa cannot live without the West, although its leaders and people will have to abandon existing habits, and development aid must be more intelligently applied.[77] Whichever view is correct, the coming decade will be critical for Africa. Even a partial recovery would give grounds for hope; on the other hand, a second decade of decline, together with a further surge in population, would result in catastrophe.

5.

From the above, it is clear that the developing countries' response to the broad forces for global change is going to be uneven. The signs are that the gap between success and failure will widen; one group enjoys interacting beneficial trends, while others suffer from linked weaknesses and deficiencies.[78]

This is most clearly the case with respect to demography. As noted earlier, the commitment of the East Asian trading states to education, manufacturing, and export-led growth produced a steady rise in living standards, and allowed those societies to make the demographic transition to smaller family sizes. This was in marked contrast to sub-Saharan Africa where, because of different cultural attitudes and social structures, improved health care and rising incomes led, *not* to a drop in population growth, but to the opposite. Just before independence in 1960, for example, the average Kenyan woman had 6.2 children, whereas by 1980 she had 8.2[79]—and that in a period when Africa's economic prospects were fading.

In Africa's case the "global trend" which drives all others is, clearly, the demographic explosion. It spills into every domain—overgrazing, local conflicts over water and wood supplies, extensive unplanned urbanization, strains upon the educational and social structures, reliance upon imported food supplies (at the cost of increasing indebtedness), ethnic tensions, domestic unrest, border wars. Only belatedly are some African governments working to persuade families to limit their size as people become aware that access to family planning, plus improved educational opportunities for women, produce sig-

nificant declines in birth rates. Against such promising indications stand the many cultural, gender-related, and economic forces described above that encourage large families. This resistance to change is aided by Africa's general lack of resources. Raising Somalia's female literacy rate (6 percent) to South Korea's (88 percent) to produce a demographic transition sounds fine until one considers how so ambitious a reform could be implemented and paid for. Unfortunately, as noted above, the projections suggest that, as Africa's population almost trebles over the next few decades, the only development curtailing it could be the rapid growth of AIDS.[80]

In many parts of Latin America, the demographic explosion will also affect the capacity to handle globally driven forces for change. While wide differences in total fertility rates exist between the moderate-climate countries and those in the tropics, the overall picture is that Latin America's population, which was roughly equal to that of United States and Canada in 1960, is increasing so swiftly that it will be more than double the latter in 2025.[81] Even if birth-rates are now declining in the larger countries, there will still be enormous increases: Mexico's population will leap to 150 million by 2025 and Brazil's to 245 million.[82] This implies a very high incidence of child poverty and malnutrition, further strain upon already inadequate health-care and educational services, the crowding of millions of human beings into a dozen or more "mega-cities," pollution, the degradation of grazing land, forests, and other natural resources. In Mexico, for example, 44 million people are without sewers and 21 million without potable water, which means that when disease (e.g., cholera) strikes, it spreads swiftly.[83] These are not strong foundations upon which to improve the region's relative standing in an increasingly competitive international economic order.

In this regard, many Muslim states are in a similar or worse position; in no Arab country is the population increasing by less than 2 percent a year,[84] and in most the rate is considerably higher. The region's total population of more than 200 million will double in less than twenty-five years and city populations are growing twice as fast as national averages. This puts enormous pressures upon scarce food, water, and land resources, and produces unbalanced populations. Already, in most Arab countries at least four out of every ten people are under the age of fifteen—the classic recipe for subsequent social unrest and political revolution. One in five Egyptian workers is jobless, as is one in four Algerian workers.[85] In what is widely regarded as the most turbulent part of the world, therefore, demography is contributing to the prospects of future unrest year by year. Even the Israeli-Palestine quarrel has become an issue of demography, with the influx of Soviet Jews seen as countering the greater fertility of the Palestinians.

There is, moreover, little likelihood that population growth will fall in the near future. Since infant mortality rates in many Muslim countries are still high, further improvements in prenatal care will produce rises in the numbers surviving, as is happening in the Gulf States and Saudi Arabia (see chart).

As elsewhere, politics intrudes; many regimes are deliberately encouraging women to have large families, arguing that this adds to the country's military strength. "Bear a child," posters in Iraq proclaim, "and you pierce an arrow in the enemy's eye."[87] Countries such as Iraq and Libya offer many incentives for larger families, as do the Gulf States and Saudi Arabia, anxious to fill their oil-rich lands with native-born rather than foreign workers. Only in Egypt are propaganda campaigns launched to curb family size, but even if that is successful—despite resistance from the Muslim Brotherhood—present numbers are disturbing. With a current population of over 55 million Egyptians, six out of ten of whom are under twenty, and with an additional one million being born every eight months, the country is in danger of bursting at the seams during the next few decades.

6.

For much the same reasons, we ought to expect a differentiated success rate among developing countries in handling environmental challenges, with the newly industrializing East Asian economies way ahead of the others. This is not to ignore significant local schemes to improve the ecology that are springing up in Africa and the interesting proposals for "sustainable development" elsewhere in the developing world,[88] or to forget that industrialization has caused environmental damage in East Asia, from choked roads to diminished forests. Yet the fact is that nations with lots of resources (capital, scientists, engineers, technology, a per capita GNP of over US $4,000) are better able to deal with environmental threats than those without money, tools, or personnel. By contrast, it is the poorer societies (Egypt, Bangladesh, Ethiopia) that, lacking financial and personnel resources, find it difficult to respond to cyclones, floods, drought, and other natural disasters—with their devastated populations augmenting the millions of refugees and migrants. Should global warming produce sea-level rises and heightened storm surges, teeming island populations from the Caribbean to the Pacific are in danger of being washed away.[89]

Finally, it is the population explosion in Latin America and South Asia and Africa that is the major cause for the overgrazing, soil erosion, salinization, and clearing of the tropical rain forests, which, while contributing to global warming, also hurts the local populations and exacerbates regional struggles for power. Elsewhere, in the Middle East for example, supplies of water are the greatest concern, especially in view of growing demographic pressures. The average Jordanian now uses only one third the amount of domestic water consumed in Israel and has little hope of increasing the supply, yet Jordan's population, which is now roughly equal to Israel's, is expected to double during the next twenty years.[90]

With all governments in the region striving to boost agricultural output and highly sensitive to famine and unrest among their peasant farmers, the search for secure water influences domestic politics, international relations, and spending priorities. Egypt worries that either the Sudan or Ethiopia might dam the Nile in order to increase irrigation. Syria and Iraq have taken alarm at Turkey's new Ataturk dam, which can interrupt the flow of the Euphrates. Jordan, Syria, and Israel quarrel over water rights in the Litani, Yarmuk, and Jordan river valleys, as do Arabs and Jews over well supplies in the occupied West Bank. Saudi Arabia's ambition to grow wheat is draining its aquifers, and the same will occur with Libya's gigantic scheme to tap water from under the Sahara.[91] As more and more people struggle for the same—or diminishing—amounts of water, grand ideas about preparing for the twenty-first century look increasingly irrelevant; surviving *this* century becomes the order of the day.

COMPARATIVE INFANT MORTALITY RATES[86] (Infant deaths per 1,000 live births)		
	1965–1970	1985–1990
Algeria	150	74
Egypt	170	85
Sudan	156	108
Yemen Arab Republic	186	116
Saudi Arabi	140	71
Kuwait	55	19
Iraq	111	69
Japan	16	5
US	22	10
Sweden	13	6

What are the implications for these societies of the new technologies being developed by Western scientists? The revolution in biotech farming, for example, is of great relevance to developing countries, even if the consequences will be mixed. Improved strains of plants and more sophisticated pesticides and fertilizers could, potentially, enhance yields in the developing world, reduce pressures upon marginal lands, restore agricultural self-sufficiency, improve the balance of payments, and raise standards of living. Since much biotech does not involve expensive enterprise, we could witness farmers' groups experimenting with new seeds, improved breeding techniques, cultivation of gene tissue, regional gene-banks, and other developments.

Yet it is also possible that giant pharmaceutical and agro-chemical firms in the "first" world may monopolize much of the knowledge—and the profits—that this transformation implies. Surpluses in global foodstuffs caused by the biotech revolution could be used to counter malnutrition. They could also undermine commodity prices and hurt societies in which most inhabitants were employed in agriculture. Removing food production from the farm to the laboratory—which is what is implied by recent breakthroughs in biotech agriculture—would undercut agrarian societies, which is why some biotech experts in the development field call for serious planning in "agricultural conversion," that is, conversion into other economic activities.[92]

While the uses of biotechnology are relatively diverse, that is not the case with robotics and automated manufacture. The requirements for an indigenous robotics industry—capital, an advanced electronics sector, design engineers, a dearth of skilled labor—suggest that countries like Taiwan and Korea may follow Japan's example out of concern that Japan's automation will make their own products uncompetitive. On the other hand, automated factories assembling goods more swiftly, regularly, and economically than human beings pose a challenge to *middle-income* economies (Malaysia, Mexico), whose comparative advantage would be undercut. As for countries without a manufacturing base, it is difficult to

see how the robotics revolution would have any meaning—except to further devalue the resource which they possess in abundance, masses of impoverished and under-educated human beings.

Finally, the global financial and communications revolution, and the emergence of multinational corporations, threatens to increase the gap between richer and poorer countries, even in the developing world. The industrial conglomerates of Korea are now positioning themselves to become multinational, and the East Asian NIEs in general are able to exploit the world economy (as can be seen in their trade balances, stock-markets, electronics industries, strategic marketing alliances, and so on). Furthermore, if the increasingly borderless world rewards en-trepreneurs, designers, brokers, patent-owners, lawyers, and dealers in high value-added services, then East Asia's commitment to education, science, and technology can only increase its lead over other developing economies.

By contrast, the relative lack of capital, high-technology, scientists, skilled workers, and export industries in the poorer countries makes it difficult for them to take part in the communications and financial revolution, although several countries (Brazil, India) clearly hope to do so. Some grimmer forecasts suggest the poorer parts of the developing world may become more marginalized, partly because of the reduced economic importance of labor, raw materials, and foodstuffs, partly because the advanced economies may concentrate upon greater knowledge-based commerce among themselves.

7.

Is there any way of turning these trends around? Obviously, a society strongly influenced by fundamentalist mullahs with a dislike of "modernization" is unlikely to join the international economy; and it does not *have* to enter the borderless world if its people believe that it would be healthier, spiritually if not economically, to remain outside. Nor ought we to expect that countries dominated by selfish, authoritarian elites bent upon enhancing their military power—developing world countries spent almost $150

billion on weapons and armies in 1988 alone—will rush to imitate Japan and Singapore.

But what about those societies that wish to improve themselves yet find that they are hampered by circumstances? There are, after all, many developing countries, the vast majority of which depend upon exporting food and raw materials. With dozens of poor countries seeking desperately to sell their cane sugar or bananas or timber or coffee in the global market, prices fall and they are made more desperate.[93] Moreover, although much international aid goes to the developing world, in fact far more money flows out of impoverished countries of Africa, Asia, and Latin America and *into* the richer economies of Europe, North America, and Japan—to the tune of at least $43 billion each year.[94] This outward flow of interest repayments, repatriated profits, capital flight, royalties, fees for patents and information services, makes it difficult for poorer countries to get to their feet; and even if they were able to increase their industrial output, the result might be a large rise in "the costs of technological dependence."[95] Like their increasing reliance upon Northern suppliers for food and medical aid, this has created another dependency relationship for poorer nations.

In sum, as we move into the next century the developed economies appear to have all the trump cards in their hands—capital, technology, control of communications, surplus foodstuffs, powerful multinational companies[96]—and, if anything, their advantages are growing because technology is eroding the value of labor and materials, the chief assets of developing countries. Although nominally independent since decolonization, these countries are probably more dependent upon Europe and the United States than they were a century ago.

Ironically, three or four decades of efforts by developing countries to gain control of their own destinies—nationalizing Western companies, setting up commodity-exporting cartels, subsidizing indigenous manufacturing to achieve import substitution, campaigning for a new world order based upon redistribution of the existing imbalances of wealth—have all failed. The "market," backed by governments of the developed economies, has proved too strong, and the struggle against it has weakened developing economies still further—except those (like Korea and Taiwan) which decided to join.

While the gap between rich and poor in today's world is disturbing, those who have argued that this gap is unjust have all too often supported heavy-handed state interventionism and a retreat from open competition, which preserved indigenous production in the short term but rendered it less efficient against those stimulated by market forces. "Scientific socialism for Africa" may still appeal to some intellectuals,[97] but by encouraging societies to look inward it made them less well equipped to move to newer technologies in order to make goods of greater sophistication and value. And a new "world communications order," as proposed a few years ago by UNESCO to balance the West's dominance, sounds superficially attractive but would in all likelihood become the pawn of bureaucratic and ideological interests rather than function as an objective source of news reporting.

On the other hand, the advocates of free market forces often ignore the vast political difficulties which governments in developing countries would encounter in abolishing price controls, selling off national industries, and reducing food subsidies. They also forget that the spectacular commercial expansion of Japan and the East Asian NIEs was carried out by strong states which eschewed laissez faire. Instead of copying either socialist or free market systems, therefore, the developing countries might imitate East Asia's "mixed strategies" which combine official controls and private enterprise.[98]

Although the idea of a mixed strategy is intriguing, how can West or Central African countries imitate East Asia without a "strong state" apparatus, and while having a weak tradition of cooperation between government and firms, far lower educational achievements, and a different set of cultural attitudes toward family size or international economics? With the global scene less welcoming to industrializing newcomers, how likely are they to achieve the same degree of success as the East Asian NIEs did, when they "took off" a quarter-century ago?[99] Even if, by an economic miracle, the world's poorest fifty nations *did* adopt the Korean style of export-led growth in manufactures, would they not create the same crisis of overproduction as exists in the commodity markets today?

How many developing nations will be able to follow East Asia's growth is impossible to tell. The latest *World Development Report* optimistically forecast significant progress across the globe, provided that poorer nations adopted "market friendly" policies and richer nations eschewed protectionism.[100] Were Taiwan and Korea to be followed by the larger states of Southeast Asia such as Malaysia and Thailand, then by South Asia and a number of Latin American countries, that would blur the North-South divide and make international economic alignments altogether more variegated. Moreover, sustained manufacturing success among developing countries *outside* East Asia might stimulate imitation elsewhere.

At the moment, however, the usual cluster of factors influencing relative economic performance—cultural attitudes, education, political stability, capacity to carry out long-term plans—suggests that while a small but growing number of countries is moving from a "have-not" to a "have" status, many more remain behind. The story of winners and losers in history will continue, therefore, only this time modern communications will remind us all of the growing disparity among the world's nations and regions.

NOTES

[1]Discussed further in my new book, *Preparing For the Twenty-First Century* (Random House, 1993).

[2]For reasons of size and organization, China and India (containing around 37 percent of the world's population) are not treated here: for coverage, see Chapter 9, "India and China," of *Preparing For the Twenty-First Century*.

[3]*World Tables 1991* (Washington, DC: World Bank, 1991), pp. 268–269, 352–353.

[4]*World Tables 1991*, pp. 268–269, 352–353.

[5]See the World Bank publication *Trends in Developing Economies*, 1990, pp. 299–303, for Korea.

[6]For descriptions, see F. Braudel, *Civilization and Capitalism: Vol. 3, The Perspective of the World* (Harper and Row, 1986), pp. 506–511.

[7]See P. Lyon, "Emergence of the Third World," in H. Bull and A. Watson, editors, *The Expansion of International Society* (Oxford University Press, 1983), p. 229 ff.; G. Barraclough, *An Introduction to Contemporary History* (Penguin, 1967), chapter 6, "The Revolt Against the West."

[8]J. Ravenhill, "The North-South Balance of Power," *International Affairs*, Vol. 66, No. 4 (1990), pp. 745–746. See also, J. Cruickshank, "The Rise and Fall of the Third World: A Concept Whose Time Has Passed," *World Review*, February 1991, pp. 28–29. Ravenhill's divisions are high-income oil-exporting countries; industrializing economies with strong states and relatively low levels of indebtedness (Taiwan, etc.); industrializing economies with the state apparatus under challenge and/or with debt problems (Argentina, Poland); potential newly industrializing countries (Malaysia, Thailand); primary commodity producers (in sub-Saharan Africa, Central America).

[9]Ravenhill, "The North-South Balance of Power," p. 732.

[10]S. Fardoust and A. Dhareshwan, *Long-Term Outlook for the World Economy: Issues and Projections for the 1990s*, a World Bank report (February 1990), p. 9, Table 3.

[11]W. L. M. Adriaansen and J. G. Waardensburg, editors, *A Dual World Economy* (Groningen: Wolters-Noordhoff, 1989).

[12]P. Drysdale, "The Pacific Basin and Its Economic Vitality," in J. W. Morley, editor, *The Pacific Basin: New Challenges for the United States* (Academy of Political Science with the

East Asian Institute and the Center on Japanese Economy and Business, 1986), p. 11.

[13]While Korea has a population of around 43 million and Taiwan about 20 million, Hong Kong possesses 5.7 million and Singapore only 2.7 million.

[14]See especially, "Taiwan and Korea: Two Paths to Prosperity," *The Economist*, July 14, 1990, pp. 19–21; also "South Korea" (survey), *The Economist*, August 18, 1990. There is a useful comparative survey in L. A. Veit, "Time of the New Asian Tigers," *Challenge*, July–August 1987, pp. 49–55.

[15]N. D. Kristof, "In Taiwan, Only the Strong Get US Degrees," *The New York Times*, March 26, 1989, p. 11.

[16]Figures taken, respectively, from J. Paxton, editor, *The Statesman's Year-book 1990–1991* (St. Martin's Press, 1990); and from R. N. Gwynne, *New Horizons? Third World Industrialization in an International Framework* (New York/London: Wiley, 1990), p. 199.

[17]Lest this 1987 figure appear too distant, note that Korea's sixth Five-Year Plan calls for a national savings rate of 33.5 percent in the early 1990s: see *Trends in Developing Economies*, p. 300. This table is taken from p. 31 (Table 10) of T. Fukuchi and M. Kagami, editors, *Perspectives on the Pacific Basin Economy: A Comparison of Asia and Latin America* (Tokyo: Asian Club Foundation, Institute of Developing Economics, 1990).

[18]The table on p. 4 (Table 1) of Fukuchi and Kagami shows the different rates of growth, and of export's share of total GDP, of the Asian Pacific nations compared with those of Latin America. See also H. Hughes, "Catching Up: The Asian Newly Industrializing Economies in the 1990s," *Asian Development Review*, Vol. 7, No. 2 (1989), p. 132 (and Table 3).

[19]"The Yen Block" (Survey), *The Economist*, July 15, 1989; "Japan Builds A New Power Base," *Business Week*, March 20, 1989, pp. 18–25.

[20]"Taiwan and Korea: Two Paths to Prosperity," *The Economist*, p. 19; "South Korea: A New Society," *The Economist*, April 15, 1989, pp. 23–25.

[21]"Development Brief," *The Economist*, May 26, 1990, p. 81, for the first two columns; the GNP per capita comes from *World Development Report*, 1990, pp. 178–179.

[22]"When a Miracle Stalls," *The Economist*, October 6, 1990, pp. 33–34

(on Taiwan); *Trends in Developing Economies*, 1990, pp. 299–300 (Korea); R. A. Scalapino, "Asia and the United States: The Challenges Ahead," *Foreign Affairs*, Vol. 69, No. 1 (1989–1990), especially pp. 107–112; "Hong Kong, In China's Sweaty Palm," *The Economist*, November 5, 1988, pp. 19–22.

[23]See the detailed forecasts in "Asia 2010: The Power of People," *Far Eastern Economist Review*, May 17, 1990, pp. 27–58. On industrial retooling, see pp. 8–9 of "South Korea" (Survey), *The Economist*, August 18, 1990.

[24]N. Sadik, editor, *Population: The UNFPA Experience*, (New York University Press, 1984), chapter 4, "Latin America and the Caribbean," pp. 51–52.

[25]A. F. Lowenthal, "Rediscovering Latin America," *Foreign Affairs*, Vol. 69, No. 4 (Fall 1990), p. 34.

[26]Figure from "Latin America's Hope," *The Economist*, December 9, 1989, p. 14.

[27]Taken from page 5 of G. W. Landau et al., *Latin America at a Crossroads*, (The Trilateral Commission, 1990), which reports the source as being *Economic and Social Progress in Latin America: 1989 Report* (Washington, DC: Inter-American Development Bank, 1989), Table B1, p. 463.

[28]As mentioned earlier, Japan and its East Asian emulators also sought to protect fledgling domestic industries, but that was in order to create a strong base from which to mount an export offensive—*not* to establish an economic bastion within which their industries would be content to remain.

[29]For details, see the various national entries in *The Statesman's Year-Book 1990–91*; and *The Economist World Atlas and Almanac* (Prentice Hall, 1989), pp. 131–157. R.N. Gwynne's *New Horizons?* has useful comments on Latin America's "inward-oriented industrialization" (chapter 11), which he then contrasts with East Asia's "outward orientation" (chapter 12).

[30]World Resources Institute, *World Resources 1990–91* (Oxford University Press, 1990), p. 39.

[31]*World Resources 1990–91*, p. 246.

[32]In 1989, the net transfer of capital leaving Latin America was around $25 billion.

[33]For the above, see pp. 33–48 of *World Resources 1990–91*: "Latin America At a Crossroads," B.J. McCormick, *The World Economy: Patterns of Growth and Change* (Oxford University Press, 1988), chapter 13;

"Latin American debt: The banks' great escape," *The Economist*, February 11, 1989, pp. 73–74.

[34]For educational details, see *The Statesman's Year-Book 1990–91*, pp. 95, 236; for literacy rates, see especially those of Uruguay, Costa Rica, Argentina, and Venezuela in the table "Development Brief," *The Economist*, May 26, 1990, p. 81.

[35]T. E. Martinez, "Argentina: Living with Hyperinflation," *The Atlantic Monthly*, December 1990, p. 36.

[36]*The Statesman's Year-Book 1990–91*, pp. 584, 605.

[37]T. Kamm, "Latin America Edges Toward Free Trade," *The Wall Street Journal*, November 30, 1990, p. A10.

[38]C. Farnsworth, "Latin American Economies Given Brighter Assessments," *The New York Times*, October 30, 1990; "Latin America's New Start," *The Economist*, June 9, 1990, p. 11; N.C. Nash, "A Breath of Fresh Economic Air Brings Change to Latin America," *The New York Times*, November 13, 1991, pp. A1, D5.

[39]"Latin America's Hope," *The Economist*, December 9, 1989, p. 15; Nash, "A Breath of Fresh Economic Air Brings Change to Latin America."

[40]J. Brooke, "Debt and Democracy," *The New York Times*, December 5, 1990, p. A16; P. Truell, "As the U.S. Slumps, Latin America Suffers," *The Wall Street Journal*, November 19, 1990, p. 1.

[41]For these arguments, see especially Lowenthal's fine summary, "Rediscovering Latin America," in *Foreign Affairs*; also G.A. Fauriol, "The Shadow of Latin American Affairs," *Foreign Affairs*, Vol. 69, No. 1 (1989–1990), pp. 116–134; and M.D. Hayes, "The U.S. and Latin America: A Lost Decade?" *Foreign Affairs*, Vol. 68, No. 1 (1988–1989), pp. 180–198.

[42]This is the subdivision preferred by *The Economist World Atlas and Almanac*, pp. 256–271, which discusses the North African states (except Egypt) in a later section, under "Africa."

[43]"The Arab World" (survey), *The Economist*, May 12, 1990.

[44]See "Religions," p. 21 of the *Hammond Comparative World Atlas* (Hammond, Inc., 1993 edition).

[45]The few oil-producing countries in Africa, such as Gabon and Nigeria, still have relatively low per capita GNPs compared with the Arab Gulf states.

[46]G. Brooks and T. Horwitz, "Shaken Sheiks," *The Wall Street Journal*, December 28, 1990, pp. A1, A4.

[47]"The Arab World," *The Economist*, p. 12.

[48]In 1985, adult female literacy in the Yemen Arab Republic was a mere 3 percent, in Saudi Arabia 12 percent, in Iran 39 percent. On the other hand, many women from the middle and upper-middle classes in Muslim countries are educated, which suggests that poverty, as much as culture, plays a role.

[49]M. A. Heller, "The Middle East: Out of Step with History," *Foreign Affairs* Vol. 69, No. 1 (1989–1990), pp. 153–171.

[50]See also the remarks by S. F. Wells and M. A. Bruzonsky, editors, *Security in the Middle East: Regional Change and Great Power Strategies* (Westview Press, 1986), pp. 1–3.

[51]D. E. Duncan, "Africa: The Long Good-bye," *The Atlantic Monthly*, July 1990, p. 20.

[52]J. A. Marcum, "Africa: A Continent Adrift," *Foreign Affairs*, Vol. 68, No. 1 (1988–1989), p. 177. See also the penetrating article by K. R. Richburg, "Why Is Black Africa Overwhelmed While East Asia Overcomes?" *The International Herald Tribune*, July 14, 1992, pp. 1, 6.

[53]C. H. Farnsworth, "Report by World Bank Sees Poverty Lessening by 2000 Except in Africa," *The New York Times*, July 16, 1990, p. A3; Marcum, "Africa: A Continent Adrift"; Duncan, "Africa: The Long Good-bye"; and "The bleak continent," *The Economist*, December 9, 1989, pp. 80–81.

[54]B. Fischer, "Developing Countries in the Process of Economic Globalisation," *Intereconomics* (March/April 1990), p. 55.

[55]J.S. Whitaker, *How Can Africa Survive?* (Council on Foreign Relations Press, 1988).

[56]As will be clear from the text, this discussion excludes the Republic of South Africa.

[57]T. J. Goliber, "Africa's Expanding Population: Old Problems, New Policies," *Population Bulletin*, Vol. 44, No. 3 (November 1989), pp. 4–49, an outstandingly good article.

[58]*World Resources 1990–91*, p. 254.

[59]*World Resources 1990–91*, p. 254 (overall population growth to 2025), and p. 258 (infant mortality). L.K. Alt-man, "W.H.O Says 40 Million Will Be Infected With AIDS by 2000," *The New York Times*, June 18, 1991, p. C3 (for percentage of GNP devoted to health care).

[60]L.K. Altman, "W.H.O. Says 40 Million Will Be Infected With AIDS Virus by 2000"; and for further figures, see Kennedy, *Preparing For the Twenty First Century*, chapter 3.

[61]K.H. Hunt, "Scenes From a Nightmare," *The New York Times Magazine*, August 12, 1990, pp. 26, 50–51.

[62]See Whitaker, *How Can Africa Survive?*, especially chapter 4, "The Blessings of Children," for a fuller analysis; and J.C. Caldwell and P. Caldwell, "High Fertility in Sub-Saharan Africa," *Scientific American*, May 1990, pp. 118–125.

[63]"The bleak continent," *The Economist*; Whitaker, *How Can Africa Survive?*, chapters 1 and 2; Goliber, "Africa's Expanding Population," pp. 12–13.

[64]Whitaker, *How Can Africa Survive?*; Duncan, "Africa: The Long Good-bye."

[65]"Fruits of Containment" (op-ed), *The Wall Street Journal*, December 18, 1990, p. A14, for the Africa-Belgium comparison; H. McRae, "Visions of tomorrow's world," *The Independent* (London), November 26, 1991, for Africa's share of world GDP.

[66]"Aid to Africa," *The Economist*, December 8, 1990, p. 48.

[67]In this regard, East Asian nations like Taiwan and Korea, possessing coherent indigenous populations, are once again more favorably situated.

[68]*The Economist World Atlas and Almanac* (Prentice Hall, 1989), p. 293.

[69]Apart from the country by country comments in *The Economist World Atlas and Almanac*, see also K. Ingham, *Politics in Modern Africa: The Uneven Tribal Dimension* (Routledge, 1990); "Africa's Internal Wars of the 1980s—Contours and Prospects," United States Institute of Peace, *In Brief*, No. 18 (May 1990).

[70]T. R. Odhiambo, "Human resources development: problems and prospects in developing countries," *Impact of Science on Society*, No. 155 (1989), p. 214.

[71]*The Statesman's Yearbook 1989*, p. 84; Goliber, "Africa's Expanding Population," p. 15.

[72]*The Statesman's Yearbook 1989*, pp. 1,159–1,160 (certain smaller groups of students are excluded from these totals).

[73]P. Lewis, "Nyere and Tanzania: No Regrets at Socialism," *The New York Times*, October 24, 1990.

[74]"Wind of change, but a different one," *The Economist*, July 14, 1990, p. 44. See also the encouraging noises made—on a country by country basis—in the World Bank's own *Trends in Developing Economies*, 1990, as well as in its 1989 publication *Sub-Saharan Africa: From Crisis to Sustainable Growth* (summarized in "The bleak continent," *The Economist*, pp. 80–81).

[75]See especially P. Pradervand, *Listening to Africa: Developing Africa from the Grassroots* (Greenwood, 1989); B. Schneider, *The Barefoot Revolution* (London: I. T. Publications, 1988); K. McAfee, "Why The Third World Goes Hungry," *Commonweal* June 15, 1990, pp. 384–385.

[76]See Edward Sheehan's article "In the Heart of Somalia," *The New York Review*, January 14, 1993. See also Duncan, "Africa: The Long Good-bye," p. 24; G. Hancock, *Lords of Poverty: The Power, Prestige, and Corruption of the International Aid* (Atlantic Monthly Press, 1989); G.B.N. Ayittey, "No More Aid for Africa," *The Wall Street Journal*, October 18, 1991 (op-ed), p. A14.

[77]Whitaker, *How Can Africa Survive?* p. 231.

[78]See, for example, the conclusions in B. Fischer, "Developing Countries in the Process of Economic Globalisation," pp. 55–63.

[79]Caldwell and Caldwell, "High Fertility in Sub-Saharan Africa," *Scientific American*, p. 88.

[80]"AIDS in Africa," *The Economist*, November 24, 1989, p. 1B; E. Eckholm and J. Tierney, "AIDS in Africa: A Killer Rages On," *The New York Times*, September 16, 1990, pp. 1, 4; C.M. Becker, "The Demo-Economic Impact of the AIDS Pandemic in Sub-Saharan Africa," *World Development*, Vol. 18, No. 12 (1990), pp. 1,599–1,619.

[81]*World Resources 1990–91*, p. 254. The US-Canada total in 1960 was 217 million to Latin America's 210 million; by 2025 it is estimated to be 332 million to 762 million.

[82]*World Resources 1990–91*, p. 254.

[83]Apart from chapters 2 and 4 above, see again *World Resources 1990–91*, pp. 33–48; T. Wicker, "Bush Ventures South," *The New York Times*, December 9, 1990, p. E17; T. Golden, "Mexico Fights Cholera But Hates to Say Its

Name," *The New York Times*, September 14, 1991, p. 2.

[84]"The Arab World," *The Economist*, p. 4.

[85]"The Arab World," p. 6; Y.F. Ibrahim, "In Algeria, Hope for Democracy But Not Economy," *The New York Times*, July 26, 1991, pp. A1, A6.

[86]*World Resources 1990–91*, pp. 258–259.

[87]As quoted in "The Arab World," p. 5.

[88]See again Pradervand, *Listening to Africa*. Also important is D. Pearce et al., *Sustainable Development: Economics and Environment in the Third World* (Gower, 1990).

[89]F. Gable, "Changing Climate and Caribbean Coastlines," *Oceanus*, Vol. 30, No. 4 (Winter 1987–1988), pp. 53–56; G. Gable and D.G. Aubrey, "Changing Climate and the Pacific," *Oceanus*, Vol. 32, No. 4 (Winter 1989–1990), pp. 71–73.

[90]"The Arab World," p. 12.

[91]*World Resources 1990–91*, pp. 176–177; *State of the World 1990*, pp. 48–49.

[92]C. Juma, *The Gene Hunters: Biotechnology and the Scramble for Seeds* (Princeton University Press, 1989).

[93]D. Pirages, *Global Technopolitics: The International Politics of Technology and Resources* (Brooks-Cole, 1989), p. 152.

[94]McAfee, "Why the Third World goes Hungry," p. 380.

[95]See P.K Ghosh, editor, *Technology Policy and Development: A Third World Perspective* (Greenwood, 1984), p. 109.

[96]C.J. Dixon et al., editors, *Multinational Corporations and the Third World* (Croom Helm, 1986).

[97]For a good example, B. Onimode, *A Political Economy of the African Crisis* (Humanities Press International, 1988), especially p. 310 ff.

[98]M. Clash, "Development Policy, Technology Assessment and the New Technologies," *Futures*, November 1990, p. 916.

[99]L. Cuyvers and D. Van den Bulcke, "Some Reflections on the 'Outward-oriented' Development Strategy of the Far Eastern Newly Industrialising Countries," especially pp. 196–197, in Adriaansen and Waardenburg, *A Dual World Economy*.

[100]*World Development Report 1991: The Challenge of Development*, a World Bank report (Oxford University Press, 1991). See also the World Bank's *Global Economic Prospects and the Developing Countries* (1991).

THE MANY FACES OF

the Future

Why we'll never have a universal civilization

By Samuel P. Huntington

Conventional wisdom tells us that we are witnessing the emergence of what V.S. Naipaul called a "universal civilization," the cultural coming together of humanity and the increasing acceptance of common values, beliefs, and institutions by people throughout the world. Critics of this trend point to the global domination of Western-style capitalism and culture (*Baywatch*, many note with alarm, is the most popular television show in the world), and the gradual erosion of distinct cultures—especially in the developing world. But there's more to universal civilization than GATT and David Hasselhoff's pecs.

If what we mean by universal culture are the assumptions, values, and doctrines currently held by the many elites who travel in international circles, that's not a viable "one world" scenario. Consider the "Davos culture." Each year about a thousand business executives, government officials, intellectuals, and journalists from scores of countries meet at the World Economic Forum in Davos, Switzerland. Almost all of them hold degrees in the physical sciences, social sciences, business, or law; are reasonably fluent in English; are employed by governments, corporations, and academic institutions with extensive international connections; and travel frequently outside of their own countries. They also generally share beliefs in individualism, market economies, and political democracy, which are also common among people in Western civilization. This core group of people controls virtually all international institutions, many of the world's governments, and the bulk of the world's economic

and military organizations. As a result, the Davos culture is tremendously important, but it is far from a universal civilization. Outside the West, these values are shared by perhaps 1 percent of the world's population.

The argument that the spread of Western consumption patterns and popular culture around the world is creating a universal civilization is also not especially profound. Innovations have been transmitted from one civilization to another throughout history. But they are usually techniques lacking in significant cultural consequences or fads that come and go without altering the underlying culture of the recipient civilization. The essence of Western civilization is the Magna Carta, not the Magna Mac. The fact that non-Westerners may bite into the latter does not necessarily mean they are more likely to accept the former. During the '70s and '80s Americans bought millions of Japanese cars and electronic gadgets without being "Japanized," and, in fact, became considerably more antagonistic toward Japan. Only naive arrogance can lead Westerners to assume that non-Westerners will become "Westernized" by acquiring Western goods.

A slightly more sophisticated version of the universal popular culture argument focuses on the media rather than consumer goods in general. Eighty-eight of the world's hundred most popular films in 1993 were produced in the United States, and four organizations based in the United States and Europe—the Associated Press, CNN, Reuters, and the French Press Agency—dominate the dissemination of news

From *Utne Reader,* May/June 1997, pp. 75-77, 102-103. Adapted from *The Clash of Civilizations and Remaking of World Order* by Samuel P. Huntington. © 1997 by Samuel P. Huntington. Reprinted by permission of Simon & Schuster.

The Real World

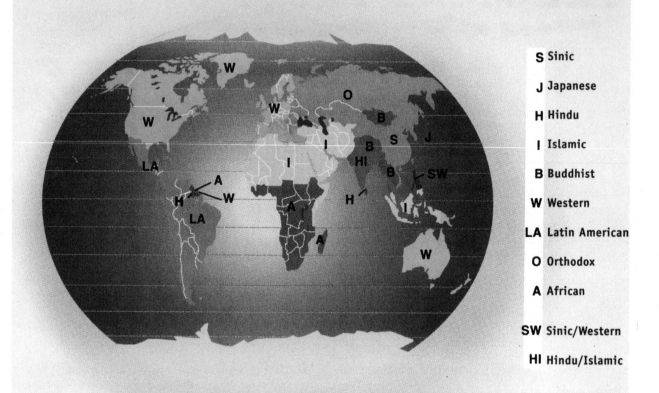

The civilizations shaping the new global order

S Sinic

J Japanese

H Hindu

I Islamic

B Buddhist

W Western

LA Latin American

O Orthodox

A African

SW Sinic/Western

HI Hindu/Islamic

worldwide. This situation simply reflects the universality of human interest in love, sex, violence, mystery, heroism, and wealth, and the ability of profit-motivated companies, primarily American, to exploit those interests to their own advantage. Little or no evidence exists, however, to support the assumption that the emergence of pervasive global communications is producing significant convergence in attitudes and beliefs around the world. Indeed, this Western hegemony encourages populist politicians in non-Western societies to denounce Western cultural imperialism and to rally their constituents to preserve their indigenous cultures. The extent to which global communications are dominated by the West is, thus, a major source of the resentment non-Western peoples have toward the West. In addition, rapid economic development in non-Western societies is leading to the emergence of local and regional media industries catering to the distinctive tastes of those societies.

The central elements of any civilization are language and religion. If a universal civilization is emerging, there should be signs of a universal language and a universal religion developing. Nothing of the sort is occurring.

Despite claims from Western business leaders that the world's language is English, no evidence exists to support this proposition, and the most reliable evidence that does exist shows just the opposite. English speakers dropped from 9.8 percent of the world's population in 1958 to 7.6 percent in 1992. Still, one can argue that English has become the world's lingua franca, or in linguistic terms, the principal language of wider communication. Diplomats, business executives, tourists, and the service professionals catering to them need some means of efficient communication, and right now that is largely in English. But this is a form of *intercultural* communication; it presupposes the existence of separate cultures. Adopting a lingua franca is a way of coping with linguistic and cultural differences, not a way of eliminating them. It is a tool for communication, not a source of identity and community.

The linguistic scholar Joshua Fishman has observed that a language is more likely to be accepted as a lingua franca if it is not identified with a particular ethnic group, religion, or ideology. In the past, English carried many of those associations. But more recently, Fishman says, it has been "de-ethnicized (or minimally ethnicized)," much like what happened to Akkadian, Aramaic, Greek, and Latin before it. As he puts it, "It is part of the relative good fortune of English as an additional language that neither its British nor its American fountainheads have been widely or deeply viewed in an ethnic or ideological context for the past quarter century or so." Resorting to English for intercultural communication helps maintain—and, indeed, reinforce—separate cultural identities. Precisely because people want to preserve their own culture, they use English to communicate with people of other cultures.

A universal religion is only slightly more likely to emerge than a universal language. The late 20th century has seen a resurgence of religions around the world, including the rise of fundamentalist movements. This trend has reinforced the differences among religions, and has not necessarily resulted in significant shifts in the distribution of religions worldwide.

Of course, there have been increases during the past century in the percentage of people practicing the two major proselytizing religions, Islam and Christianity. Western Christians accounted for 26.9 percent of the world's population in 1900 and peaked at about 30 percent in 1980, while the Muslim population increased from 12.4 percent in 1900 to as much as 18 percent in 1980. The percentage of Christians in the world will probably decline to about 25 percent by 2025. Meanwhile, because of extremely high rates of population growth, the proportion of Muslims in the world will continue to increase dramatically and represent about 30 percent of the world's population by 2025. Neither, however, qualifies as a universal religion.

If a universal civilization is emerging, there should be signs of a universal language and religion. Nothing of the sort is occurring.

The argument that some sort of universal civilization is emerging rests on one or more of three assumptions: that the collapse of Soviet communism meant the end of history and the universal victory of liberal democracy; that increased interaction among peoples through trade, investment, tourism, media, and electronic communications is creating a common world culture; and that a universal civilization is the logical result of the process of global modernization that has been going on since the 18th century.

The first assumption is rooted in the Cold War perspective that the only alternative to communism is liberal democracy, and the demise of the first inevitably produces the second. But there are many alternatives to liberal democracy—including authoritarianism, nationalism, corporatism, and market communism (as in China)—that are alive and well in today's world. And, more significantly, there are all the religious alternatives that lie outside the world of secular ideologies. In the modern world, religion is a central, perhaps *the* central, force that motivates and mobilizes people. It is sheer hubris to think that because Soviet communism has collapsed, the West has conquered the world for all time and that non-Western peoples are going to rush to embrace Western liberalism as the only alternative. The Cold War division of humanity is over. The more fundamental divisions of ethnicity, religions, and civilizations remain and will spawn new conflicts.

In today's world, the most important distinctions among people are not ideological, political, or economic. They are cultural. People identify with cultural groups: tribes, ethnic groups, religious communities, nations, and civilizations.

The new global economy is a reality. Improvements in transportation and communications technology have indeed made it easier and cheaper to move money, goods, knowledge, ideas, and images around the world. But what will be the impact of this increased economic interaction? In social psychology, distinctiveness theory holds that people define themselves by what makes them different from others in a particular context: People define their identity by what they are not. As advanced communications, trade, and travel multiply the interactions among civilizations, people will increasingly accord greater relevance to identity based on their own civilization.

Those who argue that a universal civilization is an inevitable product of modernization assume that all modern societies must become Westernized. As the first civilization to modernize, the West leads in the acquisition of the culture of modernity. And as other societies acquire similar patterns of education, work, wealth, and class structure—the argument runs—this modern Western culture will become the universal culture of the world. That significant differences exist between modern and traditional cultures is beyond dispute. It doesn't necessarily follow, however, that societies with modern cultures resemble each other more than do societies with traditional cultures. As historian Fernand Braudel writes, "Ming China . . . was assuredly closer to the France of the Valois than the China of Mao Tse-tung is to the France of the Fifth Republic."

Yet modern societies could resemble each other more than do traditional societies for two reasons. First, the increased interaction among modern societies may not generate a common culture, but it does facilitate the transfer of techniques, inventions, and practices from one society to another with a speed and to a degree that were impossible in the traditional world. Second, traditional society was based on agriculture; modern society is based on industry. Patterns of agriculture and the social structure that goes with them are much more dependent on the natural environment than are patterns of industry. Differences in industrial organization are likely to derive from differences in culture and social structure rather than geography, and the former conceivably can converge while the latter cannot.

Modern societies thus have much in common. But do they necessarily merge into homogeneity? The argument that they do rests on the assumption that modern society must approximate a single type, the Western type. This is a totally false assumption. Western civilization emerged in the 8th and 9th centuries. It did not begin to modernize until the 17th and 18th centuries. The West was the West long before it was modern. The central characteristics of the West—the classical legacy, the mix of catholicism and protestantism, and the separation of spiritual and temporal authority—distinguish it from other civilizations and antedate the modernization of the West.

In the post–Cold War world, the most important distinctions among people are not ideological, political,

The main responsibility of Western leaders is to recognize that intervention in the affairs of other civilizations is the single most dangerous source of instability in the world.

or economic. They are cultural. People and nations are attempting to answer a basic human question: Who are we? And they are answering that question in the traditional way, by reference to the things that mean the most to them: ancestry, religion, language, history, values, customs, and institutions. People identify with cultural groups: tribes, ethnic groups, religious communities, nations, and, at the broadest level, civilizations. They use politics not just to advance their interests but also to define their identity. We know who we are only when we know who we are not, and often only when we know who we are against.

Nation-states remain the principal actors in world affairs. Their behavior is shaped, as in the past, by the pursuit of power and wealth, but it is also shaped by cultural preferences and differences. The most important groupings of states are no longer the three blocs of the Cold War but rather the world's major civilizations (*See* map):

S Sinic
All scholars recognize the existence of either a single distinct Chinese civilization dating back at least to 1500 B.C., or of two civilizations—one succeeding the other—in the early centuries of the Christian epoch.

J Japanese
Some scholars combine Japanese and Chinese culture, but most recognize Japan as a distinct civilization, the offspring of Chinese civilization, that emerged between A.D. 100 and 400.

H Hindu
A civilization—or successive civilizations—has existed on the Indian subcontinent since at least 1500 B.C. In one form or another, Hinduism has been central to the culture of India since the second millennium B.C.

I Islamic
Originating on the Arabian peninsula in the 7th century A.D., Islam spread rapidly across North Africa and the Iberian Peninsula and also eastward into central Asia, the Indian subcontinent, and Southeast Asia. Many distinct cultures—including Arab, Turkic, Persian, and Malay—exist within Islam.

W Western
The emergence of Western civilization—what used to be called Western Christendom—is usually dated at about 700 A.D. It has two main components, in Europe and North America.

LA Latin American
Latin America, often considered part of the West, has a distinct identity. It has had a corporatist, authoritarian culture, which Europe had to a much lesser degree and North America did not have at all. Europe and North America both felt the effects of the Reformation and have combined Catholic and Protestant cultures, while Latin America has been primarily Catholic. Latin American civilization also incorporates indigenous cultures, which were wiped out in North America.

O Orthodox
This civilization, which combines the Orthodox tradition of Christianity with the Slav cultures of Eastern Europe and Russia, has resurfaced since the demise of the Soviet Union.

A African
There may be some argument about whether there is a distinct African civilization. North Africa and the east

coast belong to Islamic civilization. (Historically, Ethiopia constituted a civilization of its own.) Elsewhere, imperialism brought elements of Western civilization. Tribal identities are pervasive throughout Africa, but Africans are also increasingly developing a sense of African identity. Sub-Saharan Africa conceivably could cohere into a distinct civilization, with South Africa as its core.

B Buddhist

Beginning in the first century A.D., Buddhism was exported from India to China, Korea, Vietnam, and Japan, where it was assimilated by the indigenous cultures and/or suppressed. What can legitimately be described as a Buddhist civilization, however, does exist in Sri Lanka, Burma, Thailand, Laos, Cambodia; and Tibet, Mongolia, and Bhutan. Overall, however, the virtual extinction of Buddhism in India and its incorporation into existing cultures in other major countries means that it has not been the basis of a major civilization.

(Modern India represents a mix of Hindu and Islamic civilizations, while the Philippines is a unique Sinic-Western hybrid by virtue of its history of Spanish, then American rule.)

As Asian and Muslim civilizations begin to assert the universal relevance of *their* cultures, Westerners will see the connection between universalism and imperialism and appreciate the virtues of a pluralistic world. In order to preserve Western civilization, the West needs greater unity of purpose. It should incorporate into the European Union and NATO the western states of central Europe; encourage the Westernization of Latin America; slow the drift of Japan away from the West and toward accommodation with China; and accept Russia as the core state of Orthodoxy and a power with legitimate interests.

The main responsibility of Western leaders is to recognize that intervention in the affairs of other civilizations is the single most dangerous source of instability in the world. The West should attempt not to reshape other civilizations in its own image, but to preserve and renew the unique qualities of its own civilization.

Samuel P. Huntington is Albert J. Weatherhead III University Professor at Harvard University.

"The major international schisms of the twenty-first century will not always be definable in geographic terms. Many of the most severe and persistent threats to global peace and stability are arising not from conflicts between major political entities but from increased discord within states, societies, and civilizations along ethnic, racial, religious, linguistic, caste, or class lines. . . This is not to say that traditional geopolitical divisions no longer play a role in world security affairs. But it does suggest that such divisions may have been superseded in importance by the new global schisms."

Redefining Security: The New Global Schisms

MICHAEL T. KLARE

Geopolitical boundaries—notably those separating rival powers and major military blocs—have constituted the principal "fault lines" of international politics during much of the twentieth century. Throughout the cold war, the world's greatest concentrations of military strength were to be found along such key dividing lines as the Iron Curtain between East and West in Europe and the demilitarized zone between North and South Korea.

When the cold war ended, many of these boundaries quickly lost their geopolitical significance. With the reunification of Germany and the breakup of the Soviet Union, the divide between East and West in Europe ceased to have any meaning. Other key boundaries—for example, the demilitarized zone in Korea—retained their strategic importance, but elsewhere thousands of miles of previously fortified frontier became open borders with a minimal military presence. The strategic alliances associated with these divisions also lost much of their promi-

nence: the Warsaw Treaty Organization was eliminated altogether, while NATO was given new roles and missions in order to forestall a similar fate.

BATTLE LINES OF THE FUTURE

The changes associated with the cold war's end have been so dramatic and profound that it is reasonable to question whether traditional assumptions regarding the nature of global conflict will continue to prove reliable in the new, post–cold war era. In particular, one could question whether conflicts between states (or groups of states) will remain the principal form of international strife, and whether the boundaries between them will continue to constitute the world's major fault lines. Certainly the outbreak of ethnonationalist conflict in the former Yugoslavia and several other former communist states has focused fresh attention on internal warfare, as has the persistence of tribal and religious strife in such countries as Afghanistan, Burundi, Liberia, Rwanda, Somalia, Sri Lanka, and Sudan.

Nevertheless, traditional concepts retain great currency among security analysts. Although the Iron Curtain has disappeared, it is argued, similar schisms of a geographic or territorial nature will arise to take its place. Indeed, several theories have been advanced positing the likely location of these schisms.

MICHAEL T. KLARE *is a professor of peace and world security studies at Hampshire College and director of the Five College Program in Peace and World Security Studies. He is the author of* Rogue States and Nuclear Outlaws: America's Search for a New Foreign Policy *(New York: Hill and Wang, 1995).*

Some analysts contend that the territorial schisms of earlier periods—notably those produced by military competition among the major powers—will be revived in the years ahead. Professor Kenneth Waltz of the University of California at Berkeley suggests that such competition will eventually reappear, with Germany, Japan, or some other rising power such as China building its military strength in order to contest America's global paramountcy. "Countries have always competed for wealth and security, and the competition has often led to conflict," he wrote in *International Security's* summer 1993 issue. "Why should the future be different from the past?"

More novel, perhaps, is the suggestion that the principal schisms of the post–cold war era are to be found along the peripheries of the world's great civilizations: Western (including Europe and North America), Slavic-Orthodox (including Russia, Ukraine, and Serbia), Japanese, Islamic, Confucian (China), Latin American, and African. First propounded by Harvard's Samuel Huntington in the summer 1993 issue of *Foreign Affairs*, this argument holds that the economic and ideological antagonisms of the nineteenth and twentieth centuries will be superseded in the twenty-first by antagonisms over culture and cultural identity. "Nation-states will remain the most powerful actors in world affairs," Huntington wrote, "but the principal conflicts of global politics will occur between nations and groups of different civilizations." Although the boundaries between civilizations are not as precise as those between sovereign states, he noted, these loose frontiers will be the site of major conflict. "The clash of civilizations will dominate global politics. The fault lines between civilizations will be the battle lines of the future."

Others have argued that the world's future fault lines will fall not between the major states or civilizations, but between the growing nexus of democratic, market-oriented societies and those "holdout" states that have eschewed democracy or defied the world community in other ways. Such "pariah" states or "rogue" powers are said to harbor aggressive inclinations, to support terrorism, and to seek the production of nuclear or chemical weapons. "[We] must face the reality of recalcitrant and outlaw states that not only choose to remain outside the family [of nations] but also to assault its basic values," wrote President Clinton's national security adviser, Anthony Lake, in the March-April 1994 *Foreign Affairs*. Lake placed several nations in this category—Cuba, North Korea, Iran, Iraq, and

Libya—and other writers have added Sudan and Syria. But while there is disagreement about which of these states might actually fall into the "outlaw" category, Lake and other proponents of this analysis hold that the United States and its allies must work together to "contain" the rogue states and frustrate their aggressive designs.

While these assessments of the world security environment differ in many of their particulars, they share a common belief that the "battle lines of the future" (to use Huntington's expression) will fall along geographically defined boundaries, with the contending powers (and their friends and allies) arrayed on opposite sides. This, in turn, leads to similar policy recommendations that generally entail the maintenance of sufficient military strength by the United States to defeat any potential adversary or combination of adversaries.

It is certainly understandable that many analysts have proceeded from traditional assumptions regarding the nature of conflict when constructing models of future international relations, but it is not at all apparent that such assessments will prove reliable. While a number of crises since the end of the cold war appear to have followed one of the three models described, many have not. Indeed, the most intense conflicts of the current period—including those in Algeria, Angola, Bosnia, Burma, Burundi, Haiti, Kashmir, Liberia, Rwanda, Somalia, Sri Lanka, and Sudan—cannot be fully explained using these models. Moreover, other forms of contemporary violence—terrorism, racial and religious strife, gang warfare, violence against women, and criminal violence—have shown no respect for geography or civilizational identity whatsoever, erupting in virtually every corner of the world.

THE THREAT FROM WITHIN

A fresh assessment of the world security environment suggests that the major international schisms of the twenty-first century will not always be definable in geographic terms. Many of the most severe and persistent threats to global peace and stability are arising not from conflicts between major political entities but from increased discord within states, societies, and civilizations along ethnic, racial, religious, linguistic, caste, or class lines.

The intensification and spread of internal discord is a product of powerful stresses on human communities everywhere. These stresses—economic, demographic, sociological, and environmental—are exacerbating the existing divisions within societies and creating entirely new ones. As a result, we are seeing the emergence of new or deepened fissures across international society, producing multiple outbreaks of intergroup hostility and violence. These cleavages cannot be plotted on a normal map, but can be correlated with other forms of data: economic performance, class stratification, population growth, ethnic and religious composition, environmental deterioration, and so on. Where certain conditions prevail—a widening gulf between rich and poor, severe economic competition between neighboring ethnic and religious communities, the declining habitability of marginal lands—internal conflict is likely to erupt.

This is not to say that traditional geopolitical divisions no longer play a role in world security affairs. But it does suggest that such divisions may have been superseded in importance by the new global schisms.

FOR RICHER
AND POORER: THE WIDENING GAP

The world has grown much richer over the past 25 years. According to the Worldwatch Institute, the world's total annual income rose from $10.1 trillion in 1970 to approximately $20 trillion in 1994 (in constant 1987 dollars). This increase has been accompanied by an improved standard of living for many of the world's peoples. But not all nations, and not all people in the richer nations, have benefited from the global increase in wealth: some countries, mostly concentrated in Africa and Latin America, have experienced a net decline in gross domestic product over the past few decades, while many of the countries that have achieved a higher GDP have experienced an increase in the number of people living in extreme poverty. Furthermore, the gap in national income between the richest and the poorest nations continues to increase, as does the gap between rich and poor people within most societies.

These differentials in economic growth rates, along with the widening gap between rich and poor, are producing dangerous fissures in many societies. As the masses of poor see their chances of escaping acute poverty diminish, they are likely to become increasingly resentful of those whose growing wealth is evident. This resentment is especially pronounced in the impoverished shantytowns that surround many of the seemingly prosperous cities of the third world. In these inhospitable surroundings, large numbers of people—especially among the growing legions of unemployed youth—are being attracted to extremist political movements like the Shining Path of Peru and the Islamic Salvation Front of Alge-

SOURCES OF HUMAN INSECURITY	
Income	1.3 billion people in developing countries live in poverty; 200 million people live below the poverty line in industrial countries.
Clean Water	1.3 billion people in developing countries do not have access to safe water.
Literacy	900 million adults worldwide are illiterate.
Food	800 million people in developing countries have inadequate food supplies; 500 million of this number are chronically malnourished, and 175 million are under the age of five.
Housing	500 million urban dwellers worldwide are homeless or do not have adequate housing; 100 million young people are homeless.
Preventable Death	Between 15 million and 20 million people die annually because of starvation or disease aggravated by malnutrition; 10 million people die each year because of substandard housing, unsafe water, or poor sanitation in densely populated cities.

Source: Adapted from Michael Renner, *Fighting for Survival: Environmental Decline, Social Conflict, and the New Age of Insecurity* (New York: Norton, 1996), p. 81.

ria, or to street gangs and drug-trafficking syndicates. The result is an increase in urban crime and violence.

Deep economic cleavages are also emerging in China and the postcommunist states of Eastern Europe and the former Soviet Union. Until the recent introduction of market reforms in these countries, the financial gap between rich and poor was kept relatively narrow by state policy, and such wealth as did exist among the bureaucratic elite was kept well hidden from public view. With the onset of capitalism the economic plight of the lowest strata of these societies has become considerably worse, while the newly formed entrepreneurial class has been able to accumulate considerable wealth—and to display it in highly conspicuous ways. This has generated new class tensions and provided ammunition for those who, like Gennadi Zyuganov of Russia's reorganized Communist Party, seek the restoration of the old, state-dominated system.

Equally worrisome is the impact of growing income differentials on intergroup relations in multiethnic societies. In most countries the divide between rich and poor is not the only schism that matters: of far greater significance are the divisions between various strata of the poor and lower middle class. When such divisions coincide with ethnic or religious differences—that is, when one group of poor people finds itself to be making less economic progress than a similar group of a different ethnic composition—the result is likely to be increased ethnic antagonisms and, at the extreme, increased intergroup violence. This is evident in Pakistan, where violent gang warfare in Karachi has been fueled by economic competition between the indigenous inhabitants of the surrounding region and several waves of Muslim immigrants from India and Bangladesh; it is also evident in Sri Lanka, where efforts by the Sinhalese to deny employment opportunities to the Tamils helped spark a deadly civil war.

KINDLING ETHNIC STRIFE

According to information assembled by the Stockholm International Peace Research Institute (SIPRI), ethnic and religious strife figured prominently in all but 3 of the 31 major armed conflicts under way in 1994. And while several long-running ethnic and sectarian conflicts have subsided in recent years, most analysts believe that such strife is likely to erupt repeatedly in the years ahead.

It is true that many recent ethnic and religious conflicts have their roots in clashes or invasions that occurred years ago. It is also true that the violent upheavals that broke out in the former Yugoslavia and the former Soviet Union drew upon deep-seated ethnic hostilities, even if these cleavages were not generally visible during much of the communist era (when overt displays of ethnic antagonism were prohibited by government decree). In this sense, the ethnic fissures that are now receiving close attention from international policymakers are not really new phenomena. Nevertheless, many of these schisms have become more pronounced since the end of the cold war, or have exhibited characteristics that are unique to the current era.

Greatly contributing to the intensity of recent ethnic and religious strife is the erosion or even disappearance of central state authority in poor third world countries experiencing extreme economic,

political, and environmental stress. In such countries—especially Burundi, Liberia, Rwanda, Somalia, and Zaire—the flimsy state structures established after independence are simply unable to cope with the demands of housing and feeding their growing populations with the meager resources at hand. In such circumstances people lose all confidence in the state's ability to meet their basic needs and turn instead to more traditional, kinship-based forms of association for help in getting by—a process that often results in competition and conflict among groups over what remains of the nation's scarce resources. This shift in loyalty from the state to group identity is also evident in Bosnia and parts of the former Soviet Union, where various ethnic factions have attempted to seize or divide up the infrastructure (and in some cases the territory) left behind by the communist regime.

Also contributing to the intensity of intergroup conflict in the current era is the spread of mass communications and other instruments of popular mobilization. These advances have contributed to what Professor James Rosenau of George Washington University calls a "skill revolution" in which individual citizens "have become increasingly competent in assessing where they fit in international affairs and how their behavior can be aggregated into significant collective outcomes."[1] This competence can lead to calls for greater personal freedom and democracy. But it can also lead to increased popular mobilization along ethnic, religious, caste, and linguistic lines, often producing great friction and disorder within heterogeneous societies. An important case in point is India, where Hindu nationalists have proved adept at employing modern means of communication and political organization—while retaining traditional symbols and motifs—to encourage anti-Muslim sentiment and thereby erode the authority of India's largely secular government.

DEMOGRAPHIC SCHISMS

According to the most recent UN estimates, total world population is expected to soar from approximately 5.6 billion people in 1994 to somewhere between 8 billion and 12 billion by the year 2050—an increase that will undoubtedly place great strain on the earth's food production and environmental capacity. But the threat to the world's environment and food supply is not all that we have to worry about. Because population growth is occurring unevenly in different areas, with some of the highest rates of growth to be found in countries with the

---

[1]James N. Rosenau, "Security in a Turbulent World," *Current History*, May 1995, p. 194.

slowest rates of economic growth, future population increases could combine with other factors to exacerbate existing cleavages along ethnic, religious, and class lines.

Overall, the populations of the less-developed countries (LDCS) are growing at a much faster rate than those of the advanced industrial nations. As a result, the share of world population accounted for by the LDCS rose from 69 percent in 1960 to 74 percent in 1980, and is expected to jump to nearly 80 percent in the year 2000. Among third world countries, moreover, there have been marked variations in the rate of population growth: while the newly industrialized nations of East Asia have experienced a sharp decline in the rate of growth, Africa and parts of the Middle East have experienced an increase. If these trends persist, the global distribution of population will change dramatically over the next few decades, with some areas experiencing a substantial increase in total population and others moderate or even negligible growth.

This is where other factors enter the picture. If the largest increases in population were occurring in areas of rapid economic growth, the many young adults entering the job market each year would be able to find productive employment and would thus be able to feed and house their families. In many cases, however, large increases in population are coinciding with low or stagnant economic growth, meaning that future jobseekers are not likely to find adequate employment. This will have a considerable impact on the world security environment. At the very least, it is likely to produce increased human migration from rural areas (where population growth tends to be greatest) to urban centers (where most new jobs are to be found), and from poor and low-growth countries to more affluent ones. The former process is resulting in the rapid expansion of many third world cities, with an attendant increase in urban crime and intergroup friction (especially where the new urban dwellers are of a different ethnic or tribal group from the original settlers); the latter is producing huge numbers of new immigrants in the developed and high-growth countries, often sparking hostility and sometimes violence from the indigenous populations.

Rapid population growth in poor countries with slow or stagnant economic growth has other impli-

Greatly contributing to the intensity of recent ethnic and religious strife is the erosion or even disappearance of central state authority in poor third world countries experiencing extreme economic, political, and environmental stress.

cations for world security. In many societies it is leading to the hyperutilization of natural resources, particularly arable soil, grazing lands, forests, and fisheries, a process that severely complicates future economic growth (as vital raw materials are depleted) and accelerates the pace of environmental decline. It can also overwhelm the capacity of weak or divided governments to satisfy their citizens' basic needs, leading eventually to the collapse of states and to the intergroup competition and conflict described earlier. Finally, it could generate fresh international conflicts when states with slow population growth employ stringent measures to exclude immigrants from nearby countries with high rates of growth. While some of this is speculative, early signs of many of these phenomena have been detected. The 1994 United States intervention in Haiti, for instance, was partly motivated by a desire on Washington's part to curb the flow of Haitian "boat people" to the United States.

ENDANGERED BY ENVIRONMENT

As with massive population growth, the world has been bombarded in recent years with dire predictions about the consequences of further deterioration in the global environment. The continuing build-up of industrial gases in the earth's outer atmosphere, for example, is thought to be impeding the natural radiation of heat from the planet and thereby producing a gradual increase in global temperatures—a process known as "greenhouse warming." If such warming continues, global sea levels will rise, deserts will grow, and severe drought could afflict many important agricultural zones. Other forms of environmental degradation—the thinning of the earth's outer ozone layer, the depletion of arable soil through overcultivation, the persistence of acid rain caused by industrial emissions—could endanger human health and survival in other ways. As with population growth, these environmental effects will not be felt uniformly around the world but will threaten some states and groups more than others, producing new cleavages in human society.

The uneven impact of global environmental decline is being seen in many areas. The first to suffer are invariably those living in marginally habitable areas—arid grazing lands, coastal lowlands, tropical rainforests. As annual rainfall declines, sea levels rise, and forests are harvested, these lands become uninhabitable. The choice, for those living in such areas, is often grim: to migrate to the cities, with all of their attendant problems, or to move onto the lands of neighboring peoples (who may be of a different ethnicity or religion), producing new outbreaks of intergroup violence. This grim choice has fallen with particular severity on indigenous peoples, who in many cases were originally driven into these marginal habitats by more powerful groups. A conspicuous case in point is the Amazon region of Brazil, where systematic deforestation is destroying the habitat and lifestyle of the indigenous peoples and producing death, illness, and unwelcome migration to the cities.

States also vary in their capacity to cope with environmental crisis and the depletion of natural resources. While the wealthier countries can rebuild areas damaged by flooding or other disasters, relocate displaced citizens to safer regions, and import food and other commodities no longer produced locally, the poorer countries are much less capable of doing these things. As noted by Professor Thomas Homer-Dixon of the University of Toronto, "Environmental scarcity sharply raises financial and political demands on government by requiring huge spending on new infrastructure."[2] Because many third world countries cannot sustain such expenditures, he notes, "we have. . .the potential for a widening gap between demands on the state and its financial ability to meet these demands"—a gap that could lead to internal conflict between competing ethnic groups, or significant out-migration to countries better able to cope with environmental stresses.[3]

Finally, there is a danger that acute environmental scarcities will lead to armed interstate conflict over such vital resources as water, forests, and energy supplies. Some believe that the era of "resource wars" has already occurred in the form of recurring conflict over the Middle East's oil supplies and that similar conflicts will arise over control of major sources of water, such as the Nile, Euphrates, and Ganges Rivers.

THE NEW CARTOGRAPHY

These new and growing schisms are creating a map of international security that is based on economic, demographic, and environmental factors. If this map could be represented in graphic terms, it would show an elaborate network of fissures stretching across human society in all directions—producing large concentrations of rifts in some areas and smaller clusters in others, but leaving no area entirely untouched. Each line would represent a cleavage in the human community, dividing one group (however defined) from another; the deeper and wider clefts, and those composed of many fault lines, would indicate the site of current or potential conflict.

These schisms, and their continued growth, will force policymakers to rethink their approach to international security. It is no longer possible to rely on strategies of defense and diplomacy that assume a flat, two-dimensional world of contending geopolitical actors. While such units still play a significant role in world security affairs, they are not the only actors that matter; nor is their interaction the only significant threat to peace and stability. Other actors, and other modes of interaction, are equally important. Only by considering the full range of security threats will it be possible for policymakers to design effective strategies for peace.

When the principal fault lines of international security coincided with the boundaries between countries, it was always possible for individual states to attempt to solve their security problems by fortifying their borders or by joining with other nations in regional defense systems like NATO and the Warsaw Pact. When the fault lines fall *within* societies, however, there are no clear boundaries to be defended and no role for traditional alliance systems. Indeed, it is questionable whether there is a role for military power at all: any use of force by one side in these disputes, however successful, will inevitably cause damage to the body politic as a whole, eroding its capacity to overcome the problems involved and to provide for its long-term stability. Rather than fortifying and defending borders, a successful quest for peace must entail strategies for easing and erasing the rifts in society, by eliminating the causes of dissension or finding ways to peacefully bridge the gap between mutually antagonistic groups.

The new map of international security will not replace older, traditional types. The relations between states will still matter in world affairs, and their interactions may lead, as they have in the past, to major armed conflicts. But it will not be possible to promote international peace and stability without using the new map as well, and dealing with the effects of the new global schisms. Should we fail to do so, the world of the next century could prove as violent as the present one.

---

[2]Thomas Homer-Dixon, "Environmental Scarcity and Intergroup Conflict," in Michael T. Klare and Daniel C. Thomas, eds., *World Security: Challenges for a New Century* (New York: St. Martin's Press, 1994), pp. 298-299.
[3]ibid.

Population

After World War II, the world's population reached 2 billion people.

It had taken 250 years to triple to that level. In the 55 years since the end of World War II, the population has tripled again to 6 billion. When the typical reader of this book reaches the age of 50, experts estimate that the global population will have reached eight and a half billion! By 2050, or about 100 years after the second world war ended, the world may be populated by 10 to 12 billion people. A person born in 1946 (a so-called baby boomer) who lives to be 100 could see a sixfold increase in population.

Nothing like this has ever occurred before. To state this in a different way, in the next 50 years, there will have to be twice as much food produced, twice as many schools and hospitals built, and twice as much of everything else provided just to maintain the current and rather uneven standard of living. We live in an unprecedented time in human history.

One of the most interesting aspects of this unprecedented population growth is that there is little agreement about whether this is good or bad. For example, the government of China has a policy that encourages couples to have only one child. In contrast, there are a few governments that use various financial incentives to promote large families.

The lead article in this section provides a historical overview of the demographic realities of the contemporary world. The unit continues with a discussion of conflicting perspectives on the implications of population growth. Some experts view population growth as the major problem facing the world, while others see it as secondary to social, economic, and political problems. The theme of conflicting views, in short, has been carried forward from the introductory unit of the book to the more specific discussion of population.

This broad discussion is followed by a series of articles that examine specific issues such as the movement of people from developing to industrial countries. This raises interesting questions about how a culture maintains its identity when it must absorb large numbers of new people, or how will a government obtain the resources necessary to integrate these new members into the mainstream of society?

As the world approaches the new millennium, there are many population issues that transcend numerical and economic issues.

The disappearance of indigenous people is a good example of the pressures of population growth on people who live on the margins of modern society. Finally, while demographers develop various scenarios forecasting population growth, it is important to remember that there are circumstances that could lead not to growth but to a significant decline in global population. The spread of AIDS and other infectious diseases reveals that confidence in modern medicine's ability to control these scourges may be premature. Nature has its own checks and balances to the population dynamic that are not policy instruments of some governmental organization. This factor is often overlooked.

Making predictions about the future of the world's population is a complicated task, for there are a variety of forces at work and considerable variation from region to region.

The danger of oversimplification must be overcome if governments and international organizations are going to respond with meaningful policies. Perhaps one could say there is not a global population problem, but many challenges that vary from country to country and region to region.

Looking Ahead: Challenge Questions

What are the basic characteristics of the global population situation? How many people are there?

How fast is the world's population growing? What are the reasons for this growth? How do population dynamics vary from one region to the next?

What regions of the world are attracting large numbers of international immigrants?

How does rapid population growth affect the quality of the environment, social structures, and the ways in which humanity views itself?

How does a rapidly growing population affect a poor country's ability to plan its economic development?

How can economic and social policies be changed in order to reduce the impact of population growth on environmental quality?

In an era of global interdependence, how much impact can individual governments have on demographic changes?

What would be the political implications if the United States decided to end immigration?

CAN HUMANITY SURVIVE

Unrestricted Population Growth?

"As a species, we already are well in the midst of a major bio-geophysical transformation of the Earth."

Timothy C. Weiskel

Dr. Weiskel is associate director, Pacific Rim Research Center, Harvard University, Cambridge, Mass.

BIOLOGISTS are reassuring that the invertebrates and microbial species are likely to survive the current epoch relatively unscathed. This message provides small comfort when one begins to realize that the larger point is that life as we know it is undergoing massive extinction. More precisely, geologists, evolutionary biologists, and paleontologists are reporting evidence in their professional journals that the planet currently is in the midst of a global "extinction event" that equals or exceeds in scale those catastrophic episodes in the geological record which marked the end of the dinosaurs and numerous other species.

At least two important differences exist between this extinction episode and those previously documented. First, in earlier events of similar magnitude, the question of agency and the sequence of species extinctions have remained largely a mystery. In the current extinction event, however, scientists know with a high degree of certainty what the effective agent of system-wide collapse is and have a fairly good notion of the specific dynamics and sequence of these extinctions.

Second, previous events of this nature seem to have involved extraterrestrial phenomena, such as episodic meteor collisions. Alternatively, the long-term flux of incoming solar radiation that results from the harmonic convergence of the Earth's asymmetrical path around the sun and the "wobble" on its axis also drives system-wide changes generating periodic advances and retreats of continental ice sheets in high latitudes. These, too, cause system-wide transformations and have precipitated extinction events in the past.

In contrast to these extraterrestrial or celestial phenomena that served as the forcing functions behind previous mass extinctions, the current event results from an internally generated dynamic. The relatively stable exchanges among various biotic communities have shifted in a short period of time into an unstable phase of runaway, exponential growth for a small subset of the species mix—human beings, their biological symbionts (organisms living in a cooperative relationship), and their associates.

The seemingly unrestrained growth of these populations has unleashed a pattern of accentuated parasitism and predation upon a selected number of proximate species that were deemed by them to be useful. This accentuated parasitism led to the creation of human-influenced biological environments. These, in turn, drove hundreds of other species directly into extinction—sometimes within periods of only a few centuries or decades. More significantly, this pattern of unrestrained growth and subsequent collapse has repeated itself again and again, engendering in each instance a syndrome of generalized habitat destruction. Over time, it has precipitated the cumulative extinction of thousands of species as one civilization after another has devastated its environment and dispersed its remnant populations far afield in search of new resources that it can plunder and squander.

For a variety of reasons—some of them apparently related to their religious beliefs—humans remain fundamentally ignorant of or collectively indifferent toward the fate of their fellow species, insisting instead that measurements of human welfare should be the only criteria for governing human behavior. Apparently, the right to life is effectively defined as the "right to *human* life." This anthropocentric belief in human exceptionalism has characterized past civilizations and remains no less dominant today. The most pervasive form of this religiously held belief in modern times is techno-scientific salvationism. Scientists and baby boomers alike promise us that technological miracles will save us from our rapidly deteriorating ecological circumstance and that no substantial sacrifice will be required. After all, "thanks to science," there are miracle crops, miracle drugs, and Miracle Whip! What more could be needed?

The fact is, we must have a great deal more to survive as a society and a species. In reality, the true immensity of the problem is just beginning to be recognized. Consider, for instance, the truly dramatic dimensions of humans' recent growth as a species. By recent, I mean in evolutionary terms and in terms of the relatively long time scales required to engineer stable social adjustment to changing circumstances. In evolutionary terms, it took from the dawn of humanity to roughly 1945 for the human species to reach a population of about 2,000,000,000. That figure has more than doubled—indeed, nearly tripled—since 1945. Experts say that figure well could reach a total of 9,000,000,000 during the rest of our lifetimes if left to grow at projected rates.

Consider, as well, the over-all ecological "footprint" of human expansion over the millennia, particularly as humans have come to congregate in cities. Depending upon how one wishes to segment humans from their biological relatives, humans have been around for roughly 1,000,000 years. It is only in the last 1.2% of that history—roughly the last 12,000 years—that people have come to depend upon agriculture, and only the last 6,000 years or so that they have begun to transform settlement patterns into urban concentrations.

We are still in the midst of what might be called the "urban transition" in the human evolutionary experiment. It is not clear that the transition will be achieved successfully or that the human bio-evolutionary experiment will endure very much longer in evolutionary terms. Nevertheless, there is enough evidence available about the urban

transition in human history to begin generating some general statements.

The evidence of environmental archaeologists is especially sobering in this context. The history of cities has been associated with that of repeated ecological disaster. Their growth has engendered rapid regional deforestation, the depletion of groundwater aquifers, accelerated soil erosion, plant genetic simplification, periodic outbreaks of disease among pest species and domesticated animals, large-scale human malnutrition, and the development and spread of epidemics. In many cases, the individual elements of ecological decline have been linked in positive feedback processes that reinforced one another and led to precipitous collapse of particular cities.

To overcome the limitations imposed by these patterns of localized environmental collapse, cities historically have sought to dominate rural regions in their immediate vicinity and extend links of trade and alliance to similarly constituted cities further afield. As arable land and strategic water supplies became more scarce and more highly valued, violent conflict between individual city-states emerged, leading in short succession to the development of leagues of allied cities and subsequently to the formation of kingdoms and empires with organized armies for conquest and permanent defense.

Even with the limitations of pre-industrial technology, the results of these conflicts could be devastating to local or regional ecosystems, particularly when victorious groups sought to destroy the ecological viability of defeated groups with such policies as scorched-earth punishment and the sowing of salt over the arable land in defeated territory. The environmental impact of warfare and the preparation for battle has been devastating in all ages. Author C.S. Lewis' observation has proved sadly correct that "the so-called struggle of man against nature is really a struggle of man against man with nature as an instrument."

Demographic historians have added further details to the picture of repeated ecological disaster painted by environmental archaeologists. Human populations have demonstrated again and again the long-term regional tendency to expand and collapse. These undulating patterns are referred to by demographers as the "millennial long waves" (MLW), and they appear to be manifest in both the Old World and the New.

Two patterns are discernible across all cases despite the considerable differences between regions. First, the human population is both highly unstable and highly resilient. There is considerable variation in the amplitude of the population waves; therefore, human populations can not be considered stable in regional terms. Moreover, the population is resilient in the sense

that it bounces back from demographic catastrophe with an even stronger surge in reproductive performance. The second phenomena of the MLW on the regional level is that the frequency between their occurrence is shortened successively. Thus, populations seem to be collapsing and rebounding at higher and higher levels more and more frequently as we approach the present.

When we move beyond the regional evidence to a global scale, another important pattern emerges. Human populations seem to expand in spurts, corresponding to the quantities of energy they are able to harness with their available technology. This may emerge as a new way of stating the Malthusian theory of population limit. Economist Thomas Malthus focused on the relation of populations to their food supply, pointing out that, while populations tend to grow exponentially, the food supply tends to grow only arithmetically. As a result, populations ultimately are limited, as their reproductive performance outstrips the food supply needed to keep them alive and there are periodic widespread famines.

Technology fuels population growth

Since Malthus, people have come to realize that "food" itself is really a form of captured solar energy that humans can assimilate to maintain themselves and do work. If this observation is built upon to reformulate Malthus' observation in terms of energy instead of food itself, we are probably close to a broad-level truth about the human species. Simply put, the Malthusian law can be restated in these terms: Human populations tend to expand to the levels supported by the supplies of energy that they can mobilize with available technology.

The industrial era in world history marks an unprecedented period in human evolution history from this perspective. Never before have global populations experienced such high rates of growth for such sustained duration, reaching a worldwide climax with an average annual population increase of two percent during the decade from 1965 to 1975. Demographic historian Paul Demeny has described this extraordinary period quite succinctly:

"It took countless millennia to reach a global 1700 population of somewhat under 700,000,000. The next 150 years, a tiny fraction of humankind's total history, roughly matched this performance. By 1950, global human numbers doubled again to surpass 2,500,000,000. The average annual rate of population growth was 0.34% in the 18th century; it climbed to 0.54% in the 19th century and to 0.84% in the first half of the 20th. In absolute terms, the first five decades following 1700 added

41

90,000,000 to global numbers. Between 1900 and 1950, not withstanding two world wars, an influenza pandemic, and a protracted global economic crisis, the net addition to population size amounted to nearly 10 times that much."

As Demeny summarized the situation: "Clearly, viewed in an evolutionary perspective, the 250 years between 1700 and 1950 have witnessed extraordinary success of the human species in terms of expanding numbers, a success that invokes the image of swarming." For demographic historians, then, it would seem that humans in the modern era are behaving much like a plague of locusts.

What is even more striking is that the pattern of distribution of this burgeoning population is one of rapid relocation into massive urban agglomerations. In 1700, less than 10% of the total world population of 700,000,000 lived in cities. By 1950, 30% did. In North America, the urban proportion of the population had reached 64% by that time, while in Europe, it was 56%.

In 1700, only five cities had populations of 500,000 people. By 1900, that number had risen to 43. Of those, 16 had populations over 1,000,000. By now, however—in a span of less than 100 years—there are nearly 400 cities that exceed 1,000,000, and there soon will be scores of "mega-cities" with populations in excess of 10,000,000 people, particularly in the Pacific Rim.

Accordingly, it is clear that we can not avoid the problem. We have no choice. As a species, we already are well in the midst of a major bio-geophysical transformation of the Earth.

Can we survive it? Techno-boomers will assure us that of course we can. All we need is adequate incentives for investment, a sense of determination, inventiveness, and political will to make the "tough" decisions.

This well may be true, but it is essentially beside the point. The far more interesting question is: Will we survive it? Not just theoretically *can* we, but, in a very practical sense, *will* we? This only can be answered by looking carefully at what is meant by "we" and "survive." Techno-scientific salvationists—like other fundamentalists—are silent and often sadly ignorant of the social dimensions of the changes required to answer this larger set of questions.

Personally, I am not optimistic, but I remain hopeful that our political leaders will recognize that techno-scientific salvationism alone can not sustain us, especially since such a strategy to address our problems is likely to lead in the future, as it has in the past, to a growing gap between the "haves" and the "have nots." An increasingly divided human community will degrade the global environment further as factions within it struggle to dominate each other and exploit what remains of nature's resources. Political leaders must realize instead that we will need to build a compassionate sense of human community on a world scale to match the global environmental crisis that confronts everyone.

Worldwide Development or Population Explosion: Our Choice

Gerard Piel

The problem is not population; it is poverty. We can reach zero-growth population, if we expand the world economy fourfold and share the proceeds equitably. That would bring the poorest 20 percent out of poverty. The industrialized countries must climb out of their economic torpor and restart their economic engines.

GERARD PIEL, President and Publisher of *Scientific American* from 1948 to 1986, is the author of *Only One World*, W.H. Freeman & Co., 1992.

No entry on the U.S. political agenda has fewer advocates than does "foreign aid." What little of it that remains in the budget carries forward subsidies to Cold War client states which are now relegated to holding the line against Muslim fundamentalism. The poor countries of the world had their last serious mention in U.S. policy in 1961, when John F. Kennedy made his only appearance at the U.N. General Assembly. There, he proposed that the industrial nations make the 1960s the "Decade of Development," and he pledged 1.0 percent of this country's GNP to the effort. Nothing came of that speech. Nothing like it has come from any president since.

But there was a time when U. S. citizens were in favor of giving economic and technical assistance to the poorer countries. That was at the end of World War II. For a few years, as they recoiled from the horror of that war, people all around the world embraced their sense of people as global family. Freedom from want had been declared an aim of the war by the Allies. They had spelled it out in the United Nations Declaration of 1942. In the "underdeveloped countries," which were then emerging from the disbanding colonial empires of the European industrial powers, people were to be lifted out of poverty. With grants and soft loans under the Marshall Plan, U.S. taxpayers financed the economic recovery of the mother countries of those empires—allies (excepting only the USSR) and former enemies alike. In Point Four of his inaugural address to an approving electorate in 1949, Harry S Truman proposed making the Marshall Plan global.

In its interim headquarters at Lake Success, the United Nations began considering what it would take to develop the underdeveloped countries. The estimate was the work of a "Group of Experts"— respected economists from both the industrial and preindustrial worlds. Two of the Experts—Theodore W. Schultz of the University of Chicago and W. Arthur Lewis of the University of Manchester—would share the Nobel prize in Economics in 1979. In effect, they reported, it was time to get on with the industrial revolution.

In the undeveloped nations, people were still living with the technology that begat the agricultural revolution 10,000 years earlier. Given the extant population growth (1.5 percent per annum), it would be possible (and advisable) to move 1.0 percent of the population each year into nonagricultural employment. With a net increase of 1.0 percent in per capita income from industry, and another 2.0 percent increase from improved (by industrial inputs) agricultural yield, incomes could be made to improve at twice the rate of population growth.

At $2,500 for each new industrial job, the Experts estimated the total capital requirement for this enterprise in development at $19 billion per year. Some of that requirement would be filled by domestic savings within the preindustrial countries themselves. Much the greater part of it would have to come from the industrial countries. The profit and interest-bearing part of that external investment would depend, however, upon antecedent investment. It would amount to $3 billion per year, and would be spent on the building of social capital and physical infrastructure. That kind of investment is customarily financed by taxes. That $3 billion would cost the industrial countries 0.5 percent of their combined GDP, and would be generated by outright grants from their governments—a classic example of priming the investment pump. Foreign aid at that level would see the underdeveloped countries through their industrialization to self-sustained economic development by the year 2000.

Business leadership in Europe and the United States was ready to entertain this proposition. The Experts' estimate was only round one, of course. But it was of the same dimension as the ongoing, successful undertaking of the Marshall Plan. The Great Depression was still fresh in their memories. The postwar generation of business managers was receptive to imaginative ideas for countercyclical outlays by the government. But the dispatch of troops to Korea in June 1950 extinguished the vision of an organized campaign of economic development. Foreign aid never reached the 0.5 percent goal—much less the Kennedy 1.0 percent.

A GLOBAL MARSHALL PLAN

Now, in 1995, the time has come to bring the vision of a global Marshall Plan into focus again. Getting on with the industrial revolution is the most urgent challenge civilization now faces. If foreign aid was being considered an act of common humanity at mid-century, it is now dictated by the exigencies of common survival. The population of the world has more than doubled since 1950—from 2.5 billion to 5.3 billion. The number of people living in direst poverty has increased to 1.3 billion—close to the total population of the underdeveloped countries in 1950. The population is doubling now again. The number in direst poverty could equal the present world population. A doubling after that would bring the human species close to full occupation of the Earth.

The total capital requirement for the development of the pre-industrial nations is estimated at $19 billion per year. Some of that requirement would be filled by domestic savings within these countries themselves. Much the greater part of it would have to come from the industrial countries.

In order to stabilize the world's population at some sustainable level, the industrial revolution must be carried out worldwide. Natural population increase has ceased in the 20 percent of the world population that is represented by the industrialized countries. Fertility is approaching the zero-growth rate in another 20 percent of the population currently living in the pre-industrial countries. That is happening in countries that have gotten on with their industrial revolutions since 1950. The population explosion that distresses so many well-off people in the industrialized countries is confined to the countries where the revolution has lagged and is now arrested. The sooner the industrial revolution reaches people everywhere, the smaller will be the world's population.

The lack of understanding of the connection between industrial revolution and population growth is due to the baleful legacy of Thomas R. Malthus. He wrote his famous *Essay on the Principle of Population* in 1798—just about when the industrial revolution and its attendant population explosion was getting under way. He was unaware of either development. His message is easily grasped: "Population, when unchecked, increases in a geometric ratio. Subsistence increases only in an arithmetic ratio. A slight acquaintance with numbers will shew the immensity of the first power in comparison with the second." Taking the two series out nine steps, Malthus nailed down his point: "In two centuries and a quarter, the population would be to the means of subsistence as 512 to 10."

Indeed, geometric and arithmetic series do diverge. But these series do not fit the trends of the last two centuries. World population increase (now in its third doubling since Malthus published his *Essay*) has been sustained by more than five doublings of the supply of the "means of subsistence." Since 1950, industrial technology (overriding any arithmetic constraint) has twice doubled the output of material goods—even as the population has doubled. But the doubling of average per capita production was accompanied by an unprecedented increase in the per capita consumption gap. It tripled. The difference between the best-off 20 percent of the world population and the worst-off 20 percent was 20 to 1 in 1960. It rose to 60 to 1 in 1990. Of course, some people have always been rich. And most people have always been poor. But with this latest increase in disparity, the industrial revolution has starkly divided the world into two camps—rich countries and poor.

THE ISSUE IS POVERTY

The problem is not population; it is poverty. We can reach zero-growth population, if we expand the world economy fourfold and share the proceeds equitably. That would bring the poorest 20 percent out of poverty. The industrialized countries must climb out of their economic torpor and restart their economic engines. Outlays for foreign aid could help to provide the necessary stimulus. In most industrialized countries (especially in the United States), governments appear to be unwilling or unable to take the initiative.

The rich industrial country is an entirely new historical phenomenon. It is rich in the sense that none of its inhabitants need submit to toil and want. Poverty persists in the industrialized countries as a social institution. In the poor countries, rampant poverty is a familiar story. It exists as if by definition. Simply, there is not enough to go around. Even today, village people in the poor countries live very much as their forebears did when the agricultural revolution settled them in villages 10,000 years ago. They survive by the sweat of their brows. The biological energy of their bodies gets the means of subsistence to renew that energy, but not much more. With traditional tools and practice, they can increase the means of that subsistence only by bringing new land under cultivation.

Over the ten millennia of agricultural civilization, population increase proceeded at a near-zero rate. It doubled only seven times—from an estimated 5 million to 500 million around 1600. Malthus's principle of population approximately describes the equilibrium with the misery that bespoke the human condition. High birth rates offset high death rates. Through good times and bad, life expectancy hovered near twenty-five years of age. In most times and places, people could anticipate no improvement in their circumstances in the course of their lifetimes. A person could improve his circumstances only at the expense of others. Status and force served this purpose and built high civilizations on the output of the traditional technology of the agricultural revolution.

INDUSTRIAL REVOLUTION

Now, the industrial revolution has brought rich countries abruptly into history. In Europe, around 1600 (where and when the industrial revolution had its earliest beginnings), life expectancy was no greater than twenty-five years of age. With the increase of production running ahead of population growth, death rates fell and life expectancies lengthened. The high birth

> *Outlays for foreign aid could help to provide the necessary stimulus for the revitalization of the developed countries' economies. In most industrialized countries (especially in the United States), governments appear to be unwilling or unable to take the initiative.*

rates that had barely offset the formerly high death rates began to deliver net additions to the population. In the 18th century, the curve of population increased steeply. Henry Adams dated his "acceleration of history" from that period. He found he could measure it because "it took the form of utilizing heat as force, through the steam engine, and this addition of power was measurable in the coal output." By the end of the 18th century, the growth of the European population had exploded. It doubled its 50-million census (extant in 1600) four times and over to nearly 1 billion by the middle of the 20th century. It constituted one-tenth of the world population in 1600, but it grew to a full one-third of it by 1950, having avalanched on to all the other continents.

During the 19th century, birth rates began to decline in the populations which were participating in the industrial revolution. At the outset, the birth control movement in Britain, on the continent, and in America found militant supporters. They recoiled from the other existing modes of population control—infanticide, abandonment, and abortion. The foundling hospitals and baby farms were evidence of their widespread practice. Too often, these institutions had fewer alumni than matriculates. During the first half of the 20th century, declining birth rates began converging with the declining death rates in all the industrialized countries. The European population explosion was coming to an end.

THE DEMOGRAPHIC TRANSITION

By the middle of this century, demographers were recognizing an entirely new principle governing population growth—namely, that industrial revolution brings on a demographic revolution. In retrospect, it can now be seen that the population of the industrial world has made a transition since 1600 from near-zero growth at high death rates and high birth rates and life expectancy of less than thirty years to near-zero growth again at low birth rates and low death rates and life expectancy exceeding seventy years. Typically, this "demographic transition" has proceeded through two phases: (1) The population of an industrializing country sees its death rate fall first; its census then increases at rates measured by the difference between its death and birth rates; and (2) that difference narrows with the decline in the birth rate, and the rate of population growth approaches zero again.

Perfection of the technology of contraception around the middle of this century facilitated the final decline of the birth rate in the industrialized world. The total fertility rate fell everywhere to the replacement—zero-growth—rate of 2.1 infants per female reproductive lifetime. In some countries, it fell even lower. Natural population growth has all but ceased in the industrialized 20 percent of the world population. Immigration has brought most of its increase in numbers since 1950.

Figure 1 contrasts the age/sex structure of the U.S. population in 1900 and 1985. In passage through the demographic transition, the population exploded from 75 to 240 million. The 1900 0-5 cohort is the largest, but the number of those surviving into older cohorts reflects an increase in life expectancy. The 1985 structure declares the near completion of the demographic transition. The 0-5 cohort is no longer the largest. Variation in sizes of cohorts reflects reproductive preferences of parent cohorts.

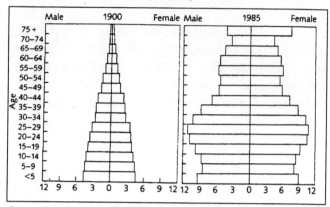

Figure 1 **Age/Sex Structure of U.S. Population, 1900–85** (millions)

Source: *Only One World*, W.H. Freeman & Co., 1992.

People, constrained to witnessing history in the short term, tend to make the simple cause-effect connection between contraceptive technology and that final decline in the fertility rate. On the other hand, as the demographer Paul Demeny has observed, "Effective methods of fertility control have always been known and available in all societies. Fertility transition implies social changes rather than merely a change in technology." The industrial revolution has surely brought such changes. It has transformed the human condition for the 25 percent of the world's population who have migrated from the farm and village to live in cities. They have exchanged the independence of self-employment for free time from wage employment. They are compelled to literacy. They get their living, not by muscular exertion in the field, but by stress on the nervous system in offices, shops, or service establishments. Women go to work (willingly or of necessity) outside the home. Sex roles de-differentiate. The mutual-aid extended-kinship family goes into decline, thereby setting its member families loose on their own. Liberated by freedom from want and toil, urban folk have been enlarging their new freedom to make their individual existence relevant to wider communities.

The lengthening of life expectancy supplies the essential condition for restraint of fertility. People who can look forward to the full biologically permitted human lifetime permit themselves to be future dwellers. Assured of survival of their first infant(s), they can plan their families. Making the inverse Malthusian calculation, they see that the fewer, the more—for each. The family in industrial civilization (and in any zero-growth population) is necessarily a small family.

Demonstrating that the knack for industrial revolution is not somehow exclusively confined to Europeans, the Japanese proceeded to their own industrialization in the last decades of the 19th century. On a smaller scale, and in a much shorter time,

> *When assured of survival of their first infant(s), people can plan their families. Making the inverse Malthusian calculation, they see that the fewer, the more. The family in industrial civilization (and in any zero-growth population) is necessarily a small family.*

they recapitulated the European demographic experience—population explosion included. They arrived at about the same time as the Europeans at the zero-growth fertility rate.

THE FIRST HUMAN POPULATION

The population of industrial civilization can be said to be the first human population. The populations of other species offer up their young in great number to the pruning process of natural selection. Survivors die away from the youngest in the largest number at each stage of development or metamorphosis—down to the minority that survives to reproduce the species. Closer to nature, such was the age-structure of populations in agricultural civilization. *Figure 2* shows that it persists in the populations of the developing countries today. Industrial civilization brings very nearly all its newborn to full human growth and capacity. The youngest may be the smallest age group. Variation in the size of age groups up to the mortal eldest reflects differences, not in survival, but in decisions taken as to child-bearing in the parental age groups ahead. As mortality continues to yield to longevity, the eldest become the most rapidly growing age group.

THE BENIGN EXPLOSION

The population explosion that is rolling over the poor countries of the world may yet be recognized as a benign event. It declares the entrance of the rest of the human family into the first phase of the demographic transition.

Population growth began to rise above the near-zero rate in those countries early in their subjugation to the colonial empires of the European industrial powers. During the present half-century, as the leading edge of industrial revolution crossed the borders of these former colonies, their population growth entered the explosive phase. The modest flows of foreign aid that emanated from the United Nations were sufficient to carry out the most portable technologies of industrial revolution. Most potent were those delivered by multilateral funding through the U.N. technical agencies. The World Health Organization brought the rudiments of preventive medicine and sanitation. The Food and Agriculture Organization brought seed and scientific practice. The Educational, Scientific, and Cultural Organization brought mass literacy campaigns. These inputs, domestic economic growth, and bilateral foreign aid from those industrial countries most interested in the country's market and resources induced a surge of development in all of the now-developing countries during the first two decades after World War II and into the 1970s. Consequently, life expectancy had lengthened by a decade on all the continents by 1990. As birth rates fell away from death rates, population-growth rates reached more than 2 percent in almost all the countries and more than 3 percent in some of them. "Explosion" is the appropriate word for this development. Comparable declines in the death rates of the existing industrialized countries transpired over the course of a century or two.

Figure 2 charts the age/sex structure of the population of Nigeria as it was in 1985 (when it was a classical "natural selection" population) and as it is projected to be in 2015. The 1985 0-5 cohort is the largest, and the numbers rapidly diminish in older

Figure 2   **Age/Sex Structure of Nigerian Population, 1985–2015** (millions)

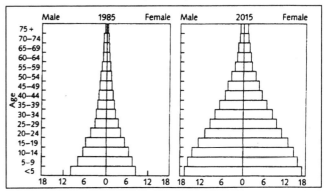

Source: *Only One World,* W.H. Freeman & Co., 1992.

cohorts. The projection shows a "population explosion" that is caused by an increase in life expectancy. The number of 0-5-year-olds is projected to double by 2015. Though the fertility rate will drop by half, four times as many women will survive to child-bearing years.

From 1950 to 1970, the world's population-growth rate climbed to just over 2 percent. This was its all-time peak. The growth rate has been in decline ever since. That turning point declares the entrance of those developing countries which are proceeding most successfully with their development into the second phase of the demographic transition. The decline in their fertility rate (and now in their birth rates) is over-taking the decline in their death rates. When industrialization has brought the rest of the developing countries into the second phase, the world population growth rate will go below 1.0 percent again, and will be headed toward zero.

BIRTH RATES DECLINE

For the present, this historic turning point is obscured from public understanding by its arithmetic. The

---

The neo-Malthusian alarm bells continue to ring. The cry is that "those people overpopulate their countries." In fact, the countries that have the highest population density—the seats of ancient civilization in Asia—have moved most decisively into the industrial revolution and through the demographic transition.

---

declining growth rate is multiplying a larger population each year. Growth proceeds, accordingly, by the largest annual increments ever—in excess of 90 million people per year. If the decline in growth rate continues on its present slope, the annual increments will begin to shrink at the turn of the next century. That depends, of course, on the rate of development—especially in the poorest countries.

The neo-Malthusian alarm bells continue to ring. The cry is that "those people overpopulate their countries." In fact, the countries that have the highest population density—the seats of ancient civilizations in Asia—have moved most decisively into the industrial revolution and through the demographic transition. Africa, with the poorest and fastest-growing popula-

tion, holds relatively the largest frontier open to human habitation.

In Latin America, disparity in income and wealth closes off another vast frontier to cultivation—the vast stretches of unused and underutilized latifundia. Meanwhile, the resources of these continents continue to fuel the economies of the industrial world. The underdeveloped countries await delivery of the less portable technologies of industrial revolution. Some day, these will permit them to develop the value of their resources for their own uses.

NEO-COLONIAL ECONOMIES

The sanctimony and controversy that have surrounded foreign aid have grossly inflated its dimensions in the public understanding. Except in the national budgets of the Nordic countries and Canada, outright grants for development have rarely exceeded 0.3 percent of the output of the industrialized world. For more than a decade, that which is properly reckoned a foreign aid in the U.S. federal budget has never exceeded 0.2 percent of the country's GDP. The percentage was higher when foreign aid served Cold War ends. Most of the flow then went to a half-dozen countries in East and Southeast Asia and to those at the eastern end of the Mediterranean. In South Korea and Taiwan, the fallout from aid and the huge military expenditure was big enough to trigger genuine development. That and the regional boom that occurred as a result of the Korean and Vietnam wars metamorphosed those countries—along with the city states of Hong Kong and Singapore. They became the celebrated "Tigers" of East Asia.

As early as the 1960s, private direct investment from the industrialized countries in plantations, mines, and oil fields began to overtake governmental outlays to foreign aid. The underdeveloped countries became the developing countries. What development most of them have seen (with the notable exceptions of India and China) is due principally to private investment. The contribution to development was indirect. Private investment (and the bilateral foreign aid it often entrained) went primarily to expedite delivery of the country's agricultural commodities, metal ores and, especially, petroleum to the dockside.

This engagement in world commerce has divided many developing countries (especially the smaller ones) into dual economies. The "modern" sectors operate in closer cultural, as well as economic, identity with the industrial powers most interested in their resources than with the traditional sectors in their own hinterlands. These countries remain in colonial status as "hewers of wood and drawers of water." They serve as sources of the raw materials most required by the industrialized world and, above all, of the petroleum that sustains industrial civilization in Europe and North America. In many countries, domestic political leadership (in half of them, military dictatorship) is content with this state of affairs.

ENTER THE TRANSNATIONALS

Over time, an ever smaller number of progressively larger corporations have made the economic connection between the developing countries and the industrial world. The 350 largest nonfinancial transnational corporations now account for 30 percent of the output of the world economy. Their combined turnover is larger by several hundred billion dollars than the total product of all the developing countries. In trade between the two worlds, from three to not more than seven of these corporations make the market for the commodity at hand. In no small measure, they owe their enormous expansion in the past three decades to their advantage in negotiation of the terms under which the developing countries have supplied every commodity—from petroleum to labor. Under the supervision of the transnationals, the imperfections of the market have caused the flow of foreign aid to run uphill—from the poor to the rich countries. For four decades, the rising trade between the two worlds has proceeded on steadily worsening terms for the poor. OPEC could hold back the tide and control the price on petroleum for no more than a few years.

The 1980 OPEC price may serve, nonetheless, as an indicator of the dimensions of the reverse flow of foreign aid. It can be argued that it expressed the true scarcity value of petroleum and, therefore, charged a fair Ricardian rent. Discounted by inflation, the price has now returned to its pre-1973 level. The difference between the two prices reflects the fact that petroleum alone carries an annual subsidy to the rich countries that approaches $200 billion. The most that OECD headquarters can claim for money flowing the other way is $50 billion.

In reaction to inflation set off by their momentary loss of control of the price of oil, the industrialized countries embraced deflation. They set aside the goal of full employment and shrank their welfare states. Even as the financial community has alternately celebrated and deplored signs of "recovery" and "reces-

sion" in the low-amplitude business cycle, the growth of the world economy has not exceeded population growth by much for two decades. Despite continued subsidy from the poor, persistent deflation in the rich countries has arrested development in the developing world. With the exceptions of China and the countries of East and Southeast Asia, economies have stopped growing and have gone into decline. The net result of four decades of trade with the industrialized world has been their combined debt of $1.4 trillion. To maintain their creditworthiness, they have been invited by the international financial institutions to "restructure" their economies in the deflated image of their creditors. In addition to their development having been aborted, restructuring has reduced their social expenditures. Progress through the demographic transition has halted in many developing countries. It has gone into reverse in the poorest countries.

One indicator of development (especially during the first two decades after World War II) was the increase in the reliability of the vital statistics kept by the developing countries. Based on these real data, the Population Division of the U.N. Secretariat has been perfecting a computer model of the world population. Confidence in the data encouraged the publication in 1980 of long-range projections, which would estimate the size of the ultimate stabilized world population. The medium-fertility projection found the population increasing to 6 billion in the year 2000 and stabilizing at 10 billion in the year 2100. The present doubling could be seen as the last. Significantly, the model showed that the present poorest billion people will contribute 4 billion descendants to that ultimate population. In the high projection, the population stabilizes at 15 billion in 2100, with still larger contributions from the poorest countries.

In 1990, with more confidence in the data and their model, the U.N. demographers ran a second long-range projection. This time, the median projection showed the population reaching 6.3 billion by the year 2000, passing 10 billion at 2100, and stabilizing at 11.5 billion in 2150. The high projection has the population growing past 28 billion in 2150. In that population, the present poorest billion will generate 14 billion descendants.

The difference between the two projections measures the ground and the time lost to persistent stagnation of the world economy. Another set of numbers suggests the reduction in the size of the ultimate population and the time that might have been gained, if an organized campaign of development had gone forward at the founding of the United Nations. The world's two most populous countries nations have achieved development on their own—with little or no foreign aid, and largely in isolation from the world economy. With the smaller populations of countries that have made similar progress added to their grand total, it can be reckoned that more than one-half of the population of the developing world has entered the second phase of the demographic transition. Birth rates in all these countries are falling. They reflect still steeper declines in their fertility rates.

Within this 2.2 billion population, a population of 100 million has actually completed the passage through the demographic transition. This includes the populations of the "Tigers" of East Asia—now classified as "newly industrializing countries"—and Thailand, which is on the verge of that classification. It also includes two countries—Sri Lanka and Cuba—that have shared the proceeds of what development they have achieved most widely in their populations. These countries have come through most of the first and all of the second phase of the demographic transition within the span of a human lifetime. That compares with the 300-year passage of the industrialized 20 percent of the world's population. The technologies which have been pioneered over the centuries by that 20 percent were, of course, there on the shelf—ready for installation in the countries that followed. With the sudden increase of life expectancy, the people of the developing countries were ready to reduce their fertility at a lower level of living than that which is enjoyed by the people of the industrial world. They are able to do so by employing the portable technology of contraception.

CHINA'S INDUSTRIAL REVOLUTION

Still more decisive for the prospect of zero population growth is the progress of China. The Chinese revolution has been no less industrial than political. In political isolation from the world economy, and from the next-door Soviet economy as well, China's industrial revolution built the world's ninth-largest economy. In the half-century since 1949, the first bridges crossed the Yangtze and the Yellow rivers, and the first dams impounded their waters for flood control, irrigation, and the generation of electrical power. Rail and highway networks tie together once-distant regions in a continental economy. China is the fifth-largest producer of steel and the largest producer of cement and nitrogen fertilizer. It had accomplished all of this

before it opened its markets and labor force to the world economy. But with a population of 1.12 billion—equal to that of all of the industrial countries combined—China remains a country of the poor. Until recently, however, China divided its increasing prod-

> *The "Tigers" of East Asia, Thailand, Sri Lanka, and Cuba have come through most of the first and all of the second phase of the demographic transition within the span of a human lifetime. That compares with the 300-year passage of the industrialized 20 percent of the world's population.*

uct with equity that was enforced by revolutionary ardor. The average GDP per capita of $370 in 1990 hovered close to the modal share in GDP—the share of most of the population. It was double that of 1949, despite the concurrent doubling of the population since then.

Much of the GDP per capita reaches the people through public expenditures on education and health. Ninety percent of the people were illiterate in 1949. Now, 75 percent are literate. Nearly all the children—equal in number to the entire population of the United States—are in school. Life expectancy—less than 40 years in 1949—now exceeds 70 years. Under-five-year-old deaths had fallen to 35 per 1,000 live births in 1992—down from more than 200 in 1949. This is the setting in which the second 20 percent of the world's population approaches full passage through the second phase of the demographic transition. In 1992, China's total fertility rate approached the zero-growth fertility rate (2.1 infants per female reproductive lifetime). It fell to 2.3.

Popular discourse, especially in the United States, attributes this astonishing development to the aggressive promotion of contraception (lately the coercive promotion of the "one-child family") by the central government. Until recently, the press has had less to say about China's economic development. The aggressive measures undoubtedly secured wide distribution of contraceptives. It hastened the "contraceptive prevalence rate" to 70 percent of the reproductive population. It cannot be shown that the coercive policies have had any result other than revival of the practice of female infanticide and increase in the rate of abortion. Upon arrival at the zero-growth fertility rate,

China will still experience huge population growth. The median age of the population is twenty-four years of age. With such a high percentage of the population in the reproductive years, the birth rate must remain high. China is bound to reach 1.5 billion population.

INDIA'S INDUSTRIALIZATION

The industrialization of India (with its 870 million population) lags behind that of China by about twenty-five years. With deference due to an already installed private industrial sector, the government of India has been constrained to a "socialist pattern of development." A succession of five-year plans, nonetheless, installed a considerable industrial infrastructure before the country lowered its barriers to foreign capital at the start of this decade. Industrial investment was dedicated, from the beginning, to increasing the productivity of agriculture. After an uncertain start, during which food aid from the United States fended off famine, India achieved self-sufficiency in food production that it maintains ahead of population growth. With an industrial plant about one-half the size of China's, and the largest railway system in Asia, India is the world's twelfth-largest economy. The average GDP per capita ($350) is close to China's, but that average is high above the modal share of about $100. Perhaps 20 percent of the population—nearly 200 million people—live comfortably in that economy—at home in an urban-industrial civilization. But the villages have had their place in the socialist pattern of development. It brought them the new technologies of agriculture, sanitation, and medicine. It enrolled the children in schools. It organized producer and marketing cooperatives. And it established the rudiments of democratic self-government against traditional landlord feudalism.

India's progress over the half-century is summed up in a total fertility rate of 4.0. That is more than halfway to the zero-growth rate from the country's fertility rate at its liberation in 1947. The combined fertility rate of the eight largest countries that have arrived at comparable GDP per capita is 5.8. The U.N. population projections schedule India's arrival at the 2.1 fertility rate in the year 2015. The low median age of the population ensures that, even at zero-growth fertility, it must increase to an ultimate census of not less than 1.6 billion. But if India's development continues on course, the present doubling of its population will be the last.

There is much more growth ahead in the rest of the world population. According to the 1990 U.N. long-range projection, Latin America will increase 2.5 times to 1.4 billion people, the rest of Asia 2.7 times to 2.8 billion, and Africa nearly five times to 3 billion. Half of the present world population will generate 7 billion of the 11.5 billion projected for the year 2150.

Today, the developing countries are being advised to develop by trade—not by aid. The international financial institutions have compelled the "restructuring" of their economies and now declare its success. The inflow of foreign private investment has increased to $40 billion from $14 billion in the early 1980s. Developing countries turn up as "players" in the financial pages. Their full incorporation in the world economy by the market process is said to be surely just a matter of time.

For two decades, however, two-thirds of private direct investment (principally by the 350 transnationals) has gone to ten countries with populations of less than 500 million. Among them are the six "newly industrializing" countries and two countries in the Japanese sphere on their way into that classification. All of them are far along on the road to industrialization under their own steam. For private investment in the ninth country now on that list—Egypt—Cold War

> *After an uncertain start, during which food aid from the United States fended off famine, India has achieved self-sufficiency in food production.*

outlays by the United States supplied the infrastructure. The combined fertility rate of these countries (3.2) puts them well on the way through the second phase of the demographic transition.

The charmed circle of ten now includes China, which had nearly completed its demographic transition before it applied for admission to the world economy. With China aboard, the combined fertility rate of the countries favored by private investment comes down to 2.6. For the rest of the developing countries (with populations totaling nearly 3 billion and a combined fertility rate in excess of 5.0), the remaining one-third of the private investment flow can scarcely move the needle of development. Most of it goes, in any case, for the extraction of resources—with no more than indirect repercussion for development. None of it goes to the poorest countries—twenty-six of them in Africa, where the fertility rate exceeds 6.0.

Poverty, of course, presents obstacles to private investment. The Group of Experts declared: ". . . the amount which can be profitably invested at a 4 percent rate of interest depends on the amount which is being spent at the same time on improving social capital, and especially on public health, on education, and on roads and communications." Because incomes inadequate to sustain current consumption cannot generate it, the necessary capital must be supplied by way of "intergovernmental grants." Nothing that has happened since 1950 puts the wisdom of this counsel in doubt.

In the long-term transitional period, most developing countries have developed technically sophisticated indigenous intelligentsias. There has been time for these people to put flesh on the bare bones of the 1950 formulation of the essential role of foreign aid. On the floor of the U.N. General Assembly, and in bilateral negotiations between developing countries and prospective donors, their ongoing labors have lent tangible reality and specificity to the need for aid and the industrial technology it is supposed to transfer.

AGENDA 21

A comprehensive sampling of this now immense body of work is available in Agenda 21 and its underlying primary data bank. As the U.S. media failed to report, Agenda 21 is the principal work product of the U.N. Conference on Environment and Development that convened in Rio de Janeiro in June 1992. Agenda 21 spells out and prices out the program of "sustainable development" that will sustain the fourfold multiplication of the global GDP that will be required in the next century to eliminate poverty in a world population that has doubled to 10-to-12 billion. It is a program of development the Earth can sustain in bringing the human species through its demographic transition.

Agenda 21 is composed of 2,500 enterprises engineered and otherwise realized by indigenous experts in the developing countries and U.N. technical agencies. They specify work to be done in environmental repair and conservation, in resource (especially agricultural resource) development, in the building of urban infrastructure, and in the development of human capital. The 2,500 enterprises constitute, of course, no more than a start on the work that must engage hundreds of millions of men and women in every developing country over the next century.

Agenda 21 shows that the task is finite and within the bounds of the Earth's resources. The developing countries are to supply most of the approximately $600-billion annual investment. From "savings" which are latent in their underemployed work forces and underutilized resources, they are committed to invest $500 billion—about 10 percent of their GDP. The industrial countries are asked to invest $125 billion—0.7 percent of their combined GDP. It will be transferred principally in the form of the technology necessary to catalyze the yield from people and resources. While the industrial countries signed the nonbinding document setting forth Agenda 21, they made no commitment to supply their 0.7 percent share.

For foreign aid there is "no money." The industrial countries were readier forty-five years ago to render economic assistance to the underdeveloped countries. Governments had retained war powers for the first tasks of peace. Now the globalized economy is in private hands. The 350 transnational corporations conduct their own foreign policies with the countries of the two worlds. Their 25 million employees and perhaps 100 million principal shareholders thrive in a financial hothouse that escapes the doldrums in which the industrial economies and populations are becalmed. The 24-hour world financial market, which conducts currency transactions at ten times the rate that facilitates the movement of goods and investment capital across national borders, disburses the credit to corporations and governments alike. A government that undertakes countercyclical fiscal measures, including outlays for foreign aid, invites trades against the value of its currency.

Agenda 21 asks, first of all, that the industrialized countries restart their economies. The electorates of those countries must soon assert their interest in the choice now being made by default. In the United States, apparently, the choice is to be deliberate. The "Contract with America" schedules the last best hope of Earth for zeroing-out to oblivion. For the survival of market economies and self-governing polities, the present doubling of the world's population must be the last. The logistics of sustaining a population of 28 billion would offer little slack for the market process and no tolerance for freedom of expression.

P. Mountzis/UNHCR

REFUGEES: THE RISING TIDE

BY RONY BRAUMAN

There have never been so many long-term refugees as there are today

Above, Somali refugees arrive in Mombasa (Kenya), 1992.

There are over sixteen million refugees in the world today. The reality behind this stark figure is the multitude of human tragedies being played out in encampments, sometimes surrounded with barbed wire, where freedom is the price paid for survival and security is maintained not by the rule of law but by enclosure. To be a refugee is to exchange one injustice for another, one form of suffering for another.

But unless we are prepared to accept the refugee's condition as a permanent one, as is sometimes unfortunately the case, it is important to understand the origins of these mass movements and the course they take. Since 1990, for example, some 10 million exiles have managed to return home and pick up the threads of a way of life they had been forced to abandon. Another important fact is that half the total number of refugees, some 8.5 million people, originate from only four countries: Palestine, Afghanistan, Rwanda, and Bosnia and Herzegovina.

This does not mean that the refugee problem is confined to the Third World and that the refugee's plight has never been known in the countries which are today industrialized. The Huguenots, the French Protestants who fled from France after the revocation of the Edict of Nantes, the law which gave them a measure of religious liberty, in 1685 were the first group of refugees to be defined as such. To avoid *dragonnades*, the quartering of Louis XIV's soldiers in their households, forcible conversion, and exclusion from professional activities, 300,000 Protestants fled the kingdom and sought refuge in neighbouring Protestant countries. They were the first exiles for whom specific responsibility was acknowledged, in this instance a duty of religious solidarity.

Horror and humanitarianism

But the age of refugees that has outstripped all others has been the twentieth century, which seems to have been divided between humane sensitivity and political terror. Constant growth of concern for human rights—both in the minds of men and women and in international conventions and regulations—has been accompanied by the appearance of new forms of oppression, social control and destruction. Modern tyrants are probably no worse than those of the past, but the technical means at their disposal have enabled them to envisage programmes of social surgery that their predecessors could never have imagined. Horror magnified by technology is a leitmotiv of the twentieth century, but it has been accompanied by a concomitant determination to react by taking humanitarian action. A year after it was founded in 1920, the League of Nations established the High Commission for Refugees under the leadership of Norway's Fridtjof Nansen, whose first task was to organize the repatriation of 1.5 million refugees and prisoners of war scattered all over Europe by the turmoil of the First World War.

In the Second World War, civilians were in the eye of the storm. At the end of the conflict there were a recorded 21 million refugees scattered across Europe. In 1951, the Office of the United Nations High Commissioner for Refugees (UNHCR) began its activities (see box). According to the 1951 Geneva Convention relating to the Status of Refugees, which was drawn up in parallel with the creation of UNHCR,

Refugees voluntarily leaving Mexico to return home to Guatemala.

Liba Taylor/UNHCR

refugee status is accorded to any person who, "owing to well-founded fear of being persecuted for reasons of race, religion, nationality or political opinion, is outside the country of his nationality and is unable, or owing to such fear, is unwilling to avail himself of the protection of that country. . . .". One necessary (but not sufficient) condition of refugee status is the crossing of an international border. This differentiates refugees from people forced out of their usual place of residence, who are considered as "displaced persons" and are without legal status.

Changing status

This definition was hammered out by Europeans in the political context of the 1950s. Since then its practical application has broadened over the years in response to changing conditions. It was a straightforward matter when a Soviet or Hungarian dissident sought protection in a democratic country in the 1960s or 1970s. It was just as straightforward when it was a question of saving Iranians or Argentines from the claws of their gaolers in the 1970s. Serious complications began to appear in the second half of the 1970s when major upheavals occurred in several parts of the Third World. Changes of regime in Southeast Asia and in southern and eastern Africa, the invasion of Afghanistan and the rise of violence in Central America

THE OFFICE OF THE UNITED NATIONS HIGH COMMISSIONER FOR REFUGEES (UNHCR)

The Office of the United Nations High Commissioner for Refugees (UNHCR) was established in 1951 with responsibilities for "providing international protection . . . and . . . seeking permanent solutions for the problems of refugees". Its work is humanitarian and entirely non-political. Initially, its mandate was limited to people outside their country of origin, but over the years it has increasingly been called on to protect or assist returnees in their home countries and particular groups of displaced people who have not crossed an international border but are in a refugee-like situation inside their country of origin.

The 1951 UN Convention relating to the Status of Refugees, which is the key to UNHCR's protection activities, is a legally binding treaty. It contains a general definition of the term "refugee" that no longer ties it to specific national groups, clearly establishes the principle of *non-refoulement,* whereby no person may be returned against his or her will to a territory where he or she may be exposed to persecution, and sets standards for the treatment of refugees, including their legal status, employment and welfare.

UNHCR endeavours:
☛ to encourage governments to ratify international and regional conventions concerning refugees, returnees and displaced people;
☛ to ensure that refugees are treated in accordance with recognized international standards and receive an appropriate legal status and the same economic and social rights as nationals of the country in which they have been given asylum;
☛ to promote the granting of asylum to refugees, i.e. to ensure that they are admitted to safety and protected against forcible return to a country where they have reason to fear persecution or other serious harm;
☛ to ensure that applications for asylum are examined fairly and that asylum-seekers are protected, while their requests are being examined, against forcible return to a country where their freedom or lives would be endangered;
☛ to help refugees to cease being refugees either through voluntary repatriation to their countries of origin, or through the eventual acquisition of the nationality of their country of residence;
☛ to help reintegrate refugees returning to their home country and to monitor amnesties, guarantees or assurances on the basis of which they have returned home;
☛ to promote the physical security of refugees, asylum-seekers and returnees.

UNHCR's material assistance activities include emergency relief, assisting efforts to promote voluntary repatriation or resettlement within new national communities, social welfare, education and legal aid.

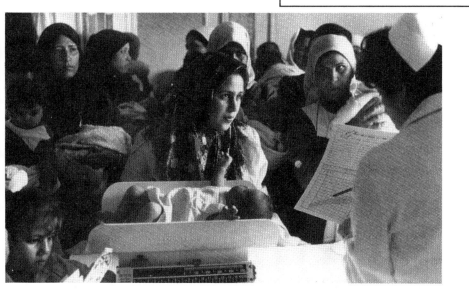

The United Nations Relief and Works Agency for Palestine Refugees in the Near East (UNRWA), established in 1949, runs 98 health units and 30 dental and special clinics. One third of the 2.39 million refugees registered with UNRWA live in crowded refugee camps. Shown here, a medical visit in Beqa'a camp.

transformed the problem, although perceptions of it and the international instruments designed to provide a response did not really change accordingly. The end of the Cold War saw the easing of a number of conflicts, enabling millions of exiles to return home. But other regions erupted into violence.

These political transformations have had profound consequences on the status of refugees. The problem was once solved by the integration of refugees in their host countries; today's solution is to provide aid in camps established along the borders of warring nations for people who hope even-

As persons displaced within their own national borders, these Chechen civilians fleeing the combat zone are of concern to UNHCR.

Below, voluntary Cambodian returnees head for a reception centre set up by UNHCR.

UNHCR:
FACTS AND FIGURES

UNHCR Public Information Section
Case postale 2500, CH-1211 Geneva 2 Dépôt
Switzerland
Tel: (41 22) 739 85 02
Fax: (41 22) 739 73 15
e-mail: hqpi00@unhcr.ch

● UNHCR programmes are financed by voluntary contributions from governments and governmental and non-governmental organizations. UNHCR's budget has increased from some $550 million in 1990 to $1.3 billion in 1995. It also receives a subsidy from the regular budget of United Nations for administrative costs.

● In 1996 UNHCR employed 5,500 staff members working in 123 countries.

● In August 1996, 131 States were Parties to the 1951 Convention relating to the Status of Refugees and/or its 1967 protocol.

● Between 1981 and 1991, the number of refugees more than doubled, rising from 8 to 17 mil-

lion persons. 26 million refugees and persons of concern to UNHCR were recorded in 1996.

● In 1994, UNHCR confronted the largest and fastest exodus in its history when more than 2 million Rwandans fled to neighbouring countries between April and August.

● The conflict in the former Yugoslavia has given rise to more than 3.7 million refugees, displaced people and others of concern to UNHCR since 1991. During this period, UNHCR spent more than $1 billion in this region alone.

M. Kobayashi/UNHCR

tually to return home. The last few years have shown that return can be possible and that exile is not inevitable.

Ethnic cleansing

A Third World phenomenon in the 1980s, refugee camps have since then reappeared in Europe for the first time for forty years. In conflicts of ethnic and political "cleansing" refugees are no longer a *consequence* of violence but its very *purpose*. Here, displacement is no longer a grim by-product of human passions but a *strategic goal* of total wars waged by armies, not against other armies, but against civilians.

Whatever the cause of the exodus may be, the international community's duty—its fundamental commitment—must be to protect these peoples, first of all by applying the principle of *non-refoulement* (see box page 55). People do not choose to uproot themselves from their land voluntarily, for reasons of opportunism. They flee to escape oppression, and the international community has a collective duty to shelter and help those deprived by force of circumstances of the means to ensure their own survival. The defence of freedom and pluralism can only be based on recognition and defence of the right of asylum. In these uncertain times, the struggle is certainly a hard one, but it is more important than ever to wage it.

WATER-BORNE KILLERS

In the global resurgence of infectious diseases, the flow of water—for drinking, sanitation, and irrigation—is playing a central role.

Anne Platt

Anne Platt authored the *World Watch* article "Why Don't We Stop Tuberculosis?" which was later published in *Censored: The News that Didn't Make the News and Why* (New York: Four Walls Eight Windows, 1995).

Along the dying Aral Sea, in central Asia, the people are dying too—of cancer, typhoid, and hepatitis. The rivers that fed the sea are now largely diverted for irrigation; the water left for drinking bears toxins and diseases. Along the Danube River in eastern Europe, communities are losing millions of dollars because the water is too polluted to support a fishing industry—or to attract tourists. In these and many other places around the world, the health of people, their societies, and the land itself is being undermined by the sickness of the water. Healing our water is therefore an essential task—for preserving both human and ecological health.

For one out of every five people in the world, having enough clean water to drink and bathe in is a life-or-death issue. Eighty percent of all disease in developing countries is spread by consuming unsafe water. In those regions, waterborne pathogens and pollution kill 25 million people every year—a toll that amounts to one-third of all developing country deaths. The diseases that do most of the killing—diseases like malaria, cholera, and typhoid—are today primarily tropical: three-quarters of the victims they claim live in the tropics. But to some degree, every population on earth is threatened by waterborne diseases, and the pollution that so often accompanies them. Globally, about 250 million new cases of infection are reported every year—that's nearly the population of the United States.

This tragedy has its roots in two very basic and very common social problems: lack of clean drinking water, and lack of sanitation. Of course, these problems are closely related: in communities without adequate sanitation, pathogen-laden human and animal wastes, food, and garbage pile up near homes, or drain into waterways to infect drinking supplies. A whole range of diarrheal diseases is transmitted through this fecal-oral route: Hepatitis A, typhoid fever, cholera, salmonella—even roundworms. In 1993, the most recent year for which data were available, there were more than 1.8 billion cases of diarrhea worldwide, predominantly in Sub-Saharan Africa. Every year, diarrhea alone kills nearly 3 million children under age five, accounting for a full quarter of the deaths in this age group.

When one of these pathogens makes its way from sewage into a freestanding body of water, the stage is set for an epidemic. All it may take is a drink, a swim, or a meal of contaminated fish to become infected. An outbreak of cholera that began in Peru in 1991, for example, gradually contaminated the water supplies of every country in Latin America except for Paraguay and Uruguay, infecting more than 500,000 people before it subsided two years later. In Peru, the disease got around the ordinary preventive measures, such as boiling drinking water, because many people were consuming the bacterium by eating *ceviche*—raw fish with lemon juice. About 90 percent of cholera outbreaks are caused by inadequate sanitation.

Other diseases work variations on the same theme. Schistosomiasis, for instance, is a snail-borne illness caused by a parasite that penetrates human skin, and causes cirrhosis of the liver, intestinal and urinary tract damage, and anemia. The disease is endemic to certain parts of Africa, Asia, and South America, where it infects farmers and fishers who spend a lot of time wading through the shallow waters favored by the snails. About 200 million people are thought to be at risk. Onchocerciasis, or river blindness, affects some 18 million people in west

Africa, especially in Cameroon and Nigeria. This parasite is carried by a blackfly that breeds along the region's slow-moving streams. It causes severe lesions around the eyes; about 10 percent of the cases result in blindness.

In addition to microbial diseases, our waters are spreading what could be called industrial diseases, as they absorb toxic chemicals from factories, nitrates from fertilizers, phosphates from household detergents—a growing list of synthetic chemicals of virtually every description. And other forms of environmental degradation are also taking a toll. Loss of forests and the resulting erosion clogs rivers with sediment; loss of wetlands disrupts nutrient cycles. These and similar stresses are greatly weakening the ability of natural waterways to absorb, filter, and process wastes naturally.

The "rivers of life" is a metaphor that must be as old as human consciousness. But now our rivers and lakes have also become reservoirs of sickness and death. In the United States, nearly 40 percent of rivers and streams are too dangerous for fishing and swimming, let alone drinking. In Russia, the Volga, the Dvina, and the Ob Rivers harbor strains of cholera, typhoid, dysentery, and viral hepatitis. (Russians depend on all of these rivers for drinking water.) In some parts of the world, rivers are so contaminated by industrial and human waste that no available treatment system could offer adequate protection. The same processes are at work in lakes, and even seas. (See "Dying Seas," January/February 1995.) The Black Sea, for instance, is choking to death from high levels of nutrient pollution. The pollution fosters algal blooms that are suffocating the fisheries, which form the basis of the region's local economy. All over the world, the health of aquatic ecosystems is deteriorating, and so is the health of their inhabitants, human and otherwise.

RUNNING JUST TO STAY IN PLACE

During a cholera outbreak in London in 1854, most people blamed their suffering on the rotting garbage in the streets or on some invisible evil in the air. But a local doctor named John Snow succeeded in tracing the infection to contaminated drinking water. That conceptual breakthrough opened the way for one of the most significant public health improvements the world had ever seen—the installation of comprehensive urban sewage systems in western Europe and the United States. By the late 19th century, improvements in water supply and sewage systems were having a dramatic effect on urban public health in these areas. In French cities, for example, such improvements correlate closely with an increase in life expectancy from about 32 years in 1850 to about 45 years by 1900.

Yet more than a century after Snow's discovery,

we have not managed to find a way to break the grip of cholera and other waterborne diseases in much of the developing world. The most significant attempt occurred during the 1980s, which the U.N. declared the "International Drinking Water Supply and Sanitation Decade." The point of this program was to move from a state of chronic crisis—during the 1960s and 1970s, one-third of the world's population had no clean water supply at all—to a world in which there would be "safe water and sanitation for all." To that end, UNICEF and World Health Organization (WHO) representatives joined forces with local governments, activists, and independent public health authorities, and more than $130 billion was spent on infrastructure projects and community-based initiatives.

In terms of absolute numbers of people helped, the program was a far greater success than the last century's infrastructure improvements. Between 1980 and 1989, more than 1.2 billion people won access to safe drinking water for the first time, and 770 million people gained an appropriate means of sanitation. And unlike its precursor, the program reached both urban and rural areas in developing countries: access to safe water increased from 73 to 85 percent in urban areas, and from 32 to 58 percent in rural areas. But at the same time, populations were exploding in most of the Third World. Despite its successes, the Decade became an object lesson in the importance of integrating family planning into programs dealing with health and resource use. According to Martin Beyer, former chief of UNICEF's water and sanitation section, officials found themselves "running very hard just to stay in place." By the end of the Decade, more than 1 billion people still had no access to clean drinking water.

Nor have the Decade's achievements been as durable as was hoped. In rural sub-Saharan Africa, for example, about 25 percent of the population had access to safe water in the late 1970s. By 1990, the program claimed that safe water was available to 32 percent in rural areas. But that is probably not a realistic figure, since more than half of the new systems had reportedly failed. In India and Pakistan, many of the new systems work only sporadically—usually for just a few hours a day. Some days they don't work at all.

But lack of clean water is more than a public health issue, and the problem cannot be expressed simply by counting faucets and pumps. In many parts of the world, lack of water has become a kind of basic cultural and environmental deficit. Water has become, in other words, an economic problem, a human rights issue, and of course, an environmental issue.

Many of the environmental problems are brutally direct. In India, for example, surveys in the northwestern state of Gujarat found water table drops in 90 percent of the wells monitored; in some wells, the water levels dropped by 9 meters. Water withdrawals on this scale are likely to have a severe impact on a region's plant and animal life, as streams dry up and plant roots can no longer find enough soil moisture. But on a global level, most of the water withdrawn does not go for drinking—it goes for watering crops. Worldwide, about 65 percent of diverted freshwater is used for irrigation, but global irrigation efficiency probably averages no better than 40 percent. All over the world, in places as diverse as the Aral Sea basin and the Colorado River basin in the southwestern United States, wasteful diversion projects are disrupting rivers and exacerbating water shortages. In China, where both agriculture and rapid industrial growth are competing for an increasingly scarce water supply, more than 300 cities are short of water for their inhabitants.

Other environmental problems are less direct. In Jakarta, Indonesia, for example, people almost never drink water straight from a tap or well if they can avoid it, because it is so contaminated. Jakartan households spend more than $50 million a year on wood and other fuels, to boil their drinking water. This exacerbates the air pollution, both indoors and outdoors, and it boosts the rate of deforestation. The loss of tree cover, in turn, further degrades the water supply.

As a social issue, the lack of clean water is perhaps best known for the familiar image of African and Asian women balancing water jugs precariously on their heads, while clutching infants to their breasts— all too apt a reminder that the burden of collecting water falls primarily on women and children. In Nigeria's Imo state, for example, the average household invests six hours a day collecting water during the dry season. The long walk out, the queue at the water source, and the hard trek home—such efforts cut greatly into time that could be spent in school or at other productive work.

And often, government intervention fails to reach those who need it most. Water utilities may provide services only to landowners or homeowners, so the large squatter populations typical of many Third World cities, or people in other types of informal settlements, may fall outside the scope of the service. A family in the top-fifth income group in Peru, the Dominican Republic, or Ghana is, respectively, three, six, or twelve times more likely to have a house water connection than a family in the bottom fifth in those countries.

Because they lack access to publicly subsidized utilities, the poor often end up paying *more* for their water than do the rich, because they must obtain it from illegal sources or private vendors. In Lima, Peru, for instance, poor people may pay a private vendor as much as $3 for a cubic meter of water— which they must then collect by bucket and which is often contaminated. The more affluent, on the other hand, pay 30 cents per cubic meter for treated water provided on tap in their houses. In Dhaka, Bangladesh, squatters pay water rates that are twelve times higher than what the local utility charges.

INFECTING OUR WATERS, POLLUTING OURSELVES

But getting access to safe drinking water is only half the problem. Without safe ways to store clean water, and safe ways to dispose of used water, any progress made can be quickly undone. Sometimes new community supplies actually contribute to the spread of disease. In crowded, urban areas, for example, seepage around hand pumps and storage facilities can create breeding sites for the mosquitoes that carry dengue fever, yellow fever, and malaria. And of course, sewage presents an even graver disease potential. In 1990, an estimated 1.7 billion people worldwide threw their sewage out untreated. The situation in rural areas of developing countries is particularly troubling. In the African countryside, only one out of five people is served by an appropriate means of sanitation, and in rural Southeast Asia, only a meager 12 percent of the population has minimal sanitation facilities. Even the simplest facilities, such as outdoor latrines or sewage pits, can make an enormous difference. In households without such facilities, children have a 60 percent higher chance of dying from diarrhea.

In more densely populated areas, waste management becomes a more complex affair. In Latin America and the Caribbean, for example, WHO reports that 41 percent of urbanites have access to sewer systems—but 90 percent of sewage is discharged directly into natural waters, completely untreated. Unfortunately, many of the urban sewage systems in the developing and former East Bloc countries are simply not up to the demands placed upon them. Crumbling sanitation systems are turning the region's rivers into sewers—or worse. Three-fourths of Poland's rivers are so contaminated by chemicals, sewage, and agricultural runoff that their water is unfit even for industrial use. Nearly half of the water and sewage treatment systems in Moscow are ineffective or malfunctioning. Many of these facilities were built in the 1950s and cannot possibly handle the assortment of heavy metals, petroleum derivatives—even radioactive waste—that finds its way into them.

This kind of infrastructure decay is creating public health threats of the highest order. According to a 1993 Russian Security Council report, 75 percent of the Republic's lake and river water is unsafe to drink because of bacterial contamination. From

1992 to 1993, Russia's incidence of bacterial dysentery jumped 128 percent. (Bacterial dysentery is a group of diseases that cause intestinal pain and bloody diarrhea; cholera is among the most severe of these.) During the same time, Russia saw its typhoid infections grow by 300 percent.

Untreated sewage can be environmentally devastating as well. Sewage contains phosphates, nitrates, and various other materials important in plant and animal metabolism—but at concentrations far higher than they would naturally occur. These excessively high nutrient levels tend to throw aquatic ecosystems out of balance. One common effect is to provoke huge algal "blooms," since algae can metabolize the nutrients more rapidly than more complex plants. The overgrowth of algae may suffocate other aquatic life, by using up much of the oxygen in the water column and blocking out sunlight. Higher plants, invertebrates, fish—all these other organisms lose out. The process is well advanced, for instance, in the Danube river. Over the past 25 years, the Danube's phosphate and nitrate concentrations have increased six- and four-fold respectively. Communities throughout the drainage basin have lost millions of dollars from declining tourism and fisheries, in large measure because of the pollution.

In more developed countries, better sewage treatment and other pollution-control technologies keep the pollution of inland surface waters fairly low **by comparison. These measures, combined with chlorination of drinking water—standard practice in Europe, North America, and Japan—have also greatly reduced the possibility of waterborne infection. But even in the richest countries, serious problems remain. Every year, for example, more than 700,000 Americans contract cryptosporidiosis, a waterborne protozoan that causes prolonged diarrhea, abdominal pain, weight loss, and fever. *Cryptosporidium* is one of the most difficult of pathogens to exclude from water supplies because it can cause infection at a very low dose and is often resistant to disinfectants at levels acceptable in drinking water. A survey in 1992 showed that nearly 40 percent of treated drinking water supplies in the United States contained either *Cryptosporidium* or *Giardia*, a protozoan that infects a small intestine, causing nausea, diarrhea, and anorexia. According to the Natural Resources Defense Council, an environmental organization based in New York City, some 53 million Americans—nearly one fifth of the U.S. population—drink tap water contaminated with lead, fecal bacteria, or other serious pollutants.**

HEALING OUR WATER

Despite the extent of the problem, a number of success stories offer solid grounds for hope. These are often based on simple techniques such as public education and local stewardship—not expensive technology. During the 1980s, for example, WHO launched a series of grassroots education campaigns in Africa to prevent guinea worm disease. Also known as dracunculiasis, this disease is caused by a parasite transmitted in larval form by a water flea. When people drink infected water, the parasite enters the body and, over the course of a year, matures into a worm from half to three-quarters of a meter in length, usually lying below the skin of the arms or legs. To soothe the ulcers the worm causes, victims often bathe their limbs in water. As the ulcers open, the worm releases a new generation of larvae into the water, continuing the cycle of disease.

Fortunately, it is relatively easy to prevent infection. The WHO programs teach people how to filter drinking water to remove the larvae and then to boil or chlorinate the water as a further precaution. These simple techniques have dropped the incidence of guinea worm dramatically in recent years. Since 1986, the global burden of guinea worm has been reduced from 3.5 million cases to less than 100,000 as a result of the WHO campaign, which aims at total eradication of the disease.

In a part of the world where so many public health and development programs have failed, the guinea worm campaign may be setting a broad social precedent. Along Africa's west coast, in Côte D'Ivoire, the campaign has been especially successful; in 1966, more than 67,000 people in the country reported guinea worm. A decade later, only 4,971 cases were reported and by 1990, fewer than 1,500 infections were discovered—despite the fact that detection and reporting had improved significantly. To the east, three nations—Nigeria, Niger, and Sudan—account for the majority of the remaining cases. Sudan presents perhaps the most difficult problem, because of its chronic civil war. But both sides have agreed to a "guinea worm truce," so the campaign can proceed. WHO officials predict that guinea worm could be eradicated within the next decade.

There are equally simple techniques for handling some other types of infection as well. For example, cholera and dysentery deaths can be reduced by as much as 80 percent with oral rehydration therapy (ORT)—an inexpensive mixture of water, sugar, and salt that is given to diarrhea patients as soon as they can drink. In sub-Saharan Africa, UNICEF has been working with families directly, supplying them with the ORT mixture and showing them how to use it. The number of families in the region practicing ORT nearly doubled from 1988 to 1993. Of course, not all diseases can be treated this simply, but the potential of this technique is enormous. In 1993 alone, ORT saved more than 1 million children's lives throughout the developing world (although 2.5 million children still died from diarrheal diseases in that year). If implemented widely, such relatively simple programs could radically improve the lives of hundreds of millions of people.

Even though the connection between water and health may seem beyond debate, a huge amount of money has been spent on programs that ignore it. A recent internal review of 120 World Bank water supply projects, for example, found that less than half of them had any provision for addressing sanitation. And even those that did have a sanitation component often dropped it when funds ran low. In many cities, the Bank did not even provide enough funds to address the increased wastewater that resulted from its own projects.

Sometimes even efforts aimed directly at the problem miss a critical link. During the 1980s, a Dutch aid project installed more than 1,000 kilometers of pipeline for 141 villages in western India. But despite the safe, reliable water supply the pipes brought in, workers could find no measurable impact on people's health. The problem proved to be what happened after the water left the pipes, so the local government hired an NGO, the Center for Health, Education, Training and Nutrition Awareness, to teach people the importance of cleaning utensils and hands in water already determined to be safe, before collecting the new supply. UNICEF's experience in developing countries suggests that by adopting the simple act of washing hands before cooking and eating, a community can reduce the incidence of severe diarrhea by as much as 40 percent.

Teaching hygiene is obviously essential—and a great deal more of it should be done. Only one-third of all developing countries reported in 1990 that health and hygiene were integrated into their primary school curriculum. But some efforts fail by providing the training without the resources to use it. Researchers in the Nigerian city of Zaria, for example, found that secondary schoolchildren knew they should wash their hands and food before eating, but the children said they did not have enough water at home to "waste" by doing so.

Despite the problems with these and other health programs, experience has left us with a fairly substantial range of sustainable technologies appropriate to local conditions and needs. During the U.N.'s International Decade, for example, water supplies were established by drilling boreholes in places like Jakarta and Manila, where groundwater is plentiful. In drier areas, such as north Africa, open wells and rain catchment systems were built. Where the service was being built from scratch, a public standpost and pump were appropriate; elsewhere, existing systems were upgraded with direct house connections. A similar approach was taken with sanitation. In Lesotho, for instance, people built latrines and raised the level of rural sanitation from zero to 23 percent.

Even with the practical lessons that hard experience has taught us, we can't afford to ignore the shortcomings of earlier efforts if we are to go beyond them. The demographic pressure that overwhelmed the U.N.'s International Decade shows perhaps the biggest procedural problem that public health authorities face: finding more effective ways to integrate their work into other types of development projects—whether they be family planning, pollution control, wetlands restoration, or irrigation. Of course, achieving this kind of integration is a huge challenge, but a number of approaches are already bearing fruit.

In the Netherlands, private water companies have begun paying farmers to reduce their use of pesticides and fertilizers. This cuts the level of chemical residues in the field run-off, which means the water companies don't have to spend as much money cleaning up their water. The public gains a more secure drinking water supply, and the health of aquatic ecosystems improves. Major benefits can often be achieved by looking for up-front ways to remove pollutants from industrial processes, rather than simply trying to filter them out after the fact.

In Britain it is estimated that one-quarter of the water that enters the distribution network is lost because of broken pipes and other system inefficiencies. By repairing distribution systems and improving irrigation techniques, huge quantities of water could be freed up for use. In this regard, water utilities may be able to learn a lesson from electric utilities: higher efficiency is often a better strategy than building extra capacity.

More efficient irrigation technology can help reconcile a city's thirst with the water needs of surrounding farmland. In California, a major water wholesaler is financing the lining of irrigation canals and other conservation projects in exchange for the water the investments will save. By paying for the irrigation improvements, the utility is essentially tapping into a new source of water for the state's cities.

Creative solutions can sometimes be found by discovering some value in the waste itself. Aquatic biologists at the New Alchemy Institute in the U.S. state of Massachusetts, for example, have developed an artificial ecosystem that uses 200 plant and two dozen fish species to clean up sewage. Waste water flows through a series of tanks and ponds, where it is exposed to a range of natural processes that break the waste down and incorporate it into natural nutrient cycles. The result is a flourishing plant and animal community—and clean water. Such low-tech sewage treatment systems are already feasible in both the industrialized and developing world. Piracicaba,

MAJOR WATER-BORNE DISEASES

DISEASE	VECTOR	NEW CASES	DEATHS
Diarrheal diseases		1.8 billion	3 million
Dengue fever	Mosquito	560,000	23,000
Yellow fever	Mosquito	200,000	30,000
Dracunculiasis (Guinea worm)	Water flea	100,000	n/a
Japanese encephalitis	Mosquito	40,000	11,000

DISEASE	VECTOR	POPULATION AT RISK	DEATHS
Malaria	Mosquito	400 million	2 million
Schistosomiasis (Bilharziasis)	Snail	200 million	200,000
Lymphatic filariasis (Elephantitis)	Mosquito	100 million	43 million (disabled)
Onchocerciasis	Blackfly	17.6 million	35,000

Sources: Report of the Director-General, WHO, The World Health Report 1995: Bridging the Gaps, (Geneva: World Health Organization, 1995); J.M. Hunter et al., eds., Parasitic Diseases in Water Resources Development: The Need for Intersectoral Negotiation (Geneva: WHO, 1993): Table 9, p. 26; Malaria data from "World Malaria Situation in 1992, Part I: Middle South Asia, Eastern Asia and Oceania," Weekly Epidemiological Record, October 21, 1994.

Brazil, for instance, processes wastewater into drinking water by using a natural treatment system that relies primarily on duckweed—a fast-growing, floating aquatic plant. Duckweed has a high protein content and is a valuable animal feed; a duckweed sewage treatment system in Bangladesh harvests the plant for fish food in an aquaculture set-up. Holistic approaches like this integrate the entire water use cycle, making wastewater a valuable resource.

This approach can be extended to the entire landscape. In various parts of the southeastern United States, for example, planners and developers are working with biologists to restore degraded wetlands, so that these natural areas can help purify wastewater. Of course, such projects must insure that wetlands receive only biodegradable waste, and that the waste arrives at a rate the wetlands can process. But wetlands restoration can be a far better social and ecological investment than artificial treatment facilities alone. Indeed, given the heavy infrastructure costs, energy inputs, and chemical monitoring necessary in conventional sewage treatment, wetlands restoration may come to be seen as an economic objective in its own right.

Perhaps the toughest challenge of all is family planning, but even here, there are encouraging signs. In light of the U.N. Population Fund's proposal to stabilize world population, which emerged from the 1994 Cairo conference on population and development, there is a growing consensus among policymakers that family planning must be part of a broad development strategy that includes health services, primary education, women's empowerment, nutrition and the provision of clean water. In a few places, perhaps, such a formula may already be working. Despite its poverty, India's state of Kerala, for example, has a birthrate of 18 per 1,000—40 percent below India's average rate and about the same as that of the United States. By some estimates, portions of Kerala will reach zero population growth before the United States will. Many factors distinguish Kerala from other parts of India, and have presumably played some role in reducing its birth rate. Among the most notable are good health care, reasonably equitable land tenure, and a high level of education—for both men and women. It is worth noting that during an immensely successful literacy push in Kerala in late the 1980s, the subjects covered included sexual equality, childhood immunizations, and the importance of clean drinking water.

A CHANGE OF ATTITUDE

There are other places in the developing world where an interdisciplinary approach, attuned to the needs of the people involved, is yielding major benefits. In Botswana, for instance, the government has resisted pressures to develop the Okavango River delta, acting instead in the interests of the delta's inhabitants, who want the wetland preserved. In place of what would probably have been a short-term economic gain, Botswana retains the long-term benefits of a rich wildlife habitat, resources for fishers and pastoralists, continued hydrological stability, and the capacity for natural wastewater treatment.

In Sudan, where the harsh, arid landscape seems a world away from the Okavango, some projects are giving farmers and nomads direct responsibility for managing what little water there is. Even though these people have little formal education and live close to the subsistence level, the strategy is working. Local people have assumed complete responsibility for water distribution facilities and established a fund to which water users must contribute. The water is managed so efficiently that the funds sometimes show surpluses. An added dividend is the enhanced status of the women, who help manage the supply; in this traditional Muslim society, women have relatively few opportunities to participate in public life.

Successes like these suggest the simple steps that could lead to tremendous change. For if the fight against waterborne diseases has taught us anything, it is that we already know how to save most of the 25 million lives those diseases claim every year. Our greatest need, therefore, may be a matter of political will. In 1992, people all over the world reacted with horror at the images on their televisions and in their newspapers, as the famine in Ethiopia killed 300,000 people in six months. We see famine as an outrage against humanity that we cannot afford to tolerate; we must learn to see cholera, malaria, and the other waterborne killers in the same light.

KEY SOURCES

Andrew Livingstone and Harry J. McPherson, "Management Strategies for Rural Water Development: A Case Study from Sudan," *Natural Resources Forum* (November 1993): 294-301.

J.M. Hunter et al., eds., *Parasitic Diseases in Water Resources Development: The Need for Intersectoral Negotiation* (Geneva: WHO, 1993).

UNICEF, *Planning for Health and Socio-Economic Benefits from Water and Environmental Sanitation Programmes: A Workshop Summary* (New York: UNICEF Water and Environmental Sanitation Section, Evaluation and Research Office, UNICEF, April 1993).

Water Solidarity Network, *Water and Health in Underprivileged Urban Areas* (Paris: 1994).

World Health Organization, *The International Drinking Water Supply and Sanitation Decade 1981-1990: End of Decade Review*, WHO/CWS/92.12 (Geneva: WHO Division of Environmental Health, August 1992).

How Many People Can the Earth Support?

The answers depend as much on social, cultural, economic and political choices as they do on constraints imposed by nature

JOEL E. COHEN

Joel E. Cohen is head of the Laboratory of Populations at Rockefeller University in New York City. His paper "Conflict Over World Population: Cairo and Beyond" recently appeared in the New York Academy of Sciences Science Policy Report SCIENCE, TECHNOLOGY AND NEW GLOBAL REALITIES: ISSUES FOR U.S. FOREIGN POLICY.

O N APR IL 25, 1679, IN DELFT, HOLLAND, the inventor of the microscope, Antoni van Leeuwenhoek, wrote down what may be the first estimate of the maximum number of people the earth can support. If all the habitable land in the world had the same population density as Holland (at that time about 120 people for every square kilometer), he calculated, the earth could support at most 13.4 billion people—far fewer than the number of spermatozoans his lenses had revealed in the milt of a cod.

In subsequent centuries, van Leeuwenhoek's estimate has been followed by dozens of similar calculations. Around 1695 a Londoner named Gregory King estimated that the earth's "Land If fully Peopled would sustain" at most 12.5 billion people. In 1765 a German regimental pastor, Johann Peter Süssmilch, compared his own figure (13.9 billion) with the estimates of van Leeuwenhoek, the French military engineer Sébastien Le Prestre de Vauban (5.5 billion) and the English writer and cartographer Thomas Templeman (11.5 billion).

In recent decades estimates of maximum population have appeared thicker and faster than ever before. Under the rubric of "carrying capacity" they crop up routinely in environmental debates, in United Nations reports and in papers by scholars or academic politicians trained in ecology, economics, sociology, geography, soil science or agronomy, among other disciplines. Demographers, however, have been strangely silent. Of the more than 200 symposiums held at the 1992 and 1993 annual meetings of the Population Association of America, not one session dealt with es-timating or defining human carrying capacity for any region of the earth. Instead, professional demographers tend to focus on the composition and growth of populations, restricting their predictions to the near term—generally a few decades into the future—and framing them in conditional terms: *If* rates of birth, death and migration (by age, sex, location, marital status and so on) are such-and-such, *then* population size and distribution will be so-and-so.

> **IF POPULATIONS CONTINUE TO GROW**
> *at 1990 rates, the world*
> *population will increase to 694 billion*
> *by the year 2150.*

Such conditional predictions, or forecasts, can be powerful tools. projections by the U.N. show dramatically that *if* human populations continued to grow at 1990 rates in each major region of the world, *then* the population would increase more than 130-fold in 160 years, from about 5.3 billion in 1990 to about 694 billion in 2150. Those figures are extremely sensitive to the future level of average fertility. If, hypothetically, from 1990 onward the average couple gradually approached a level of fertility just one-tenth of a child more than required to replace themselves, world population would grow from 5.3 billion in 1990 to 12.5 billion in 2050 and 20.8 billion in 2150. In contrast, if (again hypothetically) starting in 1990 and ever after couples bore exactly the number of children needed to replace themselves world population would grow from 5.3

billion in 1990 to 7.7 billion in 2050 and would level off at around 8.4 billion by 2150.

The clear message is that people cannot forever continue to have, on average, more children than are required to replace themselves. That is not an ideological slogan; it is a hard fact. Conventional agriculture cannot grow enough food for 694 billion people; not enough water falls from the skies. The finiteness of the earth guarantees that ceilings on human numbers do exist.

Where are those ceilings? Some people believe that any limit to human numbers is so remote that its existence is irrelevant to present concerns. Others declare that the human population has already exceeded what the earth can support in the long run (how long is usually left unspecified). Still others concede that short-term limits may exist, but they argue that technologies, institutions and values will adapt in unpredictable ways to push ceilings progressively higher so that they recede forever. The differences of opinion are buttressed by vast disparities in calculation. In the past century, experts of various stripes have made estimates of human carrying capacity ranging from less than a billion to more than 1,000 billion. Who, if anybody, is right?

For several years I have been trying to understand the question, "How many people can the earth support?" and the answers to it. In the process I came to question the question. "How many people can the earth support?" is not a question in the same sense as "How old are you?"; it cannot be answered by a number or even by a range of numbers. The earth's capacity to support people is determined partly by processes that the social and natural sciences have yet to understand, partly by choices that we and our descendants have yet to make.

I N MOST OF ITS SCIENTIFIC SENSES, *CARRYING capacity* refers to a population of wild animals within a particular ecosystem. One widely used ecology textbook defines it as follows: "Number of individuals in a population that the resources of a habitat can support; the asymptote, or plateau, of the logistic and other sigmoid equations for population growth." Even within ecology, the concept of carrying capacity has important limitations. It applies best under stable conditions and over relatively short spans of time. In the real world, climates and habitats fluctuate and change; animals adapt to their conditions and eventually evolve into new species. With each change, the carrying capacity changes, too.

When applied to human beings, the concept becomes vastly more volatile. I have collected twenty-six definitions of human carrying capacity, all published since 1975. Most of them agree on a few basic points—for instance, that the concept refers to the number of people who can be supported for some period (usually not stated) in some mode of life considered plausible or desirable. Most of the definitions recognize that ecological concepts of carrying capacity must be extended to allow for the role of technology. Most also agree that culturally and individually variable standards of living, including standards of environmental quality, set limits on population size well before the physical requirements for sheer subsistence start to become an issue.

In other respects, however, the definitions vary widely or even contradict one another. How long must a population be sustainable? Does it make sense to speak of local or regional carrying capacity—or do trade and the need for inputs from outside any specified region imply that only a global scale will do? More fundamental, how constraining are constraints? Some definitions deny the existence of any finite carrying capacity altogether, holding that human ingenuity will win out over any natural barriers; others acknowledge that the limits are real but recognize that human choices, now and in the future, will largely decide where those limits fall.

I N MY OPINION, THAT LAST POINT—THE INTERplay of natural constraints and human choices— is the key to making sense of human carrying capacity. The deceptively simple question "How many people can the earth support?" hides a host of thorny issues:

How many people at what average level of material well-being?

THE HUMAN CARRYING CAPACITY OF THE EARTH WILL OBviously depend on the typical material level at which people choose to live. Material well-being includes food (people choose variety and palatability, beyond the constraints imposed by physiological requirements); fiber (people choose cotton, wool or synthetic fibers for clothing, wood pulp or rag for paper); water (tap water or Perrier or the nearest river or mud hole for drinking, washing, cooking and watering your lawn, if you have one); housing (Auschwitz barracks, two men to a plank, or Thomas Jefferson's Monticello); manufactured goods; waste removal (for human, agricultural and industrial wastes); natural-hazard protection (against floods, storms, volcanoes and earthquakes); health (prevention, cure and care); and the entire range of amenities such as education, travel, social groups, solitude, the arts, religion and communion with nature. Not all of those features are captured well by standard economic measures.

How many people with what distribution of material well-being?

AN ECOLOGIST, AN ECONOMIST AND A STATISTICIAN WENT bow hunting in the woods and spied a deer. The ecologist shot first, and his arrow landed five meters to the left of the deer. The economist shot next, and her arrow landed five meters to the right of the deer. The statistician looked at both arrows, looked at the deer, and jumped up and down shouting: "We got it! We got it!"

Estimates of human carrying capacity rarely take into account the scatter or distribution of material well-being throughout a population. Yet paying attention to average well-being while ignoring the distribution of well-being is like using an average arrow to kill a deer. People who live in extreme poverty may not know or care that the global average is satisfactory, and the press of present needs may keep them from taking a long-term view. For example, thanks to genetic engineering, any country with a few

Ph.D.'s in molecular plant biology and a modestly equipped laboratory can insert the genes to create stronger, more disease-resistant, higher-yielding plants. If every region has the scientific and technical resources to improve its own crop plants, the earth can support more people than it can if some regions are too poor to help themselves.

How many people with what technology?

THE COMPLEXITIES OF TECHNOLOGICAL CHOICES OFTEN disappear in heated exchanges between environmental pessimists and technological optimists:

ECOLOGIST: When a natural resource is being consumed faster than it is being replenished or recycled, an asset is being depleted, to the potential harm of future generations.

TECHNOLOGIST: If new knowledge and technology can produce an equivalent or superior alternative, then future generations may turn out to be better off.

TAXPAYER: Which natural resources can be replaced by technology yet to be invented, and which cannot? Will there be enough time to develop new technology and put it to work on the required scale? Could we avoid future problems, pain and suffering by making other choices now about technology or ways of living? [*No answer from ecologist or technologist.*]

The key to the argument is time. As Richard E. Benedick, an officer of the U.S. Department of State who has also served with the World Wildlife Fund, worried:

While it is true that technology has generally been able to come up with solutions to human dilemmas, there is no guarantee that ingenuity will always rise to the task. Policymakers must contend with a nagging thought: what if it does not, or what if it is too late?

How many people with what domestic and international political institutions?

POLITICAL ORGANIZATION AND EFFECTIVENESS AFFECT human carrying capacity. For example, the United Nations Development Program estimated that developing countries could mobilize for development as much as $50 billion a year (an amount comparable to all official development assistance) if they reduced military expenditures, privatized public enterprises, eliminated corruption, made development priorities economically more rational and improved national governance. Conversely, population size, distribution and composition affect political organization and effectiveness.

How will political institutions and civic participation evolve with increasing numbers of people? As numbers increase, what will happen to people's ability to participate effectively in the political system?

What standards of personal liberty will people choose?

How will people bring about political change within existing nations? By elections and referendums, or by revolution, insurrection and civil war? How will people choose to settle differences between nations, for instance, over disputed borders, shared water resources or common fisheries? War consumes human and physical resources. Negotiation consumes patience and often requires compromise. The two options impose different constraints on human carrying capacity.

How many people with what domestic and international economic arrangements?

WHAT LEVELS OF PHYSICAL AND HUMAN CAPITAL ARE ASsumed? Tractors, lathes, computers, better health and better education all make workers in rich countries far more productive than those in poor countries. Wealthier workers make more wealth and can support more people.

What regional and international trade in finished goods and mobility in productive assets are permitted or encouraged? How will work be organized? The invention of the factory organized production to minimize idleness in the use of labor, tools and machines. What new ways of organizing work should be assumed to estimate the future human carrying capacity?

How many people with what domestic and international demographic arrangements?

ALMOST EVERY ASPECT OF DEMOGRAPHY (BIRTH, DEATH, age structure, migration, marriage, and family structure) is subject to human choices that will influence the earth's human carrying capacity.

A stationary global population will have to choose between a long average length of life and a high birthrate. It must also choose between a single average birthrate for all regions, on the one hand, and a demographic specialization of labor on the other (in which some areas have fertility above their replacement level, whereas other areas have fertility below their replacement level).

Patterns of marriage and household formation will also influence human carrying capacity. For example, the public resources that have to be devoted to the care of the young and the aged depend on the roles played by families.

POLICY MAKERS MUST WONDER:
*Will new technology
always save the day?
What if it arrives too late?*

In China national law requires families to care for and support their elderly members; in the United States each elderly person and the state are largely responsible for supporting that elderly person.

How many people in what physical, chemical and biological environments?

WHAT PHYSICAL, CHEMICAL AND BIOLOGICAL ENVIRONments will people choose for themselves and for their children? Much of the heat in the public argument over current environmental problems arises because the consequences of present and projected choices and changes are uncertain. Will global warming cause great problems, or would a global limitation on fossil-fuel consumption cause greater problems? Will toxic or nuclear wastes or ordinary sewage sludge dumped into the deep ocean come back to haunt future generations when deep currents well up in biologically productive offshore zones, or would the long-term effects of disposing of those wastes on land be worse? The choice of particular alternatives could materially affect human carrying capacity.

How many people with what variability or stability?

HOW MANY PEOPLE THE EARTH CAN SUPPORT DEPENDS ON how steadily you want the earth to support that population. If you are willing to let the human population rise and fall, depending on annual crops, decadal weather patterns and long-term shifts in climate, the average population with ups and downs would include the peaks of population size, whereas the guaranteed level would have to be adjusted to the level of the lowest valley. Similar reasoning applies to variability or stability in the level of well-being; the quality of the physical, chemical and biological environments; and many other dimensions of choice.

How many people with what risk or robustness?

HOW MANY PEOPLE THE EARTH CAN SUPPORT DEPENDS ON how controllable you want the well-being of the population to be. One possible strategy would be to maximize numbers at some given level of well-being, ignoring the risk of natural or human disaster. Another would be to accept a smaller population size in return for increased control over random events. For example, if you settle in a previously uninhabited hazardous zone (such as the flood plain of the Mississippi River or the hurricane-prone coast of the southeastern U.S.), you demand a higher carrying capacity of the hazardous zone, but you must accept a higher risk of catastrophe. When farmers do not give fields a fallow period, they extract a higher carrying capacity along with a higher risk that the soil will lose its fertility (as agronomists at the International Rice Research Institute in the Philippines discovered to their surprise).

How many people for how long?

HUMAN CARRYING CAPACITY DEPENDS STRONGLY ON THE time horizon people choose for planning. The population that the earth can support at a given level of well-being for twenty years may differ substantially from the population that can be supported for 100 or 1,000 years.

The time horizon is crucial in energy analysis. How fast oil stocks are being consumed matters little if one cares only

> IN PRACTICE, RELIGION
> *does not seem to be decisive*
> *in setting average levels of fertility*
> *for Roman Catholics.*

about the next five years. In the long term, technology can change the definition of resources, converting what was useless rock to a valuable resource; hence no one can say whether industrial society is sustainable for 500 years.

Some definitions of human carrying capacity refer to the size of a population that can be supported indefinitely. Such definitions are operationally meaningless. There is no way of knowing what human population size can be supported indefinitely (other than zero population, since the sun is expected to burn out in a few billion years, and the human species almost certainly will be extinct long before then). The concept of indefinite sustainability is a phantasm, a diversion from the difficult problems of today and the coming century.

How many people with what fashions, tastes and values?

HOW MANY PEOPLE THE EARTH CAN SUPPORT DEPENDS ON what people want from life. Many choices that appear to be economic depend heavily on individual and cultural values. Should industrial societies use the available supplies of fossil fuels in households for heating and for personal transportation, or outside of households to produce other goods and services? Do people prefer a high average wage and low employment or a low average wage and high employment (if they must choose)?

Should industrial economies seek now to develop renewable energy sources, or should they keep burning fossil fuels and leave the transition to future generations? Should women work outside their homes? Should economic analyses continue to discount future income and costs, or should they strive to even the balance between the people now living and their unborn descendants?

I am frequently asked whether organized religion, particularly Roman Catholicism, is a serious obstacle to the decline of fertility. Certainly in some countries, church policies have hindered couples' access to contraception and have posed obstacles to family planning programs. In practice, however, factors other than religion seem to be decisive in setting average levels of fertility for Roman Catholics. In 1992 two Catholic countries, Spain and Italy, were tied for the second- and third-lowest fertility rates in the world. In largely Catholic Latin America, fertility has been falling rapidly, with modern contraceptive methods playing a major role. In most of the U.S. the fertility of Catholics has gradually converged with that of Protestants, and polls show that nearly four-fifths of Catholics think that couples should make up their own minds about family planning and abortion.

Even within the church hierarchy, Catholicism shelters a diversity of views. On June 15, 1994, the Italian bishops' conference issued a report stating that falling mortality and improved medical care "have made it unthinkable to sustain indefinitely a birthrate that notably exceeds the level of two children per couple." Moreover, by promoting literacy for adults, education for children and the survival of infants in developing countries, the church has helped bring about some of the social preconditions for fertility decline.

On the whole the evidence seems to me to support the view of the ecologist William W. Murdoch of the University of California, Santa Barbara: "Religious beliefs have only small, although sometimes significant, effects on family size. Even these effects tend to disappear with rising levels of well-being and education."

IN SHORT, THE QUESTION "HOW MANY PEOPLE can the earth support?" has no single numerical answer, now or ever. Human choices about the earth's human carrying capacity are constrained by facts of nature and may have unpredictable consequences. As a result, estimates of human carrying capacity cannot aspire to be more than conditional and probable: if future choices are thus-and-so, then the human carrying capacity is likely to be so-and-so. They cannot predict the constraints or possibilities that lie in the future; their true worth may lie in their role as a goad to conscience and a guide to action in the here and now.

The following beautiful quotation from *Principles of Political Economy,* by the English philosopher John Stuart Mill, sketches the kind of shift in values such action might entail. When it was written, in 1848, the world's population was less than one-fifth its present size.

There is room in the world, no doubt, and even in old countries, for a great increase of population, supposing the arts of life to go on improving, and capital to increase. But even if innocuous, I confess I see very little reason for desiring it. The density of population necessary to enable mankind to obtain, in the greatest degree, all the advantages both of cooperation and of social intercourse, has, in all the most populous countries, been obtained. A population may be too crowded, though all be amply supplied with food and raiment. It is not good for man to be kept perforce at all times in the presence of his species. A world from which solitude is extirpated, is a very poor ideal. . . . Nor is there much satisfaction in contemplating the world with nothing left to the spontaneous activity of nature; with every rood of land brought into cultivation, which is capable of growing food for human beings; every flowery waste or natural pasture ploughed up, all quadrupeds or birds which are not domesticated for man's use exterminated as his rivals for food, every hedgerow or superfluous tree rooted out, and scarcely a place left where a wild shrub or flower could grow without being eradicated as a weed in the name of improved agriculture. If the earth must lose that great portion of its pleasantness which it owes to things that the unlimited increase of wealth and population would extirpate from it, for the mere purpose of enabling it to support a larger but not a better or a happier population, I sincerely hope, for the sake of posterity, that they will content to be stationary, long before necessity compels them to it.

It is scarcely necessary to remark that a stationary condition of capital and population implies no stationary state of human improvement. There would be as much scope as ever for all kinds of mental culture, and moral and social progress; as much room for improving the Art of Living, and much more likelihood of its being improved, when minds ceased to be engrossed by the art of getting on. Even the industrial arts might be as earnestly and as successfully cultivated, with this sole difference, that instead of serving no purpose but the increase of wealth, industrial improvements would produce their legitimate effect, that of abridging labour. . . . Only when, in addition to just institutions, the increase of mankind shall be under the deliberate guidance of judicious foresight, can the conquests made from the powers of nature by the intellect and energy of scientific discoverers, become the common property of the species, and the means of improving it and elevating the universal lot.

Natural Resources

International Dimensions (Articles 9–11)
Raw Materials (Articles 12–14)
Food and Hunger (Articles 15–18)
Energy (Articles 19–21)

In the eighteenth, nineteenth, and early twentieth centuries, the idea of the modern nation-state was conceived and developed. These legal entities were conceived of as separate, self-contained units that independently pursued their national interests. Scholars envisioned the world as an international political community of independent units, which "bounced off" each other (a concept that has often been described as a billiard ball model).

This concept of self-contained and self-directed units, however, has undergone major rethinking in the past 30 years, primarily because of the international dimensions of the demands being placed on natural resources. National boundaries are becoming less and less valid. The Middle East, for example, contains a majority of the world's known oil reserves, yet Western Europe and Japan are very dependent on this source of energy. Neither resource dependency nor such problems as air pollution recognize political boundaries on a map. Therefore, the concept that independent political units control their own destiny is becoming outdated. In order to understand why it is so, one must look at how Earth's natural resources are being utilized.

The articles in the first subsection of this unit examine the international dimensions of the uses and abuses of natural resources. The central theme in these articles is whether or not human activity is in fact bringing about fundamental changes in the functioning of Earth's self-regulating ecological systems. In many cases a nonsustainable rate of usage is under way, and, as a consequence, an alarming decline in the quality of the natural resource base is taking place. Alternative visions and policies propose alternative methods that are designed to sustain natural resource utilization.

An important concept resulting from this analysis is that these problems transcend national boundaries. Global climate changes, for example, will affect everyone, and international efforts will be required to respond to these changes. The consequences of basic human activities such as growing and cooking food are profound when multiplied billions of times every day. A single country or even a few countries working together cannot have a significant impact on redressing these problems. Solutions will have to be conceived that are truly global in scope. Just as there are shortages of natural resources, there are also shortages of new ideas for solving many of these problems.

The second subsection begins with a discussion of the issues involved in moving from a perspective of the environment as simply an economic resource to be consumed to a perspective that has been defined as "sustainable development." This change is easily called for, but in fact it goes to the core of social values and basic economic activities. Implementing it, therefore, will be a challenge of great magnitude.

The third subsection focuses on the most fundamental relationship between society and nature: food production and hunger. An overview is provided on the ability of the world's population to feed itself.

Another critical relationship between social structures and the environment is the subject of the final subsection of this unit: the production and consumption of energy. Since 1973, the fluctuations in the price and supply of energy in general and oil in particular have had a major impact on everyone. The initial price shocks of 1973 (which resulted from an Arab oil boycott of Israel's political allies) have been followed by many ups and downs, and the supply and price of oil remain at the core of the global political economy. However, many predict that the heavy dependence on oil will change as supplies dwindle and new technologies are developed. This prospect creates special problems for developing countries, for they will have to discover alternative energy sources and more efficient technologies than what is currently available.

Nature is not some object "out there" to be visited at a national park. It is the food we eat and the energy we consume. Human beings are joined in the most intimate of relationships with the natural world in order to survive from one day to the next. It is ironic how little time is spent thinking about this relationship. The pressures that rapidly growing numbers of people are placing on Earth's carrying capacity suggest that this oversight will not continue much longer.

Looking Ahead: Challenge Questions

How is the availability of natural resources affected by population growth?

Do you think that the international community has adequately responded to problems of pollution and threats to our common natural heritage? Why or why not?

What is the natural resource picture going to look like 30 years from now?

How is society, in general, likely to respond to the conflicts between economic necessity and resource conservation?

How is agricultural production a function of many different aspects of a society's economic and political structure?

Are there any similarities between the global energy shortages and food shortages?

What is the likely future of energy supplies in both the industrial world and the developing world?

What transformations will societies that are heavy users of fossil fuels have to undergo in order to meet future energy needs?

The Global Challenge

MICHAEL H. GLANTZ

Circulating freely around the planet, the atmosphere and oceans are shared resources whose resiliency is being tested by ever-growing human demands.

The atmosphere and the oceans are fluids that encircle the globe. Their movements can be described in physical and mathematical terms, or even by some popular adages: "what goes up, must come down" and "what goes around, comes around."

The atmosphere and oceans are two of Earth's truly global commons. In cycles that vary from days to centuries to millions of years, air and water circulate interactively around the globe irrespective of national boundaries and territorial claims.

With regard to the first adage, pollutants emitted into the atmosphere must come down somewhere on Earth's surface—unless, like the chlorofluorocarbons (CFCs), they can escape into the stratosphere until they are broken down by the Sun's rays. Depending on the form of the pollutant (gaseous or particulate), its size, or the height at which it has been ejected into the atmosphere, it can stay airborne for short or long periods. So, pollutants expelled into the air in one country and on one continent may make their way to other countries and continents. The same can be said of the various pollutants that are cast into the ocean. "What goes around, comes around" clearly applies to the global commons.

As human demands on the atmosphere and oceans escalate, the pressures on the commons are clearly increasing. Defining the boundaries between acceptable human impacts and crisis impacts is a demanding and rather subjective task.

The Atmosphere

The atmosphere is owned by no nation, but in a sense it belongs to all nations. Several types of human activity interact with geophysical processes to affect the atmosphere in ways that engender crisis situations. The most obvious example of local effects is urban air pollution resulting from automobile emissions, home heating and cooling, and industrial processes. The Denver "brown cloud" is a case in point, as is the extreme pollution in Mexico City. Such pollution can occur within one political jurisdiction or across state, provincial, or international borders. Air pollution is one of those problems to which almost everyone in the urban area contributes.

Acid rain is an example of pollution of a regional atmospheric commons. Industrial processes release pollutants, which can then interact with the atmosphere and be washed out by rainfall. Acid rain has caused the health of forest ecosystems to deteriorate in such locations as the northeastern part of North America, central Europe, and Scandinavia. The trajectories of airborne industrial pollutants moving from highly industrialized areas across these regions have been studied. The data tend to support the contention that while acid rain is a regional commons problem, it is also a problem of global interest.

A nation can put any chemical effluents it deems necessary for its well-being into its own airspace. But then the atmosphere's fluid motion can move those effluents across international borders. The purpose of the tall smokestack, for example, was to put effluents higher into the air, so they would be carried away and dispersed farther from their source. The tall stacks, in essence, turned local air pollution problems into regional ones. In many instances, they converted national pollution into an international problem.

Climate as a Global Commons

There is a difference between the atmosphere as a commons and the climate as a commons. Various societies have emitted a wide range of chemicals into the atmosphere, with little understanding of their potential effects on climate. For example, are industrial processes that produce large amounts of carbon dioxide (which contributes to atmospheric warming) or sulfur dioxide (which contributes to atmospheric cooling and acid rain) altering global climate? There seems to be a growing consensus among scientists that these alterations manifest themselves as regional changes in the frequencies, intensities, and even the location of extreme events such as droughts and floods.

Not all pollutants emitted in the air have an impact on the global climate system. But scientists have long known that some gases can affect global climate patterns by interacting with sunlight or the heat radiated from Earth's surface. Emission of such gases, especially CO_2, can result from human activities such as the burning of fossil fuels, tropical deforestation, and food production processes. The amount of CO_2 in the atmosphere has increased considerably since the mid 1700s and is likely to double the preindustrial level by the year 2050. Carbon dioxide is a highly effective greenhouse gas. Other greenhouse gases emitted to the atmosphere as a result of human activities include CFCs (used as refrigerants, foam-blowing agents, and cleansers for electronic components), nitrous oxide (used in fertilizers), and methane (emitted during rice production). Of these trace gases, the CFCs are produced by industrial processes alone; and others are produced by both industrial and natural processes.

The increase in greenhouse gases during the past two centuries has resulted primarily from industrial processes in which fossil fuels are burned. Thus, a large proportion of the greenhouse gases produced by human activity has resulted from economic development in the industrialized countries (a fact that developing countries are not reluctant to mention when discussing the global warming issue).

National leaders around the globe are concerned about the issue of climate change. Mandatory international limits on the emissions of greenhouse gases could substan-

tially affect their own energy policies. Today, there are scientific and diplomatic efforts to better understand and deal with the prospects of global atmospheric warming and its possible impacts on society. Many countries have, for a variety of motives, agreed that there are reasons to limit greenhouse gas emissions worldwide. National representatives of the Conference of Parties meet each year to address this concern. In the meantime, few countries, if any, want to forgo economic development to avoid a global environmental problem that is still surrounded by scientific uncertainty.

The Oceans

The oceans represent another truly global commons. Most governments have accepted this as fact by supporting the Law of the Sea Treaty, which notes that the seas, which cover almost 70 percent of Earth's surface, are "the common heritage of mankind." In the early 1940s, Athelstan Spilhaus made a projection map that clearly shows that the world's oceans are really subcomponents of one global ocean.

There are at least three commons-related issues concerning the oceans: pollution, fisheries, and sea level. Problems and possible crises have been identified in each area.

The oceans are the ultimate sink for pollutants. Whether they come from the land or the atmosphere, they are likely to end up in the oceans. But no one really owns the oceans, and coastal countries supervise only bits and pieces of the planet's coastal waters. This becomes a truly global commons problem, as currents carry pollutants from the waters of one country into the waters of others. While there are many rules and regulations governing

pollution of the oceans, enforcement is quite difficult. Outside a country's 200-mile exclusive economic zone are the high seas, which are under the jurisdiction of no single country.

In many parts of the world, fisheries represent a common property resource. The oceans provide many countries with protein for domestic food consumption or export. Obtaining the same amount of protein from the land would require that an enormous additional amount of the land's surface be put into agricultural production. Whether under the jurisdiction of one country, several countries, or no country at all, fish populations have often been exploited with incomplete understanding of the causes of variability in their numbers. As a result, most fish stocks that have been commercially sought after have collapsed under the combined pressures of natural variability in the physical environment, population dynamics, and fish catches. This is clearly a serious problem; many perceive it to be a crisis.

Bound Together by Air and Water

- What goes up must come down" describes the fate of most pollutants ejected into the atmosphere. Taller smokestacks were used to assure that the pollutants did not come down "in my backyard."

- Fish stocks that naturally straddle the boundary between a country's protected zone and the open seas are a global resource requiring international protection measures.

- Sea level in all parts of the world would quickly rise some 8 meters (26 feet) if the vast West Antarctic ice sheet broke away and slid into the sea.

- Scientific controversy still surrounds the notion that human activities can produce enough greenhouse gases to warm the global atmosphere.

In many parts of the world, fisheries represent a common property resource.

For example, an area in the Bering Sea known as the "Donut Hole" had, until recently, also been suffering from overexploitation of pollack stocks. In the midst of the Bering Sea, outside the coastal zones and jurisdictions of the United States and Russia, there is an open-access area that is subject to laws related to the high seas, a truly global commons. Fishermen from Japan and other countries were overexploiting the pollack in this area. But these stocks were part of the same population that also lived in the protected coastal waters of the United States and Russia. In other words, the pollack population was a straddling stock—it straddled the border between the controlled coastal waters and the high seas.

To protect pollack throughout the sea by limiting its exploitation, the two coastal states took responsibility for protecting the commons (namely, the Donut Hole) without having to nationalize it. They did so by threatening to close the Bering Sea to "outsiders," if the outsiders were unable to control their own exploitation of the commonly shared pollack stock. There are several other examples of the overexploitation of straddling stocks, such as the recent collapse of the cod fishery along the Georges Bank in the North Atlantic.

Another commons-related issue is the sea level rise that could result from global warming of the atmosphere. Whereas global warming, if it were to occur, could change rainfall and temperature patterns in yet-un-known ways both locally and regionally, sea level rise will occur everywhere, endangering low-lying coastal areas worldwide. Compounding the problem is the fact that the sea is also an attractor of human populations. For example, about 60 percent of the U.S. population lives within a hundred miles of the coast.

This would truly be a global commons problem because *all* coastal areas and adjoining estuaries would suffer from the consequences of global warming. Concern about sea level rise is highest among the world's small island states, many of which (e.g., the Maldives) are at risk of becoming submerged even with a modest increase in sea level. In sum, there are no winners among coastal states if sea level rises.

Antarctica always appears on the list of global commons. Although it is outside the jurisdiction of any country, some people have questioned its classification as a global commons. It is a fixed piece of territory with no indigenous human population, aside from scientific visitors. It does have a clear link to the oceans as a global commons, however. One key concern about global warming is the possible disintegration of the West Antarctic ice sheet. Unlike Arctic sea ice, which sits in water, the West Antarctic ice sheet would cause sea level to rise an estimated eight meters if it broke away and fell into the Southern Ocean. Viewed from this perspective, the continent clearly belongs on the list of global commons. It is up to the global community to protect it from the adverse influences of human activities occurring elsewhere on the globe.

What's the Problem?

Are the changes in the atmosphere and oceans really problems? And if so, are they serious enough to be considered crises?

The consequences of the green-house effect are matters that scien-

World Ocean Map
(Spilhaus Projection)

ATHELSTAN SPILHAUS / COURTESY OF CELESTIAL PRODUCTS, PHILMONT, VA

Our one-ocean world: The oceans are but one body of water, as highlighted by the World Ocean Map developed more than 50 years ago by oceanographer Athelstan Spilhaus.

In 5 or 10 years incremental changes can mount into a major environmental crisis.

tists speculate about. But changes in the environment are taking place *now*. These changes are mostly incremental: low-grade, slow-onset, long-term, but gradually accumulating. They can be referred to as "creeping environmental problems." Daily changes in the environment are not noticed, and today's environment is not much different from yesterday's. In 5 or 10 years, however, those incremental changes can mount into a major environmental crisis [see "Creeping Environmental Problems," THE WORLD & I, June 1994, p. 218].

Just about every environmental change featuring human involvement is of the creeping kind. Examples include air pollution, acid rain, global warming, ozone depletion, tropical deforestation, water pollution, and nuclear waste accumulation. For many such changes, the threshold of irreversible damage is difficult to identify until it has been crossed. It seems that we can recognize the threshold only by the consequences that become manifest

after we have crossed it. With regard to increasing amounts of atmospheric carbon dioxide, what is the critical threshold beyond which major changes in the global climate system might be expected? Although scientists regularly refer to a doubling of CO_2 from preindustrial levels, the truth of the matter is that a doubling really has little scientific significance except that it has been selected as some sort of marker or milestone.

Policymakers in industrialized and developing countries alike lack a good process for dealing with creeping environmental changes. As a result, they often delay action on such changes in favor of dealing with issues that seem more pressing. Creeping environmental problems tend to be put on the back burner; that is, they are ignored until they have emerged as full-blown crises. The ways that individuals and societies deal with slow-onset, incremental adverse changes in the environment are at the root of cop-

ing effectively with deterioration and destruction of local to global commons.

Societal concerns about human impacts on commonly owned or commonly exploited resources have been recorded for at least 2,500 years. Aristotle, for example, observed "that which is common to the greatest number has the least care bestowed upon it." How to manage a common property resource, whether it is a piece of land, a fish population, a body of water, the atmosphere, or outer space, will likely confound decisionmakers well into the future.

Michael H. Glantz is program director of the Environmental and Societal Impacts Group at the National Center for Atmospheric Research (NCAR) in Boulder, Colorado. NCAR is sponsored by the National Science Foundation.

A GLOBAL WARNING

BY ROSS GELBSPAN

lobal warming is now accepted by reputable scientists as a genuine and severe threat. The ten hottest years on record have all occurred since 1980, and the five hottest consecutive years began in 1991. In late 1995, the world's leading 2,500 climate scientists, reporting to the United Nations, declared that the recent heating of the atmosphere is caused by carbon emissions from oil and coal combustion, not by the natural variability of the climate.

As the heating of the atmosphere intensifies, it will increase sea levels by as much as three feet in the next century, causing disastrous floods. Warming surface waters will also fuel dramatically more powerful hurricanes, cyclones, and windstorms. The early stages of increased warming have already altered rainfall patterns. Spreading droughts are projected to threaten food-growing regions of continental interiors. And a number of infectious diseases are spreading as the world's insect populations—one of the most sensitive of all nature's systems to temperature change—migrate beyond traditional boundaries.

Global warming need not require a reduction of living standards, but it does demand a rapid shift in patterns of fuel consumption—reduced use of oil, coal, and the lighter-carboned natural gas to an economy more reliant on solar energy, fuel cells, hydrogen gas, wind, biomass, and other renewable energy sources. It is doubtful that market forces can bring about this shift, since the market price of fossil fuels does not incorporate their environmental costs. Nor can this adjustment be successfully delayed until its impacts become too disruptive to ignore. The most prevalent of all greenhouse gases—carbon dioxide—has an atmospheric lifetime of between 100 and 200 years. Even were the world to stop all coal and oil burning tomorrow, the new era of climatic instability would persist well into the next century.

The globalization of the economy, and attendant problems of its governability, have gotten much attention lately. But governance of the global environment may be the more serious challenge. For there is neither a polit-ical consensus about how rapidly to reduce carbon emissions, nor agreement on the appropriate regulatory mechanism.

The question of how to temper global warming divides along two axes. Commercially, it is pitting oil and coal industries against those that will bear the cost of inaction, notably the world's insurers. Geopolitically, it pits the developed countries—especially those dependent on oil and coal—against many developing nations and a few of the more enlightened European countries.

Negotiating under the United Nations Framework Convention on Climate Change, 153 countries hope to draft an international treaty to limit fossil fuel emissions in time for a final session scheduled for Kyoto, Japan, in December 1997. But there is a yawning disjunction between what may be politically feasible and the natural requirements of the planet's inflamed atmosphere. The most interventionist proposals on the diplomatic table call roughly for emissions cuts by the industrial nations of 10 or 15 percent below 1990 levels by the year 2010. Even those proposals are far greater than anything the Clinton administration is willing to endorse. By contrast, atmospheric scientists generally agree it will require emissions cuts of more than 60 percent to stabilize the global atmosphere at current climatic levels.

CORPORATIONS TO THE RESCUE?

The resistance to any mandatory emissions cuts has been led by the two-trillion-dollar oil and coal industry, in league with the governments of OPEC and other coal- and oil-exporting nations. While the fossil fuel lobby has fought to discredit each new scientific confirmation of the climate trend, the world's property insurance giants—who will pay the cost of global warming damage—are becoming more vocal in their advocacy of immediate and dramatic cuts in the burning of oil and coal.

In this decade, a series of floods, hurricanes, and other severe storms has sent property insurance losses to unprecedented levels. Insurance payouts for weather-related (non-earthquake) losses averaged less than $2 billion a year in the 1980s, totaling $17 billion for the decade, according to the German reinsurance firm of Munich Re. But between 1990 and 1995 just 16 floods, hurricanes, and storms destroyed more than $130 billion in property and insurers paid $57 billion in covered losses.

In the last 2 years, 61 of the world's largest insurance giants have signed a "Statement of Environmental Commitment," pledging themselves to incorporate considerations of climate impacts into their decisionmaking. There are early signs that the banking community is also beginning to take notice of the devastating potential of climate disruptions. At a 1995 conference on climate change for leaders of financial institutions, Sven Hansen, vice president of the Union Bank of Switzerland, called climate change the "single most important environmental problem for the world today." At the same conference, Hilary Thompson of Britain's National Westminster Bank urged bankers to "support businesses that are going to create sustainable wealth that will actually not only redress the historic harm that has [occurred] but also finance the research and development that is necessary to bring about change."

Her remarks were underscored by a recent report by London's Delphi Group, which advises large institutions on their investment policies. Delphi recommended that banks, insurers, and other large institutional investors begin to withdraw their investments from oil and coal companies, with their traditionally lucrative returns. The report noted that continuing disturbances in the global climate could easily lead to high carbon taxes and enforced reductions on oil and coal use. "As a result," noted the report's author, Mark Mansley, a former financial analyst for Chase Manhattan Bank, "climate change presents major long term risks to the carbon fuel industry [that have] not been adequately discounted by the financial markets." At the same time, the Delphi Group noted, "The alternative energy industry offers greater growth prospects than the carbon fuel industry. Diversification into this sector also offers substantial scope to offset the risks of climate change. . . ."

Last year, the Business Council for a Sustainable Energy Future took steps to position itself prominently in the international climate negotiations in order to promote development of climate-friendly alternative energy technologies. While it represents an array of small renewable energy producers, the Business Council also includes some major corporations—Honeywell, Enron, Maytag, Brooklyn Union Gas, and a number of concerned utilities.

A much more influential business group, the International Climate Change Partnership (ICCP), counts among its members such giants as General Electric, AT&T, Allied Signal, Dow Chemical, 3M, Dupont, Enron, and Electrolux. Unlike the fossil fuel industry, the ICCP accepts the findings of the world's scientists and agrees on a need for an enforceable set of carbon dioxide reductions. "The fundamental science of global warming is pretty basic," the ICCP's executive director, Kevin Fay, said in an interview. "There is some uncertainty about specific effects and impacts, but we understand that there is a long lag time for atmospheric greenhouse gases—and that it also takes a long time to develop remedies for the problem."

The ICCP wants to trade on the success of its earlier incarnation. In the 1980s its predecessor organization, composed of leading chemical companies, worked with the world's governments to achieve the Montreal Protocol, which resulted in phasing out and developing substitutes for CFCs—a class of refrigerant chemicals responsible for depleting the ozone layer. As a public-private partnership dealing with a major global environmental problem, it was a remarkable success.

Unfortunately, that same formula is not applicable to the climate crisis. For one thing, the ozone-depleting chemicals constituted a small fraction of the chemical business. Fuel for heat, energy, and transportation, by contrast, are central to our collective economic existence. For another, the same chemical companies that agreed to the ban on ozone-depleting chemicals were able to develop and market their replacements. But the world's coal and oil companies are not positioned to produce and distribute solar panels, fuel cells, hydrogen gas production facilities, and windmills.

The ICCP, unlike the world's extractive industries, thinks it can profit from the development of renewable energy technologies. But though it supports specific targets and timetables to reduce greenhouse gas emissions, it shares with the oil and coal industries a general distaste for government regulation and a preference for private-sector solutions. "Our group envisions a process that produces good information on what alternative energy technologies are out there, what developments are in the pipeline, and what the deployment of those energy sources will do to the global greenhouse gas profile," according to Fay. "The next step we need to take is to assist those technologies to become competitive."

However, market forces alone are unlikely to generate a shift to renewable, non-carbon energy, because of the global fault line between rich and poor nations. Even if the United States, Europe, and Japan were able to dramatically reduce their own oil and coal use, those reductions would shortly be overwhelmed by the next pulse of carbon from China, India, Mexico, Brazil, and all the developing countries, which need energy to feed and house their expanding populations and to keep themselves beyond the undertow of deepening poverty.

Virtually all the market-based mechanisms currently being considered by international negotiators involve, in one form or another, the sale of climate-friendly energy technologies to developing countries that are barely able to feed and house their populations. These countries, not surprisingly, observe that the industrial north did not pay much attention to the niceties of pollution control until after they attained high levels of consumption. So the world's poor countries, not unreasonably, want either free technology transfer or other forms of subsidy from the north in order to finance an energy transition without increasing the burden on their poor populations.

YOU ARE WHAT YOU HEAT

In the climate negotiations, the postures of even the most pro-environment governments are guided by pure self-interest. The strongest position was taken by a group of small island nations calling themselves AOSIS, an acronym for Alliance of Small Island States, including the Philippines, Jamaica, the Marshall Islands, and Samoa—states that understandably fear being flooded into oblivion. AOSIS proposed a stringent emissions standard for the industrial nations of the world—a reduction by 20 percent of their 1990 greenhouse gas emissions levels by the year 2005.

Among the rich nations, Germany and Britain have proposed emissions cuts in the industrialized countries by 10 percent below 1990 levels by the year 2005 and 15 percent by the year 2020. But the United States, Australia, and OPEC charge Germany with cynically playing to its domestic constituency, which includes the largest Green Party in Europe. Germany, critics say, can readily afford to sustain a large emissions cut by virtue of West Germany's reunification in 1989 with East Germany, which is far less industrial and emits far less carbon dioxide—bringing German emissions nearly within the limits of that target with no additional hardship.

Britain, likewise, readily supports the emissions targets at no cost to British consumers, critics say. In 1991 the U.K. decided for budgetary and political reasons to terminate its program of coal subsidies and to switch, instead, to far cheaper and cleaner North Sea natural gas. So the seeming German and British high-mindedness actually involves no sacrifice, according to their critics. Even worse, they charge, the German and British positions allow room for other, poorer countries of the European Union to increase their burning of fossil fuels under an aggre-

> Major corporations now recognize the danger of global warming, but market forces alone won't generate a shift to renewable energy.

gated European Union cap. That situation would allow some of the less affluent European countries—Ireland, Portugal, Spain, and Greece—relatively high emissions margins so they can continue to develop their own economies with no cuts to their own fossil fuel consumption. And if, as anticipated, the E.U. expands by another 15 countries to include a number of former communist nations in eastern Europe, the combined cap for an enlarged E.U. would also provide them even more latitude to increase greenhouse emissions.

German officials counter that their citizens are bearing a significant tax burden to help finance an environmentally friendly reindustrialization of East Germany, costs that would be unacceptable to Americans. And British officials say that, whatever their initial motivations, they have in the last two years come to regard the climate crisis as very real and worthy of strong international action. Britain's environmental secretary, John Gummer, went so far as to call for an emissions reduction target of 50 percent beginning with an end to all subsidies for oil and coal use. "There is no point," he said, "in seeking to mitigate the effects of carbon dioxide while providing an inducement for people to use more."

Other members of the E.U. have gone their own ways. Denmark has already enacted a carbon tax as well as efficiency standards for its utilities in order to attain a 20 percent emissions reduction below 1990 levels by 2005. And the Netherlands has declared it intends to stabilize its emissions at 1990 levels by 2000 and reduce them by 3 percent five years later. By contrast, Norway, with its lucrative North Sea oil reserves, wants no emissions limits at all.

But the divisions within Europe pale before the yawning split between the wealthy world and the poverty-stressed, less-developed giants like India, China, Brazil, and Mexico. While the United States, Europe, and Japan can afford to give at least lip service to the high priority of the climate issue, the large developing countries, fighting to keep their economies above water, cannot. And until the issue of international equity between the world's wealthy and poor countries is addressed with some degree of authenticity, no developing country will adhere to any agreement that restricts its energy consumption.

Many Western diplomats attribute the recalcitrance of countries like China and India to an attitude of indifference to the planet. But that cynical dismissal lets the northern countries off the hook in two respects. It ignores the fact that industrial countries consume the lion's share of fossil fuels. And it minimizes the leadership that the United States and its developed allies could exert if they chose to make a priority policies that reconcile economic development of poor countries with concerns for the global environment. The developing nations will likely reject any international agreement that does not address their own overriding issues of poverty and underdevelopment.

PROGRESS AND POVERTY

Under the terms of the United Nations Climate Convention, any target for reducing coal and oil emissions would apply, initially, to only the world's industrialized countries. But diplomats envision subsequent similar restrictions for the world's poor countries, since it is clear the developing world will not be able to continue the potentially catastrophic growth of their own fossil fuel burning.

The climate crisis requires both measures by the industrial north to reduce fossil fuel consumption, as well as a transfer of wealth—in the form of new energy technologies—to assist the poorer countries to leapfrog beyond carbon fuels to an industrialization powered by renewable energy sources. Without such assistance, there is very little hope of avoiding a doubling—and probably a tripling—of atmospheric carbon dioxide concentrations. Today, for instance, as it staggers under the pressure of an increasingly fragile food supply and diminishing water resources, the government of China at this point sees no alternative to promoting its own economic growth as rapidly as possible. While energy consumption in the United States, Europe, and Japan rose by about 28 percent between 1970 and 1990, it rose by almost 10 times that amount—208 percent—during the same period in China. Under current estimates, moreover, Chinese coal consumption—which equaled that of the United States in 1990—will more than double America's ten years from now.

The situation in China is so bad it is sparking alarm even among its government researchers, despite the regime's commitment to rapid growth powered by conventional energy. Oceanographers with China's State Oceanic Administration estimate that rising sea levels will trigger massive flooding if current trends continue. "Sea levels will rise up to three feet during the twenty-first century," said Du Bilan, an agency official. Without a massive program to build coastal-protection bulwarks and sea-walls, the researchers project that economic losses from a 12-inch rise in sea level would be devastating "since coastal areas are home to about half of China's cities and 40 percent of the country's total population of 1.2 billion," Du said.

And China, as large as it is, is only one of many sources of the emerging Asian boom in greenhouse gas emissions. In May 1996, the environment ministry of Japan estimated that emissions of carbon dioxide and other greenhouse gases from 15 Asian nations will more than double in 30 years—a projected increase of 150 percent of 1990 levels by the year 2025. Using data from other Asian countries as well as from the World Bank, the Japanese report noted that the greenhouse emissions from the region will account for 36 percent of the world's emissions by the year 2025 and for 50 percent by the end of the next century.

The massive gap in economic pressures and priorities between northern and southern countries is more than the source of diplomatic deadlock. It has provided a most useful wedge for those who most want the negotiations to fail. Throughout the ongoing negotiations, the OPEC nations and their industry allies have warned the large developing nations that the "climate scare" is based on flawed science and is basically a plot by the wealthy countries to keep them relatively poor. Consequently, they have urged those large developing giants to accept nothing but the most minimal future restrictions. At the same time, the OPEC nations and the representatives of the oil and coal industry have put the United Nations on notice that they will accept no restrictions that do not fall equally heavily on the developing world. Anything less, they argue, is fundamentally unfair to fossil fuel producers, whose income depends on their sales of oil and coal.

It is a strategy designed to guarantee the failure of the climate negotiations. The rich nations have built their industrial wealth on fossil fuel consumption. Any attempt to impose the same restrictions on the poor countries—whose per capita consumption of coal and oil has been but a fraction of

ours—amounts to "environmental colonialism," according to Sunita Narain, an Indian researcher and co-author of a report titled, "Global Warming in an Unequal World." This idea of environmental colonialism, of course, is precisely what the fossil fuel lobby pitches to developing countries. The success of the negotiating tactics of Saudi Arabia and Kuwait, in league with representatives of the U.S. oil and coal industry, has, in effect, precluded negotiators from moving forward on any truly meaningful measures.

Given this backdrop of nearly stalemated diplomatic and economic agendas, it is understandable that U.S. Undersecretary of State Timothy Wirth called it a "big deal" last July when he announced that the United States would support some level—albeit minimal—of mandatory emissions reductions. It is not only Wirth who thinks so paltry a response to the disruption of the global climate is a "big deal." Clearly the oil and coal lobby think so as well. That is why they are feverishly mobilizing key leaders in Congress to defeat the ratification of any treaty that requires those mandatory cuts.

All of this, in the end, leaves the resolution of perhaps the most ominous environmental problem ever confronting humanity to the mercy of the global marketplace. Under the current scenario, our ability to avert a climate disaster may well depend on whether we can get China to buy our conservation technologies, whether we can sell our solar panels to Brazil and our windmills to India, and whether our marketing experts can persuade the poor governments of the world to put the nutritional and medical and educational needs of their people on hold and divert their overstretched resources to revamping their national energy systems with technologies we will sell them at the right price.

Meanwhile, the world's glaciers are melting, the world's oceans are warming, plants and insects are migrating northward, the zooplankton are dying in the Pacific Ocean, the Antarctic ice shelves are breaking up, and the planet continues to heat at a faster rate than at any time in the last ten thousand years.

> The divisions within Europe pale before the yawning split between the wealthy world and poverty-stressed, less-developed countries.

ENVIRONMENT

Fire in The Sky

By Murray Hiebert with S. Jayasankaran in Kuala Lumpur and John McBeth in Jakarta

L*ocusts, frogs and hail have yet to descend upon Southeast Asia, but the woes afflicting its people already seem of Biblical proportions. Hard on the heels of tumbling currencies came a blanket of noxious smog, primarily the product of massive forest blazes in Indonesia, with some homegrown pollution among its neighbours thrown in. The fires' persistence and, for days, the lack of cleansing rain were due to dry weather, in turn attributed to the El Nino current that warms the Pacific every few years.*

Although El Nino couldn't have been prevented, the environmental crisis, like the economic one, had been preceded by plenty of warnings. Just as runaway credit growth and gaping current-account deficits set off alarm bells long ago, so did Indonesia's recurring, man-made fires and the region's rampant industrial and traffic pollution.

While some Southeast Asian leaders, most notably Malaysian Prime Minister Mahathir Mohamad, sought to pin the economic crisis on pernicious Westerners, blame for the smog falls squarely within the region. Politicians' pell-mell drive to develop their economies blinded them to the growing environmental costs. Today, wheezing lungs and wheezing markets stand as a double reminder of the need for far-sighted leadership, and perhaps as a warning that Asean's policy of noninterference doesn't always serve the region best.

Indonesian President Suharto has taken the unusual step of publicly apologizing for the smog, but that's far from the final word in the saga. In the following pages, REVIEW reporters tally the growing economic and health toll from the haze, assess the possible political fallout, and look at whether a cloud of poison can be prevented from enveloping the region again next year.

Bill Wong knew he was a pioneer when he opened a hi-tech plant in Malaysia's remote state of Sarawak, on Borneo, early last year. He never guessed that 18 months later his $115 million factory would be engulfed in smoke from some of the largest forest fires in history.

"We never planned for it," says Wong, managing director for Komag, an American maker of disk-drive components. Air-pollution readings of over 500—on a scale on which readings above 301 are considered dangerous—kept half of Komag's 800 local employees off work. They weren't all needed anyway; thick smoke and haze closed the airport and port in nearby Kuching, making it impossible for Wong to get his products to customers. The plant cut back to a single shift, and the workers who did show up were given bonuses and free meals because food prices had jumped as much as 500%.

Komag's problems are just a small fraction of the mounting costs Southeast Asia faces from the environmental disaster created by the epic forest fires still raging in Indonesia. Pollution has closed airports, forced airlines to cancel flights and prompted foreign visitors to call off vacation plans, threatening the region's multibillion-dollar tourism industry. The lack of sunlight could ravage crops, and analysts warn that poor air quality may damage the region's attractiveness as a long-term investment destination.

That's not the half of it, either. The smog has already resulted in a sharp increase in the number of patients treated for respiratory ailments. Doctors warn of short-term problems like lung and heart diseases, reduced fertility, and damage to the nervous system, blood cells and kidneys. The long-run is even scarier, they say, because the full impact of the damage probably won't be known for another decade or more.

From *Far Eastern Economic Review*, October 9, 1997, pp. 74-75, 78. © 1997 by Review Publishing Company Limited. Reprinted by permission.

Such health concerns have many Southeast Asians feeling decidedly impatient with their leaders. Indonesia's press has roundly castigated authorities for their inability to handle the raging fires. In Malaysia, Prime Minister Mahathir Mohamad raised eyebrows by flying to Cuba at the height of the emergency. "The troubling thing is that the Malaysian government isn't treating the problem seriously," says Kuala Lumpur-based environmentalist Gurmit Singh. "When it comes to hard decisions about health and the economy, they go for the economy part. They take risks with health."

In the last days of September, rain and winds brought some relief to the region, but air quality could deteriorate again before the onset of the autumn monsoons. And unless Indonesia takes steps to prevent a reoccurrence of the disastrous fires, the smog could be just as bad again next year.

At this point, it's impossible to give a full reckoning of the disaster's economic toll. But the most immediate impact is a sharp blow to Southeast Asian tourism. Numerous governments in Europe and

North America have issued advisories warning their citizens against visiting countries hit by the polluted air, particularly Malaysia, Indonesia and Singapore.

In late September, Kuching ground to a halt, its hotels empty and its tour boats idle. "Business dropped 95%-100%," says Margaret Tan, manager of Galeri M, an upmarket fine-arts gallery in the local Hilton Hotel. "For 10 days Kuching was a ghost town." She doesn't expect business to come back any time soon, either, because tourists fear the winds may shift and blow fresh clouds of smoke over the city.

This couldn't have come at a worse time, just ahead of the usually lucrative winter season. Tour operators in Germany are already offering full refunds to visitors who have booked trips to Southeast Asia. Hotels in Singapore, where tourism generates $7.2 billion a year, expect cancellations to increase in the coming weeks as images of the disaster are aired on television newscasts around the world. Reports say some athletes could skip Malaysia's Commonwealth Games, scheduled for next September, and thousands of visitors may stay away.

The smog has also affected air travel, repeatedly forcing airports in Malaysia and Indonesia to close due to poor visibility. All flights to the five airports in Indonesia's Kalimantan have been cancelled for the past two weeks, while only two of Sumatra's airports have been open through that period. On two successive days in late September, Malaysia Airlines cancelled a total of over 140 flights. The airline hasn't commented on the fallout, but according to Merrill Lynch analyst Yeoh Kait Seng, "if they keep cancelling flights, margins will be squeezed."

Decreased visibility may even be making air travel hazardous. Forest-fire smoke was dense when a Garuda Indonesia plane crashed near Medan, Sumatra, on September 26, killing all 234 people on board. Authorities haven't commented on possible causes, but the poor visibility may have compounded confusion in the cockpit following a reported miscommunication between the pilot and the control tower. Shipping in the Malacca Strait, the world's busiest waterway, hasn't been much better. At least three collisions in recent weeks may have been caused by low visibility.

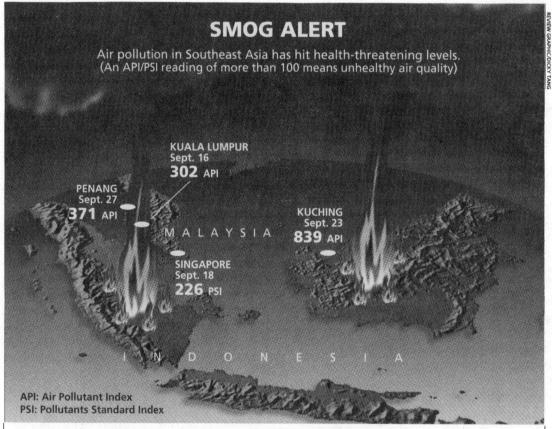

SMOG ALERT

Air pollution in Southeast Asia has hit health-threatening levels.
(An API/PSI reading of more than 100 means unhealthy air quality)

KUALA LUMPUR
Sept. 16
302 API

PENANG
Sept. 27
371 API

MALAYSIA

KUCHING
Sept. 23
839 API

SINGAPORE
Sept. 18
226 PSI

INDONESIA

API: Air Pollutant Index
PSI: Pollutants Standard Index

REVIEW GRAPHIC/DICKY TANG

The figures show air-pollution indexes in Malaysia and Singapore. While the two countries calculate their figures differently—which means Singapore's readings aren't directly comparable with, say, Kuala Lumpur's—they use the same classifications: A reading of 0-50 means air quality is good, 51-100 moderate, 101-200 unhealthy, 201-300 very unhealthy and 301-500 hazardous. And Kuching's reading of 839? Off the scale.

Source: Singapore Ministry of Environment, Malaysia Department of Environment

In Kuala Lumpur, the impact on daily life is unmistakable. Food-hawker stalls complain that business has fallen 30%. Some produce prices have risen. Taxi driver K. Loganathan says his daily income has been cut by more than a quarter. "Nobody is going out to shop, everyone is staying home," he grumbles.

That's all immediate, short-run damage—but the largest cost of the disaster will almost certainly be the long-term health effects. In Kuching, health officials say the number of patients seeking treatment for respiratory illnesses has doubled in recent weeks. In Kuala Lumpur, the number of children treated for asthma has grown seven-fold. Across Malaysia, the number of people seeking help for respiratory problems has surged 30%, according to Thambyappa Jayabalan, a doctor in Penang.

Looking ahead, physicians see potentially catastrophic effects. "In 20 to 30 years, you could see an increase in cancer and leukaemia," Jayabalan says. "The cost in the future could be phenomenal."

One problem is that no region has ever suffered through such extended exposure to pollutants from cars, factories *and* forest fires. "The bad news is we just don't have the answers we need," William Jackson, a U.S. government medical officer, told hundreds of Americans who attended a meeting organized by the U.S. Embassy in Kuala Lumpur. "The data just doesn't exist."

For the first time ever, the U.S. government has authorized the evacuation of its embassy personnel for medical reasons, and about 100 employees and dependents have left Kuala Lumpur. The crisis is also knocking some of the shine off Malaysia's reputation among foreign investors. Multinationals such as Ericsson and General Electric are evacuating expatriates from Kuala Lumpur. All in all, thousands have left Malaysia in the smog's wake.

Even the Multimedia Super Corridor—a special hi-tech zone that Malaysia hopes will attract leading multimedia firms—could be threatened. "There will be consequences if they want to turn this into a tropical Eastern Europe," says one Western diplomat, alluding to the environmental degradation in many former communist countries.

Farmers face more immediate concerns: Their crops may be affected by reduced sunlight and lower levels of oxygen. One of the hardest-hit crops could be palm oil, of which Malaysia is the world's largest exporter. Palm trees need five hours of continuous sunlight each day to produce to their capacity, says Jalani Suhaimi, deputy director of the Palm Oil Research Institute of Malaysia. Because smog reduces the intensity of sunlight, Jalani believes the output of palm trees could be reduced this year and into the future. If Malaysia's crop falters, international palm-oil prices could soar.

Fruit, vegetables and other crops could also be hit. Agronomists say the lack of sunlight inhibits photosynthesis, resulting in smaller fruit. Besides that, the shortage of sunlight is causing birds, bees and other insects to become inactive, says zoologist Idris Adbul Ghani. "If the bees aren't active, there's no pollination, and this reduces the amount of fruit," he points out.

Indonesia's mining industry is struggling to cope, too. Heavy smoke has forced intermittent shutdowns at Kelian Equatorial's gold mine in East Kalimantan. At Mt. Muro, Kalimantan's other operating gold mine, Aurora Gold, hasn't been able to get in an aircraft for more than two months and its main supply route, the Berito River, hasn't been navigable since August.

No one knows when the monsoon rains will come and put out Indonesia's raging fires. But Roger Stone, an Australian expert on the El Nino phenomenon that has delayed the annual rains, says northern Sumatra, home to many of the blazes, has a 70% chance of receiving normal rainfall over the next three months. But he puts the chances of normal rain over most of Indonesia at just 10%-30%.

The Malaysian government has refitted eight planes to spray salt solution into the clouds, hopefully creating rain to wash away the pollutants. But scientists worry that when the rains begin, they will contain dangerous levels of pollutants and cause new environmental hazards, including acid rain.

Although the Indonesian fires account for much of the smog, other countries' breakneck race to prosperity has exacerbated the problems. The region's factories were belching out pollutants and its cities were choked in traffic long before smoke from the forest fires began blotting out the sun.

Demands for development have often brushed aside environmental concerns. Three years ago, for instance, Malaysia's Department of Environment developed a plan to control vehicle emissions and develop a public-transport system. But the cabinet rejected the proposals after several ministers argued they would cost too much.

Does the airborne disaster threaten to undermine Southeast Asia's leaders? There will be political costs, observers say, though they may not be immediately apparent. "There's been currency mismanagement, economic problems and now the haze—and the prime minister is out of the country," observes an Asian diplomat in Kuala Lumpur. "There's a perception that the men at the top are out of touch. It will have no immediate effect, but it could start to add up."

As yet, there's little outlet for that frustration in Malaysia. Up to the end of September, environmentalists had organized only one small demonstration, attended by a few dozen activists.

Nonetheless, some businessmen believe the crisis could serve as a wake-up call for Southeast Asia. "Maybe this will be a blessing in disguise," says economist Ghazali Atan, head of Kompleks Metro Wangsa, a fund-management firm. "You can't ignore this. This will raise environmental consciousness, maybe even change the way we do business . . . That can only be good."

Mining the oceans

The world is just beginning to tap the mother lode
of mineral riches at the bottom of the sea.

Bjørn Sletto

• *Free-lance writer Bjørn Sletto, a frequent contributor to* THE ROTARIAN, *is based in Lawrence, Kansas, U.S.A.*

On the pitch-back floor of the Pacific Ocean, more than three miles (4.8 kilometres) below the surface, lies an area known as the Clarion-Clipperton Zone. It's a cold and hostile world, inhabited by few species, undisturbed by swirling currents, and subject to the bone-crushing atmospheric pressures. But this vast, five million-square mile (12,950,000-square kilometre) area, located 1,200 miles (1,931 kilometres) south of Hawaii, U.S.A., holds a wealth of rare minerals surpassing even the richest deposits on land.

The minerals in this zone—named because of its location between two fractures in the Earth's crust, the Clarion and the Clipperton—occur in nodules, potato-sized balls littering the flat, desolate sea floor like hail after a spring storm. What makes these mineral balls so valuable is their extremely high purity. Nickel content in nodules is one and one-half percent, compared to one-half percent in many land deposits. In nodules, the copper content is one and one-half percent; in land-based rock, the amount is commonly five-tenths of one percent.

"The Clarion-Clipperton Zone contains twice as much nickel as occurs on land," says deep-sea mining specialist Jan Magne Markussen at Norway's Fridtjof Nansen Institute, a leading international oceanographic center. "But this area is just one of many. The Pacific Ocean alone is twice the area of all land. Through seismic mapping, we have discovered enormous mineral resources on the floor of the deep seas—probably more than all mineral deposits on land combined."

But if the deposits are so vast, why aren't they being mined? Not for lack of available technology, according to deep-sea mining experts, but for economic and political reasons. Mineral prices are currently too low to justify, at least in the minds of mining executives, the huge initial costs of developing deep-sea mining fields. But perhaps most importantly, the deep seas, those areas of the ocean outside the exclusive economic zones (EEZs) of coastal countries, are under United Nations jurisdiction. Deep-sea mining is subject to the mineral exploration and mining provisions of the 1982 International Law of the Sea, a set of rules rejected as too restrictive by mining companies and world powers such as the United Kingdom and the United States.

Interest in deep-sea mining began in earnest in the 1970s, when private mining firms and research institutions such as the Woods Hole Oceanographic Institute in the United States and the Fridtjof Nansen Institute in Norway began mapping mineral resources in the ocean and testing mining methods. A high point came in 1978, when insurgents from Angola and Zambia invaded the Shaba province of Zaire. Most of the world's supply of cobalt comes from this area, and as a result of the war, prices rose sevenfold in just days. Since cobalt is an irreplaceable ingredient in high-speed power alloys such as those used in fighter plane engines, political pressure grew to develop alternative sources for strategic minerals.

Researchers discovered that deep-sea mineral deposits appeared in a variety of guises—not just as nodules—and were more difficult to mine than originally envisioned. Nodules are perhaps the easiest source to exploit, since they can be scooped up with dragline dredges or sucked up with trailing suction dredges, much like vacuuming crumbs off the kitchen floor. Formed through a process similar to silver-plating, nodules consist mostly of manganese deposited from the sea water and enriched with minor amounts of cobalt, nickel, platinum, copper, and molybdenum.

The two other types of deep-sea mineral deposits, crusts and polymetallic sulfides, need to be excavated or blasted much like in mines on land. Crusts form through a leaching process on submerged ridges or seamounts between 2,700 and 8,000 feet (824 and 2,440 metres) at a rate of between one to 2.8 millimetres per million years—a slow rate even in geologic terms. These deposits contain large amounts of cobalt, platinum, and phosphorus, and are less than 41 centimetres (16 inches) thick. They can be crushed and mined with various dredging techniques or excavated with clamshell buckets.

Polymetallic sulfides are rich sources of virtually all significant minerals, including gold, and can be excavated with dredges or liquefied into a slurry and pumped up to the surface. Sulfides form in fault zones, areas where the plates that make up the earth's surface are pulled apart. Faults—also known as rifts—are conduits for the melted rock of the earth's interior, which continually erupts in the form of lava, building sea ridges that parallel the fault.

Polymetallic sulfides form when seawater percolates down into the faults and reacts with the hot rock, dissolving the minerals contained in the rocks. As the heated seawater escapes through vents paralleling the lava flow, some of the minerals precipitate on the walls of the fault and on the sea floor. The crust deposit in one such fault zone, the Galapagos Rift off the northwestern coast of South America, is only one-half mile (.8 kilometre) long and 650 feet (198 metres) wide, but it contains an estimated 25 million U.S. tons (22.7 million metric tons) of copper and zinc—larger than some deposits currently mined on land.

After the initial flurry of deep-sea research expeditions in the 1970s, interest fizzled out during the next decade. Mineral prices fell as developing nations increased their production to earn desperately needed hard currency, and the benefits of developing ocean-bottom mining fields no longer exceeded the projected costs. A mobile manganese nodule operation, for example, would cost more than U.S. $1 billion, a hefty sum even for the leading mining conglomerates.

Still, according to some experts, economics is not the main reason mining companies are holding back. "Commodity prices are low right now," says Frank Manheim, senior research geologist and deep-sea mining expert with the United States Geological Survey. "But deep-sea mining is really precluded for political reasons. The conditions outlined in the United Nations Law of the Sea are unacceptable to the United States, the United Kingdom, and large mining companies. This has resulted in a stalemate that's slowed down exploration and mining for more than a decade."

According to the Law of the Sea, resources beyond the range of national EEZs are our common heritage. The provisions that have raised some countries' hackles state that any one country or company cannot obtain sovereign control of any part of the deep seas. Any exploration must be licensed through a UN body—the International Seabed Authority, headquartered in Jamaica—although prices are freely determined by the market. The United States and the mining giants, however, maintain that the licensing process is guided by strict environmental standards and is unnecessarily political. But proponents argue that such licensing is the only way to safeguard the deep seas from undue exploitation.

"The deep seas are the only parts of the world untouched by people," says Markussen at the Fridtjof Nansen Institute. "The Law of the Sea gives us a unique opportunity to establish regulations before the commercial development begins—instead of trying to catch up after the damage is done."

But despite the decade-long controversy surrounding the Law of the Sea—which went into effect in November 1994 over the protest of the United States—ocean mining is not dead in the water. When the commercial companies abandoned the deep seas in the 1980s, the momentum passed to a handful of newly industrialized countries, most notably India, the People's Republic of China, and South Korea, which launched extensive development programs.

Actually, ocean mining in shallow water has a long tradition in the developing world. Indonesia has dredged for tin in offshore waters since 1910. Diamonds have been dredged off the coast of Namibia since the 1960s, and a joint Sudanese-Saudi Arabian project excavated polymetallic sulfide mud in the Red Sea in the late 1980s. Countries such as Nigeria and Venezuela have developed some of the world's biggest offshore oil fields.

Throughout the 1980s, the Indian Nodule Programme developed a remotely controlled collector unit with a capacity of 100 U.S. tons (90.7 metric tons) of nodules a day, along with advanced data communication technologies and several riser systems to lift the minerals to the surface. In addition, India has conducted an extensive exploration program in the Central Indian Basin, often in cooperation with Norwegian and other Western seismic mapping firms.

In 1991, the People's Republic of China announced its intention to mine the Clarion-Clipperton area jointly with Russia and the United States. Stymied by the political reticence of the U.S. and the economic doldrums of the Russian republic, the Chinese Ocean Mineral Resources Research and Development Association (COMRA) has lately been seeking investors from Hong Kong, Macao, and Taiwan for the project. Trial mining is slated to begin in 2005, and production five years later.

According to industry insiders, several leading industrial countries—including Japan—are seeking U.S. partnership for commercial development of the Clarion-Clipperton Zone. Still, such international cooperation is probably a few years off. In the meantime, deep-sea mining may prove to be a boon to small island states that are short on capital and land-based resources but that sport enormous EEZs—many with huge mineral resources. According to Michael Cruickshank, director of the Marine Minerals Technology Center of the University of Hawaii, U.S.A., the Cook Islands may actually be the first country to develop a commercial deep-sea mining industry.

"I think it's highly probable that deep-sea mining will begin within the next couple of decades," says Cruickshank, "and then probably in a place such as the Cook Islands. Despite the political opposition from the United States, the marketplace is always stronger than the bureaucracy. Marine mining will inevitably become more competitive as the environmental effects and costs of land-based mining continue to grow. Eventually, we'll begin to deplete our resources on land, and then we'll have to move to the sea. The minerals there constitute the ultimate source for our future survival."

GREENWATCH

RED ALERT FOR THE EARTH'S GREEN BELT

FRANCE BEQUETTE

France Bequette is a Franco-American journalist specializing in environmental questions. Since 1985 she has been associated with the WANAD-UNESCO training programme for African news agency journalists.

"TROPICAL forest" is the common name for what specialists call "rainforest", a term coined in 1898 by the botanist Andreas Schimper to designate forests that grow in a perpetually humid environment, receiving more than 2,000 millimetres of rain per year. In these conditions trees with smooth trunks can grow to more than sixty metres high. Their tops join together in what is known as the canopy, a roof of thick vegetation that keeps out the light.

Like a scarf girdling the equator, rainforests cover about 9.5 million square kilometres. The largest single tropical forest zone is in South America. Only five million square kilometres of rainforest now exist in tropical Asia and central Africa. A report published by UNESCO in 1991 reveals that Côte d'Ivoire has lost 75 per cent of its forest since 1960, and Ghana 80 per cent. In 25 years the Philippines have lost 15 out of 16 million hectares. By the year 2000 the forests of Viet Nam may well be no more than a fond memory. As British ecologist Edward Goldsmith noted in his *Report on Planet Earth*,

published in 1990, the Food and Agriculture Organization of the United Nations (FAO) estimated in the early 1980s that 100,000 square kilometres of rain forest were being lost each year. The American Academy of Sciences was far more pessimistic, deploring the loss of twice that area. The situation in Brazil seems to support the Academy's claim, since Brazil lost 48,000 square kilometres in 1988 alone.

Lowland forests, by far the biggest and the most easily accessible, have suffered most from human exploitation. Although less developed because of lower temperatures, rainfall variability and poorer soil, highland forests still play a very important role in preventing soil erosion and lowland flooding. Mangroves are a kind of rainforest growing in the salt-water and silt-rich coastal regions and along the banks of rivers flowing through forests. The mangrove forests in the Sundarbans region of the Ganges delta are the world's largest.

WHO IS TO BLAME?

Although they cover only 7 per cent of the earth's surface, rainforests are the home of more than half of the planet's plant species. With massive media support, international organizations are rightly insisting on the

need to preserve biodiversity, which is threatened from all sides, most notably by competition from agriculture. Again according to FAO, some 250 million farmers live in rainforests around the world. In search of land for crop-growing and livestock raising, they occupy forest areas owned by the state, which is often unable to control access to it. These farmers have no recognized right to the areas they occupy. Alain Karsenty and Henri-Félix Maître of the forestry department of France's Centre for International Co-operation in Agronomic Research for Development (CIRAD) in a report to the XIth Directorate of the Commission of the European Communities published in 1993 stress that "recognition of property rights (not necessarily in the Western sense of the term 'property') for local communities is one of the necessary (but not sufficient) conditions for joint management of the forest with those who live in it."

Peoples who have lived for a long period in these zones are well adapted to their environment, but this is not the case with the new arrivals who grow cash crops such as cocoa and coffee. They follow the roads and trails gouged out by the loggers, thereby infiltrating the dense forest where, mainly by using fire, they create "frontiers" which push back the forest. "This interrelationship between exploitation

W O R L D

THE DIMINISHING OZONE LAYER

The World Meteorological Organization (WMO) reports that in 1993 low ozone levels were measured over most of South America. Ozone concentrations fell by 7% above Sao Paulo and by 3 to 4% above Rio de Janeiro. In March and April 1994 the depletion of the ozone layer above Europe, Siberia and the adjacent polar-ocean areas was more than 10% below long-term mean values. ∎

FUEL FOR KANGWANE'S FIRES

An American reader, Suzy Liebenberg, former co-ordinator of Ecolink's environmental community development programme, has written to tell us about an interesting project in the eastern Transvaal lowveld of South Africa, where members of the rural community of Kangwane are growing Leucaena trees around their homes and in their vegetable gardens. The species grows quickly and produces many stems from ground level rather than a single trunk. This makes it ideal for coppicing, which involves cutting a few stems from each tree annually, thus ensuring renewable supplies of wood. Tree seedlings are provided at a reasonable cost to the villagers and are planted to act as windbreaks and to provide shade and slow down evaporation in vegetable gardens. Leucaena is a legume, and its root nodules contain bacteria that extract nitrogen from the atmosphere and improve soil fertility by producing nitrates. Community members are encouraged to plant 52 seedlings because in

a 3-to-5-year period, 52 trees would supply enough fuel for a year. It also relieves women of having to carry heavy loads for great distances. ∎

ON THE SCENT OF THE MUSK DEER

The musk deer (*Moschus moschiferus*), a small hornless ruminant that lives in mountainous regions of Central Asia, China, eastern Korea and Siberia, is out of luck. The musk gland of the male is coveted both by Asian medicine and the Western perfume industry. Consisting of sexual hormones, cholesterol and a waxy substance, musk gives out a strong odour. Although musk can be collected from farm-reared specimens without killing the animal, as is done in China, poachers do not hesitate to defy measures to protect the musk deer. According to World Wide Fund for Nature (WWF) estimates, there are no more than 100,000 musk deer left in the world. ∎

SHRIMP IN CAGES

Since 1992, France's Research Institute for Exploitation of the Sea (IFREMER) has been co-operating with Brazil on a pilot project for farming shrimp in cages. The project is designed to increase production and to study the impact of aquaculture on the environment. In Ecuador, IFREMER is co-operating with the National Centre for Aquaculture and Marine Research (CENAIM) on the immunology and pathology of shrimp grown on farms. But while the cage technique is simple, the high-tech facilities being used in Ecuador have been strongly criticized by the British

ecologist Edward Goldsmith on the grounds that their products are too expensive for the needy. ∎

FIRE-LOVING FLOWERS

A rare flowering plant, the Peter's Mountain mallow (*Iliamna corei*), has made a remarkable comeback thanks to a prescribed burning programme in a Nature Conservancy Preserve in Virginia (U.S.A.). Only four such plants were known to exist when scientists discovered a large amount of dormant but viable seeds surrounding the plants. The fire-dependent plant was brought back from the brink of extinction when over 500 seeds sprouted after a controlled burn was conducted in the preserve. ∎

THE GREEN BUSES OF BRUSSELS [3]

Last March, Belgium's Ministry of Public Works and Communications and World Wildlife Fund (WWF) Belgium launched 20 new buses in Brussels that run on compressed natural gas (CNG). Although they cost almost $30,000 more than diesel buses to buy, maintenance costs are halved and a ministry subsidy keeps CNG prices even with those of diesel fuel. New York, Toronto and several other European cities including Utrecht (Netherlands) and Ravenna (Italy) already power public transport vehicles with natural gas. WWF-Belgium has sent education packs explaining the link between transportation and urban pollution to all secondary schools in Brussels. While the world waits for a miracle-fuel, CNG remains the least polluting of all. ∎

and agricultural colonization," says Alain Karsenty, "makes it difficult to apportion the responsibility borne by each activity in deforestation processes."

Edward Goldsmith has no time for those who condemn farmers for clearing land by fire, for this process has always been used, even in Europe. Its disadvantages become apparent when the population grows and the land is not left fallow for long enough, thus preventing

the forest from regenerating itself between two burnings.

Crops are greedy devourers of forest. In Ethiopia vast plantations have replaced trees: 60 per cent of the land is now given over to cotton-growing and 22 per cent to sugar cane. Central America has seen two-thirds of its forests sacrificed to live-stock-raising. Numerous developing countries that once exported timber—Nigeria, for example, but above all the Philippines, once a

major exporter—now import it. Of the last thirty exporters in the Third World today, only ten will still be exporting by the end of the century.

Another factor in deforestation is the timber industry. Until now Suriname on South America's north-eastern coast has been 90 per cent covered by virgin rainforest. But the government has just granted a concession of 150,000 hectares to an Indonesian logging company and is considering throwing in two million hectares more. Ernie Brunings, a member of Suriname's National Assembly, was quoted by *Time* magazine as saying bluntly, "We cannot have these riches and keep them for their beauty if we have children dying of hunger, as we have here." This is the crux of the matter. The logging industry creates jobs, and however low the wages may be, they provide a basic minimum.

LAND-HUNGRY FARMERS

Sustainable management of rainforests on a planetary scale is essential. This is what the United Nations Environment Programme (UNEP), the World Bank and the World Resources Institute (WRI) are trying to achieve via an ongoing process known as the Tropical Forestry Action Plan (TFAP). This is not a new plan but it is still relevant, although there has been some criticism that state authorities and sources of finance have a bigger say in it than the populations directly concerned.

"Is it possible," Alain Karsenty wonders, "both to preserve vast multifunctional forest ecosystems (protectors of biodiversity, homes to local communities, bulwarks against erosion and regulators of climate) and to allow logging activities on an industrial scale?" He goes on to ask, "How can we reconcile a business rationale that thinks largely in the short term with natural forest regeneration, a process that extends over dozens of years?"

Forest space is in high demand. Not only by logging companies but—once the loggers have pulled out—by large-scale livestock-raisers and cacao and rubber planters, who are always ready to clear the land. Forms of exploitation vary from region to region. In Africa, where highly-prized wood like mahogany is found and logging is very selective, only one tree per hectare is felled on average. This may not be much, but to reach logging sites, trails have to be cut, sometimes as much as one hundred kilometres long, and this opens the way to land-hungry farmers. In tropical

America, the opposite happens. The farmers go in first and are followed by loggers. Deforestation problems in southeast Asia result from intensive, often devastating, clear-cutting. The pockets of remaining forest are vulnerable to fires, as has been seen in Borneo.

SUSTAINABLE POSSIBILITIES

Several proposals for preserving the rainforest have been put forward. One is to limit the time period of concessions granted to logging companies and making their renewal dependent on "good behaviour". Logging companies might also be obliged by states to build on-site saw mills, as is done in Cameroon, to prevent them from clearing out once they have cut down all the valuable trees. The value of concessions could also be reasssssed by taking account of their true commercial value and granting them on a competitive basis. Skid trails must also be laid down, for, according to the World Bank, from 15 to 35 per cent of the damage to forests is caused by tractors foraging randomly in search of felled trees. Felling techniques could also be improved so that falling trees cause less damage to their neighbours. If their operating costs could be brought down and their safety ensured for both men and forest, helicopters and blimps could eventually lift timber vertically out of the forest.

The preservation of the rainforest depends above all on the political determination of states. Either states tolerate tree-felling and impose taxes on it, or they define regulations for using and managing the forests that international organizations like the FAO and the World Bank are prepared to support.

Some states, such as Indonesia, prohibit the exporting of unprocessed wood. In the process of industrializing, they have sought to add value to their timber and create jobs. Is this a solution? In Indonesia there are 500,000 jobs in plywood mills and about three million jobs in the wood industry overall. To function,

the industry requires 50 million m^3 of unprocessed wood per year, but the country can no longer supply this amount. Wood must be obtained at any price—thus encouraging illicit practices—or the mills will have to be closed down, which is politically impossible.

German, Dutch and American ecologists have proposed that the developed countries should boycott tropical wood unless it carries the "green label" awarded to wood from forests that are exploited sustainably. Even this plan is not without drawbacks. What is to prevent timber companies from reaping maximum profits before the restriction becomes universal? It might also speed up the conversion of forests into huge cacao and coffee farms that are supposedly more profitable. Or states may simply cease to manage and develop their forests, in the belief they will not be able to make money out of them.

Preservation and exploitation are not incompatible. In the tropics as in Europe, a forest that is not taken care of is a dying forest. But in managing these renewable natural resources, we must be satisfied with reaping the interest without touching the capital.

FURTHER READING:

➤ *Tropical Forests, People and Food, Man and the Biosphere series,* UNESCO and Parthenon Publishing Group, 1993.
➤ *The Last Rain Forests,* Mark Collins, IUCN and Mitchell Beasley, 1990.
➤ *Tropical Forest Ecosystems* (UNESCO, UNEP and FAO), UNESCO, 1979.
➤ *The Disappearing Tropical Forests,* MAB and the International Hydrological Programme, UNESCO, 1991.
➤ *Etude des modalités d'exploitation du bois en liaison avec une gestion durable des forêts tropicales humides,* CIRAD-Forêts, the Commission of the European Communities, XI D.G.,1993.
➤ *Bois et forêts des tropiques,* revue n° 240, CIRAD, Nogent-sur-Marne, France1994.

We *Can* Build a Sustainable Economy

The keys to securing the planet's future lie in stabilizing both human population and climate. The challenges are great, but several trends look promising.

By Lester R. Brown

The world economy is growing faster than ever, but the benefits of this rapid growth have not been evenly distributed. As population has doubled since midcentury and the global economy has nearly quintupled, the demand for natural resources has grown at a phenomenal rate.

Since 1950, the need for grain has nearly tripled. Consumption of seafood has increased more than four times. Water use has tripled. Demand for beef and mutton has tripled. Firewood demand has tripled, lumber demand has more than doubled, and paper demand has gone up sixfold. The burning of fossil fuels has increased nearly fourfold, and carbon emissions have risen accordingly.

These spiraling human demands for resources are beginning to outgrow the earth's natural systems. As this happens, the global economy is damaging the foundation on which it rests.

To build an environmentally sustainable global economy, there are many obstacles, but there are also several promising trends and factors in our favor. One is that we know what an environmentally sustainable economy would look like. In a sustainable economy:

- Human births and deaths are in balance.
- Soil erosion does not exceed the natural rate of new soil formation.
- Tree cutting does not exceed tree planting.
- The fish catch does not exceed the sustainable yield of fisheries.
- The number of cattle on a range does not exceed the range's carrying capacity.
- Water pumping does not exceed aquifer recharge.
- Carbon emissions and carbon fixation are in balance.
- The number of plant and animal species lost does not exceed the rate at which new species evolve.

We know how to build an economic system that will meet our needs without jeopardizing prospects for future generations. And with some trends already headed in the right direction, we have the cornerstones on which to build such an economy.

Stabilizing Population

With population, the challenge is to complete the demographic transition, to reestablish the balance between births and deaths that characterizes a sustainable society. Since populations are rarely ever precisely stable, a stable population is defined here as one with a growth rate below 0.3%. Populations are effectively stable if they fluctuate narrowly around zero.

Thirty countries now have stable populations, including most of those in Europe plus Japan. They provide the solid base for building a world population stabilization effort. Included in the 30 are all the larger industrialized countries of Europe—France, Germany, Italy, Russia, and the United Kingdom. Collectively, these 30 countries contain 819 million people or 14% of humanity. For this goal, one-seventh of humanity is already there.

The challenge is for the countries with the remaining 86% of the world's people to reach stability. The two large nations that could make the biggest difference in this effort are China and the United States. In both, population growth is now roughly 1% per year. If the global

From *The Futurist,* July/August 1996, pp. 8-12. © 1996 by The World Future Society, Bethesda, MD. http://www.wfs.org/wfs. Reprinted by permission.

food situation becomes desperate, both could reach stability in a decade or two if they decided it were important to do so.

The world rate of population growth, which peaked around 2% in 1970, dropped below 1.6% in 1995. Although the rate is declining, the annual addition is still close to 90 million people per year. Unless populations can be stabilized with demand below the sustainable yield of local ecosystems, these systems will be destroyed. Slowing growth may delay the eventual collapse of ecosystems, but it will not save them.

The European Union, consisting of some 15 countries and containing 360 million people, provides a model for the rest of the world of an environmentally sustainable food/population balance. At the same time that the region has reached zero population growth, movement up the food chain has come to a halt as diets have become saturated with livestock products. The result is that Europe's grain consumption has been stable for close to two decades at just under 160 million tons—a level that is within the region's carrying capacity. Indeed, there is a potential for a small but sustainable export surplus of grain that can help countries where the demand for food has surpassed the carrying capacity of their croplands.

As other countries realize that continuing on their current population trajectory will prevent them from achieving a similar food/population balance, more and more may decide to do what China has done—launch an all-out campaign to stabilize population. Like China, other governments will have to carefully balance the reproductive rights of the current generation with the survival rights of the next generation.

Very few of the group of 30 countries with stable populations had stability as an explicit policy goal. In those that reached population stability first, such as Belgium, Germany, Sweden, and the United Kingdom, it came with rising living standards and expanding employment opportunities for women. In some of the countries where population has stabilized more recently, such as Russia and other former Soviet republics, the deep economic depression accompanying economic reform has

substantially lowered birth rates, much as the Great Depression did in the United States. In addition, with the rising number of infants born with birth defects and deformities since Chernobyl, many women are simply afraid to bear children. The natural decrease of population (excluding migration) in Russia of 0.6% a year—leading to an annual population loss of 890,000—is the most rapid on record.

Not all countries are achieving population stability for the right reasons. This is true today and it may well be true in the future. As food deficits in densely populated countries expand, governments may find that there is not enough food available to import. Between fiscal year 1993 and 1996, food aid dropped from an all-time high of 15.2 million tons of grain to 7.6 million tons. This cut of exactly half in three years reflects primarily fiscal stringencies in donor countries, but also, to a lesser degree, higher grain prices in fiscal 1996. If governments fail to establish a humane balance between their people and food supplies, hunger and malnutrition may raise death rates, eventually slowing population growth.

that he wanted to provide better access to family-planning services for poor women. "It is only fair," he said, "to disseminate thoroughly the methods of family planning to everyone."

Stabilizing Climate

With climate, as with population, there is disagreement on the need to stabilize. Evidence that atmospheric carbon-dioxide levels are rising is clear-cut. So, too, is the greenhouse effect that these gases produce in the atmosphere. That is a matter of basic physics. What is debatable is the rate at which global temperatures will rise and what the precise local effects will be. Nonetheless, the consensus of the mainstream scientific community is that there is no alternative to reducing carbon emissions.

How would we phase out fossil fuels? There is now a highly successful "phase out" model in the case of chlorofluorocarbons (CFCs). After two British scientists discovered the "hole" in the ozone layer over Antarctica and published their findings in *Nature* in May 1985, the international community convened a con-

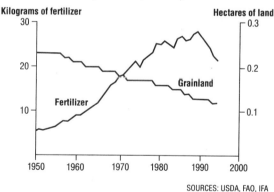

World Fertilizer and Grainland
(Per Person, 1950-94)

SOURCES: USDA, FAO, IFA

Some developing countries are beginning to adopt social policies that will encourage smaller families. Iran, facing both land hunger and water scarcity, now limits public subsidies for housing, health care, and insurance to three children per family. In Peru, President Alberto Fujimori, who was elected overwhelmingly to his second five-year term in a predominantly Catholic country, said in his inaugural address in August 1995

ference in Montreal to draft an agreement designed to reduce CFC production sharply. Subsequent meetings in London in 1990 and Copenhagen in 1992 further advanced the goals set in Montreal. After peaking in 1988 at 1.26 million tons, the manufacture of CFCs dropped to an estimated 295,000 tons in 1994—a decline of 77% in just six years.

As public understanding of the

costs associated with global warming increases, and as evidence of the effects of higher temperatures accumulates, support for reducing dependence on fossil fuels is building. As the March 1995 U.N. Climate Convention in Berlin, environmental groups were joined in lobbying for a reduction in carbon emissions by a group of 36 island communities and insurance industry representatives.

The island nations are beginning to realize that rising sea levels would, at a minimum, reduce their land area and displace people. For some low-lying island countries, it could actually threaten their survival. And the insurance industry is beginning to realize that increasing storm intensity can threaten the survival of insurance companies as well. When Hurricane Andrew tore through Florida in 1992, it took down not only thousands of buildings, but also eight insurance firms.

In September 1995, the U.S. Department of Agriculture reported a sharp drop in the estimated world grain harvest because of crop-withering heat waves in the northern tier of industrial countries. Intense late-summer heat had damaged harvests in Canada and the United States, across Europe, and in Russia. If farmers begin to see that the productivity of their land is threatened by global warming, they, too, may begin to press for a shift to renewable sources of energy.

As with CFCs, there are alternatives to fossil fuels that do not alter climate. Several solar-based energy sources, including wind power, solar cells, and solar thermal power plants, are advancing rapidly in technological sophistication, resulting in steadily falling costs. The cost of photovoltaic cells has fallen precipitously over the last few decades. In some villages in developing countries where a central grid does not yet exist, it is now cheaper to install an array of photovoltaic cells than to build a centralized power plant plus the grid needed to deliver the power.

Wind power, using the new, highly efficient wind turbines to convert wind into electricity, is poised for explosive growth in the years ahead. In California, wind farms already supply enough electricity to meet the

equivalent of San Francisco's residential needs.

The potential for wind energy is enormous, dwarfing that of hydropower, which provides a fifth of the world's electricity. In the United States, the harnessable wind poten-

World Wind Energy
(Generating Capacity, 1980-94)

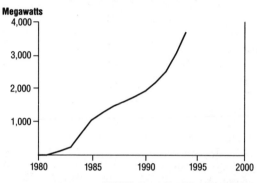

SOURCES: Gipe and Associates, BTM Consulting

tial in North Dakota, South Dakota, and Texas could easily meet national electricity needs. In Europe, wind power could theoretically satisfy all the continent's electricity needs. With scores of national governments planning to tap this vast resource, rapid growth in the years ahead appears inevitable.

A Bicycle Economy

Another trend to build on is the growing production of bicycles. Human mobility can be increased by investing in public transportation, bicycles, and automobiles. Of these, the first two are by far the most promising environmentally. Although China has announced plans to move toward an automobile-centered transportation system, and car production in India is expected to double by the end of the decade, there simply may not be enough land in these countries to support such a system and to meet the food needs of their expanding populations.

Against this backdrop, the creation of bicycle-friendly transportation systems, particularly in cities, shows great promise. Market forces alone have pushed bicycle production to an estimated 111 million in 1994, three times the level of automobile production. It is in the interest of societies everywhere to foster the use of bicycles and public transporta-

tion—to accelerate the growth in bicycle manufacturing while restricting that of automobiles. Not only will this help save cropland, but this technology can greatly increase human mobility without destabilizing climate. If food becomes increasingly scarce in the years ahead, as now seems likely, the land-saving, climate-stabilizing nature of bicycles will further tip the scales in their favor and away from automobiles.

The stabilization of population in some 30 countries, the stabilization of food/people balance in Europe, the reduction in CFC production, the dramatic growth in the world's wind power generating capacity, and the extraordinary growth in bicycle use are all trends for the world to build on. These cornerstones of an environmentally sustainable global economy provide glimpses of a sustainable future.

Regaining Control of Our Destiny

Avoiding catastrophe is going to take a far greater effort than is now being contemplated by the world's political leaders. We know what needs to be done, but politically we are unable to do it because of inertia and the investment of powerful interests in the status quo. Securing food supplies for the next generation depends on an all-out effort to stabilize population and climate, but we resist changing our reproductive behavior, and we refrain from converting our climate-destabilizing, fossil-fuel-based economy to a solar/hydrogen-based one.

As we move to the end of this century and beyond, food security may well come to dominate international affairs, national economic policy making, and—for much of humanity—personal concerns about survival. There is now evidence from enough countries that the old formula of substituting fertilizer for land is no longer working, so we need to search urgently for alternative formulas for humanly balancing our numbers with available food supplies.

Unfortunately, most national political leaders do not even seem to be aware of the fundamental shifts occurring in the world food economy, largely because the official projections by the World Bank and the U.N. Food and Agriculture Organization are essentially extrapolations of past trends.

If we are to understand the challenges facing us, the teams of economists responsible for world food supply-and-demand projections at these two organizations need to be replaced with an interdisciplinary team of analysts, including, for example, an agronomist, hydrologist, biologist, and meteorologist, along with an economist. Such a team could assess and incorporate into projections such things as the effect of soil erosion on land productivity, the effects of aquifer depletion on future irrigation water supplies, and the effect of increasingly intense heat waves on future harvests.

The World Bank team of economists argues that, because the past is the only guide we have to the future, simple extrapolations of past trends are the only reasonable way to make projections. But the past is also filled with a body of scientific literature on growth in finite environments, and it shows that biological growth trends typically conform to an S-shaped curve over time.

The risk of relying on these extrapolative projections is that they are essentially "no problem" projections. For example, the most recent World Bank projections, which use 1990 as a base and which were published in late 1993, are departing further and further from reality with each passing year. They show the world grain harvest climbing from 1.78 billion tons in 1990 to 1.97 billion tons in the year 2000. But instead of the projected gain of nearly 100 million tons since 1990, world

grain production has not grown at all. Indeed, the 1995 harvest, at 1.69 billion tons, is 90 million tons below the 1990 harvest.

One of the most obvious needs today is for a set of country-by-country carrying-capacity assessments. Assessments using an interdisciplinary team can help provide information needed to face the new realities and formulate policies to respond to them.

Setting Priorities

The world today is faced with an enormous need for change in a period of time that is all too short. Human behavior and values, and the national priorities that reflect them, change in response to either new information or new experiences. The effort now needed to reverse the environmental degradation of the planet and ensure a sustainable future for the next generation will require mobilization on a scale comparable to World War II.

Regaining control of our destiny depends on stabilizing population as well as climate. These are both key to the achievement of a wide array of social goals ranging from the restoration of a rise in food consumption per person to protection of the diversity of plant and animal species. And neither will be easy. The first depends on a revolution in human reproductive behavior; the second, on a restructuring of the global energy system.

Serving as a catalyst for these gargantuan efforts is the knowledge that if we fail our future will spiral out of control as the acceleration of history overwhelms political institu-

tions. It will almost guarantee a future of starvation, economic insecurity, and political instability. It will bring political conflict between societies and among ethnic and religious groups within societies. As these forces are unleashed, they will leave social disintegration in their wake.

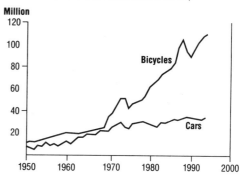

Bicycles vs. Cars
(Worldwide Production, 1950-94)

SOURCES: U.N., Interbike Directory

Offsetting the dimensions of this challenge, including the opposition to change that is coming from vested interests and the momentum of trends now headed in the wrong direction, are some valuable assets. These include a well-developed global communications network, a growing body of scientific knowledge, and the possibility of using fiscal policy—a potentially powerful instrument for change—to build an environmentally sustainable economy.

Policies for Progress

Satisfying the conditions of sustainability—whether it be reversing the deforestation of the planet, converting a throwaway economy into a reuse–recycle one, or stabilizing climate—will require new investment. Probably the single most useful instrument for converting an unsustainable world economy into one that is sustainable is fiscal policy. Here are a few proposals:

• **Eliminate subsidies for unsustainable activities.** At present, governments subsidize many of the very activities that threaten the sustainability of the economy. They support fishing fleets to the extent of some $54 billion a year, for example, even though existing fishing capacity already greatly exceeds the sustainable yield of oceanic fisheries. In

Germany, coal production is subsidized even though the country's scientific community has been outspoken in its calls for reducing carbon emissions.

• **Institute a carbon tax.** With alternative sources of energy such as wind power, photovoltaics, and solar thermal power plants becoming competitive or nearly so, a carbon tax that would reflect the cost to society of burning fossil fuels—the costs, that is, of air pollution, acid rain, and global warming—could quickly tip the scales away from further investment in fossil fuel production to investment in wind and solar energy. Today's fossil-fuel-based energy economy can be replaced with a solar/hydrogen economy that can meet all the energy needs of a modern industrial society without causing disruptive temperature rises.

• **Replace income taxes with environmental taxes.** Income taxes discourage work and savings, which are both positive activities that should be encouraged. Taxing environmentally destructive activities instead would help steer the global economy in an environmentally sustainable direction. Among the activities to be taxed are the use of pesticides, the generation of toxic wastes, the use of virgin raw materials, the conversion of cropland to nonfarm uses, and carbon emissions.

The time may have come also to limit tax deductions for children to two per couple: It may not make sense to subsidize childbearing beyond replacement level when the most pressing need facing humanity is to stabilize population.

The challenge for humanity is a profound one. We have the information, the technology, and the knowledge of what needs to be done. The question is, Can we do it? Can a species that is capable of formulating a theory that explains the birth of the universe now implement a strategy to build an environmentally sustainable economic system?

About the Author
Lester R. Brown is president of the Worldwatch Institute, 1776 Massachusetts Avenue, N.W., Washington, D.C. 20036. Telephone 202/452-1999; fax 202/296-7365.

Global Population and the Nitrogen Cycle

Feeding humankind now demands so much nitrogen-based fertilizer that the distribution of nitrogen on the earth has been changed in dramatic, and sometimes dangerous, ways

by Vaclav Smil

During the 20th century, humanity has almost quadrupled its numbers. Although many factors have fostered this unprecedented expansion, its continuation during the past generation would not have been at all possible without a widespread—yet generally unappreciated—activity: the synthesis of ammonia. The ready availability of ammonia, and other nitrogen-rich fertilizers derived from it, has effectively done away with what for ages had been a fundamental restriction on food production. The world's population now has enough to eat (on the average) because of numerous advances in modern agricultural practices. P 't human society has one key chemica. industry to thank for that abundance—the producers of nitrogen fertilizer.

Why is nitrogen so important? Compared with carbon, hydrogen and oxygen, nitrogen is only a minor constituent of living matter. But whereas the three major elements can move readily from their huge natural reservoirs through the food and water people consume to become a part of their tissues, nitrogen remains largely locked in the atmosphere. Only a puny fraction of this resource exists in a form that can be absorbed by growing plants, animals and, ultimately, human beings.

Yet nitrogen is of decisive importance. This element is needed for DNA and RNA, the molecules that store and transfer genetic information. It is also required to make proteins, those indispensable messengers, receptors, catalysts and structural components of all plant and animal cells. Humans, like other higher animals, cannot synthesize these molecules using the nitrogen found in the air and have to acquire nitrogen compounds from food. There is no substitute for this intake, because a minimum quantity (consumed as animal or plant protein) is needed for proper nutrition. Yet getting nitrogen from the atmosphere to crops is not an easy matter.

The relative scarcity of usable nitrogen can be blamed on that element's peculiar chemistry. Paired nitrogen atoms make up 78 percent of the atmosphere but they are too stable to transform easily into a reactive form that plants can take up. Lightning can cleave these strongly bonded molecules; however, most natural nitrogen "fixation" (the splitting of paired nitrogen molecules and subsequent incorporation of the element into the chemically reactive compound ammonia) is done by certain bacteria. The most important nitrogen-fixing bacteria are of the genus *Rhizobium*, symbionts that create nodules on the roots of leguminous plants, such as beans or acacia trees. To a lesser extent, cyanobacteria (living either freely or in association with certain plants) also fix nitrogen.

A Long-standing Problem

Because withdrawals caused by the growth of crops and various natural losses continually remove fixed nitrogen from the soil, that element is regularly in short supply. Traditional farmers (those in preindustrial societies) typically replaced the nitrogen lost or taken up in their harvests by enriching their fields with crop residues or with animal and human wastes. But these materials contain low concentrations of nitrogen, and so farmers had to apply massive amounts to provide a sufficient quantity.

Traditional farmers also raised peas, beans, lentils and other pulses along with cereals and some additional crops. The nitrogen-fixing bacteria living in the roots of these plants helped to enrich the fields with nitrogen. In some cases, farmers grew legumes (or, in Asia, *Azolla* ferns, which harbor nitrogen-fixing cyanobacteria) strictly for the fertilization provided. They then plowed these crops into the soil as so-called green manures without harvesting food from them at all. Organic farming of this kind during the early part of the 20th century was most intense in the lowlands of Java, across the Nile Delta, in northwestern Europe (particularly on Dutch farms) and in many regions of Japan and China.

The combination of recycling human and animal wastes along with planting green manures can, in principle, provide annually up to around 200 kilograms of nitrogen per hectare of arable land. The resulting 200 to 250 kilograms of plant protein that can be produced in this way sets the theoretical limit on population density: a hectare of farmland in places with good soil, adequate moisture and a mild climate that allows continuous cultivation throughout the year should be able to support as many as 15 people.

In practice, however, the population densities for nations dependent on organic farming were invariably much lower. China's average was between five and six people per hectare of the arable area during the early part of this century. During the last decades of purely organic farming in Japan (which occurred about the same time), the population density there was slightly higher than in China, but the Japanese reliance on fish protein from the sea complicates the comparison between these two nations. A population density of about five people per hectare was also typical for fertile farming regions in northwestern Europe during the 19th century, when those farmers still relied entirely on traditional methods.

The practical limit of about five people per hectare of farmland arose for many reasons, including environmental stresses (caused above all by severe weather and pests) and the need to raise crops that were not used for food—those that provided medicines or fibers, for example. The essential difficulty came from the closed nitrogen cycle. Traditional farming faced a fundamental problem that was especially acute in

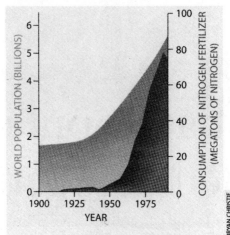

SUDDEN GROWTH in the global consumption of nitrogen fertilizer during the 20th century has been matched by a parallel increase in world population.

land-scarce countries with no uncultivated areas available for grazing or for the expansion of agriculture. In such places, the only way for farmers to break the constraints of the local nitrogen cycle and increase harvests was by planting more green manures. That strategy preempted the cultivation of a food crop. Rotation of staple cereals with leguminous food grains was thus a more fitting choice. Yet even this practice, so common in traditional farming, had its limits. Legumes have lower yields, they are often difficult to digest, and they cannot be made easily into bread or noodles. Consequently, few crops grown using the age-old methods ever had an adequate supply of nitrogen.

A Fertile Place for Science

As their knowledge of chemistry expanded, 19th-century scientists began to understand the critical role of nitrogen in food production and the scarcity of its usable forms. They learned that the other two key nutrients—potassium and phosphorus—were limiting agricultural yields much less frequently and that any shortages of these two elements were also much easier to rectify. It was a straightforward matter to mine potash deposits for potassium fertilizer, and phosphorus enrichment required only that acid be added to phosphate-rich rocks to convert them into more soluble compounds that would be taken up when the roots absorbed water. No

comparably simple procedures were available for nitrogen, and by the late 1890s there were feelings of urgency and unease among the agronomists and chemists who were aware that increasingly intensive farming faced a looming nitrogen crisis.

As a result, technologists of the era made several attempts to break through the nitrogen barrier. The use of soluble inorganic nitrates (from rock deposits found in Chilean deserts) and organic guano (from the excrement left by birds on Peru's rainless Chincha Islands) provided a temporary reprieve for some farmers. Recovery of ammonium sulfate from ovens used to transform coal to metallurgical coke also made a short-lived contribution to agricultural nitrogen supplies. This cyanamide process—whereby coke reacts with lime and pure nitrogen to produce a compound that contains calcium, carbon and nitrogen—was commercialized in Germany in 1898, but its energy requirements were too high to be practical. Producing nitrogen oxides by blowing the mixture of the two elements through an electric spark demanded extraordinary energy as well. Only Norway, with its cheap hydroelectricity, started making nitrogen fertilizer with this process in 1903, but total output remained small.

The real breakthrough came with the invention of ammonia synthesis. Carl

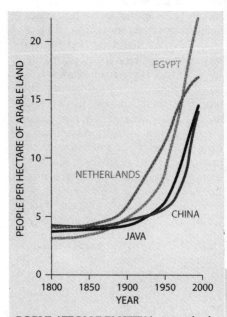

POPULATION DENSITY increased substantially in countries with intensive agriculture only after the use of nitrogen fertilizer became common.

	N₂ DINITROGEN	NH₃ AMMONIA	CO(NH₂)₂ UREA	AMINO ACIDS	PROTEINS
SPACE-FILLING MODEL					
NITROGEN SHARE	100%	82%	47%	8%–27%	~16%
BIOSPHERIC ABUNDANCE (BILLIONS OF TONS)	10,000	10	0.01	10	1

NITROGEN   HYDROGEN   OXYGEN   CARBON   SULFUR

NITROGEN COMPOUNDS permeate the biosphere. The most abundant form (N_2), which makes up 78 percent of the atmosphere, is so strongly bonded that it does not engage in most chemical reactions. Plants need reactive nitrogen compounds, such as ammonia (NH_3) and urea ($CO(NH_2)_2$), which are much more scarce. (The abundance estimates shown are valid to within a factor of 10.) Plants use these substances to fashion amino acids, the building blocks of proteins, which serve myriad functions in living cells.

BIOGRAFX

Bosch began the development of this process in 1899 at BASF, Germany's leading chemical concern. But it was Fritz Haber, from the technical university in Karlsruhe, Germany, who devised a workable scheme to synthesize ammonia from nitrogen and hydrogen. He combined these gases at a pressure of 200 atmospheres and a temperature of 500 degrees Celsius in the presence of solid osmium and uranium catalysts.

Haber's approach worked well, but converting this bench reaction to an engineering reality was an immense undertaking. Bosch eventually solved the greatest design problem: the deterioration of the interior of the steel reaction chamber at high temperatures and pressures. His work led directly to the first commercial ammonia factory in Oppau, Germany, in 1913. Its design capacity was soon doubled to 60,000 tons a year—enough to make Germany self-sufficient in the nitrogen compounds it used for the production of explosives during World War I.

Commercialization of the Haber-Bosch synthesis process was slowed by the economic difficulties that prevailed between wars, and global ammonia production remained below five million tons until the late 1940s. During the 1950s, the use of nitrogen fertilizer gradually rose to 10 million tons; then technical innovations introduced during the 1960s cut the use of electricity in the synthesis by more than 90 percent and led to larger, more economical facilities for the production of ammonia. The subsequent exponential growth in demand increased global production of this compound eightfold by the late 1980s.

This surge was accompanied by a relatively rapid shift in nitrogen use between high- and low-income countries. During the early 1960s, affluent nations accounted for over 90 percent of all fertilizer consumption, but by 1980 their share was down below 70 percent. The developed and developing worlds drew level in 1988. At present, developing countries use more than 60 percent of the global output of nitrogen fertilizer.

Just how dependent has humanity become on the production of synthetic nitrogen fertilizer? The question is difficult to answer because knowledge remains imprecise about the passage of nitrogen into and out of cultivated fields around the globe. Nevertheless, careful assessment of the various inputs indicates that around 175 million tons of nitrogen flow into the world's croplands every year, and about half this total becomes incorporated into cultivated plants. Synthetic fertilizers provide about 40 percent of all the nitrogen taken up by these crops. Because they furnish—directly as plants and indirectly as animal foods—about 75 percent of all nitrogen in consumed proteins (the rest comes from fish and from meat and dairy foodstuffs produced by grazing), about one third of the protein in humanity's diet depends on synthetic nitrogen fertilizer.

This revelation is in some ways an overestimate of the importance of the Haber-Bosch process. In Europe and North America nitrogen fertilizer has not been needed to ensure survival or even adequate nutrition. The intense use of synthetic fertilizer in such well-developed regions results from the desire to grow feed for livestock to satisfy the widespread preference for high-protein animal foods. Even if the average amount of protein consumed in these places were nearly halved (for example, by persuading people to eat less meat), North Americans and Europeans would still enjoy adequate nutrition.

Yet the statement that one third of the protein nourishing humankind depends on synthetic fertilizer also underestimates the importance of these chemicals. A number of land-scarce countries with high population density depend on synthetic fertilizer for their very existence. As they exhaust new areas to cultivate, and as traditional agricultural practices reach their limits, people in these countries must turn to ever greater applications of nitrogen fertilizer—even if their diets contain comparatively little meat. Every nation producing annually in excess of about 100 kilograms of protein per hectare falls in this category. Examples include China, Egypt, Indonesia, Bangladesh, Pakistan and the Philippines.

Too Much of a Good Thing

Massive introduction of reactive nitrogen into soils and waters has many deleterious consequences for the environment. Problems range from local health to global changes and, quite literally, extend from deep underground to high in the stratosphere. High nitrate levels can cause life-threatening methemoglobinemia ("blue baby" disease) in infants, and they have also been linked epidemiologically to some cancers. Leaching of highly soluble nitrates, which can seriously contaminate both ground and surface waters in places un-

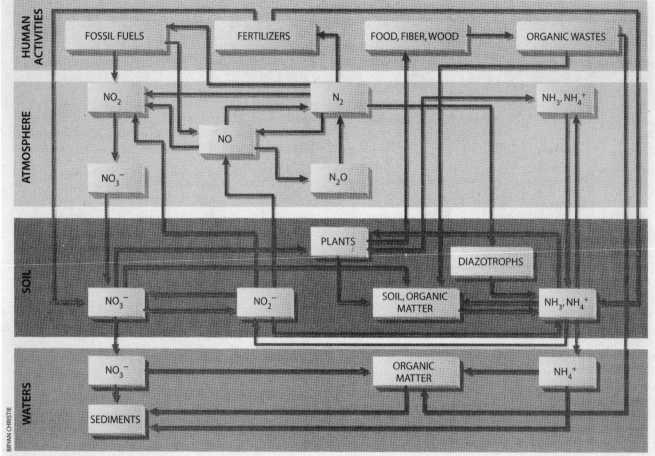

NITROGEN RESERVOIRS of many different kinds exist within the earth's waters, soil, atmosphere and biological mantle. Nitrogen moving between these temporary resting spots takes diverse forms. The advent of large-scale fertilizer production modifies natural flows of this element enormously, unbalancing the nitrogen cycle in sometimes troubling ways.

dergoing heavy fertilization, has been disturbing farming regions for some 30 years. A dangerous accumulation of nitrates is commonly found in water wells in the American corn belt and in groundwater in many parts of western Europe. Concentrations of nitrates that exceed widely accepted legal limits occur not only in the many smaller streams that drain farmed areas but also in such major rivers as the Mississippi and the Rhine.

Fertilizer nitrogen that escapes to ponds, lakes or ocean bays often causes eutrophication, the enrichment of waters by a previously scarce nutrient. As a result, algae and cyanobacteria can grow with little restraint; their subsequent decomposition robs other creatures of oxygen and reduces (or eliminates) fish and crustacean species. Eutrophication plagues such nitrogen-laden bodies as New York State's Long Island Sound and California's San Francisco Bay, and it has altered large parts of the Baltic Sea. Fertilizer runoff from the fields of Queensland also threatens parts

of Australia's Great Barrier Reef with algal overgrowth.

Whereas the problems of eutrophication arise because dissolved nitrates can travel great distances, the persistence of nitrogen-based compounds is also troublesome, because it contributes to the acidity of many arable soils. (Soils are also acidified by sulfur compounds that form during combustion and later settle out of the atmosphere.) Where people do not counteract this tendency by adding lime, excess acidification could lead to increased loss of trace nutrients and to the release of heavy metals from the ground into drinking supplies.

Excess fertilizer does not just disturb soil and water. The increasing use of nitrogen fertilizers has also sent more nitrous oxide into the atmosphere. Concentrations of this gas, generated by the action of bacteria on nitrates in the soil, are still relatively low, but the compound takes part in two worrisome processes. Reactions of nitrous oxide with excited oxygen contribute to the destruction of ozone in the

stratosphere (where these molecules serve to screen out dangerous ultraviolet light); lower, in the troposphere, nitrous oxide promotes excessive greenhouse warming. The atmospheric lifetime of nitrous oxide is longer than a century, and every one of its molecules absorbs roughly 200 times more outgoing radiation than does a single carbon dioxide molecule.

Yet another unwelcome atmospheric change is exacerbated by the nitric oxide released from microbes that act on fertilizer nitrogen. This compound (which is produced in even greater quantities by combustion) reacts in the presence of sunlight with other pollutants to produce photochemical smog. And whereas the deposition of nitrogen compounds from the atmosphere can have beneficial fertilizing effects on some grasslands or forests, higher doses may overload sensitive ecosystems.

When people began to take advantage of synthetic nitrogen fertilizers, they could not foresee any of these insults to the environment. Even now, these disturbances receive surprisingly little attention, especially in comparison to the buildup of carbon dioxide in the atmosphere. Yet the massive introduction of reactive nitrogen, like the release of carbon dioxide from fossil fuels, also amounts to an immense—and dangerous—geochemical experiment.

From Habit to Addiction

Emissions of carbon dioxide, and the accompanying threat of global warming, can be reduced through a combination of economic and technical solutions. Indeed, a transition away from the use of fossil fuels must eventually happen, even without the motivation to avoid global climate change, because these finite resources will inevitably grow scarcer and more expensive. Still, there are no means available to grow crops—and human bodies—without nitrogen, and there are no waiting substitutes to replace the Haber-Bosch synthesis.

Genetic engineers may ultimately succeed in creating symbiotic *Rhizobium* bacteria that can supply nitrogen to cereals or in endowing these grains directly with nitrogen-fixing capability. These solutions would be ideal, but neither appears imminent. Without them, human reliance on nitrogen fertilizer must further increase in order to feed the additional billions of people yet to be born before the global population finally levels off.

An early stabilization of population and the universal adoption of largely vegetarian diets could curtail nitrogen needs. But neither development is particularly likely. The best hope for reducing the growth in nitrogen use is in finding more efficient ways to fertilize

The Curious Fate of Fritz Haber

Although he was awarded the Nobel Prize in 1919 for ammonia synthesis, Fritz Haber led an essentially tragic life. As the director of the Kaiser Wilhelm Institute for Physical Chemistry during World War I, he developed the use of chlorine gas for the German general staff. Haber believed this gruesome weapon would help bring a swift victory and thus limit overall suffering. Others took a dimmer view. On the eve of the first use of the gas against Allied troops in 1915, Haber's wife committed suicide, tormented by her husband's horrific contribution to the war. And after the Armistice, the Allies considered Haber a war criminal. Haber was demoralized, but he continued to conduct research. Later, with the rise of Nazi-inspired anti-Semitism in Germany, this Jewish scientist fled and took up residence in England. Haber died in 1934 in Basel, Switzerland.   —*V.S.*

crops. Impressive results are possible when farmers monitor the amount of usable nitrogen in the soil so as to optimize the timing of applications. But several worldwide trends may negate any gains in efficiency brought about in this way. In particular, meat output has been rising rapidly in Latin America and Asia, and this growth will demand yet more nitrogen fertilizer, as it takes three to four units of feed protein to produce one unit of meat protein.

Understanding these realities allows a clearer appraisal of prospects for organic farming. Crop rotations, legume cultivation, soil conservation (which keeps more nitrogen in the soil) and the recycling of organic wastes are all desirable techniques to employ. Yet these measures will not obviate the need for more fertilizer nitrogen in land-short, populous nations. If all farmers attempted to return to purely organic farming, they would quickly find that traditional practices could not feed today's popula-

tion. There is simply not enough recyclable nitrogen to produce food for six billion people.

When the Swedish Academy of Sciences awarded a Nobel Prize for Chemistry to Fritz Haber in 1919, it noted that he created "an exceedingly important means of improving the standards of agriculture and the well-being of mankind." Even such an effusive description now seems insufficient. Currently at least two billion people are alive because the proteins in their bodies are built with nitrogen that came—via plant and animal foods—from a factory using his process.

Barring some surprising advances in bioengineering, virtually all the protein needed for the growth of another two billion people to be born during the next two generations will come from the same source—the Haber-Bosch synthesis of ammonia. In just one lifetime, humanity has indeed developed a profound chemical dependence.

The Author

VACLAV SMIL was educated at the Carolinum University in Prague in the Czech Republic and at Pennsylvania State University. He is currently a professor in the department of geography at the University of Manitoba in Canada. Smil's interdisciplinary research covers interactions between the environment, energy, food, population, economic forces and public policy.

Further Reading

POPULATION GROWTH AND NITROGEN: AN EXPLORATION OF A CRITICAL EXISTENTIAL LINK. Vaclav Smil in *Population and Development Review,* Vol. 17, No. 4, pages 569–601; December 1991.
NITROGEN FIXATION: ANTHROPOGENIC ENHANCEMENT—ENVIRONMENTAL RESPONSE. James N. Galloway, William H. Schlesinger, Hiram Levy II, Anthony Michaels and Jerald L. Schnoor in *Global Biogeochemical Cycles,* Vol. 9, No. 2, pages 235–252; June 1995.
NITROGEN POLLUTION IN THE EUROPEAN UNION: ORIGINS AND PROPOSED SOLUTIONS. Ester van der Voet, Rene Kleijn and Udo de Haes in *Environmental Conservation,* Vol. 23, No. 2, pages 120–132; 1996.
CYCLES OF LIFE: CIVILIZATION AND THE BIOSPHERE. Vaclav Smil. Scientific American Library, W. H. Freeman and Company, 1997.

How Much Food Will We Need in the 21ˢᵗ Century?

By William H. Bender

Seldom has the world faced an unfolding emergency whose dimensions are as clear as the growing imbalance between food and people.[1]

The world food situation has improved dramatically during the past 30 years and the prospects are very good that the 20 year period from 1990 to 2010 will see further gains. . . . If Malthus is ultimately to be correct in his warning that population will outstrip food production, then at least we can say: Malthus Must Wait.[2]

Ever since Malthus, society has worried periodically about whether it will be able to produce enough food to feed people in the future. Yet until recently, most of the debate surrounding the issue of food scarcity focused on the potential for increasing the food supply. The key questions were whether there would be enough land and water to produce the amount of food needed and whether technol-ogy could keep increasing the yields of food grains. Now, however, scientists are growing concerned that the intensive use of land, energy, fertil-izer, and pesticides that modern agri-culture seems to require jeopardizes the health of the environment. This anxiety has been integrated into the general debate about food scarcity, but interestingly enough, the question of the demand for food—including the specific physiological needs and die-tary desires of different peoples—has not. In fact, relatively little attention has been paid to the issue of demand despite the fact that like energy and water, food can be conserved and the de-mand for it adjusted to meet human needs and lessen the burden that modern agriculture places on the environment.

Unlike with many other forms of consumption, there are limits to the physical quantity of food that people can consume. In a number of high-income countries, that limit seems to have been reached already. If global population does double by 2050, as many have predicted, providing ev-eryone with a rich and varied diet (equivalent to that enjoyed by today's wealthiest countries) would only re-quire a tripling of food production. Alternatively, with sufficient improve-ments in efficiency and adoption of a healthier diet in high-income coun-tries, it would be possible to provide such a diet for the entire global popu-lation with just a doubling of food production. But even a doubling of current production could strain Earth's ecosystems, as critics of modern agri-culture's intensive use of resources will attest. Clearly, then, increases in food demand will have to be slowed if we hope to achieve a sustainable ag-ricultural system. Central to the issue of demand, however, is the question of how much food the world really needs.

From an analytical standpoint, the amount of food a given population (be it a country, a region, or the world) actually *needs* is the product of two factors: the number of people and the average (minimal) food requirement per person. The amount of food the

From *Environment*, March 1997, pp. 7-11, 27-28. © 1997 by the Helen Dwight Reid Educational Foundation. Reprinted by permission of Heldref Publications, 1319 Eighteenth Street, NW, Washington, DC 20036-1802.

Table 1. World population supportable under different conditions

Conditions in	Population (billions)
United States	2.3
Europe	4.1
Japan	6.1
Bangladesh	10.9
Subsistence only	15.0
Addendum: Actual 1990 population	5.3

NOTE: This table shows the number of people that could be fed at the 1990 level of agricultural production if the dietary preferences and food system efficiencies in the countries (or area) shown prevailed throughout the world. Dietary preferences reflect both income and the extent to which cereal grains are fed to animals instead of being consumed directly. Food system efficiencies reflect the extent to which food is spoiled or wasted in going from farm to mouth.

SOURCE: Author's calculations.

population *consumes*, however, is determined not only by its basic needs but also by its income and dietary preferences. This difference is particularly important in high-income countries, where crops that could be consumed directly are instead fed to animals to produce eggs, meat, and milk. Finally, the amount of food a given population *requires* (i.e., has to produce or import) depends on how much is wasted in going from farm to mouth as well as on its level of consumption. In mathematical terms,

$$Req = Pop \cdot PFR \cdot Diet \cdot Eff,$$

where *Req* is the total number of food calories that has to be produced, *Pop* is population, *PFR* is the number of calories per person that is needed to sustain life and health, *Diet* is a factor reflecting the conversion of some plant calories to animal calories, and *Eff* is the ratio of calories available in the retail market to those consumed.

This article will address the neglected issue of food demand in terms of the four variables of this equation. In the process, it will question some of the assumptions previous analysts have made, particularly with regard to desirable diets and food system efficiency. Though not definitive, the analysis strongly suggests that the right policy choices can reduce the growth in the global demand for food. Indeed, the potential scope of such a reduction appears to be substantial: As Table 1 on this page shows, vastly different numbers of people can be supported by a given amount of agricultural production depending on dietary habits and degrees of efficiency.

Population

Global population will play an important role in determining how much food we will require in the future. For this reason, attempts to calculate future food requirements depend upon projections of population growth. Although demographers generally agree that the current global population will double by the middle of the next century, considerable uncertainty accompanies these projections. The United Nations' estimates of the world's population in 2050, for example, vary from 7.9 billion to 11.9 billion. If global population reaches the higher value rather than the lower one, global food requirements will be 50 percent higher.

National and international policies that provide family planning services, maternal education, and social support systems can affect population growth, and these policies will undoubtedly have the single largest effect on food requirements in the 21st century. The availability of food will also play a role, however. Famine—the most dramatic example of lack of food—has fortunately been largely eliminated (except during wars) and no longer ranks as a major factor in global population growth. Even so, the relative abundance of food has a direct effect on the other key factors that influence population growth, and combined with the subtle influences exerted by the food and agriculture sector, it can have a significant impact. For example, in rural agricultural societies, the demand for agricultural labor affects fertility rates, while reductions in child mortality (which are influenced by food availability) usually precede reduction in fertility rates.

Physiological Requirements

Physiological food requirements, represented by PFR in the equation, are determined by several factors, including the population's age and gender distribution, its average height and weight, and its activity level. One may compute such requirements in two different ways, using either actual circumstances or normative ones (such as desired heights and weights or activity levels).[3]

Around the world, actual per capita caloric consumption varies from a low of 1,758 calories per day in Bangladesh to a high of 2,346 calories per day in the Netherlands. Caloric consumption is higher in the Netherlands for several reasons. First, the population is generally older, and adults require more food than children. Second, people in the Netherlands are on average taller and heavier than those in Bangladesh and therefore need more food. (Lower activity levels in the Netherlands partially offset these factors, however.) If the actual consumption levels in these two countries were to change, either the weights of individuals or their activity levels would have to change accordingly. Caloric consumption levels vary by no more than one-third on a national basis—far less than the variation in caloric availability.

When making future projections, normative considerations can also be very important. A population's general health, for instance, affects the amount of food it needs. Parasites and disease can substantially increase an individual's energy requirements, with fever, for example, raising his or her basal metabolic rate (the number of calories he or she uses when at rest) approximately 10 percent for every one degree C increase in body temperature.[4] Disease can also impair the body's ability to absorb nutrients, while parasites siphon away food energy for their own

Table 2. Numerical estimates for key food variables, 1991

Variable	World	High-income countries	Low- and middle-income countries	Best practice/ medically preferred
Calories per person per day				
Total food available[a]	3,939	6,964	3,007	n/a
Food available in retail markets	2,693	3,255	2,520	n/a
Physiological food requirements[b]	2,179	2,231	2,169	n/a
Ratio				
Dietary conversion factor[c]	1.46	2.14	1.19	1.5
End-use efficiency factor[d]	1.24	1.46	1.16	1.3

n/a Not applicable
[a]Includes animal feed
[b]1990 estimate
[c]Line 1 divided by line 2, except for last column, which is author's estimate
[d]Line 2 divided by line 3, except for last column, which is author's estimate
NOTE: Computational methods are described in the box on this page.
SOURCES: Line 1: Author's calculations; Line 2: United Nations Food and Agriculture Organization at http://www.fao.org; Line 3: Author's calculations.

use. Although not important globally, health factors are highly significant in certain low-income countries. In fact, in localized situations health interventions may be more effective than merely increasing the food supply in helping people to satisfy basic physiological food requirements.

Of course, to qualify as truly sustainable, the world's agricultural system has to produce enough calories to ensure food security around the globe. This is a normative concept, as is clear in the commonly accepted definition of food security: "access by all people at all times to enough food for

an active, healthy life."[5] Thus, for future projections, we could consider a world with lower levels of undernutrition and stunting, leading to higher food requirements.

Table 2 shows estimates of physiological food requirements for the world as a whole, for high-income countries, and for low-income countries, all based on current circumstances. (The box below discusses the way in which these estimates were prepared.) High-income countries use much more than twice as much food per person. This variation is not due to differences in calories actually consumed but to differences in diet and the lower efficiency of food systems in those countries.

Dietary Patterns

Diets are largely determined by economic factors, particularly prices and incomes. In Africa, for example, people derive two-thirds of their calories from less expensive starchy staples (including cereals, roots, and tubers) and only 6 percent from animal products. In Europe, on the other hand, people derive 33 percent of their calories from animal products and less than one-third from starchy staples. The global diet falls somewhere

A NOTE ON COMPUTATIONS

Physiological food requirements. Estimating the number of calories that the average person in a given population actually consumes (as distinct from the number that is available in the retail market) entails a five-step procedure.[1] The first step is to determine the age-gender structure of the population, placing children in single-year age groups and adults in five-year age groups. The second step is to estimate the basal metabolic rates for each group based on group members' average heights and weights. The third step is to estimate the different groups' physical activity patterns and combine them with their basal metabolic rates to determine each group's energy requirements. The fourth step is to make allowances for such factors as pregnancy and infection rates and then multiply the average energy requirement for each group by the

number of people in the group. The final step is to sum the energy requirements for the different groups and divide by the total population. Normative food requirements (i.e., the number of calories needed to maintain desired heights, weights, and activity levels) can then be determined by adjusting appropriately for heights, weights, and activity levels.

Dietary conversion factor. This factor reflects the number of calories "lost" in using grain to produce animal products. It is computed as the ratio of the total number of calories produced to the number available (in final form) in the retail market. The denominator is usually per capita caloric availability as estimated by the United Nations Food and Agriculture Organization (FAO).[2] The numerator is more difficult to determine because some animals graze rather than being fed grain. The procedure used in

this article was to sum three factors: the number of plant calories available, excluding cereals, starchy roots, and tubers; the number of plant calories available from cereals, starchy roots, and tubers, whether used for feed or for human consumption; and the estimated number of animal calories derived from range feeding.

End-use efficiency factor. End-use efficiency—the proportion of calories produced that actually ends up in human mouths—is computed as the ratio of calories available in the retail market (from FAO) to calories consumed (as computed above).

1. See W. P. T. James and E. C. Schofield, Human Energy Requirements (Oxford, U.K.: Oxford University Press by arrangement with the United Nations Food and Agriculture Organization, 1990).

2. Available at http://www.fao.org.

in the mid-range between these two extremes.

As people's level of income increases, the share of starchy staples in their diet declines, and the shares of animal products, oils, sweeteners, fruits, and vegetables increase.[6] In fact, the absolute quantities of these products that people eat increase even faster than the shares because caloric availability overall also increases as incomes increase. This growing dietary diversity provides a substantial health benefit for people at the low to medium income level.

The overall increase in food availability over the last several decades, while a welcome development, has created problems of its own. As people consume more animal products, they tend to consume more animal fats than recent medical research has shown to be healthy. Currently, the World Health Organization (WHO) recommends that people limit their dietary intake of fat to no more than 30 percent of calorie consumption, and some foresee a revision to no more than 25 or 20 percent in the future.[7]

At present, 16.8 percent of the global population lives in high-income countries, where, on average, fat consumption exceeds the 30 percent level. But health concerns have clearly begun to affect consumption patterns in those countries: Despite rising incomes and relatively stable prices, beef consumption has declined in a number of countries since the mid-1970s. In the United States, for instance, per capita beef consumption has dropped 25 percent.[8] (Overall meat consumption in the United States has remained approximately constant, however, because people merely shifted to eating poultry.)

Clearly, public policy that encourages people to reduce their consumption of animal fat has two benefits. It improves the health of the population while reducing the pressure that increased food production places on the global agricultural system. Table 3 on this page shows the conversion rates of grain to animal products in terms of two common measures: kilograms and calories. For the past 30 years, approximately 40 percent of all cereal grains produced globally have been used for feed, with 50 percent being used for food. (The remaining 10 percent have gone to seed, been used in processing, or ended up as waste.) As Table 2 shows, however, the use of grain for feed is much higher in high-income countries.

Efficiency

The last factor affecting global food requirements is the efficiency with which food moves from farms to human mouths. Efficiency actually has two components, one pertaining to marketing and distribution and one pertaining to "end use." Losses in marketing and distribution, such as those due to rodents and mold, are important in low-income countries but decline steadily with increases in income.[9] Inefficiencies in end use, which include losses due to spoilage, processing and preparation waste, and plate waste, are most significant in high-income countries, however.

The United Nations Food and Agriculture Organization (FAO) estimates that per capita caloric availability (i.e., the amount of food that appears in the retail market) ranges from a low of 1,667 calories in Ethiopia to a high of 3,902 calories in Belgium-Luxembourg. These two figures differ by 234 percent—much more than the 33 percent difference in physiological consumption. Because it is physiologically impossible for the population of an entire country to consume an average of 3,902 calories, we know that a substantial amount of food in high-income countries is never consumed. According to estimates, losses from end-use inefficiencies equal 30 to 70 percent of the amount of food actually consumed.[10] With the exception of Belgium-Luxembourg, it is middle-income countries such as Greece, Ireland, Yugoslavia, Hungary, Bulgaria, Egypt, and Libya that have the highest levels of waste. But in every country where per capita income is more than $1,500 (U.S.), at least 20 percent more food is used than is consumed. The computed values for the end-use efficiency factor in Table 2 also reflect the discrepancy between high- and low-income countries.

It is unclear to what extent these losses are a necessary component of increased standards of living because little analysis has been done on the sources of this waste. Some intercountry comparisons provide useful insights, however. The Netherlands, Finland, Japan, and Sweden, which have comparable levels of income, waste only about 35 percent (on a per capita caloric basis), while the United States, Belgium-Luxembourg, Switzerland,

Table 3. Conversion rates of grain to animal products

Animal product	Kilograms of feed/ kilograms of output	Calories of feed/ calories of output
Beef	7.0	9.8
Pork	6.5	7.1
Poultry	2.7	5.7
Milk	1.0	4.9

NOTE: These conversions are very approximate, as the caloric density of both feeds and animal products can vary greatly. Furthermore, data units are often not specified or precisely comparable.

SOURCES: Column 1: Office of Technology Assessment, *A New Technological Era for American Agriculture*, OTA-F-474 (Washington, D.C., 1992); Column 2: Author's estimates.

and Italy waste nearly 60 percent.[11] This suggests that there is scope for reducing food requirements without lowering standards of living, much as high-income countries have done with energy use since the 1970s.

Given the current distribution of food consumption and food system efficiency, if every middle- and high-income country were to reduce its level of waste to 30 percent, global food requirements would decline 7.4 percent. (If consumption of animal products were to decrease in proportion, requirements would decline 12.5 percent owing to the lower demand for feed.) Clearly, as global incomes increase and the number of people living in countries with low food system efficiency continues to grow, the level of end-use waste will become an increasingly important part of overall food requirements.[12]

Final Thoughts

By its very nature, agricultural production has significant impacts upon natural ecosystems and the environment. There is little question that agricultural production must increase to meet population growth, but the magnitude of the increase necessary to improve human welfare is very much a question of policy tradeoffs between demand management and supply promotion.

Food is the only sector of the economy that has reached satiation for a large portion of the world's population. Tripling world food production would provide sufficient food for a doubled global population to have a varied, nutritious, and healthy diet comparable to today's European diet. The same goal could be reached by slightly more than doubling agricultural production if an effort were made to improve food system efficiencies and if diets low in fat became commonplace. This change will only take place if public policy creates explicit incentives for healthier diets and more efficient food systems, however.

It is environmentally and medically prudent to prevent the levels of waste and fat consumption in the wealthier developing economies from rising to those seen in North America today. It is also fiscally prudent: Grain imports tend to rise rapidly in maturing developing economies, so that decreased food system efficiency and increased fat consumption can lead directly to the loss of vital foreign exchange. Therefore, self-interest can be used to dramatically improve the long-term sustainability of the global agricultural system.

William H. Bender is an economist with extensive international experience in food and nutrition. He has consulted with the United Nations Children's Fund, the United Nations Food and Agriculture Organization, the World Bank, the United States Agency for International Development, the European Community, and many other organizations. His address is P.O. Box 66036, Auburndale, MA 02166 (telephone: (617) 647-9210; e-mail: bender@tiac.net).

NOTES

1. L. Brown et al., *State of the World, 1994* (New York: W. W. Norton & Company, 1994), 196.

2. D. O. Mitchell and M. D. Ingco, *The World Food Outlook* (Washington, D.C.: World Bank, 1993), 232.

3. Requirements are usually measured in terms of calories, both because food analysts tend to focus on producing sufficient calories and because even with a cereal-based diet, people can get adequate protein if they consume enough calories. (The exception to this rule lies in groups, such as infants, who have special nutritional needs.) Of course, consuming enough calories does not guarantee getting enough micronutrients such as iron, vitamin A, and iodine. To obtain those nutrients, people have to eat fruit, vegetables, and fat in addition to starchy staples. However, the inputs (e.g., land, water, and fertilizer) needed to provide a diverse diet are minor compared with those needed to provide enough calories.

4. R. E. Behrman and V. C. Vaughn, *Nelson Textbook of Pediatrics*, 13th ed. (Philadelphia: W. B. Saunders Company, 1987).

5. World Bank, *Poverty and Hunger: Issues and Options for Food Security in Developing Countries* (Washington, D.C., 1986), 1.

6. Calculations of income elasticities reflect how consumption patterns change as income increases. Income elasticity is the percentage change in the demand for a particular good that results from a 1 percent increase in income. Demand is considered elastic when the percentage change is greater than 1, inelastic when it is less than 1. Animal products, for instance, are income-elastic goods because their share in diets tends to increase more rapidly than income. Researchers at organizations like the World Bank, the International Food Policy Research Institute, and the International Institute for Applied Systems Analysis use such elasticities in global models that attempt to simulate future developments in the world agricultural system. Models like these can help provide insight into questions such as the effect increased demand for animal products is likely to have on grain production.

7. World Health Organization Study Group on Diet, Nutrition and Prevention of Noncommunicable Diseases, *Diet, Nutrition and the Prevention of Chronic Diseases: Report of a WHO Study Group*, World Health Organization Technical Report Series 797 (Geneva: World Health Organization, 1992), 109.

8. L. A. Duewer, K. R. Krause, and K. E. Nelson, *U.S. Poultry and Red Meat Consumption, Prices, Spreads, and Margins*, Agriculture Information Bulletin Number 684 (Washington, D.C.: United States Department of Agriculture, Economic Research Service, 1993).

9. In low-income countries, such losses are as high as 15 percent for cereals and 25 percent for roots and tubers; in high-income countries they are less than 4 percent. See, for example, D. Norse, "A New Strategy for Feeding a Crowded Planet," *Environment*, June 1992, 6; and W. Bender, "An End Use Analysis of Global Food Requirements," *Food Policy* 19, no. 4 (1994): 381.

10. Bender, note 9 above, pages 388–90. In these countries, of course, data accuracy is also highest, giving us the most confidence in these estimates.

11. Ibid.

12. Ibid.

ENVIRONMENT

THE FISH CRISIS

The oceans that once seemed a bottomless source of high-protein, low-fat food are rapidly being depleted

By J. MADELEINE NASH

THICK SWORDFISH STEAKS. ORANGE roughy fillets. Great mounds of red-fleshed tuna. Judging from the seafood sections of local supermarkets, there would seem to be plenty of fish left in the oceans. But this appearance of abundance is an illusion, says Sylvia Earle, former chief scientist for the National Oceanic and Atmospheric Administration. Already, Earle fears, an international armada of fishing vessels is on the verge of exhausting a storehouse of protein so vast that it once appeared to be infinite. "It's a horrible thing to contemplate," shudders Earle. "What makes it even worse is that we know better. Yet here we go, making the same mistake over and over again."

If fishermen around the world soon start hauling back empty nets and fishing lines, it will not be for lack of warning. In the 1990s, after increasing for nearly four decades, the wild catch of marine fish leveled off worldwide and in some years actually declined. "We are reaching, and in many cases have exceeded, the oceans' limits," declare the authors of a sobering report released by the Natural Resources Defense Council earlier this year. "We are no longer living off the income but eating deeply into the capital."

Fights have already started to break out over the dwindling supply. Two weeks ago, hundreds of Canadian fishermen blockaded a British Columbia port for several days to keep an Alaskan ferry from leaving. The reason for their protest? Alaskan trawlers were sweeping up the salmon that spawn in Canada's rivers. Now the Canadians are threatening to do to the salmon runs of Washington State what U.S. fishermen have done to theirs.

Of course, overfishing is not the only human activity that is jeopardizing life in the oceans. Coastal pollution and habitat destruction—filling in wetlands, building dams—are contributing to the crisis. But it is overfishing, the NRDC report makes plain, that constitutes the most urgent threat and demands the most immediate action.

Until now, the worst threat most creatures of the sea had faced at fishermen's hands was so-called commercial extinction. Whenever local populations of a particular fish plummeted, boats simply targeted some other species or moved to more distant waters. The depleted stocks almost always recovered. But now, experts warn, unprecedented forces—among them, industrial-scale fishing gear and a burgeoning global seafood market—are altering this age-old cycle. The economic and technological barriers that have kept overfishing within bounds appear increasingly shaky, like dikes along a river that floodwaters have undermined. Should these barriers collapse, commercial extinction could escalate into biological catastrophe.

In most imminent peril are the giant predators of the oceans—sharks, of course, but also marlin, sailfish, swordfish and bluefin tuna, the magnificent swimming machines that have earned the nickname "Porsches of the sea." In the western Atlantic, the breeding population of northern bluefin, the largest tuna species, is thought to consist of perhaps 40,000 adults, down from some 250,000 two decades ago. Reason: the flourishing airfreight industry that allows fish brokers to deliver Atlantic Ocean bluefin overnight to Tokyo's sashimi market, where a single fish can fetch $80,000 or more at auction. "To a fisherman, catching a bluefin is a lot like winning the lottery," sighs Stanford University marine biologist Barbara Block.

The crash of commercially important fisheries is not new. What is new is how quickly fisheries arise and how quickly they are exploited. In recent years, piked dogfish, a small spiny shark, has begun to stand in for cod in the fish and chips served by British pubs, and the Patagonian toothfish has become a popular substitute for sablefish in Japan. But environmental groups are concerned about the long-term viability of the fisheries that are serving up these quaintly named piscine treats. This year, for example, ships from around the world have converged on the Southern Ocean, where the toothfish makes its home. "At this rate," predicts Beth Clark, a scientist with the Antarctica Project, "the entire fishery will be gone in 18 months."

UNFORTUNATELY, IT TAKES LONGER to rebuild a fishery than it does to ruin one. Consider the present state of the orange roughy on New Zealand's Challenger Plateau. Discovered in 1979, this deep-water fishing hole took off

From *Time*, August 11, 1997, pp. 65-67. © 1997 by Time Inc. Magazine Company. Reprinted by permission.

in the 1980s when the mild-tasting, white-fleshed fish became popular with U.S. chefs. Happy to stoke the surging demand, fishermen are believed to have reduced the biomass of orange roughy as much as 80% before officials stepped in. Now, says Yale University ichthyologist Jon Moore, it may take centuries before the fishery rebounds. As scientists have belatedly learned, orange roughy grow extremely slowly, live 100 years or more and take 25 to 30 years to reach sexual maturity.

How can a fishing fleet do so much damage so quickly? Until recently, many fish, especially deep-water fish, were too hard to find to make tempting commercial targets. But technical advances have given fishermen the power to peer beneath the waves and plot their position with unprecedented accuracy. Sonar makes it possible to locate large shoals of fish that would otherwise remain concealed beneath tens, even hundreds of feet of water. And once a fishing hot spot is pinpointed by sonar, satellite-navigation systems enable vessels to return unerringly to the same location year after year. In this fashion, fishermen from New Zealand to the Philippines have been able to home in on orange roughy and giant groupers as they gather to spawn, in some cases virtually eliminating entire generations of reproducing adults.

But what has amplified the destructive power of modern fishing more than anything else is its gargantuan scale. Trawling for pollock in the Bering Sea and the Gulf of Alaska, for example, are computerized ships as large as football fields. Their nets—wide enough to swallow a dozen Boeing 747s—can gather up 130 tons of fish in a single sweep. Along with pollock and other groundfish, these nets indiscriminately draw in the creatures that swim or crawl alongside, including halibut, Pacific herring, Pacific salmon and king crab. In similar fashion, so-called longlines—which stretch for tens of miles and bristle with thousands of hooks—snag not just tuna and swordfish but also hapless sea turtles and albatrosses, marlin and sharks.

What happens to the dead and dying animals that constitute this so-called by-catch? Most are simply dumped overboard, either because they are unwanted or because fishery regulations require it. In 1993, for example, shrimp trawlers in the Gulf of Mexico caught and threw away an estimated 34 million red snappers, including many juveniles. By contrast, the annual catch of red snapper from the Gulf averages only around 3 million fish. Indeed, so many snappers are being scooped up as by-catch that the productivity of the fishery has been compromised. Fortunately, there is a solution. Shrimp nets can be outfitted with devices that afford larger animals like snappers and sea turtles a trapdoor escape hatch.

To a surprising extent, solutions to the problem of overfishing also exist, at least on paper, and that's what critics of the fishing industry find so encouraging—and so frustrating. Last year, for example, Congress passed landmark legislation that requires fishery managers to crack down on overfishing in U.S. waters. Perhaps even more impressive, the U.N. has produced a tough-minded treaty that promises to protect stocks of fish that straddle the coastal zones of two or more countries or migrate, as bluefin tuna and swordfish do, through international waters in the wide-open oceans. The treaty will take effect, however, only after 30 or more nations ratify it—and even then, some question how diligently its provisions will be enforced.

What has been missing is a willingness to take action. Consumers no less than politicians bear some of the blame. Simply by refusing to buy bluefin tuna in Tokyo, grouper in Hong Kong or swordfish in Chicago, consumers could relieve the pressure on some of the world's most beleaguered fisheries and allow them the time they need to recover. To help shoppers become more selective about what they put on the dinner table, the Worldwide Fund for Nature and Unilever, one of the world's largest purveyors of frozen seafood, have launched a joint venture that in 1998 will start putting labels on fish and fish products caught in environmentally responsible ways.

A sign that consumers are worried about the world's fisheries could provide the jolt political leaders need. For the past half-century, billions of dollars have been spent by maritime nations to expand their domestic fishing fleets, subsidizing everything from fuel costs to the construction of factory trawlers. And until countries like Canada, China, Japan, South Korea, New Zealand, Norway, Spain and, yes, the U.S. are willing to confront this monster of their own making, attempts to control overfishing are likely to prove ineffectual. The problem, as Carl Safina, director of the National Audubon Society's Living Oceans Program, observes, is as politically intractable as it is intellectually simple: there is just too much fishing power chasing too few fish.

Angling for 'aquaculture'

Fish farms emerge as a viable alternative to dwindling sea harvests.

by Gary Turbak

For centuries, many viewed the seas as an inexhaustible source of food. High-tech breakthroughs increased the amount of fish harvested worldwide from 1959 to 1989 almost five-fold to nearly 100 million tons (90.7 million metric tons). Then suddenly, once abundant stocks of cod, bluefin tuna, salmon, and other species began disappearing from fish finder screens. The world's fishing fleets had accomplished the unthinkable—they had virtually depleted the oceans.

According to the Food and Agriculture Organizations (FAO) of the United Nations, 70 percent of the world's fish stocks are fully exploited, depleted, or in the process of rebuilding. It calls the situation "globally nonsustainable" and says that "major ecological and economic damage is already visible." Current shortages have resulted in fishing bans, antagonism among fishermen and nations for territorial rights, and the use of habitat-damaging harvesting methods like dynamite. But most worrisome is the potential loss of protein for a rising human population.

With oceans becoming increasingly barren, dinner plates are being filled by an industry almost as ancient as fishing itself—aquaculture, or fish farming. Since 1991, aquaculture's output has shot up from a million (907,000 metric) tons annually to more than 16 million

Examples of fish farming: salmon hatchery in Maine, U.S.A., salmon farm off Norway's coast.

(14.5 million metric) tons in 1994. Globally, this $26 billion industry already accounts for 22 percent of all fish production, and by 2010, will account for four of every five fish consumed. Among freshwater species, farms already produce more fish than traditional harvesting methods.

Culturing fish is actually a centuries-old practice. The Egyptians raised tilapia 4,000 years ago, and Roman fish reservoirs predate the birth of Christ. In 460 B.C., a Chinese entrepreneur named Fen Li wrote "Fish Culture Classics" to describe his country's carp-raising endeavors. European noblemen often kept fish in the moats encircling their castles, and pools near the Washington Monument in the U.S. capital once harbored carp.

Modern aquaculture encompasses a variety of marine animal life. Carp and shrimp are common crops in many Asian countries, while salmon, crawfish, trout, bass, and the "king"—catfish—are popular in the U.S. Other underwater livestock include oysters, clams, redfish, tilapia, abalone, turbot, cod, and lobster. Virtually no aquatic creature is exempt—even eel ranching is big business in Japan and Taiwan. The Japanese annually eat 150 million pounds (68 million kilograms) of these snake-like creatures, and gastronomes in Europe and elsewhere are developing a taste for them.

Various species have been added to the roster as ocean stocks decline and technology improves. Salmon farming, for example, started in the 1960s in Norway, when researchers dammed some estuaries and turned loose a few million fingerlings. The practice later spread to other nations such as Chile, Canada, the United Kingdom, and the United States. Canada and Norway are now in the process of building efficient halibut-growing operations.

Fish farming booms in developing nations—especially those in Asia, home to more than 80 percent of the global total. China alone is responsible for half the worldwide production, followed by India and Japan. Europe produces about nine percent of the total, North America about four percent, and South America about three percent.

But even in regions with relatively low production, aquaculture boosts national economies. Chile has become the world's second leading producer of domestic salmon (after Norway), producing nearly 200 million pounds (90.8 million kilograms) annually. In Ecuador, exports of commercially raised shrimp now surpass even coffee, bananas, and cocoa. And for the last two decades, fish farming has been the fastest growing agricultural industry in the U.S.

Fish can be raised in various manmade habitats—flooded natural lowlands, inland ponds filled with well water, or coastal enclosures anchored near shore. Aquaculture even exists in the open sea (where it is referred to as "mariculture"). In the Gulf of Mexico, Sea Pride Industries plans a futuristic, sunken cage-like system capable of producing five million pounds (2.7 million kilograms) of red snapper, bass, and other species annually. Configured like spokes on a wheel, the tubular cages will be 40 feet (12.2 metres) in diameter and 172 feet (52.4 metres) long. Feeding pipes will run the length of each spoke, and air tanks at the hub will permit the entire apparatus to be raised and lowered. Gulf growers have even experimented with stretching tent-shaped net enclosures around the legs of offshore oil rigs.

Other methods feature high technology. In California, Solar Aquafarms raises tilapia in a sprawling operation covered by greenhouses and warmed by solar heaters. Computers control feeding, water temperatures, and levels of oxygen and nitrogen. The water is continually cleaned and reused with the resulting waste products turned into fertilizer.

Some growers breed fish using a hormone supplement that produces predominantly female offspring, which grow faster and produce better filets. Norwegian aquaculturists have even developed gene-altering techniques that make fish grow faster, help them better withstand disease, and produce a higher-quality taste. Another technique alters genes so that fish can survive in colder temperatures.

Retailers and restaurateurs like farm-raised fish for their standard reliable quality and year-round availability. Due to regulations or migratory behavior, some wild stocks—Alaskan salmon for example—can only be purchased during certain months.

Farm fish also stand head and fin above other livestock when it comes to efficiency. Chickens require five and a half pounds of feed to produce a single pound of meat. For pigs, the ratio is seven to one; for cattle, it's 15 to 1. Salmon, however, will produce a pound of filets from just two pounds of feed.

Although epicures argue about the taste of cultured versus wild fish, the former are generally thought to possess piscatorial palatability because they are raised in a controlled environment, fed a prescribed diet, and treated for diseases. Cultured fish can be processed in minutes, instantly frozen or shipped immediately to market. Many consumers, especially Americans, prefer their relatively mild flavor and "non-fishy" taste.

But not everything is rosy down on the old fish farm. "Much of the current expansion of aquaculture is creating an expensive product which only richer people and nations can afford," writes investigative journalist Alex Wilks in the British journal The Ecologist. One specific problem is that predatory fish such as salmon, trout, shrimp, bass, and others require a diet high in animal protein, which invariably comes from fish meal composed of herring and other less profitable species. Consequently, the raising of carnivorous fish may actually reduce the amount of fish protein available for human consumption.

Then there is the environmental issue. Fish farming requires large quantities of clean water, another endan-

'King' Catfish

In the United States, catfish is the king of aquaculture. Today, this species accounts for more of the U.S. industry than all other fish combined—an annual production of nearly 500 million pounds (227 million kilograms). At one time a southern specialty, catfish is now available nationwide and per-capita consumption has doubled since 1985.

As with other livestock, catfish production begins with the mating of selected breeding animals. The resulting eggs are placed in environmentally controlled hatching tanks, where a week later they become infant catfish called fry. After two or three weeks, the fry have grown to an inch (2.5 centimetres) in length and become hardy enough to survive in outdoor maturing ponds.

Maturing ponds vary in size from a few to more than 20 acres (8.1 hectares), and a large farm operation may have several such reservoirs. A one-acre (.405 hectare) pond that is four to five feet (1.2 to 1.5 metres) deep can hold from 70,000 to 200,000 fry. In four states (Mississippi, Alabama, Arkansas, and Louisiana), there are an estimated 144,000 such ponds.

Catfish generally dine on commercially prepared pellets served via a computerized machine. This high-protein food consists of fish meal combined with ground soybeans or corn and a smattering of other nutrients. The pellets float, keeping the fish from feeding off the pond's bottom and allowing ranchers to see their herd.

After 18 months, catfish reach their ideal weight of one and a quarter to one and a half pounds (.56 to .68 kilograms). They are then scooped from the water into tank trucks for live shipment to processing plants. A few of the fish go into a frying pan immediately upon arriving. If they pass muster with taste testers, the entire load is processed; if not, they go back to the pond for a few days of "flavor improvement."

Renowned for their mild flavor, firm texture, and versatility as a cooking ingredient, catfish can be baked, grilled, stewed, broiled, poached—or batter-dipped and deep-fried, as nature intended.

—G.T.

gered commodity. A 20-acre (8.1-hectare) salmon operation can produce as much organic waste as a city of 10,000 people. Disposal at sea can pollute surrounding waters and has in some cases made the area inhabitable for native species.

Shrimp are typically raised in flooded coastal areas, but in some places this practice has destroyed thousands of acres of mangroves. "Half the world's mangrove forests have now been cut down, and in many cases, aquaculture is the lead cause," says Wilks. Such destruction is especially acute in Ecuador and Thailand.

Another problem occurs when farm fish escape and pollute the natural gene pool by breeding with their wild kin. And even in confinement, captive fish can spread diseases to their free-swimming cousins. Researchers in Ireland, for example, traced the demise of local trout fisheries to lice larvae coming from nearby salmon farms. When growers attacked the problem with a pesticide, it killed off much of the wild shellfish population.

Environmental questions notwithstanding, fish will continue to play an important role in human nutrition. Most seafood is low in cholesterol and high in calcium, phosphorous, potassium, and Vitamin A. "Worldwide, people eat more fish than beef and chicken combined," says Worldwatch Institute researcher Hal Kane, "and in many low-income countries fish provide most of the protein people get from animal sources." Advocates describe fish farming as a "blue revolution" that will do for aquatic food production what the green revolution did for terrestrial agriculture.

Currently, every man, woman, and child on the planet consumes an average of more than 30 pounds (13.6 kilograms) of seafood per year. With the human population expected to grow by more than eight billion over the next few decades, the demand will only increase. Thanks to aquaculture, much of that sustenance will come not from the ocean but from "down on the farm."

• Frequent contributor Gary Turbak lives and fishes in Missoula, Montana, U.S.A.

By Robert W. Fisher

The Future of Energy

Changing our fuel sources requires changing our values, but it's happened before and may already be happening again.

Since the first Earth Day in 1970, we have made important moves to clean up energy production and use: Drilling for oil and gas and mining coal are now done less harmfully, power plants burn coal more cleanly, and vehicles get better gas mileage and emit far fewer pollutants. But these changes do not get at the root of the problem—our use of "dirty" fossil fuels.

The numbers tell the story: In 1971, the world consumed 4,722 million tons of oil equivalent (MTOE). Twenty years later, consumption was up to 7,074 MTOE, and it still was almost all fossil fuels—97% in 1971 and 90% in 1991. The 7% drop was captured by nuclear power. By 2010, consumption is projected to rise to 11,500 MTOE, with fossil fuels still accounting for 90% of that demand. Our energy choices simply do not reflect our concerns about the environment and sustainability of our supply.

Concerns about Fossil Fuel Supply

Many people are worried that we are going to run out of fossil fuels, especially oil and natural gas. Running out of oil has been a worry ever

since people first began to use it in large quantities. In 1908, the U.S. Geological Survey (USGS) predicted that total future supply of U.S. oil would not exceed 23 billion barrels. In 1914, the U.S. Bureau of Mines was even more pessimistic, putting the limit at 5.7 billion barrels. In 1920, the USGS proclaimed the peak in

U.S. oil production was almost reached. In 1939, the Department of Interior declared that there was only 13 years of production remaining. In 1977, President Jimmy Carter said, "We are now running out of oil." Despite these gloomy projections, the United States has produced over 200 billion barrels of oil since the early 1900s.

Belying the forecasts, the oil industry keeps on finding new producing regions, developing more effective methods of finding oil fields, reducing costs, and coming up with innovative technology that lets them produce oil in places they could not even look before, such as very deep water.

The future for oil supplies looks promising as well. [Editor's note: For another viewpoint, see "Get Ready for Another Oil Shock!" by L.F. Ivanhoe in the January-February 1997 issue of THE FUTURIST.] Saudi Arabia has just begun to explore in older, deeper rocks that produce oil in surrounding countries. Iraq has the potential to surpass Saudi Arabia in oil reserves once exploration and development work is restarted there. Khazakstan and Eastern Siberia are relatively unexplored potential oil-producing giants. Deep water technology is opening up large areas of the Gulf of Mexico for exploration and production. And some recent testing suggests there are oil deposits in the abyssal depths of the Atlantic Ocean. Then we have immense tar sand deposits in Canada and very heavy oil in the Orinoco Belt of Venezuela, both of which contain hundreds of billions of barrels of oil.

The industry is also improving the recovery rates from established fields. On average, producers get only 35% of the oil out of a reservoir before they abandon it. The remaining oil is either too difficult or too expensive to recover. But one producer in the North Sea now claims to be able to recover 40% and expects to recover up to 60% in a few years.

Natural gas resources have also been subjected to pessimistic forecasts, partly because, in the United States, government-controlled prices were so low that few companies were willing to explore for gas fields. Today, the conservative estimate is that there is at least a 100-year supply of standard gas resources in North America. In addition, there are large deposits of gas hydrates that the industry doesn't yet know how to use economically.

Internationally, the natural gas supply is even larger. Europe hasn't used much natural gas because it had an infrastructure in place to mine, transport, and burn coal and did not see any advantage to going to the expense of building a gas pipeline system. Southeast Asia has only recently begun to tap and use its gas resources.

Coal will last much longer than either oil or natural gas. Known deposits of coal are huge, and there is a massive infrastructure in place to mine, deliver, and burn it. And it is the cheapest of fossil fuels.

So sustainability of supply is not an issue today. Does that mean we will continue to rely on fossil fuels for the next 30 years or longer? Unless we change our values, the answer is yes.

Changing Values and Changing Energy Sources

Before discussing that needed change in values, I want to make a historic connection between changes in value systems and shifts in energy use. The underlying motivation for technological development has primarily been to gain wealth and power—that is not to disparage the thrill of discovery or of innovation for its own sake, but to acknowledge its secondary importance.

> "The prime motivation behind energy choice has been to increase wealth and power."

Wood was the primary source of energy for humans up to 1880, when coal gained first place. Wind, water, and solar power were also used. What happened to trigger the switch from wood to coal to oil as our main source of energy? And why did wind and water power, which for centuries had ranked right behind wood as major sources of energy, fall so far behind?

The transition from wood to coal to oil began because of shifts in the economy and two shifts in thinking that occurred in late Medieval Europe: First, people who were engaged in manufacturing, trade, and creating innovative technology were given a higher human value than those who could fight. Second, it became acceptable for the elite to become involved in devising practical applications from scientific knowledge.

The elite of the age were heavily focused on wealth and power. But people at all levels began to look with less favor on fighting, raiding, and plundering as the primary means of acquiring and enhancing wealth and power. Grain-grinding water mills became important profit centers as innovations enabled them to saw logs, make paper and gunpowder, full woolens, and perform other manufacturing tasks. People who could make machines, run mills, and engage in expanded trading were bringing in more profits than the lords could gain from maintaining a retinue of knights. The other values change that occurred about the same time was that highly educated philosophers and scientists began to get involved in developing practical mechanical devices. Up to that time, such activity was considered beneath their dignity.

Change began in earnest following these economic and value shifts. Better manufacturing processes required better machines, which needed more efficient fuels. Coke made from coal was a more efficient fuel for smelting iron than was charcoal made from wood, but the surface outcrops of coal soon became exhausted. Mines had to go deeper, and that made flooding a problem. Steam engines, which also burned coal, were developed to pump water out of mines.

The improved steam engines suggested steam-powered locomotives on iron rails as a solution to roads that were being constantly torn up from transporting coal. Railroading was born, pushing coal demand higher still, and by 1880, coal became the most used energy source. Water power and wind power for mills gave way to coal-fired steam engines that were more efficient, provided for greater flexibility of use, and produced greater profits. Sailing ships yielded to coal-fired steam ships for the same reasons.

Steam-powered road carriages using external combustion engines

From petroleum to wind, from coal to solar. Whether or not there is enough fossil fuel to keep us going, we should switch to renewables for the sake of the environment, says author Fisher.

were in use even before railroading began, but they required a separate furnace and boiler, making them too heavy and bulky for practical road use. Internal combustion was seen as the solution. Gunpowder, hydrogen explosions, and benzene made from coal tar were tried without much success, but gasoline distilled from oil made internal combustion a commercial success. This stimulated the development of the automobile industry, a major consumer of oil.

Better cars required better engines, which needed higher performance fuels. The performance spiral went up until it was possible to build a gasoline engine powerful enough but still light and small enough to power an airplane. Air travel was born, and by 1950 oil passed coal as

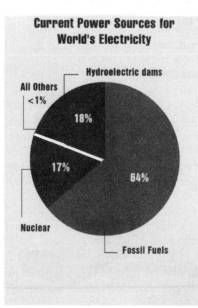

Current Power Sources for World's Electricity

Hydroelectric dams

All Others <1%

18%

17%

64%

Nuclear

Fossil Fuels

Source: International Energy Agency

the most used energy source in the world.

Energy Choices Reflect Our Values

The prime motivation behind energy choice has been to increase wealth and power. We continue to rely on fossil fuels today because they are cheap, efficient, and bring the most profit to their developers. Today, 64% of the world's electricity is generated by burning fossil fuels, mostly coal; 18% comes from hydroelectric dams, 17% from nuclear power plants, and less than 1% from all other sources, including geothermal, biomass, wind, and solar. For the next couple of decades, the outlook of the International Energy Agency is for most expansion of electrical generating capacity to be met by fossil fuels. Nuclear power use is projected to decline and to be replaced by fossil fuel plants. Hydropower and the other renewable sources are projected to increase only slightly.

Wind turbines, photovoltaic arrays on Earth and in space, solar thermal plants, ocean thermal generators, biomass, and tidal power are renewable sources of energy that we know will work. But we use these renewable sources only in special situations, because fossil fuels are cheaper when environmental and health costs are ignored.

It will take a major shift in thinking today to move us away from fossil fuels and into renewable resources. It will be a shift away from placing our highest human value on becoming rich and powerful to giving our highest esteem to those who improve how we relate to each other. That shift has begun and needs nurturing.

Signs of Change

The numerous human rights movements indicate that we are beginning to value people more highly than we have in the past. As these movements gain momentum, people as people will move higher on the priority list, while the personal accumulation of wealth and power will decline.

Another promising development is the rise of ISO 14000, a set of internationally accepted standards for environmental management systems

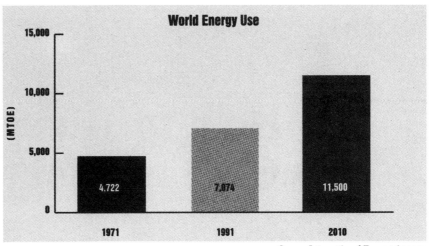

World Energy Use

(MTOE)

1971	1991	2010
4,722	7,074	11,500

Source: International Energy Agency

being promoted by the International Organization for Standardization in Geneva. The drive to adopt ISO 14000 standards comes from consumers, not from government command-and-control regulations. Retailers are beginning to tell their suppliers, who are in turn telling their suppliers, that they will buy only from those who manufacture or produce in an environmentally sound manner. ISO 14000 certification assures all customers that the company not only is operating cleanly, but is committed to continual improvement of its environmental performance. The shift in thinking here is that we are beginning to accept responsibility for our part in the environmental impact of a product through its entire life cycle.

With these changes in our value system, our choices of energy sources will no longer be based solely on their ability to produce immediate profits for someone, but rather on how well they fit into the overall quality of life for everyone—employees, customers, and neighbors. But until we make such changes, the world will continue to rely most heavily on fossil fuels for its future energy needs.

About the Author

Robert W. Fisher, an energy analyst, is president of The Consortium International, Apartado Postal #1, Marfil, Guanajuato C.P. 36251, Mexico. E-mail consintl@redes.int.com.mx.

The International Energy Agency is located at 9, rue de la Federation, 75739 Paris Cedex 15, France. Telephone 33-1 4057 6554; fax 33-1 4057 6559; e-mail info@iea.org.

How to Divvy Up Caspian Bonanza

The landlocked sea holds extraordinary reserves of gas, oil

Thomas Orszag-Land

Thomas Orszag-Land is an author and foreign correspondent who writes on global affairs from London.

RUSSIA and Kazakstan hope they have found a compromise over the status of the Caspian Sea that could resolve a stubborn conflict delaying the development of its enormous offshore hydrocarbon reserves.

The resolution of the issue may well create a dependable new oil and gas industry supplying the needs of Western Europe from resources that dwarf even those of the Persian Gulf. Last week, the deputy foreign ministers of the five Caspian countries completed three days of talks on the legal status of the Caspian Sea. It will be followed by a ministerial conference in November. The fundamental issue is whether the enclosed, salt-water "sea" is a sea or a lake.

If it is a sea, then the five countries bordering its shores must be entitled to exploit individually their separate seabed resources without any say in each other's affairs. If it is a lake, they must act together in a collaborative enterprise.

Time is an increasingly urgent factor because the Caspian neighbors—Russia and Kazakstan, as well as Azerbaijan, Turkmenistan, and Iran—are anxious to exploit their seabed riches. Indeed, the latest discoveries are beyond their wildest dreams.

A seismic survey just carried out on behalf of the Caspian Sea Consortium (CSC), an oil industry group, in the sea-bed near the Kazakstan shore has indicated the presence of crude-oil reserves estimated at 10 billion tons, as well as 2 trillion cubic meters of natural gas.

If confirmed, these offshore reserves, overshadowed by the controversy between the Caspian neighbors, would be 10 times bigger than Kazakstan's fabulously rich Tengiz oilfield, and they would easily exceed Russia's entire proven oil reserves of 6.7 billion tons.

These and other resources in the Caspian region would be ideally suited for the hungry and prosperous energy markets of Europe.

The legal status of the Caspian, which divides the Caucasus region from Central Asia, has arisen since the collapse of the Soviet Union in 1991.

To Russia and Iran, it's a lake

Russia and Iran argue that the Caspian is a lake, as defined by international law, and its resources should therefore be jointly and equally exploited by the littoral states. The three Central Asian republics of the former Soviet Union regard it as a sea; they have invited their powerful neighbors to the north and south to mind their own business.

But this is no way to generate business confidence among Western investors whose contribution is essential to the development of the Caspian hydrocarbon reserves.

A compromise negotiated by Russian President Boris Yeltsin and Kazak leader Nursultan Nazarbayev calls on all parties to sign a convention "respecting sovereignty, territorial integrity, and political independence." The joint statement describes the completion of a Caspian convention opening the way to industrial development at full speed as a "top priority and urgent task."

A key clause in such an accord would allow all countries in the region to carry out their own exploration and production projects while allowing for cooperation in international waters.

Mr. Nazarbayev, a former Soviet Communist Party Politburo member, carefully balances his country's fragile independence between the rival forces of Russia, which would like to restore its former economic control over the region, and nearby Iran, which is intent on spreading its brand of religious fundamentalism among its Islamic neighbors.

Landlocked Kazakstan is about the size of Western Europe, but has a population of just 17 million people. About half are Turkish-speaking Kazaks, who live with a huge Russian ethnic minority.

Their plentiful natural resources and stable politics have attracted 39 percent of the committed foreign investment flow ($117.8 billion) directed to all of the former Soviet Union. The country is believed to hold more oil resources than Iran and Iraq combined and more natural gas reserves than in Norway's continental shelf.

It has a fifth of the former Soviet Union's arable land, nine-tenths of its chrome reserves, and half of its copper, lead, and zinc. It also holds substantial deposits of gold, tungsten, molybdenum, iron ore, manganese, chromite, potash, phosphate, borates, barite, fluorite, and uranium. But it cannot export much because of its long and expensive supply routes restricted by the separatist conflicts in southern Russia. Its only open outlet is the Caspian Sea—which is also landlocked.

Vyacheslav Gizatov, the Kazak deputy foreign minister, told a press conference that his country's compromise with Russia should defuse all problems affecting the CSC. The consortium, involved in the biggest offshore seismic survey in the history of oil exploration, was rewarded by the latest giant discovery. CSC comprises Agip SpA of Italy, British Gas Plc., British Petroleum Co. Plc., Den Norske Stats Oljeselskap SA (Statoil) of Norway, America's Mobil Corp., Shell, and Total SA of France.

Drilling could start in 1998

Intensive seismic work on behalf of CSC began in 1994. Drilling for oil may well commence in 1998.

Some Russian oil companies have also begun searching for hydrocarbon reserves in the Caspian, creating what Mr. Gizatov describes as separate "theoretical conflicts of interest" in the area.

Yet Moscow also seems to have put its faith in the accord with Kazakstan. Vladimir Andreyev, the chief spokesman for the Russian Foreign Ministry, has announced that an expert working group has been assembled already to see the bilateral statement through the difficult negotiating stages into a formal Caspian convention. But he insists that Russia has not altered its view that the resources of the Caspian—a lake—should be held and developed in common by the littoral states.

Moscow does not object in principle to the exploitation of Caspian offshore hydrocarbon reserves in the absence of a convention—but it would also not recognize any production contract contrary to its perception of international law. As Mr. Andreyev put it, "We view such contracts signed by non-Caspian states or even a Russian oil company as agreements concerning only their participants."

These are tough words. But analysts believe that they may have been measured to leave room for further compromise in the face of tough negotiations ahead.

[As] we talk about changing the world's energy systems we have to realize that the industrial North is glutted with energy, using seven times as much per capita as the South consumes. The South is starved of the cheap energy it desperately needs to fuel economic growth and haul itself out of poverty. So Northern and Southern priorities are likely to be quite different.

To explore this tension [*New Internationalist*] used a fictional device and created two characters, Gloria Thembisa from South Africa and Claire Green from England [and] follows them in their exploration of various energy paths. The device is fictive but the substance is factual.

[This article is one excerpt from *New Internationalist*'s "Energy" report.]

Vanessa Baird, *Editor*
New Internationalist

Here comes the **sun...**
and the **wind** and the **rain**

A tour around the possible future... some passion
from **Claire**... but will it dent **Gloria's** scepticism?

UP A NARROW LANE they went until they reached The Quarry, a disused slate works, on a hill outside the small Welsh town of Machynlleth.

It was here that in the 1970s a handful of hippies and idealists tried to create an alternative way of living. They wanted an entirely self-sufficient community – and that meant devising their own energy systems.

'Have you been here before?' asked Gloria.

'Oh yes.' Claire's eyes misted over slightly.

A romantic connection, wondered Gloria? Or was it just that she was a romantic? 'And have you been back there recently?' she asked.

'Oh yes,' she replied in a more matter-of-fact voice.

'Has it changed much?'

'Yes. It's... um... matured. It's now a Centre for Alternative Technology, the foremost in Europe. About 80,000 people pass through a year, including lots of school groups. They run residential courses on eco-building or on how to generate your own power. There are eco-cabins where people can stay and a restaurant and shop...'

'And the politics?'

'Less purist. More pragmatic. There aren't the endless debates there used to be about whether one could use

ready-made nails or whether one had to make one's own. They still run the place as a co-operative, though...'

The pace of life seemed to slow right down as they came up the hill. They walked through organic gardens, past the bee house, past a solar-powered telephone kiosk. 'Shall I call South Africa?!' Gloria was about to say but Claire had already marched ahead in the direction of a wind turbine, poking out above the trees.

'So,' said Gloria, catching up, 'what I want to know is if I had this in my backyard could it I run my house on it?'

'You'd have to have a good windsite, in the country probably.'

'And if I didn't... If I lived in a city or a suburb?'

'You might be better getting your power from a windfarm...'

'And where might I find one of those.'

'There are a few in this country. But California and Denmark are the places where windpower's really taken off. In California windfarms already supply the equivalent of all of San Francisco's domestic power needs. What they are doing in Denmark is really interesting. People get together in groups and buy a wind turbine or group of turbines which provides them with the electricity they need, and they sell off any surplus

to the national grid. About half of Denmark's wind turbines are owned and operated in this way.'

'Mmm . . . But is it a real option as a main source of energy? Can wind power ever really produce enough energy to supply an industrialized nation, for example?'

'Well, it's reckoned that in Europe windpower could meet all the continent's electricity needs. The European Wind Energy Association's proposal is rather more modest. They reckon it would be quite feasible to meet ten percent of the European Union's needs by 2030 using turbines, and if you put them all together - not that you would - they would occupy an area about the size of Crete.'

'Ha! So they occupy land that could be used for agriculture . . .'

'And could still - 99 per cent of the land would still be available to agriculture around the windmills.' Touché, thought Claire, but managed to stop herself saying it. But just as she basked, Gloria was coming back with another point.

'One thing that seems to get missed out by you renewable energy people is employment. What about all the jobs that are going to be lost in the energy industry?'

'Well, I'm not sure about that,' Claire twitched. 'I mean, look at this European

Wind Energy proposal. The manufacture of turbines will employ about 50,000 people and operation and maintenance of windpower will create another 100,000 rural jobs. . . '

'It's not like coal mining though. . . '

'It's something that will have to be addressed. . . I'm not sure how. But don't underestimate the new energy jobs that will be created by renewables - safer, healthier jobs too.'

'Some people would argue that an unsafe job is better than no job.'

They meandered on and came across a windpowered water pump, devised by Dulas, a local alternative engineering company, for a group of Eritreans who visited the Centre in the 1980s.

'This system has really taken off in Africa. It's good for irrigation.'

Gloria nodded, now looking at a water turbine powered by a nearby lake. 'So what's the power source being used in this Centre, then?'

'Everything you see. Let's go to the power house, I'll show you how it works.'

They walked past a biomass wood-chip burner and came to a big board on which all the energy systems were displayed: there was micro-hydro, windpower, solar, biomass, diesel. . .

'Diesel!' shouted Gloria. 'But that's sacrilege!' She looked aghast.

Claire couldn't help laughing. 'Yes, fossil fuels come on as a stop-gap. And actually I think it's okay to use a little, in a limited way.'

'Huh!'

Claire explained the series of computerized trips and switches in the power house, how the most productive source of power was automatically selected to come on stream depending on the weather or water level conditions.

'So in your renewable future are we all expected to have a great power house in our backyards and half a dozen different energy systems..?'

'No. This is not a model to be repeated on this scale. It just demonstrates the different energy options available on a far larger scale.'

'Mmm... And what's this about solar? Where's that?'

Claire led her to the solar installation. 'Now there is one unfortunate thing about this installation,' said Claire once they reached the panels. 'It is built in what is probably the least sunny spot in Europe! But anyway, it seems to be producing power today.'

'How can you tell?'

Claire showed her a miniature fairground roundabout being driven by power from the panels.

'Sweet,' commented Gloria, 'but it's

hardly going to power a steel plant.'

'No, for that you need a big installation in an area that gets lots of direct sunlight, like they have in the Mojave desert in California or in Israel.'

Gloria looked at the clouds passing across the sky, reflected in the panels.

'You know I'm not at all convinced by solar power. I don't think it's got the potential...'

'Potential!' Claire exploded. 'It has enormous potential... it has greater potential than anything else! Just a quarter of an hour of sunlight offers more energy than humanity consumes in a whole year! Now not all that is usable but what is is still 1,000 times more than the world currently consumes . . . '

'And how much of our energy comes from solar power at the moment?'

'Just 0.001 percent.'

'What? If solar is so great why isn't everyone using it?'

'The simple answer is it's still much more expensive to generate electricity from solar than from conventional systems. And the reason for that is that the funding for research and development has been pathetic. While fossil fuels get huge amounts of research and development money, solar gets peanuts.'

She fumbled in her bag. 'I've got some figures somewhere. It really beggars belief. Ah, here! Do you know that the US spent less on solar research in a year than it costs to buy just one fighter plane? Worldwide more than $200 billion is spent on direct subsidies to fossil fuels to help keep the prices down. Solar gets nothing! No wonder fossil fuels appear cheaper. But it's a false economy. We are just paying for them out of another pocket. Not to mention the environmental price!'

Claire was well away by now: 'The whole world's energy system is skewed in favour of the fossil fuels and the multinationals that control them. It's scandalous really. What's amazing is how much solar research has achieved with so little help. It's got much more efficient and the price of photovoltaic panels has gone down tenfold in the past 20 years!'

Gloria was somewhat quietened by Claire's passionate outburst. They both sat looking at the panels. Gloria went over to them and read what was written there:

If you were asked to design the ideal energy conversion system it would be pretty difficult to come up with anything better than the solar photovoltaic cell. It harnesses the energy source that is by far the most abundant of those available on the planet. It's clean - very

small amounts of toxic chemicals are used in the manufacture of cells, but that's all; there are no emissions. The photovoltaic cell itself is made from the second most abundant element after oxygen in the earth's crust – silicon. It has no moving parts and cannot therefore, in theory, wear out. And its output is electricity, probably the most useful of all forms of energy.

She then looked at charts showing the decline in price. The average market price of PV cells plunged dramatically from $30 in 1975 to around $3.5 per peak watt hour now. In a few years time, analysts reckoned, it would be no more expensive than electricity produced by nuclear power.

'I suppose the technology is controlled by the North,' Gloria remarked to Claire who had come up alongside her.

'At the moment most cells are being made in the US, Japan, Germany and France, but Brazil, China, India and Pakistan have started making their own. What tends to happen is that countries start by importing modules to assemble themselves – they are doing that in parts of Africa now – and then move on to actually making the cells themselves.'

When they got back to their Bed & Breakfast Claire eagerly presented Gloria with another stack of papers. 'I thought you might like...'

'What, more reading matter!'

'Well... of course you don't have to...' muttered Claire, feeling suddenly embarrassed by her own evangelism.

But Gloria was already taking the bundle from her. 'We'll see. If those moaning eco-friendly windmills keep me awake all night I might welcome something to read...'

That night Gloria was not kept awake by windmills, but she read all the same. First she picked up a newspaper clipping:

SCHEER'S REVOLUTION

'I have no doubt that the day will come when the only energy used on this earth will be solar,' says Hermann Scheer, the charismatic German former Energy Minister and founder of the pressure group Eurosolar.

He is calling for a 'Solar Revolution' with the replacement of all nuclear and fossil fuels within the next four decades. 'Only a fully solar global energy economy can preserve the ecosphere,' he maintains.

Scheer wants an international 'solar proliferation treaty' that will bring us into the Solar Age and break the reactionary stranglehold of vested interests, both corporate and government. And his views are rapidly gaining ground in his native Germany.

The main opposition SPD party has said that an ecological economy based on renewable energies will be the main plank of its policy.

Scheer, who is the SPD spokesperson on Agriculture and the Environment, has introduced a Solar Initiative Bill in the German Parliament designed to finance the conversion of 100,000 roofs to photovoltaics. This would mark the beginning of a whole new industry and employ 30,000 people...'

GLORIA PICKED UP Scheer's book *A Solar Manifesto*. She read his scathing critique of the small-mindedness of the decision-making élites who slashed research on renewable energy the moment oil prices went down in the 1980s. In the US the 1990 research and development budget for renewables was a mere 12 per cent of the 1981 budget. In Canada it fell to 16 per cent, in the UK to 50 per cent and in Australia and Aotearoa/ New Zealand it dwindled to almost nothing.

Scheer wrote:

'...it is obvious that support for solar energy was kept deliberately small, even though it is the newest and most wide-reaching area of publicly supported energy research... Disinformation was spread about the efficiency of solar energy technologies and positive results were downplayed... As this has been happening in virtually all countries, it leads one to conclude that this is due to a colluding international opinion Mafia.'

GLORIA WONDERED how much she had been influenced by the 'colluding international opinion Mafia'.

She picked up another book, entitled *The Hydrogen Solar Future* by John O'M Bockris and T Nejat Veziroglu, Professor of Chemistry at Texas A&M University, and Director of the Clean Energy Research Institute in Miami, respectively. The subtitle was: *The power to save the earth. Fuel forever.*

'Well, they can't be accused of underselling their own theory,' she remarked. But she found it intriguing all the same:

SOLAR HYDROGEN COUPLING
'The solar energy scheme we are putting forward here is sometimes called the solar-hydrogen energy system. Put simply, solar energy is converted to electricity; to get the electricity over long distances or for use at night the electricity is used to elec-

trolyze water to produce hydrogen... The hydrogen is sent through pipelines, just as natural gas is today, to cities and towns.

The benefit of this system is that by putting excess electricity to work by producing hydrogen, it is not wasted. In addition it is cheaper and more efficient to transport through pipelines than to send the excess electricity over wires and through cables. Finally, and most beneficial of all, hydrogen and solar energy do not pollute: when hydrogen is used to supply heat or energy, water is the by-product.

Our solar energy will be around for a few billion more years – it is everlasting as far as we are concerned – and we would obtain hydrogen from water, and that won't run out either as water is the by-product of burning hydrogen. Thus solar hydrogen is a clean and renewable system.

So many of the natural processes on our planet are self-sustaining – the circulatory systems of animals and humans, the respiratory system of animals, humans and plants, the food chain, and the earth's water cycle. Doesn't it make sense that our energy should be derived from a renewable system too?'

'NEAT,' SHE THOUGHT. 'And convincing.' She closed her eyes and tried to imagine how a renewable energy future would look. Would there be huge solar power installations in the Sahara or massive windfarms covering hillsides or stretched along coastlines. Or would it be each individual household with its own system?

She picked out a personal testimony from a young North American woman called **Sara Chamberlain**:

OFF THE GRID
We moved to Northern California in 1976, when I was eight. My parents' idealistic plan was to build a cabin in the woods and live self-sufficiently off the land. Although they soon realized that it was cheaper to buy lentils than grow them, they managed to make their dream of a solar and hydro energy-powered house a reality – and said goodbye to electricity bills forever.

Our solar power system developed thanks to the experiments of our landpartner, John Harnish. In 1980 he discovered Real Goods: a small local store that sold a variety of solar panels and alternative energy equipment, which today is one of the largest alternative power hardware retailers in North America.

Initially John bought one solar panel, capable of producing approximately 30

watts of power per hour of sunlight, for $260. He also bought two 12-volt golf-cart batteries (for $60 each) to store the power generated by the solar panels, and 12 feet of household electrical wire to link them together.

He hung the solar panel on the sunny side of his house, using a few nails, connected the batteries and ran some wires into the house. Now he could plug in three 15-watt halogen bulbs (which give off three times as much light as regular bulbs) for six hours a night. That night, as the stars of the Big Dipper came out one by one above the oak trees, John read the *Tao of Physics* by the bright light of an electric lamp.

My parents followed suit. They bought one 30-watt solar panel for $260, and one 70-watt panel for $385, and six golf-cart batteries for $360. Seventeen years later, this $1,110 solar system still faithfully powers 12 lights, a blender, fan, and answering machine; and allows my 69-year-old father and 64-year-old mother to surf the Internet on their computer and download information on their printer. Satisfied with these basic amenities, my parents haven't ever needed to expand their solar system.

However, 1979 brought a succession of monsoon-style storms. Weeks of non-stop rain climaxed in a snowstorm. The panels stopped functioning, we drained the batteries dead, and were forced to re-light our kerosene lamps. Attempting to decipher *A Tale of Two Cities* in semi-darkness, we realized we needed a winter-weather alternative.

John came to our rescue. Over the years he had struck up a friendship with a man called Ross Burkhart, who had invented one of the first micro-hydro energy systems, the 'Burkhart pelton wheel'. When the wheel was put in a box, and water fed through it, the wheel would spin around turning a shaft which powered an alternator and generated electricity. All it needed was water that dropped at least 200 feet before entering the box.

John bought one of Ross's pelton wheels, some piping, wire and batteries, and rigged it up at the edge of a nearby creek. The Burkhart pelton wheel, which can now be purchased from Real Goods for $265, produces 1,000 to 10,000 watts of power per day during the winter, which is more than enough electricity to satisfy even the most power-hungry....

Today, come rain or shine, my parents can read the *New York Times* on the Internet, and John's eight-year-old son Bodhi can play computer games without ever having had to connect to the grid.

'CRAZY AMERICANS,' Gloria conclud-ed. Though she had to admit they did make things sound so easy...

She thought of the remote rural communities in South Africa, desperate to link up to the National Grid, as though this were the be-all and end-all. She also knew in her heart of hearts that they would have to wait a very long time, and in the meantime they could be generating their own power.

She picked out another piece, also about inventive ways of adapting to change in rural North America. This article was written by Canadian **Stephen Leahy**:

With cuts to income-support programs and the increasing globalization of agri-culture, North American farmers are looking to their past to find ways to survive in the future. Often forming new co-operative enterprises, farmers are turning waste straw into building materials, corn into fuel, wheat starch into plastics, soybeans into inks and milk into paints and glues.

Farmers are also growing non-tradi-tional crops like kenaf to make paper, milkweed to replace goose down in pil-lows and, now that it is legal in Canada, hemp. The strong, breathable fibre of the non-narcotic hemp plant has hun-dreds of uses from jeans to linens. When the full environmental cost of using petrochemicals is considered, it's clear the next century belongs to living plants, not long-dead ones.

GLORIA LIKED THAT idea. It made her think about possible building materials for South Africa's housing program.

Traditional adobe or mud was in many ways the best material, but it was con-sidered insufficiently 'modern'. She'd enjoy telling people back home that North Americans were building houses with straw stubble!

The idea of renewables was growing on her.

'Maybe that place has had an effect on me,' she mused as she was dropping off to sleep and recalling the quietly inventive atmosphere of the Centre. Meanwhile in the next room Claire was lying awake thinking: 'Oh my God, why is she so resistant? I really wasn't prepared for such scepticism. I doubt my thinking has had any impact on her whatsoever. She obviously thinks I'm just some wet, white, greenie liberal. Oh well... only a couple more days to go...'

Political Economy

Globalization Debate (Articles 22–25)
Case Studies (Articles 26–34)

The twentieth century will be remembered for many significant historical events. The scientific and technological breakthroughs that resulted in the advent of nuclear power and extraterrestrial flight, the rapid end of colonialism, and two devastating world wars are just some of the most notable of these.

An underlying debate that shaped much of the century's social history focused on dramatically opposing views about how economic systems should be organized and what role government should play in the management of a country's economy. For some, the dominant capitalist economic system appeared to be organized for the benefit of the few, with the masses trapped in poverty, supplying cheap labor to further enrich the wealthy. This economic system, they argued, only could be changed by gaining control of the political system and radically changing the ownership of the means of production. In striking contrast to this perspective, others argued that the best way to create wealth and eliminate poverty was to encourage entrepreneurs with the motivation of profits and to allow a competitive marketplace to make decisions about production and distribution. Government interference in market processes was generally to be avoided, according to advocates of this view.

The debate between socialism/communism on the one hand and capitalism on the other (with variations in between) has been characterized by both abstract theorizing and very pragmatic and often violent political conflict. Countless lives have been lost and rivers of blood shed in the struggle between these conflicting views. The Russian and Chinese revolutions overthrew the old social order and created radical changes in the political and economic systems in these two giant countries. The Soviet experiment in state farms and the Chinese experiment in collective farms are examples of efforts to fundamentally alter one of the most basic economic activities. The political structures created to support these new systems of agricultural production, along with the planning of all other aspects of economic activity, eliminated most private ownership of property; they were, in short, unparalleled experiments in social engineering. The end of the colonial system often resulted in bloodshed as political factions fought to chart a new course in the newly independent countries of the world.

The collapse of the Soviet Union and the dramatic reforms that have taken place in China have recast the debate about how to best structure contemporary economics. Some believe that with the end of communism and the resulting participation of hundreds of millions of new consumers in the global market economy, an unprecedented era has been entered. Rather than a world divided between two differing economic systems, proponents of this view argue that a new global economy is emerging, setting into motion a series of processes that will ultimately result in a single economic system characterized by interdependence and increased prosperity.

Many have noted that this process of "globalization" is being accelerated by the revolution in communication and computer technologies. Some have even predicted that the end result of these processes will be a single, global culture, eliminating many of the differences among people that have been the sources of conflict and warfare.

Others are less optimistic about the prospects of globalization. They argue that the creation of a single economic system where there are no boundaries to impede the flow of capital does not mean a closing of the gap between the world's rich and poor. They contend that quite the opposite is already taking place.

The use of the term "political economy" for the title of this unit is a recognition that modern economic and political systems are not separable. All economic systems have some type of marketplace where goods and services are bought and sold. The government in most cases regulates these transactions, that is, it sets the rules that govern the marketplace. In addition, the government's power to tax in order to pay for defense and other political activities directly affects all economic activities (i.e., by determining how much money remains for other expenditures).

One of the most important concepts in thinking about the contemporary political economy is "development." Television talk shows, scholarly publications, political speeches, and countless other forums echo this term. Yet, if a group of experts were gathered to discuss this concept, it would soon be apparent that many define the word "development" in various ways. For some, development means becoming industrialized—like the United States or Japan. To others, development means having a growing economy, which is usually measured in terms of the expansion of the so-called gross domestic product (GDP). To still others, development is primarily a political phenomenon. They question how a society can change its economy if it cannot first establish collective goals and successfully administer their implementation. And to still others, development means attaining a certain quality of

UNIT 4

is resulting in increased development, not only for a few people but for most of those participating in the global political economy.

The unit is organized into two subsections. The first is a general discussion of the concept of globalization. How do different people define the term, and what are their various perspectives on it? For example, is the idea of a global economy merely wishful thinking by those who sit on top of the power hierarchy, self-deluded into believing that globalization is an inexorable force that will evolve in its own way, following its own rules? Or will there always be traditional issues of power politics between the rich, those who are ascending in power, and the ever-present poor, which will result in clashes of interests just like those that have characterized history since the early years of civilization?

The second subsection focuses on case studies. These have been selected to help the reader draw his or her own conclusions about the validity of the globalization concept. What in fact is taking place in countries that have not participated directly in the industrial revolution? In addition, can countries like China and India find a significant economic role in the contemporary world? Does the contemporary political economy result in winners and losers, or can all benefit from its system of wealth creation and distribution?

Looking Ahead: Challenge Questions

Are those who argue that there is in fact a process of globalization overly optimistic? Why or why not?

What are some of the impediments to a truly global political economy?

How are the political economies of traditional societies different from those of the consumer-oriented societies of the West?

How are the developing countries dependent on the highly developed industrialized nations?

What are some of the barriers that make it difficult for nonindustrial countries to develop?

The international political economy is faced with unprecedented problems. What are some of these, and what are some of the proposals for addressing these problems?

How are China, India, and other newly industrialized countries trying to alter their ways of doing business in order to meet the challenges of globalization? Are they likely to succeed?

life, based on the establishment of adequate health care, leisure time, and a system of public education, among other things.

For purposes of this unit, the term "development" will be defined as an improvement in the basic aspects of life: lower infant mortality rates, greater life expectancy, lower disease rates, higher rates of literacy, healthier diets, and improved sanitation. While it is obvious that, judged by these standards, some groups of people are more developed than others, the process of development is an ongoing one for all countries. As a result, a fundamental question that the thoughtful reader must consider is whether the apparent trend toward greater globalization

Globalization, we are told, is what every business should be pursuing, and what every nation should welcome. But what, exactly, is it? James Rosenau offers a nuanced understanding of a process that is much more real, and transforming, than the language of the marketplace expresses.

The Complexities and Contradictions of Globalization

JAMES N. ROSENAU

The mall at Singapore's airport has a food court with 15 food outlets, all but one of which offering menus that cater to local tastes; the lone standout, McDonald's, is also the only one crowded with customers. In New York City, experts in *feng shui,* an ancient Chinese craft aimed at harmonizing the placement of man-made structures in nature, are sought after by real estate developers in order to attract a growing influx of Asian buyers who would not be interested in purchasing buildings unless their structures were properly harmonized.

Most people confronted with these examples would probably not be surprised by them. They might even view them as commonplace features of day-to-day life late in the twentieth century, instances in which local practices have spread to new and distant sites. In the first case the spread is from West to East and in the second it is from East to West, but both share a process in which practices spread and become established in profoundly different cultures. And what immediately comes to mind when contemplating this process? The answer can be summed up in one word: globalization, a label that is presently in vogue to account for peoples, activities, norms, ideas, goods, services, and currencies that are decreasingly confined to a particular geographic space and its local and established practices.

Indeed, some might contend that "globalization" is the latest buzzword to which observers resort when things seem different and they cannot other-

JAMES N. ROSENAU *is University Professor of International Affairs at George Washington University. His latest book is* Along the Domestic-Foreign Frontier: Exploring Governance in a Turbulent World *(Cambridge: Cambridge University Press, 1997). This article draws on the author's* "New Dimensions of Security: The Interaction of Globalizing and Localizing Dynamics," Security Dialogue, *September 1994, and* "The Dynamics of Globalization: Toward an Operational Formulation," Security Dialogue, *September 1996.*

wise readily account for them. That is why, it is reasoned, a great variety of activities are labeled as globalization, with the result that no widely accepted formulation of the concept has evolved. Different observers use it to describe different phenomena, and often there is little overlap among the various usages. Even worse, the elusiveness of the concept of globalization is seen as underlying the use of a variety of other, similar terms—world society, interdependence, centralizing tendencies, world system, globalism, universalism, internationalization, globality—that come into play when efforts are made to grasp why public affairs today seem significantly different from those of the past.

Such reasoning is misleading. The proliferation of diverse and loose definitions of globalization as well as the readiness to use a variety of seemingly comparable labels are not so much a reflection of evasive confusion as they are an early stage in a profound ontological shift, a restless search for new ways of understanding unfamiliar phenomena. The lack of precise formulations may suggest the presence of buzzwords for the inexplicable, but a more convincing interpretation is that such words are voiced in so many different contexts because of a shared sense that the human condition is presently undergoing profound transformations in all of its aspects.

WHAT IS GLOBALIZATION?

Let us first make clear where globalization fits among the many buzzwords that indicate something new in world affairs that is moving important activities and concerns beyond the national seats of power that have long served as the foundations of economic, political, and social life. While all the buzzwords seem to cluster around the same dimension of the present human condition, useful distinctions can be drawn among them. Most notably, if it is presumed that the prime characteristic of this dimension is change—a transformation of practices and norms—then the term "globalization" seems appropriate to denote the "something" that is changing humankind's preoccupation with territoriality and the traditional arrangements of the state system. It is a term that directly implies change, and thus differentiates the phenomenon as a process rather than as a prevailing condition or a desirable end state.

Conceived as an underlying process, in other words, globalization is not the same as globalism, which points to aspirations for a state of affairs where values are shared by or pertinent to all the world's more than 5 billion people, their environment, and their role as citizens, consumers, or producers with an interest in collective action to solve common problems. And it can also be distinguished from universalism, which refers to those values that embrace all of humanity (such as the values that science or religion draws on), at any time or place. Nor is it coterminous with complex interdependence, which signifies structures that link people and communities in various parts of the world.

Although related to these other concepts, the idea of globalization developed here is narrower in scope. It refers neither to values nor to structures, but to sequences that unfold either in the mind or in behavior, to processes that evolve as people and organizations go about their daily tasks and seek to realize their particular goals. What distinguishes globalizing processes is that they are not hindered or prevented by territorial or jurisdictional barriers. As indicated by the two examples presented at the outset, such processes can readily spread in many directions across national boundaries, and are capable of reaching into any community anywhere in the world. They consist of all those forces that impel individuals, groups, and institutions to engage in similar forms of behavior or to participate in more encompassing and coherent processes, organizations, or systems.

Contrariwise, localization derives from all those pressures that lead individuals, groups, and institutions to narrow their horizons, participate in dissimilar forms of behavior, and withdraw to less encompassing processes, organizations, or systems. In other words, any technological, psychological, social, economic, or political developments that foster the expansion of interests and practices beyond established boundaries are both sources and expressions of the processes of globalization, just as any developments in these realms that limit or reduce interests are both sources and expressions of localizing processes.

Note that the processes of globalization are conceived as only *capable* of being worldwide in scale. In fact, the activities of no group, government, society, or company have ever been planetary in magnitude, and few cascading sequences actually encircle and encompass the entire globe. Televised events such as civil wars and famines in Africa or protests against governments in Eastern Europe may sustain a spread that is worldwide in scope, but such a scope is not viewed as a prerequisite of globalizing dynamics. As long as it has the potential of an unlimited spread that can readily transgress national jurisdictions, any interaction sequence is considered to reflect the operation of globalization.

Obviously, the differences between globalizing and localizing forces give rise to contrary conceptions of territoriality. Globalization is rendering boundaries and identity with the land less salient while localization, being driven by pressures to narrow and withdraw, is highlighting borders and intensifying the deep attachments to land that can dominate emotion and reasoning.

In short, globalization is boundary-broadening and localization is boundary-heightening. The former allows people, goods, information, norms, practices, and institutions to move about oblivious to or despite boundaries. The boundary-heightening processes of localization are designed to inhibit or prevent the movement of people, goods, information, norms, practices, and institutions. Efforts along this line, however, can be only partially successful. Community and state boundaries can be heightened to a considerable extent, but they cannot be rendered impervious. Authoritarian governments try to make them so, but their policies are bound to be undermined in a shrinking world with increasingly interdependent economies and communications technologies that are not easily monitored. Thus it is hardly surprising that some of the world's most durable tensions flow from the fact that no geographic borders can be made so airtight to prevent the infiltration of ideas and goods. Stated more emphatically, some globalizing dynamics are bound, at least in the long run, to prevail.

The boundary-expanding dynamics of globalization have become highly salient precisely because recent decades have witnessed a mushrooming of the facilities, interests, and markets through which a potential for worldwide spread can be realized. Likewise, the boundary-contracting dynamics of localization have also become increasingly significant, not least because some people and cultures feel threatened by the incursions of globalization. Their jobs, their icons, their belief systems, and their communities seem at risk as the boundaries that have sealed them off from the outside world in the past no longer assure protection. And there is, of course, a basis of truth in these fears. Globalization does intrude; its processes do shift jobs elsewhere; its norms do undermine traditional mores. Responses to these threats can vary considerably. At one extreme are adaptations that accept the boundary-broadening processes and make the best of them by integrating them into local customs and practices. At the other extreme are responses intended to ward off the globalizing processes by resort to ideological purities, closed borders, and economic isolation.

THE DYNAMICS OF FRAGMEGRATION

The core of world affairs today thus consists of tensions between the dynamics of globalization and localization. Moreover, the two sets of dynamics are causally linked, almost as if every increment of globalization gives rise to an increment of localization, and vice versa. To account for these tensions I have long used the term "fragmegration," an awkward and perhaps even grating label that has the virtue of capturing the pervasive interactions between the fragmenting forces of localization and the integrative forces of globalization.[1] One can readily observe the unfolding of fragmegrative dynamics in the struggle of the European Union to cope with proposals for monetary unification or in the electoral campaigns and successes of Jean-Marie Le Pen in France, Patrick Buchanan in the United States, and Pauline Hanson in Australia—to mention only three examples.

It is important to keep in mind that fragmegration is not a single dynamic. Both globalization and localization are clusters of forces that, as they interact in different ways and through different channels, contribute to more encompassing processes in the case of globalization and to less encompassing processes in the case of localization. These various dynamics, moreover, operate in all realms of human activity, from the cultural and social to the economic and political.

In the political realm, globalizing dynamics underlie any developments that facilitate the expansion of authority, policies, and interests beyond

There is no inherent contradiction between localizing and globalizing tendencies.

existing socially constructed territorial boundaries, whereas the politics of localization involves any trends in which the scope of authority and policies undergoes contraction and reverts to concerns, issues, groups, and institutions that are less extensive than the prevailing socially constructed territorial boundaries. In the economic realm, globalization encompasses the expansion of production, trade, and investments beyond their prior locales, while localizing dynamics are at work when the activities of producers and consumers are constricted to narrower boundaries. In the social and cultural realms, globalization operates to extend ideas, norms, and practices beyond the settings in which they originated, while localization highlights or compresses the original settings and thereby inhibits the inroad of new ideas, norms, and practices.

It must be stressed that the dynamics unfolding in all these realms are long-term processes. They involve fundamental human needs and thus span all of human history. Globalizing dynamics derive from peoples' need to enlarge the scope of their self-created orders so as to increase the goods, services, and ideas available for their well-being. The agricultural revolution, followed by the industrial and postindustrial transformations, are among the major sources that have sustained globalization. Yet even as these forces have been operating, so have contrary tendencies toward contraction been continuously at work. Localizing dynamics derive from people's need for the psychic comforts of close-at-hand, reliable support—for the family and neighborhood, for local cultural practices, for a sense of "us" that is distinguished from "them." Put differently, globalizing dynamics have long fostered large-scale order, whereas localizing dynamics have long created pressure for small-scale order. Fragmegration, in short, has always been an integral part of the human condition.

GLOBALIZATION'S EVENTUAL PREDOMINANCE

Notwithstanding the complexities inherent in the emergent structures of world affairs, observers have not hesitated to anticipate what lies beyond fragmegration as global history unfolds. All agree that while the contest between globalizing and localizing dynamics is bound to be marked by fluctuating surges in both directions, the underlying tendency is for the former to prevail over the latter. Eventually, that is, the dynamics of globalization are expected to serve as the bases around which the course of events is organized.

[1]For an extensive discussion of the dynamics of fragmegration, see James N. Rosenau, *Along the Domestic-Foreign Frontier: Exploring Governance in a Turbulent World* (Cambridge: Cambridge University Press, 1997), ch. 6.

Consensus along these lines breaks down, however, over whether the predominance of globalization is likely to have desirable or noxious consequences. Those who welcome globalizing processes stress the power of economic variables. In this view the globalization of national economies through the diffusion of technology and consumer products, the rapid transfer of financial resources, and the efforts of transnational companies to extend their market shares is seen as so forceful and durable as to withstand and eventually surmount any and all pressures toward fragmentation. This line acknowledges that the diffusion that sustains the processes of globalization is a centuries-old dynamic, but the difference is that the present era has achieved a level of economic development in which it is possible for innovations occurring in any sector of any country's economy to be instantaneously transferred to and adapted in any other country or sector. As a consequence,

> when this process of diffusion collides with cultural or political protectionism, it is culture and protectionism that wind up in the shop for repairs. Innovation accelerates. Productivity increases. Standards of living improve. There are setbacks, of course. The newspaper headlines are full of them. But we believe that the time required to override these setbacks has shortened dramatically in the developed world. Indeed, recent experience suggests that, in most cases, economic factors prevail in less than a generation. . .
>
> Thus understood, globalization—the spread of economic innovations around the world and the political and cultural adjustments that accompany this diffusion—cannot be stopped. . . As history teaches, the political organizations and ideologies that yield superior economic performance survive, flourish, and replace those that are less productive.[2]

While it is surely the case that robust economic incentives sustain and quicken the processes of globalization, this line of theorizing nevertheless suffers from not allowing for its own negation. The theory offers no alternative interpretations as to

how the interaction of economic, political, and social dynamics will play out. One cannot demonstrate the falsity—if falsity it is—of the theory because any contrary evidence is seen merely as "setbacks," as expectable but temporary deviations from the predicted course. The day may come, of course, when events so perfectly conform to the predicted patterns of globalization that one is inclined to conclude that the theory has been affirmed. But in the absence of alternative scenarios, the theory offers little guidance as to how to interpret intervening events, especially those that highlight the tendencies toward fragmentation. Viewed in this way, it is less a theory and more an article of faith to which one can cling.

Other observers are much less sanguine about the future development of fragmegration. They highlight a litany of noxious consequences that they see as following from the eventual predominance of globalization: "its economism; its economic reductionism; its technological determinism; its political cynicism, defeatism, and immobilism; its de-socialization of the subject and resocialization of risk; its teleological subtext of inexorable global 'logic' driven exclusively by capital accumulation and the market; and its ritual exclusion of factors, causes, or goals other than capital accumulation and the market from the priority of values to be pursued by social action."[3]

Still another approach, allowing for either desirable or noxious outcomes, has been developed by Michael Zurn. He identifies a mismatch between the rapid extension of boundary-crossing activities and the scope of effective governance. Consequently, states are undergoing what is labeled "uneven denationalization," a primary process in which "the rise of international governance is still remarkable, but not accompanied by mechanisms for. . .democratic control; people, in addition, become alienated from the remote political process. . . The democratic state in the Western world is confronted with a situation in which it is undermined by the process of globalization and overarched by the rise of international institutions."[4]

While readily acknowledging the difficulties of anticipating where the process of uneven denationalization is driving the world, Zurn is able to derive two scenarios that may unfold: "Whereas the pessimistic scenario points to instances of fragmentation and emphasizes the disruption caused by the transition, the optimistic scenario predicts, at least in the long run, the triumph of centralization." The latter scenario rests on the presumption that the increased interdependence of societies will propel them to develop ever more effective democratic

[2]William W. Lewis and Marvin Harris, "Why Globalization Must Prevail," *The McKinsey Quarterly*, no. 2 (1992), p. 115.

[3]Barry K. Gills, "Editorial: 'Globalization' and the 'Politics of Resistance,'" *New Political Economy*, vol. 2 (March 1997), p. 12.

[4]Michael Zurn, "What Has Changed in Europe? The Challenge of Globalization and Individualization," paper presented at a meeting on What Has Changed? Competing Perspectives on World Order (Copenhagen, May 14-16, 1993), p. 40.

controls over the very complex arrangements on which international institutions must be founded.

UNEVEN FRAGMEGRATION

My own approach to theorizing about the fragmegrative process builds on these other perspectives and a key presumption of my own—that there is no inherent contradiction between localizing and globalizing tendencies—to develop an overall hypothesis that anticipates fragmegrative outcomes and that allows for its own negation: *the more pervasive globalizing tendencies become, the less resistant localizing reactions will be to further globalization.* In other words, globalization and localization will coexist, but the former will continue to set the context for the latter. Since the degree of coexistence will vary from situation to situation (depending on the salience of the global economy and the extent to which ethnic and other noneconomic factors actively contribute to localization), I refer, borrowing from Zurn, to the processes depicted by the hypothesis as *uneven fragmegration.* The hypothesis allows for continuing pockets of antagonism between globalizing and localizing tendencies even as increasingly (but unevenly) the two accommodate each other. It does not deny the pessimistic scenario wherein fragmentation disrupts globalizing tendencies; rather it treats fragmentation as more and more confined to particular situations that may eventually be led by the opportunities and requirements of greater interdependence to conform to globalization.

For globalizing and localizing tendencies to accommodate each other, individuals have to come to appreciate that they can achieve psychic comfort in collectivities through multiple memberships and multiple loyalties, that they can advance both local and global values without either detracting from the other. The hypothesis of uneven fragmegration anticipates a growing appreciation along these lines because the contrary premise, that psychic comfort can only be realized by having a highest loyalty, is becoming increasingly antiquated. To be sure, people have long been accustomed to presuming that, in order to derive the psychic comfort they need through collective identities, they had to have a hierarchy of loyalties and that, consequently, they had to have a highest loyalty that could only be attached to a single collectivity. Such reasoning, however, is a legacy of the state system, of centuries of crises that made people feel they had to place nation-state loyalties above all others. It is a logic that long served to reinforce the predominance of the state as the "natural" unit of political organization and that probably reached new heights during the intense years of the cold war.

But if it is the case, as the foregoing analysis stresses, that conceptions of territoriality are in flux and that the failure of states to solve pressing problems has led to a decline in their capabilities and a loss of legitimacy, it follows that the notion that people must have a "highest loyalty" will also decline and give way to the development of multiple loyalties and an understanding that local, national, and transnational affiliations need not be mutually exclusive. For the reality is that human affairs are organized at all these levels for good reasons; people have needs that can only be filled by close-at-hand organizations and other needs that are best served by distant entities at the national or transnational level.

In addition, not only is an appreciation of the reality that allows for multiple loyalties and memberships likely to grow as the effectiveness of states and the salience of national loyalties diminish, but it also seems likely to widen as the benefits of the global economy expand and people become increasingly aware of the extent to which their well-being is dependent on events and trends elsewhere in the world. At the same time, the distant economic processes serving their needs are impersonal and hardly capable of advancing the need to share with others in a collective affiliation. This need was long served by the nation-state, but with fragmegrative dynamics having undermined the national level as a source of psychic comfort and with transnational entities seeming too distant to provide the psychic benefits of affiliation, the satisfactions to be gained through more close-at-hand affiliations are likely to seem ever more attractive.

THE STAKES

It seems clear that fragmegration has become an enduring feature of global life; it is also evident that globalization is not merely a buzzword, that it encompasses pervasive complexities and contradictions that have the potential both to enlarge and to degrade our humanity. In order to ensure that the enlargement is more prevalent than the degradation, it is important that people and their institutions become accustomed to the multiple dimensions and nuances as our world undergoes profound and enduring transformations. To deny the complexities and contradictions in order to cling to a singular conception of what globalization involves is to risk the many dangers that accompany oversimplification.

Spreading the Wealth

How 'globalization' is helping shift cash from rich nations to poor ones

First of a series

By Keith B. Richburg

Washington Post Foreign Service

ROSARIO, Philippines

Not so long go, Manila Bay was the life sustenance for Arnulfo Plocios and the other small fishermen in this struggling coastal village of stilted nipa huts and dirt-floored shanties, just on the edge of the capital. And then the fishing industry started dying.

Plocios now lives a Spartan existence in a one-room, tin-roofed squatter's shack with no electricity. The daily meal is rice and a little dried fish; the children's only toys are the shells that wash up on the shore. It is a life of little joy and little hope, the life of the poorest of the poor in the Philippines.

Like Plocios, Reynaldo S. Bernal is a small-scale fisherman, in nearby Naic town, and he too says he can barely make enough from the sea to survive. But something important has changed for Bernal: His family lives comfortably because two of Bernal's four daughters have jobs in the new, foreign-owned factories that have sprung up nearby. The sisters recently pooled their savings and surprised their parents with a new $1,500 Gold Star television; they shop for clothes in one of the province's new retail malls. Dinner at the Bernal house typically means meat and vegetables along with rice.

The gulf between Arnulfo Plocios and Reynaldo Bernal—between a dark one-room shack and a two-story house with a TV and an electric fan—is one measure of how the massive increase in world trade and private foreign investment in the post-Cold War world is affecting the lives of the world's poorest people.

More than any government program, more than any aid agency or any international bank, the rapid spread of free trade, free markets and investment across borders by private companies and individual investors—a phenomenon economists are calling "globalization"—is proving to be an effective weapon against poverty in many nations around the world and, in some places, arguably the most effective anti-poverty measure ever known.

Driven by the search for new customers and cheap and plentiful labor, companies large and small, from the United States, South Korea and other economic powerhouses, have been scouring long-neglected parts of the world that were ruled for most of this century by colonial powers or dictatorships that greatly restricted trade and foreign investment. Increasingly since 1990, they have been welcomed by democratic governments, or at least by pragmatic authoritarians who have opened up domestic markets, sold off state-owned industries, removed tariffs and trade barriers, and welcomed foreign investors.

The result has been an unprecedented flow of money from rich to poor nations: About $422 billion worth of new factories, supplies and equipment came into developing countries such as this one between 1988 and 1995, according to the United Nations. In 1995 alone, the flow of private capital into the Third World totaled $170 billion, a 200 percent increase over 1990.

▣

THE STREAM OF DOLLARS HAS LIFTED HUNDREDS of millions of people out of absolute poverty, according to the

World Bank and other international institutions. In the Philippines and other Asian countries, including China, Malaysia, Thailand and Indonesia, the pace of change has been breathtaking—one of the largest, fastest improvements in living standards ever recorded. Between 1987 and 1994 alone, according to the World Bank, the number of poor people in China decreased by more than 50 million.

But the effects of globalization have been neither consistent nor unambiguous. Large parts of the developing world, including most of Africa and Latin America, either have been bypassed by the flows of private money or have yet to see its effects among the poor. Many workers in developed countries, including the United States, have suffered a decline in living standards that they blame on the growth of trade with the Third World and the new factories there. And around the world, the gap between the richest people and the poorest is growing, even in those countries where poverty is decreasing.

According to the World Bank, the percentage of people categorized as the world's poorest—meaning those earning less than the equivalent of $1 a day—declined somewhat from 1987 to 1993 in East Asia, South Asia and North Africa. According to the United Nations Food and Agriculture Organization, there are 200 million fewer hungry people in the world than there were in 1975, though 840 million remain malnourished.

But, the World Bank says, poverty increased slightly in Latin America, the Caribbean and sub-Saharan Africa between 1987 and 1993.

Overall, the bank says, the percentage of the world's population living on less than $1 a day declined from 30 to 29 percent from 1987 to 1993, but, because of the increase in world population, the total number of people in that category continued to rise, to more than 1.3 billion.

Despite the mixed results, free markets and foreign investment have become the new orthodoxy of development, eagerly embraced around the developing world even by Communist governments in China, Cuba and Vietnam. "The whole international aid climate has changed, and now the name of the game is bringing in foreign investment," says Farooq Sobhan, the foreign secretary of Bangladesh. "We are competing for investors just as we are competing for markets. The cost of failure is too frightening to contemplate."

❂

BUT THE GLOBALIZATION TREND IS NOT WITHOUT critics, and a backlash against free trade and investment motivates political movements and trade unions in both rich and poor countries. Nationalists in the developing world argue that governments racing to attract foreign investment end up selling off national resources and crippling indigenous industries. In agricultural countries, opponents say the influx of foreign factories is destroying valuable farmland and traditional farming economies.

"Even as we are concerned with growth, we stress that having growth is not enough," says one publication of the Philippine Peasant Institute, a left-leaning nongovernmental group.

The group criticizes the Philippine government's "rush to embrace globalization" and instead advocates more investment in health care, education and developing self-sufficiency in agriculture.

While Third World dissidents argue that the trend primarily benefits the rich, North American critics, such as 1996 presidential candidates H. Ross Perot and Patrick J. Buchanan, say poor countries are benefiting at the expense of U.S. workers.

The skewed impact of foreign investment is clearly evident in countries such as the Philippines that receive large amounts of investment capital. Communities like Rosario that get foreign factories show the obvious benefits—new shopping areas and restaurants, and a boom in sales of consumer items such as television sets. And those lucky enough to get jobs at foreign factories—usually single young people with a high school education—can and do become better off economically.

"There's been a big increase in our livelihood, especially for our public school youth," says Jose del Rosario, 69, a retired teacher here in Cavite Province. "Before, they had no incentive to stay in school. Now they can be hired by the factories."

PHOTOS BY MICHAEL WILLIAMSON—THE WASHINGTON POST
The poor live alongside Manila's new wealth; residents of tin shacks have a view of fancy hotels.

But therein lies a central problem: The factories generally hire only workers with specific skills, or those who have attained at least a high school diploma. In Cavite Province, few in a largely poor population of farmers and fishermen have any chance of qualifying for one of the new jobs, although some, such as Bernal, can see their better-educated children make the transition to factory work.

Bernal, a soft-spoken man who, at 49, has silver streaks in his hair, is a proud man who does not like the idea of taking money from his children. "I didn't ask a single centavo of them," he boasts. But he realizes that between his family and the hard fate of other fishermen, such as Plocios, now lie the foreign factories—and his daughters' ability to work for them. "Maybe I'm just more okay than the others," he says.

The economic turning point for the Philippines—and for millions of families like Bernal's—came in 1992, when Fidel Ramos, the general who saved former president Corazon Aquino from a half-dozen coup attempts, won the presidency in his own right.

Ramos inherited a country wracked by endemic poverty, a legacy of Ferdinand Marcos's corruption-ridden 20-year dictatorship and of an economic backslide that turned a robust economy into what was viewed as "the sick man of Asia." With nearly 40 percent of the population living at or below the poverty line when he took office, Ramos developed a plan called Philippines 2000, whose cornerstone is to lure foreign investment to designated industrial enclaves, managed by the Export Processing Zone Authority.

◘

TO WIN OVER INVESTORS, RAMOS FIRST PERSUADED A reluctant legislature to approve laws making it easier for foreign firms to invest in the Philippines, then traveled the world as the country's salesman in chief.

Cavite is home to one of the oldest zone authority enclaves. The Marcos dictatorship launched it more than a decade ago by carving an area out of former farmland and setting it aside for industrial use.

But only recently, with the Ramos government's concerted efforts, has the zone taken off. Some 199 companies are now operating in the 682-acre zone, directly employing 50,000 workers. Most of the firms are foreign-owned or owned jointly with foreigners, with the biggest investors coming from South Korea and Taiwan, and a few from the United States.

JRA Philippines, which makes Jordache jeans for sale in U.S. department stores, transferred to Cavite from Manila three years ago, and the firm's experience makes clear the lure of this export-processing zone. "There's very little red tape in here," says Antonio Caballero, the company's director. "I got my import permit in half an hour. Same with my export permit."

JRA employs 350 workers, who are paid a base salary of about $6.30 a day, the minimum wage, plus a piece-rate incentive determined by how much they produce. With the incentive, the workers can earn as much as $480 a month, which is more than schoolteachers or government office workers

make. In addition, there is retirement pay, a health plan and other benefits, sports competitions and a Christmas raffle with 100 prizes.

Romeo Gil M. Santos, 38, is a production manager who considers himself lucky to have a job with JRA. "We have the social security, we have the 13th-month pay, we have accident insurance also," he says. The factory is so well known for good wages and benefits, he says, that the demand for jobs far exceeds the number of openings. "If, for example, we need five additional sewers, we'll put a notice up outside," he says. "We'll get 100 people standing outside the gates, because they know [we] pay well in this company."

Santos is typical of the JRA work force: He is not a native of Cavite Province, but of elsewhere on Luzon Island, and his family lives in Manila. During the workweek, he stays in one of the cramped boardinghouses outside the industrial zone's gates, going home only on weekends.

Santos is experienced in the garment business, also typical, having worked for another garment factory before transferring here. Workers without previous experience in the garment business have little chance of getting a job with JRA.

◘

ARMANDO RODRIGUEZ DOES NOT KNOW HOW TO operate machines. Rodriguez, 38, is a fisherman and owns a small boat. He remembers the days when bay fishing was good and he could earn about $120 a month in the peak season. But that was long ago, before the waters were over-fished and before factory pollutants forced fishermen to travel farther and farther from the shore for good hauls.

These days, Rodriguez says, "there are times when we have a good catch. But most of the time, not much." The Rodriguez family of five survives on what little money his wife can make selling dried fish in the marketplace—but when there's little catch, there's little to sell.

Rodriguez is ambivalent about the influx of foreign factories into the nearby export-processing zone. On the one hand, he understands the benefits for some, including his younger sister, Nerissa, 28. For four years she has worked at the Youngshin Korean electronics factory and uses her $6.30-a-day salary to support their aging mother, an unemployed younger brother and at least three nieces and nephews.

"It's beautiful!" Nerissa Rodriguez says of her job. She lives within walking distance of her brother's shack, in a spacious house with some modern luxuries, such as an electric fan. She complains that her salary is too low and not enough for food sometimes, though every two weeks, on payday, she treats herself and the children she supports to a container of Pringle's or Cheez'ums potato chips; she keeps the colorful, empty cans lined on a shelf like books in a library.

But Armando Rodriguez feels little effect of the export-processing plants on his own life. "The [zone authority] helps, because it is able to provide jobs, especially for my sister," he says. "But we small fisherfolk feel threatened, especially if the [authority] is going to expand and cover other areas. And because of the pollution."

For those whose sons or daughters, or they themselves, work in the zone, "it's great," he says. "But for the fishermen, it's not good."

Statistically speaking, Armando Rodriguez should be better off than he was a decade ago, and far better off than his father, who fished the waters off the Visayan Islands, about 250 miles south of here. Daily life is hard in Cavite, as it is all over the Philippines. But according to the numbers, poverty is declining, and even the poorest are said to be marginally better off than they were a decade ago, before the flood of new foreign investment.

According to a recent World Bank study on the Philippines, the proportion of people here living below the official poverty line was 59 percent in 1961; 39 percent in 1991; and 36 percent in 1994. But while the gains in the war on poverty have been substantial, the real story, according to the report, is the improved lot of those considered poor. Between 1961 and 1991, the bank found, the gap between the average income of the poor and the official poverty line closed by 40 percent.

"This means that although the proportion of the poor in the total population has declined modestly, the poor are better off than before, and the income disparities among the poor have declined noticeably since 1961," the bank report says.

The changes in the Philippines mirror the trend for areas such as East Asia and the Indian subcontinent that have received the lion's share of foreign investment; poverty is down overall, and the poor are markedly less poor than they were a few decades ago.

Infant mortality rates in East Asia dropped from 44 deaths per 1,000 live births in 1987 to 35 deaths per thousand in 1993; life expectancy rose from 67 to 68 years; and the number of people in poverty, which the bank defines as living on less than $1 a day, dropped from 573 million to 519 million, it reports.

As the living standards of the very poor have risen, so have their expectations. But so, too, has a sense among some poor that their lives are more difficult as well as more affluent.

Nelia Don, for example, knows something about foreign investment, living as she does here in Rosario, in the shadow of the sprawling industrial zone. She even worked briefly in a foreign factory, making children's dresses for less than minimum wage.

She left after six months because her pay was not enough to support herself, her two children and her husband, who works as a driver. A few weeks ago, her son, Renanta, was hired at one of the foreign factories. The zone "is good, especially for the young people to be able to have a job," she says. "But for a family, it's not so good, because the salary can't meet the needs of a family."

Don, the daughter of a fisherman, came to Cavite from Bicol, farther south, on a fishing boat 20 years ago, partly to find a better life in a province just outside Manila. But, she says, the relatives who stayed in Bicol have fared better, and the life of the poor two decades ago was easier and simpler than now. "Superficially, you can say people are better off [now] because of the material things they didn't used to have," she says. "But . . . people are very much in debt. Some families, yes, they have a TV, but they don't have food to eat for the day.

"It's difficult to compare, because family life before, and the kind of development we had to keep up with, was different," she says. "During my parents' time, there was no electricity. Now families have to put up with whatever is held up as this drumbeat of development, like [having] a TV or an electric fan. And if you don't have them, it means you are way behind civilization."

> "Globalization is not making the world less diverse and more equal. . . [True,] more and more people across the planet have become increasingly exposed to the amenities of the global marketplace, although mostly as permanent window-shoppers and silent spectators. The large majority of humankind, however, is rapidly being left outside and far behind."

Prosper or Perish?
Development in the Age of Global Capital

BLANCA HEREDIA

Dominant thinking about development today sees globalization as a matter of life or death for less developed countries. If embraced, it is argued, globalization will quickly propel developing nations into modernity and affluence; if resisted it will either crush them or throw them by the wayside. The matter, unfortunately, is not so clear and simple. The recent experience of much of sub-Saharan Africa shows that failure to catch the global train can prove deadly for underdeveloped countries. But a ride on that train does not provide a sure ticket to fast, stable, and equitable growth. Globalization may allow a few poor countries to leapfrog out of the backwater; but as the recent financial troubles in East Asia suggest, embracing global financial markets can also be treacherous, and costly.

The sharply unequal effects of globalized finance and production across and within developing countries stand in sharp contrast to the widely shared image of globalization as a formidable equalizer of tastes, incomes, outlooks, and lifestyles. Greater economic openness has made small parts of the developing world full-fledged members of the global village. But in many developing nations, globalized islands of prosperity are thriving alongside vast and growing expanses of economic stagnation and human deprivation. Nothing is more common for an upper-middle-class professional in a large emerging market such as Brazil or Mexico than to switch off the Internet and, before stepping out the door, to switch on a heightened awareness of his or her surroundings in order to survive the dangers of the darker side of the global village.

Rather than allowing developing nations to quickly catch up, globalization has greatly exacerbated inequalities among and within them. Its mixed record at century's end has dampened the euphoric optimism of the 1980s and given rise to a more sober mood. Advocates of globalization continue to see it as essentially good news for lagging economies. While still calling for greater openness, they have also begun to recognize globalization's many costs and admit to the importance of effective state institutions in allowing developing nations to actually profit from it. Most illustrative of this new mood is the World Bank's tempered rehabilitation of the centrality of the state in its latest *World Development Report*.

The belated recognition by free marketeers of the importance of effective state institutions in mediating globalization's impact on economic development—a bit ironic given their committed efforts throughout the 1980s to dismantle state institutions—is a welcome sign. Heightened exposure to world markets will only become a true lever of economic development in the presence of institutions able to mitigate market failures and manage the competitive challenges and domestic dislocations produced by openness. Contrary to conventional wisdom, however, the absence of the requisite institutional conditions is not necessarily self-correcting.

In countries lacking the institutional capacity to regulate markets and compensate losers, openness does not necessarily lead to economic stagnation or social collapse. Exposure to global markets can promote exclusionary types of growth based on

BLANCA HEREDIA *is a professor in the department of international studies and academic dean at the Center for Research and Teaching in Economics in Mexico City.*

dynamic export enclaves and highly profitable—albeit volatile—domestic financial markets. Supported rather than punished by failure-prone global financial markets, and buttressed by political arrangements that limit losers' ability to organize, these disjointed and exclusionary varieties of outward-oriented growth may persist for long periods of time.

Liberalization and globalization are unlikely to promote stable and equitable development. The type of growth and the kind of society produced by economic openness hinge more on the number and the quality of a given nation's institutional resources. The problem for less developed countries is that exposure to unbridled international financial markets will not automatically generate the correct—let alone the best—institutions and may make efforts to assemble and pay for them increasingly costly and difficult.

GLOBALIZATION LAID BARE

Among the images associated with globalization, the most popular portrays it as a worldwide process of converging incomes and lifestyles driven by ever larger international flows of goods, images, capital, and people. In throwing hamburgers, money, and television shows into the same global hodgepodge, this conventional and immensely seductive view fails to single out what is truly distinctive about globalization.

The basic engine behind the emergence of a globalized world economy lies not in goods, people, money, and ideas becoming increasingly and similarly transportable across national frontiers. It lies, rather, in capital becoming historically more portable and more internationally mobile than anything else. Capital, moreover, is not only winning the international mobility race: it is also largely driving the globalization of all the rest.

Successive waves of financial deregulation in advanced economies along with new information and communication technologies helped power the dizzying growth experienced by international finance over the last 30 years. Initially fueled by the dramatic expansion of world trade and by growing competition among United States, European, and Japanese firms for one another's domestic markets, financial deregulation accelerated in the 1970s in the midst of the petrodollar boom, leading to a truly phenomenal resurrection of international finance. Cross-border transactions in equities and bonds in major advanced economies, for example, jumped from less than 10 percent of GDP in 1980 to well over 100 percent in 1995. Relative to world GDP, total foreign direct investment (FDI) flows doubled between 1980 and 1994. The most explosive growth has occurred in the foreign exchange market, where the average *daily* turnover surged from about $200 billion in the mid-1980s to around $1.2 trillion in 1995—approximately 85 percent of total world reserves.

The growth of international finance has radically reshaped the structural and institutional makeup of the world economy. Few areas have been left untouched. Capital mobility and technological change have allowed production to become more transnationally integrated, which has introduced major changes in international trade. The share of world commerce channeled and managed by global corporations has spiraled upward. As a result, trade and investment have ceased to be substitutes for one another and have become mutually reinforcing. The mounting importance of intrafirm trade has contributed to the continued expansion of world commerce. Since intrafirm trade is less sensitive than arm's length trade to exchange rate movements as well as to a variety of trade policy instruments, the ability of governments to shape trade flows has declined.

Globalized financial markets have greatly heightened the structural power of capital holders and have drastically reduced the policy options open to governments. Room for sustaining, let alone building, the kinds of extensive welfare systems that allowed small open economies in Europe to reconcile high trade openness with domestic social stability during the postwar period has dramatically narrowed. The same holds for the activist industrial and financial policy strategies employed by the miracle economies of East Asia from the 1960s through the 1980s. Thus, with untrammeled capital mobility the highly interventionist credit allocation schemes deployed by the South Korean government during the era of super-high growth have become unworkable and unthinkable.

The newest developmental orthodoxy of free markets and sound money has yet to prove its merits. Ever more fierce competition for financial resources and export markets can help limit monetary and fiscal folly and may well generate important efficiency and productivity gains. But the kind of growth promoted by the disciplining embrace of global markets is not necessarily high, stable, balanced, and equitable; unfortunately, not all good things go together. A country—such as Mexico during the first half of the 1990s—may open up but then experience slow, polarizing, and unstable growth. Or take Thailand, furiously embracing free and open finance in the early 1990s only to find itself saddled in 1997 with a banking system on the brink of collapse, the prospect of slower growth, and no option but to cut back on investment as well as on attempts to reduce poverty or upgrade human capital.

As United States Treasury Secretary Robert Rubin kindly reminded us during his appearance this September in Hong Kong at the IMF-World Bank joint annual meeting, the root of the recent financial malaise in East Asia—and the root of all the troubles spurred by globalization across the developing world, for that matter—may well lie in poor nations not opening up deep and fast enough. The problem with the "more openness, less government intervention" solution is that it pushes the issue, once again, into the unknown future. Judging from the record so far, what more of the same is likely to mean for developing nations is less and less room for building or sustaining the kinds of institutions that are necessary to ensure that the developmental benefits of globalization materialize.

INEQUALITIES WITHOUT. . .

Developing countries today are a much more heterogeneous group than at the beginning of the postwar period. Globalization is not helping them become more equal; the poorest are not catching up the fastest. Instead, globalization is making the differences between developing countries increasingly deep and wide.

Contrary to the predictions of neoclassical economic theory, the freeing up of international capital flows is not benefiting countries where capital is most scarce. The lion's share of private international financial flows has continued to go to capital-abundant nations. In 1995, for example, 65 percent of FDI inflows went to the developed world. The bulk of the recent growth of capital inflows into developing countries, moreover, has been concentrated in a handful of relatively rich emerging markets.

Still, international financial flows to developing countries have grown significantly in recent years; their composition has also changed. Throughout most of the postwar period, private foreign financing for developing nations was relatively small and tended to be heavily dominated by FDI. In the 1970s,

The lion's share of private international financial flows has continued to go to capital-abundant nations.

international bank lending to less advanced countries resumed on a grand scale, but after the global debt crisis fell sharply. Starting in the late 1980s, and fueled by deregulation in the North as well as by major episodes of financial liberalization and privatization in many developing countries, FDI and especially portfolio investment flows underwent a formidable expansion. The share of world FDI going to developing countries jumped from an average of 24 percent between 1983 and 1987 to 32 percent in 1995. Equity and bond flows grew even faster, rising from 0.5 percent of GDP in 1983 to 1989 to between 2 and 4 percent from 1994 to 1996.

The developing countries' expanded access to international private financing has been unevenly distributed. Between 1989 and 1992, for example, 72 percent of total FDI flows to developing countries went to only 10 countries (China, Mexico, Malaysia, Argentina, Thailand, Indonesia, Brazil, Nigeria, Venezuela, and South Korea). The distribution of portfolio investment flows has been even more heavily skewed. Between 1989 and 1993, only 10 countries received 90 percent of the total gross portfolio investments flowing to the developing world (Mexico, Brazil, Argentina, Hungary, South Korea, Greece, Turkey, China, Venezuela, and Thailand).

The poorest countries have seen little profit from the recent boom in international financial flows, while suffering a great deal from major cuts and reorientations in aid flows from advanced nations. Net official development assistance over the past decade has stagnated in terms of value and has declined as a share of donors' GDP, reaching in 1994 its lowest level since 1973. Given the strong reorientation in favor of disaster relief and peacekeeping operations, aid flows for supporting economic development have actually contracted. Meanwhile, and largely due to deteriorating terms of trade since the early 1980s, aid dependence among least developed nations has risen sharply in the past few years.

The gains for those developing countries that have benefited from greater access to international financial resources have come at a significant price. International financial integration has entailed an important loss of policy autonomy and has increased host countries' vulnerabilities to external financial shocks. The rapidly growing importance of highly mobile and liquid portfolio investment flows has proved, in this sense, especially challenging.

Heightened dependence on larger volumes of short-term external capital flows has vastly complicated monetary and exchange rate management and has severely limited governments' ability to use exchange rate and monetary policy in ways conducive to growth in the real economy. Globalized finance has also contributed to the increasing fragility of domestic financial systems in developing countries. Since 1980, more than 100 developing nations have experienced serious banking crises. The public cost of these crises has been extremely high. In Mexico, for example, the 1995 collapse of the banking system—which came in the wake of fast financial liberalization—has cost the Mexican public around 12 percent of GDP.

Much of the cost of heightened exposure to global financial markets has resulted from the lack of appropriate regulatory capacities as well as domestic institutions able to ensure the sound use and the proper management of larger volumes of external financial flows. Much of it, though, has stemmed from the tendency of global financial markets to wait until the crisis hits to impose their discipline stringently—and then to impose it with a vengeance. In short, domestic government failures have certainly magnified the costs of financial openness. Global market failures—such as the propensity of global investors to engage in euphoric rides followed by equally intense panic attacks—have also been a major contributor.

. . .AND INEQUALITIES WITHIN

Globalization has exacerbated differences not only among developing nations, but also within them. Heightened exposure to global markets has magnified and multiplied domestic inequalities. It is true that in a handful of countries, liberalization and expanded access to global finance have resulted in significant advances in poverty reduction. The most notable among this select group is China, where over the past 15 years poor people as a share of total population fell from 33 percent to 10 percent. The bulk of the developing world has not been as fortunate.

Since the 1980s, poverty has grown in absolute terms throughout developing countries and has increased in both absolute and relative terms in much of Africa and Latin America. In the latter, after a sharp rise in the 1980s, the proportion of poor people started to slowly decrease from the early 1990s onward, but in only two countries: Chile and Colombia. In the rest of the region poverty has continued to grow and, if current trends persist, will

continue to do so in the next 10 years at the rate of two more poor people per minute.

The rush to free markets and openness has also coincided with increasing inequality throughout the developing world. Even in Southeast Asia's fastest-growing economies, income differentials have been widening slowly since the early 1990s. It is, again, in Latin America where inequalities have recently become larger and most glaring. Income inequality has grown significantly in the region as a whole over the past few decades. In 1995, 15 of the region's 17 countries had levels of income inequality exceeding those normally associated with their level of development.

High levels of poverty and extreme income inequality are not new to Latin America. Economic theory would predict, though, that greater openness should have helped alleviate both: trade openness by promoting labor-intensive export growth and financial openness by expanding the pool of capital available for productive investment, especially in those sectors and regions where capital is scarce. But extremely fast-paced trade and financial liberalization in Latin America has not helped reduce poverty or inequality.

Latin America's faster and deeper economic liberalization has thus coincided with a significant widening of income differentials as well as increasing poverty. As a result, initially large social deformities in many Latin American countries have become, over the past decade, larger still. In much of the region, the globalizing 1980s and 1990s have brought more Mercedes and more homeless children to the streets; they have also brought more Norwegian salmon, more youngsters involved in crime, more Nike sneakers to dream about, and more violence in and outside the home. In the midst of growing poverty and inequality, life, even for those fully wired into the global mall, has become much more harsh.

Other aspects of Latin America's recent economic performance have also left much to be desired. Despite more radical liberalization than in other developing regions, between 1990 and 1995 Latin America's average annual GDP grew 3.2 percent; in South Asia and East Asia the corresponding figures were 4.6 percent and 10.3 percent, respectively. More important, average total factor productivity between 1989 and 1994 has, with the exception of Chile and Argentina, fallen in all major Latin American economies compared to the period between 1950 and 1980, and has remained lower than in East Asia.

In most Latin American countries, the resumed growth of recent years has been based in a very small number of sectors, regions, and firms. The two most dynamic sectors have been exports and finance, but even here the number of winners has been small. Though with important cross-national variations, export growth has tended to be highly concentrated and heavily dominated by transnational firms. In 1995, for example, the share in total exports of the top 25 exporting firms—many of them transnationals—was 44 percent in Argentina, 26 percent in Brazil, and 56 percent in Mexico.

Foreign financial inflows and domestic financial sectors, on the other hand, have experienced impressive, if unstable, growth. Latin American stock markets have grown rapidly in the past few years. Between 1990 and 1995, market capitalization as a percentage of GDP jumped from 2.3 to 13.5 in Argentina, from 3.4 to 21.8 in Brazil, and from 13.2 to 36.3 in Mexico. In contrast to Southeast Asia, where stock exchange growth has been accompanied by a significant increase in the number of participating firms, the number of listed domestic companies has remained remarkably small in most Latin American countries. Particularly noteworthy is the contrast between Indonesia, with almost 8,000 listed firms in 1995, and Brazil, with only 543. The benefits of greater access to foreign financial funds have also been unevenly shared. In Mexico, 10 firms received over 50 percent of total foreign investment in equities in 1993.

The most important exception to these regional economic trends is Chile. After the 1982 economic collapse associated with the dogmatic monetarism employed during the initial years of General Augusto Pinochet's dictatorship, the Chilean government adopted a more pragmatic economic policy approach. Most of the structural reforms pushed through in the 1970s—trade liberalization and privatization—were left in place, but a series of important adjustments was introduced. These included controls on short-term financial inflows, fiscal policies oriented to raising domestic savings, pension system reform, large poverty alleviation programs, and a flexible exchange rate regime that was used to maintain a high real exchange rate.

Through this mix of openness, moderately interventionist financial and exchange rate policies, and compensatory schemes for the most vulnerable, Chile has managed to combine over the last 10 years relatively high and stable growth rates that have averaged 6 percent annually, along with important advances in poverty reduction. While Chile's recent performance has been less spectacular than that of East Asia's superachievers, its record remains significantly brighter than that of its more financially liberal, more overvaluation-prone, and less welfare proactive regional neighbors.

INSTITUTIONS AND TYPES OF GROWTH

Globalization is not making the world less diverse and more equal. A growing but still small part of the world's population is becoming more similar in what it eats, buys, wears, and thinks. And more and more people across the planet have become increasingly exposed to the amenities of the global marketplace, although mostly as permanent window-shoppers and silent spectators. The large majority of humankind, however, is rapidly being left outside and far behind.

The drastic unevenness of globalization's effects among less developed countries can be traced to major cross-national differences in preexisting social and economic conditions as well as to the depth and breadth of recent market-oriented reforms. Crucial in accounting for the widely diverse kinds of growth spurred by globalization are the differing state capacities and institutional resources through which these countries have dealt with the manifold challenges and opportunities posed by globalized capital.

The bulk of the developing world has not been as fortunate [as China].

The strongest message coming from international financial institutions, development agencies, and professional economists over the past 15 years is that state intervention is bad for economic growth. Though views on the issue have become more tempered and balanced in recent years, the central idea remains firmly in place: reducing state intervention is the most effective and efficient way to kindle growth. Sophisticated modeling and endless repetition of this dictum notwithstanding, recent experience suggests that matters are much more complicated.

Differences in the size of state intervention (as measured by central government spending as a percentage of GDP) are not very good at explaining variations in rates of economic growth or levels of domestic welfare. Between 1980 and 1994, extensive state intervention in the Middle East and North Africa was associated with poor growth, while lower—though still very high—state intervention produced an even worse growth record in sub-

Saharan Africa. During this same period, government intervention in Latin America—which was smaller than its counterpart in East Asia—did not lead to higher growth rates or higher levels of welfare. The reverse turned out to be the case.

It is not the size of the government that appears to determine the different cross-national growth trajectories of developing nations in the recent past; more important than size in mediating the growth and welfare effects of globalization have been the large variations in the type and quality of government intervention. In accounting for why liberalization and globalization have led to unstable, slow, and exclusionary growth in some poor countries, high and inequitable growth in others, and extremely rapid, stable, and widely shared growth in a small number of developing nations, one must move beyond the quantity of state intervention and focus on its quality instead.

Classifications of state institutional capacities and resources can easily get complicated, as can typologies of different kinds and qualities of economic growth. The typology of state functions provided by the 1997 *World Development Report* offers a useful first attempt at addressing the issue. The report singles out three basic types of state functions: minimal (the provision of pure public goods, such as law and order, property rights, and macroeconomic stability); intermediate (interventions to address market failures such as externalities and monopolies); and activist (coordination of market activity and redistribution of assets).

What does this typology tell us about recent economic performance in developing countries? We can make the following preliminary observations. Countries where the state was able to fulfill all three functions—notably the star performers in East Asia—did best. For them, and only for them, the winds of global openness have delivered the full bundle of goodies: very high, very stable, and widely shared growth. In those countries where the state managed to fulfill only minimal and intermediate functions—Chile, for example—growth has been high and stable and has been accompanied, if not by a lessening of inequality, at least by a signif-

icant reduction in poverty. In those developing nations, such as most of Latin America, where greater openness has been managed by states that fulfill only minimal functions—and unevenly so at that—growth has been slower, less stable, and much more inequitable.

THE CHALLENGES

The good news coming out of the admittedly sketchy picture that has been presented is that focusing on sustaining or enhancing state institutional capacities can make a huge difference in allowing developing countries to profit from closer international economic integration. The bad news?

First, following the World Bank's advice to states—namely, restricting state intervention to those areas in which state capabilities exist—is unlikely to make developing nations richer and nicer places to live in. Given the limited state capabilities in most developing countries, and based on the record so far, following the bank's recommendation will tend to promote only the least desirable kinds of growth (as in Bolivia, where profound market reform during the 1980s led to 1.7 percent annual average growth between 1985 and 1994).

Second, continued fast-paced liberalization and globalization are likely to make it more difficult for states to maintain or acquire the capacity to translate openness into an effective springboard into greater prosperity for most of a country's people. Further financial deregulation in the absence of effective international discipline and domestic regulation could be especially costly. An ever more frantic competition among nations to retain and attract private investors would not necessarily benefit anybody except private globalized investors themselves. Rather than promoting a race to the top, more unbridled competition for mobile funds may well fuel a race to the bottom in regulatory standards and fiscal burdens on capital. If unchecked, such a race is likely to severely erode the fiscal and institutional capacities required to allow developing countries not only to grow, but to grow in ways that allow them to become more livable places.

The false promise of globalization.

AN ILLUSION FOR OUR TIME

By Peter Beinart

"Iinternational finance has become so interdependent and so interwoven with trade and industry that ... political and military power can in reality do nothing.... These little recognized facts, mainly the outcome of purely modern conditions (rapidity of communication creating a greater complexity and delicacy of the credit system), have rendered the problems of modern international politics profoundly and essentially different from the ancient." These words come from perhaps the best-selling book on international relations ever written. That book, *The Great Illusion*, sold more than a million copies in seventeen languages. Its author, Norman Angell, was knighted, and won the Nobel Peace Prize. In the years following the book's publication, close to 100 organizations arose to spread its message: that the world had entered a new era in which economic interdependence made war unthinkable. *The Great Illusion* was published in 1910.

On March 20, 1997, *New York Times* columnist Thomas Friedman wrote that we have entered a "new world of globalization—a world in which the integration of financial networks, information and trade is binding the globe together and shifting power from governments to markets." In his December 8, 1996, column, Friedman wondered whether "a country, by integrating with the global economy, opening itself up to foreign investment and empowering its consumers, permanently restricts its capacity for troublemaking and promotes gradual democratization and widening peace." And on February 14, 1996, in a column on the impending Russian elections, he wrote: "Sure, a Communist or radical populist in the Kremlin would be worrying. But their room for maneuver would be constricted—much more than we realize and much, much more than they realize. Russia today is connected with the global economy."

The conventional wisdom about post-cold war American foreign policy is that there is no conventional wisdom—no unifying theory that traces disparate phenomena to a single source. But one candidate for conceptual preeminence may be breaking from the pack, and it is Friedman's candidate, globalization. The idea is that technology has led to unprecedented and irreversible economic integration among countries. The only way governments can survive is to do what global business demands: observe the rule of law at home, and act peacefully abroad. For the United States that means abiding by the imperatives of the global economy and informing others that they must do the same. It is a foreign policy vision for a world where politics barely matters.

And it is a vision that the Clinton administration has embraced. On June 19, in a speech prior to the summit of the eight industrial powers in Denver, President Clinton said, "Protectionism is simply not an option because globalization is irreversible." On June 6, in a speech arguing that trading with China would make it less dangerous, National Security Adviser Samuel Berger explained that "the fellow travelers of the new global economy—computers and modems, faxes and photocopiers, increased contacts and binding contracts—carry with them the seeds of change." A couple of years ago an unnamed State Department official told *The Washington Post*: "People who trade don't fight. They have shared interests in a way that autarchic economies do not."

The globalization doctrine builds on an idea popular in the early years of the Clinton administration: that American foreign policy should seek to widen the international community of democracies because democracies don't go to war with one another. But it goes a crucial step further. The earlier idea implied American pressure on democratization's behalf. For that reason, as the Clintonites discovered when they tried to apply it to China, it provoked real conflicts. The new doctrine, by contrast, does not require the United States to levy sanctions and create diplomatic rows. Globalization—powered by the inexorable march of technology and trade—will do democratization's work more effectively than State Department pressure ever could. America need simply warn renegades that if they menace neighbors or torture dissidents, they will be disciplined by the all-powerful global market. Foreign policy becomes an exercise not in coercion but in education.

This is globalization's appeal to a country both obligated to keep the world safe and increasingly reluctant to do so. It allows American elites to imagine that the security won for this country in struggle is now protected by a force both unstoppable and benign. And it allows them to imagine that rising and aggrieved powers will embrace a world governed by free trade as well, even though it locks them into a position of political and military subservience. Globalization is the narcissism of a superpower in a one superpower world. It allows America to look at the world and see its own contentment and its own fatigue. And it has provided the same false comfort to lone superpowers in the past. That's where Norman Angell comes in.

It is obvious to any casual observer of international affairs that today's world is far more interdependent than ever before. But it is not true. International trade and investment have indeed been increasing since the 1950s. Yet after four decades of growing interdependence, the world is just now becoming as economically integrated as it was when Norman Angell wrote *The Great Illusion*. According to Paul Bairoch of the Center for International Economic History at the University of Geneva, merchandise exports by the industrial countries were 13 percent of their Gross Domestic Product in 1913. In 1992, they were 14 percent.

As for financial integration, Bairoch estimates that by 1993 Foreign Direct Investment as a percentage of gross product had risen to roughly the level of 1914: around 11 percent for the industrial countries. A more elaborate study by the U.S. Trust Company's Robert Zevin, which examines financial integration by measuring "cross-market correlations between asset price movements" concludes that "every available descriptor of financial markets in the late nineteenth and early twentieth centuries suggests that they were more fully integrated than they were before or have been since."

So Norman Angell was right that he lived in a highly interdependent world. He considered this the result of technology, of "the incredible progress of rapidity in communication." All around him he saw technology forging a global economy that forced states to fit a single, fiscally responsible mold. "Just note what is taking place in South America," he wrote. "States in which [debt] repudiation was a commonplace of everyday politics have of recent years become as stable and as respectable as the City of London." "[C]ircumstances stronger than ourselves are pushing us," he insisted, and for those countries that resisted, "punishment is generally swift and sure."

But Angell's interest in the global economy was not merely descriptive. He sought to convince his fellow Britons, some of whom feared the outbreak of war with Germany, that the German threat was an illusion. After all, Britain and Germany were probably the two most economically interdependent nations on earth. Germany was Britain's second largest trading partner, and Germany sold more goods to the United Kingdom than to any other country. And even trade doesn't reveal the true depth of Anglo-German economic ties, since the City of London largely financed German industry. A Committee of Imperial Defence study noted that, since Lloyds insured the German merchant marine, it would have to pay the Kaiser for any lost ships, even if they were sunk by the British navy.

Under such circumstances, Angell argued, the key to preventing war was awakening people to their self-interest. He rejected suggestions that Britain contain Germany through military preparation and balance-of-power diplomacy. Any German penchant for aggression, he insisted, was "founded upon illusions which she would be bound sooner or later to shed." To speed up this inevitable process, Britons should forge ever deeper economic links with Germany while teaching people in both countries that war was self-defeating.

In Britain, a country ideologically committed to free trade, Angell's educational campaign struck a chord within the ruling elite. Of the 100 societies which sprang up to do the job, the most prominent included former Conservative Party Prime Minister Arthur Balfour, and Lord Esher, chairman of the Committee of Imperial Defence. If Germany was challenging Britain's industrial supremacy, Britain remained the world's undisputed financial capital, and London's powerful financiers more than counterbalanced the few farmers and manufacturers who wanted tariffs against German imports. Even Benjamin Disraeli, whose Conservative Party had fought for the Corn Laws in the mid-nineteenth century, announced that the Tories were now free traders. "Musty phrases of mine forty years ago," he said, were no longer relevant.

The British elite's enthusiasm for globalization implicitly rested on their country's privileged international position. Britain had been the world's leading military and economic power for close to a century. The relatively open trading system of the late nineteenth century, of which Britain was the chief beneficiary, was sustained by the protective power of the British navy. But Britain's military primacy had gone unchallenged for so long that many in Britain had lost sight of its importance. So Norman Angell, and others in the British establishment, saw globalization not as a fact of politics based on a security system, but as a fact of technology, independent of politics.

In Germany, however, which had been recently weak, divided, and at war, security concerns didn't seem so irrelevant. From Berlin, globalization did not look like a panacea; it looked like British hegemony. Britain's navy controlled the waterways on which German ships traveled, and Britain, through its empire, controlled many of the raw materials Germany's burgeoning industries needed. Britain saw the continent's division as evidence of a stable international order. Germany, which believed it deserved a central European sphere of influence, saw that division as a sign of British domination.

Quite aware that Britain had industrialized before the era of free trade, many Germans regarded London's continual preaching about the immorality of protectionism as rank hypocrisy. Starting in the 1870s, German governments began protecting their industries behind a tariff wall. As Paul Kennedy shows in *The Rise of the Anglo-German Antagonism*, Germany's reigning ideology was mercantilism. Its leaders knew that trade could be a means to wealth and power. But they also believed that, for a rising power beset by deep social conflicts, unregulated free trade could be a threat to political stability and governmental control. While Norman Angell followed in the tradition of Adam Smith and Richard Cobden, Germany in the late nineteenth century saw a revival of interest in the works of Friedrich List, who wrote in his 1841 classic *The National System of Political Economy* that the ideology of free trade was a "clever device that when anyone has attained the summit of greatness, he kicks away the ladder by which he has climbed up, in order to deprive others of the means of climbing up after him."

For Germany to climb up, it would have to be strong enough to integrate with the world economy on its terms. So while many Britons argued that globalization was rendering military power irrelevant, the German elite believed globalization made it all the more crucial. Concerned that its trade routes were at the mercy of the British navy, Germany embarked in 1897 on a massive ship-building program. This naval challenge pushed Britain gradually closer to France and Russia, and set in place the alliance system that would turn a local squabble into World War I.

The United States in 1997 differs from Britain in 1897 in obvious ways. Its empire is informal, not formal; its democracy is mature, not embryonic. But its elite shares turn-of-the-century Britain's fascination with economic interdependence. Today, as then, globalization suggests a world in which the imperatives of economic integration overwhelm those of politics. And in today's America, as in Norman Angell's Britain, there is a strong, intuitive sense that globalization is connected to wondrous new developments in communications technology: satellites, faxes, the Internet.

But if technological progress by itself produced integration, globalization would have risen steadily during the twentieth century. It has not. The period between 1914 and 1950 saw a revolution in both transportation and communication. The automobile assembly line was introduced in 1913; the first transatlantic flight took place in 1919; and the first commercial radio broadcast was in 1920. But during that time interdependence decreased dramatically. The reasons, of course, were World War I, World War II, and the economic depression in between. The era's technological breakthroughs did not prevent the rise of aggressive, expansionist ideologies in Germany and Japan. And those forces swamped the supposedly inevitable trend toward a more peaceful, globalized world.

Similarly, the rise in global integration since World War II stems more from politics than from technology. In particular, it stems from two institutional shifts, both made possible by American political and military power. The first was the establishment of a liberal trading and monetary regime in the 1940s. America built the regime—whose key components were the International Monetary Fund, the General Agreement on Tariffs and Trade, the Marshall Plan, and the American nuclear umbrella—both because free trade was in the U.S.'s self-interest, and because the U.S. wanted to help Western Europe and Japan recover so they would not fall prey to communism. Economic integration grew because the GATT reduced tariffs, the International Monetary Fund stabilized world currencies, and the Marshall plan rebuilt European industry. From 1950 to 1975, trade among the industrial countries grew twice as fast as their economies.

In 1974, the United States made the second key decision: it abolished its controls on the movement of foreign capital. This decision, like the first, can be traced to American self-interest. Declining U.S. productivity had spawned a trade deficit, which was pushing the dollar down and threatening the fixed exchange rate system. Abandoning both the fixed exchange rate and capital controls allowed the dollar to drop to its natural level, and let in the foreign capital America needed to finance its trade deficit. The decision was possible because Western Europe and Japan had grown strong enough that they no longer needed fixed exchange rates to stabilize their economies and fend off communism. Deregulating its capital market cemented the United States' position as the world's financial center, and it eventually forced America's competitors to end their capital control as well.

To be sure, by the time America scrapped capital controls, advances in telecommunications technology had already rendered them less effective. But as Eric Helleiner of York University in Toronto argues in *States and the Reemergence of Global Finance*, the United States could have restored their efficacy had it wanted to. It did not, and the result was an explosion of globalized finance that dwarfs even the rise in trade. In the late 1970s, the industrial nations invested $34 billion a year overseas. By 1990, that figure had reached $214 billion.

So we too live in a highly interdependent world. The problem is the widespread American belief that economic integration, because it stems from technology, is both all-powerful and politically neutral—that is, not identified with the interests of any one country. This leads to soothing assumptions about the restraints the global market imposes on potential aggressors, restraints that only exist if the potential aggressors also see globalization as both inevitable and benign.

Consider the way globalization looks from Beijing. Americans often see East Asia as the vanguard of the new economics-dominated world. But Japan, South Korea, and Taiwan all emerged as major world traders and investors under the protection of the American military. The U.S. Navy guarantees the South and East China Sea trade routes on which all three rely. Each has profited from access to U.S. markets, access granted in part to foster prosperity, and thereby to ensure they remained on the American side during the cold war. The United States has promoted growth and economic integration in East Asia, but as part of a broader American strategy to prevent any Asian power from gaining regional hegemony.

If Americans sometimes forget this, the leadership in Beijing—which seeks exactly that regional sphere of influence—does not. What Washington calls globalization, Beijing calls American hegemony, and this difference of perspective helps explain why China is violating globalization's core imperative. Like Imperial Germany before World War I, China's links to the world economy are making its leaders more interested in the accumulation and projection of military power, not less.

As Princeton's Kent E. Calder wrote last year in *Foreign Affairs*, China's growing international trade has led to a tremendous boom in manufacturing, and in air and car travel. This in turn has made China a net importer of energy. Shell China Petroleum Development estimates that by 2015 Beijing will need to import as much oil as the United States does today. This is one reason China has in recent years tried hard to establish a sphere of influence in the South and East China Seas. In January 1995, the Chinese navy forced a group of Filipino fisherman off Mischief Reef, part of the disputed Spratly Islands. The Spratlys contain considerable oil reserves, and sit astride the South China Sea, through which Middle Eastern oil travels on its way to China (as well as to Japan, South Korea, and Taiwan). In December 1995, Chinese ships were spotted encroaching on the Senkaku Islands (the Chinese call them the Diauyutai) in the East China Sea. The Senkakus, claimed by both China and Japan, are also oil-rich and near key international shipping routes.

Just as China's growing economic interdependence may foster, rather than restrain, military aggression, many of Beijing's economic reformers are also its biggest hawks. The People's Liberation Army, which has grown more powerful within the political hierarchy since the Tiananmen Square massacre, strongly favors economic reform. In his book *China After Deng Xiaoping*, Hong Kong journalist Willy Wo-Lap Lam estimates that there are perhaps 50,000 PLA-owned businesses, in which foreigners have invested over $1 billion. But Lam also shows that the army is one of the most expansionist elements within the Chinese leadership. The PLA pushed the government to be aggressive in the Spratlys, and in November 1992, a group of retired generals reportedly wrote Jiang Zemin and Li Peng a letter demanding a "stern reaction" to American and French sales of fighter jets to Taiwan. In early twentieth-century Germany, many industrialists encouraged their government's challenge to British naval dominance. In China, the industrialists and the admirals are often one and the same.

According to the theory of globalization, it is irrational for China to keep demanding that the U.S. Navy vacate the South China Sea. After all, it is there protecting free trade, which benefits everyone. But to China today, as to Germany in 1900, free trade looks less like a universal good, and more like the expression of a hegemon's self-interest. From Beijing's perspective, it is dangerous to have the U.S. military patrolling its trade routes—not necessarily because China fears the U.S. will cut off access to its key imports, but because it fears America might use the threat to force China to acquiesce in the total opening of its market (something China was forced to do in the nineteenth century).

To see how "American" free trade can look, consider Beijing's relations with multinational corporations. In America it has become fashionable to say that today's multinationals have no national identity. On this view, it is self-defeating for the Chinese to insist, as they do, that, as a condition of selling in China, multinationals transfer technology to Chinese companies. After all, this raises the cost of imports for the Chinese consumer.

But the men who run Beijing don't think multinational corporations lack a national identity. They see them as the agents of the United States and its allies, which is not altogether unreasonable. In 1991, only 2 percent of the corporate directors of American multinationals were non-American. As Louis W. Pauly of the University of Toronto and Simon Reich of the University of Pittsburgh have shown, multinationals are deeply tied to their home countries in corporate style, ownership, and the production of their highest value components. Beijing knows this, and it fears Western multinationals will not give it the knowledge it needs to move from making toys to making microchips unless China insists on technology transfer as the price of increased trade.

China's rulers are mercantilists. They believe economic engagement can help make their country powerful, but they also believe unregulated commerce can sow instability. They know tariffs played a key role in the industrialization of the United States and Japan, and they suspect that American insistence on free trade today is a clever attempt to prevent China from adopting the same tested formula for national greatness. That's what Beijing hears when American officials say that free trade will undermine Beijing's current authoritarian regime and foment a democratic revolution.

This raises a question that Thomas Friedman and other globalization enthusiasts seldom bother to ask: Why is globalization such an attractive theory in this country at this time? The answer is that the U.S. is in a position only one other country has known in the last two centuries. Like Victorian Great Britain, the U.S. today is the world's lone superpower. Its old rivals are dead, and its new ones are not yet born. Its security is so assured that it suspects military power has become irrelevant. And so America can afford to dream of a world without conflict, of an end to History.

But globalization reflects not only America's success. It also bespeaks its quiet fears. It is possible to be the world's only superpower and also be in decline. That decline has been impressively obscured in the past decade, by the Soviet Union's collapse and by economic troubles in competitors like Germany, France, and Japan. Most of all, it has been obscured by American industry's return to international preeminence over the past decade. But from a long-term perspective, America's economic decline relative to other nations is indisputable. In 1950, the United States represented 39 percent of world GNP. In 1995, it represented 26 percent. In 1953, the United States accounted for 45 percent of the world's manufacturing output. In 1990, it accounted for 22 percent.

This decline in global economic dominance is making it harder for the United States to sustain its apparatus of political and military power, even though the challenges to that apparatus are currently quite minor. America has recently closed a number of embassies and consulates. According to a recent study by UNICEF, it now ranks lowest among twenty-one industrial countries in the percentage of GNP it devotes to foreign aid. The percentage of World Bank lending underwritten by the U.S. has fallen by half since the institution was founded. Between 1989 and 1995, America's troop strength in the Pacific fell 15 percent.

To the superpower's worry that it cannot maintain its security system with declining resources, globalization offers a reassuring answer: it isn't the security system that keeps the peace, but rather the global market. And while military power waxes and wanes, the expansion of the global market—as Thomas Friedman and Bill Clinton never tire of saying—is unstoppable. American foreign policy can content itself with helping globalization along, and with reminding other countries of the restraints it imposes.

This is the story of the Clinton administration's policy toward China. In 1993, Bill Clinton took office threatening sanctions to force China to be less repressive at home and less aggressive abroad. In 1994, Warren Christopher took this message with him on a trip to Beijing, and was publicly humiliated. America's allies and American business rejected any effort to isolate China, and the United States backed down. The Clintonites realized that they lacked the power to change China's behavior, at least its domestic behavior. From this realization came "engage-ment"—globalization in policy form. The policy assumes that China's growing integration with the world economy will tame it, even without U.S. pressure. This is what Friedman means when he writes that, "Hong Kong will be a largely self-sanctioning diplomatic problem." When Christopher returned to China in November 1996, he told his hosts that, "history shows that nations with accountable governments and open societies make for … better places for foreign investment and economic growth." In other words, China's desire for wealth will improve its behavior, and keep it from becoming a threat.

These are dangerous assumptions. The better response to America's relative decline would be to get our increasingly wealthy allies to accept a greater share of maintaining the security system from which they benefit. In East Asia, that means putting trade conflicts with countries like Japan, South Korea, and Indonesia on the back burner, and giving them more say in how the U.S. deals with China. Since those countries have no interest in China's internal affairs, America would have to downplay human rights considerations. But it has done so anyway. This is a price worth paying in order to convince China's neighbors to assume more of the burden of thwarting China's hegemonic push. America would base its policy not on the imperatives of the global market, but on a renewed balance of power. And this would mean accepting, though we would rather not, that neither the march of technology nor the spread of wealth can keep us safe absent the mobilization of national resources and national will.

In 1939, with one world war past and another looming, the renowned British historian E.H. Carr reflected on why events had proved Norman Angell wrong. He wrote in *The Twenty Years' Crisis*: "To make the harmonisation of interests the goal of political action is not the same thing as to postulate that a natural harmony of interests exists; and it is this latter postulate which has caused so much confusion in international thinking." The theorists of globalization, then and now, are not wrong because they believe peace is possible. They are wrong because they believe peace is possible without politics.

High Noon in Europe

Big Wall St. Banks Gallop In, Guns Ablaze

By EDMUND L. ANDREWS

FRANKFURT

The 7,000 metalworkers were full of righteous rage on March 25 as they marched past the headquarters of Deutsche Bank, Germany's biggest bank. Roaring protests against "Wild West" bankers and "Las Vegas" tactics, union leaders accused the bank of destroying social peace by promoting a cold-blooded hostile takeover.

The galvanizing event for the protest had occurred a week earlier: the Krupp-Hoesch consortium, Germany's second-largest steel manufacturer, had mounted an unprecedented hostile takeover attempt against Germany's top steel company, Thyssen A.G. Never before had Germany seen a hostile takeover even close to that magnitude, or one aimed so clearly at eliminating thousands of jobs and

shutting down redundant factories. Even worse, in the minds of union workers, this affront had been supported and financed by two pillars of Germany's own financial establishment, Deutsche Bank and Dresdner Bank.

"Casino capitalism is a danger to our society," roared Klaus Zwickel, head of the nation's metalworkers union, his amplified voice echoing off the twin glass towers of Deutsche Bank headquarters. "Who governs us? The democratically elected Government or the uncontrolled financial centers of the big banks?"

Yet there was something strangely amiss. No one mentioned the real mastermind: Goldman, Sachs & Company, of Wall Street renown. It was Goldman that Krupp had first approached with its plans. It was Goldman that had mapped the strategy for an all-cash tender offer, Goldman that had proposed what it

hoped would be an irresistible "bear hug" and Goldman that had agreed to lend up to $3 billion of its own money, if needed, to the war effort. Only after the basic plan was conceived were Deutsche Bank and Dresdner asked to participate.

Anybody in search of financial villains, moreover, would have quickly discovered that Wall Street banks like Goldman and Morgan Stanley have collectively engineered far more European mega-mergers than home-grown powerhouses like Deutsche Bank, Lazard Frères of France and even SBC Warburg of Switzerland.

Indeed, Wall Street investment banks are at the epicenter of a restructuring boom sweeping corporate Europe. European mergers and acquisitions hit a record $400.6 billion in 1996—just over half the volume of deals in the United States but double the European level just two years earlier. And American investment banks advised companies in two-thirds of those deals.

Wall Street deal makers are cold-calling prospective clients, an almost unheard-of tactic in European finance. They are luring top talent from prestigious European banks. They are introducing hostile takeovers, which had been almost non-existent in Europe, except in Britain. They have imported infamous tools from American corporate warfare: the "white knight," the "poison pill" and even junk bonds. The role of "haus-banks," the big German banks that earned money by owning big stakes in companies like Daimler-Benz while handling their money, is crumbling. Today, those banks are losing billions of dollars in business to deal makers who demand—and receive—hundreds of millions of dollars in advisory fees on one deal and then are free to disappear in search of the next.

All this is changing the rules by which continental Europe does business. As corporations here raise progressively more investment capital outside Europe, they are trading in traditional loyalties to hometowns and unions in favor of a brasher American-style priority on profits and stock prices. And, perhaps most profoundly, Europe's biggest banks have begun to fight back with the same tools that the Wall Street invaders use. Even if deal makers from the United States end up losing market share, the rougher American playbook appears here to stay.

Few Wall Street firms have built their European businesses more aggressively in the last few years than Goldman, Sachs.

Measured by the value of mergers in which it had an advisory role, Goldman outran the top French banks in France and the top German banks in Germany in 1996.

In France, Goldman advised companies in six of the seven biggest mergers of the last year—including several between French companies. In 1990, the firm had virtually no presence in continental Europe. To-

day, it has about 50 people in Paris and 220 in Frankfurt.

"Goldman was everywhere," said Renault Belleville, a business editor for Les Echoes, a French newspaper. "They went only for the big clients and they were involved in all the deals that everyone was talking about."

And not just in mergers and acquisitions. Goldman has also advised the French Government on privatizing and selling off state-owned companies from Pechiney to Crédit Lyonnais.

"Five years ago, it would have been totally unthinkable for French companies to share their strategic plans with a bank other than Lazard, Rothschild or Bank Paribas," said Sylvain Hefes, managing director in charge of Goldman's Paris office.

To be sure, Goldman is not alone in Europe. J. P. Morgan and Morgan Stanley were the principal advisers last year in the $30 billion merger of two Swiss pharmaceutical giants, Ciba-Geigy A.G. and Sandoz A.G. Merrill Lynch is a lead adviser to the French Government on the $5 billion to $7 billion privatization of France Télécom. And Lehman Brothers has been a central adviser to Hoechst A.G., the big German chemical concern that has bought and sold a slew of companies as part of a corporate restructuring. Beyond that, an investment bank's success is often as cyclical as that of a sports team: one year it seems to win all the big games, only to lose a few key players and slip back in the rankings a few years later.

But the broad trend is unmistakable. And Goldman's activities provide a revealing glimpse of how American deal makers on the Continent have imported the new rules by which European companies must increasingly play. Goldman's success has hardly been without blemishes—the Krupp mega-merger sank in a political firestorm the company clearly did not expect. But Europe has been a huge growth center for the firm, generating about 25 per-

cent of its profits, up from almost nothing in 1990.

Cold-Calling in France

Sylvain Hefes took one look at his computer screen and immediately knew it was time to put aside manners and resort to an old Wall Street tactic: the cold call.

It was May 15, 1996, and what caught Mr. Hefes's eye was a report that Auchan, one of the biggest supermarket chains in France, had just acquired 11.6 percent of Docks de France, a big chain of variety stores similar to Kmart or Wal-Mart.

It looked suspiciously like the start of a hostile takeover—an exceedingly rare event in France. Mr. Hefes knew almost nothing about Docks de France, but that did not stop him from picking up the phone to call the chairman, Michael Deroy.

"We had never had any relationship with the company, and I didn't even know what city they were in," Mr. Hefes, 44, said.

At first, Mr. Deroy refused to return Mr. Hefes's repeated calls. When he did, he quickly assured the investment banker that hostile takeovers simply didn't occur in France. Beyond that, 36 percent of the voting stock was held by three families descended from the company's founder.

A few years ago, that might have been the end of the matter. But Mr. Hefes had already crashed through the clubby confines of French finance. A former managing director at Rothschild & Company, he essentially started Goldman's French practice from scratch in 1991. Along with Mr. Hefes, Goldman had recruited as an "international adviser" one of the most respected figures in French banking, Jacques Mayoux, who had previously been chairman of two big French banks, Société Générale and Crédit Agricole.

Despite his skepticism, Mr. Deroy, the family patriarch, agreed to meet Mr. Hefes two weeks later.

There, the Goldman banker outlined the reasons that Docks de France might have a problem. For starters, a new French environmental law had all but prohibited any company from building big new "hypermarkets," which meant that the only way Auchan could grow was through acquisition.

More important, the family-held shares were spread among many people who no longer had much personal stake in owning the company. Family solidarity, Mr. Hefes said, was no guarantee against a takeover.

Unfortunately for Mr. Deroy and other family members, Goldman was right about Auchan but unable to do much about it. Mr. Deroy hired Goldman, which promptly began looking for a "white knight" investor who could buy enough Docks shares to fend off a takeover. It also held some inconclusive talks directly with Auchan, a privately held company that was itself being advised by a foreign investment bank, the Morgan Grenfell subsidiary of Deutsche Bank.

On June 24, 1996, Auchan surprised both the company and most investors by issuing an unsolicited tender offer to buy all shares in Docks de France for more than $3 billion. Family members were deeply split, with those who still worked for the company more inclined to fight a takeover and those who did not work for it more inclined to cash out. Goldman and Banque Nationale de Paris—more often than not, French companies still insist on having a French bank along for the ride—opened talks with several possible investors who might keep control in friendly hands, but those efforts failed. Goldman then resorted to bargaining for more money by threatening to adopt a "poison pill" defense that would deflate the value of the shares. But that did not get far either. A month later, after Auchan increased its offer by about 10 percent, Docks agreed to sell out.

Those sympathetic to Goldman say it cannot be blamed for the outcome, any more than a brain surgeon can be faulted for losing an ill patient. But some family members remain furious, given the steep advisory fee that Goldman earned and the relatively modest premium that Auchan ultimately paid. Auchan ultimately dismissed virtually all the top executives of Docks, eliminated the Docks name on most stores and changed the stores' look.

"I am not at all happy with the way Goldman handled this, not at all happy with the result," said one family member, who spoke on the condition of anonymity.

But that was not the only deal with a hostile edge that involved Goldman. Axa Group had been chafing for months to merge with Union des Assurances de Paris, yet talks between the companies had broken off early last summer. In November, Axa's chief executive, Henri de Castries, decided to play hardball and arranged for himself and Axa's chairman, Claude Bebear, to have a weekend meeting at the headquarters of Union des Assurances with that company's chairman and chief executive, Jacques Friedmann.

There, with Mr. Hefes of Goldman in the room, Mr. de Castries outlined a choice: either reach an agreement on a friendly merger or prepare for an unsolicited tender offer of cash and securities that Goldman had helped prepare. A $10 billion agreement was reached and the "friendly" merger was announced two days later, with all sides declaring it a triumphant step toward a much stronger company.

"The whole world is restructuring, so why shouldn't the most dynamic French companies do so as well?" Mr. de Castries said.

Mr. de Castries said his 20-year friendship with Mr. Hefes had little to do with why he used Goldman, along with Bank Paribas, to advise him on the deal.

"The key to all this is that global companies need a global investment banker," he said. "One of Goldman's strengths is that their partners work very well together, and we don't need to explain our case 5 or 10 or 15 times. They have a very good ability to circulate information throughout their organization and to investors."

Wearing the Black Hat in Germany

Paul Achleitner, the Austrian-born head of Goldman's office in Frankfurt, knew he faced a possible explosion.

It was early January, and Gerhard Cromme, the no-nonsense chairman of the Krupp-Hoesch steel conglomerate, wanted to acquire Thyssen, the country's biggest steel producer. Both companies had been swamped by competition, and Thyssen had run up huge losses to modernize and restructure.

The two had more than enough capacity between them, and could easily shut down mills in Germany employing well over 10,000 people. Analysts, both European and American, had argued for years that a merger would save the companies hundreds of millions of dollars a year.

Mr. Achleitner, who was a consultant in Boston before joining Goldman in New York, began setting up an office in Germany in the early 1990's. It had begun almost by accident. Mr. Achleitner started by advising the German agency in charge of selling off old state-owned companies in the former East Germany, then moved on to advise medium-sized concerns, among them the Hugo Boss clothing company.

But by last year, Goldman had managed to crack into the highest ranks of German business. Along with hometown rivals like Deutsche Bank and Dresdner, it had advised Daimler-Benz as that conglomerate frenetically began shedding companies and refocusing on its core automobile business. With Deutsche and Dresdner, Goldman was one of the three global managers of Deutsche Telekom's worldwide $12 billion initial public stock offering last year.

And, not insignificantly, Mr. Achleitner had advised Mr. Cromme on a global stock offering as well as on acquiring a Mexican stainless-steel manufacturer.

"German companies need more money than they can get from local capital markets," Mr. Achleitner remarked recently. "Therefore they need to play by the rules of the international capital market."

By the time Mr. Cromme trained his sights on Thyssen, Mr. Achleitner was overseeing an office of 220 people high atop the Messe Turm skyscraper.

Mr. Cromme wanted to carry off a peaceful merger, convinced that the two companies desperately needed each other if they were going to survive. But he was a veteran of hostile takeovers—he had used one in 1991 to win control of the steelmaker Hoesch A.G. for $1.6 billion. He was ready to do it again if need be.

Still, everybody knew that a forced merger here would hit almost every political hot button. With exceptions like Mr. Cromme's own takeover of Hoesch, hostile takeovers in Germany were nonexistent. Beyond that, Germany's jobless rates were higher than at any time since 1933, and hundreds of thousands of metalworkers had already lost their jobs as companies fled Germany's high costs and rigid work rules. And steelmaking, in Germany as in many other countries, has always had a special symbolic resonance of industrial prowess.

For Mr. Achleitner, as well as for Goldman partners in New York, there was yet another risk. With a few exceptions, Goldman had generally refused to advise the acquirers in a hostile takeover—only the defenders. The partners hoped this deal would not turn hostile, but Mr. Achleitner also knew that Krupp needed ammunition if Thyssen proved resistant.

"It was a bear hug more than a hostile takeover," Mr. Achleitner said. "We decided to approach Thyssen, but in order to be taken seriously, we knew we would have to go with a pretty well-thought-out concept."

So Goldman devised an all-cash tender offer that Mr. Cromme could

present to the chairman of Thyssen, Dieter H. Vogel. Mr. Cromme hired Deutsche Bank and Dresdner to join Goldman, and each of the banks pledged to finance the offer with about $3 billion of its own money, essentially gunpowder that Goldman hoped it would not need to ignite.

The plan never got off the ground. Thyssen managers got wind of the strategy, which they promptly made public amid dire warnings that tens of thousands of jobs would be lost. Unions immediately organized protests at Krupp mills around Germany, and Mr. Cromme was forced to speak behind a bulletproof shield when he tried to outline his plan in public. Then German politicians went on the attack, particularly those from the steelmaking regions. Finally, Chancellor Helmut Kohl himself telephoned Deutsche Bank's chairman, Hilmar Kopper, demanding that he find some sort of peaceful resolution.

In response, Krupp withdrew the threat of a tender offer and the two companies agreed on a plan to merge the steel operations, leaving their other industrial businesses separate. While that is expected to lead to a loss of about 7,000 jobs, the number is far smaller than a full merger might have brought. What's more, the cuts will come over five years and are expected to take the form of voluntary buyouts and attrition.

Goldman and the two German banks wound up with almost no fees—advisory fees for banks representing the acquirer are contingent on the success of a proposed deal, and this outcome was not considered a success.

Goldman, though, actually emerged from the whole affair relatively unscathed.

While politicians and unions confined their scolding to the German banks, Goldman has gone on to yet more deals in Germany.

Just two weeks ago, Daimler-Benz announced that Goldman would be its sole adviser in selling a software company worth nearly $1

billion. The move was striking because it was the first time Daimler had decided not to use Deutsche Bank even as a junior partner, even though the bank owns about a quarter of Daimler's stock.

"If you are an investment banker, you are a catalyst of change," Mr. Achleitner said. "There is more change going on in Germany than people sometimes credit it with."

Raiding the Raiders

Even as American investment banks have taken Europe by storm, their rivals in France and Germany have been aggressively responding in kind.

Big Wall Street firms still have a definite edge, thanks to their huge retail sales networks and their experience with the kinds of deals that are still new here. But that edge may already be eroding, simply because Wall Street techniques are not immune to copying. As a result, the competition has increasingly focused on luring the right kind of talent—the handful of "rainmakers" who have both a strong European pedigree and the requisite American expertise to drum up billion-dollar corporate clients.

A result has been a two-way brain drain, with high-profile bankers being recruited as aggressively and lucratively as ballplayers.

American companies like Goldman and Merrill Lynch have concentrated on buying European cachet—prestigious French or German or Italian bankers with good connections and an innate feel for the way France or Germany or Italy works.

Goldman hired Mr. Mayoux, one of the most respected figures in French banking, as an "international adviser" just as he was ready to retire. Mr. Mayoux, though not a partner, has helped bring in several of Goldman's biggest deals in France.

In Italy, Goldman recruited none other than Romano Prodi as an international adviser before Mr. Prodi went on to become Prime Minister.

And in 1995, it hired Sir Peter Sutherland, formerly head of the World Trade Organization, as its vice chairman.

Last week, Goldman recruited Simon Robertson, who had recently quit as head of Kleinwort Benson, the London-based investment bank owned by Dresdner.

European firms, meanwhile, have been recruiting in exactly the opposite direction: American or British deal makers steeped in the ego-driven and hyper-competitive style of drumming up business that is typical of both Wall Street and London.

Deutsche Bank, for example, bought Morgan Grenfell in the early 1990's, and transferred virtually all of Deutsche Bank's investment banking business to London, where Morgan Grenfell was based.

It also went on an eye-popping recruiting drive, buying up much of Morgan Stanley's high-technology practice in Silicon Valley and luring a top Merrill Lynch executive—Edson Mitchell, born in New York—to build up its global bond-trading business.

"The era of the closed shop is terminated," said Jean-Claude Meyer, vice chairman of Rothschild's European operations. "American banks have enlarged their presence, but we have also improved. The competition has been good. It has been very stimulating."

The techniques, though, are growing more and more similar.

"Globally, what is taking place is the Americanization of finance, because American firms are by their nature both global and local," said Michel Fleuriet, the very French head of Merrill Lynch's office in Paris.

The question in the next few years will be whether European bankers can outperform the Americans at their own game.

Piling Into Central Europe

Stability and big economic gains are luring investors to Poland, Hungary, and the Czech Republic

It has been a quiet revolution. While the turmoil in Russia has held the world's attention for months, another part of the old Soviet bloc has been reshaping itself. Thanks to a combination of political stability, an able labor force, and consistent economic reform, Poland, Hungary, and the Czech Republic are managing to outshine other countries in Eastern Europe and the former Soviet Union.

Inflation has tapered off, once-gyrating currencies are now stable, output is rising at a brisk pace, and unemployment has leveled off. Poland's gross domestic product increased by 7% in 1995, rivaling Taiwan's 6% and Indonesia's 8.1%. This year, Poland and the Czech Republic are forecast to expand by 5.5%, placing them among Europe's most robust economies.

Such growth is producing a prosperity that no one wants to endanger. Thus, even the former communists who rule in Poland and Hungary are dedicated to promoting the flow of investment. And Milos Zeman, the Czech Social Democrat who did surprisingly well against free-marketer Václav Klaus in the recent election, is emphatic in his defense of the fundamental direction of the economy.

INDUSTRIAL MIGHT. The clearest sign of this stability is a wave of foreign investment in everything from auto assembly to retailing. Direct foreign investment in Poland, Hungary, and the Czech Republic doubled in 1995, bringing the total since 1990 to $23.5 billion. Cumulative investment is expected to jump an additional 29%, to $30.4 billion by yearend. Says Dan Lubash, head of European emerging-markets research at Merrill Lynch &

Co.: "Give these countries two more years, and they'll be like the Asian tigers."

That kind of optimism is finally attracting investors from Asia who had long viewed the region as too risky. In January, Matsushita Electric Industrial Co. said it would build a $66 million TV plant in the Czech Republic. Daewoo Motor has pledged $1.47 billion for two plants to assemble cars and vans in Poland. In March, Sony Corp. chose Hungary for its newest European factory, a $20.4 million plant that will make CD players, stereos, and color TVs for sale throughout Europe. "These countries have become dependable," says Jack Schmuckli, chairman of European operations at Sony. "They will keep our European manufacturing competitive."

Certainly, problems remain. Central Europe must still repair the

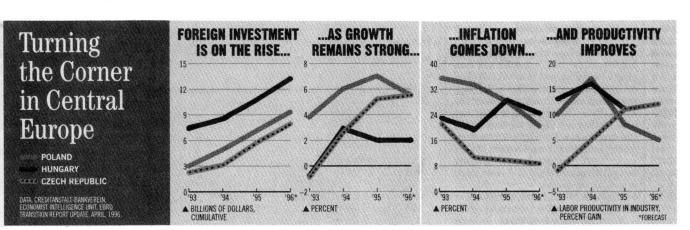

Turning the Corner in Central Europe

POLAND
HUNGARY
CZECH REPUBLIC

DATA: CREDITANSTALT-BANKVEREIN, ECONOMIST INTELLIGENCE UNIT, EBRD TRANSITION REPORT UPDATE, APRIL 1996

FOREIGN INVESTMENT IS ON THE RISE...
▲ BILLIONS OF DOLLARS, CUMULATIVE

...AS GROWTH REMAINS STRONG...
▲ PERCENT

...INFLATION COMES DOWN...
▲ PERCENT

...AND PRODUCTIVITY IMPROVES
▲ LABOR PRODUCTIVITY IN INDUSTRY, PERCENT GAIN   *FORECAST

damage left by four decades of mismanagement—from bloated pension systems to inefficient factories in need of overhaul. Former Communist Party bureaucrats at state-owned companies in Poland have managed to bog down privatization: In recent weeks, the high-profile bankers and policymakers who disagreed with a controversial plan to consolidate banks were fired—a blatant act of interference.

Despite these irritations, more and more global companies are convinced they can earn a healthy return on their investments. Productivity in the region is rising fast enough to outweigh wage increases. For example, Creditanstalt-Bankverein calculates that unit labor costs in Hungary in dollar terms will drop 10% in 1996, even as wages paid in forints are increasing. To attract more investors and prepare for membership in the European Union, Czech, Polish, and Hungarian leaders are steadily aligning tax, labor, investment, and banking codes with those in the West and relinquishing controls on hard currency.

The new rules are making it much easier for corporations to raise cash. ING Bank and Citibank have issued corporate bonds and commercial paper totaling more than $2 billion since the start of 1995. In April, Standard & Poor's Corp. rated Poland's debt investment-grade, a status the Czechs have enjoyed since 1993. "There is now a first tier for investors to target," says Susanne Gahler, an economist at J. P. Morgan & Co. Hungary's stock market has surged 73% in dollar terms this year, while Poland's is up 44%.

One of the biggest surprises for investors has been how much local talent there is to bankroll. Take Imre Somody, who a decade ago hit upon the idea of a vitamin-C tablet that dissolves in water to become a fizzy drink. The state drugmaker where he worked rejected it, so in 1988, Somody and a few colleagues founded Pharmavit. They created Hungary's best-known brand: Plusssz vitamins. Pharmavit also makes generic drugs

at its two modern plants outside Budapest. By 1995, sales had soared fivefold, to about $42 million. Bristol-Myers Squibb Co. recently paid $110 million for Pharmavit and put Somody in charge of all products in Hungary, from cancer drugs to Clairol hair care.

Other outsiders see big potential in creating world-class financial services for Central Europe's consumers. GE Capital Corp. is moving into the region as part of its global expansion. After buying a small Polish bank last year, GE Capital teamed up with the European Bank for Reconstruction & Development (EBRD) in December to pay $87 million for a 60% stake in Budapest Bank, Hungary's sixth-largest. The EBRD wants a 15% return on equity, similar to what a healthy Western bank brings in. Bela Singlovics, chief executive of Budapest Bank, is keen on pushing the auto loans and credit cards, which are now found in only 8% of Hungarian wallets. "With GE, we can be a major player in consumer finance," he says.

The region's consumers are now on a lot of radar screens. Poland, for example, has seen per capita GDP rise by more than $2,000 in six years, to about $3,500. A group of U.S. and Canadian investors wants to set up a network of U.S.-style shopping malls, starting in Hungary on a former Soviet army base. France's E. LeClerc opened a hypermarket, a vast French-style emporium, in Warsaw in November and plans an additional 50 in Poland, aiming to snare a good portion of the $34 the average Pole spends on groceries each month.

CABBAGE AND SAUSAGE. Judging from the crowd one Thursday at 6:30 p.m., it looks like an easy task. Some 2,000 shoppers jam the vast, high-ceilinged hypermarket in Jolibosz, the heart of a working-class borough north of downtown Warsaw. Polish cabbages rest alongside Argentinian oranges and fresh fish filets, while four tall shelves stock sausages in every shape, size, and flavor. A few meters away are auto

A Flood of Foreign Investment

ADAM OPEL Plans to build a $340 million car plant in southern Poland

DAEWOO MOTOR Edged out General Motors to buy 70% of Poland's FSO auto maker for $440 million

IBM Plans to spend $40 million to triple the capacity of its disk-drive plant in Hungary

MATSUSHITA Announced a new $66 million TV plant in the Czech Republic

GE CAPITAL Bought a 27.5% stake in Budapest Bank for $39.9 million

AGIP, CONOCO, ROYAL DUTCH/SHELL Bought 49% of Czech Refining for $149 million; pledged an additional $480 million over five years

DATA: BUSINESS WEEK

and office supplies, videos, and vacuum cleaners. About 90% of the 15,000 products for sale are Polish.

Demand is growing slowly in Western Europe, but it's surging in Eastern markets

But it's the heavy-duty manufacturing investments that are reshaping the industrial map. Siemens was among the first to move to a facility across the Czech border, where rows of women hand-weave multicolored wiring destined for BMW cars. Inexpensive labor often gives these countries an edge over eastern Germany, where employers must pay nearly the same high wages and taxes as in western Germany.

Besides exporting cheap industrial goods, Central Europe is turning into a large market. To meet the demand, Goodyear Tire & Rubber Co. last year offered $115 million for a controlling stake in tiremaker TC Debica in southeastern Poland. Goodyear says it has already boosted daily output by 25% to 30%. While demand is growing by no more than 3% in Western Europe, it is surging by at least 15% in Eastern markets. Poland is the place to be "if you're looking to where you can have an overnight market," says Sylvain G. Valensi, vice-president in charge of Goodyear Europe.

"BACKBONE." Cars are probably Central Europe's hottest spot. That's why Daewoo Motor pushed so hard to take a 70% stake in Poland's state-owned car-maker, FSO, last November, edging out General Motors. Kim Woo Choong, Daewoo Corp.'s chairman, aims to export $1.5 billion worth of cars and car parts from Poland within three years. GM's Adam Opel will build a $340 million factory in southwestern Poland to make a low-cost version of the family-size Astra.

The billions invested by the likes of Opel nourish new supply networks throughout the region. By the end of the decade, GM aims to derive $1 billion worth of parts from Central Europe every year. Volkswagen's presence at Skoda has led to 46 auto-parts joint ventures and 28 new factories. Skoda buys parts from a total of 234 Czech companies. "The strength of the Czech supply industry is the backbone of our success," says Volkhard Köhler, Skoda's vice-chairman and chief financial officer.

Such dynamism will guarantee Central Europe's growth for the next few years. It will be hard-pressed to match Southeast Asia's scorching rates of 8% to 10%. But Poland, Hungary, and the Czech Republic are nonetheless pulling away from the frontier capitalism of their region and offering a safe zone for investors. As global investors contemplate where to spend their dollars, marks, yen, and won, Central Europe is a more competitive choice than ever.

By Karen Lowry Miller in Prague, with Peggy Simpson in Warsaw and Zachary Schiller in Cleveland

THE MARKETS ▰▰▰▰▰▰▰

Where Asia Goes From Here

*The great Asian stock market crash—
over $400 billion in losses so far this year—
has had little effect on politicians from Tokyo
to Jakarta. Are they dreaming?*

By Neel Chowdhury and Anthony Paul

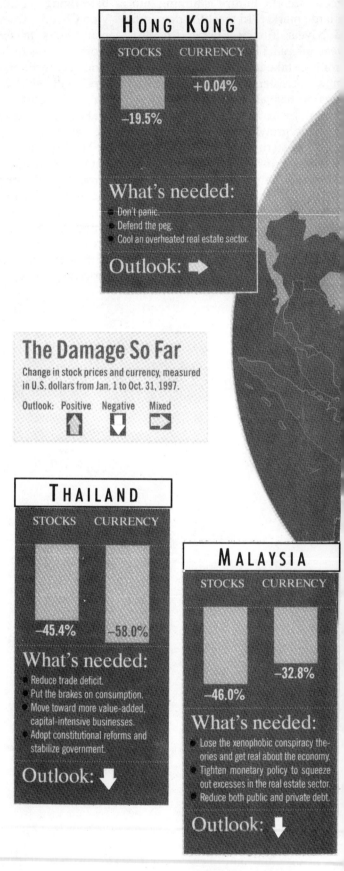

A s far as the citizens of Hong Kong were concerned, Wednesday, Oct. 23, couldn't have been a more inauspicious day. In the city's financial center, a plumbing fault suddenly drained an ornamental pool holding a school of carp, a Chinese symbol of prosperity. As the fish lay gasping, the local stock market was reaching the low point of its heaviest drubbing ever—the loss of nearly a quarter of its value in four days.

But then, it hardly requires faith in signs and portents to believe these are scary times in Asia—the raw numbers are apocalyptic enough. Since the beginning of the year, Asian stock markets have collectively lost an amazing $400 billion in value. As everyone from New York to London to Buenos Aires is now well aware, it was the shock waves emanating from Hong Kong in mid-October that set financial markets reeling across the globe. No one knows when all this volatility will end, but one thing is clear: It will stop only when Asian politicians finally push their countries to get their battered economic houses back in order. And that requires making some very tough choices. As Singapore's Senior Minister Lee Kuan Yew recently observed, addressing a top group of U.S. CEOs at the FORTUNE 500 Forum in Boston: "In nearly every economic crisis, the root cause is political, not economic."

Even if all goes well, it will take as much as two years for most of these ex–miracle makers to work their way out of their current problems. In the meantime economists agree that growth in Southeast Asia will slow from around 8% this year to 5% or less next. While that slowdown is bad news for Western

---

TAIWAN

STOCKS **+6.9%**
CURRENCY **−12.1%**

What's needed:
- Keep adding value to high-tech exports.
- Seek greater investment opportunities in mainland China.

Outlook: ⬆

SOUTH KOREA

STOCKS **−28.0%**
CURRENCY **−14.3%**

What's needed:
- Restructure the troubled *chaebol.*
- Deregulate the economy to facilitate mergers and acquisitions.
- Open financial markets to foreign investors.
- Recapitalize banks battered by corporate bankruptcies.

Outlook: ➡

PHILIPPINES

STOCKS **−42.4%**
CURRENCY **−33.4%**

What's needed:
- Keep a lid on inflation.
- Try to let some air out of the growing property bubble.
- Move faster into high-end industries.

Outlook: ➡

SINGAPORE

STOCKS **−28.7%**
CURRENCY **−12.3%**

What's needed:
- Not much. Stick to strong economic fundamentals—no debt and a balanced budget.

Outlook: ⬆

INDONESIA

STOCKS **−21.6%**
CURRENCY **−53.0%**

What's needed:
- Take IMF medicine and cut the national budget.
- Deregulate this highly protected economy.
- Curb pricey pet projects of President Suharto's family.

Outlook: ⬇

AUSTRALIA

STOCKS **+2.2%**
CURRENCY **+11.0%**

What's needed:
- Take advantage of the Asian currency crash by ramping up direct investment in regional markets.
- Tackle flagging growth by spurring domestic demand.

Outlook: ⬆

FORTUNE MAP BY RENEE KLEIN

Japan: A Model for What *Not* to Do

Asia's richest economy saw its asset bubble burst six years ago. Since then it has avoided major deregulation, corporate restructuring—and gone nowhere fast.

Stocks plunge. Real estate goes bust. Consumers get tightfisted. That scenario is a cold, new reality in much of Asia, but to Japan it's a familiar story. Ever since Japan's financial and real estate bubble burst in the early 1990s, the economy has limped along, with annual GDP growth averaging just over 1%. Indeed the Tokyo market has been down so long—the Nikkei index has yet to climb back to more than 58% of its 1989 peak of 38,916—that the shock from October's stockquake was no big deal. In contrast to double-digit swings in much of Asia, the Nikkei fell just 4.3%.

Even so, Asia's continued tailspin poses the most serious danger to Japan since the yen rose to 80 to the dollar in 1995, threatening to fatally throttle the sole sustaining force in Japan's economy—the competitiveness of its blue-chip exporters. Buoyed by a weaker yen over the past two years, Japan's exporters have made Asia their fastest-growing market. Today 44% of Japanese exports go to Asia, vs. just 25% to the U.S. Now with those markets stalling out, sales of Japanese cars and electronics are set to sink.

Making matters worse, up to 70% of Japan's Asia-bound exports are capital goods, like factory machinery, that are headed for an especially sharp fall. Most Asian countries have already significantly overinvested in new factories and capacity. Fearing the worst, economists in Tokyo are cutting their growth forecasts for Japan in the current fiscal year to zero or a bit above. "We had a financial and a real estate bust already in Japan," says Geoffrey Barker, chief of Asian research at Schroders Securities Asia in Hong Kong. "Now we may be about to have an industrial bust." Nor can Japanese companies expect to make up much of the slack by shifting exports to the U.S.—especially not with a newly vigilant Washington on the lookout for dumpers.

Japan had appeared to be on the road to recovery last spring. Then Prime Minister Ryutaro Hashimoto decided to both raise taxes and reduce government spending to shrink Japan's huge budget deficit (7% of GDP). Bad call. Consumption collapsed and growth plunged 2.9% in the second quarter of 1997, the worse quarterly showing in 23 years.

Now the stakes are rising. If the stock market takes another dive (it remained just under 16,500 at October's end, when FORTUNE went to press), Hashimoto may have to rethink his austerity drive—simply to avoid a new crisis. Still suffering from the collapse of asset values in Japan, the insurance companies—and to a lesser extent the banks—will be in a sweat if the market goes much below 16,000. A drop to that level would wipe out most of the unrealized stock gains in their portfolios, making the future more desperate for imperiled insurers and complicating the banks' efforts to set aside required reserves. One major insurance company, Nissan Mutual Life Insurance, collapsed in April this year, and there is widespread expectation in Tokyo that it will not be the last.

Even with those risks, many economists question whether Japan can afford to apply any new Keynesian or supply-side tonics, given the size of its budget deficit and the huge burden it faces in caring for the world's most rapidly aging population. "Japan's policymakers are adopting a fatalistic approach," says Peter Tasker, a strategist at Dresdner Kleinwort Benson. "They managed to prevent heavy unemployment and bankruptcies of major corporations in the 1990s. Now they feel the economy may just have to take its lumps."

If the setbacks roiling the rest of Asia make it impossible to dodge a contraction, Japan can only hope that its coming slump will at least force it to deregulate and restructure the way it should have ten years ago. That, of course, is a lesson its neighbors would do well to ponder too.

—Edward W. Desmond

multinationals that have been banking on Asia for a big profit boost—one reason stock markets got so spooked—there is a potential payoff: The crisis may finally force much needed structural economic reform in the region. As Hong Kong Monetary Authority Chief Executive Joseph Yam Chi-kwong puts it, all the turmoil is just a "painful but necessary adjustment to the new world of greater competition."

Painful is right. Especially vulnerable countries such as Thailand, Malaysia, and Indonesia must now swallow the International Monetary Fund's bitter medicine and move quickly to acknowledge bad bank loans, cut subsidies, raise interest rates, and bring down their trade and budget deficits. So far the prospects look bleak. Says Douglas Johnson, a senior international investment strategist at Merrill Lynch: "No country in the region has stepped up to the plate—they've been in denial."

Nor are austerity measures alone enough. The tigers and would-be tigers of Asia must also radically reshape their entire economic infrastructures to get in step with the information standard demanded by the new global capitalism. If their corporations and banks don't, in the lingo of economists, make their financial reporting more transparent—that is, if foreign and local investors can't understand where their money is and what they're earning on it—then these institutions can expect to see that capital pick up and move elsewhere. Finally, these nations must continue to deregulate their industries and forgo their penchant for handing valuable business franchises to "friends" of the ruling party. Such protectionism and cronyism ulti-

REPORTER ASSOCIATES *Jeremy Kahn and Rajiv M. Rao*

mately prevents a nation and its corporations from becoming truly competitive with the best of the world's multinationals.

This doesn't mean, however, that every country in Asia will follow the same road to recovery. The Asia-Pacific region is an extraordinary mix of political and economic arrangements and companies in search of production sites and markets. Understandably, a regional tour uncovers many local peculiarities. Of all the nations in the region, Singapore, Australia, and Taiwan seem the soundest. Yes, their markets may experience some scary swings, but their debt is low, their inflation mild, and their currencies are relatively strong. (Singapore, for example, with zero foreign debt and $80 billion in reserves, so far has had to devalue its dollar by only 12%.) In a sense, all these countries need to do is stay the course.

Singapore, in fact, could stand as a model for other Southeast Asian nations. Over the years it has invested heavily in education and training to move local industries up the technological ladder. It is also taking advantage of cheap labor in foreign markets. In information technology, for instance, Singapore builds industrial parks in Suzhou, China, and Vietnam that manufacture things like telephones. At the same time it has made itself a logistics and shipment hub for the region's electronic trade.

In the long run, the experts argue, countries like Singapore, along with Taiwan and Australia, should actually benefit from the current troubles. Why? It's now cheaper for them to build and operate factories in Southeast Asian countries like Thailand and Malaysia that have dramatically devalued their currencies.

Nearer term, however, the Asian crisis will take a toll. For one thing, it may crimp Australia's growth. Recently, Australian Prime Minister John Howard told FORTUNE that he was expecting a very welcome 3.75% growth for 1997–98, high for his country's developed economy (and perhaps enough to begin making a dent in a stubborn 8.7% unemployment rate). By late last month, however, Southeast Asia's travail plus the El Niño–driven drought were threatening to cut growth to below 3%, which could create even higher unemployment. And if the turmoil were to spread to Japan and South Korea, which take 50% of Australia's exports, even those reduced growth figures will look optimistic.

China, conspicuously immune so far during this crisis, won't escape unscathed either. Beijing's industrial modernization drive is largely financed by investors from Hong Kong, Southeast Asia, and Taiwan—where many companies suddenly have less capital to put into the mainland. Adding to the squeeze, sharp currency devaluations are making such countries as Thailand and Indonesia more formidable export competitors to China. Thailand's 54% surge in exports in September may well be a hint of what lies ahead for the region as a whole.

After stalwarts like Singapore, Taiwan, and Australia, the countries in the best shape in the region seem to be Hong Kong, the Philippines, and South Korea. While the members of this trio all enjoy basically healthy economies, they are struggling with problems in real estate and banking in the cases of Manila and Hong Kong, and with shaky conglomerates in the case of Seoul. Compared with Southeast Asia, South Korea has an advanced industrial economy, much more like Japan's. But its *chaebol* (large conglomerates such as Samsung and Daewoo) are grappling with stunted profits and debts that, on average, exceed four times their equity capital. They have borrowed relentlessly to expand capacity in a few industries that are now saturated—including petrochemicals and autos. Already several *chaebol*, notably the automaker Kia, have collapsed under the weight of debts. Says Thomas Dongho Lee, an attorney with the New York law firm Winthrop Stimson Putnam & Roberts: "Korea needs to rationalize its corporations by freely allowing mergers and acquisitions."

Beyond too many factories is another problem. If growth slows in the region, who will fill the hundreds of office towers and luxury condos going up all over the region? Nowhere is this more evident than in the Philippines. One number tells the story: Starting in 1993, annual loan growth to Filipinos surged 40%, then 30%, 41%, and 54%. The result: an alarming property bubble. A glut looms. Though office vacancy rates are low now, they may well hit 15% to 20% in two years. Given how highly linked the entire economy is to the property market, that could be devastating.

If the problems of South Korea and the Philippines are worrisome, those of the shakiest of the Southeast Asian nations—Indonesia, Malaysia, and Thailand—are downright unnerving. That's because all three are suffering from endemic, system-wide economic problems: high debt, corporate cronyism, and overcapacity. Says Rob Reiner, co-manager of the BT Investment International Equity Fund: "There doesn't seem to be a short-term resolution, because for many of these countries, it really is a structural issue."

The first order of business for these nations is to get their fiscal and monetary houses in order. In Malaysia, for instance, Prime Minister Mahathir Mohamad, oversees a nation that has invested heavily—some say overinvested—in real estate and infrastructure projects, yet he refuses to raise interest rates to wring excess capacity out of the system (see box, next page).

An absence of political will is what's also plaguing Thailand. There a revolving-door government has allowed the nation to drift into its current crisis. Morgan Stanley predicts that Thailand, which is the most troubled Southeast Asian country, will enter a recession next year with a negative 1.5% growth rate. That's a far cry from only a few years ago when the spunky nation was barreling along at a double-digit pace.

The root cause of Thailand's problems is its current political system. Thai politicians spend millions of dollars getting elected in hopes of recouping while in office. As Singapore's Lee Kuan Yew recently pointed out, Thai politicians, who held personal stakes in many troubled financial institutions, have displayed "a natural reluctance to discipline them."

To the Thais' credit, committees representing a broad range of the kingdom's subjects have come up with practical constitutional reforms that, among other things, would reduce the role of money in politics. And very late in the game, the Thais have finally suspended operations of 58 financial institutions, though the increasingly unpopular Prime Minister Chavalit Yongchaiyudh continues to shrink from other crucial moves.

His reluctance is understandable. Already the prospect of hundreds of thousands of urban workers facing unemployment has raised the worry that civil disorder may soon erupt. Politicians have begun maneuvering for elections, which are now expected early next year. They can't come too soon. As Sutichai Yoon, director of the Nation Group, a leading media company, puts it, "It's difficult to imagine any real resolution of Thailand's economic problems until we have a new, much cleaner, more competent cabinet."

At the heart of most such cleanups is Asia's endemic political cronyism, which leads to monopoly power and protectionism. Nowhere is this more of a problem than in Indonesia, Southeast Asia's largest nation. President Suharto, 76, has ruled for 32

More Malaise in Malaysia

Despite growing warning signs, the man who built up modern Malaysia is sticking to a risky policy path that may well lead to a Thai-like economic meltdown.

It's no secret that international investors, whom Malaysian Prime Minister Mahathir Mohamad has derided as "criminals" and "morons" for making a run on his currency, would draw deep satisfaction from seeing him fail. The irony: Mahathir may be helping them get their wish. In the midst of modern East Asia's most serious financial crisis, he has chosen not to heed the market's forceful demand for structural reform but is instead making a huge bet on the status quo. If the bet goes wrong—and the odds are that it will—the now relatively calm Malaysian economy will by next spring be plunged into chaos of Thai-like proportions, with even worse political turmoil.

Mahathir is in a position to take his reckless gamble because, after Singapore, Malaysia has Southeast Asia's strongest banks. Balance sheets are firm, nonperforming loans are low, and the quality of banking supervision is at least a notch above the regional norm. None of these virtues can be boasted by the financial systems of Thailand, Indonesia, or the Philippines, all of which have already been driven to accept that strict discipline of the IMF. Mahathir would, as one opposition politician puts it, "rather shoot himself than go to the IMF," and he is relying on the financial might of Malaysia's banks to make sure he has to do neither.

At first glance, Mahathir is not badly positioned to make his escape. Unlike Thailand and Indonesia, Malaysia has no overwhelming foreign-debt problem. Its total foreign-bank debt is a relatively modest $27 billion: As a share of GDP, that's less than half as big as Thailand's foreign-bank debt.

But Malaysia does have a bad and worsening problem with domestic debt. Loans as a share of GDP will reach at least 140% by the end of this year, the biggest such percentage in Asia. There is nothing wrong with debt, of course, provided the loans go for things that will eventually produce a stream of income to pay them off. But it is never a good sign when so much government money is going to build the "world's tallest" building or the "world's biggest" dam. Moreover, a lot of credit has been extended for speculative investments. Analysts at Jardine Fleming in Singapore estimate that half Malaysia's domestic bank loans in 1995–97 went for property, consumption, and equity investment, with only 16% going into manufacturing.

A more prudent government might react by squeezing its budget, tightening liquidity, and deregulating industry. Malaysia will have none of that. Although some white-elephant monuments such as the Bakun Dam have been postponed, the mid-October budget was only mildly contractive; GDP growth in 1998 is projected to fall to a "mere" 7% from more than 8% last year. Real interest rates remain at zero or below.

This is where those robust banks come in. Malaysia can put off its day of reckoning by provisionally shoving every failure onto the books of the financial system. The country's 61 brokerages had, as of late September, made very few margin calls, even though they're sitting on around $2.5 billion in margin losses. Nor do commercial banks seem to be calling in loans. Thanks to such flimflam, Jardine Fleming reckons that nonperforming loans as a share of all loans in Malaysia will quadruple and that the country will be left with a higher share of bad debts relative to GDP than even Thailand.

For his bet to succeed, Mahathir is banking on four things: that exports will rise, that consumer spending will rise, that the stock market will recover, and that the currency will stop falling. Some combination of these might mount a successful rescue. Overall, this economic strategy represents a wild throw of the dice. Like everywhere else in Asia, Malaysia needs deep reforms. Unlike everywhere else in Asia, Malaysia denies it. — *Jim Rohwer*

years and is about to get another five-year term, but he suffers from a dangerous myopia. He simply doesn't see anything wrong with the vast business empires his sons and daughters are incessantly building with generous financing from government banks and special tax breaks. Example: the $1.3 billion "national car" venture called the Timor, which is run by his youngest son, Tommy. Despite that massive investment, the poorly made Timor has proved a flop with local consumers.

What exactly should Indonesia and its neighbors do? BT's Reiner says: "They need to let poor or laggard companies go bankrupt. Close down inefficient operations, reduce capacity, and cancel big projects that are unnecessary." That, however, is easier said than done. Essentially, Suharto has gained legitimacy for his highly authoritarian regime by steadily improving living standards. But average income is still a modest $1,200 annually, so even a little belt-tightening could hurt. A slowdown in economic growth (Indonesia expects GDP to rise 5% this year) would seriously curb job opportunities for its large population—a tinder box for potential trouble. Adding to the growing uncertainty, Suharto has avoided picking a political successor. Rumors swirl that he may try to install his eldest daughter, Tutut, whose credentials beyond her family link are minimal.

On Oct. 31, after lengthy negotiations, the IMF, World Bank and Asian Development Bank finally came forward with a $23 billion aid package for Indonesia. But right up until the last minute there had been disturbing signs that Suharto, in order to preserve his political maneuvering room and family fortunes, was trying to avoid such strict discipline. Instead he appears to have hoped that rich neighbors like Singapore, Malaysia, and Australia would provide billions of dollars to bail out Indonesia—with ew strings attached. Those hopes were dashed when Singapore declared that its minimum pledge of $5 billion in aid was firmly tied to the IMF plan, which, among other things, requires Indonesia to sharply cut fiscal spending and save money by eliminating various food subsidies and import controls covering wheat, flour, and soybeans.

The latter may sound like no big deal, but in Indonesia the politics of food is highly sensitive—and extremely lucrative. Before the IMF put its foot down, an Indonesian state agency, known as Bulog, set the price of rice and handed out lucrative licenses to Suharto cronies like the Salim family, which gave them control over agro-businesses like flour milling. "The reduction in Bulog's role is excellent," says P.K. Basu, regional economist for UBS Securities in Singapore. "There will be more volatility in food prices in Indonesia, but it should result in lower prices overall."

"In nearly every economic crisis, the cause is political, not economic."

— Lee Kuan Yew

What's unclear is whether Suharto will really observe the details of the IMF's plan. If not—and many analysts fear this is a distinct possibility—Indonesia's stock and currency markets will continue to be pounded by foreign investors. That could be a fatal blow to Indonesian corporations already reeling from the damaging effects of the 53% drop in the rupiah to date. According to UBS Securities in Jakarta, the entire 1997 net profit of Indofood, another Salim family holding and one of the nation's largest corporations, would be wiped out by a further fall in the currency.

Beyond their struggles with political reform, Thailand and Indonesia, like the other nations of Southeast Asia, are debat-

ing which industries are most likely to lead them back to real prosperity. What they should not do is count on a revival of that old mainstay of the Asian miracle—low-end manufacturing. In many countries businesses like textile weaving, toy manufacturing, or shoemaking have gone, possibly forever. Today lower-cost producers like Bangladesh or Vietnam enjoy the competitive edge. One good illustration: In 1989 Thailand was Nike's second-largest manufacturing source. Today Vietnam and China are primary sources. Why? Simple. Since 1989, Thai wages have increased 79%.

At the same time, much of Southeast Asia's high-end manufacturing—industries like petrochemicals, steel, automobile manufacturing, and computer software—is foundering. The region's greatest weakness is skilled labor. Since it takes years to produce intrepid engineers or innovative software designers, Indonesia, Malaysia, and Thailand are, for now, all net importers of industrial managers, engineers, accountants, and software designers from the U.S., Europe, and India.

Are there any quick-fix solutions to the current slump? In a limited way, yes. At least three countries reeling from the economic meltdown—Malaysia, Indonesia, Thailand—are blessed with oil and other natural resources that can be easily converted into exports. Thanks to the currency devaluations, these products now look like real bargains. Tourism, a great way to generate cash even in hard times, is another critical industry that's automatically bolstered by softer currencies.

It would be a mistake, though, for these nations to think of commodity exports and tourism as anything but temporary cushions. When it comes to long-term cures, Southeast Asia needs to continue pursuing the new industries being generated by the inexorable rise of the global electronics and information industries. That's where the real value lies.

Will Asia be able to capitalize on these opportunities? Again, despite some advantages such as high savings and a strong work ethic, it all comes down to political will. The financial meltdown has underscored the need for aging leaders in Thailand, Malaysia, and Indonesia to prepare for orderly political succession rather than cling to office until they die. Governments should focus more sharply on what has made the region so successful in the past—including honest administration, prudent use of debt, and a respect for market forces. If Asia's nations pursue that course, argues Singapore's Lee, "in two to three years [Western investors] will be kicking themselves for not having seized the great opportunities and bargains that now exist here." One reason to think Asia will eventually take the right path is simply that the alternative is too bleak to contemplate—an end to the miracle, with countries flapping like carp in an empty pool.

Ignored Warnings

Long before the deluge, storm clouds were gathering over Asia's economy

By Keith B. Richburg and Steven Mufson

Washington Post Foreign Service

One year ago, as Asia finished another year of sky-high growth and its leaders boasted of a dawning Pacific Century, a little-noticed bank scandal in Thailand provided a hint of the shock the region was about to receive. The scandal, at the Bangkok Bank of Commerce, involved billions of dollars in questionable loans, including one to a convicted swindler known as the "Biscuit King." The bank's managers disguised their malfeasance using financial shell games, such as backing loans with vastly overvalued property.

The mess at the Bangkok bank exposed the weakness of Thailand's banks and the lack of government oversight in a deregulated financial system run amok. And though few guessed it at the time, that obscure and complex scandal was the portent for a larger economic meltdown that not only would send Thailand reeling into recession, but later would sweep through Indonesia, Malaysia, the Philippines and, eventually, South Korea, the world's 11th-largest economy.

By the end of 1997, the crisis had left behind bankrupt corporations and failed financial institutions across Asia, and a pile of regional currencies worth up to 40 percent less than before. It exposed a mountain of bad debt wrought by shoddy lending practices, and it underscored a generation of corrupt political and business practices long concealed by high growth figures. And perhaps most importantly, the crisis pierced the bubble of confidence that has allowed Asia to prosper for a decade on foreign investment.

Few can claim to have seen Asia's dramatic change in economic fortune coming. Indeed, at the start of 1997, most economists, regional analysts, and Asian academics and politicians were saying that the region's "miracle" growth was destined to continue well into the next millennium.

Looking back, however, the Thai bank scandal was the first—and perhaps the most glaring—of many warning signs that Asia's bubble of prosperity was about to burst. This story, reported with the benefit of hindsight, looks at how the gathering storm clouds in two key places—Thailand and South Ko-rea—for more than a year signaled the eventual, region-wide economic crisis to come.

In many cases, the warnings were ignored by government officials anxious to conceal unfavorable news, by foreign investors anxious to keep the funds flowing and by an international community eager to keep the myth of the miracle alive.

"The relative complacency across the globe in the initial stages of the crisis was probably a contributing factor to the crisis," says Andy Tan, a Singapore-based analyst. After the Mexican currency crisis of 1994, Tan says, "there was a sense of complacency that this would be the same."

"If you look at all of these countries," says Bruce Gale, regional manager of the Political and Economic Risk Consultancy, "the problems were known, but there wasn't the political will to do anything about them."

Most analysts in the region say Asia is in a position to pick up the pieces from the shambles of 1997, as governments to varying degrees show a willingness to recognize the size of the crisis and make the necessary reforms, particularly in the banking and financial sector. As with the savings and loan scandal in the United States, which led to a shakeout of the American finance sector and greater regulation, so too might Asia retool by cleaning up its banking mess.

In most cases, the cleanup will involve shutting down banks and finance companies whose operations already have been suspended—16 banks in Indonesia, 14 merchant banks in South Korea, 56 finance companies in Thailand. Other banks will be forced to merge, and laws are being changed from Jakarta to Seoul to allow still other banks to merge with foreign partners.

But the process is likely to be longer than initially thought, and more painful, according to regional analysts, economists and investors. Asia is likely to face recession, more bankruptcies, higher unemployment and perhaps social unrest, they say. Where initially the turnaround seemed likely to come by the end of this year, most analysts now suspect Asia's troubles could last to the year 2000.

In addition, changes in global trade and investment patterns could slow recovery. Asia now is competing more with Latin America and Eastern Europe, and it may find it difficult to recapture its role as the favori region for foreign capital. China, with i endless supply of low-wage labor, will cha lenge Southeast Asians increasingly in the traditional export fields. And perhaps mo fundamentally, the crisis of 1997 has sappe investors confidence in the region.

THAILAND, WHERE THE ASIAN COI lapse began last summer, holds the first clue of its origin and shows how warning sigr along the road to disaster either were misse entirely or deliberately ignored.

One year ago, Thailand was coming ov of a decade of unparalleled economi growth, averaging 8 percent annually. Fe nine years in a row, the country reported balanced budget. The technocrats in charg of financial and economic policy were cor sidered among the most professional in th region; the history of political noninterfer ence in economic management seemed wel entrenched; and the country boasted relatively open, liberal investment policy.

"Every single person has been caught b surprise by the rapidity of the crisis and th depth of the crisis," a Western embass economist in Bangkok says.

But Dominique Maire had his doubts. I 1996, Maire was a regional economist for UBS Securities based in Singapore. In September c that year, he and other UBS analysts spent tw days in Bangkok talking with officials i charge of economic policy. "We asked wha was going on," Maire recalls. "I told them ex ports were weakening, everyone was still con centrating on strong economic growth investment plans were still high—but can yo do something to prevent a slowdown?

"I remember in our case, after two day of meetings, I said, that's it—it's a majo slowdown. That was the trigger point, afte which I started cutting major forecasts."

Key to that 1996 reassessment were fig ures showing export performance for the las quarter of the year as sluggish at best. At th Beginning of 1996, the government had pre dicted an 18 percent growth in exports, hu at midyear Thailand's export growth was ir the single digits. Government officials in sisted that the earlier growth projections were on target and that Thailand simply was experiencing a brief cyclical downturn that had no long-term implications. And many foreign economists followed that line.

"Everyone was scurrying around trying to find cyclical explanations," says a hedge fund manager with long experience in Thailand. "But the drop in exports was crucial."

In fact, a long-term shift was underway, with profound implications for Thailand and the region. Thailand's traditional exports—footwear, garments, seafood—"got creamed," as one U.S. economist indelicately puts it. The main problem was increased competition from relative newcomers India, Burma and Vietnam, and from China, whose exports expanded as Thailand's contracted. In addition, higher labor costs and the relatively high value of Thailand's currency, the baht, compared with the U.S. dollar, meant Thais had "priced themselves out of the market," the U.S. economist says.

While exports were collapsing, trouble was brewing on an unrelated front: The country was embroiled in its biggest banking scandal. The issue received little outside attention; because some ministers in the government of then-Prime Minister Banharn Silpa-archa were touched by the scandal, the government tried to hide the depth of the problem.

The Bangkok Bank of Commerce, or BBC as it is widely known, was taken over by a government committee in summer 1996 after it was revealed in parliament that the bank was insolvent because of some $3 billion in outstanding loans, many of them with inadequate collateral. The beneficiaries included the late Rajan Pillai, a biscuit-maker and convicted swindler known as the "Biscuit King," who got 3 billion Thai baht (about $117 million at 1996 conversion rates), and members of Banharn's Chart Thai political party.

The bank's former president and treasury adviser have been accused of running the bank into the ground. The ex-president is fighting the charges in Thailand, while the ex-treasury adviser is fighting extradition from Canada.

The BBC mess led to the resignation of Vijit Supinit as governor of the Bank of Thailand, the country's central bank, eroding confidence in that institution. More importantly, it focused attention on a banking sector that was seriously out of control.

After Thailand allowed offshore banks in 1993–94 and began offering high interest rates on deposits, foreigners poured in money, attracted by the relatively stable exchange rates. Flush with foreign cash, the proliferating banks "went out and loaned shamelessly," one Western diplomat says. Facing liquidity problems, and with lax government oversight, the banks covered up their increasing volume of bad loans by making still more loans and, as the economist says, "that's where we were in mid-'96 when the rot started."

By early 1997, the bad news on exports and the worries over BBC combined to put heavy foreign pressure on the baht. Analysts say they now believe the central bank was intervening in the futures currency markets even earlier than first revealed, in spring 1997. On Feb. 12, 1997, the Singapore-based Political and Economic Risk Consultancy group published its "Asian Intelligence" newsletter that for the first time warned of the extent of the impending crisis.

The pressure on the baht in January "betrayed worries not just about the gloomy run of Thailand's macroeconomic results, but also about the health of the country's financial institutions," the report said. "Serious surgery is needed to invigorate the country's financial institutions," it said, warning, "If panic takes hold of the market, reform may have to come to stave off, or respond to, a meltdown."

The meltdown did come in August, with the government suspending the operations of 58 ailing financial firms and going to the International Monetary Fund for a bailout.

JUST AS THE CRISIS IN THAILAND BEgan quietly with the mess at BBC, in South Korea the scandal had another name: Hanbo. In what should have been a warning sign of South Korea's coming financial crisis, the giant Hanbo Group went bankrupt in January 1997 with a debt of about $6 billion—the first of the big conglomerates to go under. The scandal caused South Korea's normally pliant banks to mutter publicly about the conglomerates' high debt levels.

The Hanbo Group's chairman and his son were convicted of siphoning $400 million from the group to bribe government officials and bankers in a futile attempt to keep the group afloat. To many analysts, the mess at Hanbo appeared unique. But others say Hanbo's crisis was indicative of the rot at the core of Korea's financial and industrial base.

In its February 1997 report, the Political and Economic Risk Consultancy group had rated Korea's banks among the region's most worrisome. "The recent Hanbo crisis has underlined just how much South Korea's banking system needs serious reform," the report said, adding that, among other things, the scandal exposed how Korean banks suffered under the "suffocating embrace from government" that made them "vulnerable to corrupt government officials."

As in Thailand, the banking scandal was the most visible and dramatic warning sign, but the roots of the economic problem were long in the making.

In Korea's case, double-digit growth in plant capacity since 1995 flooded markets with too many products, which then spurred a growth in inventories and price-slashing. This in turn caused a drop in profits for Korean firms, leaving them helpless in the face of crushing debts. With debts commonly equal to three to six times the cash invested in their firms, companies were having trouble finding cash to make interest payments. The amount of corporate debt reached nearly twice the annual gross national product.

Even in fiscal year 1996, when Korea's economy grew at 7.1 percent (similar to Thailand's stunning growth that same year), 13 of the top 30 conglomerates were losing money, including four of the top 10. The loans mounted as investment slowed, indicating that from mid-1996, the firms were using borrowed money to cover operating costs.

BORROWING MONEY AND AMASSING debt seemed an attractive alternative to South Korea's corporate chiefs. It allowed them to navigate lean times while retaining control of their companies, rather than raising cash by issuing new stock and diluting their own stakes.

Merchant banks, relatively new in Korea, also played a role. They were, says Kim Kihwan, ambassador-at-large for economic affairs, "used literally as private coffers" by the conglomerates that owned them. The problems were compounded when companies went abroad for their borrowing, making them vulnerable to the collapse in the currency later in the year, after Thailand's currency troubles spread.

After the Hanbo mess was exposed, banks began taking a closer look at their loan portfolios, and started calling in loans to the most indebted firms. That created a domino effect of more companies failing.

The biggest blow to confidence came with the July collapse of Kia Motors, the country's eighth-largest conglomerate. Its debts were bigger than Hanbo's, and it brought down one of the country's premier banks, the Korea First Bank.

The crisis deepened as Southeast Asian currencies began collapsing in July and August. Many Korean merchant banks had borrowed U.S. dollars to buy high-risk bonds in Thailand. In addition, the loss of value of Southeast Asian currencies meant a loss of purchasing power for Korean goods.

Yet as late as September, many analysts, including the IMF, were making optimistic forecasts about Korea and its growth. And as late as November, with more big companies collapsing and the central bank spending half-a-billion dollars each day to prop up the sagging won, the government was still trying to cover up the extent of the crisis.

When on Nov. 12, Stephen Marvin, research chief for SsangYong Investment and Securities, issued a report to investors warning that "no beacon of light is visible" in Korea's financial mess, the finance ministry threatened to slap sanctions on SsangYong if it didn't halt distribution of the document.

Richburg reported from Bangkok and Hong Kong, Mufson from Seoul.

ECONOMIES

No More Free Lunch

China's economic reforms have left money-losing state firms unable to care for millions of workers. As Beijing speeds up reform of the state sector, it also has to put in place a new welfare net.

By Matt Forney in Beijing and
Pamela Yatsko in Shanghai

"Life was much better under Mao Zedong," huffs Xu Baofang, shaking his head with its shock of unkempt hair. "He cared about us."

Try telling the 40-year-old that he lost his job at a state-run Shanghai construction company because the economy needs structural reform. Or that his monthly 230 renminbi ($35) in unemployment benefit is more than many get. Tell him that state enterprises simply can't afford the old "iron rice bowl" and he spits back: "If we get sick now, they just let us die."

Xu's bitterness is shared by millions. In Chairman Mao's economy, he and other Chinese in big state firms could expect to be born in a factory hospital, study in a factory school, live in a factory apartment, inherit a factory job, and be reduced to ash in a factory crematorium. But the Communist Party's 15th Congress last month sent the clear message that the crib-to-coffin security of the socialist welfare state is gone forever.

The party outlined plans to sell or merge tens of thousands of inefficient state enterprises; those that are beyond redemption will go bankrupt. The whole idea is to invigorate Chinese industry so it can compete in the global economy. As a result, roughly 30 million surplus industrial workers could lose their jobs; those that remain can forget about receiving lifelong social benefits free of charge. At the congress, party chief Jiang Zemin told them: "Workers should change their ideas about employment."

If Beijing's economic reforms are the key to China's future, weaving a new welfare net for workers is a key to those reforms. The new net won't be fully in place for another 10 to 15 years, but China cannot afford to put off reforming its state sector any longer. As the old system unravels and the new one is patched together, China seems to be rely-

ing on a job-creating private sector, ad hoc measures and the capacity of its people to *chi ku* (eat bitterness) to see it through the transition.

But amid such stoicism, there's a volatile group that still remembers the party's promises of "working-class rule." Small-scale demonstrations are common outside city halls across China. "The government can't rely on coercion when old ladies at the gates are demanding their pensions," says British sinologist Gordon White. "It actually has to solve the problems."

The worst-case scenario is awful. About a million factory workers are in the military reserve, often with armouries on factory grounds. During the Tiananmen uprising, a Western diplomat notes, "workers threw gasoline-soaked blankets over the air ducts of tanks and incinerated them, because that's what they'd been trained to do. You don't want these people turning against you."

That's one reason why Beijing needs to remake its welfare net. The goal is to move from an enterprise-based to a government-run social-security system that will also allow firms to hire and fire, and workers to change jobs, more easily. The aim is also to get employees, the government and all types of enterprises—not just state-owned behemoths—to share the welfare burden. That means workers will have to pay for more of their pensions, medical care, unemployment insurance and housing. Experiments in several cities are already being repeated across the country.

These will allow China to start saving now for social costs it will incur in the future, instead of mortgaging the present to pay bills already due. It is a tremendously complicated, expensive and politically hazardous undertaking that must proceed in

lock-step with state-enterprise reform. If works, China's leaders will have gone fron socialism to secure capitalism in one genera tion, pulling off one of the greatest polic reversals in economic history. . . .

Obstacles to the reforms are huge, star ing with the primary problem of coming u with the money for the new welfare systen For chronic loss-making state firms it's a v cious cycle: They can't smoothly liquidat merge or form joint ventures without ne welfare schemes to help bear their social ob ligations; yet they have no money to partic pate in the new schemes. "We need a welfar net so that state enterprises can go bankrup but state enterprises must fund the welfar net," says Tang Xiaoli of the State Commis

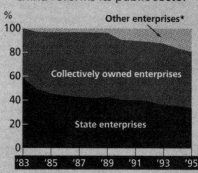

Behemoth's Share

State-owned enterprises' share of employment is falling as China reforms its public sector

*Includes private and individually owned firms as well as joint ventures and foreign-funded firms

Source: World Bank

sion for Restructuring the Economy. "It's all linked."

Take state-run Shenyang Internal Combustion, which makes tractors. As of September, the heavy loss-maker had not paid its 4,500 workers in 10 months, let alone provide them adequate benefits. It tried to declare bankruptcy, which would have given its workers first claim on any liquidated assets. Local officials denied approval, possibly because no alternative arrangements could be made for the factory's welfare burdens. Yet because the firm has no money, it can't participate in new social-security schemes.

So it's been selling land, leasing equipment and doing what it can to keep things going. It gave retirees, who had been pensionless for two months, 150 renminbi each in September. To its very sickest employees, it hands out at most 500 renminbi a month. And it no longer collects rent from unpaid workers living in its deteriorating apartments.

Another obstacle: turf wars. Nine bureaucracies have a say in social-security reforms, and infighting is intense because the money involved will run into billions of dollars. Pension funds alone could amass $60 billion a year by 2030, the World Bank estimates. In cities unable to meet government payrolls, the temptation to misuse the funds, which are administered locally, will be enormous.

More troubles to ponder: In a country with no experienced fund managers, who will control all that money? If companies begin paying into a fund for future pensioners, who will pay all the people who have already retired? How will younger companies be induced to pay into the fund, since their pension and medical bills are negligible for now?

Beijing is trying to manage expectations in order to stave off unrest while it crafts the new welfare system. During the transition, its propagandists are spreading a self-help message. The "Love Industry Centre" in Shenyang, for example, has been widely reported in the national press. A laid-off worker, Wang Yujiang, founded the centre—actually a toilet-paper factory—in 1995. Wang insists on hiring only workers fired by state firms.

But it will take more than propaganda. Whereas most economists think the only way to help workers in industrial rust-zones is to encourage them to find work elsewhere, the traditional system locks them where they are. In Harbin, thousands of people gather every morning in labour markets hoping for a few hours' work. Yet any who move to more successful Dalian will lose their pensions, medical benefits, even their homes.

Beijing is betting that as the private economy outpaces its state counterpart, it will increasingly absorb these workers. In wealthier places like Shanghai, this has a better chance of working. Laid-off worker Xu Baofang now drives a taxi. In depressed places like Shenyang, however, the job switch is not so easily made. Without a safety net that provides for security, mobility and health, China's worst labour upheavals are before it.

This is the first in a series of reports on China's efforts to build a new welfare safety net. [See REVIEW, October 23, 1997, for additional information. **Ed.**]

A NEW TIGER

India used to pride itself on poverty-stricken self-sufficiency. Now it seeks growth, exports and foreign investment, and the economy is booming.

BY STEVEN STRASSER AND SUDIP MAZUMDAR

TRAVEL INTO THE DEPTHS OF Bihar, India's poorest state, along the dirt paths that connect its stagnant pools of humanity, past government signs touting chimerical health and education programs, into the hopeless heart of a subcontinent where the squalid villages might remind you of sub-Saharan Africa—except that the poorest Africans fare better than the destitute of Bihar. Eventually you will stumble onto the village of Kalipahari, blessed with electricity thanks to a nearby hydroelectric dam. Here you will see, in practically every hovel, an incongruous sight: a television set, pulling down American soap operas and Scotch whisky ads from Hong Kong. This is the Indian dream at ground level. As the vision of "Baywatch" filters through Bihar, so even the poorest of the poor finally begin to rise from the depths of rotted isolation.

And so does poor old India. For 50 years the national identity has depended on isolation from perceived enemies—from plotting neocolonialists in the West, from greedy multinational companies, even from those intrepid Indians who resisted the official creed of self-sufficiency. But now satellite TV has come to Bihar, and Coca-Cola, too. Health and education will one day follow. The leaders in New Delhi have a new national ideal—rapid growth—and, at least in spirit, they have thrown open the doors to multinationals everywhere. More important, they are forging a national identity more suited to modern times. India, at last, has begun to see itself as another Asian nation dedicated to the accumulation of wealth and the spread of prosperity. In the next century that vision will hold infinitely more power than the old asceticism. "Perhaps our industrialization is not complete," says Srini Rajam, head of the Texas Instruments branch in booming Bangalore, "but we can leapfrog into the Information Age."

India has always had pride. Now it has ambition. In the early years of independence, Jawaharlal Nehru's government rejoiced in standing apart, the epitome of the "nonaligned" nation. As a conglomeration of peoples with seven major religions and 18 official languages, India made its own rules: a democracy on a continent ruled by despots, a planned economy whose bureaucratic stewards were satisfied to creep along at a 3 or 4 percent "Hindu rate of growth." Only when the New Delhi elite squarely acknowledged that its hubris had put the nation on the sidelines of the global economy—while India's great rival China was getting rich—did real reforms begin. Now, six years into India's opening to the world, the economy is growing by nearly 7 percent a year, a rate that by 2020 will transform its economy into the world's fourth largest (after China, the United States and Japan). "There is a lot of political cacophony," says Finance Minister P. Chidambaram, who has served under two coalition governments in the last 14 months. "But we are on course."

There is no lilt to his optimism. A visitor to urban China (which is churning along at a growth rate of 9.5 percent a year) can almost hear the hum of enterprise in a nation that is fairly bursting to build a better life. The reformers of India, by contrast, tend to bow under the weight of their nation's great poverty. Even now, 52 percent of their people still live on incomes of less than $1 a day, according to World Bank figures. Nearly two thirds of Indian children younger than 5 are malnourished, and those who reach school age can count on an average of only 3.5 years of education if they are boys, 1.5 if they are girls. By the time they reach adulthood, half are still illiterate. Think of it: India is trying to accelerate onto the Information Superhighway with nearly 300 million adults who cannot read road signs.

Comparisons between India and the economic tigers of East Asia are equally dismal. Pacific Rim economies that once ranked far below India and its South Asian neighbors now enjoy per capita incomes 27 times greater, according to the Human Development Centre, a Pakistani think tank that studies regional economic trends. The blunt reality of India's failures is now driving its reforms, and most Indians agree on what must be done. From the Marxists running Calcutta to the Hindu nationals running Bombay (they call it Mumbai), the bywords of the new India are growth, foreign investment and, most hallowed of all, exports.

The strategy, formed in 1991 by the then prime minister P. V. Narasimha Rao and his finance minister, Manmohan Singh, was ruthlessly simple: to dismantle the stifling bureaucracy that once ruled India as intrusively as Moscow's planners once ran the Soviet Union. Rao and Singh cut much of the bureaucracy's "license raj" of red tape, then went on to simplify taxes, reduce the scope of the state sector (which provided everything from power to motor scooters), liberalize foreign investment and cut tariffs. From the earliest days, says Singh, "our goal has been to show the world that India can compete with any country in Southeast Asia in our hospitality to investment and our spirit of enterprise."

India's culture has also been a force for reaching out to the world. The film industry turns out both masterpieces and tawdry B movies in astonishing profusion. Using the imported English language in their own unique way, novelists like Arundhati Roy, 37, a former actress and screenwriter, have become international best sellers. The literary tradition has deep roots; Hindu poet and philosopher Rabindranath Tagore won the Nobel Prize in Literature as long ago as 1913.

Neither culture nor industry has done anything yet for the dregs of Indian society, the 200 million or so people at the very bottom of the ladder. But for the first time in history, economic growth and the spread of communications are working a revolution among many millions of India's other poor. New Delhi's program of teaming with foreign investors to string out copper wire for telephones is proceeding in fits and starts. Even in the capital, the wait for a new phone can still stretch to three years. Nonetheless, the government's decision to let in foreign satellite television has led to an explosion of more than 20 million cable-TV connections within the last two years. That alone had helped to spur demand among low-income consumers to unprecedented levels. A manufacturer of $1.20 bottles of shampoo for middle-class Indians found a huge new market for two-cent packets of the brand in poor areas. The race is on to produce cheap television sets and appliances. One entrepreneur found a way to convert devices for making *lassi* (a yogurt drink) into cheap washing machines. And the first developer of a good $50 refrigerator, suggests economist S. L. Rao, would now find a huge new market in rural India.

More important, India's poor are beginning to find their political voice. Indian democracy has always been hobbled by the primitive state of its grass-roots politics. Too many local leaders bubbled up to national power on their ability to buy votes and deliver favors—and subsequently used their national platforms mainly to enrich themselves. But the rural awakening that came with reform also has revived state and local politics. State competition for the spoils of reform is now common. Tamil Nadu attracted a Ford plant by waiving state sales taxes and offering land at a concessionary price. Uttar Pradesh won the battle to lure an electronics project set up by the Korean giant Daewoo.

The southern city of Bangalore, India's Silicon Valley, stands as the glittering tiara of the new India. Indians themselves own only 1.8 million installed personal computers—about a third the number in New York City. But what the info-tech companies stand for is vitally important. The homegrown firms and those allied with all the big names, from IBM to Intel, have exuberantly cut through red tape and protectionism, welcoming competition while becoming successful software exporters themselves. "If we can't compete with international brands in our own country, we can't hope to ever compete in other countries," says software-industry spokesman Dewang Mehta.

As India streamlines its bureaucracy and unclogs its courts, New Delhi and Mumbai may become more attractive to multinational corporations than the regulatory wilds of Beijing and Shanghai. If India can mobilize its hundreds of millions of young, cheap workers at a time when the work force of the developed world is aging, a boom of Chinese magnitude might not be out of the question. "Just think of the economic output we can generate from this population when our per capita income of $330 doubles early in the next century," says Mukesh Ambani, vice chairman of Mumbai's Reliance Industries. "That will clearly boost us into range of becoming an economic superpower."

Somehow the mantle of "superpower" does not quite fit the personality of a huge, poor country that will continue to regard itself, culturally and politically, as the world's great exception. Nor will India likely become a classic Asian tiger. As a vibrant democracy that must always tend to its own first, the nation will never produce a Deng Xiaoping to dictate its strategy from on high. The new Indian dynamo will muddle along, sure of its direction but never of its strategy, obsessed always with the myriad demands from within. "We will take one sector at a time, show that it works and build confidence," says Manmohan Singh. "There can be no big-bang theory of growth."

An outsider can gauge India's progress by measuring the market's success at shifting resources to the government's neediest constituents—something the centralized bureaucracy never could accomplish. How will life change in the most desolate regions of Bihar? At the absolute end of the line, in the village of Devnagra, a foreign donor recently gave $7,000 for a new well, the kind of gesture that short-circuits India's inefficiencies (to put it politely) rather than validating reform. Nonetheless, once fresh water comes to the village, it will be less hard to imagine a school, a clinic, even a road—and along that road, a thin copper wire connecting the darkest corner of India to the riches of the world.

With RON MOREAU *in Mumbai,*
TONY CLIFTON *in New Delhi and*
JOSHUA KWAN *in Hong Kong*

VILLAGE BANKING: A REPORT FROM 5 COUNTRIES

BY RUPERT SCOFIELD

In Latin America, Africa and Asia, an international nonprofit foundation has created a 3,000-strong network of autonomous village banks

■ HONDURAS ■

For as long as anyone can remember, the women of Siguatepeque, a rural pueblo in central Honduras, have produced ceramics. You can see them for sale on the side of the highway that runs between the capital city of Tegucigalpa and the northern city of San Pedro Sula: great stacks of flower pots, urns, plates and ornamental pieces in the shapes of roosters, parrots, dogs, cats and caimans.

Six years ago, most of the women worked for a man—let's call him Don Alejandro—who purchased the pottery the women made, and resold them to a wholesaler who trucked them to retail markets in Tegucigalpa. The women of Siguatepeque were poor, and disorganized. Most of them sold the pieces as fast as they made them, for a fraction of what Don Alejandro and the retailers earned on them. They had no choice: they needed the money to buy their daily food.

In 1990, when I was looking for a suitable place for the first village bank to be organized by the Foundation for International Community Assistance (FINCA) in Honduras, a friend of mine suggested I go to Siguatepeque. The organizational meeting took place with about thirty women, in Don Alejandro's house. Our host was quite chagrined when, halfway through the meeting, I explained that the bank was for women only. Still, Don Alejandro was a good sport, and supported the idea that FINCA would make $50 loans to the assembled women to invest however they felt best, and that, four months later, they would repay the loan with interest of 3 per cent per month. Another condition of the loan, I explained, was that they would save at least 20 per cent of it, or $10.

I kept waiting for some of the women to drift away, or to be scared off by the interest or the savings requirement, but they all remained, nodding solemnly, as if they understood and were in complete agreement. I didn't tell them it was only the second time I had organized a village bank. But as I was to learn from this and subsequent organizing meetings, they all go this way. It was as if the women already knew how the system worked. It was that simple.

In those days, FINCA had few resources, and I was unable to return to Siguatepeque to conduct the follow-up meetings with the women. Fortunately, the village banking manual I had left behind with the women fell into the hands of an enterprising Peace Corps volunteer, and one month after I had left I received a letter from the women of Siguatepeque which read: "Dear Mr. Scofield: Carolina, the volunteer, has helped us organize our village bank, which we have named "Pinos del Porvenir" ("Pines of the Future"). We have had our four meetings, and we all understand how the bank works. Please send us a check for $1,500."

It was almost four months before I could return to Siguatepeque. I watched as the President, Graciela, ran the meeting. The first thing I noticed was the palpable change in attitude. In sharp contrast to my first meeting with the women, today they were all smiles. Checking the books, I saw that all the loans were current, and that the group had savings of almost $1,000, after only three months.

I asked the women what they had done with the loans. "I spent it on food for my family," woman after woman said. I was appalled. "But how can you be paying off the loans?" Graciela explained to me that the FINCA loans had enabled them to purchase a month's supply of

Reprinted with permission from *The UNESCO Courier,* January 1997, pp. 32-36.

food, which had taken the pressure off them to sell their ceramics as fast as they produced them. Instead, they produced a month's stock, withholding it from Don Alejandro and the other middlemen until the price was more favourable. The village bank loans had given them power in the marketplace.

Today, "Pinos del Porvenir" is independent of FINCA, and has several thousands of dollars in savings, which capitalize the bank's loans to its members. The women no longer sell to middlemen, but have their own retail store.

FINCA Honduras, meanwhile, has grown from a shoestring operation to a financially self-sufficient lending institution servicing 13,000 low-income borrowers in several regions of the country. The experience of the women of Siguatepeque has been repeated many times. Some of the village banks in Siguatepeque, in fact, went on to "graduate" and become clients of the local commercial bank.

FINCA has derived a number of lessons from the Siguatepeque experience. Most important, perhaps, is the fact that a mere $50 loan can catalyze a process of individual and community development, which appears to be self-sustaining. Second, is the idea that the borrowers, in possession of far more information regarding local conditions than we outside "experts", are better prepared to determine how to invest that loan. Finally, there is the evidence that village banking can create a three-tiered self-sufficiency: at the borrower, community, and even national levels. If this kind of result can be replicated on a massive, worldwide scale, then rescuing many of the over one billion people living in poverty today may not be as daunting a challenge as we imagined.

PERU

The village bank "Union y Progreso" ("Union and Progress") is located in a crime-ridden shanty town on the southern border of Lima (Peru). Like many other "pueblos jovenes" ("young towns") surrounding the Peruvian capital, this one was established by squatters fleeing the violence of the "Shining Path" Guerrillas, and the impossibility of scratching out a living from agriculture on the rapidly eroding, parched soils of the Andean highlands. From the outside, the village bank President's house bears little resemblance to a bank. The walls are a conglomeration of scavenged lumber, cardboard, and corrugated metal, and the roof is a patchwork of the same, weighted by stones to prevent the strong winds from blowing them away. As a deterrent to housebreakers, the top of the wall is crested with an intimidating glaze of broken glass, barbed wire and nails.

Inside, the eighteen members of "Union and Progress" are holding their meeting. The Treasurer and President are giving the financial report, with the aid of two large sheets of paper, upon which the bank's "vital signs" have been recorded with a pink magic marker. After two years, the eighteen members of "Union and Progress" have saved a total $12,322, or almost $700 apiece. An examination of the bank's records reveals that, through active relending of their savings, the members have generated an additional $55,278 in loans over the past four months. This dwarfs the mere $7,200 which FINCA Peru has lent to the group. The interest income from these "internal account" loans is $1,100.

Other income has been generated from fines on borrowers whose payments were made late. A late payment on either an internal account loan or external account carries a fine of 10 *soles* (about $4.50). This goes into a pot shared by only those who had perfect payment records. The women of "Union and Progress" came up with this carrot-stick system themselves. It strikes me as ingenious. An institutional approach would be to focus exclusively on the punitive side, the fines. I intend to see that this idea gets disseminated to the other 3,000 village banks in the FINCA network. Most of the good ideas incorporated into village banking methodology have arisen in this way, from the borrowers themselves. The concept of the "internal account"—the relending of the borrowers' savings, among themselves and to the community at large—came from a village bank in the border town of Sasabe, Mexico.

Now it is the turn of the borrowers, to ask questions or to make comments. I listen to the testimony of Maria Ponte, aged sixty-five, who is leaving the bank, returning to the mountain town of Puno to live with her son. She thanks FINCA Peru for bringing the village bank to their community, and the members for trusting and supporting her. "I used to be thin as a stick. Now, thanks to FINCA, I have meat on my bones (she holds up her biceps and squeezes her flesh). I can afford to take vitamins. I have $683 in savings. I used to be afraid to borrow money. When I got my first loan from FINCA, I was shaking. This cycle, I borrowed and repaid $1,867 from the internal account in four months. We used to be afraid of dollars. In FINCA, I learned to save and borrow."

With an average savings rate of $281.57 per member, Peru has the largest savings-to-loans ratio in the FINCA network. In all, FINCA's

68,000 borrowers have saved $3.6 million over the past ten years, up 80 per cent from just two years ago. This money has not been funneled off to commercial banks in the capital, or sent offshore to Miami or Switzerland. It remains in the poorest communities of the world, working to create jobs and income on the bottom floor of the economy. Clearly, microenterprise has great potential for what my economics professor used to call "capital formation: the engine of development."

■ EL SALVADOR ■

In 1991, Maribel Escobar Avalos' situation seemed desperate. Having witnessed the destruction of her first home in an earthquake in 1985, and her second in a guerrilla offensive in 1989, she had few possessions other than the clothes on her back. At the same time, she was supporting a family of nine, including an unemployed male companion, her seventy-three-year-old father, an invalid brother, two daughters, a son, a son-in-law, and a niece. But Maribel had learned from her mother in the markets of El Salvador how to sell. In a bold gamble, she sold what little she had left to make the down payment on a corner house lot in the western El Salvador town of El Sunsa.

The first year in El Sunsa was one of sacrifice and struggle. Totally decapitalized, the Escobar family spent the year in a makeshift shack of cardboard, with palm fronds for a roof. Their food budget was so small that often their only nutrition came from a concoction Maribel calls *sopa de monte* ("weed soup").

It was in these conditions that Maribel discovered the FINCA Micro-Enterprise Support Center. The MSC made Maribel the first loan of her life, $50, which she invested in the purchase and sale of used clothing. Over the next two years, through her skill in selling, and access to ever-larger loans, Maribel began to diversify. First she established a small grocery store. Then a restaurant. Finally, she began to supply fruit and vegetables to other traders in El Sunsa. Eventually, these activities provided employment for the entire family. Along the way, Maribel accumulated $805 in cash savings in her village bank. Today, on the corner lot which used to host a ramshackle *choza* of cardboard and palm fronds, a comfortable four bedroom brick house stands. The store front room houses the store and restaurant, with an electrified "Orange Crush" sign featuring the name "Restaurante y Pupuseria El Canalito."

As she sends her children off to high school (she herself never progressed beyond third grade), Maribel explains her formula for success. "My whole life, I've worked hard, getting up at 5 a.m. and going to bed at 9 p.m. But the difference is, now we are saving. The more we save, the more we can borrow. The more we borrow, the more we can sell. The more we can sell, the greater our income."

■ UGANDA ■

Prior to 1992, the women of Kimantu village in southeastern Uganda, near the sources of the Nile, had never managed their own money or run a business, let alone received credit. What little money did pass through their hands had to be begged from their husbands, even to buy food for their children. When I first described how the village bank would work, one of the women in the village asked me how much money FINCA would lend them. "Fifty thousand shillings," I replied, which was the equivalent of $50. This was a tense moment for me: I had been assured by the Executive Director of another non-governmental organization working in Uganda that the women would turn up their noses at such a paltry sum.

The woman gasped and nearly fainted. She assured me that 50,000 shillings was too much; she could never take responsibility for paying back such a princely sum. In the end, at the urging of her neighbours, she agreed to accept half that amount, splitting the loan with another woman in the bank.

When I returned to Kimantu, four months later, I found the women, and the village, transformed. They had repaid their loans, 100 per cent. They had saved in excess of the required 20 per cent. "The thing I like best about the village bank," one woman told me, "is that I have learned to start a business and to manage money." The woman who had been too timid to borrow 50,000 shillings now told me she intended to borrow 100,000.

The men in the village, who had initially viewed the village bank with suspicion, now welcomed it. As the Kimantu village chief told me: "When the women first started to hold their meetings, we men were concerned. We thought they were talking about divorcing us. But then, when we saw them earning money, and they no longer came to us for money to buy salt, and pay school fees, we saw that the village bank was a good thing. But Mr. Scofield, I have one question." "And what is that?" I asked. The chief grinned. "Can you create a village bank for us men?"

In many communities of Uganda, Aids has left its brutal imprint, sweeping away husbands, wives, and sometimes entire families. In most cases, however, the children survive, to be raised by the village as a whole. Many Ugandan village bankers are supporting not only their own children, but those orphaned by deceased relatives and neighbours. It is an intensely sad, but at the same time inspiring experience to meet these selfless, struggling mothers. "Women who are in village banks are seen as the most responsible members of the community," was the way one observer put it. "It is natural that people look to them, when they want a secure future for the children they leave behind."

▓ KYRGYZSTAN ▓

Can microenterprise succeed in a country where, until recently, private enterprise was officially discouraged, considered immoral, and, in some cases, even outlawed? In 1994, FINCA established the first village banks in the newly independent state of Kyrgyzstan, Central Asia, in the capital city of Bishkek.

With the snow-capped Himalayas as a backdrop, Bishkek is a city just coming to life, economically, after years of surviving on subsidies from mother Russia. Today, an estimated 15 per cent of the population is unemployed, and more expected as state-run enterprises are privatized or closed altogether. Increasingly, the population is moving to self-employment as an alternative to the meagre wages of the public sector.

Today, the village bank *Bereke* ("Blessing") is receiving its first loan. Village banks are smaller in Kyrgyzstan than in other countries in the FINCA network, reflecting an added cautiousness on the part of the members towards their neighbours, the vast majority of whom have never operated a business. FINCA has learned to respect the members' appreciation of local conditions as being far superior to its own, and seldom intervenes in decisions regarding the selection of the bank's members, or in the loan approval process. In this case, most of the fifteen borrowers will be investing their loans in consumer goods, to be sold in the local market. A great feast for the visitors was laid out on a gorgeous, hand-woven rug in the village bank president's living room. Other rugs, of equally dazzling patterns, adorned the walls. These rugs, which sell domestically for less than $10, can command over $100 in export markets. Though it was only mid morning, glasses of brandy were offered and accepted.

The meeting began, presided over by a democratically elected President, Treasurer and Secretary. The President followed the standard village bank agenda: financial report, approval and disbursement of loans, and collection of obligatory and voluntary savings. Besides the small size of the village banks, the methodology has suffered little modification in its adaptation to the Kyrgyz context. Contrary to initial warnings that no one would be interested in small loans in Kyrgyzstan, FINCA has found the demand to be strong. To date, FINCA Kyrgyzstan has reached 2,300 borrowers, and, in a country of five million, the word is just beginning to spread.

Child Labour:
Rights, risks, and realities

by Carol Bellamy

"Dust from the chemical powders and strong vapours in both the storeroom and the boiler room were obvious...We found 250 children, mostly below 10 years of age, working in a long hall, filling in a slotted frame with sticks. Row upon row of children, some barely five years old, were involved in the work."

The description could come from an observer appalled at the working conditions endured by children in the 19th century in British mills and factories.

But the quote is from a report on the matchstick-making industry of modern day Sivakasi, in India.

Similar descriptions of children at work in hazardous conditions can be gathered from countries across the world. In Malaysia, children may work up to 17-hour days on rubber plantations, exposed to insect- and snakebites. In the United Republic of Tanzania, they pick coffee beans, inhaling pesticides. In Portugal, children as young as 12 are subject to heavy labour and the myriad dangers of the construction industry. In Morocco, they hunch at looms for long hours and little pay, knotting the strands of luxury carpets for export. In the United States, children are exploited in garment-industry sweatshops. In the Philippines, young boys dive in dangerous conditions to help set nets for deep-sea fishing. Statistical data on child labour is scarce, but our most reliable estimates indicate about 250 million child labourers (ages 10-14) in developing countries alone.

The world should, indeed, have outgrown the many forms of abuse that labouring children endure. But it hasn't, although not for lack of effort. Child labour was one of the first and most important issues addressed by the international community, resulting in the 1919 Minimum Age Convention of the International Labour Organization.

Early efforts were hobbled, in part, because campaigners struggling to end child labour appealed to morality and ethics, values easily sidelined by the drive for profit and hard realities of commercial life. Child labourers were objects of charity and humanitarian concern, but they had no rights.

Today's world is somewhat different. Children have rights established in international laws, not least in the Convention on the Rights of the Child, which has now been ratified by 191 countries—all but the U.S. and Somalia—making it the most universally embraced human rights instrument in history. One provision —Article 32—obligates governments to protect children "from economic exploitation and from performing any work that is likely to be hazardous or to interfere with the child's education, and/or to be harmful to the child's health or physical, mental, spiritual, moral, or social development."

Children's exploitation in work also contravenes many more of the rights enshrined in the Convention, among them children's rights to parental care, to compulsory and free primary education, to the highest attainable standard of health, to social security, and to provisions for rest and recreation.

Looking at children's work through the lens of the Convention on the Rights of the Child offers not only new ways

A domestic servant in Mauritania

C-8E UNICEF/L. GOODSMITH

From *The Rotarian*, September 1997, pp. 26-29. Adapted from *The State of the World's Children* by Carol Bellamy. © 1997 by Oxford University Press. Reprinted by permission.

Herding cattle in Kenya

of understanding the problem of child labour, but also provides new impetus and direction to the movement against it.

Child labour is often a complex issue. Powerful forces sustain it, including many employers, vested interest groups, economists proposing that the market must be free at all costs, and traditionalists who believe that the low caste or class of certain children denudes them of rights.

The overriding consideration must always be the best interests of the child. It can never be in the best interests of a child to be exploited or to perform heavy and dangerous forms of work. No child should labour under hazardous and exploitative conditions, just as no child should die of causes that are preventable.

Work that endangers children's physical, mental, spiritual, moral, or social development must end. Hazardous child labour is a betrayal of every child's rights as a human being and is an offence against civilization.

Most children who work do not have the power of free choice. They do not choose between career options with varying advantages,

drawbacks, and levels of pay. A fortunate minority have sufficient material means behind them to be pulled toward work as an attractive option offering them even more economic advantages.

But the vast majority are pushed into work that is often damaging to their development for three reasons: the exploitation of poverty, the absence of education, and the restrictions of tradition.

The exploitation of poverty

The most powerful force driving children into hazardous, debilitating labour is the exploitation of poverty. Where society is characterized by poverty and inequity, the incidence of child labour is likely to increase, as does the risk that it is exploitative.

For poor families, the small contribution of a child's income or assistance at home that allows the parents to work can make the difference between hunger and a bare sufficiency. Survey after survey makes this clear. A high proportion of child employees give all their wages to their parents. Children's work is considered essential to maintaining the economic level of the household.

If employers were not prepared to exploit children, there would be no child labour. The parents of child labourers are often unemployed or underemployed, desperate for secure employment and income. Yet it is not they but their children who are offered the jobs. Why? Because children can be paid less, of course. (In Latin America, for example, children ages 13 to 17 earn on average half the pay of a wage-earning adult with seven years of education.) Because children are more malleable, they will do what they are told without questioning authority. Because children are largely powerless before adults, they are less likely to organize against oppression and can be physically abused without striking back.

Put simply, children are employed because they are easier to exploit.

Exploitation of the poor and the powerless not only means that adults are denied jobs that could better have sustained their families. It not only means that children are required to work in arduous, dangerous conditions. It also means a life of unskilled work and ignorance not only for the child, but often for the

167

children of generations to come. Any small, short-term financial gain for the family is at the cost of an incalculable long-term loss. Poverty begets child labour begets lack of education begets poverty.

A serious attack on poverty will reduce the number of children vulnerable to exploitation at work. Social safety nets are essential for the poor, as are access to credit and income-generating schemes, technology, education, and basic health services. Budgetary priorities need to be re-examined in this light.

Tackling the exploitation itself does not have to wait until some future day when world poverty has been brought to an end. Hazardous child labour provides the most powerful of arguments for equality and social justice. It can and must be abolished here and now.

The lack of relevant education

Cuts in social spending worldwide have hit education—the most important single factor in ending child labour—particularly hard.

In all regions, spending per student for higher education fell during the 1980s, and in Africa and Latin America, spending per pupil also fell for primary education.

A pilot survey, sponsored by the United Nations Educational, Scientific, and Cultural Organization (UNESCO) and the United Nations Children's Fund (UNICEF) and carried out in 1994 in 14 of the world's least-developed countries, reinforced concerns about the actual conditions of primary schools. In half of these countries, classrooms for the equivalent of first grade have sitting places for only four in 10 pupils. Half the pupils have no textbooks and half the classrooms have no chalkboards. Teachers commonly have to attempt to handle huge classes—an average of 67 pupils per teacher in Bangladesh and nearly 90 per teacher in Equatorial Guinea. In 10 of the 14 countries, most children are taught in a language not spoken at home. And most homes, of course, have no books or magazines in any language.

Education everywhere is clearly underfunded, but the school system as it stands in most developing countries of the world is blighted by more than just a lack of resources. It is often too rigid and uninspiring in approach, promoting a curriculum that is irrelevant to and remote from children's lives.

Education has become part of the

problem. It has to be reborn as part of the solution.

Traditional expectations

The economic forces that propel children into hazardous work may be the most powerful of all. But traditions and entrenched social patterns play a part, too.

In industrialized countries, it is now almost universally accepted that if children are to develop normally and healthily, they must not perform disabling work. In theory at least, education, play and leisure, friends, good health, and proper rest must all have an important place in their lives. This idea emerged only relatively recently. In the early decades of industrialization, work was thought to be the most effective way of teaching children about life and the world. Some residue of this notion remains in the widespread expectation that teenage children should take on casual jobs alongside school, both to gain an understanding of the way the world functions and to earn spending money of their own.

There is a darker side to the expectations about children's work. The harder and more hazardous the jobs become, the more they are likely to

Picking cotton in El Salvador

88-002 UNICEF/ASLAK AARBUS

be considered traditionally the province of the poor and disadvantaged, the lower classes, and ethnic minorities. In India, for example, the view has been that some people are born to rule and to work with their minds while others, the vast majority, are born to work with their bodies. Many traditionalists have been unperturbed about lower-caste children failing to enroll in or dropping out of school. And if those children end up doing hazardous labour, it is likely to be seen as their lot in life.

Understanding all the various cultural factors that lead children into work is essential. But deference to tradition is often cited as a reason for not acting against intolerable forms of child labour. Children have an absolute, unnegotiable right to freedom from hazardous labour—a right now established in international law and accepted by every country that has ratified the Convention on the Rights of the Child. Respect for diverse cultures should not deflect us from using all the means at our disposal to make every society, every economy, every corporation, regard the exploitation of children as unthinkable.

Mobilizing society

Nongovernmental organizations, such as Rotary International, have a vital role to play both in raising levels of public concern and in protecting children. You can monitor the conditions in which children work and help launch the long, indispensable process of changing public attitudes.

R.I. President Glen W. Kinross has asked Rotarians this year to "strike out at the root causes of child abuse and abandonment and child labour. Children are our most precious treasure and the future belongs to them." And we know that today many Rotary clubs are working to improve the lives of children by striving to fight poverty and hunger, provide education, and prevent child abuse and exploitation. On behalf of the world's children, thank you, Rotarians, for your concern and actions.

As we step into the next millennium, hazardous child labour must be left behind, consigned to history as completely as those other forms of slavery that it so closely resembles.

Above: Selling vegetables in Nepal. Below: Making bricks in Mexico

• *Carol Bellamy is Executive Director of the United Nations Children's Fund (UNICEF).*

The Burden of Womanhood

Too often in the Third World, a female's life is hardly worth living

John Ward Anderson and Molly Moore

Washington Post Foreign Service

GANDHI NAGAR, India

When Rani returned home from the hospital cradling her newborn daughter, the men in the family slipped out of her mud hut while she and her mother-in-law mashed poisonous oleander seeds into a dollop of oil and forced it down the infant's throat. As soon as darkness fell, Rani crept into a nearby field and buried her baby girl in a shallow, unmarked grave next to a small stream.

"I never felt any sorrow," Rani, a farm laborer with a weather-beaten face, said through an interpreter. "There was a lot of bitterness in my heart toward the baby because the gods should have given me a son."

Each year hundreds and perhaps thousands of newborn girls in India are murdered by their mothers simply because they are female. Some women believe that sacrificing a daughter guarantees a son in the next pregnancy. In other cases, the family cannot afford the dowry that would eventually be demanded for a girl's marriage.

And for many mothers, sentencing a daughter to death is better than condemning her to life as a woman in the Third World, with cradle-to-grave discrimination, poverty, sickness and drudgery.

"In a culture that idolizes sons and dreads the birth of a daughter, to be born female comes perilously close to being born less than human," the Indian government conceded in a recent report by its Department of Women and Child Development.

While women in the United States and Europe—after decades of struggling for equal rights—often measure sex discrimination by pay scales and seats in corporate board rooms, women in the Third World gauge discrimination by mortality rates and poverty levels.

"Women are the most exploited among the oppressed," says Karuna Chanana Ahmed, a New Delhi anthropologist who has studied the role of women in developing countries. "I don't think it's even possible to eradicate discrimination, it's so deeply ingrained."

This is the first in a series that will examine the lives of women in developing countries around the globe where culture, religion and the law often deprive women of basic human rights and sometimes relegate them to almost subhuman status. From South America to South Asia, women are often subjected to a lifetime of discrimination with little or no hope of relief.

As children, they are fed less, denied education and refused hospitalization. As teenagers, many are forced into marriage, sometimes bought and sold like animals for prostitution and slave labor. As wives and mothers, they are often treated little better than farmhands and baby machines. Should they outlive their husbands, they frequently are denied inheritance, banished from their homes and forced to live as beggars on the streets.

The scores of women interviewed for this series—from destitute villagers in Brazil and Bangladesh, to young professionals in Cairo, to factory workers in China—blamed centuries-old cultural and religious traditions for institutionalizing and giving legitimacy to gender discrimination.

Although, the forms of discrimination vary tremendously among regions, ethnic groups and age levels in the developing world, Shahla Zia, an attorney and women's activist in Islamabad, Pakistan, says there is a theme: "Overall, there is a social and cultural attitude where women are inferior—and discrimination tends to start at birth."

In many countries, a woman's greatest challenge is an elemental one: simply surviving through a normal life cycle. In South Asia and China, the perils begin at birth, with the threat of infanticide.

Like many rural Indian women, Rani, now 31, believed that killing her daughter 3 ½ years ago would guarantee that her next baby would be a boy. Instead, she had another daughter.

"I wanted to kill this child also," she says, brushing strands of hair from the face of the 2-year-old girl she named Asha, or Hope. "But my husband got scared because all these social workers came and said, 'Give us the child.'" Ultimately, Rani was allowed to keep her. She pauses. "Now I have killed, and I still haven't had any sons."

Amravati, who lives in a village near Rani in the Indian state of Tamil Nadu, says she killed two of her own day-old daughters by pouring scalding chicken soup down their throats, one of the most widely practiced methods of infanticide in southern India. She showed where she buried their bodies—under piles of cow dung in the tiny courtyard of her home.

"My mother-in-law and father-in-law are bedridden," says Amravati, who has two living daughters. "I have no land and no salary, and my husband met with an accident and can't work. Of course it was the right decision. I need

a boy. Even though I have to buy clothes and food for a son, he will grow on his own and take care of himself. I don't have to buy him jewelry or give him a 10,000-rupee [$350] dowry."

Sociologists and government officials began documenting sporadic examples of female infanticide in India about 10 years ago. The practice of killing newborn girls is largely a rural phenomenon in India; although its extent has not been documented, one indication came in a recent survey by the Community Services Guild of Madras, a city in Tamil Nadu. Of the 1,250 women questioned, the survey concluded that more than half had killed baby daughters.

In urban areas, easier access to modern medical technology enables women to act before birth. Through amniocentesis, women can learn the sex of a fetus and undergo sex-selective abortions. At one clinic in Bombay, of 8,000 abortions performed after amniocentesis, 7,999 were of female fetuses, according to a recent report by the Indian government. To be sure, female infanticide and sex-selective abortion are not unique to India. Social workers in other South Asian states believe that some communities also condone the practice. In China, one province has had so many cases of female infanticide that a half-million bachelors cannot find wives because they outnumber women their age by 10 to 1, according to the official New China News Agency.

The root problems, according to village women, sociologists and other experts, are cultural and economic. In India, a young woman is regarded as a temporary member of her natural family and a drain on its wealth. Her parents are considered caretakers whose main responsibility is to deliver a chaste daughter, along with a sizable dowry, to her husband's family.

"They say bringing up a girl is like watering a neighbor's plant," says R. Venkatachalam, director of the Community Services Guild of Madras. "From birth to death, the expenditure is there." The dowry, he says, often wipes out a family's life savings but is necessary to arrange a proper marriage and maintain the honor of the bride's family.

After giving birth to a daughter, village women "immediately start thinking, 'Do we have the money to support her through life?' and if they don't, they kill her," according to Vasanthai, 20, the mother of an 18-month-old girl and a resident of the village where Rani lives. "You definitely do it after two or three daughters. Why would you want more?"

Few activists or government officials in India see female infanticide as a law-and-order issue, viewing it instead as a social problem that should be eradicated through better education, family planning and job programs. Police officials say few cases are reported and witnesses seldom cooperate.

"There are more pressing issues," says a top police official in Madras. "Very few cases come to our attention. Very few people care."

Surviving childbirth is itself an achievement in South Asia for both mother and baby. One of every 18 women dies of a pregnancy-related cause, and more than one of every 10 babies dies during delivery.

For female children, the survival odds are even worse. Almost one in every five girls born in Nepal and Bangladesh dies before age 5. In India, about one-fourth of the 12 million girls born each year die by age 15.

The high death rates are not coincidental. Across the developing world, female children are fed less, pulled out of school earlier, forced into hard labor sooner and given less medical care than boys. According to numerous studies, girls are handicapped not only by the perception that they are temporary members of a family, but also by the belief that males are the chief breadwinners and therefore more deserving of scarce resources.

Boys are generally breast-fed longer. In many cultures, women and girls eat leftovers after the men and boys have finished their meals. According to a joint report by the United Nations Children's Fund and the government of Pakistan, some tribal groups do not feed high-protein foods such as eggs and meat to girls because of the fear it will lead to early puberty.

Women are often hospitalized only when they have reached a critical stage of illness, which is one reason so many mothers die in childbirth. Female children, on the other hand, often are not hospitalized at all. A 1990 study of patient records at Islamabad Children's Hospital in Pakistan found that 71 percent of the babies admitted under age 2 were boys. For all age groups, twice as many boys as girls were admitted to the hospital's surgery, pediatric intensive care and diarrhea units.

Mary Okumu, an official with the African Medical and Research Foundation in Nairobi, says that when a worker in drought-ravaged northern Kenya asked why only boys were lined up at a clinic, the worker was told that in times of drought, many families let their daughters die.

"Nobody will even take them to a clinic," Okumu says. "They prefer the boy to survive."

For most girls, however, the biggest barrier—and the one that locks generations of women into a cycle of discrimination—is lack of education.

Across the developing world, girls are withdrawn from school years before boys so they can remain at home and lug water, work the fields, raise younger siblings and help with other domestic chores. By the time girls are 10 or 12 years old, they may put in as much as an eight-hour work day, studies show. One survey found that a young girl in rural India spends 30 percent of her waking hours doing household work, 29 percent gathering fuel and 20 percent fetching water.

Statistics from Pakistan demonstrate the low priority given to female education: Only one-third of the country's schools—which are sexually segregated—are for women, and one-third of those have no building. Almost 90 percent of the women over age 25 are illiterate. In the predominantly rural state of Baluchistan, less than 2 percent of women can read and write.

In Islamic countries such as Pakistan and Bangladesh, religious concern about interaction with males adds further restrictions to females' mobility. Frequently, girls are taken out of school when they reach puberty to limit their contact with males—though there exists a strong impetus for early marriages. In Bangladesh, according to the United Nations, 73 percent of girls are married by age 15, and 21 percent have had at least one child.

Across South Asia, arranged marriages are the norm and can sometimes be the most demeaning rite of passage a woman endures. Two types are common—bride wealth, in which the bride's family essentially gives her to the highest bidder, and dowry, in which the bride's family pays exorbitant amounts to the husband's family.

In India, many men resort to killing their wives—often by setting them afire—if they are unhappy with the dowry. According to the country's Ministry of Human Resource Development, there were 5,157 dowry murders in 1991—one every hour and 42 minutes.

After being bartered off to a new family, with little education, limited access to health care and no knowledge of birth control, young brides soon become young mothers. A woman's adulthood is often spent in a near constant state of pregnancy, hoping for sons.

According to a 1988 report by India's Department of Women and Child Development: "The Indian woman on an average has eight to nine pregnancies, resulting in a little over six live births, of which four or five survive. She is estimated to spend 80 percent of her reproductive years in pregnancy and lactation." Because of poor nutrition and a hard workload, she puts on about nine pounds during pregnancy, compared with 22 pounds for a typical pregnant woman in a developed country.

A recent study of the small Himalayan village of Bemru by the New Delhi-based Center for Science and the Environment found that "birth in most cases takes place in the cattle shed," where villagers believe that holy cows protect the mother and newborn from evil spirits. Childbirth is considered unclean, and the mother and their newborn are treated as "untouchables" for about two weeks after delivery.

"It does not matter if the woman is young, old or pregnant, she has no rest, Sunday or otherwise," the study said, noting that women in the village did 59 percent of the work, often laboring 14 hours a day and lugging loads 1 1/2 times their body weight. "After two or three . . . pregnancies, their stamina gives up, they get weaker, and by the late thirties are spent out, old and tired, and soon die."

Studies show that in developing countries, women in remote areas can spend more than two hours a day carrying water for cooking, drinking, cleaning and bathing, and in some rural areas they spend the equivaent of more than 200 days a year gathering firewood. That presents an additional hazard: The International Labor Organization found that women using wood fuels in India inhaled carcinogenic pollutants that are the equivalent of smoking 20 packs of cigarettes a day.

Because of laws relegating them to a secondary status, women have few outlets for relaxation or recreation. In many Islamic countries, they are not allowed to drive cars, and their appearance in public is so restricted that they are banned from such recreational and athletic activities as swimming and gymnastics.

In Kenya and Tanzania, laws prohibit women from owning houses. In Pakistan, a daughter legally is entitled to half the inheritance a son gets when their parents die. In some criminal cases, testimony by women is legally given half the weight of a man's testimony, and compensation for the wrongful death of a woman is half that for the wrongful death of a man.

After a lifetime of brutal physical labor, multiple births, discrimination and sheer tedium, what should be a woman's golden years often hold the worst indignities. In India, a woman's identity is so intertwined and subservient to her husband's that if she outlives him, her years as a widow are spent as a virtual nonentity. In previous generations, many women were tied to their husband's funeral pyres and burned to death, a practice called *suttee* that now rarely occurs.

Today, some widows voluntarily shave their heads and withdraw from society, but more often a spartan lifestyle is forced upon them by families and a society that place no value on old, single women. Widowhood carries such a stigma that remarriage is extremely rare, even for women who are widowed as teenagers.

In some areas of the country, women are forced to marry their dead husband's brother to ensure that any property remains in the family. Often they cannot wear jewelry or a *bindi*—the beauty spot women put on their foreheads—or they must shave their heads and wear a white sari. Frequently, they cannot eat fish or meat, garlic or onions.

"The life of a widow is miserable," says Aparna Basu, general secretary of the All India Women's Conference, citing a recent study showing that more than half the women in India age 60 and older are widows, and their mortality rate is three times higher than that of married women of the same age.

In South Asia, women have few property or inheritance rights, and a husband's belongings usually go to sons and occasionally daughters. A widow must rely on the largess of her children, who often cast their mothers on the streets.

Thousands of destitute Indian widows make the pilgrimage to Vrindaban, a town on the outskirts of Agra where they hope to achieve salvation by praying to the god Krishna. About 1,500 widows show up each day at the Shri Bhagwan prayer house, where in exchange for singing "Hare Rama, Hare Krishna" for eight hours, they are given a handful of rice and beans and 1.5 rupees, or about 5 cents.

Some widows claim that when they stop singing, they are poked with sticks by monitors, and social workers allege that younger widows have been sexually assaulted by temple custodians and priests.

On a street there, an elderly woman with a *tilak* on her forehead—white chalk lines signifying that she is a devout Hindu widow—waves a begging cup at passing strangers.

"I have nobody," says Paddo Chowdhury, 65, who became a widow at 18 and has been in Vrindaban for 30 years. "I sit here, shed my tears and get enough food one way or another."

Conflict

Do you lock your door at night? Do you secure your personal property to avoid theft? These are basic questions that have to do with your sense of personal safety and security. Most people take steps to protect what they have, including their lives. The same is true for groups of people, Including countries. In the international arena, governments pursue their national security the majority of the time by entering into mutually agreeable deals with others. Social scientists call these "exchanges"(i.e., giving up something in order to gain something that one values more). It usually goes something like this: "I have oil that you need. I will sell you my oil if you will sell me agricultural products that I lack." Whether on a personal level ("You help me with my homework and I will drive you home this weekend") or on the governmental level, this is the process used by most individuals and groups to "secure" and protect what is of value. The exchange process, however, can break down. When threats and punishments replace mutual exchanges, conflict ensues. Neither side benefits, and there are costs to both. Each side may use threats and hope the other will capitulate, but if efforts at coercion fail, the conflict may escalate into violent confrontation.

With the end of the cold war, the issues of national security are changing for the world's major powers. Old alliances are changing, not only in Europe, but in the Middle East as well. These changes have great policy implications not only for the major powers but also for participants in regional conflicts. Agreements between the leadership of the now-defunct Soviet Union and the United States led to the elimination of support for participants in low-intensity conflicts in Central America, Africa, and Southeast Asia. Fighting the cold war by proxy is now a thing of the past. Nevertheless, there is no shortage of conflicts in the world today.

The unit begins with a discussion of the growing importance of low-intensity conflicts. This is followed by a summary of the types of conflicts that are likely to dominate and the challenges of keeping them from escalating into warfare. Then, specific case studies address ethnic violence, terrorism, China and Russia's security problems, and the spread of nuclear weapons.

The unit concludes by examining one of the most important issues in history—the avoidance of nuclear war. Many experts initially predicted that the collapse of the Soviet Union would decrease the threat of nuclear war. However, many now believe that the threat has increased as control of nuclear weapons has become less centralized and the command structure less reliable. What these dramatically different circumstances mean for strategic weapons policy in the United States is also a topic of considerable debate. With this changing political context as the backdrop, the prospects for arms control and increased international cooperation are reviewed.

Like all the other global issues described in this anthology, international conflict is a dynamic problem. It is important to understand that it is not a random event, but there are patterns and trends. Forty-five years of cold war established a variety of patterns of international conflict as the superpowers contained each other with vast expenditures of money and technological know-how. The consequence of this stalemate was a shift to the developing world as the arena of conflict. With the end of the cold war, these patterns are changing. Will there be more nuclear proliferation, or will there be less? Will the emphasis be shifted to low-intensity conflicts related to the interdiction of drugs?

Or will economic problems turn the industrial world inward and allow a new round of ethnically motivated conflicts to become brutally violent, as we have seen in Yugoslavia and its former republic, Bosnia-Herzegovina? The answers to these and related questions will determine the patterns of conflict in the post–cold war era.

Looking Ahead: Challenge Questions

Are violent conflicts and warfare increasing or decreasing today? Explain your response.

What changes have taken place in recent years in the types of conflicts that occur and in who participates?

How is military doctrine changing to reflect new political realities?

How is the role of the United States in global security likely to change? What about Russia and China?

Are nuclear weapons more or less likely to proliferate in the post–cold war era? Why?

What institutional structures can be developed to reduce the danger of nuclear war?

> "Because of the global upsurge in ethnic and sectarian conflict, policymakers have become more attuned to the role played by [light] arms in sparking and sustaining low-level warfare and have begun to consider new constraints on trade in these munitions. . . Although heavy weapons sometimes play a role, most of the day-to-day fighting is performed by irregular forces armed only with rifles, grenades, machine guns, light mortars, and other 'man-portable' munitions."

The New Arms Race:
Light Weapons and International Security

MICHAEL T. KLARE

For most of the past 50 years, analysts and policymakers have largely ignored the role of small arms and other light weapons in international security affairs, considering them too insignificant to have an impact on the global balance of power or the outcome of major conflicts. Nuclear weapons, ballistic missiles, and major conventional weapons (tanks, heavy artillery, jet planes) are assumed to be all that matter when calculating the strength of potential belligerents. As a result, international efforts to reduce global weapons stockpiles and to curb the trade in arms have been focused almost exclusively on major weapons systems. At no point since World War II have international policymakers met to consider curbs on trade in light weapons, or to restrict their production.

Recently, world leaders have begun to take a fresh interest in small arms and light weapons. Because of the global upsurge in ethnic and sectarian conflict, policymakers have become more attuned to the role played by such arms in sparking and sustaining low-level warfare, and have begun to consider new constraints on trade in these munitions. "I wish to concentrate on what might be called 'micro-disarmament,'" United Nations Secretary General Boutros Boutros-Ghali declared in January 1995. By that, he explained, "I mean practical disarmament in the context of the conflicts the United Nations *is actually dealing with*, and of the weapons, most of them

MICHAEL T. KLARE *is a professor of peace and world security studies at Hampshire College and director of the Five College Program in Peace and World Security Studies. He is the author of* Rogue States and Nuclear Outlaws: America's Search for a New Foreign Policy *(New York: Hill and Wang, 1995).*

light weapons, that are actually killing people in the hundreds of thousands" (emphasis added).

This focus on the conflicts the United Nations is "actually dealing with" represents a major shift in global priorities. During the cold war, most world leaders were understandably preoccupied with the potential threat of nuclear war or an East-West conflict in Europe. Today policymakers are more concerned about the immediate threat of ethnic and sectarian warfare. While such violence does not threaten world security in the same catastrophic manner as nuclear conflict or another major war in Europe, it could, if left unchecked, introduce severe instabilities into the international system.

This inevitably leads, as suggested by Boutros-Ghali, to a concern with small arms, land mines, and other light munitions; these are the weapons, he notes, that "are probably responsible for most of the deaths in current conflicts." This is true, for instance, of the conflicts in Afghanistan, Algeria, Angola, Bosnia, Burma, Burundi, Cambodia, Kashmir, Liberia, Rwanda, Somalia, Sri Lanka, Sudan, Tajikistan, and Zaire. Although heavy weapons sometimes play a role, most of the day-to-day fighting is performed by irregular forces armed only with rifles, grenades, machine guns, light mortars, and other "man-portable" munitions.

SMALL ARMS, GLOBAL PROBLEMS

The centrality of light weapons in contemporary warfare is especially evident in the conflicts in Liberia and Somalia. In Liberia, rival bands of guerrillas—armed, for the most part, with AK-47 assault rifles—have been fighting among themselves for

Light Weapons in Worldwide Circulation

ASSAULT RIFLES:
- Russian/Soviet AK-47 and its successors
- U.S. M-16
- German G3
- Belgian FAL
- Chinese Type 56 (a copy of the AK-47)
- Israeli Galil (also a copy of the AK-47)

MACHINE GUNS:
- U.S. M-2 and M-60
- Russian/Soviet RPK and DShK
- German MG3
- Belgian MAG
- Chinese Type 67

LIGHT ANTITANK WEAPONS:
- U.S. M-20 and M-72 rocket launchers
- U.S. Dragon and TOW antitank missiles
- Russian/Soviet RPG-2 and RPG-7 rocket-propelled grenades (and Chinese variants, Types 56 and 69)
- French-German MILAN antitank missiles

LIGHT MORTARS:
- Produced by many countries in a variety of calibers, including 60 mm, 81 mm, 107 mm, and 120 mm.

ANTIPERSONNEL LAND MINES:
- U.S. M-18A1 "Claymore"
- Russian/Soviet PMN/PMN-2 & POMZ-2
- Belgian PRB-409
- Italian VS-50 and VS-69
- Chinese Types 69 and 72

SHOULDER-FIRED ANTI-AIRCRAFT MISSILES:
- U.S. Stinger
- Russian/Soviet SAM-7
- British Blowpipe
- Swedish RBS-70

stepped on or driven over) is a common feature of many of these conflicts. These munitions, which can cost as little as $10 apiece, are planted in roads, markets, pastures, and fields to hinder agriculture and otherwise disrupt normal life. An estimated 85 million to 110 million uncleared mines are thought to remain in the soil of some 60 nations, with the largest concentrations in Afghanistan, Angola, Cambodia, and the former Yugoslavia. Each year some 25,000 civilians are killed, wounded, or maimed by land mines, and many more are driven from their homes and fields.

There are many reasons why small arms, mines, and other light weapons figure so prominently in contemporary conflicts. The belligerents involved tend to be insurgents, ethnic separatists, brigands, and local warlords with modest resources and limited access to the international arms market. While usually able to obtain a variety of light weapons from black-market sources or through theft from government arsenals, they can rarely afford or gain access to major weapons systems. Furthermore, such forces are usually composed of ill-trained volunteers who can be equipped with simple infantry weapons but who lack the expertise to operate and maintain heavier and more sophisticated equipment.

Logistical considerations also mitigate against the acquisition of heavy weapons. Lacking access to major ports or airfields and operating largely in secrecy, these forces must rely on clandestine and often unreliable methods of supply that usually entail the use of small boats, pack animals, civilian vehicles, and light planes. These methods are suitable for delivering small arms and ammunition, but not heavy weapons. Tanks, planes, and other major weapons also require large quantities of fuel, which is not easily transported by such rudimentary methods.

The character of ethnic and sectarian warfare further reinforces the predominance of light weapons. The usual objective of armed combat between established states is the defeat and destruction of an adversary's military forces; the goal of ethnic warfare, however, is not so much victory on the battlefield as it is the slaughter or the intimidation of members of another group and their forced abandonment of homes and villages ("ethnic cleansing"). In many cases a key objective is to exact retribution from the other group for past crimes and atrocities, a task best achieved through close-up violence that typically calls for the use of handheld weapons: guns, grenades, and machetes.

While the weapons employed in these clashes are relatively light and unsophisticated, their use can

control of the country, bringing commerce to a standstill and driving an estimated 2.3 million people from their homes and villages. In Somalia, lightly armed militias have been similarly engaged, ravaging the major cities, paralyzing rural agriculture, and at one point pushing millions to the brink of starvation. In both countries, UN-sponsored peacekeeping missions have proved unable to stop the fighting or disarm the major factions.

The widespread use of antipersonnel land mines (small explosive devices that detonate when result in human carnage of horrendous proportions. The 1994 upheaval in Rwanda resulted in the deaths of as many as 1 million people and forced millions more to flee their homeland. Similarly, the fighting in Bosnia is believed to have taken the lives of 200,000 people and has produced millions of refugees.

Although the availability of arms is not in itself a cause of war, the fact that likely belligerents in internal conflicts are able to procure significant supplies of light weapons has certainly contributed to the duration and intensity of these contests. Before the outbreak of violence in Rwanda, for example, the Hutu-dominated government spent millions of dollars on rifles, grenades, machine guns, and machetes that were distributed to the army and militia forces later implicated in the systematic slaughter of Tutsi civilians. In Afghanistan, the fact that the various factions were provided with so many weapons by the two superpowers during the cold war has meant that bloody internecine warfare could continue long after Moscow and Washington discontinued their supply operations. The ready availability of light weapons has also contributed to the persistence of violence in Angola, Kashmir, Liberia, Sri Lanka, and Sudan.

The widespread diffusion of light weapons in conflict areas has also posed a significant hazard to UN peacekeeping forces sent to police cease-fires or deliver humanitarian aid. Even when the leaders of major factions have agreed to the introduction of peacekeepers, local warlords and militia chieftains have continued to fight to control their territory. Fighting persisted in Somalia long after American and Pakistani UN peacekeepers arrived in 1992, leading to periodic clashes with UN forces and, following a particularly harrowing firefight in October 1993, to the withdrawal of American forces. Skirmishes like these were also a conspicuous feature of the combat environment in Bosnia before the signing of the Dayton peace accords, and remain a major worry for the NATO forces stationed there today.

---

[1]Three basic sources constitute a provisional database on the topic: Jeffrey Boutwell, Michael T. Klare, and Laura W. Reed, eds., *Lethal Commerce: The Global Trade in Small Arms and Light Weapons* (Cambridge, Mass.: American Academy of Arts and Sciences, 1995); Michael Klare and David Andersen, *A Scourge of Guns: The Diffusion of Small Arms and Light Weapons in Latin America* (Washington, D.C.: Federation of American Scientists, 1996); and Jasjit Singh, ed., *Light Weapons and International Security* (New Delhi: Indian Pugwash Society and British-American Security Information Council, 1995).

Even when formal hostilities have ceased, the diffusion of light weapons poses a continuing threat to international security. In those war-torn areas where jobs are few and the economy is in ruins, many demobilized soldiers have turned to crime to survive, often using the weapons they acquired during wartime for criminal purposes or selling them to combatants in other countries. During the 1980s, South African authorities provided thousands of guns to antigovernment guerrillas in Angola and Mozambique; these same guns, which are no longer needed for insurgent operations, are now being smuggled back into South Africa by their former owners and sold to criminal gangs. Some of the guns provided by the United States to the Nicaraguan contras have reportedly been sold to drug syndicates in Colombia.

MAIMING PROGRESS

It is no longer possible to ignore the role of small arms and light weapons in sustaining international conflict. Although efforts to address this problem are at an early stage, policymakers have begun to consider the imposition of new international constraints on light weapons trafficking. The UN, for example, has established a special commission—the Panel of Governmental Experts on Small Arms—to look into the problem, while representatives of the major industrial powers have met under the auspices of the Wassenaar Arrangement (a group set up in 1996 to devise new international controls on the spread of dangerous military technologies) to consider similar efforts. Despite growing interest, movement toward the adoption of new controls is likely to proceed slowly because of the many obstacles that must be overcome. (Only in one area—the establishment of an international ban on the production and use of antipersonnel land mines—is rapid progress possible.)

One of the greatest obstacles to progress is the lack of detailed information on the international trade in small arms and light weapons. Although various organizations, including the United States Arms Control and Disarmament Agency (ACDA) and the Stockholm International Peace Research Institute (SIPRI) have long compiled data on transfers of major weapons systems, no organization currently provides such information on light weapons. Those who want to study this topic must begin by producing new reservoirs of data on the basis of fragmentary and anecdotal evidence. Fortunately, this process is now well under way, and so it is possible to develop a rough portrait of the light weapons traffic.[1]

SUPPLY AND DEMAND

There is no precise definition of light weapons. In general, they can be characterized as conventional weapons that can be carried by an individual soldier or by a light vehicle operating on back-country roads. This category includes pistols and revolvers, rifles, hand grenades, machine guns, light mortars, shoulder-fired antitank and anti-aircraft missiles, and antipersonnel land mines. Anything heavier is excluded: tanks, heavy artillery, planes, ships, and large missiles, along with weapons of mass destruction.

Small arms and light weapons of the types shown in the table on page 174 can be acquired in several ways. All the major industrial powers manufacture light weapons of various types, and tend to rely on domestic production for their basic military needs. Another group of countries, including some in the third world, has undertaken the licensed manufacture of weapons originally developed by the major arms-producing states. The Belgian FAL assault rifle has been manufactured in Argentina, Australia, Austria, Brazil, Canada, India, Israel, Mexico, South Africa, and Venezuela, while the Russian/Soviet AK-47 (and its variants) has been manufactured in China, the former East Germany, Egypt, Finland, Hungary, Iraq, North Korea, Poland, Romania, and Yugoslavia. All told, about 40 countries manufacture at least some light weapons in their own factories. All other nations, and those countries that cannot satisfy all of their military requirements through domestic production, must rely on the military aid programs of the major powers or the commercial arms market.

Historically, the military aid programs of the United States and the Soviet Union were an important source of light weapons for developing nations. In addition to the major weapons supplied by the superpowers to their favored allies, both Moscow and Washington also provided vast quantities of small arms, grenades, machine guns, and other light weapons. Today, direct giveaways of light weapons are relatively rare (although the United States still supplies some surplus arms to some allies), so most developing nations must supply their needs through direct purchases on the global arms market.

Unfortunately, there are no published statistics on the annual trade in light weapons. However, the ACDA has estimated that approximately 13 percent of all international arms transfers (when measured in dollars) is comprised of small arms and ammunition. Applying this percentage to ACDA figures on the value of total world arms transfers in 1993 and 1994 would put global small arms exports at approximately $3.6 billion and $2.9 billion, respectively (in current dollars). Adding machine guns, light artillery, and antitank weapons to the small arms category would probably double these figures to some $6 billion per year, which is about one-fourth the total value of global arms transfers.

Further data on the sale of small arms and light weapons through commercial channels are simply not available. Most states do not disclose such information, and the UN Register of Conventional Arms (an annual listing of member states' arms imports and exports) covers major weapons only. However, some indication of the scope of this trade can be obtained from the information in *Jane's Infantry Weapons* on the military inventories of individual states. The FAL assault rifle is found in the inventories of 53 third world states; the Israeli Uzi submachine gun is found in 39 such states; the German G3 rifle in 43 states; and the Belgian MAG machine gun in 54 states.

For established nation-states (except those subject to UN arms embargoes), the commercial arms trade provides an ample and reliable source of small arms and light weapons. For nonstate actors, however, the global arms market is usually closed off. Most countries provide arms only to other governments, or to private agencies that employ or distribute arms with the recipient government's approval. (Such approval is sometimes given to private security firms that seek to import firearms for their own use, or to gun stores that sell imported weapons to individual citizens for hunting or self-defense.) All other groups, including insurgents, brigands, and ethnic militias, must rely on extralegal sources for their arms and ammunition.

THE OTHER ARMS MARKETS

Nonstate entities that want weapons for operations against the military forces of the state or against rival organizations can obtain arms in three ways: through theft from government stockpiles; through purchases on the international black market; and through ties to government agencies or expatriate communities in other countries.

Theft is an important source of arms for insurgents and ethnic militias in most countries, especially in the early stages of conflict. The fledgling armies of Croatia and Slovenia were largely equipped with weapons that had been "liberated" from Yugoslav government arsenals. Weapons seized from dead or captured soldiers also figure prominently in the arms inventories of many insurgent forces. Thus the mujahideen of Afghanistan relied largely on captured Soviet weapons until they began receiving arms in large quantities from outside sources. Many of the guerrilla groups in Latin America have long operated in a similar fashion.

For those insurgent and militia groups with access to hard currency or negotiable commodities (such as diamonds, drugs, and ivory), a large variety of light weapons can be procured on the international black market. This market is composed of private dealers who acquire weapons from corrupt military officials or surplus government stockpiles and ship them through circuitous routes—usually passing through a number of transit points known for their lax customs controls—to obscure ports or airstrips where they can be surreptitiously delivered to the insurgents' representatives. Transactions of this sort have become a prominent feature of the global arms traffic, supplying belligerents around the world. The various factions in Bosnia, for example, reportedly obtained billions of dollars in arms through such channels between 1993 and 1995. Many other groups, including the drug cartels in Colombia and the guerrilla groups in Liberia, have also obtained arms in this fashion.

Finally, insurgents and ethnic militias can turn to sympathetic government officials or expatriate communities in other countries for weapons (or for the funds to procure them from black-market suppliers). During the cold war, both the United States and the Soviet Union—usually operating through intelligence agencies like the CIA and the KGB—supplied weapons to insurgent groups in countries ruled by governments allied with the opposing superpower. At the onset of the 1975 war in Angola, for example, the CIA provided anticommunist insurgents with 20,900 rifles, 41,900 anti-tank rockets, and 622 mortars; later, during the Reagan administration, the United States supplied even larger quantities of arms to the contras in Nicaragua and the mujahideen in Afghanistan. The KGB also supplied insurgent groups with arms of these types, often routing them through friendly countries such as Cuba and Vietnam.

Superpower intervention has largely ceased with the end of the cold war, but other nations are thought to be engaged in similar activities. The Inter-Services Intelligence (ISI) agency of Pakistan is believed to be aiding in the covert delivery of arms to antigovernment insurgents in Kashmir. Likewise, the government of Iran has been accused of supplying arms to Kurdish separatists in Turkey, while Burkina Faso has been charged with aiding some of the guerrilla factions in Liberia. Expatriate groups have also been known to supply arms to associated groups in their country of origin. Americans of Irish descent have smuggled arms to the Irish Republican Army in Northern Ireland, while Tamil expatriates in Canada, Europe, and India are thought to be sending arms (or the funds to procure them) to the Tamil Tigers in Sri Lanka.

A DUAL STRATEGY FOR ARMS CONTROL

What are the implications of all this for the development of new international restraints on light weapons trafficking? We are dealing with two separate, if related, phenomena: the overt, legal transfer of arms to states and state-sanctioned agencies, and the largely covert, illicit transfer of arms to insurgents, ethnic militias, and other nonstate entities. While there is obviously some overlap between the two systems of trade, it is probably not feasible to deal with both through a single set of controls.

Any effort to control the light weapons trade between established states (or their constituent parts) will run into the problem that most government leaders believe the acquisition of such weaponry is essential to the preservation of their sovereignty and therefore sanctioned by the United Nations charter. Many states are also engaged in the sale of light weapons and would resist any new constraints on their commercial activities. It is unlikely, therefore, that the world community will adopt anything resembling an outright ban on light weapons exports or even a significant reduction in such transfers.

This does not mean that progress is impossible. It should be possible to insist on some degree of international transparency in this field. At present, governments are under no obligation to make available information on their imports and exports of light weapons. By contrast, most states have agreed to supply such data on major weapons systems, for release through the UN Register of Conventional Arms. Although compiling data on transfers of small arms and light weapons would undoubtedly prove more difficult than keeping track of heavy

> *For those. . .with access to hard currency or negotiable commodities (such as diamonds, drugs, and ivory), a large variety of light weapons can be procured on the international black market.*

weapons (because small arms are normally transferred far more frequently, and with less government oversight, than heavy weapons), there is no technical reason why the UN register could not be extended over time to include a wider range of systems. Including light weapons in the register would enable the world community to detect any unusual or provocative activity in this area (for example, significant purchases of arms and ammunition by a government that is supposedly downsizing its military establishment in accordance with a UN-brokered peace agreement) and to respond appropriately.

The major arms suppliers could also be required to abide by certain specified human rights considerations when considering the transfer of small arms and light weapons to governments involved in violent internal conflicts. Such sales could be prohibited in the case of governments that have suspended the democratic process and employed brutal force against unarmed civilians. An obvious candidate for such action is Burma, whose military leadership has usurped national power, jailed pro-democracy activists, and fought an unrelenting military campaign against autonomy-seeking minority groups. Human rights considerations have already figured in a number of UN arms embargoes—such as that imposed on the apartheid regime in South Africa—and so it should be possible to develop comprehensive restrictions of this type.

Finally, the world community could adopt restrictions or a prohibition on the transfer of certain types of weapons that are deemed to be especially cruel or barbaric in their effects. The first target should be the trade in antipersonnel land mines. President Bill Clinton called for a worldwide ban on the production, transfer, and use of such munitions in May 1996. Many other leaders have promised to support such a measure, but more effort is needed to persuade holdout states to agree. In addition to land mines, a ban could be imposed on bullets that tumble in flight or otherwise reproduce the effects of dumdum bullets (a type of soft-nosed projectile that expands on impact and produces severe damage to the human body). Bullets of this type where outlawed by the Hague Convention of 1899, but have reappeared in other forms.

STOPPING BLACK-MARKET TRAFFIC

An entirely different approach will be needed to control the black-market traffic in arms. Since such trafficking violates, by definition, national and international norms regarding arms transfers, there is no point in trying to persuade the suppliers and recipients involved to abide by new international restraints on the munitions trade. Instead, governments should be asked to tighten their own internal controls on arms trafficking and to cooperate with other states in identifying, monitoring, and suppressing illegal gun traffickers.

As a first step, all the nations in a particular region—such as Europe or the Western Hemisphere—should agree to uniform export restrictions and establish electronic connections between their respective customs agencies to permit the instantaneous exchange of data on suspect arms transactions. These measures should prohibit the export of arms to any agency or firm not subject to government oversight in the recipient nation, and the use of transshipment points in third countries that do not adhere to the uniform standards. At the same time, the law enforcement agencies of these countries should cooperate in tracking down and prosecuting dealers found to have engaged in illicit arms transfers. Eventually these measures could be extended on a worldwide basis, making it much more difficult for would-be traffickers to circumvent government controls.

It is unrealistic, of course, to assume that these measures will prevent all unwanted and illicit arms trafficking—there are simply too many channels for determined suppliers to employ. Nor should airtight control be the goal of international action. Rather, the goal should be to so constrict the flow of weapons that potential belligerents (including nonstate actors) are discouraged from achieving their objectives through force of arms and seek instead a negotiated settlement. Such controls should also be designed to reduce the death and displacement of civilians trapped in conflict areas, and to impede the activities of terrorist and criminal organizations.

Obviously, it will not be possible to make progress so long as policymakers view the trade in small arms and light weapons as a relatively insignificant problem. Educating world leaders about the dangerous consequences of this trade in an era of intensifying ethnic and sectarian conflict is a major arms control priority. Once these consequences are widely appreciated, it should be possible for the world community to devise the necessary controls and make substantial progress in curbing this trade.

ORGANISED CHAOS: NOT THE NEW WORLD WE ORDERED

David Keen

Under threat from warlords, profiteers, privatisers and ethnic nationalists, can the state be helped to survive? And what is the function of war for the warriors?

HAVING SEEN THE COLD WAR RECEDE, elements of the American right have now come out in a cold sweat. A combination of real and imagined threats has created something of a moral panic in the vacuum left by the collapse of communism, as analysts have highlighted the perils of disintegrating states, of 'Islamic fundamentalism', the 'clash of civilisations', of 'mindless tribal violence' and ethnic nationalism. For those afflicted by a rather bizarre nostalgia for the days of nuclear brinkmanship, the Soviet Union may have been the Red Devil, but at least it was the Red Devil we knew. Now the threats are seemingly more diffuse, more invisible, more difficult to comprehend. It is as if, thirty years after the United States entered the Vietnam war, the enemy has once more taken to the jungle.

In his widely read article 'The Coming Anarchy', which drew on West African examples in particular, Robert Kaplan outlined a nightmarish vision of young men as a seething mass of 'loose molecules' waiting to ignite into violence.[1]

His vision of order and chaos was well summed up in a *Panorama* programme on

DAVID KEEN is a Research Officer at Queen Elizabeth House, Oxford University, and author of *The Benefits of Famine: A Political Economy of Famine Relief in Southwestern Sudan, 1983 – 89*, published by Princeton University Press.

BBC Television in March 1995, when he observed: 'You have a lot of people in London and Washington who fly all over the world, who stay in luxury hotels, who think that English is dominating every place, but yet they have no idea what is out there. Out there is that thin membrane of luxury hotels, of things that work, of civil order, which is proportionately getting thinner and thinner and thinner.'

Both Kaplan and the influential military historian Martin van Creveld have often portrayed violence as essentially irrational. In *The Transformation of War*,[2] van Creveld noted that '...the reason why fighting can never be a question of interest is – to put it bluntly – that dead men have no interests... Warfare constitutes the great proof that man is not motivated by selfish interest.' Meanwhile, Kaplan's 'Balkan ghosts' emphasised the long-standing ethnic enmities underpinning conflict in the Balkans.

This kind of analysis can easily feed into rightist political agendas, notably the idea that 'we in the West' need somehow to steel ourselves against the coming anarchy, whether through isolationism, or a strong military, or both. Kaplan and van Creveld have both been warmly received by the US military and foreign-policy establishment. Kaplan's analysis of the Balkans was taken by some as justifying Western inaction in the face of allegedly entrenched antagonisms. Van Creveld's talk of the need for the military to adapt to new and diverse forms of conflict has found a receptive ear in Washington.

Meanwhile, the 'Fortress Europe' and 'Fortress America' lobbies have been lent a degree of intellectual, or quasi-intellectual, support. Van Creveld suggested, on

Panorama, that gathering chaos would lead to attempts at mass emigration and that Western governments might want to 'blow a couple of those boats out of the water' as an example to the rest. In reference to the recent Italian conflict with Albanian immigrants, van Creveld added: 'This may be in the long run a more humane solution both for the Italians... and for the immigrants.'

AN ALTERNATIVE SYSTEM OF PROFIT AND POWER

Of course, it is undeniable that the thawing of the Cold War has indeed contributed to a variety of recent conflicts, and that ethnic nationalism, in particular, has proved to be a major source of violence with the collapse of the communist bloc. To put it mildly, this is not quite the new world that we ordered.

But at least two elements of the new moral panic need questioning. The first is the perception that contemporary patterns of violence somehow represent a kind of chaos, a kind of irrationalism, that is breaking through previous patterns of order and repression based on Cold War antagonisms. The second is the (related) suggestion that this new and somehow incomprehensible threat is best met by some combination of fight and flight – in other words, by arming ourselves against the gathering chaos, while at the same time attempting to isolate ourselves from it as much as possible.

What is most conspicuously missing from many accounts of the 'new world disorder' is any sense of the vested interests, political and economic, which are driving the apparent 'chaos' – and indeed the vested interests that may be driving its depiction as chaos. Also damagingly absent is any adequate attention to what might be done to counter or cajole those who have a vested interest in violence and disorder.

Part of the problem is that we tend to regard conflict as, simply, a breakdown in a particular system, rather than as the emergence of another, alternative system of profit and power. For example, the emergence of 'warlords' in many countries does not equate to 'chaos'; rather, it is likely to represent a reconstituted system in which some of the activities previously conducted by the state – protection, taxation – are taken over by regional warlords.

Michel Foucault's analysis of the Gulag in the former Soviet Union can also be applied to violence more generally: the problem of causes cannot be dissociated from that of function.[3] In other words, it is not enough to enumerate the many causes of violence (as Kaplan does in an exhaustive list in his 'Coming Anarchy' article); we need also to understand the functions of violence, and to wonder what can be done in the light of these functions.

MINDLESS VIOLENCE... MINDLESS ANALYSIS

Nor is it enough to point despairingly to 'the collapse of the state' without understanding how international financial institutions have often wilfully undermined the state in favour of the 'market economy', or how the state – from Sudan to former Yugoslavia to Sierra Leone – has sometimes sponsored its own demise, with elites attempting to foment violence to prop up their own positions of privilege. In these circumstances, labels like 'chaos' and 'mindless violence' can be actively – and even sometimes intentionally – disabling.

Faced with international analysts' depictions of 'mindless violence' in troublespots around the globe, we need to ask whether it is the violence that is mindless or the analysis. Violence leading to devastating famine in southern Sudan in the late 1980s was typically depicted by the Sudanese government – and to a large extent by the US State Department – as arising from 'long-standing ethnic hostility' between the Arab-speaking Baggara peoples of the north and the Dinka and Nuer in the south. Superimposed on this misleading portrayal was a habitual emphasis in the international media on the religious origins of a civil war between the 'Islamic north' and the 'Christian south'.

What was damagingly absent was any coherent account of the role of the Sudanese government in supplying arms and granting immunity from prosecution to northern Baggara militias, who were encouraged to attack southern Sudanese occupying areas that were rich in fertile land and, critically, oil. Facing pressure to repay escalating international debts and unable to afford a large, salaried army, the Sudanese government resorted to a strategy of turning the dissatisfaction of the economically marginalised Baggara against the Dinka and the Nuer. Partly through inducing man-made famine, this strategy offered the prospect of depopulating oil-rich lands and decimating the principal supporters of the rebel Sudan People's Liberation Army (SPLA). It also offered an opportunity to confuse the international community, and deflect recriminations from the Sudanese government.

In the course of this violence and famine, the state had not so much collapsed as attempted to compensate for its economic weakness by dividing and manipulating civil society. At the same time, the violence, so far from being completely irrational, served a range of mundane functions, not only for central government but also for elements of the Baggara, who stood to gain from access to grazing land, stolen cattle and the cheap – or even free – labour of southern Sudanese captives and famine migrants.

This is not to say that these processes were not, in some sense, 'evil'. However, this was an evil that was driven by a complex

> WARFARE MAY COME TO RESEMBLE A VIRUS WHICH 'MUTATES', MAKING IT MUCH MORE DIFFICULT FOR OUTSIDERS TO TACKLE THE VIRUS

set of economic and political pressures, including the exclusion of the (western Sudanese) Baggara cattle herders from the bulk of the benefits of a highly uneven pattern of development centring on Sudan's central-eastern region. Moreover – and in this respect the evolution of evil was not totally different from the famine in the Jew-

ish ghettos of Poland – this was an evil which began as a plan for resettlement and dovetailed into the starvation of the displaced when it was found that local authorities were not keen, for a variety of pragmatic reasons, to receive waves of refugees.

A failure to get to grips with the rational aspects of this violence in Sudan tended to obscure the opportunities for reducing human suffering, while allowing the government, as later in Rwanda, to get away with the portrayal of violence as irrational and 'tribal'. Major international donors pressured the government on its macroeconomic policy, but largely turned a blind eye to the abuses of militias the government was arming and manipulating. The pattern of famine relief – concentrating on refugee camps in Ethiopia and on government garrison towns in the south – tended to speed up the process of depopulating rural areas of the south, while at the same time giving the SPLA a reason to attack relief shipments. Meanwhile, the provision of inadequate relief to Baggara drought victims in the north tended to encourage them to turn south in search of a remedy for their own destitution.

In Sierra Leone, after an initial period of vacillation when rebellion broke out in 1991, the government responded by rapidly expanding its military from some 3,000 to around 14,000. It recruited militiamen who had spilled over from the conflict in Liberia, as well as Sierra Leonean boys as young as eight. This ragtag Sierra Leonean army, underpaid and under-trained, was sent to do battle with the rebels, who were concentrated in the fertile and diamond-rich south and east of the country. One of the results has been that government soldiers have repeatedly resorted to raiding and to illegal mining to supplement their inadequate incomes. They have tended to avoid pitched battles with the rebels, and have even sold arms, ammunition and uniforms to them, apparently in a bid to keep the conflict going – whilst at the same time making short-term cash.

Presently, according to evidence of eye witnesses during my visit to the country in the summer of 1995, Sierra Leonean civilians are threatened not only by rebels but also by government soldiers, who sometimes seem to be acting in concert with the rebels to control and partially depopulate resource-rich areas and divide the spoils between them. Although the government claimed to have retaken the diamond-rich eastern district of Kono from the rebels, these raids continued throughout the autumn of 1995, suggesting continuing government soldier involvement in the violence against civilians.

Among the reasons why the rebellion in Sierra Leone originally gathered force were the poor social services and a notable decline in educational opportunities, which were themselves a reflection of international pressures for financial austerity. Thus, although the conflict in Sierra Leone has led to a partial collapse of the state, with 'government' increasingly confined to the capital, Freetown, the conflict was also partly caused by a collapsing state administration—most notably, a tottering educational system and an inadequately trained and funded army.

PRIVATISING WAR

In effect, in many African countries, in particular, it is not just the social services which have been partially privatised as a result of pressure from international creditors, but also war itself. That is, financially strapped governments have delegated the right to inflict violence to unpaid or underpaid fighters who have made up for the lack of salary with an abundance of loot. In these circumstances, warfare threatens to veer out of the control even of the government which seeks to manipulate it. In Sudan, the Baggara have to some extent followed their own economic agenda, raiding Muslim and semi-Muslim groups in the north, fostering opposition rather than quelling it, and reaching an accommodation with the SPLA that allows the Baggara access to contested grazing lands. For government troops in Sierra Leone, the business of defeating the rebels has often taken second place to the business of making money.

Thus, the functions of war, for those carrying out the violence, may diverge from the military to the economic. If this happens, warfare may come to resemble a virus which 'mutates', making it much more difficult for outsiders to tackle the virus, particularly if they do not understand the nature of this mutation.

Given the importance of pillage in warfare, the boundaries between war and crime may be quite indistinct. Stephen Ellis has shown how, in Liberia, young militiamen –

few of whom have been paid or trained – have tended to base themselves in areas that are rich in diamonds, or where villagers were still producing crops, or where humanitarian convoys could be looted.[4] Looting of civilians and commandeering of slave labour has been commonplace. 'Only rarely did the militias attack each other head-on. For the most part, they preyed on civilians,' Ellis recently wrote in *African Affairs*. Meanwhile, senior commanders – adults – have preyed on the boy militiamen, duplicating the generally unhappy experience of boy soldiers in Sierra Leone.

The West African experience shows clearly how violence may be used to create or preserve trade monopolies, a goal that Lenin saw as feeding into international wars but which may also feed into civil wars. Having created a trading monopoly and a geographical area that can be taxed, rebel 'warlords' may then be in a position to fund the increased use of violence, allowing them to preserve or enlarge their 'mini-states'. In Somalia, the ability of a particular clan to gain control of critical ports and roads has sometimes allowed it to increase its revenue and strengthen its military muscle, permitting a further expansion in the geographical territory it controls.[5]

The phenomenon of government forces 'going soft' on the rebels has echoes around the world. For example, elements of the military in both Cambodia and Thailand appear to have an economic interest in collaborating with the Khmer Rouge, which occupies an area of Cambodia rich in diamonds and timber. In Peru, as John Simpson's book *In the Forests of the Night* demonstrates,[6] government soldiers have habitually set free rebel fighters from the Shining Path guerrilla movement, apparently in order to perpetuate insecurity in areas where officers can benefit from illegal trading – in this case, principally the trade in cocaine.

Many contemporary conflicts are reminiscent of medieval warfare, which tended to see widespread pillage and an avoidance of pitched battles. In those days too, pillage was particularly likely when soldiers' provisions ran out or their pay was in arrears. In her account of the fourteenth-century, *A Distant Mirror*, Barbara Tuchman notes: 'Above all, war was made to pay for itself through pillage. Booty and ransom were not just a bonus, but a necessity to take the place of arrears in pay and to induce enlistment.'[7]

Although we have come to regard strong states capable of commanding a disciplined army as somehow 'normal', these states only emerged in Europe from a long and difficult struggle with local warlords, as central rulers were handicapped by their own underpaid soldiers. In many parts of the world, a modern bureaucratic state has never been properly established; in others, the modern state is extremely fragile. Insofar as the resources available to states in Africa are diminishing – not least through programmes of structural adjustment – the opportunities for prospective warlords to challenge state sovereignty would appear to be considerable.

If many of the characteristics of contemporary wars are not confined simply to the contemporary era, neither are they confined to countries at war. Indeed, the blurring of war and crime may increasingly call into question the traditional distinction between countries at war and countries at peace. Just as poorly paid and trained soldiers may prove unable or unwilling to confront rebel forces in resource-rich areas, so also may poorly paid and trained policemen be unable or unwilling to confront criminals, particularly where these criminals are operating within a lucrative illegal economy such as drugs or prostitution.

In the Polish capital Warsaw, police officers may be offered the equivalent of three years' pay to turn a blind eye to activities in the drug and prostitution sectors. As with the Khmer Rouge and the international timber and diamond trade, the Polish criminals' links with international trading networks provide them with resources that give them a degree of immunity to suppression.

PEOPLE PROTECTING PEOPLE

In Sierra Leone, faced with the twin threat of rebel and government soldier attacks, many civilians are providing funding and personnel for nascent 'civil defence groups'. Although badly equipped, such groups have sometimes managed to intimidate undisciplined gunmen, including government soldiers, into tempering their abuses. Again, this is not a trend confined to 'countries at war'. In South Africa, we have seen the emergence of citizens' vigilante groups in response to soaring crime and a perceived weak response by poorly paid, poorly trained policemen. Both crime and the vigilante groups appear to provide a role and activity for under-employed young men half-trained by the resistance movement.

Even in Western countries like Britain, France and – notably – the United States, we have seen the emergence of areas of the inner city where the law cannot properly be enforced, not least because of the control which certain criminals are able to exert over the community on which the police depend for tip-offs and witnesses.

Where the state gives up – or is forced to give up – its responsibilities for protecting people, they will seek their own protection, and the consequences may not be good. Self-protection may mean throwing in your lot with a particular ethnic group, as has happened in former Yugoslavia. It will certainly mean securing some kind of arms, either, as Hans Magnus Enzensberger notes,[8] through the obliging international market or through access to existing arsenals, like those that have fuelled conflict in the Balkans and the Caucasus. Such violence may feed on intense fear, and may lurch in unpredictable directions.

The point, perhaps, is not to mourn the collapse of the state but to counteract it. For example, the Rwandan state requires a major injection of resources if it is to stand any chance of convincing Hutus and Tutsis alike that it is capable of administering measured punishment and measured clemency in the wake of the genocide. Earlier, as argued by the London-based human rights organisation African Rights, the international drive towards democratisation in Rwanda appeared to have run aground, in part due to the resource shortages brought about by internationally generated austerity packages.[9] Extremist Hutu factions defended their privileged position with a ruthlessness that embraced carefully planned genocide.

BATTLES AGAINST THE STATE

In some ways, both right and left seem to have been waging a battle against the state. For the right, the principal enemies have been public services and state control of the economy. A critical blind-spot at home and abroad has been the fuelling of violence through lack of economic and educational opportunities. For the left, the state's instruments of 'repression' – the army and police – have come in for attack, while left-leaning non-governmental organisations have tended to place 'civil society' on a pedestal. Moreover, while the needs and, belatedly, the strategies of disaster victims have come under examination from the aid community – notably *after* large-scale human rights abuses have taken place – the needs and strategies of those carrying out human rights abuses have been largely ignored. As a result, opportunities for influencing the perpetrators have been missed. Prevention has been neglected in favour of cure or, more accurately, in favour of the band-aid of humanitarian relief.

It is true, particularly in the poorer parts of the world, that states have tended to act in the interests of a narrow elite, and that the police and army have often been instruments of repression. But perhaps, in the days of ethnic militias and unpaid soldiers, we are now realising more and more that 'civil society' is not necessarily particularly civil, especially when it is manipulated by an elite that finds itself threatened by democracy and austerity. Properly salaried state officials, for all their faults, may have their uses. At the same time, we need to be aware of the covert manipulation of private militias outside state structures. The challenge, perhaps, is to rebuild the institutions of the state in such a way that do not recreate the resentments that have encouraged states to promote their own decline by fuelling the tensions in civil society.

The fall of communism in the eastern bloc has been hailed as a triumph for capitalism, peace and democracy. Yet it is by no means clear that these three 'brothers' will ride together into the sunset at the 'End of History'. Whilst Marx predicted that socialism would lead to the withering away of the state, it may ultimately be capitalism that proves more effective in leading us towards that dubious goal, with all the attendant dangers to both peace and democracy. The more arms are being sold for profit, the more decentralised the means of violence are likely to become. And with large groups effectively excluded from the promised benefits of the free market, the temptation to resort to these arms – as in Sierra Leone – will be great.

The 'anti-welfarist' culture is built on the assumption that, deprived of state support, people will use their own initiative; unfortunately, this is already proving to be all too true, as disgruntled young men demonstrate their 'initiative' with the use of guns.

Of course, initiative can also include participation in other 'free' markets, the – often international – markets in illegal drugs, illegal mining and resource-depletion, and prostitution. Meanwhile underpaid government officials, who in countries like Sierra Leone have always tended to have an ambiguous relationship with the illegal economy, may increasingly follow the culture of individual initiative to the extent of accepting kickbacks that allow criminal gangs, and even 'rebels,' to operate with impunity. If capitalism, as Max Weber famously argued, was built on a set of moral values— the so-called 'Protestant ethic' of working and saving—is it not quite possible that capitalism is destroying the moral values on which its continued existence, at least in forms compatible with peace and democracy, depends?

Notes

1 Robert Kaplan, *Atlantic Monthly*, February 1994, pp. 44–76.

2 Martin van Creveld, *The Transformation of War* (New York: The Free Press, 1991).

3 *Power/Knowledge: Selected Interviews and other writings 1972–1977*, edited by C. Gordon (Brighton: Harvester Press, 1988).

4 Stephen Ellis, 'Liberia 1989–1994: a study of ethnic and spiritual violence, *African Affairs*, April 1995.

5 For essential information, see Mark Bradbury, *The Somali Conflict: Prospects for Peace*, Oxfam Research Paper No. 9.

6 John Simpson, *In the Forests of the Night: Encounters in Peru with Terrorism, Drug-running and Military Oppression* (London: Arrow, 1994).

7 Barbara Tuchman, *A Distant Mirror: The Calamitous 14th Century* (London and Basingstoke: Papermack, 1989).

8 Hans Magnus Enzensberger, *Civil War* (London: Granta Books, 1994).

9 *Rwanda: Death, Despair and Defiance*, London, 1994.

TOWARDS THE GLOBAL MILLENNIUM.
THE CHALLENGE OF ISLAM

Akbar S. Ahmed

Because we are approaching a millennium that promises to accelerate the processes of globalisation, already irreversible and advancing dizzily before our eyes to envelope even the most remote people of the world in a suffocating embrace, we seek global answers as to how best we can adjust to one another. How can different world cultures learn to live with each other? How can local cultures retain their sense of identity and dignity in the face of the onslaught of globalisation – non-stop satellite television, instant high-tech communications and so on?

GIVEN THE HIGH DEGREE OF UNCERTAINTY SURROUNDING THESE questions, it is not surprising that we are often given superficial and shoddy answers. Even the experts can get it wrong. The relationship between Islam and the West is an example. While using the terms Islam and the West as a short-hand, we need to add the caveat that reducing the two highly complex and internally diverse civilisations to such simplistic terms may create more problems than it solves. We will continue to colour in grey, however great the compulsion to use black and white. But for our discussion, let us use Islam to mean Muslims, wherever they live, especially in those

Professor AKBAR S. AHMED is a Fellow of Selwyn College, Cambridge, and author of *Living Islam; From Samarkand to Stornoway* (BBC-Penguin, 1995). This is a version of a lecture he gave at Chatham House.

countries which have a Muslim majority; by the West we mean North America and Western Europe, with its leadership clearly residing with the United States.

I will point out why some of the most influential current global theories about Islam's relations with the West are inadequate. I will then explore an alternative method of understanding what is happening in the Muslim world through a discussion of Muslim political structures and leadership. This will help explain Islam's present predicament and its sometimes thorny relations with the West. In conclusion, I will suggest ways to improve mutual understanding.

In the process a host of important questions will be raised, not all of which will find answers in this paper: Who speaks for Islam? Saladin, the model of a chivalric and heroic figure, or Saddam, the modern military dictator? We recognise the same words hastily stitched by Saddam on his flag when the Gulf crisis developed on the headbands of the Chechen warriors in the Caucasus, and on the posters of Hamas in Israel and ask: Why is Islam such a potent symbol of resistance in our times? Is the clash between Islam and the West then inevitable?

An understanding of Islam is important in our world because there are forty-four Muslim states and Islam has over one billion followers with abundant vitality and passion whose span is now truly global. Besides, Muslims control much of the oil and gas reserves of the world; Muslims live in the West in large numbers as permanent citizens. The challenge to Western-backed Israel from Islamic organisations like Hamas, the resurgence of Islam in countries that matter strategically to the West like Turkey, Egypt and Algeria, and the nuclear ambitions of several Muslim countries make Islam important.

More Muslims have made an impact on the global media – positively (Benazir Bhutto) or negatively (Saddam Hussein, Muammar Qaddafi, Yasser Arafat) – than those of any other non-Western civili

Reprinted with permission from *The World Today,* August/September 1996, pp. 212-216. © 1996 by *The World Today,* a publication of the Royal Institute of International Affairs.

sation. Can the Western man or woman in the street name any Russian leader apart from Gorbachev and Yeltsin, and any black African except Mandela? And how many can name any Latin American, Japanese, Indian or Chinese leader?

We saw how during the Gulf war a regional Muslim crisis drew in the West, economically, politically and militarily; a Muslim crisis rapidly escalated into a world crisis.

Global theories

In the last few years Muslims have simplified global issues and interpreted a series of developments, on the surface clearly unconnected, as a well-laid plan by the West and its allies to humiliate them: the controversy over *The Satanic Verses*, the collapse of the BCCI Bank, the Gulf war, the rape and death camps of Bosnia and the slaughter of the civilian population of Lebanon.

In this atmosphere of suspicion, even scholarly exercises providing global explanations of our times – Professor Samuel Huntington's essay, 'The Clash of Civilisations?',[1] Francis Fukuyama's *The End of History and the Last Man*[2] and Felipe Fernandez-Armesto's *Millennium*[3] – are seen as part of the conspiracy against Islam, part of a bludgeon-Islam-out-of-existence school of thought. Even post-modernist gurus such as Jean Baudrillard see the rich West confronting 'the distress and catastrophe' of Africa, Asia (which is the Muslim world) and Latin America in a mutually self-destructive, symbiotic relationship.[4]

Not all books on Islam are sensationalist. In spite of its alarmist title, *A Sense of Siege: The Geopolitics of Islam and the West* by Graham Fuller and Ian Lesser,[5] is level-headed and objective. Benjamin Barber's, *Jihad versus McWorld*,[6] explains how all, not just Islamic, ethnic and religious communities, feel threatened by globalisation – hence the 'Mc' in the title.

The theses suggesting conflict are cause and effect of an end-of-millennium mood, reflecting in part, I suspect, the nervous twitching of a civilisation predisposed to entering a new millennium with heightened anxiety; and we need to be reminded that the concept is a Christian one, however global its impact through the media. Ideas of dramatic, apocalyptic happenings are in the air: perhaps a major, all but inevitable, final show-down between Islam and the West?

A clash of civilisations?

Huntington's essay, 'The Clash of Civilisations?' was influential because it struck a responsive chord in the West. The Harvard Professor argued that future conflicts will be cultural, not ideological or economic, in content. Islam was singled out as a potential enemy civilisation in an argument that was as deterministic as it was simplistic. Huntington's thesis derived from established Orientalist thinking: 'We are facing a mood and a movement far transcending the level of issues and policies and the governments that pursue them. This is no less than a clash of civilisations,' wrote Bernard Lewis in September 1990.[7] 'Islam has bloody borders,' concluded Huntington.[8] But so do Christianity, Judaism and Hinduism – ask, respectively, the Bosnians and Chechens, the Palestinians and the Kashmiris. And where does this dangerously deterministic argument take us except to a clash of civilisations? Is this merely a self-fulfilling prophecy?

Isn't the real clash, the root cause of the turmoil, to be located within Islam, whether in Algeria, Egypt, Afghanistan or Pakistan? Isn't the target the Muslim leadership? For Muslims, their leadership has failed. It is caricatured by stories of the hidden, illegal wealth

looted from the people, to be kept abroad, and the corruption and cruelty at home. Hence the depth of their despair, the extent of their anger and the desperation of their response.

Who bludgeoned out of existence large parts of Hama in Syria to crush the Muslim Brothers? Who slaughtered the Kurds in Halabja and the Shia in southern Iraq? Bombs in bus stops and bazaars which kill innocent citizens are deplorable acts and not Islamic. But they will continue to take place as long as justice is denied.

Besides, the global strategic and security interests of the West are directly related to Muslim lands, and many Muslim nations are seen as important allies. Of the nine 'pivotal states' identified in a recent article by Western experts around which America forms its foreign policy, five were Muslim – Algeria, Turkey, Egypt, Pakistan, and Indonesia.[9] Strategic imperatives scramble Huntington's neat theory.

What about the twenty million Muslims permanently settled in the West conveniently ignored by Huntington? Where do they line up? Surely they are a bridge between the two civilisations? Huntington needs to recognise that an entire generation of young Muslims is coming of age in the West. There is a strong middle-class component among them in America, and they are integrated into the social and political structure. Black Muslims too are now emerging as a force in the United States. Into the millennium we can expect influential figures in public life – members of Congress and Senators in the United States and Members of Parliament in Britain – from this generation. Perhaps what is most significant is that they see themselves as both Muslim and American, or Muslim and British.

We need also to point out the serious efforts – at global level, and perhaps for the first time on this scale and with this frequency – by influential individuals to increase mutual understanding. Although the reputation of individuals is vulnerable in an age of intense, even perverse, iconoclasm, several have spoken of the need to view Islam on its own terms, in terms of the global community and not as the 'other' or, more simplistically, as the new enemy after communism.

The laudable attempts of the Pope and the Prince of Wales find an echo in King Hassan of Morocco, King Hussein and his brother, Crown Prince Hassan, of Jordan, Benazir Bhutto of Pakistan, Muhammad Mahathir of Malaysia and the Aga Khan.

The end of history?

If Huntington sees Islam as a world threat, Fukuyama has a solution. He has simply written Islam – which is a threat to the triumphant liberal practice, consumerism and democracy of the West, a force of disruption in the tranquillity at the end of history – out of history.[10]

Fukuyama outrageously equates Islam to 'European fascism'.[11] The main entry in the reference to Islam in his index is under 'Islamic Fundamentalism' and then, in case anyone has missed the point, cross-referenced to 'Fundamentalist Islam'. There is no other entry under Fundamentalist – no Christians, Jews, Hindus, in spite of the clear global evidence of exuberant fundamentalism in these religions – except that of Islam. 'Fundamentalism' is equated to fanaticism, extremism and violence.

Fukuyama does not help himself: there is not a single Muslim author in his bibliography nor, surprisingly for an expert working in Washington, such acknowledged American experts as Professors

John Esposito, Clifford Geertz, Roy Mottahedeh, James Piscatori and Edward Said. To compound matters, Huntington has five entries in the bibliography.

Felipe Fernandez-Armesto in *Millennium* also echoes Fukuyama: 'As the end of the millennium approaches, the Islamic revolution seems to be over and Islamic revival seems stymied.'[12] Khomeini and the violence in Iran dominate the discussion.

A *Quranic model*

We are still left searching for an explanation to what is happening in the Muslim world, for a general theory. Let us look for a model that will explain Muslim behaviour in the Quran, the Muslim holy book. No self-respecting political or social scientist, reared in the secular or liberal tradition of the West, would dream of looking in the Quran for explanations of behaviour. Muslim social scientists themselves remain in awe of Western social theories and look around for easy answers in Ivy League or Oxbridge or London university departments – that is why so much of their work appears to be second-rate.

But ours is not entirely an original route. Max Weber persuasively showed the way in explaining the influence of the Protestant ethic on economic behaviour, in contrast to Karl Marx, who emphasised economic and material factors as all-important. Inherent in Weber's models of authority is the assumption that societies move along a secular path, that leadership would be provided by a rational bureaucracy set in a working democracy. But even Weber could not foresee the collapse of the civilised veneer and easy reversion to primordial tribalism and savagery in Europe. Germany half a century ago, just decades after Weber was writing, and the Balkans in the 1990s illustrate for us how fragile the notion of a staid and safe European civilisation, based on respect for human life and liberty, really is.

Our thesis is that if the political leadership in its behaviour, ideas and politics is close to the Islamic ideal as laid out in the Quran and the life of the Prophet, friction in society is minimal; the further from the Islamic ideal, the greater the tension in society.[13]

The first and greatest model for Muslims is the holy Prophet. His life provides the balance between action and spirit, between this world and the next: he is the perfect person, *insan-i-kamil*. Imitating him were those disciples who were closest to him, such as Umar and Ali, great religious figures. But others too – not seen as religious figures – have attempted to live up to the ideal Islamic model. Saladin is one such name, which explains why Saddam Hussein encouraged the comparison during the Gulf war.

We can refine our thesis by constructing socio-political categories, however crude, of Muslim leadership. To do so we cut through the confusing conflation, overlap and collision of several traditions now functioning in the Muslim world – tribal, dynastic, European and Islamic.

● The first of our four categories is that of the clerical rulers. Iran provides an example. With the global media explosion through organs like the CNN and BBC from the 1980s onwards, images of this category became the image of the Muslim cleric; indeed of Islam itself: a dark, scowling, evil-looking, bearded figure in black robes. The image neatly echoed Hollywood ideas and popular cartoons of the wicked wizard.

Iran, however much the West is transfixed by it, remains a one-off example, largely explained by its Shia culture and tradition. Whenever given a choice through the polls, the people have

> THE IMAGE OF THE MUSLIM CLERIC: A DARK, SCOWLING, EVIL-LOOKING, BEARDED FIGURE IN BLACK ROBES, NEATLY ECHOED HOLLYWOOD IDEAS AND CARTOONS OF THE WICKED WIZARD.

rejected the religious parties in countries like Pakistan. The Jamat-i-Islami, perhaps the best organised and with the most coherent and sophisticated view of the modern world, has never had more than a few members in Parliament. The answer to this mystery is simple. Islam does not encourage a priesthood. 'There is no monkery in Islam,' said the Prophet.

● The second category is that of the military rulers and monarchies. Of the former, General Zia in Pakistan used Islam; Saddam did not until the Gulf war. Of the latter, the Saudis parade Islam; the Shah of Iran did not. In many countries in this category, the already existing tribal structures provided the bare bones of the state structure. Thus the dominant tribal clan of the last century simply became the royal rulers, senior administrators and entrepreneurs of this one. Saudi Arabia and the Gulf States are examples of this. Even the military dictators rely on tribal politics. Both Assad and Saddam trust, as far as leaders of this kind can trust, their own sect or tribal clan.

● The third category is the democratic one, which includes countries such as Egypt, Pakistan, Turkey and Bangladesh. Governments in this category are democratic and elections are held, although there is a history of lapsing back to martial law in times of crisis. Stories of corruption, mismanagement and evidence of the collapse of law and order create a general disillusionment with this category.

Such Muslim leaders skilfully exploit the fears of the West regarding Muslim fundamentalists. Their argument is simple: we are all that stands between you and your worst nightmare – that is, Muslim fanatics, the dreaded fundamentalists of the media – in power with itchy Islamic fingers. With the nuclear ambitions of many Muslim countries and the nuclear potential of others – e.g. Pakistan – this is a genuine concern of the West.

However, this category needs to be developed and strengthened for the future. It reflects the Islamic spirit of egalitarianism, the need for tolerance in plural societies (again reflecting Islam), and larger global trends. In spite of the present faulty interpretation of democracy and the running of the nation-state, this is the most viable category for our times.

● The fourth, rather unsuccessful, category is that of the socialist/communist leader, modelled on Stalin and the Soviet experience, whose appeal lies mainly in a rhetoric of care for the poor. Brutal dictators with little hint of Islamic compassion and justice have ruled in this category through the secret police. After the Cold War, this category has little backing or appeal.

But we must be cautious with our categories. Pakistan illustrates that one country can at different times adopt different categories: under Jinnah, it was democratic; under Ayub, a military dictatorship; and under Zia, Islamic. Each category presents problems for the future.

An end to demonising

In the short term, the prospects for a harmonious relationship between Islam and the West look uncertain, even pessimistic. In the longer term, a great deal will depend on whether those who encourage dialogue and understanding will succeed or not.

What can be done to improve matters? The first steps are to stop demonising each other; for Muslims to stop seeing a global conspiracy all around them – Christian, Jew and Hindu germs every time they sneeze. They need to improve their understanding of the West beyond the stereotype of the great Satan determined to exterminate Islam who spends his spare time in an orgy of sex and violence.

Muslims need to put themselves in the place of the non-Muslims who see them as a threat; of Jews, surrounded by what they see as millions of Arabs united on one thing alone – their destruction; of Hindus in India, flanked by Pakistan and Bangladesh; and just beyond this circle, Iran and the Middle East – Muslim societies that to them appear in the grip of Islamic fervour.

We need also to point out what Muslims sometimes gloss over or refuse to acknowledge. There are far too many complaints about human rights violations, including that of non-Muslim minorities, in Muslim countries. This is because there is too little of the Islamic spirit of tolerance and compassion. Why are Muslims ignoring the Quranic instructions in Surahs 2 and 109? Why are they forgetting that God's greatest names are 'the Beneficient, the Merciful'?

The kidnapping, hijacking, torture and blowing up of ordinary people in buses and bazaars – where are the young men getting their inspiration from? Why are the gentle teachers and mystics of Islam not heard? Why have Muslims abandoned one of the most powerful and endearing features of Islam? Why is the resistance invariably expressed in violence, as in Iran, Afghanistan, Algeria, Pakistan and Egypt?

Muslims also face another, greater challenge, an internal one. They need to rebuild an idea of Islam which includes justice, integrity, tolerance and the quest for knowledge – the classic Islamic civilisation, not just the insistence on the rituals; not just the five pillars of Islam but the entire building. Reducing a sophisticated civilisation to simple rituals encourages simple answers: reaching for guns and explosives, for instance. Today, piety and virtue are judged by political action, often equated to violence – not sustained spirituality.

Figures of concern

Muslim leaders also need to worry about the social, demographic and educational trends in their countries. Muslim population growth is among the highest in the world, the literacy rates among the lowest, the figures for health facilities poor and the life expectancy below average.

> THE WEST NEEDS
> TO DISCOURAGE
> THE KNEE-JERK
> 'NUKE 'EM' RESPONSE
> TO MUSLIMS AND
> THE LABELLING OF
> ANY MUSLIM ACT
> AS 'FUNDAMENTALIST'.

The uneven spread of per capita income between countries like the Arab Gulf states and Bangladesh reflects the uneven picture within most Muslim countries. Affluent corrupt elites are living the extravagant and wasteful high life in the capital cities alongside the miserable squalor of the shanty towns. The gap between rich and poor is growing ominously wide. All this when a large percentage of the population is young, jobless and restless for radical change. For many, Islam is the only natural way out.

Because of the global power of the West, the initiatives in understanding must come from the West. The West must back off; it must treat Islam in its reporting and in its handling with the dignity due to a world religion. The problems of the unhappy people of Bosnia, Palestine, Chechnya and Kashmir have not been solved. There is little hope of permanent peace unless this happens. Violence is possible at any time as young men give way to desperation and anger, whatever the surface movement towards normality.

The West must put pressure on Muslim governments – and it interacts with most of them overtly or covertly – to get their act together, to ensure justice and provide clean administration. It must send serious signals to the ordinary Muslim people, through its media, through seminars, conferences, meetings, that it does not consider Islam as the enemy, however much it may disagree with certain aspects of Muslim behaviour. The West needs to understand the Islamic expressions of revolt as movements against corruption and lack of justice, not as anti-Western.

A fundamental question

The West needs to discourage the knee-jerk 'nuke 'em' response to Muslims and the labelling of any Muslim act as 'fundamentalist'. The generalised and intense contempt of the Western media towards Islam pushes many Muslims into an anti-Western stance. It also makes the position of those who talk of dialogue and moderation more vulnerable.

Because the world media equate the word fundamentalist with an extremist, fanatic terrorist who is – invariably – Muslim, we need to ask how many media people raise the question: Can we legitimately use a term devised to describe something in one culture – a certain brand of Christian behaviour and thought – to another distinct culture? As Muslims by definition believe in the Quran, however actively or not they may follow its instructions, they are technically all fundamentalists. So, is every Muslim on earth then today an extremist, a fanatic and a terrorist?

How many know – and this question is also put to Muslims – that the notion of the greater *jihad*, commonly misunderstood as an aggressive act of religious war in the West, which derives from the word to strive, was explained by the Prophet as the attempt to control our own base instincts and work towards a better, more harmonious world? The lesser *jihad* is to battle physically for Islam; that, too, is only directed against tyranny and injustice.

The common problems in this shrinking world need to be identified: drug and alcohol abuse; divorce, teenage violence and crime; ethnic and racist prejudice; the problems of the aged and the poor; the challenge of the growing sense of anarchy and rampant materialism; the sexual debasement of women and children; the depletion of our natural resources; and ecological concerns. On all these issues Islam takes a strong, enlightened position. This is the real Islamic *jihad*, and if it is properly harnessed and understood, it can provide fresh, sorely needed strength to these most crucial of global issues.

We have seen how some of the most eminent Western global thinkers have got it so wrong where Islam is concerned. While pointing out their inadequacies, we have suggested an alternative method of examining Islam and thereby understanding its relations with the West. Serious and urgent rethinking is required by the policy-planners and policy-makers in the corridors of power, not only in Washington, London, Moscow and Paris but also in Cairo, Kabul and Tehran.

We conclude with a formula for the millennium. If justice flourishes – and is seen to flourish – in the Muslim world, if its rulers are people of integrity, and if Muslims are allowed to practise their faith with honour, then Islam provides its followers with the most viable, stable and legitimate force for political action. It will be a good neighbour to non-Muslims living outside its borders and provide a benevolent and compassionate environment to those living inside them. But it will continue to resist attempts to subvert its identity or dignity. That resistance can take the form of a Saladin or a Saddam.

In its October 1996 issue, *The World Today* printed the article, "Unfinished Struggle for Freedom" by Benazir Bhutto and Crown Prince Hussan of Jordan, in response to this article.

NOTES

1 Samuel Huntington, 'The Clash of Civilisations?', *Foreign Affairs*, Vol. 72, No 3, 1993, pp. 22–49.

2 Francis Fukuyama, *The End of History and the Last Man* (New York: Avon Books, 1993).

3 Felipe Fernandez-Amesto, *Millenium: a history of the last thousand years* (New York: Scribner, 1995).

4 Jean Baudrillard, *The Illusion of the End* (Oxford: Polity Press, 1994).

5 Graham Fuller and Ian Lesser, *A Sense of Seige: The Geopolitics of Islam and the West* (Boulder, CO.: Westview Press, 1995).

6 Benjamin Barber, *Jihad vs. McWorld* (New York: Times Books, 1995).

7 Bernard Lewis, 'The Roots of Muslim Rage', *Atlantic Monthly*, September 1990.

8 Huntington, op. cit.

9 Robert Chase et al., 'Pivotal States and U.S. Strategy', *Foreign Affairs*, Vol. 74. No 1, 1996, pp. 33–51.

10 Fukuyama, op. cit., pp, 45–46.

11 Ibid., p. 236.

12 Fernandez-Armesto, op. cit., p. 574.

13 This idea was first explored in a general sense in *Discovering Islam: Making Sense of Muslim History and Society*, by Akbar S. Ahmed (London: Routledge, 1988).

> "[D]espite China's undoubted ambition to become a full-fledged great military power, . . .there is no evidence that Beijing has embarked on a crash course to correct all its well-known deficiencies. . . China's defense modernization strategy remains long-term and incremental."

Uncertainty, Insecurity, and China's Military Power

PAUL H. B. GODWIN

When Deng Xiaoping came to power in 1978, he inherited a defense establishment that was little more than a lumbering giant. In the 20 years following the Sino-Soviet split of 1959–1960 and Moscow's termination of military assistance, China's military power had eroded into obsolescence. The country's defense industrial base was incapable of producing anything more than copies of Soviet designs from the 1950s, and the defense research and development (R&D) infrastructure was equally backward. Even the nuclear weapons program, developed at great cost and to the neglect of conventional weaponry, had produced only crude strategic systems, including a single nuclear-powered ballistic missile submarine that had yet to launch a missile. Moreover, during this time the Chinese armed forces had become intensely involved in Mao Zedong's domestic political campaigns, especially the Cultural Revolution, and were no longer an effective combat force, a reality demonstrated by their poor performance in the 1979 incursion into Vietnam.

Deng Xiaoping's long-term objective for the military reforms he introduced in 1979 was to build a self-sustaining defense establishment so that China could not be intimidated by any military power, and Beijing's foreign policies would not be constrained by military weakness. Rebuilding military strength, however, was not given first priority in Deng's strategy for modernizing China. In the "four modernizations" that defined his program for transforming China into a nation capable of assuming a leading role in world politics, renovating national defense came fourth, after the modernization of agriculture, industry, and science and technology.

Apprehension in Asia and the United States that China's military power was becoming potentially dangerous to the region did not emerge until the cold war's end. Four major developments in Beijing's defense policies intersected to create the image of potential peril. First, in 1985 Beijing transformed its national military strategy: China's armed forces were directed no longer to prepare for a major, possibly nuclear, war with the Soviet Union but for local, limited wars on China's borders. Second, annual double-digit percentage increases in Beijing's defense budgets began in 1989 (and continue), sustained by the dramatic growth in China's economy, which suggested a potential change in priorities. Third, the armament and military technology linkage established with the Soviet Union in 1990, and upheld by Russia after the Soviet Union's disintegration, was viewed as potentially revitalizing China's defense industrial base in addition to providing advanced weaponry. Finally, in the early 1990s, improvements in China's conventional forces were joined by the development of a new series of short-range, tactical battlefield ballistic missiles and land- and submarine-based strategic missiles.

These four elements converged as China's military security, in Beijing's own assessment, became more assured than at any time in the previous 150 years. Even as the threat to China's security diminished, Beijing demonstrated an assertive, if not aggressive, nationalism in its approach to territorial claims in the South and East China Seas. An assertive, nationalistic China, facing no major military threat but with growing military muscle bolstered by a rapidly expanding economy and

PAUL H. B. GODWIN *is a professor of international affairs in the department of military strategy at the National War College in Washington, D.C., where he specializes in China's defense and security policies. The views expressed in this essay are those of the author.*

Reprinted with permission from *Current History,* September 1997, pp. 252–257. © 1997 by Current History, Inc.

increasing military expenditures, raised serious questions about Beijing's long-term international intentions. Beijing's belligerent use of military exercises to intimidate Taiwan in the summer of 1995 and the spring of 1996, leading to United States deployment of two aircraft carrier battle groups near Taiwan, served only to exacerbate these concerns.

CHINA'S MILITARY STRENGTH IN CONTEXT

Military power is relative, not absolute; any evaluation of a state's military strength must be comparative and placed in context. Despite widespread apprehension in Asia and the United States that Beijing's military modernization programs could overturn East Asia's balance of power early in the twenty-first century, China's military leadership has no such confidence. To the contrary, it looks forward to the twenty-first century with uncertainty and a sense of insecurity, knowing that the Chinese People's Liberation Army (PLA), as all four services and branches are collectively named, will enter the next century with armaments and equipment just beginning to incorporate technologies from the 1970s and 1980s. It is not that Beijing perceives an immediate military threat to China, but that in an uncertain future with military technology evolving quickly, the PLA's relative obsolescence is becoming increasingly difficult to overcome.

Even apart from America's overwhelming military strength, Beijing looks out on an Asia undergoing major military renovation that in many areas exceeds the PLA's current capabilities and will continue to outmatch China's programs for at least a decade. As Beijing examines Asia's defense modernization programs, its concerns can be fully understood. Notwithstanding Tokyo's long-standing security relationship with the United States, including the protection provided by American nuclear forces and ongoing discussions about joining the United States theater missile defense program, Japan's euphemistically named Self-Defense Forces (SDF) are technologically the most sophisticated in the region and supported by Asia's most advanced defense industrial base. Nor are these forces small. Japan's maritime Self-Defense Forces constitute the region's largest modern navy, with 63 major surface combatants and 17 submarines; many of these are armed with the most advanced military technology in the world. With the capability to operate up to 1,000 nautical miles from the home islands, Japan's navy is supported by a land-based air arm deploying cutting-edge antisubmarine and antiship weapons on 110 aircraft and 99 armed helicopters.

Japan's air Self-Defense Forces are equally powerful, deploying 90 American F-4Es, 189 domestically produced copies of the United States F-15 (considered the world's finest interceptor), and 50 indigenous F-1 ground attack fighters, all supported by airborne warning and control system (AWACS) aircraft. Furthermore, Tokyo's current plans call for continued modernization of its air, ground, and naval forces with a defense budget, $46.8 billion, that is the third largest in the world.

Tokyo clearly intends to sustain Asia's most powerful navy and air force, even though the Soviet Union no longer exists to threaten Japan and its security ties with the United States are politically strong. Further heightening Beijing's insecurity is the fact that the PLA and Japan's SDF began their modernization programs at about the same time (Tokyo's National Defense Program Outline that guided the SDF to its current status was announced in 1976, and Deng Xiaoping's military reforms were initiated in 1979). In the two decades since China and Japan began modernizing their armed forces and defense industries, Tokyo has clearly made the most progress, and its edge will continue into the foreseeable future.

In addition to Japan, throughout East Asia most defense establishments have been rapidly modernizing their armed forces with advanced combat aircraft, ships, and submarines. Thailand is about to deploy the region's first aircraft carrier—the Spanish-built *Chakkrinareubet*. Displacing only about 11,500 tons, and intended for search-and-rescue and humanitarian operations, this carrier nevertheless can embark a small number of helicopters and aircraft, and thus represents East Asia's first sea-based airpower.

In Southeast Asia, naval forces are being acquired that, in combination with modernizing air forces deploying a variety of United States F-16 and F/A-18 combat aircraft and Russian MiG-29s, will be better able to defend territorial and maritime interests. Taiwan in particular continues programs to extensively upgrade its air and naval forces, including air defense capabilities highlighted by the deployment of Patriot surface-to-air missiles. Taiwan is also acquiring French and American combat aircraft, ships, and air defense systems that will be on line within the decade.

From Beijing's perspective, the renovation of China's armed forces is part of a pattern of Asian military modernization that began in the late 1970s and continues, with few exceptions, today. Furthermore, United States defense alliances and forward-deployed military forces provide an added complication to any net assessment Beijing would make of its regional capabilities. This is true not only of formal United States treaty relationships but also of America's less formal commitments. Beijing could not ignore the fact that the first of two United States aircraft carrier battle groups to arrive off Taiwan during the March 1996 crisis was based in Japan. Similarly, it is American technology and research that threaten to erode the credibility of China's small nuclear deterrent force and tactical battlefield missiles through the promise of theater missile defense systems and national missile defenses, both plausible in the next century. Once again, Japan's defense industrial and R&D capabilities are highlighted by United States pressure on Tokyo to join the theater missile defense research program and agree to future deployment.

RETHINKING NATIONAL MILITARY STRATEGY

When the Soviet Union was China's principal threat and Beijing's military strategy was based on defending continental China, most of the PLA's technological weaknesses could be overcome by a strategy of protraction, attrition, and the threat of nuclear retaliation—the so-called people's war under modern conditions. Continental defense, including the ability to conduct offensive operations short distances beyond China's borders, benefited from the sheer size of the 4 million-man PLA and the ultimate strategy of falling back into China's vast interior and simply exhausting an adversary through protracted war.

As the cold war ended, China began preparing for local, limited war on its periphery, including the defense of maritime borders and territorial claims in the East and South China Seas; this new orientation accentuated the obsolescence of the PLA's arms and equipment far more than had the requirements for continental defense. Beijing's new national military strategy required the PLA to prepare for early, offensive operations designed to defeat an adversary quickly and decisively, and potentially at some distance from the mainland. In modern warfare, these operations depend on the synergistic effect of ground, air, and naval forces operating together for common military objectives. China's armed forces had no experience with these complex operations, and therefore lacked the joint service command, staff, and logistic sup-

---

[1]See the June 1996 issue of *The China Quarterly*, which is devoted to a thorough analytic survey of China's military affairs. Much of my assessment draws on this issue.

port to prepare them for the demands of the new military strategy.

Moreover, existing and emerging warfare technologies make defense against a sudden attack or a preemptive military operation far more difficult than in the past. Standoff weaponry has become significantly more accurate and lethal, offers precision targeting at far greater ranges, and can be used at night and in other low-visibility conditions. Limited war involving high-technology weapons and equipment raises the importance of the initial engagement far beyond what it was a decade ago. Equally important for military operations, the development of surveillance technology is making the battlefield increasingly transparent. The significance of contemporary military technologies was underlined by the devastatingly swift defeat of Iraqi forces by the United States–led coalition in 1991. While the PLA knows it is extremely unlikely it will face such capabilities in the near future, it recognizes that China's military environment is becoming more demanding with the spread of advanced weapons and equipment throughout East Asia. In a direct response to the Gulf War's demonstration of high-technology warfare, China's military leadership modified its definition of future military contingencies from "limited, local war" to "limited war under high-tech conditions."

THE PLA'S EMERGING CAPABILITIES

The PLA is undoubtedly seeking to overcome the deficiencies highlighted by the demands of China's revised national military strategy.[1] It is also the case that access to Russian military technology and weapons, and Israeli technological and design support, have hastened the day when China's defense industries and the PLA will be more competent and capable. The difficulty is determining when that day will arrive, and to what extent China's capabilities will exceed those of its neighbors—nearly all of whom are committed to continued modernization of their defense forces. The question for Asia, however, is not whether the PLA will be better able to defend China in the improbable event of an attack on its mainland; apprehension within the region is instead based on China's potential force projection capabilities, especially as they apply to the future of Taiwan's and Beijing's territorial claims in the East and South China Seas. Thus, it is not the sheer size of China's armed forces and the vast amounts of largely obsolescent equipment it deploys, but the direction and intent of current modernization programs that are the source of anxiety.

Beijing has not sought to hide its recent focus on air and naval power. The PLA also has not tried to obscure its concentration on building "crack troops" capable of responding effectively to the kinds of military contingencies outlined in China's new national military strategy. For the past decade, but especially during the past five years, the PLA has focused on training and equipping selected ground units for quick-reaction and amphibious warfare roles. These are the "fist" (*quantou*) and "rapid response" (*kuaisu*) units, such as the 15th Group Army (Airborne) and the PLA navy's brigade-strength marine corps. Similarly, the PLA is attempting to establish command-and-control and logistic support systems that can effectively coordinate and sustain operations involving ground, air, and naval units. Training and exercises are explicitly concentrated on joint service operations. This training includes amphibious warfare exercises and naval maneuvers involving underway replenishment, as task forces train for surface combat and antisubmarine warfare.

Beijing's current weapons, equipment, and technology acquisition programs support the needs of its national military strategy. Air and naval forces answer the demand to defend far-flung maritime sovereignty claims, including Taiwan and those in the South China Sea. Strategic weapons are being replaced because of their age and the need to make new systems more survivable and accurate in the next century. Analyzing these acquisitions within the operational doctrine of today's PLA and Asia's military environment provides a measure of capability. There are, nonetheless, specific constraints that must be kept in mind as part of such an assessment.

Before Moscow began military technology transfers in 1990, the Western powers had placed stringent limits on what they would sell China. Following the Tiananmen tragedy of 1989, the West—with the exception of Israel—essentially embargoed all arms and military technology transfers to China. Because of these constraints, China's experience with advanced military technology is limited to, at most, the past five years, when the PLA began receiving Russian arms. Until China's defense industries place advanced weapons and equipment into series production, they cannot be considered an effective defense industrial base for China's armed forces. Equally important, the small number of weapons purchased and the time it takes to train the first crews and mainte-

It will be many years before the PLA can be considered modern.

nance personnel mean that it will be many years before the PLA can be considered modern.

ACQUIRING AND PROJECTING POWER

China has pursued programs designed to update obsolescent equipment with foreign technologies and develop new indigenous designs. The failure of these programs to meet the PLA's needs can be seen in acquisitions from Russia. The 1994 purchase of four Kilo-class diesel-electric-powered attack submarines from Russia indicates that China's own submarine programs were unsatisfactory. The submarine force is large, but 50 percent of the 50 or so deployed are based on outdated Soviet Romeo-types from the 1950s. China's newer designs are the 12 Romeo-derived Ming-class, and a single Song-class of more modern design currently undergoing operational evaluation. These ships are supplemented by 5 Han-class nuclear-powered submarines based on older technologies, and therefore undoubtedly very noisy and easily targeted by modern antisubmarine warfare systems. Similarly, the purchase in 1997 of 2 Russian Sovremenny-class destroyers is a strong indication that the new Luhu-class destroyer and Jiangwei-class frigate developed by China using primarily Western technologies are less than successful. Only 2 Luhus and 4 Jiangweis have been built in the past five years.

Long-standing efforts to improve the PLA air force and navy fleet air arm include the F-8, now operational but at best representing early 1960s technologies, and the FB-7, originally developed for the navy but not yet in series production. The future of China's airpower is tied to the F-10 that is being developed with Israeli assistance, and to the agreement for licensed production of Russia's Su-27 following the purchase of 72 completed aircraft. Over time these new aircraft will replace, but in much smaller numbers, China's obsolescent airpower composed primarily of about 4,400 fighter and ground attack aircraft derived from Soviet MiG-17, MiG-19, and MiG-21 designs. There is as yet no sign that the bomber force of some 420 aircraft derived from 1950s Soviet Il-28 and Tu-16 designs is to be replaced.

Forty-eight of the 72 Su-27s purchased from Russia have been delivered. Licensed production of these aircraft from complete kits supplied by Russia could begin in a year or so, but full Chinese-content Su-27s cannot be built for many years. It is unclear when the Israeli-assisted F-10 will enter production; even after years of development there is as yet no flying prototype. Two of the Kilo-class diesel-electric submarines have been delivered, and their first crews are completing Russian training programs. The two Sovremenny destroyers may be delivered by the end of this century and could be operational around 2004. Thus, from the PLA's point of view, true modernization of its weapons and the process of integrating them into operational and tactical doctrine have only just begun.

Military power projection requires the ability to sustain expeditionary forces in combat some distance from their home base. For the PLA, as with any other military, time and distance are critical variables in offensive operations. Should the PLA be called on to defend China's sovereignty claims in the South China Sea, military operations would require sustaining forces in combat as far as 600 miles (960 kilometers) from Hainan Island. If China sought to invade Taiwan, it would require an amphibious and/or air assault some 100 miles (160 km) from the mainland—essentially the distance covered by the allied invasion of France in 1944. At least for the next decade, China's armed forces will be incapable of successfully performing either operation against determined resistance.

With the exception of its ancient bomber fleet, combat operations in the South China Sea are beyond the effective range of China's airpower, which is entirely land-based and has no aerial refueling capability. Furthermore, Beijing's naval forces lack effective defenses against cruise missiles and air attack. Deployed naval air defenses consist of surface-to-air missiles (SAM) with a range of seven miles (11 km), providing an adversary the opportunity to launch antiship missiles beyond the range of the defending SAMs. Chinese warships have no defense against cruise missiles, since they do not mount radar-controlled close-in weapons systems designed for this purpose. Moreover, even with recent improvements, Chinese warships do not deploy antisubmarine warfare (ASW) systems capable of defeating modern, quiet submarines.

Should Beijing attempt combat air patrols over the South China Sea without aerial refueling, even its most modern fighter-bombers would have at most five minutes of loiter time. Without AWACS aircraft to detect and assign targets, the combat air patrols would be ineffective. Any of China's obsolescent long-range bombers deployed would be dangerously exposed to SAM defenses and modern interceptors firing medium-range air-to-air missiles. China can maintain a naval presence in the South China Sea, but it cannot conduct sustained combat

operations like those rehearsed for three weeks this April in the region by Australia, Singapore, Malaysia, Brunei, and Britain (the British Commonwealth's Five-Power Defense Arrangement group). This exercise, dubbed "Flying Fish," involved the deployment of 160 aircraft and 36 ships, including a British aircraft carrier and nuclear-powered submarine.

An assault on Taiwan would be perhaps even more difficult for the PLA because of improvements in the island's defenses. Taipei is acquiring 60 French Mirage 2000 fighter-bombers, 150 United States F-16s, and 4 American E-2 AWACS aircraft, making it extremely difficult for the PLA to gain air superiority over the Taiwan Strait. Taipei's acquisition of 6 French La Fayette-class frigates, the construction of 6 improved United States Perry-class frigates, and the lease of 6 modernized United States Knox frigates (which augment 22 updated older American destroyers) provide Taiwan's navy with far more advanced ships than those currently deployed by the PLA. In particular, the Perry's SAM defenses have a range of at least 60 miles (97 km), and defense against cruise missiles is provided by close-in weapons systems. These ships also employ very effective ASW systems and surface-to-surface missiles. On a ship-to-ship basis, Taiwan's navy can outshoot China's. An amphibious assault across the 100 miles (160 km) of the Taiwan Strait would require air superiority and sea control. Even with a large submarine force, it is doubtful the PLA could achieve such predominance except at great cost and over a considerable period of time.

Time is an extremely important consideration for Beijing. By deploying two carrier battle groups off Taiwan in response to China's aggressive military exercises, the United States clarified its commitment and added a clear complication to any PLA planning. Put simply, the PLA cannot plan military operations designed to subdue Taiwan without including the contingency of United States involvement. To the extent that Taiwan can prevent the PLA from rapidly achieving air superiority and sea control, American military support in the defense of Taiwan becomes more probable.

THE NUCLEAR DIMENSION

Beijing's strategy for nuclear deterrence is straightforward: China shall have the capability to respond to any nuclear attack with a second strike lethal enough to seriously harm the attacker. Beijing believes that this strategy can deter the kinds of nuclear threats made by the United States during the Korean War and the Taiwan Strait crises of the

1950s, and faced from the Soviet Union in the 1960s, 1970s, and 1980s.

China's small, aging, liquid-fueled intercontinental ballistic missile (ICBM) force of some 17 missiles was initially deployed in the mid-1970s and early 1980s. Deployment of its intermediate-range ballistic missile (IRBM) force of perhaps 70 weapons began in the late 1960s. To provide a survivable, quicker-reacting nuclear deterrent in an era when the United States and Russia continue to deploy thousands of strategic weapons and when missile defense is on the horizon, this force had to be modernized. Survivability is being sought through tactical mobility, with both the new solid-fueled 7,500-mile (12,000-km)-range DF-41 ICBM and the 5,000-mile (8,000-km)-range DF-31 designed to be road- and rail-mobile. The DF-41 is not anticipated to be operational before 2010, but the DF-31 will perhaps begin deployment in a year or two.

Solid fuels improve booster reliability and provide quicker response time, thereby reducing the missiles' vulnerability to a counterforce first strike. Solid propellants, however, have less boost power than liquid fuels, which means that the change to solid fuels required smaller warheads with greater yield-to-weight ratios. Smaller warheads have also been developed to prepare for the time when China masters multiple reentry vehicle technologies and missile defenses require penetration aids.

China's single nuclear-powered submarine (SSBN) entered service in 1983. This ship is not known to have test-launched a missile in a decade and may not be operational, if it ever was. Nonetheless, a new submarine-launched missile—the JL-2—has been derived from the DF-31, and it is assumed that a follow-on SSBN is under construction to take the weapon.

There are indications that some of Beijing's military strategists believe China's strategic forces are too small to be considered a credible deterrent. They would have China change from minimum deterrence, where a relatively small number of warheads capable of inflicting considerable damage in a second strike are considered sufficient, to a more robust strategy that calls for the deployment of a larger number of strategic forces. In an era when missile defenses are likely to be put in place, there will be continuing pressure on China to deploy more systems, with warheads equipped with multiple reentry vehicles, including penetration aids. Development of these technologies is almost certainly under way, but some years of testing will be required before they can be employed. This will provide sufficient lead time

to determine that a major shift in nuclear strategy has occurred and that the number and capability of China's strategic systems is increasing.

A MIRROR-IMAGE FUTURE

Beijing's military planners face an increasingly difficult dilemma. Rapid advances in military technologies have created requirements that China's defense R&D infrastructure and industrial base cannot meet. Beijing's national military strategy and the proliferation of high-technology arms and equipment nonetheless accentuate the role of advanced technologies in operations conducted by China's conventional forces, especially offensive operations, and in maintaining a viable nuclear deterrent. Yet, despite China's undoubted ambition to become a full-fledged great military power and its quest for Russian assistance in achieving this objective, there is no evidence that Beijing has embarked on a crash course to correct all its well-known deficiencies. Rather, Beijing's limited purchase of advanced weapons and equipment, and its continued preference for technology over end-use items, demonstrate that China's defense modernization strategy remains long-term and incremental. Modernization of China's defense industrial base and R&D, as this term is understood in the United States, Europe, Russia, and Japan, remains at least two decades into the future—decades during which the rest of Asia will not be standing still, least of all Japan.

Need East Asia worry? Of course. Although China's capabilities are currently limited, Beijing's ambition to achieve the status of a major military power has never been hidden. Two or three decades from now, assuming China's economy can continue to support the long-term strategy of building a largely self-reliant defense establishment, Asia could have in its midst a new primary military power. How Beijing will choose to use this power is the critical uncertainty. Hence, the central question for East Asia's security analysts is how long the United States will continue to deploy the military forces that are such a crucial element in the region's military balance. Despite Washington's constant reiteration that significant United States forces will remain, much of the buildup in East Asia reflects uncertainty about the American commitment and the misgiving that in a decade or two the region will contain two giants, China and Japan, each potentially seeking dominance. Thus, in an ironic twist, the uncertainty and consequent insecurity marking the PLA's perception of the twenty-first century is mirror-imaged by the rest of the region.

> Talk of a post-Soviet empire "has resurfaced and Western policymakers are considering whether an enlarged NATO will have to stand once again as a bastion against Russian expansion. In the weak and divided international community of the early 1920s, the Soviet Union succeeded in establishing itself and incorporating by force many of the territories of the former Russian empire. Would the international community allow a similar process to repeat itself today?"

Russian Foreign Policy in the Near Abroad and Beyond

Karen Dawisha

Boris Yeltsin's victory in the 1996 presidential election marked further progress in Russia's consolidation of democracy and movement toward a free-market economy. Yeltsin won, however, not least by shifting to the right in foreign policy and by advocating the pursuit of Russia's great power interests in the neighboring former Soviet republics—the so-called Near Abroad. In so doing he prevented the Communists from taking over the presidency, but his rightward shift was too late to prevent them or their allies from gaining control of the Duma, the Russian parliament, in the December 1995 elections. Thus, even with Boris Yeltsin as president, Russian foreign policy for the foreseeable future can be expected to be more assertive toward the West and more oriented toward reestablishing Russian primacy on the Eurasian continent.

Russia, however, currently lacks the capacity to reassert imperial control over the newly independent states of its former empire. The Russian military doctrine adopted in 1993 emphasizes war prevention and the maintenance of military sufficiency and eschews earlier doctrinal commitments to war fighting in forward areas and conventional superiority. The new doctrine sees two major roles for the Russian military: preventing local wars that

KAREN DAWISHA *is a professor in the department of government and politics at the University of Maryland and director of its Center for the Study of Post-Communist Societies. Her most recent book is* Foreign Policy-Making in Russia and the New States of Eurasia *(Armonk, N.Y.: M. E. Sharpe, 1995). The author would like to thank Darya Pushkina for research assistance. A version of this paper was presented at the Aspen Institute's congressional program meeting in St. Petersburg, Russia, in August.*

might arise from secessionist claims (as in the fight for independence by the breakaway Chechen republic in southern Russia) and de-escalating conflicts in lands adjacent to Russian territory that could imperil Russian interests and spill over into Russia proper (as in the conflicts in the Georgian provinces of Abkhazia and South Ossetia). Moreover, in the five years since the break up of the Soviet Union, the Russian military has shrunk by more than half its peak level in the mid-1980s, and the call-up to go to war in Chechnya and other hot spots has produced widespread draft dodging.

Although Russia's ability to achieve imperial aims by force is currently limited, observers worry that the imperial idea may nevertheless be reborn, presaging a future round of expansion. While neither elite nor public opinion presently favors such a resurgence, there are minority currents in both that deserve examining.

THE DRIFT TO THE RIGHT

Beginning in 1993, the liberal, pro-Western orientation of Russian foreign policy, which had virtually ignored the Near Abroad in favor of reliance on ties with Europe and America, gave way. The 1993 and 1995 Duma elections and the two rounds of this summer's presidential election showcased right-wing leaders and parties that supported the expansion of Russian borders; these included the Liberal Democrats (led by Vladimir Zhirinovsky), the Communists (led by Gennadi Zyuganov), and the Congress of Russian Communities (led by retired General Aleksandr Lebed).

Under unrelenting pressure from the right, liberal and centrist politicians have increasingly had to concede that the Near Abroad should be a zone of Russian rights and interests. Even President Yeltsin's election platform stated that the two top priorities of Russian foreign policy were "the achievement of the utmost integration of the CIS [the Commonwealth of Independent States—the regional organization to which most of the former Soviet republics acceded after the Soviet Union collapsed] countries on a voluntary and mutually advantageous basis and the active protection of the rights and interests of fellow-countrymen in the near and far abroad." In contrast, the improvement of Russian-American relations was not even mentioned among his priorities if elected, reflecting the political sensitivity of his prior commitment to that relationship.

After the first round of the presidential election, Yeltsin boosted his chances in the runoff by turning to the right and appointing General Lebed as his national security adviser. It had been Lebed's charisma and his reputation as an incorruptible supporter of law and order more than his hawkish stance on foreign policy that had won him over a sixth of the popular vote in the first round. Yet his new position undoubtedly assured his ability to shape future policy toward the Near Abroad.

The problem for Yeltsin in allying with Lebed and other rightist leaders is that many of them vehemently support the redrawing of borders by force and have only a lukewarm commitment to democracy and the rule of law. In 1991 and 1993, Communist and right-wing leaders attempted to take power by force, and they have remained active on the political stage. Even after being appointed national security adviser, Lebed labeled himself only a semidemocrat, and Yeltsin's own inner circle includes advisers who have favored both a get-tough policy toward Russia's neighbors and the use of extralegal means to ensure that Yeltsin stays in control. Given the connection between the antidemocratic and pro-imperial ideas of these groups, the further entrenchment of the latter could undermine democracy. Conversely, the further institutionalization of democracy should also weaken the force of imperial ideology.

Yet the institutionalization of democracy will not automatically or immediately decrease the influence of these groups since they do control the Duma. Although the Duma's powers are limited, it can and has passed any number of nonbinding resolutions that force a government response and shape the general political environment in which policy is made. Duma actions have included calls for military-basing agreements with all countries on Russia's borders; promotion of dual-citizenship agreements with Russia's neighbors; denunciation of preferences for the titular nationality in neighbors' citizenship laws; the elimination of Belarus's central bank as a precondition for accepting Belarus's request for economic union with Russia; a declaration of Russian sovereignty over Sevastopol, the Ukrainian port in the Crimea where the contested Black Sea Fleet is headquartered; and a resolution annulling the agreements that brought about the end of the Soviet Union.

The Duma's failure to deal with what are seen as more pressing domestic concerns has led to a decline in its reputation among the populace. Public opinion polls have consistently shown the people's low interest in foreign policy as compared to their concern with the rule of law, the fight against crime, and, above all, domestic economic recovery. In the December 1995 Duma elections, parties that were perceived as capable of dealing with foreign policy but less capable of addressing the country's economic ills (such as Lebed's Congress of Russian Communities) typically did not receive the 5 percent of the vote that would allow representation in the Duma.

Public opinion has also shown that while nostalgia for the Soviet era is widespread, the people are completely unwilling to use Russian troops to forcibly restore the Union. The revulsion at the loss of Russian life in the fight against the Chechens has shaped popular sentiment against imperial expansion abroad: polls repeatedly have shown that almost three-quarters of the population reject any form of reestablishment of the Union, and among those who support such an end, only 5 percent would sanction the use of force.

RUSSIA'S "NATIONAL SECURITY ZONE" DEFINED

While Russia is unlikely to seek the forcible reestablishment of empire, the country's leaders have moved clearly to mark out the Near Abroad as their "national security zone." As the largest and strongest country of the former Soviet Union, and the one that has benefited most from the institutional inheritance of the Soviet state, Russia has enormous comparative advantage. Thus, Russia has used its position as the least dependent economy in the former Soviet space to exert economic pressure, especially through the supply or withholding of energy or access to Russian-controlled pipelines. Because of the comparative weakness of most of the new states, Russia is able to exert enormous leverage with relatively little effort. The way Russia has been able to shift between the Armenians and the

Azerbaijanis—supplying energy to one side and then the other—shows that it can punish and reward without suffering significant or proportionate losses.

That Russia has been willing to provide substantial energy and trade subsidies makes clear the extent to which it is concerned about not destabilizing the newly independent countries. According to IMF estimates, Russia provided $17 billion in goods at concessionary and subsidized prices in 1993 alone—making it the single largest aid donor to the other newly independent states in that year. Furthermore, in February 1996 Russia and Belarus signed an agreement renouncing mutual debts, including the $600 million (plus the millions in penalties) Belarus owed to the Russian natural gas monopoly Gazprom.

Russian leaders encouraged all the former republics to join the Commonwealth of Independent States, which originally included a joint military command dominated by Russia. While currently incapable of mounting and maintaining a large-scale military operation beyond Russia's borders, the Russian military—via a network of formal basing agreements, contingents "temporarily" stationed abroad, a unified air defense system controlled by Moscow, and peacekeeping missions sanctioned by regional treaties—is the only force in the Eurasian space capable of sustained significant influence in the other states of the Near Abroad.

Russia's commitment of 25,000 troops to Tajikistan, its legal claims to Crimea, and its pledge to protect ethnic Russians living abroad are issues that spring from different situations and political motivations. But they reflect an overall consensus in Russia that the former Soviet area constitutes a natural russophone zone over which Moscow has "always" been able to exercise influence. Even President Yeltsin, whose initial foreign policy views emphasized international and Western links, has come to embrace the notion that "the sphere of Russia's economic, political, and humanitarian interests extends to the entire post-Soviet space."

One reason for this stance is that Russia lacks a regional alternative to cooperation with the other new states. While it is abundantly richer in natural resources than its neighbors, the psychological and organizational detritus of the Soviet era has created barriers to cooperation with new partners. Whereas in the 1960s Britain and France could simultaneously pursue decolonization in Africa and Asia and integration in Europe, Russia has little alternative but to pursue decolonization in Eurasia even as it seeks regional reintegration with countries in the region. Naturally, such a policy is fraught with the potential for misunderstanding.

Indeed it is difficult to read the official "Strategic Course of the Russian Federation" with the CIS countries without wondering whether the successful pursuit of this course could pave the way for a de facto imperial reassertion. The document is a clear statement of Russia's assertion of great power status over the other states. It asserts that Russia's main objective toward the CIS is the creation of "an economically and politically integrated association of states capable of claiming its proper place in the world community"; that Russia should be "the leading force in the formation of a new system of interstate political and economic relations"; and that when working with the UN and the Organization for Security and Cooperation in Europe on peacekeeping in the CIS, "it is necessary to seek their agreement that this region is primarily a zone of Russian interests."

CONTINUED COEXISTENCE

Many of Moscow's actions toward the Near Abroad since independence have met a stern rebuff. Indeed, it could be said that a central feature in the national identity of many of the new states is the imperative of resistance to any renewed Russian drive.

This resistance to Russian control is especially apparent in Latvia and Estonia, western Ukraine, western Moldova, Azerbaijan, and within Russia itself in the North Caucasus. It is less prevalent in Central Asia, Armenia, Georgia, eastern and southern Ukraine, eastern Moldova, Belarus, and Lithuania. In the first group there is a solid consensus among the elites and the population that independence means independence from Russia; the situation in the latter group is not so clear cut. Historic memories of Russia as a savior of local populations, common Slavic and Orthodox roots, an economic infrastructure still centered in Moscow, and russophone elites or large numbers of Russian nationals settled in and intermarried with the local population all lend themselves to Russia's continued coexistence with these countries.

This coexistence has under certain circumstances translated into significant Russian influence. In Georgia both the Abkhaz separatists and the Georgian state authorities called on Russia for military support to tip the balance in their favor and then to maintain the peace once the threat of separatism had subsided. In the process, the Georgian government acceded to Russian demands for military-basing rights in the country, bases that could be used both to support President Eduard Shevardnadze's embattled position and to promote Russia's interests in the Caucasus if needed.

In Armenia, the government has repeatedly enlisted Russian military support in its conflict with Azerbaijan over the Armenian-populated enclave of Nagorno-Karabakh in Azerbaijan. It received critical supplies of oil for its 1994 offensive into Azerbaijan and relies on those supplies for its continued occupation of western Azerbaijan. Both Armenia and Russia have sought to weaken Azerbaijan: Armenia wants to promote its own claims to Nagorno-Karabakh, and Russia wants to gain access to Azerbaijan's oil and weaken Baku's potential to reclaim its historic role as the beacon for the spread of pan-Turkic and Islamic appeals north and east from the Middle East.

Azerbaijan has been thrown onto the defensive in the face of this dual pressure. The Azerbaijani Popular Front and its leader, former President Abulfaz Elchibey, long an object of Russian concern, lost power to Gaidar Aliev, a former Soviet apparatchik. Since becoming president, Aliev has tried to protect the country from Armenia by acceding to virtually all Russian demands, including granting ever-larger percentages of stock in Azerbaijan's oil industry to Russian firms and guaranteeing that Azerbaijani aid would continue to be exported to the outside world through Russian pipelines. The Azerbaijanis have decided that the only way to buy security from Armenian attacks is to recognize Russian economic interests in the area.

None of the states in the Caucasus have become colonies of Russia; they have only accepted an increased Russian presence in return for the economic and security benefits it provides. In so doing, however, they have become more dependent on Russia and made it possible for Russia to exert pressure on the politics of the region at a lower cost than if Caucasian elites had not so easily accepted an increased Russian presence.

In Belarus the situation is different. While other states, including Kazakstan and Kyrgyzstan, have sought stronger ties with Russia, Belarus stands alone among the new states in actively favoring reunification. Opinion polls in Belarus have shown support from almost half the population for significantly closer relations with Russia—including sup-

A central feature in the national identity of many of the new states is the imperative of resistance to any renewed Russian drive.

port among a small minority for the complete restoration of the Soviet Union—and a popular referendum supported by the president called for union as well. (Indeed, President Alexander Lukashenko ran on a platform that promised complete union with Moscow.) Belarus has dismantled border posts along the frontier with Russia, restored Russian as the official language, promised to maintain its army's preparedness, agreed to continue paying pensions to the thousands of retired Soviet-era officers residing in Belarus, established a joint parliamentary assembly with the Russian Duma, and granted Russia leases for two bases.

Despite President Lukashenko's assurances that the two countries would soon become a single "unified state," a treaty creating only a "Community of Sovereign Republics" was signed in April 1996. Lawmakers in both countries expressed skepticism that Russia would undertake the economic burden of reincorporating Belarus and that authorities in Minsk would surrender the country's sovereignty completely.

In Central Asia, elites were clearly unprepared for independence and spent much of the first year trying to convince Russia to form a commonwealth. In contrast to elites in the Caucasus and the Baltics, most post-independence Central Asian leaders had not been involved in pre-independence national struggles, undergone any period of imprisonment, or formed or led popular fronts. The exception, of course, was Tajikistan; there, after a brief but bloody civil war, pro-Moscow elites gained the ascendancy and established a regime strongly in favor of a continued Russian presence.

In the region as a whole, elites have been unable or unwilling to act on their economic independence from Russia. Elites trained in central planning have continued to see Moscow as the center, and Russia has maintained its economic advantage; a treaty between Russia, Belarus, Kazakstan, and Kyrgyzstan signed in March 1996 called for the "deepening of integration" in the economic field.

However, in none of the Central Asian countries is there an indigenous trend favoring the surrender of political sovereignty. Most national elites (Tajikistan is the exception) have become more and not less committed to maintaining their countries' formal independence while continuing to rely on Moscow for economic and military support. Their reaction to Moscow's rhetoric that the Belarus-

Russia treaty would be a model for future Russian relations with other CIS countries was almost uniformly negative.

Given the speed and circumstances of the Soviet collapse, the initial unpreparedness of so many elites and populations for independence is historically unique. With the passage of time their countries have come to value independence more, particularly since they have been able to enjoy its economic, security, psychological, and cultural benefits. Yet many of these new states, however hostile to Russia, are weaker and more fragile than Russia and will therefore remain dependent on it. Consequently, Russia is unlikely to recede as an economic or geopolitical presence in the area, and the temptation to empire will have to be contained by more than the varying will and ability of peoples in the bordering states.

RUSSIA AND THE WORLD

During the course of the twentieth century, the Russian empire was replaced by a Soviet empire; that empire has fallen, but talk of another has resurfaced and Western policymakers are considering whether an enlarged NATO will have to stand once again as a bastion against Russian expansion. In the weak and divided international community of the early 1920s, the Soviet Union succeeded in establishing itself and incorporating by force many of the territories of the former Russian empire. Would the international community allow a similar process to repeat itself today?

Several important factors make such a repetition unlikely. First, elites in neighboring countries have a greater awareness of the nature and potential of Russian power. For example, reabsorbing Kazakstan today, with its cities, educated elite, developed infrastructure, and communications links to the outside world would be a far more difficult task than it was in the 1920s, when the indigenous peoples were nomadic, illiterate, geographically isolated, and had no history of independent statehood. Moreover, if Russia attempted to forcibly re-integrate them, these states would undoubtedly seek and receive support from the international community for a renewed policy of containment. Regional security organizations of the kind developed during the early years of the cold war, such as NATO, SEATO, and CENTO, could be expanded to include not only new East-Central European members but also states of the former Soviet Union itself.

Current restraints on forward basing of United States and Western European troops would also presumably be lifted under such circumstances.

Second, the post-1945 international system has largely come to accept the principles of state sovereignty, national self-determination, and the inadmissibility of the use of force to change boundaries of legitimate, popularly elected governments. At the close of the nineteenth century, the golden age of empires imposed a normative logic on the international system. A century later the defense of the nation-state (not the imperial state) and the promotion of decolonization, democracy, and human rights—and not the reestablishment of empire and authoritarian regimes—are the dominant norms upheld by the international community and from which international institutions derive their legitimacy. To the extent that force has been sanctioned by the international community through the United Nations, it has been to uphold these norms (as in Kuwait, Haiti, or Bosnia). It is virtually impossible to foresee a situation in which the clear use of Russian force against the wishes of a legitimately elected government would be formally sanctioned by the international community and its organizations.

Should there be a resurgence of imperial fervor, Russia's options will also be limited geopolitically. Eastern Europe and the West would undoubtedly move to expand NATO without taking Russian sensitivities into account, and any possibility of establishing joint committees from Russia and NATO states on foreign affairs or defense would vanish. While the Soviet Union could leapfrog over the American-sponsored regional security organizations that ringed it during the Cold War by establishing ties with leftist regimes in the third world, most of these regimes have now become integrated into the global economy. They would not gain by establishing relations with a right-wing Russia that would threaten their connections with other trading partners.

Finally, the entrenchment of democracy in Russia and among its neighbors will decrease civil strife, diminish the influence of antidemocratic forces, increase the ability of the legislatures, courts, and media to oversee the "power ministries," and create growing incentives to respect international norms. Russia's size and wealth will ensure its continued preeminence in Eurasia, but it is its commitment to democracy and its new institutions, if sustained, that will ensure it a respected place in the international arena.

Nuclear Deterrence and Regional Proliferators

Robert G. Joseph

BELOW ARE FIVE general propositions regarding the deterrence of chemical and biological weapons (CBW) use by regional adversaries, focusing specifically on the contribution of nuclear weapons in strengthening the U.S. deterrent posture. This article is drawn from a larger, ongoing effort to assess the continuing rationale for nuclear weapons in the contemporary security environment. The results of this related work will be published separately.

1. The prospect of CW and BW employment is increasing. This is due in part to the fact that barriers to both possession and use of these weapons have been substantially undermined in recent years, despite an unprecedented effort, led by the United States, to strengthen international norms against proliferation. In terms of acquisition, export controls and supplier groups—although they make an important contribution—will not always be effective. Over time, a determined state or non-state actor with even modest resources will most likely succeed, given easy access to dual-use technologies, the willingness of some suppliers—such as China—to provide sensitive equipment and expertise, the emergence of indigenous capabilities, and the growth in illicit, black market transfers.

In terms of barriers to use, here again, international norms are important but will not likely affect the calculations of those who ignore legal impediments. One of the main lessons learned from the employment of chemical weapons in recent conflicts is that the use of CW can have dramatic military effects on the battlefield and a significant impact on the enemy's strategic calculations, as it did in persuading the Ayatollahs of Iran to accept peace with Iraq. Moreover, another equally unfortunate lesson learned was that the use of chemicals against even unarmed civilians, such as the Kurds, did not lead the international community to impose effective sanctions;

Robert G. Joseph is director of the Center for Counterproliferation Research at the National Defense University and is on the faculty of the National War College. This article draws on a number of ongoing Center research projects examining the implications for U.S. security of the proliferation of nuclear, biological and chemical weapons.

it protested loudly but did nothing that would dissuade the next outlaw from committing a similarly horrific act.

2. Even for conflicts in regions of vital U.S. interest and directly involving U.S. military forces, deterrence of adversaries armed with CW and BW capabilities is significantly more likely to fail than during the Cold War. Several factors reinforce this proposition.

First, unlike in the bipolar context, regional states are now more free to pursue their own aggressive political, ideological, and, in some cases, religious objectives through the use of force. For the United States, this lack of discipline is compounded by the fact that proliferation is occurring in regions in which we have security commitments and forward-based forces.

Second, the conditions necessary for deterrence to succeed are likely not to pertain. These include such essentials as mutual understandings and effective communications with the adversaries. We thought these conditions existed in the East–West deterrent relationship, but they are not likely to be present when dealing with threats such as a desperate North Korea.

Third, the strategic profiles of regional adversaries are fundamentally different from those assumed about Soviet leadership. Based on empirical studies by RAND and others of leadership risk propensities, those often referred to as rogue regimes are considered more prone to take risks and more willing to sacrifice the lives of their citizens for personal, territorial, or other objectives.

Fourth, regional adversaries' concepts of weapons employment are also likely to be much different than those assumed about the Soviet Union. In the Cold War, nuclear weapons and even chemical weapons were viewed by the West as weapons of last resort. We assumed the Russians held the same view. Today, regional proliferators see nuclear, biological, and chemical (NBC) weapons much differently—as weapons of the weak against the strong, as the only weapons that can counter the conventional superiority of the West. NBC weapons and missiles are viewed not as weapons of last resort but as weapons of choice—to be threatened or even used early in a conflict for political, psychological, and military purposes.

Reprinted with permission from *The Washington Quarterly*, Summer 1997, pp. 167-175. © 1997 by the Center for Strategic and International Studies (CSIS) and the Massachusetts Institute of Technology.

3. Despite this pessimistic view, deterrence must remain our first line of defense in regional conflicts. Deterrence—that is, convincing an opponent not to undertake a specific action by posing the prospect that the costs of that action will outweigh the benefits—continues to be a valid concept. The fundamentals of deterrence—that is, the possession of capabilities and the perceived will to make the threat of retaliation credible in the mind of the enemy—also remain critical to success.

Yet, it is essential to recognize that deterrence has changed. The standard Cold War doctrine of deterrence based on punishment and retaliation alone no longer appears relevant, especially for regional adversaries armed with chemical and biological weapons and the means to deliver them inside and outside the theater of conflict, perhaps with unconventional forces and without attribution. In this context, we need to take into account that the deterrence equation in a regional setting is likely not to be one of symmetry as in the East–West relationship, where we put the very survival of the United States and the Soviet Union at stake. In a regional context, there is likely to be an asymmetry of interests, where our survival is not at risk but the enemy is likely to see his own survival—or at least that of his regime—at stake, perhaps prompting him to use CBW with less concern or fear about the consequences.

Also different is that, in the Cold War, nuclear deterrence was an essential part of our broader containment policy. The primary mission of our nuclear forces was to deter the Soviet Union from projecting power or expanding outward. In a regional setting, our adversaries tell us they will use "weapons of mass destruction" to keep us from intervening or projecting our power into their area. In other words, deterrence is even more of a two way street and, as a result, more problematic.

Clearly, we need to reconsider how we think about implementing deterrence under these conditions. We will need to adjust our statements and deployments to fit the regional circumstances and the nature of the adversary. The one-size-fits-all approach will no longer be sufficient. We need to develop regional and regime-specific deterrence strategies taking into account the political, military, and cultural dynamics that are critical to success. We must also think about more effective ways to communicate resolve and make known our capabilities, through declaratory policy, private channels, exercises, and presence.

4. In terms of forces, the major challenge for the United States and our coalition partners is to acquire military capabilities specifically tailored to deny the enemy any benefit from using chemical and biological weapons. The ability to retaliate and punish with overwhelming force will remain an important ingredient in our deterrent posture—as evidenced by Iraq's concern that the United States and Israel would respond to CBW use with nuclear weapons. Yet, given the nature of the adversaries we face—including their incentives to employ chemical and biological weapons for political and military advantages—we need to shift the focus to deterrence through denial—that is, developing and deploying the national capability to deny the enemy any advantages from the use of these weapons. We must have the ability to defend against the threat both to bolster deterrence and to provide the best hedge should deterrence fail.

If the United States and our allies develop and deploy such capabilities—active defenses, passive defenses, and counter-force capabilities—and if we effectively integrate these capabilities into our forces through appropriate refinements in doctrine, training, and leadership development, potential enemies will have less incentive to use or even to acquire chemical and biological weapons. This, in fact, may be the most critical impact that robust U.S. military capabilities can have on the proliferation problem.

5. Turning more specifically to the contribution of nuclear weapons in this new deterrent framework, nuclear weapons will continue to play an essential deterrent role in a counter-proliferation context. Here, one can draw on the real world case mentioned earlier. Iraqi leaders attribute their decision not to use CW—and we now know BW as well—to the U.S. threat of massive retaliation: the warning of "catastrophic consequences" if Iraq were to use chemical weapons. Of course we need to consider the source, but clearly it seems that there was significant mirror imaging present and that the Iraqis interpreted this warning to mean that Baghdad would be destroyed by nuclear weapons. It would be very difficult for Saddam Hussein to believe that the United States would not use nuclear weapons, or at least that the Israelis would not, given his view of the world and his own demonstrated absence of constraints in the use of force to achieve his personal objectives.

Additional factors may have weighed in the Iraqi decision: practical operational considerations such as the perceived preparedness of U.S. forces to protect themselves—perhaps even more effectively than Iraqi forces—from the effects of CW use on the battlefield. Some individuals have cited interviews with Iraqi prisoners of war who mention this perceived preparedness as the rationale behind Iraqi non-use of chemicals in Operation Desert Storm. If accurate, this would reinforce the need for improved denial capabilities in the future as a means of strengthening deterrence.

The most valid explanation of why deterrence worked in the Gulf will almost certainly include more than one cause. Yet, most of the policy-level participants in that conflict, at least on the U.S. side, consider the contribution of the threat of a nuclear response to have been key—although the word nuclear was deliberately avoided. Although several of President George Bush's senior officials have since stated and written that the United States would never actually have employed nuclear weapons, they make this statement not to suggest that nuclear weapons were unimportant as a deterrent but rather that there appeared to be no operational role for these weapons, especially given the stunningly rapid victory of our conventional forces.

Yet, what was important for deterrence was what Saddam believed. In this context, Defense Secretary Dick Cheney's position is the most thoughtful, and risks far less in terms of undermining deterrence in future conflicts. Cheney states that nuclear weapons use was never seriously considered but that, had CW or BW been used against us, a nuclear response may have become a consideration. This is clearly the right message if we desire to strengthen deterrence.

The False Goal of Denuclearization

It has become a popular sport to question and, in fact, deny the utility of nuclear weapons, despite our knowledge of widespread CBW proliferation. Some argue that radical reductions and even denuclearization will translate into regimes such as Iraq forgoing nuclear weapons, and perhaps even chemical and biological weapons. This is simply astonishing.

When the United States gave up BW as an option for retaliation, we heard similar assertions that we now know were empty. We now hear the same assertions in the context of giving up U.S. CW capabilities. Interestingly, we also heard from many of these same sources that we could risk the consequences of being wrong about BW and CW because the massive U.S. nuclear retaliatory capability would remain a strong deterrent.

How can we believe that by drastically reducing or giving up our nuclear weapons, one of the most important deterrent tools we possess, we will strengthen deterrence? The opposite is surely the predictable outcome. For countries like Iraq, Iran, Libya, and North Korea, weapons of mass destruction are their best counter to our conventional superiority. Again, this is what they tell us and their own people.

Why would these states grant us the overwhelming advantage of competing and conducting conflict on solely conventional terms? The answer is simple: they would not. As much as we would like to believe it would be otherwise, all evidence is to the contrary.

Another means of calling into question the utility of nuclear weapons is to imply that there are no "appropriate" targets for such weapons. In this context, we often hear that all relevant targets can be destroyed by advanced conventional weapons. Here again, the evidence contradicts the assertion. Despite the great superiority of the West's conventional forces in Desert Storm, we were unable to defeat the mobile Scuds, notwithstanding a massive effort by coalition air forces. This stands as a clear lesson for future adversaries. Coalition forces were also unsuccessful against deep underground targets, which simply cannot in many cases be destroyed by air attack. The technology just does not exist today.

In response to CW use against U.S. troops or BW use against U.S. population centers, with perhaps massive loss of life, we well may want to destroy such targets promptly and with absolute certainty, rather than leave them operational even for a short time. We may also want to strike other military targets, perhaps even those we could attack with conventional forces, to cause shock and to send a clear signal that CBW use will be severely punished. What is essential is that we retain the option to respond and that this capability is known to our adversaries. If we rule out these options, we undercut deterrence and raise the likelihood of conflict occurring, as well as the likelihood that chemical and biological weapons will be used against us.

Nuclear Weapons as a Hedge

The rationale for maintaining a credible and effective nuclear weapon posture is only in part based on the counterproliferation role. Of greater importance is the need to provide a hedge—an insurance policy—against a reversal in our relations with Russia and China. Both of these nuclear weapon states have demonstrated a tendency for radical shifts in their political orientation, as well as an enduring commitment to possess nuclear weapons both for the status they afford and as an essential part of their security.

Neither Russia nor China would seriously consider eliminating their nuclear arsenals, although they would both likely see real value in a nuclear emaciated United States. Indeed, while we in the United States debate the pros and cons of dramatic reductions in our nuclear forces, and in fact whether we should go to zero nuclear weapons, these two states are modernizing their nuclear forces. In the case of China, this entails building new missiles and warheads, recently tested.

In the case of Russia, whose conventional forces are in desperate condition, nuclear modernization includes not only new missiles but elaborate, hardened command-and-control facilities. In fact, Russian security doctrine today places much more emphasis on nuclear weapons than did Soviet doctrine, as evidenced by Moscow's reversal of the no-first-use policy. More recently, President Boris Yeltsin's rhetoric on the eve of the Helsinki summit, although primarily intended for domestic consumption and negotiating capital, makes evident the wide gap between official Russia and those in the United States advocating the elimination of nuclear weapons or even drastic reductions "to a few hundred." Yeltsin's response to a fanciful question on the prospect of a North Atlantic Treaty Organization (NATO) attack on Russia, in which he explicitly emphasized the importance of "nuclear means," perhaps best underscores this gap.

The obvious point is that, given the inability to control or even predict where these two states will be in 5 to 10 years, we need to hedge against a reversal in our relations. Nuclear weapons are an important element of this hedge. Few in the U.S. want to return to the past, and even fewer in Russia desire a turn to the hard right, but what we want and what occurs are seldom the same.

Those who promote the movement toward a nuclear-free world often see nuclear weapons as an evil in and of themselves; some even argue that the elimination of these weapons is a precondition for a peaceful international order. This, as Samuel Johnson once said of second marriages, is the clear "triumph of hope over experience." The enduring lessons from World War II—particularly the need to avoid simplistic approaches which contributed to the most deadly conflict in our history—have again become blurred. Deterrence, rather than disarmament through denuclearization, is the basis for sound policy, as deterrence has worked in the past to save countless lives by making the prospect of war horrific.

The optimism of the nuclear abolitionists—some would say their naiveté—appears to be uniquely American. Notwithstanding the usual cacophony emanating from the United Nations

General Assembly, the currency of nuclear weapons may have increased outside of the United States. In Europe, France has been actively playing the nuclear card in the continental political context. In South Asia, India and Pakistan give no indication of change in their deadly collision course, one that potentially involves nuclear confrontation. In the Middle East, one hears little talk in Israel about giving up the nuclear option. The call to nuclear disarmament is perceived at best as academically interesting, but of little relevance to a state whose very existence could be threatened by CBW proliferation in its immediate neighborhood. One can only wonder about the amusement that the debate in the United States must invoke in Iran, Iraq, and other proliferant states aggressively pursuing nuclear weapons.

Turning to numbers, it is clear that setting force levels has never been an exact science, nor can it be. Further reductions that are implemented in a mutual and verifiable way might be the most appropriate outcome. But we should not rush to lower levels just for the sake of lower levels. And this guessing game to pick a number between a few thousand and a few hundred is fundamentally uninteresting, given the nature of the assumptions one must make, especially as the desired number gets lower. These assumptions, whether political or technical—such as an ability to monitor warhead inventory levels with confidence—simply do not correspond to real world conditions.

Moreover, the strategic consequences of drastic reductions in the U.S. nuclear force structure appear not to have been thought through, even though they could be profound. What would be the effect on crisis stability in the event of a reversal in our relations with Russia? What would be the effect on potential regional adversaries who might see nuclear parity with the United States as desirable and achievable? What would be the effect on our allies who have long relied on the U.S. nuclear guarantee for their security? In short, could the move to abolish nuclear weapons lead to their further proliferation?

The Next Step

If nuclear weapons cannot be disinvented, what can be done to build on the substantial progress made in the recent past to control these weapons? As an essential next step, we should implement **START II** and eliminate the heavy land-based **MIRVs** (multiple independently targetable re-entry vehicles), a missile whose only purpose was to conduct a first strike against the United States. This negotiating achievement was perhaps the most significant gain for strategic stability in 30 years of arms control negotiations. Rushing to the next agreement could well reverse this success, a success whose outcome is today far from certain. This would be the latest irony of an arms control process that in the past has often approached treaty making as an end in itself, rather than what it should be: part of our national security strategy.

Finally, two summary observations seem appropriate. The first is that, for deterrence to work, the adversary must be convinced of our will and capability to respond decisively. On this score, ambiguity and uncertainty play very much against us.

The second observation is that, even at the height of the Cold War, no one possessed an exact understanding of how deterrence worked. In the end, it may have been the very uncertainty that surrounded the nuclear enterprise—the how, the when, and the where of our nuclear response—that imbued it with the greatest deterrent value. An adversary who knew, or thought he knew, what our exact response to a given provocation would be could work actively to undermine that course of action. This may be the case with deterrence today. We may not have a precisely drawn nuclear response to CW or BW use against us. We may not be able to tell our adversary—or even ourselves—what targets would be put at risk to nuclear response if he unleashed CW or BW against us. Yet this very uncertainty, coupled with the certainty that we will respond decisively, should prey on the minds of adversaries and ultimately provide the rationale for nuclear weapons.

The opinions, conclusions, and recommendations expressed or implied in this article are solely those of the author, and do not necessarily represent the views of the National Defense University, the Department of Defense, or any other government agency.

Taking Nuclear Weapons off Hair-Trigger Alert

It is time to end the practice of keeping nuclear missiles constantly ready to fire. This change would greatly reduce the possibility of a mistaken launch

by Bruce G. Blair, Harold A. Feiveson and Frank N. von Hippel

O n January 25, 1995, military technicians at a handful of radar stations across northern Russia saw a troubling blip suddenly appear on their screens. A rocket, launched from somewhere off the coast of Norway, was rising rapidly through the night sky. Well aware that a single missile from a U.S. submarine plying those waters could scatter eight nuclear bombs over Moscow within 15 minutes, the radar operators immediately alerted their superiors. The message passed swiftly from Russian military authorities to President Boris Yeltsin, who, holding the electronic case that could order the firing of nuclear missiles in response, hurriedly conferred by telephone with his top advisers. For the first time ever, that "nuclear briefcase" was activated for emergency use.

For a few tense minutes, the trajectory of the mysterious rocket remained unknown to the worried Russian officials. Anxiety mounted when the separation of multiple rocket stages created an impression of a possible attack by several missiles. But the radar crews continued to track their targets, and after about eight minutes (just a few minutes short of the procedural deadline to respond to an impending nuclear attack), senior military officers determined that the rocket was headed far out to sea and posed no threat to Russia. The unidentified rocket in this case turned out to be a U.S. scientific probe, sent up to investigate the northern lights. Weeks earlier the Norwegians had duly informed

Russian authorities of the planned launch from the offshore island of Andoya, but somehow word of the high-altitude experiment had not reached the right ears.

That frightening incident (like some previous false alarms that activated U.S. strategic forces) aptly demonstrates the danger of maintaining nuclear arsenals in a state of hair-trigger alert. Doing so heightens the possibility that one day someone will mistakenly launch nuclear-tipped missiles, either because of a technical failure or a human error—a mistake made, perhaps, in the rush to respond to false indications of an attack.

Both the U.S. and Russian military have long instituted procedures to prevent such a calamity from happening. Designers of command systems in Russia have gone to extraordinary lengths to ensure strict central control over nuclear weapons. But their equipment is not foolproof, and Russia's early-warning and nuclear command systems are deteriorating. This past February the institute responsible for designing the sophisticated control systems for the Strategic Rocket Forces (the military unit that operates Russian intercontinental ballistic missiles) staged a one-day strike to protest pay arrears and the lack of resources to upgrade their equipment. Three days later Russia's defense minister, Igor Rodionov, asserted that "if the shortage of funds persists ... Russia may soon approach a threshold beyond which its missiles and nuclear systems become uncontrollable."

Rodionov's warning may have been,

in part, a maneuver to muster political support for greater defense spending. But recent reports by the U.S. Central Intelligence Agency confirm that Russia's Strategic Rocket Forces have indeed fallen on hard times. Local utility managers have repeatedly shut off the power to various nuclear weapons installations after the military authorities there failed to pay their electric bills. Worse yet, the equipment that controls nuclear weapons frequently malfunctions, and critical electronic devices and computers sometimes switch to a combat mode for no apparent reason. On seven occasions during the fall of 1996, operations at some nuclear weapons centers were severely disrupted when thieves tried to "mine" critical communications cables for their copper.

Many of the radars constructed by the former Soviet Union to detect a ballistic-missile attack no longer operate, so information provided by these installations is becoming increasingly unreliable. Even the nuclear suitcases that accompany the president, defense minister and chief of the General Staff are reportedly falling into disrepair. In short, the systems built to control Russian nuclear weapons are now crumbling.

In addition to these many technical difficulties, Russia's nuclear weapons establishment suffers from a host of human and organizational problems. Crews receive less training than they did formerly and are consequently less proficient in the safe handling of nuclear weapons. And despite President Yeltsin's promises to improve conditions, endemic housing and food shortages have led to demoralization and disaffection within the elite Strategic Rocket Forces, the strategic submarine fleet and the custodians of Russia's stockpiles of nuclear warheads. As a result, the likelihood increases that desperate low-level commanders might disregard safety rules or, worse still, that they might take unauthorized control of nuclear weapons—something a deteriorating central command might be unable to prevent or counter. Although most Russian launch crews would need to receive special codes held by the General Staff before they could fire their missiles, one recent CIA report warned that some submarine crews may be able to launch the ballistic missiles on board their vessels without having to obtain such information first.

Gorbachev, top-level allegiances suddenly shifted, and the normal chain of command for Russia's nuclear weapons was broken. For three days, the power to launch nuclear weapons rested in the hands of Defense Minister Dmitri Yazov and the chief of the General Staff, Mikhail Moiseyev. Given the dire conditions in Russia, something similar could happen again.

The Nuclear Hair Trigger

Although international relations have changed drastically since the end of the cold war, both Russia and the U.S. continue to keep the bulk of their nuclear missiles on high-level alert. So within just a few minutes of receiving instructions to fire, a large fraction of the U.S. and Russian land-based rockets

a total of more than 5,000 nuclear weapons at each other within half an hour.

Why do two countries at peace retain such aggressive postures, ones that perpetuate the danger of a mistaken or unauthorized launch? Because military planners on both sides remain fixated on the remote specter of a deliberate nuclear surprise attack from their former adversary. They assume that such a "first strike" would be aimed against their own strategic nuclear weapons and the command centers that direct them. To deter such an assault, each country strives to ensure that it could respond with a forceful counterattack against the full spectrum of military targets on its opponent's territory, including all nuclear weapons installations. This requirement saddles military planners with a task virtually identical in scope to mounting a first strike: they must be able to guarantee the rapid destruction of thousands of targets spread across a distant continent.

In order to meet this demand, both the U.S. and Russia rely on a launch-on-warning strategy—that is, each side is poised to release a massive retaliatory missile salvo after detecting an enemy missile attack but before the incoming warheads arrive (which might take just 15 minutes if they were fired from submarines nearby). Although it has thousands of warheads securely deployed at sea, the U.S. adheres to this quick-draw stance because of the vulnerability of its missile silos and command apparatus, including its political and military leadership in Washington, D.C.

Russian officials perceive an even greater need to launch their missiles on warning. The General Staff evidently fears that if its nuclear missiles are not launched immediately, then only tens of them would be able to respond after absorbing a systematic U.S. attack. Russian command posts and missile silos are as vulnerable as those of the U.S. to a massive assault.

Russia's current inability to deploy many of its most survivable forces—submarines at sea and mobile land-based rockets—amplifies this worry. A lack of resources and qualified personnel has forced the Russian navy to cut back operations considerably. At present, the Russian navy typically keeps only two of its 26 ballistic missile submarines at sea on combat patrol at any one time. Similar constraints prevent Russia from hiding more than one or two regiments

Submarine-Launched Missiles

To achieve START II limits, the U.S. plans to eliminate four of its 18 ballistic-missile submarines and to reduce the count of warheads on submarine-launched missiles from eight to five. Later, to meet the START III goals, the U.S. would most likely eliminate an additional four submarines and reduce the number of warheads on each missile to four. All these actions should be taken at once. Russia could then immediately remove the warheads from the submarines it plans to eliminate under the START agreements.

Without rather elaborate verification arrangements, neither country could determine the status of the other's submarines at sea. Both nations, however, should lower launch readiness. Approximately half the submarines that the U.S. has at sea today are traveling to their launch stations in a state of modified alert: the crew needs about 18 hours to perform the procedures, such as removing the flood plates from the launch tubes, that bring a submarine to full alert. Most U.S. submarines at sea could simply stay on modified alert. Their readiness could be reduced further by removing their missiles' guidance systems and storing them on board. Russian submarines lack this option; their missiles are not accessible from inside the vessel.

Russia should also pledge to keep its missiles on submarines in port off launch-ready alert. (The U.S. does not maintain submarines in port on alert.) The U.S. may be able to monitor the alert condition of these Russian submarines, but Russia should make their status obvious. —*B.G.B., H.A.F. and F.N. von H.*

Even at the top, control over nuclear weapons could splinter along various political fault lines. Relations between politicians and military leaders in Russia are strained, and physical control of the launch codes remains in the hands of the military. Thus, the authority to fire ballistic missiles could be usurped by military commanders during an internal crisis. In fact, during the August 1991 coup against President Mikhail S.

(which are armed with about 2,000 and 3,500 warheads, respectively) could begin their 25-minute flights over the North Pole to their wartime targets. Less than 15 minutes after receiving the order to attack, six U.S. Trident submarines at sea could loft roughly 1,000 warheads, and several Russian ballistic-missile submarines could dispatch between 300 and 400. In sum, the two nuclear superpowers remain ready to fire

Silo-Based Missiles

The START II ban on multiple-warhead, land-based missiles does not go into effect for a decade, but the U.S. and Russia could act earlier to take most of their silo-based warheads off alert. The easiest method would be to physically "pin" open the switches that allow the rocket engines to ignite. Maintenance crews would then have to enter each silo, manually remove the safety pins and close these switches before the missiles would be ready to fire remotely.

Negotiators at the Helsinki Summit envisioned actions that would take even longer to reverse. They agreed that Russia and the U.S. would have five extra years to dismantle the multiple-warhead missiles slated to be eliminated under START II, as long as these missiles are "deactivated by removing their nuclear warheads or taking other jointly agreed steps." The U.S. prefers that Russia deactivate missiles by removing warheads, an act that would take weeks to reverse. Such efforts would be apparent to surveillance satellites, and the absence of the warheads on the missiles could be checked during the inspections permitted under START.

Yet Russian experts argue that their country does not have adequate facilities to store a large number of warheads taken from missiles. They are now considering other options: immobilizing the massive silo lids so that heavy equipment would be required to open them, or removing the battery that operates the missile-guidance system during flight. A third possibility would be to replace the aerodynamic missile nose cones with flat-faced covers, which would shelter the warheads but not allow the missiles to fly. —*B.G.B., H.A.F. and F.N. von H.*

RUSSIAN SILO LID would require a large crane to tilt upward if the device that generates high-pressure gas for its pneumatically operated hinge were purposefully removed.

These vulnerabilities have led Russia to ready some of its submarines in port and mobile missiles in garages to launch on warning, along with the missiles in silos. The time available for deciding to launch these weapons is shortened by the presence of American, British and French submarines cruising in the North Atlantic, only about 2,000 miles (3,200 kilometers) from Moscow. This proximity means that the nuclear-release procedures in Russia require a response time of less than 15 minutes: a few minutes for detecting an attack, another few minutes for top-level decision making and a few minutes for disseminating the launch order. Russian leaders and missile controllers are geared to work within this brief time frame and practice regularly with drills. U.S. nuclear forces operate with a similarly short fuse.

It is obvious that the rushed nature of this process, from warning to decision to action, risks causing a catastrophic mistake. The danger is compounded by the erosion of Russia's ability to distinguish reliably between natural phenomena or peaceful ventures into space and a true missile attack. Only one third of its modern early-warning radars are working at all, and at least two of the nine slots in its constellation of missile-warning satellites are empty.

The dangers stemming from this decline in Russia's technical capabilities are offset, to some extent, by the relaxation of tensions that has come with the end of the cold war. Given the milder political climate, decision makers on both sides should be more inclined to question the validity of any reports they receive of an impending missile attack. Nevertheless, the coupling of two arsenals geared for rapid response carries the inherent danger of producing a mistaken launch and an escalating volley of missiles in return. The possibility of such an apocalyptic accident cannot be ruled out even under normal conditions. And if the control of Russian nuclear weapons were to be stressed by an internal or international political crisis, the danger could suddenly become much more acute.

During the cold war, such risks were subordinated to the overriding requirement to deter an enemy believed to be willing to launch a nuclear attack. This rationalization is no longer defensible, if ever it was. Today, when both coun-

of its truck-mounted mobile missiles by dispersing them in the field. The remaining 40 or so regiments, each controlling nine single-warhead missiles, keep their trucks parked in garages. These missiles are more exposed to attack than those housed in underground silos. Russia also has 36 10-warhead nuclear missiles carried on railway cars, which were designed to be hidden along Russia's vast rail network. But these railcars remain confined to fixed garrisons in keeping with a decision made by President Gorbachev in 1991.

Land-Mobile Missiles

De-alerting" Russia's mobile land-based missiles (the U.S. has none) could begin with removing warheads from the 36 rail-mobile missiles to be eliminated under START II. For the truck-mobile missiles, one possibility might be to alter their garages. Currently the roofs of these shelters are designed to slide open, allowing the launcher inside to tilt upright and fire the missile. Other measures might incapacitate the launcher itself in ways that would take at lease some hours to restore. —*B.G.B., H.A.F. and F.N. von H.*

tries seek normal economic relations and cooperative security arrangements, perpetuating the readiness to launch nuclear weapons on the mere warning of an attack constitutes reckless behavior. Yet this thinking is so entrenched that it will yield only to steady pressure from the public on political leaders—especially presidents—to replace it with a safer policy.

"De-alerting" Missiles

The cuts in nuclear arms set by the Strategic Arms Reduction Treaties (START) should lessen the threat of an accidental nuclear exchange, but those changes will come only gradually. Under the START III framework, endorsed in Helsinki this past spring by President Yeltsin and President Bill Clinton, the U.S. and Russian strategic arsenals would shrink to about 2,000 warheads on each side by the year 2007. But if current practices are not revised, 10 years from now half of those nuclear weapons could still remain ready to launch on a few minutes' notice.

The chance of an accidental launch could be reduced much more rapidly by "de-alerting" the missiles—increasing the amount of time needed to prepare them for launch. The U.S. and Russia should move independently down this path to a safer world, preferably taking quick strides in parallel. Two prominent proponents of this approach are former senator Sam Nunn of Georgia and retired general George L. Butler, commander in chief of the U.S. Strategic Command from 1991 to 1994. This proposal is also gaining support in the community of nongovernmental organizations involved in nuclear security and from some members of the U.S. Congress. In Russia, the Ministry of Defense is seriously studying such an alteration.

President George Bush set a notable precedent for de-alerting nuclear weapons at the end of September 1991, when the Soviet Union began to split apart in the wake of the August coup attempt. On the advice of General Butler, President Bush ordered an immediate standdown of the many U.S. strategic bombers that had remained ready for decades to take off with only a few minutes' warning. Soon afterward, air force personnel unloaded and stored the many nuclear weapons carried on these planes.

In addition, President Bush ended the alert for the strategic missiles destined to be eliminated under START I, a set composed of 450 silo-based Minuteman II rockets, along with the missiles on 10 Poseidon submarines. These important actions took only a few days.

President Gorbachev reciprocated a week later by ordering the deactivation of more than 500 land-based rockets and six strategic submarines, by promising to keep his strategic bombers at a low level of readiness and by putting the rail-based missiles in garrison. In the subsequent months, both countries also withdrew many thousands of shorter-range tactical nuclear warheads that had been deployed with their armies and navies and placed these weapons in central storage depots.

Presidents Clinton and Yeltsin took a further step together in 1994, when they agreed to stop aiming strategic missiles at each other's country. This change, though a welcome gesture, has little military significance. Missile commanders can reload target coordinates into guidance computers within seconds. In fact, the 1994 pact does not even alleviate the concern about an accidental Russian launch, because an unprogrammed missile would automatically switch back to its primary wartime target, which might be a Minuteman silo in Montana or a command center in Washington, London, Paris or Beijing. And Russian missiles, like their American counterparts, cannot be ordered to self-destruct once they are launched.

Possessing the most robust forces and cohesive command system, the U.S. government should take the lead in a new round of voluntary actions by an-

STRATEGIC MISSILE TOTALS for the U.S. and Russia should shrink over the next decade in compliance with the Strategic Arms Reduction Treaties (START). Still, each country could hold from 500 to 1,000 warheads ready to fire under these agreements. (Striped areas indicate the number of warheads kept on constant alert.)

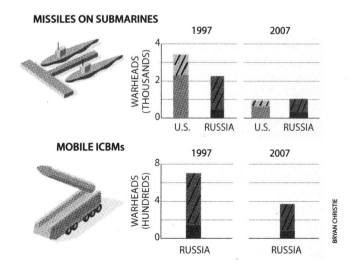

MISSILES ON SUBMARINES

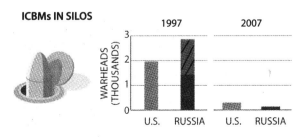

ICBMs IN SILOS

MOBILE ICBMs

A Prescription for Change

To reduce concerns that have driven Russia to maintain its missiles ready to launch on warning, the U.S. president should order the following:

1 Immediately remove to storage the warheads of the MX missiles (which will, in any event, be retired under START II).

2 Disable all Minuteman III missiles by having their safety switches pinned open (as was done for the Minuteman IIs in 1991). If Russia reciprocates, these missiles should be immobilized in a manner that would take much longer to reverse.

3 Remove to storage the warheads on the eight Trident submarines that are to be retired under START III and reduce the number of warheads on each remaining submarine missile from eight to four.

4 Take the W88 warheads off the Trident II missiles, place those warheads in storage and replace them with lower-yield weapons.

5 Allow Russia to verify these actions by using some of their annual inspections permitted by START I. Accept a greater number of inspections if Russia will also do so.

6 Put all U.S. ballistic-missile submarines at sea on a low level of alert, so that it would take at least 24 hours to prepare them to launch their missiles, and keep most submarines out of range of Russian targets. Consider ways to make these changes verifiable in the future and discuss possible reciprocal arrangements with Russian officials.

Even after these actions are taken, six submarines carrying up to 576 warheads would remain undetectable at sea, and the immobilized Minuteman IIIs could be destroyed only by a massive attack on about 500 silos.

In response to the U.S. initiative, the Russian president could order the following:

1 Remove the warheads from all 46 SS-24 rail- and silo-based missiles (which will, in any event, be retired under START II).

2 Immobilize all other silo-based missiles that are to be retired under START II.

3 Remove the warheads from the 15 ballistic-missile submarines most likely to be retired under the START agreements.

4 Place all ballistic-missile submarines (in port and at sea) in a condition such that their missiles could not be launched for at least 24 hours.

5 Disable the launchers of all truck-mobile ballistic missiles so that they cannot be activated for at least a few hours.

After these actions are taken, 128 to 400 warheads on two submarines will remain undetectable at sea, and nine to 18 SS-25 warheads on truck-mobile launchers will remain securely hidden in the field. In addition, about 2,700 warheads on silo-based ICBMs could be destroyed only by mounting successful attacks on some 340 missile silos. —*B.G.B., H.A.F. and F.N. von H.*

---

nouncing that it will withdraw the U.S. warheads that most threaten Russia's nuclear deterrent (particularly those capable of hitting Russia's missile silos and underground command posts). The most menacing warheads are those deployed on the 50 MX silo-based missiles, which are armed with 10 warheads each, and the 400 high-yield W88 warheads fitted atop some of the missiles on Trident submarines. We also recommend immobilizing all of the land-based Minuteman IIIs (about 500 missiles), which are armed with three warheads each, halving the number of submarines deployed in peacetime and cutting the number of warheads on each submarine-borne missile from eight to four. The operation of ballistic-missile submarines should also be altered so that crews would require approximately one day to ready missiles for launching.

These measures would leave almost 600 U.S. warheads remaining invulnerable at sea, each capable of destroying the heart of a great city. With such a force, the U.S. would preserve ample capacity to deter any nuclear aggressor. Such a dramatic shift by the U.S. would fully establish its intention not to pose a first-strike threat to Russia. We believe this change in policy would persuade Russia to follow suit and take most of its missiles off hair-trigger alert. These changes would also help accelerate the implementation of agreements for disarmament already negotiated under START II and START III. We estimate that most of the job could be completed within a year or two.

Capabilities already exist to confirm that nuclear weapons have been taken off alert. For instance, the number of ballistic-missile submarines in port can be monitored using satellites, and most other measures could be checked during the random on-site inspections permitted by START I. Over the longer term, additional technical means could be engineered to provide more frequent checks that nuclear missiles posed no immediate threat. For example, electronic "seals" could be used to ensure that a component removed from a missile had not been replaced. The integrity of such seals could be verified remotely through satellite relay using encrypted communications.

Global Zero Alert

This blueprint for taking U.S. and Russian nuclear forces off alert would substantially diminish the ability of either country to mount a first strike. Thus, it would eliminate both the capacity and rationale for keeping missiles ready to fire on warning. Leaders would have to wait out any alarm of an attack before deciding how to respond, drastically reducing the risk of a mistaken or unauthorized launch.

We recognize that military leaders in the U.S. and Russia might insist on maintaining small portions of their current arsenals on high alert, perhaps hundreds of warheads each, until the other nuclear-weapon states—Britain, France and China—joined in adopting similar measures to reduce the readiness of their nuclear arsenals. But if the U.S. and Russia aspire to establish the highest possible standards of safety for their nuclear armaments, they should move as rapidly as possible to take all their missiles off alert and then follow with further steps to increase the time required to reactivate these weapons.

The ultimate goal would be to separate most, if not all, nuclear warheads from their missiles and then, eventually, to eliminate most of the stored warheads and missiles. To implement such

ar state would know whether another an extensive program fully, the means for verification would have to be strengthened to ensure that every nuclecountry was making nuclear missiles launch-ready.

Moving toward a global stand-down of nuclear arms will undoubtedly encounter strong resistance from those

whose dominant fear remains a secretly prepared surprise attack. The design of procedures to take nuclear missiles off constant alert needs to take into account this already remote possibility. But these plans must urgently go forward to remove the much more immediate hazard—the mistaken or unauthorized launch of nuclear missiles.

The Authors

BRUCE G. BLAIR, HAROLD A. FEIVESON and FRANK N. VON HIPPEL have studied nuclear arms policy intensively. Blair served for four years in the U.S. Air Force Strategic Air Command before earning a Ph.D. in operations research in 1984 from Yale University. He is currently a defense analyst at the Brookings Institution in Washington, D.C. Feiveson received a master's degree in theoretical physics in 1959 from the University of California, Los Angeles. He worked in the U.S. Arms Control and Disarmament Agency for four years before moving to Princeton University to study public and international affairs. Feiveson received his Ph.D. in 1972 and joined the Princeton faculty in 1974. Von Hippel, who received a doctorate in theoretical physics from the University of Oxford in 1962, served in the office of the president's science adviser in 1993 and 1994 as assistant director for national security. He is currently a professor of public and international affairs at Princeton.

Further Reading

THE LOGIC OF ACCIDENTAL NUCLEAR WAR. Bruce G. Blair. Brookings Institution, 1993.
GLOBAL ZERO ALERT FOR NUCLEAR FORCES. Bruce G. Blair. Brookings Institution, 1995.
CAGING THE NUCLEAR GENIE: AN AMERICAN CHALLENGE FOR GLOBAL SECURITY. Stansfield Turner. Westview Press, Boulder, Colo., 1997.
THE FUTURE OF U.S. NUCLEAR WEAPONS POLICY. National Academy of Sciences. National Academy Press, 1997.

Cooperation

An individual at just about any location in the world can write a letter to another person just about anywhere else, and if it is properly addressed, the sender can be relatively certain that the letter will be delivered. This is true even though the sender pays for postage only in the country of origin and not in the country where it is delivered. A similar pattern of international cooperation is true when an individual boards an airplane in one country and never gives a second thought to the issues of potential language and technical barriers, even though the flight's destination is halfway around the world.

Many of the most basic activities of our lives are the result of international cooperation. International organizational structures to monitor public health on a global scale or scientifically evaluate changing weather conditions are additional examples of governments recognizing that their self-interest directly benefits from cooperation (i.e., the creation of international governmental organizations, or IGOs).

Transnational activities, furthermore, are not limited to the governmental level. There are now literally tens of thousands of international nongovernmental organizations (INGOs). These organizations stage the Olympic Games or actively discourage the hunting of whales and seals, to illustrate just two of the diverse activities of INGOs. The number of these international organizations along with their influence has grown tremendously in the past 40 years.

In the same time period in which we have witnessed the growth in importance of IGOs and INGOs, there has been a parallel expansion of corporate activity across international borders. Most consumers are as familiar with products with a Japanese brand name as they are with products made in the United States, Germany, or elsewhere. The multinational corporation (MNC) is an important non-state actor in the world today. The value of goods and services produced by the biggest MNCs is far greater than the gross domestic product (GDP) of many countries. The international structures that make it possible to buy a Swedish automobile in Sacramento or a Swiss watch in Singapore have been developed over many years. They are the result of governments negotiating trea-

ties and creating IGOs to implement these agreements. The manufacturers engaged in these activities have created networks of sales, distribution, and service, which grow more complex with each passing day.

These trends at a variety of levels indicate to many observers that the era of the nation-state as the dominant player in international politics is passing. Others have observed these trends and have concluded that the state system has a monopoly of power and that the diverse transnational organizations depend on the state system and in significant ways perpetuate it.

In many of the articles that appear elsewhere in this book, the authors have concluded by calling for greater international cooperation to solve our world's most pressing problems. The articles in this section show examples of successful cooperation. In the midst of a lot of bad news in the world, it is easy to overlook the fact that we are surrounded by international cooperation and that day-to-day activities in our lives often benefit from it.

Looking Ahead: Challenge Questions

Itemize the products you own that were manufactured in another country.

What recent contacts have you had with people from other countries? How was it possible for you to have these contacts?

How can the conflict and rivalry between the United States and Russia be transformed into meaningful cooperation?

What are the prospects for international governance? How would a trend in this direction enhance or threaten American values and constitutional rights?

The First Fifty Years
The Main Achievements

By Diogo Freitas do Amaral
President of the Fiftieth General Assembly

UN Photo 146677

The Palais des Nations in Geneva was originally the home of the League of Nations.

The League of Nations lasted a little more than 20 years; the United Nations has now lasted half a century. The League of Nations did not manage to achieve its principal objective: to avoid the Second World War; the United Nations has managed to achieve its principal goal: to avoid a third world war. The League of Nations concentrated all its peacemaking efforts on disarmament; the United Nations understood from the start that disarmament, while very important, was not the only way to prevent war, and strengthened its collective security system with a range of policies for economic, social and educational development.

Our "founding fathers" were endowed with foresight: the establishment in 1945 of the UN represented great hope for all people of good will throughout the world. It is true that these past 50 years have not been marked exclusively by successes and victories. The existence of the UN, like that of any organization, has been marked by many errors and defeats. But was that not inevitable, given the very nature of human beings, society and the world as it is?

In this connection, I should like to quote a remark about the UN which I consider apposite. It was made by a great President of the United States, John F. Kennedy, who said in 1962:

"Our instrument and our hope is the United Nations, and I see little merit in the impatience of those who would abandon this imperfect world instrument because they dislike our imperfect world."

Today, after our Organization has been in existence for 50 years, should our assessment of its activities be positive or negative? We are all well aware of the Organization's failures, especially its most recent ones. And the critics have not ceased their criticism. So, in the interest of balance, it is only fair to enumerate the main achievements of the UN.

Avoiding a new world war

The first, of which I have already spoken, but to which I wish to return because of its exceptional importance and which can never be stressed too much, is the following: the UN succeeded in avoiding what many deemed inevitable—the outbreak of a third world war. Although this result cannot be ascribed solely to the UN, the Organization did play a primary role in the prevention of armed East-West conflict which would have been fatal for mankind.

Three very important elements demonstrate that the international community has rightfully valued the actions carried out by the UN over the last 50 years. First, five Nobel prizes were awarded to the Organization or to one of its elements. Secondly, the number of Member States has increased from 51 in 1945 to 185 in 1995. The fact that this number has more than tripled is because the great majority of countries of the world believe that the UN has more qualities and advantages than flaws and drawbacks. Thirdly, a decision was taken to hold in October a large meeting, with the participation of more than 150 Heads of State or Government from the entire world. And, indeed, it is obvious that if so many outstanding leaders have decided to come to New York to commemorate a mere anniversary, it is because this anniversary is unquestionably the occasion for celebrating a series of important events.

I have already spoken of that global peace which fortunately has been maintained successfully for some 50 years now despite numerous local or regional conflicts which it has been impossible to avoid. But here, even in that difficult area of war and peace, the UN can pride itself on having made a decisive contribution to noticeable progress in the fields of disarmament and nuclear non-proliferation, and on having conducted negotiations and concluded agreements within the framework of the peace process for which the outcome was positive as, for example, in Cambodia, El Salvador, Nicaragua, Eritrea, Mozambique and, we hope, also in Angola.

Secondly, the UN, more than any other institution, has contributed to establishing and attempting to guarantee in practice the primacy of international law, and it is well known that, without a state of law, a human being cannot know that peace, freedom or security, which allows him to lead a normal existence in a civilized society. We will never forget the nightmare of

From *UN Chronicle,* December 1995, pp. 66-67. Reprinted by permission of *UN Chronicle,* a publication of the United Nations Department of Public Information.

"man who is a wolf to man" described with insight in the "state of nature" of the *Leviathan* of Thomas Hobbes. And, in speaking of the contribution of the UN to the recognition of the primacy of international law, I wish to hail the outstanding action and lofty prestige achieved by one of its major bodies, the International Court of Justice, to which I wish to pay a very sincere tribute.

Thirdly, also to the credit of the UN, is the attention and importance which it attaches to human rights. It is the UN which has universalized them; it is the UN that has led States to accept, through the recognition of human rights, the fact that the State is at the service of man and not man at the service of the State. It is the UN which, not limiting itself to those classical human rights born of the American and the French revolutions, consecrated the fundamental rights of the second generation and, in particular, economic, social and cultural rights. And, once again, it is the UN which today is playing a leading role in the struggle for the respect of the fundamental rights of the third generation, in particular, rights dealing with the protection of nature and of the environment, an area in which, for the first time in the history of mankind, it is no longer exclusively a question of recognizing or establishing rights governing the relations of human beings among themselves or *vis-à-vis* the State, but also to attempt to establish and implement machinery which will lead to the recognition of the rights of animals and of nature in the face of acts of aggression perpetrated by the human being himself.

Conventions: Glorious landmarks

A major reason for pride and satisfaction is the fact that it has been possible, once again thanks to the UN, to draw up and implement international conventions which do honour mankind and which will form glorious landmarks in the history of the first 50 years of the Organization and will rank among its justified achievements. I am thinking, in particular, of the Convention on the Rights of the Child, the Convention on the Elimination of all Forms of Discrimination against Women, and the Convention against Torture and Other Cruel, Inhuman or Degrading Treatment or Punishment. What would mankind be without these basic texts? Would they ever have been produced without the intervention of the UN?

It is the UN to which we owe the contribution to universal awareness of the idea that our world is formed of equal beings all enjoying the same fundamental rights to human dignity. This ideal is already long-standing. Saint Paul affirmed that with the "new man" ... "there is neither Greek nor Jew, ... barbarian, Scythian, bond nor free" (*The Holy Bible, Colossians* 3:10-11).

> "
> **The establishment in 1945 of the UN represented great hope for all people of good will throughout the world**
> "

But while that ideal is indeed an ancient one, nevertheless 20 centuries were required to enshrine it in a legal declaration of universal scope and here the credit is due to the UN. That ideal must never be forgotten nor must we fail to mention it, whether or not we adhere to the religious tradition of which it was born.

Fourthly, the UN certainly has the right to claim the major credit linked with two other victories won by mankind in the twentieth century, namely, decolonization and the end of apartheid. The fact that the number of States Members of the Organization has increased from 51 to 185 is due basically to decolonization. And the fact is that if an end was put to the un-acceptable regime in South Africa, this is in great part due to the condemnations and criticisms levelled by the UN.

It is interesting to emphasize that the leaders who succeeded in bringing about decolonization, like those who put an end to apartheid, had the most wide-ranging political convictions, a fact which clearly demonstrates that the ideals enshrined in the Charter of the UN are neither partisan nor ideological, nor religious, but purely and simply humanitarian, and that it suffices to believe in the dignity of all human beings and to respect it in practice in order to be a law-abiding and consistent Member of the UN.

Consolidating internal democratization

Fifthly, the UN has contributed, especially since the end of the cold war, to consolidating and concretizing the process of internal democratization on which many countries have embarked, countries that have decided of their own will to move from a one-party regime to a multi-party system.

It is not for the UN to dictate to a Member State the form of government the latter must adopt in its political constitution. On the other hand, the UN can and must assist those who decide on their own to embark upon a process of democratization. This is what it has done to this very day in more than 45 countries, providing assistance not only in the electoral sphere, but in other fields as well. Those who are convinced, as I am, of the superiority of the pluralistic democratic model must stress this fact and welcome it.

Sixthly—and lastly—I should like to draw attention to one of the most relevant and positive aspects of the UN, one which in most cases the Organization's detractors, and even impartial observers, frequently overlook. Here, I am referring to the outstandingly commendable part played by a large number of autonomous UN agencies and bodies in promoting the economic, social and cultural development of the poorest and most disadvantaged of the world's peoples.

—Excerpted from his speech to the General Assembly on 19 September

A Watchful Eye

Monitoring the Conventional Arms Trade

By Jordan Singer

Jordan Singer is a Staff Writer for the Harvard International Review.

ONE OF THE GREATEST LESSONS learned by the international community in the aftermath of the Persian Gulf War was that the unchecked proliferation of conventional armaments during the Cold War had left rogue nations in possession of significant destructive capabilities. Both the United States and the Soviet Union from the late 1940s onward exported conventional arms to satellite states in the developing world in hopes of influencing regional conflicts. However, the danger inherent in distributing conventional weapons to such states became manifestly apparent after the Iraqi invasion of Kuwait in August 1990. The Gulf War served as a testament to conventional weapons sales that had escalated largely without control during the Cold War. Indeed, so many arms had been sold to the regime of Saddam Hussein by so many Soviet bloc and Western nations that the members of the coalition that liberated Kuwait were unaware of the full array of weaponry that the Iraqi military held until after the war had concluded. An international debate emerged following the war as states sought to develop mutual strategies to curb the transfer of arms to unstable regimes. As the curtailment of the international arms trade itself would be both difficult to enforce and a violation of the right of nations to defend themselves, an alternative solution became necessary to prevent a repeat of the events that led to the build-up of the Iraqi military.

The concept of transparency in armaments is a compromise solution to this dilemma. Arms transparency monitors all arms transfers between states rather than regulating them. States are requested to make public information describing the type and number of arms that they export to, or import from, other states. The common goal of arms transparency is for states to increase international security by simultaneously sharing information on their own weapons acquisitions and gaining access to information on the weapons systems of other countries.

The primary mechanism for arms transparency measures in the 1990s has been the UN Register of Conventional Arms, established by the General Assembly on the recommendation of the First Committee on Disarmament and International Security in December 1991. The First Committee's recommendation was issued just months after the end of the Persian Gulf War. The draft resolution creating the Register, jointly sponsored by the European Community and Japan, drew heavily from a 1991 study that suggested the implementation of a non-discriminatory, universal register of conventional arms transfers. On November 15, 1991, the draft resolution passed the First Committee by a vote of 106-1-8. General Assembly Resolution 46/36 L, "Transparency in Armaments," was passed three weeks later by an overwhelming 150-0-2 vote. Under the resolution, the Secretary-General was invested with the responsibility of establishing the Register and convening a Panel of Government Experts (PGE) for the following year to evaluate its functioning.

Methods and Mechanisms

The UN Register of Conventional Arms requests transfer information for seven distinct categories of weapons: main battle tanks, armored combat vehicles, large-caliber artillery systems, combat aircraft, attack helicopters, warships, missiles, and missile launchers. States report transfers via a one-page form for imports and a similar form for exports. The forms are designed to be as simple to complete as possible in order to promote maximum possible participation in the registration process; they ask only for the state(s) of origin and destination of the weapons, the names of any intermediary transit states, and the number of items being transferred in each weapons category. Should participating states wish to divulge further information concerning the type or value of the weapons listed, a "Remarks" section on the form allows for more detailed description. The "Remarks" section may also be used to divulge information not specifically requested by the United Nations, including statistics on national arms holdings and armed forces. According to Dutch Ambassador to the United Nations Hendrik Wagenmakers, the driving force behind the creation and development of the Register, the sensitive nature of these latter statistics compels the Register form to include a disclaimer that "such information [as] might be affected by security or other relevant concerns...should be filled-in at the Member State's discretion."

States are asked to submit data for a given calendar year by April 30 of the following year. Thus, while the Register was established in January 1992, it was not considered to hold pertinent data until May 1, 1993. While the April 30 date of each year is not a true deadline for submitting information (several states submitted 1992 information in late 1993 and even into 1994), efforts have been made to stress the importance of punctual submission. The calendar year format takes into account only arms that were physically imported or exported during any given calendar year, not weapons that were ordered or purchased in that given year but not yet delivered. After data are sent to the United Nations, experts cross-check the information to establish whether the data submitted by importing states matches that submitted by arms exporters. The information is then compiled into an annual report issued by the Secretary-General.

The Panel of Government Experts

In accordance with the directives of the First Committee, the Secretary-General has twice convened a Panel of Government Experts to make minor modifications to the Register and suggest more significant changes. The 1992 Panel concerned itself with two major tasks: revising the definitions of the weapons categories outlined in Resolution 46/36 L, and assessing the feasibility of expanding the Register to include data on additional military holdings.

Of these two agenda items, the former carried a greater sense of urgency, as the Panel needed to solidify definitions for arms categories before the reporting forms could be finalized. The Panel deliberated extensively over the final definitions. Although some members argued for the inclusion of small arms in one of the original categories as they are seen as a major source of destabilization in many regions, the Panel ultimately decided to retain the original seven weapons categories. The PGE did, however, make several modifications of widely varying significance. First, the definition of armored combat vehicles was broadened from the General Assembly's resolution to include all vehicles with an armament caliber of 12.5 millimeters or greater. The standard had previously been 20 millimeters. Second, the original anti-tank missile launcher category was expanded to include all types of missile launchers. Third, the scope of combat aircraft and attack helicopters was broadened to encompass armed reconnaissance aircraft, but fell short of including unarmed vehicles that performed the same mission. The most major changes in definitions, however, were focused on the remaining two weapons categories: warships and missiles. The tonnage threshold of warships was lowered from 800 tons to 750 tons, although many countries involved in the Panel favored either lowering the threshold even further or eliminating it altogether. The missiles category was expanded to cover unguided rockets as well as remotely piloted vehicles, but ground-to-air missiles were eliminated on the basis that they were designed to serve purely defensive purposes. The Panel also made other significant changes in the interpretation of existing definitions and terminology for the Register. For example, certain types of leases, grants, and long-term loans were for the first time construed as being arms transfers. Ironically, although these changes were intended to clarify definitions and ease reporting, it was later speculated that the existence of two sets of formal definitions (one from the General Assembly resolution and one from the Panel of Experts) made several states more reluctant to report the arms transfers in which they had participated.

As part of its mission, the 1992 Panel also sought to evaluate expansion of the arms register to include other types of armaments. To this effect, the members of the Panel posed a series of questions for their successors in 1994. Chiefly, these questions involved the issue of whether data on military holdings arising from domestic arms production should be requested. The main rationale motivating this action was one of fairness. Under current conditions, states that assemble their arsenals almost exclusively through arms imports effectively divulge their entire arms capacity to neighboring states by participating in the Register; by contrast, net arms-producing states, due to domestic production for domestic military use, are regularly able to avoid reporting the full extent of their national armed forces. The 1992 Panel felt that this inequality should be rectified by requesting information on domestic arms production for domestic use as well as the total number and type of armaments in the possession of a nation's military forces.

Non-Compliance and Discrepancies

Formally titled the Group of Government Experts (GGE), the 1994 Panel engaged in a comprehensive study of the Register's functionality, evaluated the formal suggestions of the 1992 Panel, and reviewed the first two years of data submitted to the Register. After many months of research and evaluation, the GGE submitted its own recommendations to the Secretary-General in the fall of 1994. These recommendations fell into three major categories: participation and reporting, further development of the Register, and regional considerations. First, the GGE noted that it was encouraged by the fact that participation in the Arms Register during 1993 and 1994 was extremely high when compared to similar international reporting instruments. The GGE also asserted that most major arms exporters had submitted data to the Register; as a result, the majority of international arms transfers could be accounted for from at least the exporter's side.

At the same time, however, the GGE concluded that there still existed much work to be done in terms of increasing the level of state participation. By August 1, 1993, only 71 members of the United Nations—or 40 percent of member states—had submitted reports to the register for calendar year 1992. By August 1, 1994, the number of participants for 1993 had reached 77 states—or 42 percent of the total UN membership. Based upon these experiences, the GGE was guardedly optimistic that the slow growth of the number of participants in the UN Register of Conventional Arms would continue in the future. Principally, the GGE noted that once a nation has submitted to the Register once, it is politically more difficult to justify to the international community a termination of submissions than to justify never having participated at all. Therefore, the GGE argued that it seemed likely that the 28 states that filed reports in 1992 but not in 1993 would resume submitting reports soon under targeted international pressure.

Even more disturbing to the GGE than non-submission of arms data was the fact that much of the arms data submitted by exporters and importers did not match. For the calendar year 1993, for example, exporters reported the transfer of 2,921 battle tanks and 2,060 armored combat vehicles, but importers reported less than half of these totals in the same categories. Similarly, exporters showed transfers of almost 68,000 missiles and missile launchers for calendar year 1992, but importers showed less than 9,000 for the same year. In only 22 percent of cases did the reported items match. Nine percent of transfers were reported by both exporter and importer, but with inconsistent amounts of weaponry. Thirty-three percent of arms transfers were only reported by one party because the other party did not participate in the Register. In the remaining 36 percent of cases, transfers were reported by only one party even though the other party completed a report.

Such discrepancies in reporting are clearly troubling. First, there is the question of what figures, if any, are accurate. Currently, only in the relatively few cases in which both parties reported a transfer with corresponding figures can the information be considered truly correct. Second, if one party's figures are accurate, there remains the question of why the other party refused to provide correct figures.

Attempts at Reform

The 1994 GGE also attempted to address each of the terminology questions left unanswered by its predecessor. The GGE claimed that there existed "three dimensions to be considered: adjustments to the existing definitions for the seven categories of equipment; the addition of new categories for conventional weapons; and the early expansion of the scope of the Register as called for in General Assembly Resolution 46/36 L." In terms of the first dimension, the Group discussed possible adjustments to current weapons definitions, but decided not to alter them for the time being. The Group did reserve the right to review the definitions at a later date, however.

Several proposals were submitted regarding the addition of new weapons categories, including small arms and antipersonnel land mines. As in 1992, the various proposals to include small arms were eventually rejected; this occurred largely due to concern from small arms importing states that if small arms were added to the Register, no part of the composition of their arsenals would be shielded from becoming a part of the public domain. The inclusion of land mines under the UN Arms Register standards was debated at length, but also ultimately rejected. In the final analysis, the Secretary-General reported that "The Group's view was that the issue of anti-personnel land mines is largely one of international legal regulation."

Finally, the Group considered the directive of Resolution 46/36 L with regards to expanding the scope of the Register to include all military holdings and domestic arms production. The Group maintained that early expansion of the Register remained a valuable goal, but could not agree on the best way to include such information on the same basis as arms transfers. The final conclusion was that more consideration of the issue was necessary. Likewise, the related question of whether to expand the Register to include weapons of mass destruction or to establish separate registers for this purpose was debated but left unsettled pending further consideration.

In the final part of the GGE's evaluation, it noted that some regions participated in the Register of Conventional Arms with much greater frequency than other regions. The GGE concluded that this pattern of participation was a result of the varying security concerns present in each region. Participation in two regions was particularly dismal: three months after the deadline for 1992 reports, only 12 percent of African nations had submitted data, as had only 32 percent of Asian states. For the following year, these numbers had modestly increased to 17 percent and 40 percent, respectively. Although participation was high in Europe and North America, the percentage of submissions in these areas declined from 1993 to 1994. To combat this decline, the Group reaffirmed the need for regional and sub-regional registers that "should complement and not detract from the operation of the universal and global United Nations Register of Conventional Arms." Efforts to create regional registers have already begun under the jurisdiction of the Organization of American States (OAS) and the Organization for Security and Cooperation in Europe (OSCE).

The failure of the GGE to arrive at a plan of action to remedy inconsistencies in current reporting practices represents an important and disturbing development in international arms transparency efforts. Complete and accurate reporting lies at the heart of transparency theory; if states do not report information in a thorough and timely manner, international confidence in the validity of transparency measures such as the Register plummets, and thus overall security declines. In order to promote consistent and valuable reporting, concerted efforts must be made to diminish the "security excuse" of small arms-importing states for not reporting data. Under the UN Register of Conventional Arms, states need not report information that they feel jeopardizes their national or international security. For many states, especially arms importers, however, divulging any information may be considered a security threat primarily because there is no guarantee that its neighbors and adversaries will similarly comply with requests to submit information.

While there are admittedly no easy steps to resolving this conundrum, some measures can be taken almost immediately to improve international confidence. The first of these is to specifically request domestic arms production information from states. Requesting this information places net exporting states and net importing states alike on level ground. The General Assembly might also seek to coordinate its efforts with outside organizations that independently collect similar information. For example, SIPRI, a Swedish research institute, currently publishes an annual yearbook detailing international arms transfers. Coordinating UN and SIPRI data (after the standardization of definitions, timetables, and weapons categories has taken place) offers the United Nations an independent source of verification for its Register of Conventional Arms. Yet, given all of the technical and security challenges that have surfaced since the initiation of the United Nations Register of Conventional Arms in 1992, the current functioning of the system stands in part as a tribute to the resolve of the international community to avoid a repetition of the situation that coalition forces encountered in the Persian Gulf War against Iraq. Deliberate attempts to bring about full participation and consistent reporting will render the Register more than a useful tool for enhancing arms transparency. A fully functioning Arms Register would likely build trust between neighboring states. First, however, further efforts by the international community are necessary to bring the present Arms Register closer to its intended form.

LIKE NO OTHER PARLIAMENT ON EARTH

Alan Osborn is EUROPE's Luxembourg correspondent.

Alan Osborn

You've heard of the House of Commons. You've heard of the French Assembly and the German Bundestag. But the *European* Parliament? A Parliament for 15 countries with 11 languages and scores of political parties between them? Surely it's just a part-time consultative body, a kind of UN-style debating shop? Think again.

Imagine, in particular, a kind of very young Senate composed of people with fierce ambition, constantly chafing at the limits of their powers. The judgment should be not on what it is now so much as what it will be in, say, 15 years.

But if you feel that you can ignore it until then, Hollywood will tell you differently. in February the European Parliament (EP) voted to force European television broadcasters to devote a minimum of 51 percent of air time to European produced programs.

It's not that the members of the European Parliament (MEPs) don't like *Cheers* or *Dallas*, they just think that Europeans get too many American shows and not enough home-made programs.

This campaign will provide an important test of the balance of power in the European Union (EU) since it directly pits the EP against the 15 member governments. The latter aren't necessarily great lovers of American soaps, but they believe television stations should be free to put on whatever their viewers want.

Who are they and how do they operate, these 626 MEPs with their say in the spending of some $90 billion this year, their growing ability to influence the lives of 370 million Europeans, and their high-flung ambition?

The average American congressman or congresswoman would be dismayed at the rigors of political life in Strasbourg. Your MEP has no sweeteners to offer constituents, no ministers to lobby on a voter's behalf, no stick to take to awkward officials. "Pork-barrel" is not a term that the EP's squad of interpreters is very often called to translate.

Don't expect to hear much wit, irony, or grandeur in the EP chamber. If there is a Winston Churchill among the ranks of the MEPs, his oratory will be turned into pablum by the interpreters.

None of this makes an EP's official business very entertaining, and debates are seldom reported in the newspapers. Boondoggles are another matter. For much of its early history the EP had a spendthrift reputation in the press for excessive traveling by some members. This situation has changed, partly because the EP's leadership has taken a grip on its excesses and partly because the quality of its members has improved sharply.

Lord Plumb, a former president of the EP and now the leader of the British Conservatives, puts it this way, "Politicians used to see the EP as a stepping stone into national politics. Now we're beginning to see the reverse. I believe after the next British election we'll see a number of members who have lost their seats looking for seats in Europe."

Lord Plumb, who once memorably said that he was "born an Englishman and will die a European," is one of the few politicians to have made a national reputation through his service in the EP. But several of the present MEPs were conspicuous for other reasons before coming to Strasbourg.

There's the international financier and conservationist Sir James Goldsmith, for instance, who flies in regularly to Strasbourg in his private aircraft to deliver majestic utterances on trade and the environment.

THERE ARE A LOT OF WOMEN IN THE EP—A QUARTER OF ALL MEMBERS, THOUGH IT CAN SEEM MORE AT TIMES. IN DECEMBER ONE SESSION FEATURED AN HOUR OF DEBATE ON DIRECT SELLING DURING WHICH 12 WOMEN AND NOT ONE MAN SPOKE.

Remember Dany Cohn-Bendit—or "Danny the Red"—who achieved worldwide notoriety as a militant student leader during the Paris riots in 1968? He's now a middle-aged member of the German Green party in the EP, though not entirely a reformed character. He's been heard threatening to smoke marijuana in the chamber in support of drug legislation.

The famously bespectacled Greek folk singer Nana Mouscouri sits quietly as a member of her country's right-wing

New Democratic party. She's now a great deal more *sotto voce* now than her millions of admirers remember her.

IN THE 15 YEARS IT HAS EXISTED IN ITS DIRECTLY ELECTED FORM, THE EP HAS EXTENDED ITS POWERS FROM THE ESSENTIALLY NEGATIVE ONES OF AN UPPER HOUSE—CONSULTATION, DELAY, VETO—INTO THE MORE ACTIVE ONES OF A TRUE PARLIAMENT.

There are a lot of women in the EP—a quarter of all members, though it can seem more at times. In December one session featured an hour of debate on direct selling during which 12 women and not one man spoke. It's been remarked that the EP offers a unique forum for politically ambitious women barred by tradition and prejudice from high office in their national Parliaments.

Pauline Green, a 47 year old former policewoman from London, leads the Party of European Socialists, which with 217 seats is the EP's largest political group. She is as close as you could get to being a House Majority Leader. Strasbourg, she says, "has a very female feel to it. It's young, dynamic and not at all like the male clubby atmosphere at Westminster."

If there are more Socialists than any others in the EP, the center-right European Peoples Party is not far behind. In practice the members divide fairly equally into right and left, though political alignments tend to be unfocused. The dynamism often seems to be a perennial desire by MEPs of all parties to extend their powers at the expense of the EU governments, which often lends a bland, consensual character to debates and texts.

Such dramas as do exist are played out five days a month in Strasbourg, a city of addictive charm but a site which exacts a huge physical and financial toll on the Parliament. MEPs hold their party and committee meetings in Brussels, while much of the EP's administration takes place in Luxembourg, where, absurdly, the library is located. It would make sense to have everything under the same roof but attack the agreement under which Strasbourg is the headquarters and one might as well attack the honor of France itself.

In the 15 years it has existed in its directly elected form, the EP has extended its powers from the essentially negative ones of an upper house—consultation, delay, veto—into the more active ones of a true Parliament. It surely has much further to go and perhaps important steps will be taken this year at the EU's intergovernmental conference.

Germany will press for the EP to have a much bigger say, Britain will oppose. But Dr. Martyn Bond, head of the EP's UK office, is optimistic, "Back in the 1950s, Dean Acheson said Britain had lost an empire and not yet found a role. It's

---

The European Parliament From Left to Right

With nine political groups ranging from neo-fascists to former communists, what kind of political identity does the European Parliament have? Is it, in a word, Republican or Democrat, or something else?

Following the 1994 elections and the 1995 enlargement of the EU with the addition of Finland, Austria, and Sweden, the largest group in the European Parliament is the Party of European Socialists (PES) with 217 of the 626 seats, followed by the center-right European Peoples Party (EPP) with 173.

Then comes the newly formed right-wing alliance of the Union for Europe (UFE) composed of French Gaullists and Italian Forza Europa members, with a strength of 54.

The Liberals (ELDR) hold 52 seats and the European United Left/Nordic Green Left (EUL/NGL) 33. Next largest is the Green Party with 27. The European Radical Alliance (ERA) has 20; Sir James Goldsmith's Europe of Nations Party (EN) has 19; and there are 31 independent members.

In practice, there is a remarkably precise balance of power between the Socialists and their allies on the one hand and the forces of the right on the other. Compared to the 15 EU member governments, the EP would be ranked as middle-of-the-road politically.

It probably seems left-wing to American observers. Even the supposedly center-right governments of the UK, Germany, and France, for instance, are pledged to a degree of state-financed welfare, regulation, and interventionism that mainstream American political parties would find bordering on the extreme.

But the EP has neither the power nor the will to involve itself in grass-roots partisan politics. Outside of a few extremists there is broad support for the consensus view taken by most EU governments on such matters as immigration, law and order, taxation policy, and social security.

The EP may one day be in a position to bring about real change in the way the EU member countries are governed, but for the time being its fire is largely concentrated on building up its own powers. It can't afford to be bossy or politically extreme. It's true that a number of MEPs fiercely oppose any further advance toward European union, but the sense of the assembly is overwhelmingly in favor of it.

This consensus tends to make its debates relatively non-combative and its resolutions moderate. If the Socialists and the PPE both oppose a measure, it will never carry. If they approve it, it will. It's not surprising that political differences are very often glossed over for the sake of getting an agreed text on the record.

—Alan Osborn

quite clear that Europe is that role, and slowly but surely public and political opinion is coming round to that. The European Parliament plays a key part in that new structure."

What is the European Parliament?

The European Parliament is like no other legislative body on earth. It has 626 members from 15 countries, divides into nine political groups, does its work in three different countries and uses 11 languages.

The EP's size, powers, and procedures have grown dramatically since it was created in its present form in 1979. Those are expected to grow further in the next 15 years.

Each of the EP members (MEPs) has been directly elected by voters representing in total 370 million people. Elections take place every five years, and the next will be in 1999. The number of members assigned to each country is broadly determined by population. Germany, since reunification, has 99; the UK, France, and Italy each have 87; and so down to the tiny Luxembourg with just 6 MEPs.

In earlier years the European Commission in Brussels had the sole right to propose initiatives while the EU member governments, acting through the Council of Ministers, made the final decisions. Following reforms introduced in 1987 and 1992, the EP has been entrusted with a complex and important range of powers, including the right to co-decision with the Council on many matters and the right to initiate legislation in a few areas.

Depending on the subject, the EP exercises its powers under four main headings: consultation, cooperation, co-decision, and assent.

Under the co-decision procedure a proposal cannot be adopted without the EP's approval. In effect this means that government ministers have to agree on an acceptable text with MEPs beforehand. This procedure is used for decisions covering the free movement of workers, the internal market, technological research and development, the environment, consumer protection, education, culture, and health.

The Parliament's assent is required for decisions on the entry of new member countries and international agreements by the EU, among other things.

In the key area of spending by the EU, the member governments decide on the level of compulsory expenditure (chiefly farm spending and payments arising from international agreements) while the Parliament decides on the rest. The distinction between the two is not always clear.

The Parliament's fundamental role is dictated by its brief to exercise democratic supervision over all EU operations. MEPs have the right to censure and even dismiss the Brussels Commission.

EP members speak and vote according to political affiliation rather than nationality. Following the 1994 elections, the largest group is the European Socialist Party, with 221 seats, followed by the center-right European Peoples Party with 173 and the Liberal Democrats with 52.

MEPs are paid the same basic salary as national MPs in their home country. The annual budget of the Parliament is some $800 million, of which a fifth represents the costs of transferring members, staff, and equipment between the three operational centers of Strasbourg, Luxembourg, and Brussels. Running costs are also highly inflated by the expenses of translation.

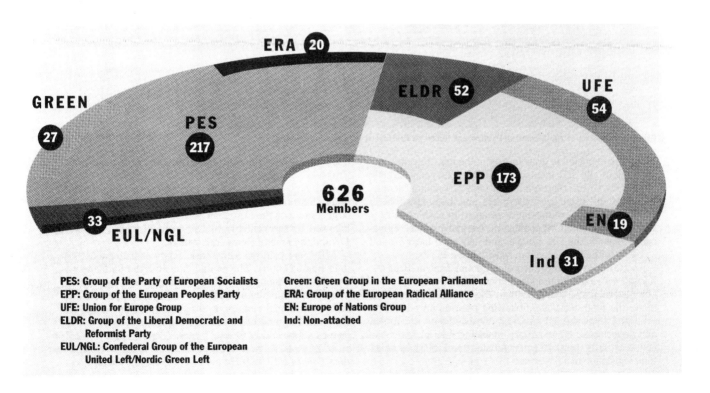

PES: Group of the Party of European Socialists
EPP: Group of the European Peoples Party
UFE: Union for Europe Group
ELDR: Group of the Liberal Democratic and Reformist Party
EUL/NGL: Confederal Group of the European United Left/Nordic Green Left

Green: Green Group in the European Parliament
ERA: Group of the European Radical Alliance
EN: Europe of Nations Group
Ind: Non-attached

From GATT to WTO

The Institutionalization of World Trade

OVER THE PAST FEW DECADES, a system of relatively open exchange, particularly in merchandise trade, has prevailed in the world under the auspices of the General Agreement on Tariffs and Trade (GATT). Today, most economists acknowledge this trading system as one of the greatest contributors to the world's rapid recovery from the desolation of the second World War, and to the phenomenal growth in world output thereafter. Through all of those years, however, GATT has served

SALIL S. PITRODA

Salil S. Pitroda is a Staff Writer for the Harvard International Review.

its member countries through a loose and informal structure, with all the inevitable problems that accompany a weak and ill-defined authority. With the passage of the Uruguay Round of trade talks, this trading system is poised to take on a new shape in a permanent institution known as the World Trade Organization (WTO). Although much skepticism and controversy have surrounded the birth of WTO, it is the hope of all free-traders that the new WTO will be able to amend what went amiss with GATT.

A Brief History of Trade

At the beginning of the nineteenth century, economists began to make advances in interpreting why human beings had always engaged in economic exchange. The theory of comparative advantage posited that countries specialize in those goods and services that they can produce more efficiently relative to other countries. When nations concentrate their production on commodities in which they have a comparative advantage, consumers as a whole benefit from lower prices and a greater range of consumption possibilities. Because each good is produced by the country that is best at producing it, scarce world resources are allocated efficiently. Like all economic activities, the distribution of the benefits of trade is not uniform; yet in general and in the long run, trade leads to a more optimal economic outcome with greater competition and greater productivity—a rising tide on which all boats float.

In 1947, such a view of the benefits of international cooperation inspired a group of visionaries gathered in Bretton Woods, New Hampshire, to erect a new economic world order from the ravages of the second World War. The Bretton Woods Accords, which celebrated their fiftieth anniversary last year, established the World Bank and the International Monetary Fund and led to the creation of GATT. These structures, albeit not always true to the visionary spirit in which they were founded, have formed the underpinnings of world economic development for the past half century.

GATT has become the framework for international trade in our time. The body was formed as an interim secretariat for trade negotiations after the United States, bowing to protectionist sentiment, refused to ratify the charter of the stillborn International Trade Organization, a full-fledged institution of the stature of the World Bank and the IMF. Based in Geneva and currently encompassing over 120 member nations, GATT has acted as a conduit for multilateral negotiations on a variety of international trade issues, including tariff and quota policy and trading practices. It has sponsored several rounds of protracted, though eventually fruitful, trade talks where members gathered to hammer out the details of the set of rules governing economic exchange. GATT panels make recommendations on changes in trade regulations and review complaints against member countries.

Despite GATT's success in coordinating international trade policy, it must be remembered that GATT is only an interim body without a fully defined institutional structure and with little legal enforcement power. For instance, many loopholes exist in the mechanism dealing with disputes regarding unfair trade practices. If a country complains of unfair trading practices on the part of another country and a GATT panel concurs with the complaint, the accused country can dissent from the finding, effectively vetoing it and preventing the complaining country from retaliation within the GATT framework. Another increasingly popular way of doing business in an extra-GATT environment is through the creation of regional trade blocs, such as the European Union (EU), the North American Free Trade Agreement (NAFTA) and the impending Association of Southeast Asian Nations (ASEAN) free trade agreement. These regional agreements, in effect, set their own rules of trade, encouraging cooperative exchange within a bloc but hinting of protectionism against countries outside the region. Non-tariff trade barriers (NTBs), such as a German requirement that, for health reasons, beer sold in Germany be made with German water, are also another device for bending GATT rules. Another way of eschewing GATT policy through these regional trading arrangements is to manipulate the rules of origin stipulation. By raising the requirement of local content value, aspiring profiteers and vested interests can turn an ostensible reduction in a tariff into an actual increase by subjecting formerly tariff-exempt goods to duties, thus circumventing the GATT guideline that for any free trade agreement the new common external tariff be no higher than the average tariff of the constituent states before the accord. Without any institutional framework or legal authority, the most that GATT can do, when confronted with such adroit legerdemain with its regulations, is to urge and exhort a spirit of cooperation among member states, each of whom has an individual incentive to cater to local interests by eschewing a rule here and raising a protectionist wall there.

Seeking to address some of these problems, the Uruguay Round of negotiations was launched nearly nine years ago. Under the leadership of GATT Director-General Peter Sutherland, this latest round of trade talks has arrived at a consensus on implementing changes to the international framework that will encourage greater openness and trade integration among the world's nations. First and foremost, the Uruguay Round promises a lowering of trade barriers and a slashing of tariffs by an average of one-third. It broadens the scope of liberalization to include traditionally protected industries such as textiles and apparel. Reflecting the changing nature of world trade, the Uruguay Round will open up exchange in the previously closed but rapidly emerging areas of agriculture, services, and intellectual property. It imposes a new discipline on NTBs and government procurement and offers clarification on subsidies, dumping regulations, quota restrictions and voluntary export restraints. It also lays the foundation for further talks dealing with important trade issues including the treatment of foreign direct investment, labor and environmental concerns, and capital and currency market fluctuations. Most importantly, the Uruguay Round of accords has boldly moved the world a step closer to global free trade by calling for the establishment of the WTO to succeed the GATT secretariat.

The Birth of WTO

The WTO will be a new international institution, on par with the World Bank and the IMF, that will outline a framework for all areas of international trade and will have the legal authority to settle trade disputes. In legal terms, it represents the maturation of the GATT secretariat into a full-fledged, permanent international entity. The supreme decision-making body will be a biannual ministerial meeting, affording the organization more political clout and a higher international profile. This WTO council will then have subsidiary working bodies that specialize in areas of trade including goods, services and intellectual property. Unlike GATT, the WTO will have a clearly defined dispute settlement mechanism. Independent panel reports will automatically be adopted by the WTO council unless there is a clear consensus to reject them. Countries who are accused of engaging in unfair trade practices can appeal to a permanent appellate body, but the verdict of this body will be ultimately binding. If an offending nation fails to comply with WTO panel recommendations, its trading partners will be guaranteed the right to compensation as determined by the panel or, as a final resort, be given the right to impose countervailing sanctions. All members of the WTO will have legal access to these multilateral dispute settlement mechanisms, and all stages of WTO deliberation will be time-limited, ensuring efficiency in dispute settlement. The World Trade Organization will be akin to an International Court of Justice for world trade, with the institutional strength and legal mandate to ensure fair trade and global economic integration.

Who will be the pioneering leader of this newly constructed international organization? The ideal candidate must possess a strategic global vision of world trade while being comfortable with technical complexity. He or she must combine the finesse of a diplomat, the organizational acumen of an experienced administrator and the leadership qualities of a seasoned statesman.

Since Peter Sutherland, the incumbent Director-General of GATT has indicated his wish to stand down in favor of fresh leadership, the competition to be the head of the WTO has been opened up to three dynamic candidates. Renato Ruggiero, the favored candidate of the EU, is a former trade minister of Italy and has also been suggested in the past as a possible president of the European Commission. He has emphasized his experience as a capable administrator with international experience in Brussels, the GATT, and world economic summits. Carlos Salinas de Gortari, who during his tenure as the President of

Mexico defined the paradigm for economic liberalization in developing countries, is the candidate favored by the Americas. His international stature as a head of state and his commitment to free trade—as evinced by his personal crusade for NAFTA—are Salinas's most important assets. The South Korean trade minister, Kim Chul-Su, has proven international experience and is naturally supported by countries in Asia and Australia, the fastest growing region in the world. In the end, politics will most likely decide who heads the WTO. Similar leadership positions are opening up at the Organization for Economic Cooperation and Development (OECD) and other international organizations, with political horse-trading sure to play an integral role in determining the new leaders of these organizations.

There are various other strategic issues relating to the establishment of the WTO. At least for the initial transition stage, the new organization is expected to grow by expanding on the existing GATT structure. The WTO will most probably be situated in the existing GATT building in Geneva and will require an increase in GATT's present budget and staff. Yet even with this augmentation in resources, the WTO will still remain far smaller in size than either the World Bank or the IMF.

Aside from such logistical matters, however, the precise nature of the transition between GATT and WTO remains more nebulous. Some countries, such as the United States, have already announced that they will terminate their GATT membership within sixty days of joining the WTO. Such a strict view of WTO's successor status to GATT raises interesting questions about US obligations to GATT members who have yet to ratify their entry into WTO.

Other countries envision the two organizations operating in tandem for a period of two years, with GATT still binding, to ease the transition to the WTO. There is also the question of new memberships. Will Slovenia and Croatia, for instance, who have just applied for GATT membership, be granted direct membership in the WTO? If the WTO does not completely supersede GATT immediately, where does that leave a country like the Sudan, which is not a GATT member, but has applied directly for WTO membership?

Of course, there is also the thorny problem of China, which has just been denied the opportunity of being a founding member of WTO, and Taiwan, whose competing applications will surely pose more dilemmas of politics and protocol. Certainly, careful deliberation will be needed to work out the multitude of implementational, organizational and transitional issues.

The Foundation of the New Order

Given these birth pangs, what are the fundamental qualities upon which the WTO must lay its foundation? As Carlos Salinas de Gortari has outlined in a recent article in *The Financial Times*, the WTO must be representative, reliable and responsive. It must embrace all countries, regardless of their level of economic development, and ensure their prompt and satisfactory integration into a multilateral trading system. Reliability is a much tougher criterion to satisfy. The WTO must clarify GATT rules, broaden its mandate and improve its dispute settlement mechanisms to demonstrate to all member nations that they have a stake in abiding by a rules-based trade regime. Finally, flexibility and responsiveness to the evolving changes of the international economy will ensure that the WTO retains the political support necessary to carrying out its work.

As an organization that has ambitions of leading the global economy into the next millennium, the WTO needs to legitimize its standing in the eyes of politicians and economists wearied by decades of trade negotiations by confronting some concrete and difficult problems. One of the first tasks it might have to face is deciding whether or not it should extend the rules regulating conduct in international trade to cover national competition policies. Ideally, countries should have roughly comparable standards on anti-trust legislation so that greater competition from all-comers, whether domestic or foreign, can be welcomed. But by treading on such sensitive territories, the WTO may stray too far from the trade-related issues at the core of its mandate. The animosities which it incurs in those confrontations may permanently impair its ability to unite its membership on other, arguably even more important, issues in the long run.

One of the most crucial tasks of the WTO will be presiding over the economic and political integration of the former socialist economies. It must provide stable and expanding outlets for these countries' products to encourage the liberalization of their economies and to help them attract much needed foreign direct investment. In fact, all the newly open economies in Latin America, Africa and Asia must be nurtured by a transparent, rules-based and mutually beneficial trading system. In particular, the WTO must encourage the reversal of the growing lethargy in North-South cooperation, especially with regard to Sub-Saharan African countries, which

desperately need open international markets for their growth. The organization also has a special responsibility to bring the nearly two billion citizens of China and India, 40 percent of the planet's population, into the world trading regime as full and active members.

On a more macroscopic level, the WTO must effectively coordinate regional free trade agreements to ensure that they do not conflict in goals or create islands of protectionism, but are instead regional building blocks toward the eventual realization of global free trade which almost every economic theory praises as the ideal for future world economic relations. Pursuant to this objective of regional coordination, the institution must stiffen its regulations and their enforcement so that less and less protectionism can be veiled behind devices such as NTBs, rules of origins requirements and other technical loopholes. It must convince member nations that their greatest economic interest is to cooperate with the other nations of the world and not bow to vested interests by taking short-sighted unilateral action. The best means for guaranteeing this end is a vigorous and binding dispute settlement mechanism. In planning for the future, the organization must also proactively embrace the changing nature of the global economy from trade in manufactured goods to trade in information-intensive services and intellectual property. The technical complexity of those issues and the administrative difficulty that will inevitably accompany any rules governing them will be a challenge to WTO's energy, resourcefulness and resolve.

Finally, and very importantly, the WTO must acknowledge and deal with some of the local pains that uncompetitive industries in member nations will feel. In order to avoid the image of an elitist other-worldliness to which so many other well-intentioned international organizations have fallen prey, the WTO must ensure that the gains from trade are trickled down to the populace. Without at least some semblance of equity to compensate for the sacrifices that the working poor will be asked to make in any transition, it will be difficult for WTO to maintain the political and moral support that it needs to push through its vision of world-wide free trade. Ideally, some sort of structural adjustment fund and a common program for retraining displaced workers should be a pillar of the WTO, so that humanity and compassion, as well as hard-nosed efficiency, may be integrated into the organization's founding philosophy. There are undoubtedly a host of other important issues the new WTO should con-

sider, but careful deliberation upon the fundamentals outlined here will be a major step toward solidifying and validating a global free trade system.

Positive Sums from Cooperation

The bottom line of the emergence of the new WTO from GATT is that world trade will be institutionalized in the formal legal structure of an international organization. The more formal status of the WTO will allow it to give more focus and publicity to efforts that attempt to create greater global cooperation in international trade. The institutionalization of trade through the WTO will give some bite to the bark of a well-articulated set of trading rules and policies. With its creation, there will exist an independent political entity that can view the world trading system from a holistic perspective and to check and balance competing interests that seek to bend the trading rules in their national or sectoral favor. By paying judicious attention to the fundamental issues in international trade, the WTO has the potential of becoming a visionary organization that outlines a bold path for international trade and leads the world into a new economic renaissance.

Recent studies have released estimates of the global economic effects of the ratification of the GATT Uruguay Round and the creation of the World Trade Organization. A GATT report released in November 1994 prognosticated that implementation of the Uruguay Round will spur an increase of $510 billion a year in world income by the year 2005. This figure is a vast underestimate, for it does not account for the impact of strengthened procedures and rules in the services trade or better dispute settlement mechanisms. Breaking up the gains by region, the report predicted that by 2005 the annual income gain will be $122 billion for the United States, $164 billion for the European Union, $27 billion for Japan and $116 billion for the developing and transitional socialist economies as a group. Figures estimating the increase in volume in the goods trade range from nine to 24 percent once the liberalization of the Uruguay Round comes into effect. In 1992 dollars, this gain represents an increase in trade flows of upwards of $670 billion. The report also suggests that Uruguay Round provisions for developing and transition economies will have the intended result of encouraging rapid growth, as exports and imports from this group are likely to be 50 percent over and beyond the increase for the rest of the world as a whole. The economic impact of a well-structured and credible institutionalization of international trade is likely to be enormous.

What remains to be done is the actual construction of this economic structure. Nowhere has the debate over GATT and the WTO been more pronounced than in the world's economic leader, the United States. As is to be expected before embarking upon any bold new initiative, those who stand to suffer short-term losses are trying to stand in the way of long-term progress. Protectionist concerns and irresponsible exaggeration have been vociferously fed to the press and the deliberative bodies of the government. One example of such red herrings is a concern about a loss of US sovereignty in becoming a member of the WTO. In truth, any changes in the law of the United States or any other nation will have to be ratified by proper legislative bodies in that country, and so the practical encroachment on national sovereignty is little more than negligible. Of course, there is a germ of truth in

All nations, the US in particular, must realize that partnerships are more advantageous than going it alone.

this argument, for when any nation enters into an international treaty, it must lose some "sovereignty" to the extent that it agrees to abide by the terms of the agreement. Some kind of consensus, such as the sensitive balance that needs to be achieved by the WTO, must be reached to preserve a predictable and liberal international trade regime. To carp at the WTO for having the potential to compromise national sovereignty is little different from saying that national sovereignty is compromised because a country has to abide by any international treaty.

All nations, the US in particular, must realize that partnerships are more advantageous than going it alone, and that economic cooperation is not a zero-sum game. Free trade makes each and every nation more prosperous because it makes the entire world more prosperous. Government leaders around the world would do well to hearken to the words of Rufus Yerxa, Deputy US Trade Representative and Ambassador to GATT: "International cooperation will bring about the economic growth of the future. We cannot survive as an island in a sea of change. If we don't embrace this change, it will be our enemy rather than our friend. Cooperation is in our own self-interest. "

Peace Prize Goes to Land-Mine Opponents

By CAREY GOLDBERG

PUTNEY, Vt., Oct. 10—The Nobel Peace Prize was bestowed today on the International Campaign to Ban Landmines and on Jody Williams, an American who coordinates it—and the newly minted laureate immediately wielded the award to step up political pressure on recalcitrant countries, including the United States.

Barefoot in her rustic yard here, and bare-knuckled as ever in her approach, Ms. Williams taunted President Clinton today, saying he would be branded a coward if the United States continued to refuse to sign the international treaty banning land mines.

"If President Clinton wants the legacy of his administration to be that he did not have the courage to be the Commander in Chief of his military, that is his legacy, and I feel sorry for him," she said. "I think it's tragic that President Clinton does not want to be on the side of humanity."

Just hours after the award was announced, President Boris N. Yeltsin unexpectedly declared that Russia had decided to sign the accord.

But the United States and China remain the big holdouts, and the White House spokesman said today that President Clinton's refusal to sign the treaty, based on his insistence that it contain exceptions for the Korean peninsula, still stands.

In awarding the prize to the group and to Ms. Williams, the Nobel committee said it was openly trying to influence the treaty process. "This could be interpreted as a message to the great powers that we hope they also will eventually choose to sign the treaty," Francis Sejersted, the committee chairman, said in Oslo.

He and others also praised the anti-land-mine campaign as an exciting new form of post-cold-war political action in which a broad, grassroots coalition of citizens' groups and smaller nations, working on their own outside the bounds of major institutions like the United Nations, led to world change.

The agreement would outlaw land mines, which are estimated to kill or maim 26,000 people a year, and require countries to clean up those already on their soil. Nearly 100 governments approved a draft of the treaty last month, and world figures ranging from Diana, Princess of Wales, to President Nelson Mandela of South Africa have supported the campaign.

The treaty, to be signed in Ottawa in December, is to go into effect after 40 nations have ratified it.

The International Campaign to Ban Landmines is a coalition of more than 1,000 organizations in more than 60 countries, and argues that with more than 100 million buried mines around the world taking such a high human toll, they must be banned.

Ms. Williams, 47, first became politically active protesting the Vietnam War, and later focused her efforts on influencing American policy in Central America and providing aid there. She joined the Vietnam Veterans of America Foundation, which began the land mines campaign, at the end of 1991.

The campaign is a descendant of the anti-war movement. It was the idea of Robert Muller, a Marine veteran who lost the use of his legs during the Vietnam War and started organizing to improve conditions at the veterans' hospitals where he was treated. He then moved into anti-war activism, and also fought for compensation for veterans who had been exposed to Agent Orange.

During the 1980's he returned to Vietnam and set up projects to provide wounded Vietnamese veterans with prosthetics. When he went to Cambodia to do similar work in 1991, Mr. Muller found that the victims were largely civilians and that their injuries were more recent—from land mines still embedded in the countryside.

He realized, he said, "that there is more we got to do—just putting on legs don't cut it." And the campaign to ban land mines was born.

Men and Women of Peace, 1971–1997

By The Associated Press

1997—The International Campaign to Ban Landmines.

1996—Filipe Ximenes Belo and José Ramos-Horta of East Timor.

1995—Joseph Rotblat and the Pugwash Conference on Science and World Affairs, Britain.

1994—Yasir Arafat of the Palestine Liberation Organization and Yitzhak Rabin and Shimon Peres of Israel.

1993—Nelson Mandela and F. W. de Klerk, South Africa.

1992—Rigoberta Menchu, Guatemala.

1991—Aung San Suu Kyi, Burma.

1990—Mikhail S. Gorbachev, Soviet Union.

1989—The Dalai Lama, Tibet.

1988—The United Nations peacekeeping operations.

1987—Oscar Arias Sanchez, Costa Rica.

1986—Elie Wiesel, United States.

1985—International Physicians for the Prevention of Nuclear War.

1984—Bishop Desmond Tutu, South Africa.

1983—Lech Walesa, Poland.

1982—Alva Myrdal, Sweden, and Alfonso Garcia Robles, Mexico.

1981—The United Nations High Commission for Refugees.

1980—Adolfo Pérez Esquivel, Argentina.

1979—Mother Teresa, Calcutta.

1978—Anwar el-Sadat, Egypt, and Menachem Begin, Israel.

1977—Amnesty International, London.

1976—Betty Williams and Mairead Corrigan, Northern Ireland.

1975—Andrei Sakharov, Soviet Union.

1974—Sean MacBride, Ireland, and Eisaku Sato, Japan.

1973—Henry A. Kissinger, United States, and Le Duc Tho, North Vietnam.

1972—No prize awarded.

1971—Willy Brandt, Germany.

It started with Mr. Muller and the Vietnam Veterans of America Foundation and a German group. "That way, we could call ourselves international," Mr. Muller said. Soon the movement was growing quickly enough to hire a coordinator, Ms. Williams.

While efforts in the United Nations stagnated, the anti-land-mine campaign found support from such figures as Lloyd Axworthy, the Canadian Foreign Minister; Senator Patrick J. Leahy, Democrat of Vermont, and Gen. Norman Schwarzkopf. The International Committee of the Red Cross also helped, with a worldwide publicity campaign beginning in 1995.

The campaign and Ms. Williams are to share the $1 million Nobel monetary award equally.

Today Ms. Williams was praised by Susannah Sirkin, deputy director of Physicians for Human Rights, a campaign member, as "an extraordinarily determined individual."

"She is fearless," Ms. Sirkin said. "She has never been reluctant to stand in front of a general or world leader with a conviction that she was right on this issue, and tell them what needs to be done."

But at her Vermont home, set near a beaver pond among trees glowing ruby and gold in the autumn sunlight, Ms. Williams adamantly refused to take the prize as a personal tribute, focusing her remarks instead on the campaign's progress and the work it has yet to do.

The group plans to focus its pressure on hold-out countries, she said, and hopes to have all countries on board by 2000. She has not decided what issue she will work on next, she said, but assumes something will evolve.

The overall message of the campaign against land mines, she said, was not only the damage the mines cause but also the concept that in this post-cold-war world, "the military cannot operate with impunity."

"I hope to educate the world that while war may not go away in our lifetime, that there are rules about how you conduct yourself in war," she said, "that if the military think they have to fight with each other, they should point the guns at each other; they should not involve all of civil society."

And entire countries should not become battlefields, she said, citing Cambodia and Angola. Cambodia is believed to harbor more than 10 million land mines, Angola 9 million.

For all her serious arguments, however, and for all her solemn appreciation of the honor inherent in joining the ranks of Nobel recipients, Ms. Williams retains a streak of irrepressible irreverence, particularly in regard to the President of the United States, whom she referred to as "Billy" and "a weenie."

When, by midafternoon, he still had not called to congratulate her, she complained comically, "He has time to call the winners of the Super Bowl, but the winner of the Nobel Peace Prize he can't call?"

Of course, she added, he probably had not called because, "If he calls me, he knows I'm going to say, 'What's your problem?'"

Values and Visions

The final unit of this book considers how humanity's view of itself is changing. Values, like all other elements discussed in this anthology, are dynamic. Visionary people with new ideas can have a profound impact on how a society deals with problems and adapts to changing circumstances. Therefore, to understand the forces at work in the world today, values, visions, and new ideas must be examined.

Novelist Herman Wouk, in his book *War and Remembrance*, observed that many institutions have been so embedded in the social fabric of their time that people assumed that they were part of human nature. Slavery and human sacrifice are two examples. However, forward-thinking people opposed these institutions. Many knew that they would never see the abolition of these social systems within their own lifetimes, but they pressed on in the hope that someday these institutions would be eliminated.

Wouk believes the same is true for warfare. He states, "Either we are finished with war or war will finish us." Aspects of society such as warfare, slavery, racism, and the secondary status of women are creations of the human mind; history suggests that they can be changed by the human spirit.

The articles of this unit have been selected with the previous six units in mind. Each explores some aspect of world affairs from the perspective of values and alternative visions of the future.

New ideas are critical to meeting these challenges. The examination of well-known issues from new perspectives can yield new insights into old problems. It was feminist Susan B. Anthony who once remarked that "social change is never made by the masses, only by educated minorities." The redefinition of human values (which, by necessity, will accompany the successful confrontation of other global issues) is a task that few people take on willingly.

Nevertheless, in order to deal with the dangers of nuclear war, overpopulation, and environmental degradation, educated people must take a broad view of history. This is going to require considerable effort and much personal sacrifice.

When people first begin to consider the challenges of contemporary global problems, they often become disheartened and depressed. They might ask: What can I do? What does it matter? Who cares? There are no easy answers to these questions, but people need only look around to see good news as well as bad. How individuals react to the world in which they live is not a function of that world but a reflection of themselves. Different people react differently to the same world. The study of global issues, therefore, is the study of people, and the study of people is the study of values. Ideally, people's reactions to these issues will help provide them with some insight into themselves as well as the world at large.

Looking Ahead: Challenge Questions

Comment on the idea that it is naive to speak of international politics and economics in terms of ethics. What role can governments, international organizations, and the individual play in making the world a more ethical place?

How easily are the values of democracy transferred to new settings such as Russia?

What are the characteristics of leadership?

In addition to the ideas presented here, what other new ideas are being expressed, and how likely are they to be widely accepted?

How do the contemporary arts reflect changes in the way humanity views itself?

How will the world be different in the year 2030? What factors will contribute to these changes? What does your analysis reveal about your own value system?

UNIVERSAL HUMAN VALUES

Finding an Ethical Common Ground

Rushworth M. Kidder

Rushworth M. Kidder, former senior columnist for The Christian Science Monitor, *is president of the Institute for Global Ethics, Box 563, Camden, Maine 04843. Telephone 207/236-6658. He has spoken at several World Future Society conferences and at "Toward the New Millennium: Living, Learning, and Working," July 24–26, 1994, in Cambridge, Massachusetts.*

In the remote New Zealand village of Panguru, tucked into the mountains at the end of a winding gravel road, a Maori woman nearly a century old pauses for a moment as she talks about the moral values of her people. "This is God's country!" says Dame Whina Cooper with great feeling, gesturing toward the flowers blooming among the bird songs outside her modest frame house. "Only, we the people running it must be doing something wrong."

Halfway around the world, in a United Nations office perched under the eaves of a fifteenth-century building in Florence, a leading journalist from Sri Lanka is asked what will happen if the world enters the twenty-first century with the ethics of the twentieth. "I feel it will be disastrous," Varindra Tarzie Vittachi replies simply.

Midway between, in his well-appointed residence in San Jose, Costa Rica, former president Oscar Arias explains that our global survival "will become more complicated and precarious than ever before, and the ethics required of us must be correspondingly sophisticated."

Turn where you will in the world and the refrain is the same. The ethical barometer is falling, and the consequences appear to be grave. That, at least, is one of the impressions to be drawn from the two dozen individuals from 16 nations interviewed over the past few years by the Institute for Global Ethics.

These interviews did not seek to discover the ethical failings of various nations, but rather to find the moral glue that will bind us together in the twenty-first century. These voices speak powerfully of an underlying moral presence shared by all humanity—a set of precepts so fundamental that they dissolve borders, transcend races, and outlast cultural traditions.

There is a pressing need for shared values in our age of global interdependence without consensus. But there is one very real question unanswered: Is there in fact a single set of values that wise, ethical people around the world might agree on? Can there be a global code of ethics? If there is a common core of values "out there" in the world, it ought to be identifiable through examination of contemporary modes of thought in various cultures around the world. Can it be found?

On that topic, the two dozen "men and women of conscience" interviewed had a clear point of view. "Yes," they said, "there is such a code, and it can be clearly articulated." These interviewees were chosen not because they necessarily know more about ethics than their peers—although some do, having made it a lifelong study. Nor were they chosen because they are the single most exemplary person of their nation or community—though some could easily be nominated for that honor. They are, however, ethical thought-leaders within their different cultures, each viewed by his or her peers as a kind of ethical standard-bearer, a keeper of the conscience of the community, a center of moral gravity.

Each of the interviews began with a common question: If you could help create a global code of ethics, what would be on it? What moral values, in other words, would you bring to the table from your own culture and background?

In an ideal world, one would have assembled all the interviewees around a table, had each talk for an hour, had each listen intently to all the others, and finally had them arrive at a consensus. If they could have done so, here's the core of moral values upon which they probably would have agreed:

LOVE

Despite the concern of foundation executive James A. Joseph in Washington that "the L-word, Love," is falling sadly into disuse, it figured prominently in these interviews. "Love, yes," said children's author Astrid Lindgren in Stockholm. "This is the main word for what we need—love on all stages and with all people."

"The base of moral behavior is first of all solidarity, love, and mutual assistance," said former first lady Graça Machel of Mozambique. Buddhist monk Shojun Bando in Tokyo agreed, detailing three different kinds of love and insisting that "it shouldn't be that *others* should tell you to love others: It should just come of its own will, spontaneously." Or, as author Nien Cheng from China put it, "You cannot guide without love."

For tribal chief Reuben Snake of Nebraska, the central word is *compassion*. "We have to be compassionate with one another and help one another, to hold each other up, support one another down the road of

life," he recalled his grandfather telling him. Thinking back on her dealings with a global spectrum of cultures at the United Nations, former ambassador Jeane Kirkpatrick in Washington noted that, no matter how severe the political differences, "there was a kind of assumption, on the part of almost everyone, that people would help one another at the personal level."

TRUTHFULNESS

Of the four theses that form Harvard University ex-president Derek Bok's code of ethics, two center on truth. "You should not obtain your ends through lying and deceitful practices," he said, and you have a "responsibility to keep [your] promises." Astrid Lindgren put it with equal clarity when she spoke of the need to "be honest, not lying, not afraid to say your opinion."

Looking through the lens of science, the late economist Kenneth Boulding of Colorado also put "a very high value on veracity—telling the truth. The thing that gets you run out of the scientific community is being caught out telling a lie." Fortunately, said Bangladeshi banker Muhammad Yunus, the spread of technology makes it increasingly difficult for the truth to be hidden. In the future, "people will be forced to reveal themselves," he said. "Nothing can be kept hidden or secret—not in computers, not in the halls of government, nothing. People will feel much more comfortable when they're dealing in truth. You converge around and in truth."

Here, however, as with many of these global values, there was also a residue of concern—a fear that trust, which is central to honesty and truthfulness, seems to be falling into abeyance. "The idea that you ought to be able to trust somebody is out of fashion," worried Katharine Whitehorn, columnist for *The Observer* of London. That's a point seconded by corporate executive James K. Baker of Indiana. "Little by little," he said, "if we let that trust go out of our personal dealings with one another, then I think the system really begins to have trouble."

FAIRNESS

Elevating the concept of justice to the top of his list, philosopher and author John W. Gardner of Stanford University said, "I consider that probably the number-one candidate

---

24 MEN AND WOMEN OF CONSCIENCE

Dame Whina Cooper: founding president of Maori Women's Welfare League in New Zealand; presented with the Order of Dame Commander of the British Empire by Queen Elizabeth.

"God wants us to be one people."

Varindra Tarzie Vittachi: Sri Lankan journalist and author; assistant secretary-general of the United Nations.

"One man in the twentieth century . . . led us back into morality as a practical thing and not as a cloud-cuckoo-land idea, and that was Mohandas Gandhi."

Oscar Arias: former president of Costa Rica; 1987 winner of the Nobel Peace Prize.

"The effect of one upright individual is incalculable."

James A. Joseph: former undersecretary of the U.S. Department of the Interior.

"I relate fairness to treating other people as I would want to be treated."

---

for your common ground." By *justice*, he meant "fair play, or some word for even-handedness."

"Here, one could get caught up in the very complicated theories of social justice," warned James A. Joseph. "Or one could simply look at the Golden Rule. I relate fairness to treating other people as I would want to be treated. I think that [rule] serves humanity well. It ought to be a part of any ethic for the future."

For many, the concern for fairness goes hand in hand with the concept of equality. "The pursuit of equality is basic," said columnist and editor Sergio Muñoz of Mexico City and

---

Astrid Lindgren: Swedish author of *Pippi Longstocking.*

"Love, yes. This is the main word for what we need—love on all stages and with all people."

Graça Machel: former first lady of Mozambique.

"The base of moral behavior is first of all solidarity, love, and mutual assistance."

Shojun Bando: Japanese Buddhist monk, studied under Zen scholar D. T. Suzuki.

"[Parents'] actions speak more than words. Their everyday doings teach the kids how to behave."

Nien Cheng: author of *Life and Death in Shanghai;* suffered over six years of solitary confinement and torture at the hands of Chinese Communists.

"You cannot guide without love."

Reuben Snake: former chairman of the American Indian Movement.

"The spirit that makes you stand up and walk and talk and see and hear and think is the same spirit that exists in me."

Los Angeles. "The people who come from Mexico and El Salvador have the same values, in my point of view, as the person who comes from Minnesota or from Alabama or from California—those basic principles that are common to all civilizations."

For some, like Joseph, the concept of fairness and equality focuses strongly on racial issues. Others, like author Jill Ker Conway from Australia, see the need for "greater equity between the sexes." Still others, like UNESCO Director-General Federico Mayor of Spain, see the problem as one of international relations: Despite the groundswell of interest in democracy arising within the former East Bloc nations, Westerners "have not reacted as humans, but only as economic individuals. . . . Even equity—the most important value in all the world—has collapsed."

FREEDOM

Very early in human history, said John Gardner, "the concept of degrees of freedom of my action—as against excessive constraints on my action by a tyrant or by military conquerors—emerged." Even the earliest peoples "knew when they were subjugated"—and didn't like it. That desire for liberty, he said, persists to the present as one of the defining values of humanity.

But liberty requires a sense of individuality and the right of that individual to express ideas freely, many of the interviewees said. "Without the principle of individual conscience, every attempt to institutionalize ethics must necessarily collapse" said Oscar Arias. "The effect of one upright individual is incalculable. World leaders may see their effect in headlines, but the ultimate course of the globe will be determined by the efforts of innumerable individuals acting on their consciences."

Such action, for many of these thinkers, is synonymous with democracy. "I think democracy is a must for all over the world," said Salim El Hoss, former prime minister of Lebanon. He defined the ingredients of democracy as "freedom of expression plus accountability plus equal opportunity." While he worried that the latter two are lacking in many countries, he noted that the first condition, freedom of expression, is increasingly becoming available to "all peoples."

UNITY

As a counterbalance to the needs of individual conscience, however, stands the value that embraces the individual's role in a larger collective. Of the multitude of similar terms used for that concept in these interviews (*fraternity, solidarity, cooperation, community, group allegiance, oneness*) *unity* seems the most encompassing and the least open to misconstruction. For some, it is a simple *cri de coeur* in a world that seems close to coming undone. "I want unity," said Dame Whina Cooper of New Zealand, adding that "God wants us to be one people." For Tarzie Vittachi of Sri Lanka, the idea of unity embraces a global vision capable of moving humanity from "unbridled competition" to cooperation. "That is what is demanded of us now: putting our community first, meaning the earth first, and all living things."

The problem arises when the common good is interpreted "by seeing the relation between the individual and the common in individualistic terms," said Father Bernard Przewozny of Rome. Carried to the extreme, individualism is "destructive of social life, destructive of communal sharing, destructive of participation," he said, adding that "the earth and its natural goods are the inheritance of all peoples."

TOLERANCE

"If you're serious about values," said John Gardner, "then you have to add tolerance very early—*very* early. Because you have to have constraints. The more you say, 'Values are important,' the more you have to say, 'There are limits to which you can impose your values on me.'"

"It is a question of respect for the dignity of each of us," said Graça Machel. "If you have a different idea from mine, it's not because you're worse than me. You have the right to think differently." Agreeing, Derek Bok defined tolerance as "a decent respect for the right of other people to have ideas, an obligation or at least a strong desirability of listening to different points of view and at-

empting to understand why they
are held."

"You have your own job, you eat
your own food," said Vietnamese
writer and activist Le Ly Hayslip.
"How you make that food is up to you,
and how I live my life is up to me."

Jeane Kirkpatrick: former U.S.
ambassador to the United
Nations.

*"I don't think life is the supreme
good. It's very nearly the supreme
good, but quality of life matters a lot,
too. And freedom matters a lot—prosperity, a decent standard of living,
possibilities for self-development."*

Derek Bok: president of Harvard
University, 1971–1991.

*"A decent respect for the right of
other people to have ideas."*

Kenneth Boulding: author of over
30 books; professor at the University of Colorado.

*"[I put] a very high value on ve-
racity—telling the truth."*

Muhammad Yunus: managing director of the Grameen Bank,
Dhaka, Bangladesh.

*"The oneness of human beings is the
basic ethical thread that holds us
together."*

Katharine Whitehorn: senior columnist for the London Sunday
newspaper *The Observer.*

*"I don't think that people habitually
do anything unless they are programmed so that they are appalled
with themselves when they don't."*

Reuben Snake traced the idea of
tolerance back to a religious basis.
"The spirit that makes you stand up
and walk and talk and see and hear
and think is the same spirit that exists in me—there's no difference," he
said. "So when you look at me,
you're looking at yourself—and I'm
seeing me in you."

Abstracting from the idea of tolerance the core principle of respect for
variety, Kenneth Boulding linked it
to the environmentalist's urgency
over the depletion of species. "If the
blue whale is endangered, we feel
worried about this, because we love
the variety of the world," he explained. "In some sense I feel about
the Catholic Church the way I feel
about the blue whale: I don't think
I'll be one, but I would feel diminished if it became extinct."

RESPONSIBILITY

Oxford don A.H. Halsey placed
the sense of responsibility high on
his list of values because of its impact on our common future. "We are
responsible for our grandchildren,"
he explained, "and we will make
[the world] easier or more difficult
for our grandchildren to be good
people by what we do right here and
now." This was a point made in a
different way by Katharine Whitehorn, who noted that, while as a
youth "it's fun to break away," it's
very much harder to "grow up and
have to put it together again."

For Nien Cheng, the spotlight falls
not so much on the actions of the future as on the sense of self-respect in
the present. "This is Confucius'
teaching," she said. "You must take
care of yourself. To rely on others is a
great shame."

Responsibility also demands caring for others, Hayslip said. But, under the complex interactions of medicine, insurance, and law that exists
in the West, "If you come into my
house and see me lying here very
sick, you don't dare move me, because you're not a doctor," she
pointed out. "So where is your human obligation? Where is your human instinct to try to save me? You
don't have it. You lost it, because
there are too many rules."

Yet, paradoxically, "responsibility
is not often mentioned in discussions
of world politics or ethics," said Oscar
Arias. "There, the talk is all of rights,
demands, and desires." Human rights
are "an unquestionable and critical
priority for political societies and an
indispensable lever for genuine development," he said. "But the impor-

tant thing is not just to assert rights,
but to ensure that they be protected.
Achieving this protection rests wholly
on the principle of responsibility."

Chicago attorney Newton Minow
agreed. "I believe the basic reason
we got off the track was that rights
became more important than respon-

James K. Baker: former president
of U.S. Chamber of Commerce.

*"There's only one 'ethics.' . . . Let's
not think you've got to adhere to one
standard at home and another standard at work."*

John W. Gardner: philosopher;
founder of Common Cause; author; Stanford University
professor.

*"[Even the earliest peoples] knew
when they were subjugated."*

Sergio Muñoz: executive editor,
La Opinion, the largest Spanish-
language daily newspaper in the
United States.

"The pursuit of equality is basic."

Jill Ker Conway: Australian author of *The Road from Coorain;*
feminist historian and former
president of Smith College.

"Greater equality between the sexes."

Federico Mayor: director-general
of UNESCO.

*"There are a lot of fundamental
values that are reflected in the Universal Declaration of Human Rights
that nobody opposes."*

---

sibilities, that individuals became
more important than community interests. We've gotten to the point
where everybody's got a right and
nobody's got a responsibility."

At its ultimate, this sense of responsibility extends to the concept of
the right use of force. "You shouldn't
perpetrate violence," said Derek Bok
simply, finding agreement with

Jeane Kirkpatrick's insistence that "war is always undesirable" and that "any resort to force should be a very late option, never a first option."

RESPECT FOR LIFE

Growing out of this idea of the responsible use of force, but separate from and extending beyond it, is a value known most widely in the West from the Ten Commandments: Thou shalt not kill. For Shojun Bando, it is an inflexible principle: Even if ordered in wartime to defend his homeland by killing, he said, "I would refuse. I would say, 'I cannot do this.'"

Such an idea, expressed in today's peaceable Japan, may seem almost naive when examined through the lens of such war-riddled areas as the Middle East. Yet, Salim El Hoss took much the same view. "I was a prime minister [of Lebanon] for seven and a half years. I can't imagine myself signing a death penalty for anybody in the world. I think that is completely illegitimate, and I think that is the kind of thing a code of ethics should deal with."

Reuben Snake, noting that the North American Indians have a warlike reputation, said, "Probably the most serious shortcoming of tribal governments is their inability to effectively resolve conflict within the tribe and externally." He described earlier Indian traditions, however, in which great efforts were made by the tribal elders to prevent killing. That's a point with which Tarzie Vittachi—himself from the much-bloodied nation of Sri Lanka—felt perfectly at home. The first element of the Buddhist "daily prayer" under which he was raised, he recalled, is "I shall not kill." It is also central to the Ten Commandments of the Jewish decalogue under which Newton Minow was raised and which he said he still feels form the basis for the world's code of ethics.

Salim El Hoss: former head of state of Lebanon.

"I can't imagine myself signing a death penalty for anybody in the world."

Bernard Przewozny: professor of Christology at the Pontifical Theological Faculty of St. Bonaventure in Rome.

"The earth and its natural goods are the inheritance of all peoples."

Le Ly Hayslip: survivor of Vietnam War; author; founder of the East Meets West Foundation.

"What are we here for? We're here so that we can help each other to grow."

A. H. Halsey: professor of social and administrative studies at Oxford University.

"We will make [the world] easier or more difficult for our grandchildren to be good people by what we do right here and now."

Newton Minow: chairman of the Federal Communications Commission; chairman of the board of the Carnegie Corporation.

"We've gotten to the point where everybody's got a right and nobody's got a responsibility."

OTHER SHARED VALUES

There were, of course, other significant values that surfaced in these interviews. Nien Cheng, for instance, pointed to *courage*. "One should basically know what is right and what is wrong," she said, "and, when you know that, be courageous enough to stand for what is right."

Figuring strongly in Shojun Bando's pantheon was *wisdom*, which he defined as "attaining detachment, getting away from being too attached to things."

Whina Cooper put *hospitality* high on her list, recalling that her father said, "If you see any strangers going past, you call them—*Kia Ora*—that means to call them to come here." Astrid Lindgren put an emphasis on *obedience*—a quality that runs throughout the life of her most famous character, Pippi Longstocking, though usually in reverse.

Kenneth Boulding pointed to *peace*, which he defined simply as "well-managed conflict." Thinking of peace brought Salim El Hoss to the concept of *stability*. "Peace is equivalent to stability," he said, adding that "stability means a long-term perspective of no problems." These and other values, while they don't find broad support, had firm proponents among those we interviewed and deserve serious attention.

Other values mentioned included the burning public concerns for racial harmony, respect for women's place, and the protection of the environment. Many of the interviewees touched on them, and some elevated them to high priority. Speaking of the need for racial harmony, James Joseph put at the top of his list a sense of "respect for the cultures of other communities, respect for the need to begin to integrate into our collective memory appreciation of the contributions and traditions of those who are different." Jill Conway topped her list with a warning about the "increasing exploitation of women" around the world. And of the many human rights identified by Father Bernard Przewozny, the one to which he has dedicated his life is the "right to a healthy environment."

So what good is this code of values? It gives us a foundation for building goals, plans, and tactics where things really happen and the world really changes. It unifies us, giving us a home territory of consensus and agreement. And it gives us a way—not *the* way, but *a* way—to reply when we're asked, "Whose values will you teach?" Answering this last question, as we tumble into the twenty-first century with the twentieth's sense of ethics, may be one of the most valuable mental activities of our time.

Women in Power: From Tokenism to Critical Mass

by Jane S. Jaquette

Never before have so many women held so much power. The growing participation and representation of woman in politics is one of the most remarkable developments of the late twentieth century. For the first time, women in all countries and social classes are becoming politically active, achieving dramatic gains in the number and kind of offices they hold. Why is political power, off limits for so long, suddenly becoming accessible to women? And what are the implications of this trend for domestic and foreign policy?

Women have been gaining the right to vote and run for office since New Zealand became the first country to authorize women's suffrage in 1893. By 1920, the year the United States amended the Constitution to allow women to vote, 10 countries had already granted women the franchise. Yet many European countries did not allow women to vote until after World War II, including France, Greece, Italy, and Switzerland. In Latin America, Ecuador was the first to recognize women's political rights, in 1929; but women could not vote in Mexico until 1953. In Asia, women voted first in Mongolia, in 1923; then, with the U.S. occupation after 1945, women secured the right to vote in Japan and South Korea. The former European colonies in Af-

rica and Asia enfranchised women when they gained independence, from the late 1940s into the 1970s.

Historically, women began to demand the right to vote by claiming their equality: If all men are created equal, why not women? The American and British suffrage movements inspired "women's emancipation" efforts among educated female (and sometimes male) elites worldwide, and most contemporary feminist movements trace their roots to these stirrings at the turn of the century. The nineteenth-century European movements had a strong influence on the thinking of Friedrich Engels, who made gender equality a central tenet of socialist doctrine. A similar movement among the Russian intelligentsia ensured that the equality of women in political and economic life would be an important goal of the Soviet state—and subsequently of its Central and Eastern European satellites.

> *Historically, a country's level of economic development has not been a reliable indicator of women's representation.*

But if the logic existed to support women's claims to political equality, the facts on the ground did not. As educated women mobilized to demand the right to vote, men in all

JANE S. JAQUETTE *is chair of the department of diplomacy and world affairs and B. H. Orr professor of liberal arts at Occidental College. Her latest book* Trying Democracy: Women in Post–Authoritarian Politics in Latin America and Central and Eastern Europe *will be published by The Johns Hopkins University Press in 1998.*

countries largely resisted, with the result that most of the world's women gained this basic right of citizenship only in the last 50 years. Before women could vote, they organized to influence legislation, from the marriage and property rights acts of the mid-nineteenth century to the early twentieth century wave of Progressive legislation in the United States and Western Europe's generous maternal and protective labor laws.

However, the vote itself did not bring women into politics. On the contrary, some countries gave women the right to vote but not to run for office. In virtually every nation, women who tried to enter politics were subject to popular ridicule. Political parties routinely excluded women from decision-making positions, resisted nominating them as candidates, and denied their female candidates adequate campaign support.

Cultural factors partially explain the varying degrees of women's representation from region to region and country to country. Predictably, women in the Nordic and northern European countries, with long traditions of gender equality, have been the most successful in breaking through traditional resistance and increasing their representation. In contrast, those in Arab countries, with curbs against women in public life and contemporary pressures to abandon secular laws for religious rules, have consistently registered the lowest levels of female participation (and the lowest levels of democratization).

But "culture" does not fully explain why women in the United States and Great Britain, which rank high on various measures of gender equality, accounted for less than 7 percent of all parliamentarians as late as 1987. Nor have women been excluded from politics in all Islamic nations. The legislatures of Syria and Indonesia, while decidedly undemocratic, are composed of 10 to 12 percent women. Former prime ministers Benazir Bhutto of Pakistan and Khaleda Zia of Bangladesh have wielded major power in Muslim societies.

Historically, a country's level of development has not been a reliable indicator of women's representation. Of the 32 most developed countries that reported electoral data in 1975, 19 had fewer than 10 percent female legislators and 11 had fewer than 5 percent. In France, Greece, and Japan—all developed, industrialized countries—female members accounted for 2 percent or less of their legislatures.

Although more women than ever are working for wages, even an increase in female participation in the work force does not necessarily translate into greater political clout for women. In recent years, for example, much of the growth in participation has been in low-wage labor. And although women's managerial participation has increased dramatically in many countries, from New Zealand to Peru, women are still rarely found at the highest levels of corporate management and ownership. Their underrepresentation in top management limits the number of private sector women invited to enter government as high-level appointees; women's lower salaries, in turn, restrict an important source of financial support for female candidates.

One can, however, discern significant worldwide increases in female representation beginning in 1975, the year in which the United Nations held its first international women's conference. From 1975 to 1995, the number of women legislators doubled in the developed West; the global average rose from 7.4 percent to nearly 11 percent.

Between 1987 and 1995 in particular, women's representation registered a dramatic increase

Percent of Women in National Legislatures, by region, 1975–97

	1975	1987	1997*
Arab States	3.5	2.8	3.3
Asia	8.4	9.7	13.4
(Asia excluding China, Mongolia, N. Korea, Vietnam)†	(3.8)	(6.2)	(6.3)
Central and Eastern Europe and Former Soviet Union	23.3	23.1	11.5
Developed countries (excluding East Asia)	5.1	9.6	14.7
Latin America and the Caribbean	6.0	6.9	10.5
Nordic Countries	16.1	28.8	36.4

* 1997 statistics for lower houses and single house systems. (Mongolia excluded.)
† women's representation under party control

Sources: *Democracy Still in the Making: A World Comparative Study* (Geneva: Inter-Parliamentary Union, 1997) and *The World's Women, 1970–1990: Trends and Statistics* (New York: United Nations, 1991).

in the developed countries, Africa, and Latin America. Of the 32 women who have served as presidents or prime ministers during the twentieth century, 24 were in power in the 1990s. In the United States, women now make up 11.2 percent of Congress, about one-third the proportion in Nordic countries, but substantially higher than the 5 percent in 1987. And although only 23 women won seats in the Diet in Japan's 1996 elections, an unprecedented 153 women ran for office. In 1997, the Inter-Parliamentary Union reported only nine countries with no women in their legislatures. From 1987 to 1995, the number of countries without any women ministers dropped from 93 to 47, and 10 countries reported that women held more than 20 percent of all ministerial-level positions, although generally in "female" portfolios like health, education, and environment rather than the "power ministries" like finance and defense.

The only exception to the global acceleration in women's representation during the past decade is in the New Independent States of the former Soviet Union and the former members of the Eastern bloc. Here, representation has dropped from earlier highs under communist rule of 25 to 35 percent women (although they exercised little real power) to around 8 to 15 percent today, and numbers are lower in the largely Muslim states of Central Asia. Where women's representation is still under Communist Party control, as in China, North Korea, and Vietnam, women still account for about 20 percent of the national legislators.

THE GLOBALIZATION OF THE WOMEN'S MOVEMENT

Why the surge in women officeholders in the last 10 years?

Three interconnected reasons seem to stand out: First, the rise of women's movements worldwide has heightened women's awareness of their political potential and developed new issues for which women are ready to mobilize. Second, a new willingness by political parties and states to ease the constraints on women's access to politics, from increasing their recruitment pools to modifying electoral systems and adopting quotas. And third, as social issues supplant security concerns in the post–Cold War political environment, opportunities have opened for new styles of leadership and have reordered political priorities.

The recent wave of female mobilization is a response to a series of political and economic crises—and opportunities—over the last two decades. On the political front, women's groups like the Madres de la Plaza de Mayo (Argentine mothers who demonstrated on behalf of their "disappeared" husbands and children) helped to inspire the defense of human rights in Latin America and beyond. Women were also recognized as valued participants in the opposition to authoritarian rule in the former Soviet bloc, where they took up the cause of human rights when their husbands and sons were arrested—dissident Andrei Sakharov's wife, Yelena Bonner, is just one example. In Africa and Asia, women are increasingly regarded as important opposition figures. In South Africa, for example, women were among prominent anti-apartheid leaders and have helped to lead the new government-sponsored effort to develop a women's charter for the post–apartheid period. In Iran, women have played an impor-

---

Women on Women

"A man, who during the course of his life has never been elected anywhere, and who is named prime minister (it was the case with George Pompidou and Raymond Barre, who had never been elected to any position)—everyone found that absolutely normal. A woman who has been elected for 10 years at the National Assembly . . . at the regional level, who is the mayor of a city, it is as if she were coming out of nowhere."

—**Edith Cresson, former prime minister of France**

"I really do think that women are more cautious in adopting . . . decisions [to go to war]. . . . But I don't think that the woman will ever sacrifice the interests of the nation or the interest of the state due to . . . weakness."

—**Kazimiera Prunskiene,
former prime minister of Lithuania**

"The traditional issues we were steered into—child care, health care, and education—have now become the sexy issues of the decade."

—**Nancy K. Kopp, former speaker pro tem.
of the Maryland House of Delegates**

"Women cannot lead without men, but men have to this day considered themselves capable of leading without women. Women would always take men into consideration. That's the difference."

—**Vigdis Finnbogadóttir,
former president of Iceland**

"Do I have an option?"

—**Patricia Schroeder, former U.S. representative,
when asked by the press if she
was "running as a woman."**

Sources: Laura Liswood, *Women Word Leaders* (London: HarperCollins, 1994); Linda Witt, Karen M. Paget, & Glenna Matthews, *Running as a Woman: Gender and Power in American Politics* (New York: Free Press, 1994).

tant role in defining electoral outcomes, despite the conventional wisdom that they are powerless.

On the economic front, the widespread adoption of market-oriented reforms, often accompanied by austerity programs, has had a severe impact on many women, who in turn have organized against price rises and the loss of health care and other public services. Women created communal kitchens in Chile and Peru to help feed their communities. Other small-scale, self-help programs like the Grameen Bank in Bangladesh and the Self-Employed Women's Association in India were

---

The Old Girls Network

Historically, one of the greatest barriers to elected office for women has been inadequate financial support. Often lacking incumbent status or access to financial networks, they have had to build their own fund-raising networks from scratch.

One of the most successful such groups has been EMILY's List (EMILY stands for Early Money is Like Yeast), the first partisan organization set up to fund women candidates in the United States. Ironically for an organization that is now America's largest political action committee (PAC), its roots lie in a political defeat. In 1982, Harriet Woods won the Democratic primary for a Senate seat in Missouri but then received only token financial backing from her party. She called on Washington, D.C., philanthropist Ellen Malcolm for help. But the money proved to be too little and too late to counter her male opponent's negative advertising campaign. Stung by this defeat, Malcolm went on to found EMILY's List in 1985 to raise money for Democratic women candidates who support abortion rights (a.k.a., "pro-choice").

EMILY's List received a major boost in 1992, when the all-male Senate Judiciary Committee confirmed Clarence Thomas to the U.S. Supreme Court despite law professor Anita Hill's accusations of sexual harassment. A torrent of female outrage turned into a record flood of financial support for female candidates in that year's elections. EMILY's List grew from 3,000 to 23,000 members and raised $6 million. It also inspired several state-level imitators, including May's List in Washington State and the Minnesota $$ Million. And EMILY's List now has a number of Republican competitors, including WISH (Women in the Senate and House), which supports pro-choice female candidates, and the Women's Leadership Fund.

According to Rutgers University's Center for the American Woman and Politics, 11 national and 47 state or local PACs and donor networks now either give money predominantly to women or receive most of their contributions from women. Organizations to fund women candidates have been established in several other nations as well. In 1993, Britain's Labour Party launched EMILY's List U.K. In 1995, the Australian Labor Party decided to form its own version of EMILY's List to meet its target of a 35 percent female Parliament by 2002.

---

developed to meet women's needs for credit. The war in Bosnia put an international spotlight on rape as a weapon of war and led to the demand that "women's rights" be considered "human rights" rather than some different or lesser category of concern.

These efforts were reinforced by international connections, many of which were created by the U.N. Decade for Women (1976–85). Three times during the decade (in 1975, 1980, and 1985) and again in 1995, the United Nations convened official delegations from member countries to report on the status of women and to commit governments to remedy women's lack of access to political, economic, and educational resources. Not only did these conferences encourage a flurry of local and national organizing, but they produced parallel meetings of nongovernmental organizations (NGOs), including the nearly 30,000 women who participated in the NGO conference in Beijing in 1995.

The Decade for Women originally meant that women's issues were geared to the U.N. agenda, which in the 1970s focused on the creation of a "new international economic order" and a more equitable sharing of resources between North and South. By the mid-1980s, however, attention had shifted from integrating women into world development efforts to enhancing roles for women in the promotion of market economics and democracy. The turn toward democracy made it easier for women to seek explicitly political goals, and the footdragging by the U.N. and its member countries on implementing their international pledges helped to stimulate women's interest in increasing their political power.

BREAKING THE POLITICAL CLASS CEILING

Since some of the public policies holding women back from greater political power—particularly women's access to education—have been easing rapidly, attention has turned to other barriers. Chief among them have been the constraints on the pool of women available to run for office. Although women constitute a growing proportion of the rank and file in political parties, unions, and civil services, they still account for only a small proportion of the higher echelons that provide a springboard to higher political office.

Although women participate more actively in local government than they do at the national level, many more men make the jump from local to national leadership. One problem has been a lack of campaign funds. In the United States, women began to address that obstacle in the 1980s through innovative fund-raising strategies. In other countries, women have organized voting blocs to support female candidates. Yet there is only one women's political party, in Iceland, that has succeeded over time in electing women to office. By the mid-1990s, the European-based Inter-Parliamentary Union was holding meetings twice a year for female parliamentarians aimed at improving their electoral skills as well as their abilities to perform more effectively in office. In another innovative effort, a group called Women of Russia organized to stem the decline in women's representation under the new democratic electoral rules. Women of Russia surprised everyone by gathering over 100,000 signatures and winning 8 percent of the vote in the 1993 Duma elections, but in the 1995 elections they failed to maintain the minimum level of support necessary under Russian electoral rules. As a result of Women in Russia's initial success, however, other Russian parties are nominating more women.

Research has shown that different kinds of voting systems can dramatically affect women's chances of election. The widely accepted explanation for the relatively low numbers of female legislators in the United States and Britain is their "single-member district" electoral systems. When each district elects only one candidate, minority votes are lost. Significantly more women are elected in countries with electoral systems based on proportional representation (in which candidates are elected from party lists according to the percentage of total votes the party receives) or on at-large districts ("multi-member constituencies"). Several countries have experimented with different electoral systems, including mixed single-member and multi-member district systems, to improve the participation of underrepresented groups, particularly women.

The surest way to achieve an increased number of women in national legislatures is to adopt a quota system that requires a certain percentage of women to be nominated or elected. Although the issue of quotas is scarcely open to debate in the United States—where Lani Guinier's nomination for U.S. attorney general in 1993 was torpedoed by detractors' interpretations of essays she had written in support of "group" representation—many political parties (especially on the Left) and national legislatures around the world are experimenting with gender quotas. Quotas account for the high levels of female representation in the Nordic countries and for the recent doubling (to 18 percent) of the number of women in the House of Commons in Britain when the Labour Party swept the election. A quota law in Argentina increased the women in its house of representatives from 4 percent in 1991 to over 16 percent in 1993 and 28 percent in 1995. In Brazil, when quotas were used in the 1997 congressional elections, the number of women legislators increased by nearly 40 percent since the last elections.

Quotas are used in Taiwan, by some of the political parties in Chile, and are under active discussion in Costa Rica, Ecuador, Paraguay, South Korea, and several other countries. The Indian constitution now mandates that one-third of the seats in local government bodies be "reserved" for women, and Pakistan is debating a similar measure. In Mexico, the Institutional Revolutionary Party (PRI) and its leftist opposition have adopted quotas, while the right-of-center party accepts the goal but maintains that it can promote women as effectively without them. Japan has adopted measures to ensure that more women are appointed to ministerial posts, and Bangladesh, among other countries, is experimenting with quotas for top civil service jobs.

It is obvious that quotas increase the number of women officeholders, but why are they being adopted now? Even where quotas are not seen to violate fundamental notions of democracy, as they appear to be in the United States, there are powerful arguments against them. Some insist that they will ghettoize women legislators and their issues. Others object that quotas lead to "proxy" representation, where women legislators run as "fronts" for their husbands or other male interests. In India, for example, there are many anecdotal cases of this phenomenon, and in Argentina there are complaints that many of the women nominated by the majority Peronist Party (which pushed through the quota law) have been chosen because of their unquestioning loyalty to President Carlos Saul Menem rather than because of their qualifications as candidates—as if only women could be considered party hacks.

Despite the controversy quotas raise, they have become popular not only because women

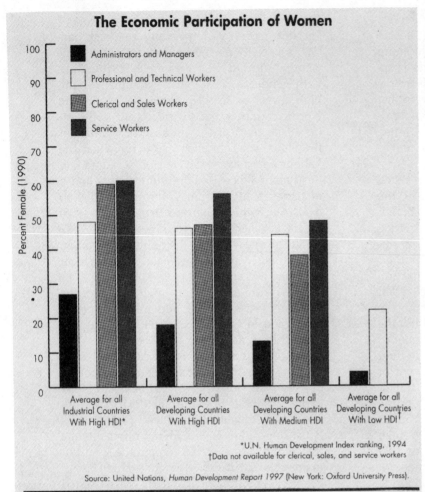

The Economic Participation of Women

- Administrators and Managers
- Professional and Technical Workers
- Clerical and Sales Workers
- Service Workers

Percent Female (1990)

Average for all Industrial Countries With High HDI*

Average for all Developing Countries With High HDI

Average for all Developing Countries With Medium HDI

Average for all Developing Countries With Low HDI†

*U.N. Human Development Index ranking, 1994
†Data not available for clerical, sales, and service workers

Source: United Nations, *Human Development Report 1997* (New York: Oxford University Press).

have organized to push for them, but—importantly—because more men have become convinced that quotas serve useful political goals in a more democratic environment. A sea change in attitudes about women in public office is occurring at a time when the number of countries under some form of democratic governance is expanding rapidly, giving new salience to the question of whether national legislatures are truly representative of pluralistic societies. Adequate representation of all groups could strengthen the consolidation of democracies that are open and responsive—and thus make them more durable.

WHAT DO WOMEN WANT?

The post–Cold War shift in national priorities from defense and security concerns to social and environmental issues also plays to women's strong suits. So do the negative impacts of economic globalization and structural adjustment policies, which have put the need for effective social safety nets high on domestic agendas. Many observers argue that the rejec-

tion of "unbridled capitalism" and the desire to retain social welfare policies explain the victories of the Labour Party in Britain, the socialists in France, and the electoral loss of the PRI in Mexico last July. Rightly or wrongly, many voters also associate market reforms with a rise in corruption. Despite accusations of corruption against leaders such as Pakistan's Bhutto and Tansu Ciller in Turkey, women's perceived "purity" and their status as outsiders, once considered political weaknesses, are now seen as strengths. In the last 10 years, it is not so much the case that women have come to politics; rather, politics has come to women.

If the trend continues, quotas will soon produce a quantum leap in women's political power. For the first time, women will form a "critical mass" of legislators in many countries, able to set new agendas and perhaps create new styles of leadership. How will women use their growing political influence?

One way to predict the direction of change is to look at how the political attitudes of women differ from those of men. Surveys show that one of the most persistent gender differences regards attitudes toward peace and war: Women are more pacifistic than men, less likely to favor defense spending, or to support aggressive policies abroad. Recent interviews of women heads of state show that most believe that they are more committed to peace than their male counterparts. Historically and today, women and women leaders are more interested in the so-called "soft" issues, including the environment and social welfare. On some measures, women are more conservative than men: They are less likely to vote for the parties on the Left, and rather than pursue their own self-interests, they more often mobilize for defensive reasons—namely to protect the interests of the family. As a result, these tendencies will probably place more focus on policies to support the family and to strengthen local communities.

But women are far from conservative in one important sense: Women are more likely than men to support state regulation of business to protect the consumer and the environment and to assure that the needs of society's weakest members are addressed. Because women are often more skeptical than men about the effectiveness of market reforms, the election of more women may signal a softening of some of reform's harsher aspects. The market's continued dominance in global politics will reinforce women s efforts to improve their access to the resources that count, from education and credit to the ownership of land and housing.

Women who find themselves experiencing real power for the first time may decide to try out blanket initiatives in areas that they believe male leaders have traditionally neglected: declarations banning war and legislation on children's rights and social or political morality.

However, radical change is unlikely. Predictions that women will act as a bloc have never been borne out in the past. Like their male counterparts, female officeholders come from all parts of the ideological spectrum and depend on the support of diverse and often divided constituencies. Women leaders are not necessarily pacificists or environmentally oriented. While former prime minister Gro Harlem Brundtland of Norway or Ireland's president Mary Robinson may support the "soft" issues, Indira Gandhi or Margaret Thatcher is capable of using force to achieve her ends.

Further, few of the initiatives on those social issues mobilizing women today directly confront male power. Global support for efforts to stem violence against women is an important exception. Antidiscrimination legislation has been developed at the international level through the U.N. Convention on the Elimination of All Forms of Discrimination Against Women—which has been ratified by 160 countries, but not the United States. The implementation of the instrument by signatories, however, lags far behind. And women leaders themselves disagree on many of the issues affecting women most, from reproductive rights and family law to genital mutilation.

Today, women are recruited aggressively into politics not to right past inequities or to recognize their equal citizenship—but to bring a different, explicitly female perspective to the political arena and to appeal to the women's vote. Whether the rationale for increasing female representation is equality or difference, women will have an unprecedented opportunity to put their stamp on politics and to increase the range of alternatives available to policymakers across the globe.

WANT TO KNOW MORE?

Merilee Karl's compendium *Women and Empowerment: Participation and Decision-Making* (London: Zed Books, 1995) discusses women's participation in a range of institutional settings from an activist perspective. A rich and thoughtful treatment of women's political participation covering a variety of cases is *Women and Politics Worldwide,* Barbara Nelson & Najma Chowdhury, eds. (New Haven: Yale University Press, 1994). Laura Liswood interviews 15 female politicians in *Women World Leaders* (London: Pandora, 1994). For information on the impact of electoral systems, consult Wilma Rule & Joseph F. Zimmerman's *Electoral Systems in Comparative Perspective: Their Impact on Women and Minorities* (Westport, Connecticut: Greenwood Press, 1994). The story of women's ascent into U.S. politics is found in Linda Witt, Karen M. Paget, & Clenna Matthews' *Running as a Woman: Gender and Power in American Politics* (New York: The Free Press, 1994). Nancy Adler & Dafna Izraeli, on the other hand, present notable research on women in the private sector in *Competitive Frontiers: Women Managers in a Global Economy* (Cambridge: Blackwell, 1994).

A key source for data on women in power is the United Nations' *Human Development Report 1995* (New York: Oxford University Press, 1995), which is dedicated to gender comparisons. For some historical statistics, see *The World's Women, 1970–1990: Trends and Statistics* (New York: United Nations, 1991). Updates and special studies on women's political participation are available through the Inter-Parliamentary Union's Web page. Access this site and others on women in political and economic power through **www.foreign-policy.com.**

The End of the Hunting Season in History

SHIMON PERES *has been at the center of Israeli political life for decades. He has not only been both foreign minister and prime minister, but also the shepherd of Israel's nuclear capacity and the architect of peace with Israel's Arab neighbors. In the following essay Shimon Peres displays the visionary prowess that has made him one of the late 20th century's leading statesmen. His most recent book is* Battling for Peace *(1995).*

JERUSALEM — The transition from the 20th century to the 21st century will be more than a chronological event. It will involve a change of historical period, a change of era.

The key events of the last decade, which failed to obey the standard rules of change, are a premonition of the times to come. Classic political instruments, such as the army, parties, or even superpowers, have had no role to play at all.

Thus, communism collapsed in the Soviet Union without aid from the Red Army — neither for those that supported it, nor for those who wished to rid themselves of it. As the Soviet Union was overthrown, the army remained neutral, or more precisely, on the sidelines.

One of the most captivating images during the attempted revolution against Mikhail Gorbachev was that of a battalion of Red Army soldiers in front of the Russian Parliament, Moscow's "White House." The soldiers were indifferent, with a "who cares" attitude, when suddenly an old Russian woman, a *babushka,* went up to them and said, "Children, what are you doing here? Go home!" It was almost as if the *babushka* were the sole commander of the Red Army.

Also, the Communist party was not beaten by another party opposing it. The Communist party was beaten by its own children and not by its rivals. The Soviet Union did not come apart under the impact of American pressure, European intervention, or a Chinese threat. The pressure did not come from without; it sprang from within. This gigantic change in human organization occurred without the army's guns, without political parties' banners, and without superpower threats.

Science knows no borders, technology has no flag, information has no passport.

The same is true of apartheid in South Africa. Also, what happened in the Israeli-Palestinian conflict is very similar. It began in the darkness of calm Norwegian nights, without a single gunshot, without a single demonstration, without the dictates of a superpower. Conversely, traditional political instruments have proven completely ineffective in Bosnia, Somalia or Burundi. The superpowers, armies, and parties which have intervened in these countries have not been successful. Is it merely chance, or are we observing the first signs of a new world which works according to rules as yet unknown to us?

Why have traditional political instruments not worked? What were the alternative means that enabled these profound changes? Is it possible to answer that it is not the instruments which have changed but rather the substance?

The armies did not move because their means of action had lost its effect. In the three above-mentioned cases — Russia, Africa, and the Middle East — the conflict was not territorial; it was not an issue of protecting the motherland, or taking land from other peoples. The issue was a struggle for a fundamental change, a change in the very content of existence. The army understood that it was not capable of protecting the supposed "status quo," because it could no longer withstand the test of reality, it could no longer endure, and there was no point in defending it. Yet, the army in and of itself was not able to bring about a new situation.

The Red Army was well aware that it could not ensure Russia's place in the new situation because nuclear missiles and weapons had to a large extent eliminated the military

 From *New Pespectives Quarterly*, Fall 1995, pp. 49-52. © 1995 by Blackwell Publishers. Reprinted by permission.

option from the list of possible actions to take in order to secure a definitive advantage. The Red Army knew what the American and all other armies around the world know: missiles do not take the time factor into account (they move at a staggering speed), nor do they take into account the land factor (they care not for mountains, snow, rivers, borders or buildings); missiles move at a height well above that of strategic space. The nuclear weapon is an absolute weapon, against which there is no defense, and no one is prepared to accept the damage that this weapon can cause.

The elimination of weapons-based strategies has been caused by more than the new military means. The strategic objectives themselves have been profoundly changed. Power and well-being no longer stem from material sources — territorial area, natural resources, population size, geographic location — but from intellectual dimensions — science, technology, information. Armies can conquer only material things, and not those which are knowledge-based.

True, there are still generals who don the uniforms of the past, but they are hard pressed to find fronts where their armies can be used. I am not arguing that danger no longer exists, or that there will be no more wars. However, I believe that the wars to come will be not those of the strong against the weak—wars of conquest—but rather wars of the weak against the strong—wars of protest. These wars will be more popular than "professional." The weapons are more likely to be stones rather than tanks and knives rather than cannons. Whether the traditional army will play a central role is doubtful.

A FUTURE WITHOUT PARTIES OR SUPERPOWERS | Political parties also find themselves in an unexpected situation. I do not think that ideology is dead. Mankind needs ideology and belief for the elevation of its intellect. However, current ideologies, which pit East against West and North against South, are no longer pertinent. While armies exist in order to provide protection against external threats, parties must ensure internal security, be it based on justice or on economic efficiency. Justice or the realization of efficiency thus no longer depend on the status quo but on that which remains to be created.

Further, it has become clear that the great challenges of our era transcend national frameworks. Science knows no borders, technology has no flag, information has no passport. The new elements are above and beyond states. All countries have access, and can decide that knowledge is more important than material things, that markets are more important than states, that iron or silk curtains can no longer stop currents of information from arriving at our doorstep. Information moves today like the air that we breathe, and it is impossible to stop it.

The lot of the superpowers is similar to those ideological parties that have become obsolete. When the Soviet Union collapsed, the United States lost its main enemy, or rather its main challenge. It is even possible to go so far as to say that the very basis of the foreign policy of the superpower that is America has been shaken, since it was centered on the communist enemy. Foreign policy was mainly concerned with enemies. Yet, the world of enemies has disappeared and the world of dangers has taken its place. The superpowers were accustomed to fighting enemies, large or small. They were not organized properly to cope with danger, be it from human poverty or environmental pollution.

The American president can well persuade the American people and Congress to give him the soldiers and means to fight an enemy of flesh and bone, with a known location, size, strength and identity. Yet, the American president cannot convince his people to send soldiers to the contorted

Markets are more important than states. Iron or silk curtains can no longer stop currents of information.

battlefield in Bosnia, just as he has difficulty in marshaling the means to fight hunger, terror, drugs, air pollution, desertification, or even the proliferation of nuclear weapons. It is possible to mobilize superpower scale means, but only against another superpower. Yet, the dangers do not hail from superpowers. They seem far off and poorly defined.

THE MEDIA AND LEADERS | With the change in the role of the army in our era, the lack of ideological pertinence and the increasing evidence of the weaknesses of the superpowers comes a loss of confidence in leaders and a decrease in their importance. This is true of both those leaders that sought to arouse their people and those that sought to dazzle them. The people no longer look up, but rather, straight at the tables of knowledge.

Increasingly, public opinion tends to view leaders as if they were characters in a television program, and no longer see them as guides capable of pointing out the path of this new era. Yet, the aspirations and needs of the people haven't disappeared. On the contrary, contemporary change is a result of bottom-up movement. It is not imposed from the top down. If neither the armies, nor the parties, nor the superpowers, have eliminated communism or apartheid, or resolved the conflict between Israel and the Palestinians, then who is responsible for these immense changes? It would not be an exaggeration to answer that it is television, radio and newspaper audiences. In other words, it is the people themselves.

The Romanian cameras were intended to magnify the rituals of dictatorship. Yet, on television, Nicolae Ceaucescu ceased to be frightening. When, one day in 1989, a few people dared to spurn the dictator on TV, it was a revelation for those who hated from a distance that true power was on their side. Ceaucescu's stupor left them dumbfounded. They had not pondered any alternatives. But, he understood that his only alternative was to flee.

No doubt, in the beginning of his career, Gorbachev had a great deal of support because he was the first leader who didn't place blame for the failure of communism on his predecessors. He made the system responsible. The young people of Moscow and Leningrad sensed that he was telling the truth when he blamed the system.

This negative truth did the job, but Gorbachev had no positive truth. Neither he nor his partisans were able to provide an alternative. They thought that the simple fact of liberation from the existing situation was somehow enough. No doubt they believed the old Marxist slogan that "philosophers have interpreted the world in different ways, what is important is to transform it."

It has become apparent that a fair economy is not purely mechanical. The economy is also based on deep human values. There can be no flourishing economy without an education system for the entire population.

Outside the Soviet Union, what played an important role was not NATO's strength, but what was called with a hint of mockery, "human rights." This subject suddenly became the cornerstone of the Helsinki Conference. This subject found itself at the heart of the East-West conflict. The communists did not know how to defend themselves against Western accusations of human rights violations. What started as a little religious ritual quickly ended up as a powerful movement of strategic importance.

This was also true of South Africa. Frederik De Klerk, a man of strong religious sentiment, felt that he was going against divine will by continuing to impose the white minority on the black majority. In Israel too, the starting point for the negotiations with the Palestinians was a moral issue. Many of us were not prepared to lend a permanent status to our domination of another people against its will. Never in our history have we dominated another people. We have

always thought that the highest expression for a people is self-mastery. To us, the true hero is the person who can master his instincts.

The power of governments was largely due to the monopoly they had over the flow of knowledge. But, ever since knowledge has become available to all, a new dynamic has been set in motion which can no longer be stopped. Each and every citizen can become his own diplomat, his own administrator, his own governor. The knowledge to do so is available to him. Also, he is no longer inclined to accept directives from on high as self-evident. He judges for himself.

Today, it is over the radio — or TV, cable and the Internet — that revolutions are made. They are broadcast, modemed, cabled and faxed directly into people's homes. Governments are not always aware of the fire that is smoldering, or the smoke rising from the flames.

This revolution is a perpetual one, not an institutional one. It cannot be stopped and does not rest for a minute. It moves forward changing things that have been set since time immemorial.

The poor peoples of Asia have understood that by adopting new economic rules, they too can soar to economic peaks as successfully as the peoples of North America and Europe. They have learned that there was no "southern" or "northern" economy, that there was not white, black or yellow people's economy. There is a good economy and a bad economy. All can and must choose the good. Rather than putting politics above the economy, they have understood that it is better to put the economy at the very heart of politics.

This is because the economy is in the service of people while, in most cases, politics serves states and ruling elites. This is especially so since it has become apparent that a fair economy is not purely mechanical. The economy is also based on deep human values. There can be no flourishing economy without an education system for the entire population. There can be no flourishing economy without an ever increasing level of science and technology; there can be no flourishing economy without freedom of research, without freedom of movement, and freedom of speech. There can be no flourishing economy without equality of men and women — because if only half the population participates in development, compared to economies where the majority of the population cooperates in the effort, there will be no economic prosperity. There can be no flourishing economy without democracy. The economy is first and foremost a human issue.

THE CHALLENGE OF IMAGINATION | For all of these mind-bending transformations, we have seen not the end of change, but only the beginning. The extraordinary revolution which appeared during the 20th century started with the technological revolution which carries the electronic revolution at its core: Both have had consequences at a strategic, political level and at an economic one. However, it is already obvious that yet another revolution awaits us, even more laden with consequences: that of genetic engineering.

Genes are being mastered in order to change man, to change the environment, to change the world. The electronic and technological revolution caught us short. We were not intellectually prepared, and we still hesitate to get our feet wet. The genetic engineering revolution will find us even more perplexed. Morally and intellectually we have been primarily concerned with what should be done with these new technologies. Henceforth, it will be necessary to consider what we will do with ourselves.

It is difficult to rid ourselves of preconceived ideas, to accept the new situation. It is so pleasant to yield to memories. What we remember is that of which we are conscious. If something is unpleasant, one quite simply forgets it. It is much more difficult to imagine. He who thinks along the lines of the future realizes that he is impotent because he does not know. Furthermore, where the future is concerned, one must never forget anything. It could be dangerous. We probably have no choice but to leave the places in history that we have known and move into the exhibition halls of the new world, even when it is difficult to know what awaits us there. One thing is certain: Anyone who wishes to buy a ticket for the 21st century need not arm himself with a bow and arrow, or even a cannon and guns. The hunting season is over.

There is no longer any need to hunt because the real attractions are no longer venison, so to speak, but our spirit of creation. The real calories we need to live as human beings will be created by our ability to innovate. To enter the 21st century, we must go as human beings, flashing not our hunting permit, but our act of birth.

During the hunting era, food was lacking. Man had to dominate beasts to put food on the table. We also had to fight our fellow hunters to ensure a larger share of the food. Today, we are discovering that the breadth of material and spiritual sustenance is a function of our intellectual capacity. We are no longer on hunting ground, but rather in a scientific space. Poor peoples can help themselves if they know how to eliminate preconceived notions, obsolete wars and their backwardness in the area of education. They can help themselves more than can the rich peoples, as long as they avoid waste and gear their resources to their true potential.

Public opinion views leaders as if they were characters on TV and no longer sees them as guides capable of pointing out the path of this new era.

The great wastes of our times are the arms race, government by dictators and cultural blindness. It is no longer possible to get rich through war: Dictatorship is a waste of resources to glorify the head of state. Cultural blindness prevents the young from tasting the fruit of the tree of science.

There is not much left to learn from the blood of Abel shed by Cain, nor from the adventures of Nimrod the hunter. Perhaps the few lines engraved on the tablets of law brought down from Mount Sinai by Moses may still truly be of help to us. Even the tablets were broken—their message floats on the winds of the future. In the 21st century mankind will have to face conditions unknown to him. Yet, it is only then that he will be able to fully play the role for which he is destined.

Reassessing the Economic Assumption

Our goals of a clean environment and a good quality of life for all cannot possibly be met by a world system bent on unlimited economic growth.

By Willis W. Harman

Is it rational for the economy to be the paramount institution in modern society? And for social decisions to be influenced predominantly by economic logic and economic values?

During the twentieth century, the scientific world view increasingly challenged the tenets of the Judeo-Christian tradition. Meanings, values, and goals stemming from that tradition grew weaker, and the market became increasingly recognized as an efficient decision maker.

As materialistic, economic values and goals came to replace more-transcendentally based values, market-oriented decision makers made increasingly poorer decisions. For example, tremendous pressures are placed on corporate CEOs by the markets to make decisions that are smart in terms of short-run financial return but socially and ecologically ill-advised in the long run.

There is now a growing disparity between the values of modern society and the goals it purports to accept. Consider these widely accepted goals: to meet basic human needs of all people; to have a healthful environment; to guarantee liberty, fairness, equity, and the rule of law throughout the world; and to eliminate poverty.

Now consider what our behaviors and policies imply about our basic assumptions: that the economy is and should be the dominant institution in modern society, that sustained economic growth is necessary to provide jobs and to provide the resources to clean up the environment, that steady increase in productivity is necessary for continued gains in standards of living, that technological advance and competition are essential for progress, and that free, unregulated markets generally result in the most efficient and socially optimal allocation of resources.

These underlying assumptions are now completely incompatible with our goals, even if they seemed to work well in the past. For example, there is a strong correlation between economic product and environmental deterioration, as evidenced by pollution, toxic chemical concentrations, forest depletion, desertification, thinning ozone layer, global warming, and so on.

Diversity of plant and animal species in an ecosystem leads to resilience, while an ecosystem consisting primarily of one species is fragile, susceptible to being wiped out by disease or invader. But the modern economy is steadily reducing biodiversity. The species that survive will be those that are useful in terms of the economy. We can be reasonably certain that this will prove to be an inadequate criterion for a healthy ecosystem.

An example can be seen in agriculture. Unlike other industries, which extract, use, and discard resources, agriculture replenishes resources—it takes, uses, and returns. But modern agriculture is treated like other industries. It is extremely productive in terms of output per person-hour or per acre of land, but it is also extremely expensive in terms of soil loss, water and soil pollution, alienation of farmers, decay of rural communities, and increasing vulnerability of the food-supply system due to reliance on single crops. The market is unable to assign a value to many factors vital to sound agriculture, such as topsoil, ecosystem, family, and community. And the excessive

From *The Futurist*, July/August 1996, pp. 13-15. © 1996 by The World Future Society, Bethesda, MD. http://www.wfs.org/wfs. Reprinted by permission.

emphasis on productivity causes overproduction, which leads to low prices and economic ruin.

More! More! More!

Ever-increasing productivity is seen as essential to economic health, with competition as the main driving force. But increased productivity is failing to meet the goal of improving the quality of life for the average citizen. This is partly because so much of the productivity increase is eaten up by the peripheral support structure. As the service sector becomes larger and larger, it dilutes the productivity increases of the sector that is producing tangible goods. In addition, a large part of the increased productivity goes into servicing corporate debt.

In an economy-dominated value system there is a pervasive belief that quality of life is to be measured in technological terms, that technological advance equals societal progress.

Some technological advance does indeed add to quality of life. But new technology is often developed and applied without being guided by a strong moral sense and social vision. Technological advance often replaces high-paid, low-tech workers with low-cost automated processes and low-wage foreign labor. It pushes those formerly high-paid production workers into low-paying service jobs and shifts wealth from displaced workers to those who own or control the technology.

Progress is the driving force behind all the assumptions at the heart of our economy-dominated society. Material progress assumes that what we have is never enough. We must continue to accumulate and consume forever, with no upper limit. But the idea of progress loses all meaning if progress no longer implies the democratization of affluence—improving the quality of life *for all*. It was the prospect of universal abundance that made progress a morally compelling ideology in the past.

In a modern industrial democracy, the tendency for power to accumulate in the hands of a mighty few is held in check by a variety of regulating measures, such as antitrust laws, fair trade agreements, graduated income tax, collective bargaining, regulatory commissions, and so forth. But these mechanisms have proven inadequate to combat the forces bringing about an increasingly inequitable distribution.

This failure is partly due to the growth of giant transnational corporations with enormous economic power and geographic spread. But more fundamentally, the mechanisms fail because the basic materialistic paradigm itself contains no rationale or incentive for more

> *"The penchant of the modern world to judge all things in terms of economics ... is rooted in the materialism of the scientific world view."*

equitable distribution of power and resources—a rationale that was once provided by society's altruistic, religious ethic.

It is obvious that extending Western consumption patterns to the rest of the world would have a staggering impact on the earth. But continuing the present patterns of the enormous and growing disparity between the world's rich and poor peoples will lay the groundwork for worldwide conflict and eventual social carnage. On no grounds are the industrial paradigm and late-twentieth-century capitalism more bitterly challenged.

The Global Development Dilemma

There is perhaps no more misused word in the English language than "development." We speak of land development and typically mean stripping the land of vegetation and paving it over with asphalt. We speak of human development and typically mean destroying traditional community and conditioning people to survive in an urban environment. We speak of economic development or improving well-being, but typically we mean increasing economic production and consumption.

Clearly these concepts of development do not lead to a long-term viable global future, or to shared well-being even in the medium term. There is, indeed, a development dilemma of global proportions.

The dilemma is that the global system in its present form is incompatible with an ecologically sustainable global society; it is incapable of resolving the plight of the poorest countries. The possible paths of global development that seem to be economically feasible are not ecologically or socially plausible, and those that are ecologically feasible and humanistically desirable are not economically or politically feasible.

To illustrate this dilemma, let us imagine three possible futures.

Scenario 1: All developing countries succeed in following the example of the industrialized and newly industrialized countries. The result: The planet is hard-pressed to accommodate six or eight billion people living high-consumption lifestyles; intense political battles arise over environmental and quality-of-life issues.

Scenario 2: The high-consumption societies continue to be high-consumption, while the poorer countries remain low-consumption (i.e., poor), with low per capita demand on resources and the environment. The result: a global system with such persisting disparity of income and wealth that vicious "wars of redistribution" (with terrorism as the main weapon) are unavoidable.

Scenario 3: High-consumption societies voluntarily cut consumption to ameliorate some of the problems. The result: severe unemployment problems in the formerly high-consumption societies.

The fact is, all past assumptions about the future of the planet are being challenged by the present reality. There is no consensus on what constitutes a viable pattern of global development, but it is increasingly clear that present trends do not: The present domination of economic values is incompatible with a wise relationship to the earth and its resources; the materialistic paradigm systematically marginalizes people who have no meaningful roles in the society—i.e., with no jobs; it results in a society that habitually confuses means (e.g., economic and technological achievement) with goals; and it persistently endangers the future of the human species with arms races that appear to be endemic to the system.

What has led to this global dilemma? We treat knowledge and an ever-increasing fraction of overall human activity as commodities in the mainstream economy. We assume that an individual's primary relationship to society is through a job. Our social thinking is dominated by concepts of competition, commercial secrecy, money exchange, and scarcity, when in fact one of our main "problems" for the future is our capacity to overproduce.

What Is Our Purpose?

The key issue as we look ahead is not how we can stimulate more demand for goods and services and information. It is not about creating more jobs in the mainstream economy. The key question is much more fundamental: *What is the central purpose of highly industrialized societies?*

The answer becomes apparent from the emerging values and beliefs

about the nature of human beings. *The central purpose of highly industrialized societies is to advance human growth and development to the fullest extent, to promote human learning in the broadest possible definition.* The key task is to find our deepest meaning in the quality of all our relationships, with one another and with nature.

Granted, up to now it has been extremely difficult for a society or a nation to pursue a development path different from the path dictated by the mainstream world economic system. However, several factors will make diverse development paths more feasible in the future.

One of these factors is the growing realization that the past ways of development are, in the end, not good for the planet and not even good for people. The highly industrialized countries are going to have to find some development path for themselves that, without unduly sacrificing quality of life, does not make such voracious demands upon the resource base and effect such gross insults to the ecological and life-support systems of the planet.

A second important factor is the growing crisis in meaning in the developed world. Just as individual riches are not always found to produce a happy life, so the allurements of affluent industrial society fail to provide the kind of shared meanings that make a society cohesive and inspire mutual loyalty.

The penchant of the modern world to judge all things in terms of economics, with its inherent short-term

focus, is rooted in the materialism of the present scientific world view. In that picture, higher values have little force, since they are not judged to be reality based. Fortunately, there is now a movement toward a more transcendental world view. As that movement continues to gain force, the legitimacy of the old order will be increasingly withdrawn.

There is nothing more crucial to this time of transition than sharing with one another our interpretations of why the transformation is necessary or seems to be happening. There is no conversation more critical today than that around these questions: Growth—in what sense, and to what end? Development—for what? What is the right development for this society? What is viable global development? What is a "world that works for everyone"? What are the requisites for achieving that goal? What are the costs of not achieving it?

About the Author
Willis W. Harman is president of the Institute of Noetic Sciences, P.O. Box 909, Sausalito, California 94966. Telephone 415/331-5650; fax 415/331-5673.

This article is based on a longer monograph, "Our Hopeful Future: Creating a Sustainable Global Society," which is available for $10 ($12 outside the United States) from Maya Porter, Porter McGinn Associates, 11828 Smoketree Road, Potomac, Maryland 20854. Telephone 301/983-8198.

Glossary

Absolute poverty: The condition of people whose incomes are insufficient to keep them at a subsistence level.

Adjudication: The legal process of deciding an issue through the courts.

African, Caribbean, and Pacific Countries (ACP): Fifty-eight countries associated with the European Community.

African National Congress (ANC): South African organization founded in 1912 in response to the taking of land from Africans and the restrictions on their employment and movement. Following attempts at peaceful resistance, its leaders were tried for treason and imprisoned. In 1990, ANC de facto leader Nelson Mandela was released from prison, and a continued resistance against the apartheid state grew. The ANC was legalized in 1991.

Airborne Warning and Control System (AWACS): Flying radar stations that instantaneously identify all devices in the air within a radius of 240 miles and detect movement of land vehicles.

Air-launched cruise missile (ALCM): A cruise missile carried by and launched from an aircraft.

Antiballistic missile (ABM): A missile that seeks out and destroys an incoming enemy missile in flight before the latter reaches its target. It is not effective against MIRVs.

Apartheid: A system of laws in the Republic of South Africa that segregates and politically and economically discriminates against non-European groups.

Appropriate technology: Also known as intermediate technology. It aims at using existing resources by making their usage more efficient or productive but adaptable to the local population.

Arms control: Any measure limiting or reducing forces, regulating armaments, and/or restricting the deployment of troops or weapons.

Arms race: The competitive or cumulative improvement of weapons stocks (qualitatively or quantitatively), or the buildup of armed forces based on the conviction of two or more actors that only by trying to stay ahead in military power can they avoid falling behind.

Association of Southeast Asian Nations (ASEAN): A regional regrouping made up of Indonesia, the Philippines, Singapore, and Thailand.

Atomic bomb: A weapon based on the rapid splitting of fissionable materials, thereby inducing an explosion with three deadly results: blast, heat, and radiation.

Autarky: Establishing economic independence.

Balance of payments: A figure that represents the net flow of money into and out of a country due to trade, tourist expenditures, sale of services (such as consulting), foreign aid, profits, and so forth.

Balance of trade: The relationship between imports and exports.

Ballistic missile: A payload propelled by a rocket, which assumes a free-fall trajectory when thrust is terminated. Ballistic missiles could be of short range (SRBM), intermediate range (IRBM), medium range (MRBM), and intercontinental (ICBM).

Bantustans: Ten designated geographical areas or "homelands" for each African ethnic group created under the apartheid government of South Africa. Beginning in the late 1970s, South Africa instituted a policy offering "independence" to the tribal leaders of these homelands. The leaders of four homeland governments accepted independent status, but no outside actors recognized these artificial entities as independent nation-states. Under the terms of the new constitution, all homeland citizens are now considered to be citizens of South Africa.

Barrel: A standard measure for petroleum, equivalent to 42 gallons or 158.86 liters.

Basic human needs: Adequate food intake (in terms of calories, proteins, and vitamins), drinking water free of disease-carrying organisms and toxins, minimum clothing and shelter, literacy, sanitation, health care, employment, and dignity.

Bilateral diplomacy: Negotiations between two countries.

Bilateral (foreign) aid: Foreign aid given by one country directly to another.

Binary (chemical) munitions/weapons: Nerve gas canisters composed of two separate chambers containing chemicals that become lethal when mixed. The mixing is done when the canister is fired. Binary gas is preferred for its relative safety in storage and transportation.

Biosphere: The environment of life and living processes at or near Earth's surface, extending from the ocean floors to about 75 kilometers into the atmosphere. It is being endangered by consequences of human activities such as air and water pollution, acid rain, radioactive fallout, desertification, toxic and nuclear wastes, and the depletion of nonrenewable resources.

Bipolar system: A world political system in which power is primarily held by two international actors.

Buffer stocks: Reserves of commodities that are either increased or decreased whenever necessary to maintain relative stability of supply and prices.

Camp David Agreements/Accords: Agreements signed on September 17, 1978, at Camp David—a mountain retreat for the U.S. president in Maryland—by President Anwar al-Sadat of Egypt and Prime Minister Menachem Begin of Israel, and witnessed by President Jimmy Carter.

Capitalism: An economic system based on the private ownership of real property and commercial enterprise, competition for profits, and limited government interference in the marketplace.

Cartel: An international agreement among producers of a commodity that attempts to control the production and pricing of that commodity.

CBN weapons: Chemical, biological, and nuclear weapons.

Chemical Weapons Convention Treaty: Signed in 1993, the treaty requires its 130 signatories to eliminate all chemical weapons by the year 2005 and to submit to rigorous inspection.

Cold war: A condition of hostility that existed between the U.S. and the Soviet Union in their struggle to dominate the world scene following World War II. It ended with the collapse of the Soviet Union in 1991.

Collective security: The original theory behind UN peacekeeping. It holds that aggression against one state is aggression against all and should be defeated by the collective action of all.

Commodity: The unprocessed products of mining and agriculture.

Common Heritage of Mankind: A 1970 UN declaration that states that the "seabed and ocean floor, and the subsoil thereof, beyond the limits of national jurisdiction . . . , as well as the resources of the area, are the common heritage of mankind."

Common Market: A customs union that eliminates trade barriers within a group and establishes a common external tariff on imports from nonmember countries.

Commonwealth of Independent States (CIS): In December 1991 the Soviet Union was dissolved and fifteen independent countries were formed: Armenia, Azerbaijan, Byelorussia (Belarus), Estonia, Georgia, Kazakhstan, Kirghizia (Kyrgyzstan), Latvia, Lithuania, Moldavia (Moldova), Russia, Tadzhikistan (Tajikistan), Turkmenistan, Ukraine, and Uzbekistan. Some of the republics have since changed their names. CIS represents a collective term for the group of republics.

Compensatory Financing Facility: An IMF program established in 1963 to finance temporary export shortfalls, as in coffee, sugar, or other cyclically prone export items.

Concessional loans: Loans given to LLDCs by MBDs that can be repaid in soft (nonconvertible) currencies and with nominal or no interest over a long period of time.

Conditionality: A series of measures that must be taken by a country before it could qualify for loans from the International Monetary Fund.

Conference on International Economic Cooperation (CIEC): A conference of 8 industrial nations, 7 oil-producing nations, and 12 developing countries held in several sessions between December 1975 and June 1977. It is composed of four separate commissions (energy, raw materials, development, and financing). It is the forum of the North-South dialogue between rich and poor countries.

Conference on Security and Cooperation in Europe (CSCE): Series of conferences among 51 NATO, former Soviet bloc, and neutral European countries (52 counting Serbia or rump Yugoslavia). Established by 1976 Helsinki Accords. There are plans to establish a small, permanent CSCE headquarters and staff.

Consensus: In conference diplomacy, a way of reaching agreements by negotiations and without a formal vote.

Counterforce: The use of strategic nuclear weapons for strikes on selected military capabilities of an enemy force.

Countervalue: The use of strategic nuclear weapons for strikes on an enemy's population centers.

Cruise missile: A small, highly maneuverable, low-flying, pilotless aircraft equipped with accurate guidance systems that periodically readjusts its trajectory. It can carry conventional or nuclear warheads, can be short-range or long-range, and can be launched from the air (ALLUM), the ground (GLCM), or the sea (SLCM).

Cultural imperialism: The attempt to impose your own value systems on others, including judging others by how closely they conform to your norms.

Current dollars: The value of the dollar in the year for which it is being reported. Sometimes called inflated dollars. Any currency can be expressed in current value. *See* **Real dollars.**

Decision making: The process by which humans choose which policy to pursue and which actions to take in support of policy goals. The study of decision making seeks to identify patterns in the way that humans make decisions. This includes gathering information, analyzing information, and making choices. Decision making is a complex process that relates to personality and other human traits, to the sociopolitical setting in which decision makers function, and to the organizational structures involved.

Declaration of Talloires: A statement issued in 1981 by Western journalists who opposed the UNESCO-sponsored New World Information and Communication Order, at a meeting in Talloires, France.

Delivery systems or vehicles or launchers: Land-based missiles (ICBMs), submarine-launched missiles (SLBMs), and long-range bombers capable of delivering nuclear weapons.

Dependencia model: The belief that the industrialized North has created a neocolonial relationship with the South in which the LDCs are dependent on and disadvantaged by their economic relations with the capitalist industrial countries.

Deployment: The actual positioning of weapons systems in a combat-ready status.

Détente: A relaxation of tensions or a decrease in the level of hostility between opponents on the world scene.

Deterrence: Persuading an opponent not to attack by having enough forces to disable the attack and/or launch a punishing counterattack.

Developed countries (DCs): Countries with relatively high per capita GNP, education, levels of industrial development and production, health and welfare, and agricultural productivity.

Developing countries (also called less developed countries): These countries are mainly raw materials producers for export with high growth rates and inadequate infrastructures in transportation, educational systems, and the like. There is, however, a wide variation in living standards, GNPs, and per capita incomes among LCDs.

Development: The process through which a society becomes increasingly able to meet basic human needs and ensure the physical quality of life of its people.

Direct investment: Buying stock, real estate, and other assets in another country with the aim of gaining a controlling interest in foreign economic enterprises. Different from portfolio investment, which involves investment solely to gain capital appreciation through market fluctuations.

Disinformation: The spreading of false propaganda and forged documents to confuse counterintelligence or to create political confusion, unrest, and scandal.

Dumping: A special case of price discrimination, selling to foreign buyers at a lower price than that charged to buyers in the home market.

Duty: Special tax applied to imported goods, based on tariff rates and schedules.

East (as in the East–West struggle)**:** A shorthand, nongeographic term that included nonmarket, centrally planned (communist) countries.

East–West axis: The cold war conflict between the former Soviet Union and its allies and the United States and its allies.

Economic cooperation among developing countries (ECDC): Also referred to as intra-South, or South-South cooperation, it is a way for LCDs to help each other with appropriate technology.

Economic statecraft: The practice of states utilizing economic instruments, such as sanctions, to gain their political ends. Economic statecraft is closely related to "mercantilism," or the use of political power to advance a country's economic fortunes.

Economically developing countries (EDCs): The relatively wealthy and industrialized countries that lie mainly in the Northern Hemisphere (the North).

Escalation: Increasing the level of fighting.

Essential equivalence: Comparing military capabilities of two would-be belligerents, not in terms of identical mix of forces, but in terms of how well two dissimilarly organized forces could achieve a strategic stalemate.

Eurodollars: U.S. dollar holdings of European banks; a liability for the U.S. Treasury.

Euromissiles: Shorthand for long-range theatre nuclear forces stationed in Europe or aimed at targets in Europe.

Europe 1992: A term that represents the European Community's decision to eliminate by the end of 1992 all internal barriers (between member countries) to the movement of trade, financial resources, workers, and services (banking, insurance, etc.).

European Community (EC): The Western European regional organization established in 1967 that includes the European Coal and Steel Community (ECSC), the European Economic Community (EEC), and the European Atomic Energy Community (EURATOM).

European Currency Unit (ECU): The common unit of valuation among the eight members of the European Monetary System (EMS).

European Economic Community (EEC). *See* **European Union.**

European Free Trade Association (EFTA): Austria, Finland, Iceland, Liechtenstein, Norway, Portugal, Sweden, and Switzerland. Each member keeps its own external tariff schedule, but free trade prevails among the members.

European Monetary System (EMS): Established in 1979 as a preliminary stage toward an economic and monetary union in the European Community. Fluctuations in the exchange rate value of the currencies of the participating countries are kept with a 2¼ percent limit of divergence from the strongest currency among them. The system collapsed in 1993, thus slowing progress toward monetary integration in Europe.

European Union: Known as the European Economic Community, and also the Common Market, until 1994, the European Union has 12 full members: Belgium, Denmark, France, Germany, Greece, Ireland, Italy, Luxembourg, Netherlands, Portugal, Spain, and the United Kingdom. (Austria, Finland, Norway, and Sweden are expected to enter the Union in 1995.) Originally established by the Treaty of Rome in 1958, the Union nations work toward establishing common defense and foreign policies and a common market.

Exchange rate: The values of two currencies relative to each other—for example, how many yen equal a dollar or how many lira equal a pound.

Export subsidies: Special incentives, including direct payments to exporters, to encourage increased foreign sales.

Exports: Products shipped to foreign countries.

Finlandization: A condition of nominal neutrality, but one of actual subservience to the former Soviet Union in foreign and security policies, as is the case with Finland.

First strike: The first offensive move of a general nuclear war. It implies an intention to knock out the opponent's ability to retaliate.

Fissionable or nuclear materials: Isotopes of certain elements, such as plutonium, thorium, and uranium, that emit neutrons in such large numbers that a sufficient concentration will be self-sustaining until it explodes.

Foreign policy: The sum of a country's goals and actions on the world stage. The study of foreign policy is synonymous with state-level analysis and examines how countries define their interests, establish goals, decide on specific policies, and attempt to implement those policies.

Forward-based system (FBS or FoBS): A military installation, maintained on foreign soil or in international waters, and conveniently located near a theatre of war.

Fourth World: An expression arising from the world economic crisis that began in 1973–74 with the quadrupling in price of petroleum. It encompasses the least developed countries (LLDCs) and the most seriously affected countries (MSAs).

Free trade: The international movement of goods unrestricted by tariffs or nontariff barriers.

Functionalism: International cooperation in specific areas such as communications, trade, travel, health, or environmental protection activity. Often symbolized by the specialized agencies, such as the World Health Organization, associated with the United Nations.

General Agreement on Tariffs and Trade (GATT): Created in 1947, this organizaiton is the major global forum for negotiations of tariff reductions and other measures to expand world trade. Its members account for four-fifths of the world's trade.

General Assembly: The main representative body of the United Nations, composed of all member states.

Generalized System of Preferences (GSP): A system approved by GATT in 1971, which authorizes DCs to give preferential tariff treatment to LCDs.

Global: Pertaining to the world as a whole; worldwide.

Global commons: The Antarctic, the ocean floor under international waters, and celestial bodies within reach of planet Earth. All of these areas and bodies are considered the common heritage of mankind.

Global negotiations: A new round of international economic negotiations started in 1980 over raw materials, energy, trade, development, money, and finance.

Golan Heights: Syrian territory adjacent to Israel, which has occupied it since the 1967 war and that annexed it unilaterally in 1981.

Gross domestic product (GDP): A measure of income within a country that excludes foreign earnings.

Gross national product (GNP): A measure of the sum of all goods and services produced by a country's nationals, whether they are in the country or abroad.

Group of Seven (G-7): The seven economically largest free market countries: Canada, France, Great Britain, Italy, Japan, the United States, and Germany.

Group of 77: Group of 77 Third World countries that co-sponsored the Joint Declaration of Developing Countries in 1963 calling for greater equity in North–South trade. This group has come to include more than 120 members and represents the interests of the less developed countries of the South.

Hegemonism: Any attempt by a larger power to interfere, threaten, intervene against, and dominate a smaller power or a region of the world.

Hegemony: Domination by a major power over smaller, subordinate ones within its sphere of influence.

Helsinki Agreement. *See* **Conference on Security and Cooperation In Europe.**

Horn of Africa: The northeast corner of Africa that includes Ethiopia, Djibouti, and Somalia. It is separated from the Arabian peninsula by the Gulf of Aden and the Red Sea. It is plagued with tribal conflicts between Ethiopia and Eritrea, and between Ethiopia and Somalia over the Ogaden desert. These conflicts generated a large number of refugees who faced mass starvation.

Human rights: Rights inherent to human beings, including but not limited to the right of dignity; the integrity of the person; the inviolability of the person's body and mind; civil and political rights (freedom of religion, speech, press, assembly, association, the right to privacy, habeas corpus, due process of law, the right to vote or not to vote, the right to run for election, and the right to be protected from reprisals for acts of peaceful dissent); social, economic, and cultural rights. The most glaring violations of human rights are torture, disappearance, and the general phenomenon of state terrorism.

Imports: Products brought into a country from abroad.

Inkatha Freedom Party (IFP): A Zulu-based political and cultural movement led by Mangosuthu Buthelezi. It is a main rival of the African National Congress in South Africa.

Innocent passage: In a nation's territorial sea, passage by a foreign ship is innocent so long as it is not prejudicial to the peace, good order, or security of the coastal state. Submarines must surface and show their flag.

Intercontinental ballistic missile (ICBM): A land-based, rocket-propelled vehicle capable of delivering a warhead to targets at 6,000 or more nautical miles.

Interdependence (economic): The close interrelationship and mutual dependence of two or more domestic economies on each other.

Intergovernmental organizations (IGOs): International/transnational actors comprised of member countries.

Intermediate-range ballistic missile (IRBM): A missile with a range from 1,500 to 4,000 nautical miles.

Intermediate-range nuclear forces: Nuclear arms that are based in Europe with a deployment range that easily encompasses the former USSR.

Intermediate-range Nuclear Forces Treaty (INF): The treaty between the former USSR and the United States that limits the dispersion of nuclear warheads in Europe.

International: Between or among sovereign states.

International Atomic Energy Agency (IAEA): An agency created in 1946 by the UN to limit the use of nuclear technology to peaceful purposes.

International Court of Justice (ICJ): The World Court, which sits in The Hague with 15 judges and which is associated with the United Nations.

International Development Association (IDA): An affiliate of the World Bank that provides interest-free, long-term loans to developing countries.

International Energy Agency (IEA): An arm of OECD that attempts to coordinate member countries' oil imports and reallocate stocks among members in case of disruptions in the world's oil supply.

International Finance Corporation: Created in 1956 to finance overseas investments by private companies without necessarily requiring government guarantees. The IFC borrows from the World Bank, provides loans, and invests directly in private industry in the development of capital projects.

International Monetary Fund (IMF): The world's primary organization devoted to maintaining monetary stability by helping countries fund balance-of-payments deficits. Established in 1947, it now has 170 members.

International political economy (IPE): A term that encapsulates the totality of international economic interdependence and exchange in the political setting of the international system. Trade, investment, monetary relations, transnational business activities, aid, loans, and other aspects of international economic interchange (and the reciprocal impacts between these activities and politics) are all part of the study of IPE.

Interstate: International, intergovernmental.

Intifada (literally, resurgence): A series of minor clashes between Palestinian youths and Israeli security forces that escalated into a full-scale revolt in December 1987.

Intra-South. *See* **Economic Cooperation among Developing Countries.**

Islamic fundamentalism: Early nineteenth-century movements of fundamentalism sought to revitalize Islam through internal reform, thus enabling Islamic societies to resist foreign control. Some of these movements sought peaceful change, while other were more militant. The common ground of twentieth-century reform movements and groups is their fundamental opposition to the onslaught of materialistic Western culture and their desire to reassert a distinct Islamic identity for the societies they claim to represent.

Kampuchea: The new name for Cambodia since April 1975.

KGB: Security police and intelligence apparatus in the former Soviet Union, engaged in espionage, counterespionage, antisubversion, and control of political dissidents.

Khmer Rouge: Literally "Red Cambodians," the communist organization ruling Kampuchea between April 1975 and January 1979 under Pol Pot and Leng Saray.

Kiloton: A thousand tons of explosive force. A measure of the yield of a nuclear weapon equivalent to 1,000 tons of TNT (trinitrotoluene). The bomb detonated at Hiroshima in World War II had an approximate yield of 14 kilotons.

Launcher. *See* **Delivery systems.**

League of Nations: The first true general international organization. It existed between the end of World War I and the beginning of World War II and was the immediate predecessor of the United Nations.

Least developed countries: Those countries in the poorest of economic circumstances. Frequently it includes those countries with a per capita GNP of less than $400 in 1985 dollars.

Less developed countries (LDCs): Countries, located mainly in Africa, Asia, and Latin America, with economies that rely heavily on the production of agriculture and raw material and whose per capita GNP and standard of living are substantially below Western standards.

Linkage diplomacy: The practice of considering another country's general international behavior as well as the specifics of the question when deciding whether or not to reach an agreement on an issue.

Lisbon Protocol: Signed in 1992, it is an agreement between ex-Soviet republics Kazakhstan and Belarus to eliminate nuclear weapons from their territories.

Lome Convention: An agreement concluded between the European Community and 58 African, Caribbean, and Pacific countries (ACP), allowing the latter preferential trade relations and greater economic and technical assistance.

Long-range theatre nuclear forces (LRTNF): Nuclear weapon systems with a range greater than 1,000 kilometers (or 600 miles), such as the U.S. Pershing II missile or the Soviet SS-20.

Maastricht Treaty: Signed by the European Community's 12-member countries in December 1991, the Maastricht Treaty outlines steps toward further political/economic integration. At this time, following several narrow ratification votes and monetary crises, it is too early to foretell the future evolution of EC political integration.

Medium-range ballistic missile (MRBM): A missile with a range from 500 to 1,500 nautical miles.

Megaton: The yield of a nuclear weapon equivalent to 1 million tons of TNT (approximately equivalent to 79 Hiroshima bombs).

Microstates: Very small countries, usually with a population of less than one million.

Missile experimental (MX): A mobile, land-based missile that is shuttled among different launching sites, making it more difficult to locate and destroy.

Most favored nation (MFN): In international trade agreements, a country grants most-favored-nation status to another country in regard to tariffs and other trade regulations.

Multilateral: Involving many nations.

Multinational: Doing business in many nations.

Multinational corporations (MNCs): Private enterprises doing business in more than one country.

Multiple independently targetable reentry vehicle (MIRV): Two or more warheads carried by a single missile and capable of being guided to separate targets on reentry.

Munich syndrome: A lesson that was drawn by post-World War II leaders that one should not compromise with aggression.

Mutual and Balanced Force Reductions (MBFR): The 19-nation Conference on Mutual Reduction of Forces and Armaments and Associated Measures in Central Europe that has been held intermittently from 1973 to the end of the 1980s.

Mutual Assured Destruction (MAD): The basic ingredient of the doctrine of strategic deterrence that no country can escape destruction in a nuclear exchange even if it engages in a preemptive strike.

Namibia: African name for South-West Africa.

National Intelligence Estimate (NIE): The final assessment of global problems and capabilities by the intelligence community for use by the National Security Council and the president in making foreign and military decisions.

Nation-state: A political unit that is sovereign and has a population that supports and identifies with it politically.

Nautical mile: 1,853 meters.

Neocolonialism: A perjorative term describing the economic exploitation of Third World countries by the industrialized countries, in particular through the activities of multinational corporations.

Neutron bomb: Enhanced radiation bomb giving out lower blast and heat but concentrated radiation, thus killing people and living things while reducing damage to physical structures.

New International Economic Order (NIEO): The statement of development policies and objectives adopted at the Sixth Special Session of the UN General Assembly in 1974. NIEO calls for equal participation of LDCs in the international economic policy-making process, better known as the North-South dialogue.

New world order: A term that refers to the structure and operation of the post-cold war world. Following the Persian Gulf War, President George Bush referred to a world order based on nonaggression and on international law and organization.

Nonaligned movement (NAM): A group of Third World countries interested in promoting economic cooperation and development.

Nongovernmental organizations (NGOs or INGOs): Transnational (international) organizations made up of private organizations and individuals instead of member states.

Nonproliferation of Nuclear Weapons Treaty (NPT): Nuclear weapon states, party to the NPT, who pledge not to transfer nuclear explosive devices to any recipient and not to assist any nonnuclear weapon state in the manufacture of nuclear explosive devices.

Nontariff barriers (NTB): Subtle, informal impediments to free trade designed for the purpose of making importation of foreign goods into a country very difficult on such grounds as health and safety regulations.

Normalization of relations: The reestablishment of full diplomatic relations, including de jure recognition and the exchange of ambassadors between two countries that either did not have diplomatic relations or had broken them.

North: (as in North–South dialogue): (a) A shorthand, nongeographic term for the industrialized countries of high income, both East and West; (b) Often means only the industrialized, high-income countries of the West.

North Atlantic Cooperation Council (NACC): Consists of 37 members, including all members of NATO, the former Warsaw Pact members, and former Soviet republics (Russia, Ukraine, Belarus, Georgia, Moldova, Armenia, Azerbaijan, Kazakhstan, Uzbekistan, Kyrgyzstan, Turkmentistan, and Tajikistan), the Czech Republic, Slovakia, Poland, Hungary, Romania, Bulgaria, Estonia, Latvia, Lithuania, and Albania.

North Atlantic Treaty Organization (NATO): Also known as the Atlantic Alliance, NATO was formed in 1949 to provide collective defense against the perceived Soviet threat to Western Europe. It consists of the United States, Canada, 13 Western European countries, and Turkey.

North-South axis: A growing tension that is developing between the North (economically developed countries) and the South (economically deprived countries). The South is insisting that the North share part of its wealth and terminate economic and political domination.

Nuclear Nonproliferation Treaty (NPT): A treaty that prohibits the sale, acquisition, or production of nuclear weapons.

Nuclear proliferation: The process by which one country after another comes into possession of some form of nuclear weaponry, and with it develops the potential of launching a nuclear attack on other countries.

Nuclear reprocessing: The separation of radioactive waste (spent fuel) from a nuclear-powered plant into its fissile constituent materials. One such material is plutonium, which can then be used in the production of atomic bombs.

Nuclear terrorism: The use (or threatened use) of nuclear weapons or radioactive materials as a means of coercion.

Nuclear Utilization Theory (NUT): Advocates of this nuclear strategy position want to destroy enemy weapons before the weapons explode on one's own territory and forces. The best way to do this, according to this theory, is to destroy an enemy's weapons before they are launched.

Nuclear-free zone: A stretch of territory from which all nuclear weapons are banned.

Official Development Aid (ODA): Government contributions to projects and programs aimed at developing the productivity of poorer countries. This is to be distinguished from private, voluntary assistance, humanitarian assistance for disasters, and, most importantly, from military assistance.

Ogaden: A piece of Ethiopian desert populated by ethnic Somalis. It was a bone of contention between Ethiopia and Somalia that continued until 1988 when a peace agreement was reached.

Organization of Arab Petroleum Exporting Countries (OAPEC): A component of OPEC, with Saudi Arabia, Kuwait, the United Arab Emirates, Qatar, Iraq, Algeria, and Libya as members.

Organization of Economic Cooperation and Development (OECD): An organization of 24 members that serves to promote economic coordination among the Western industrialized countries.

Organization of Petroleum Exporting Countries (OPEC): A producers' cartel setting price floors and production ceilings of crude petroleum. It consists of Venezuela and others such as Ecuador, Gabon, Nigeria, and Indonesia, as well as the Arab oil-producing countries.

Palestine: "Palestine" does not exist today as an entity. It refers to the historical and geographical entity administered by the British under the League of Nations mandate from 1918 to 1947. It also refers to a future entity in the aspirations of Palestinians who, as was the case of the Jews before the founding of the State of Israel, are stateless nationalists. Whether Palestinians will have an autonomous or independent homeland is an ongoing issue.

Palestine Liberation Organization (PLO): A coalition of Palestinian groups united by the goal of a Palestinian state through the destruction of Israel as a state.

Partnership for Peace Program: A U.S.-backed policy initiative for NATO formulated by the Clinton administration in 1994. The proposal was designed to rejuvenate the Atlantic Alliance and contribute to the stability of recent independent countries in Eastern Europe and the former Soviet Union. No NATO security guarantees or eventual membership in the alliance are specifically mentioned.

Payload: Warheads attached to delivery vehicles.

Peacekeeping: Occurs when an international organization such as the United Nations uses military means to prevent hostilities, usually by serving as a buffer between combatants. This international force will remain neutral between the opposing forces and must be invited by at least one of the combatants. *See* **Collective security.**

People's Republic of China (PRC): Communist or mainland China.

Petrodollars: U.S. dollar holdings of capital-surplus OPEC countries; a liability for the U.S. Treasury.

Physical Quality of Life Index (PQLI): Developed by the Overseas Development Council, the PQLI is presented as a more significant measurement of the well-being of inhabitants of a geographic entity than the solely monetary measurement of per capita income. It consists of the following measurements: life expectancy, infant mortality, and literacy figures that are each rated on an index of 1-100, within which each country is ranked according to its performance. A composite index is obtained by averaging these three measures, giving the PQLI.

Polisario: The liberation front of Western Sahara (formerly Spanish Sahara). After years of bitter fighting over Western Sahara, Polisario guerrillas signed a cease-fire agreement with Morocco in 1990. The UN has yet to conduct a referendum in Western Sahara on whether the territory should become independent or remain part of Morocco.

Postindustrial: Characteristic of a society where a large portion of the workforce is directed to nonagricultural and nonmanufacturing tasks such as servicing and processing.

Precision-guided munitions (PGM): Popularly known as "smart bombs." Electronically programmed and controlled weapons that can accurately hit a moving or stationary target.

Proliferation: Quick spread, as in the case of nuclear weapons.

Protectionism: Using tariffs and nontariff barriers to control or restrict the flow of imports into a country.

Protocol: A preliminary memorandum often signed by diplomatic negotiators as a basis for a final convention or treaty.

Quota: Quantitative limits, usually imposed on imports or immigrants.

Rapprochement: The coming together of two countries that had been hostile to each other.

Real dollars (uninflated dollars): The report of currency in terms of what it would have been worth in a stated year.

Regionalism: A concept of cooperation among geographically adjacent states to foster region-wide political, military, and economic interests.

Reprocessing of nuclear waste: A process of recovery of fissionable materials among which is weapons-grade plutonium.

Resolution: Formal decisions of UN bodies; they may simply register an opinion or may recommend action to be taken by a UN body or agency.

Resolution 242: Passed by the UN Security Council on November 22, 1967, calling for the withdrawal of Israeli troops from territories they captured from Egypt (Sinai), Jordan (West Bank and East Jerusalem), and Syria (Golan Heights) in the 1967 war, and for the right of all nations in the Middle East to live in peace in secure and recognized borders.

Resolution 435: Passed by the UN Security Council in 1978, it called for a cease-fire between belligerents in the Namibian conflict (namely SWAPO, Angola and other frontline states on the one side, and South Africa on the other) and an internationally supervised transition process to independence and free elections.

Resolution 678: Passed by the UN in November 1990 demanding that Iraq withdraw from Kuwait. It authorized the use of all necessary force to restore Kuwait's sovereignty after January 15, 1991.

SALT I: The Strategic Arms Limitation Treaty that was signed in 1972 between the U.S. and the former Soviet Union on the limitation of strategic armaments.

SALT II: The Strategic Arms Limitation Treaty was signed in 1979. SALT II was to limit the number and types of former Soviet Union and U.S. strategic weapons. It never went into effect, as it was not ratified by the U.S. Senate.

Second strike: A nuclear attack in response to an adversary's first strike. A second-strike capability is the ability to absorb the full force of a first strike and still inflict heavy damage in retaliation.

Secretariat: (a) The administrative organ of the United Nations, headed by the secretary-general; (b) An administrative element of any IGO; this is headed by a secretary-general.

Short-range ballistic missiles (SRBM): A missile with a range up to 500 nautical miles.

Solidarity: Independent self-governing trade union movement started in Poland in 1980. It was terminated in December 1981 after radical members of its Presidum passed a resolution calling for a national referendum to determine if the communist government of Poland should continue to govern.

South (as in North-South axis): A shorthand, nongeographic term that includes economically less developed countries, often represented by the Group of 77.

Sovereignty: The ability to carry out laws and policies within national borders without interference from outside.

Special Drawing Rights (SDRs): Also known as paper gold. A new form of international liquid reserves to be used in the settlement of international payments among member governments of the International Monetary Fund.

State: Regarding international relations, it means a country having territory, population, government, and sovereignty, e.g., the United States is a state, while California is not a state in this sense.

State terrorism: The use of state power, including the police, the armed forces, and the secret police to throw fear among the population against any act of dissent or protest against a political regime.

"Stealth": A code name for a proposed "invisible" aircraft, supposedly not detectable by hostile forces, that would be the main U.S. strategic fighter-bomber of the 1990s.

Strategic Arms Limitation Talks. See **SALT I** and **SALT II.**

Strategic Defense Initiative (SDI): A space-based defense system designed to destroy incoming missiles. It is highly criticized because the technological possibility of such a system is questionable, not to mention the enormous cost.

Strategic minerals: Minerals needed in the fabrication of advanced military and industrial equipment. Examples are uranium, platinum, titanium, vanadium, tungsten, nickel, chromium, etc.

Strategic nuclear weapons: Long-range weapons carried on either intercontinental ballistic missiles (ICBMs) or submarine-launched ballistic missiles (SLBMs) or long-range bombers.

Strategic stockpile: Reserves of certain commodities established to ensure that in time of national emergency such commodities are readily available.

Structural Adjustment Program. See **Conditionality.**

Submarine-launched ballistic missile (SLBM): A ballistic missile carried in and launched from a submarine.

Superpowers: Countries so powerful militarily (the United States and Russia), demographically (Pacific Rim countries), or economically (Japan) as to be in a class by themselves.

Supranational: Above nation-states.

Tactical nuclear weapons: Kiloton-range weapons for theatre use. The bomb dropped on Hiroshima would be in this category today.

Tariff: A tax levied on imports.

Technetronic: Shorthand for technological-electronic.

Territorial sea: The territorial sea, air space above, seabed, and subsoil are part of sovereign territory of a coastal state, except that ships (not aircraft) enjoy right of innocent passage. As proposed, a coastal state's sovereignty would extend 12 nautical miles beyond its land territory.

Terrorism: The systematic use of terror as a means of coercion.

Theatre: In nuclear strategy, it refers to a localized combat area such as Europe, as opposed to global warfare that would have involved the United States and the former Soviet Union in a nuclear exchange.

Theatre nuclear forces (TNF): Nuclear weapons systems for operations in a region such as Europe, including artillery, cruise missiles, SRBMs, IRBMs, and MRBMs.

Third World: Often used interchangeably with the terms less developed countries, developing countries, or the South, its two main institutions are the nonaligned movement (which acts primarily as the political caucus of the Third World) and the Group of 77 (which functions as the economic voice of the Third World).

Tokyo Round: The sixth round of GATT trade negotiations, begun in 1973 and ended in 1979. About 100 nations, including nonmembers of the GATT, participated.

Torture: The deliberate inflicting of pain, whether physical or psychological, to degrade, intimidate, and induce submission of its victims to the will of the torturer. It is a heinous practice used frequently in most dictatorial regimes in the world, irrespective of their ideological leanings.

Transnational: An adjective indicating that a nongovernmental movement, organization, or ideology transcends national borders and is operative in dissimilar political, economic, and social systems.

Transnational enterprise (TNE) or corporation (TNC). See **Multinational corporations.**

Triad (nuclear): The three-pronged U.S. strategic weapons arsenal, composed of land-based ICBMs, underwater SLBMs, and long-range manned bombers.

Trilateral: Between three countries or groups of countries, e.g., United States, Western Europe, and Japan; United States, Russia, and China.

Unilateral: One-sided, as opposed to bilateral or multilateral.

United Nations Conference on Trade and Development (UNCTAD): A coalition of disadvantaged countries that met in 1964 in response to their effort to bridge the standard-of-living gap between themselves and developed countries.

Verification: The process of determining that the other side is complying with an agreement.

Vietnam syndrome: An aversion to foreign armed intervention, especially in Third World conflicts involving guerrillas. This is an attitude that is especially common among those who were opposed to U.S. participation in the Vietnam War.

Visegrad Group: Term used to refer to Poland, Hungary, Slovakia, and the Czech Republic. These countries were subject to the same conditions and status in their recent application to participate in NATO's Partnership for Peace initiative.

Walesa, Lech: Leader of the independent trade union movement known as Solidarity, which came into existence in August 1980 and was dissolved in December 1981 by martial law decree. He was elected president of Poland in December 1990.

Warhead: That part of a missile, projectile, or torpedo that contains the explosive intended to inflict damage.

Warsaw Pact or Warsaw Treaty Organization: Established in 1955 by the Soviet Union to promote mutual defense. It was dissolved in July 1991. Member countries at time of dissolution were: the Soviet Union, Bulgaria, Czechoslovakia, Hungary, Poland, and Romania.

West (as in the East–West conflict): Basically the market-economy, industrialized, and high-income countries that are committed to a political system of representative democracy. The three main anchors of the West today are North America, Western Europe, and Japan, also known as the Trilateral countries. Australia and New Zealand are also parts of the West.

"Window of vulnerability": An expression often used, but not consistently defined, by President Ronald Reagan and his administration during the 1980s. Military specialists used the word to refer to a period of time in the late 1980s when it was predicted that the United States silo-based ICBMs could be accurately hit by Soviet missiles while the mobile MX system (now scrapped) would not yet be operational, and when the aging B-52 bombers would no longer be serviceable while the Stealth aircraft would not yet be operational. President Reagan planned to close this "window" by MIRVing the silo-based ICBMs, by hardening their concrete covers, by building B-1 bombers, and by the "Star Wars" initiative.

World Bank (International Bank for Reconstruction and Development [IBRD]): Makes loans, either directly to governments or with governments as the guarantors, and through its affiliates, the International Finance Corporation and the International Development Association.

Xenophobia: A dislike, fear, or suspicion of other nationalities.

Yield: The explosive force, in terms of TNT equivalence, of a warhead.

Zimbabwe: Formerly Rhodesia.

Zionism: An international movement for the establishment of a Jewish nation or religious community in Palestine and later for the support of modern Israel.

SOURCES

International Politics on the World Stage, Sixth Edition, 1997, Dushkin/McGraw-Hill.

Global Studies: Africa, Seventh Edition, 1997, Dushkin/McGraw-Hill.

Global Studies: Russia, The Eurasian Republics, and Central/Eastern Europe, Seventh Edition, 1998, Dushkin/McGraw-Hill.

Global Studies: The Middle East, Seventh Edition, 1998, Dushkin/McGraw-Hill.

Index

Credits/Acknowledgments

Cover design by Charles Vitelli

1. A Clash of Views
Facing overview—© 1998 by PhotoDisc, Inc.

2. Population
Facing overview—United Nations photo by J. P. Laffont.

3. Natural Resources
Facing overview—United Nations photo by John Isaac.

4. Political Economy
Facing overview—United Nations photo by Ian Steele. 147—*Business Week* chart by Rob Doyle.

5. Conflict
Facing overview—AP/Wide World photo.

6. Cooperation
Facing overview—United Nations photo by John Isaac.

7. Values and Visions
Facing overview—United Nations photo by John Isaac.

ANNUAL EDITIONS ARTICLE REVIEW FORM

■ NAME: _____ DATE: _____

■ TITLE AND NUMBER OF ARTICLE: _____

■ BRIEFLY STATE THE MAIN IDEA OF THIS ARTICLE: _____

_____

■ LIST THREE IMPORTANT FACTS THAT THE AUTHOR USES TO SUPPORT THE MAIN IDEA:

_____

_____

_____

_____

■ WHAT INFORMATION OR IDEAS DISCUSSED IN THIS ARTICLE ARE ALSO DISCUSSED IN YOUR TEXTBOOK OR OTHER READINGS THAT YOU HAVE DONE? LIST THE TEXTBOOK CHAPTERS AND PAGE NUMBERS:

_____

_____

_____

_____

_____

■ LIST ANY EXAMPLES OF BIAS OR FAULTY REASONING THAT YOU FOUND IN THE ARTICLE:

_____

_____

_____

_____

■ LIST ANY NEW TERMS/CONCEPTS THAT WERE DISCUSSED IN THE ARTICLE, AND WRITE A SHORT DEFINITION:

_____

_____

_____

_____

We Want Your Advice

ANNUAL EDITIONS revisions depend on two major opinion sources: one is our Advisory Board, listed in the front of this volume, which works with us in scanning the thousands of articles published in the public press each year; the other is you—the person actually using the book. Please help us and the users of the next edition by completing the prepaid article rating form on this page and returning it to us. Thank you for your help!

ANNUAL EDITIONS: GLOBAL ISSUES 98/99
Article Rating Form

Here is an opportunity for you to have direct input into the next revision of this volume. We would like you to rate each of the 50 articles listed below, using the following scale:

1. **Excellent: should definitely be retained**
2. **Above average: should probably be retained**
3. **Below average: should probably be deleted**
4. **Poor: should definitely be deleted**

Your ratings will play a vital part in the next revision. So please mail this prepaid form to us just as soon as you complete it.
Thanks for your help!

Rating	Article	Rating	Article
	1. Preparing for the 21st Century: Winners and Losers		27. Piling into Central Europe
	2. The Many Faces of the Future		28. Where Asia Goes from Here
	3. Redefining Security: The New Global Schisms		29. Ignored Warnings
	4. Can Humanity Survive Unrestricted Population Growth?		30. No More Free Lunch
			31. A New Tiger
	5. Worldwide Development or Population Explosion: Our Choice		32. Village Banking: A Report from 5 Countries
			33. Child Labour: Rights, Risks, and Realities
	6. Refugees: The Rising Tide		34. The Burden of Womanhood
	7. Water-Borne Killers		35. The New Arms Race: Light Weapons and International Security
	8. How Many People Can the Earth Support?		
	9. The Global Challenge		36. Organised Chaos: Not the New World We Ordered
	10. A Global Warning		37. Towards the Global Millennium: The Challenge of Islam
	11. Fire in the Sky		
	12. Mining the Oceans		38. Uncertainty, Insecurity, and China's Military Power
	13. Greenwatch: Red Alert for the Earth's Green Belt		39. Russian Foreign Policy in the Near Abroad and Beyond
	14. We *Can* Build a Sustainable Economy		
	15. Global Population and the Nitrogen Cycle		40. Nuclear Deterrence and Regional Proliferators
	16. How Much Food Will We Need in the 21st Century?		41. Taking Nuclear Weapons Off Hair-Trigger Alert
	17. The Fish Crisis		42. The First Fifty Years: The Main Achievements
	18. Angling For 'Aquaculture'		43. A Watchful Eye: Monitoring the Conventional Arms Trade
	19. The Future of Energy		
	20. How to Divvy Up Caspian Bonanza		44. Like No Other Parliament on Earth
	21. Here Comes the Sun . . . and the Wind and the Rain		45. From GATT to WTO: The Institutionalization of World Trade
	22. The Complexities and Contradictions of Globalization		
	23. Spreading the Wealth: How 'Globalization' Is Helping Shift Cash from Rich Nations to Poor Ones		46. Peace Prize Goes to Land-Mine Opponents
			47. Universal Human Values: Finding an Ethical Common Ground
	24. Prosper or Perish? Development in the Age of Global Capital		
			48. Women in Power: From Tokenism to Critical Mass
	25. An Illusion for Our Time		49. The End of the Hunting Season in History
	26. High Noon in Europe		50. Reassessing the Economic Assumption

(Continued on next page)

ABOUT YOU

Name _____ Date _____

Are you a teacher? ❑ Or a student? ❑

Your school name _____

Department _____

Address _____

City _____ State _____ Zip _____

School telephone # _____

YOUR COMMENTS ARE IMPORTANT TO US !

Please fill in the following information:

For which course did you use this book? _____

Did you use a text with this *ANNUAL EDITION*? ❑ yes ❑ no

What was the title of the text? _____

What are your general reactions to the *Annual Editions* concept?

Have you read any particular articles recently that you think should be included in the next edition?

Are there any articles you feel should be replaced in the next edition? Why?

Are there any World Wide Web sites you feel should be included in the next edition? Please annotate.

May we contact you for editorial input?

May we quote your comments?

ANNUAL EDITIONS: GLOBAL ISSUES 98/99

BUSINESS REPLY MAIL		
First Class	Permit No. 84	Guilford, CT

Postage will be paid by addressee

Dushkin/McGraw·Hill
Sluice Dock
Guilford, CT 06437

No Postage
Necessary
if Mailed
in the
United States